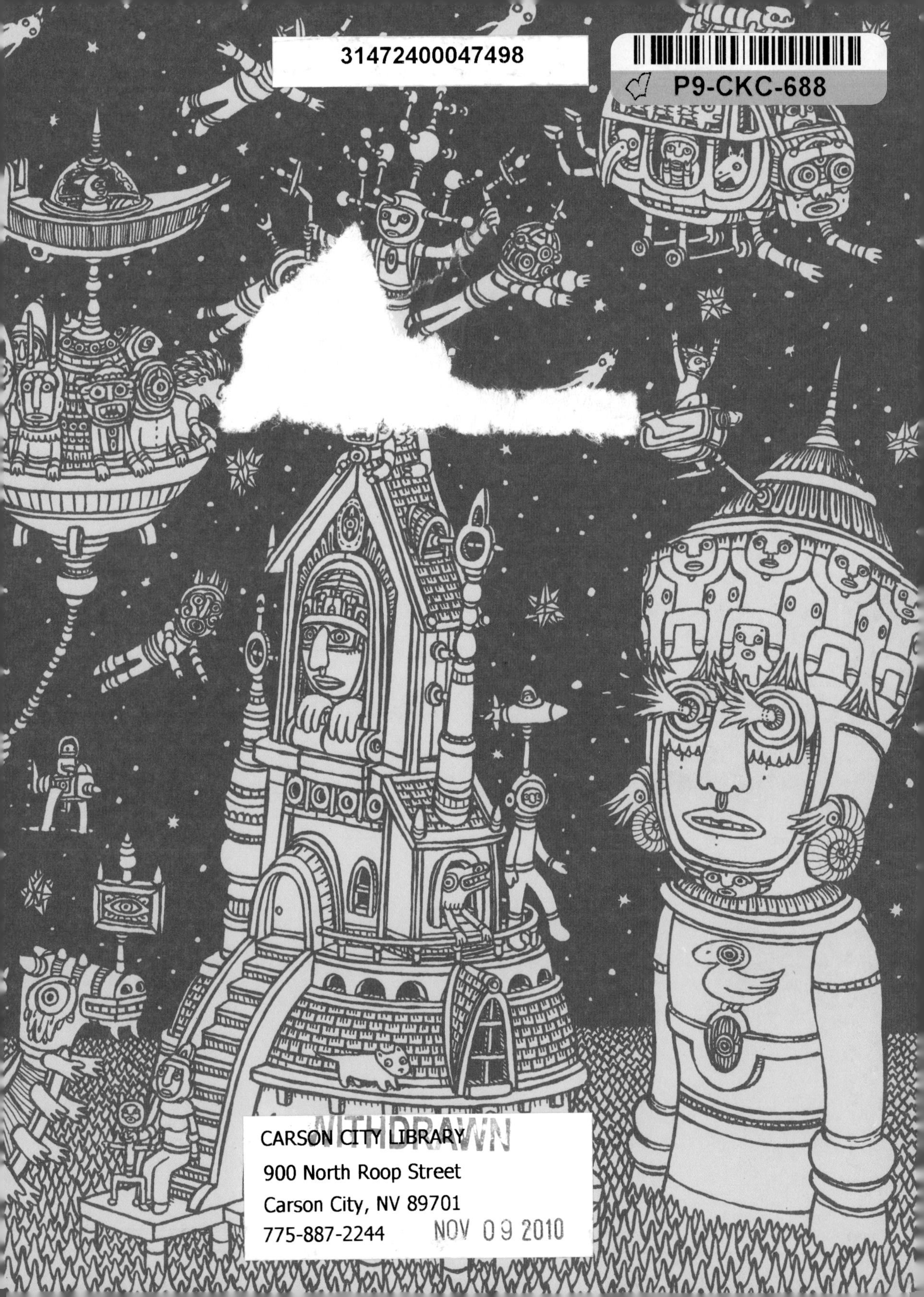

THE BEST AMERICAN

Comics 2010

GUEST EDITORS OF
THE BEST AMERICAN COMICS

2006 HARVEY PEKAR
2007 CHRIS WARE
2008 LYNDA BARRY
2009 CHARLES BURNS
2010 NEIL GAIMAN

THE BEST AMERICAN

Comics

2010

EDITED *and with an*

INTRODUCTION *by* Neil Gaiman

JESSICA ABEL & MATT MADDEN,
series editors

HOUGHTON MIFFLIN HARCOURT

BOSTON ▪ NEW YORK   2010

www.hmhbooks.com

ISBN 978-0-547-24177-7

Book design: Robert Overholtzer   Cover design: Michael Cho   Endpaper art: Theo Ellsworth

PRINTED IN THE UNITED STATES OF AMERICA

DOC 10 9 8 7 6 5 4 3 2 1

Permissions credits are located on page 329.

Contents

Foreword

THERE WAS A TIME not so long ago when a trip to the comics store was a relatively brief, straightforward affair: you went in to look at the "new releases" shelf and, no matter how eclectic your tastes, you would wind up with a reasonably sized stack of pamphlet comics (that's what we in the biz call what you probably think of as "comic books"). Maybe you'd even wander around the store a bit to look for back issues or comics that escaped your notice the first time around. And in this not-too-distant past, a trip to a regular bookstore in search of comics was even briefer; you were unlikely to find any at all, other than maybe the odd independent-press collection or superhero paperback wedged into the "humor" section, or perhaps one of the few books such as *Maus* or Larry Gonick's *Cartoon History of the Universe* that had achieved that elusive cultural stamp of approval.

Things have changed, to put it mildly. Over the last decade, a variety of publishing events and trends have catapulted comics (or graphic novels, or manga, or graphica, or webcomics, or whatever label they're given) into a new and—most would agree— higher echelon in American culture (globally as well, but let's stick to this continent, in keeping with this series' title). The seeds were numerous and were planted over the years: the publication and wide acceptance of *Maus* and *Watchmen* in the eighties; Hollywood blockbusters based on superhero franchises as well as indy film hits such as *Crumb* and *American Splendor;* and the slow-growing but now prevalent influence of all things Japanese.

There wasn't any one key moment, no shot heard 'round the world. By the time most people noticed it, the growth spurt of our medium was already well under way. But there were notable turning points. One of which was certainly the publishing of our former guest editor Chris Ware's *Jimmy Corrigan—the Smartest Kid on Earth* in 2000. That book's success across the spectrum—in the comics world, of course, but also in the literary, fine art, and design worlds—seemed to finally prove to big prose publishers that comics could sell and be a viable part of their business. For the first time, we saw some of the major publishing houses such as Random House, Macmillan, and Abrams dipping a toe—and then a whole leg—into comics, both as parts of their regular publishing catalogs in addition to, for the first time, dedicating collections and even whole imprints to comics. At the other end of the spectrum, the cluster of successful superhero films from *Spider-Man* to *Hellboy* raised the profile of comics both among those who count the numbers, yes, but also to those who are attuned to epicenters of our popular culture. Meanwhile, manga and animé reached a kind of turning point in the culture and seemed to grow overnight from cult obsession to mainstream passion.

All of which brings us back to our weekly comic-book store visit. These days, you actually quake with anxiety when you step into a comic book store, the anxiety of seeing more great and intriguing books hit the "new arrivals" shelf every week than you could finish reading by the time next week comes around—even assuming you had the money to buy them all. There is a "rising tide floats all boats" effect in the world of comics today. Everyone seems to be pushing to outdo themselves and to live up to comics' new status as a Medium That Matters. You'll find a bewildering variety of mainstream titles, often featuring the same or overlapping combinations of superheroes; beautiful book-as-art-objects from independent publishers; possibly (if you're lucky) a pile of photocopied and silkscreened mini-comics by local artists; hardcover collections of beautifully reprinted, near-forgotten newspaper strips; stacks of manga paperbacks; other international comics in translation ... the list goes on. A very notable development of this period, too, is that you can go into a chain bookstore or a savvy independent bookshop and find a large selection of all of this work there as well. For those of us who remember the way our hearts used to sink at finding our favorite cartoonists' books stuck between joke anthologies and Madlib collections, it is simply remarkable to now find multiple bookcases of comics of all sorts in our local bookstore.

It's a golden age we are living in: not only is there more and more to read, but comics are also seeing an unprecedented growth in quality. But when you're the series editor of the *Best American Comics* and your job is to read all of this stuff, well, that anxiety comes back again, believe you us! The stacks of books in our house get more intimidating every year. And for every book we decide is clearly good enough to send along to our guest editor, we come across a handful more that are nearly there—diamonds in the rough are everywhere we look. It's becoming increasingly difficult to keep track of all the great stuff that comes out, even from the major comics publishers, not to mention small houses and self-publishers. Yet we do our best, and so far we haven't made any major oversights ("What? Robert Crumb drew the Bible?!"). We keep in touch with publishers and editors, we scour the blogs (thanks, bloggers, for all your annual "best of" lists!), we canvass our peers, our students—and it's a lot of work. That's where you can help. Below, we go over our submissions procedures, and we hope you'll be in touch, whether you make a comic, publish it, or just know about something great that we might otherwise miss. Let's bring some crowdsourcing to our little corner of the world!

The Best American Comics 2010 represents a selection of the outstanding comics published in North America between September 1, 2008, and August 31, 2009. As series editors, we search out and review comics in as many formats and publications as we can find, from hand-produced mini-comics to individual pamphlet issues to graphic novels and collections to webcomics. Our goal is to put as much interesting and worthwhile material in front of our guest editors as they can stand to read through. This includes works that we consider to be excellent by reasonable objective standards, but it also includes comics we have a particular fondness for, as well as left-field choices that may not be our cup of tea but may turn out to be someone else's "best"—in particular, the guest editor's. Guest editors will sometimes seek out material on their own as well. The guest editor makes the final selections from this large and varied pool of titles. Idiosyncrasy is encouraged. One of the things we love most about this series is the way it changes from year to year. Each volume is indisputably the best of that year—as seen through one particular pair of eyes. And that vision of the guest editor is the most valuable and intriguing aspect of the ongoing series. This is now our fifth outing, and each time a new guest editor turns in his or her choices, we are surprised and pleased anew.

Even more than in the past, we were impressed this year with the strength of the submissions. We had a hard time narrowing down our choices to the required number but knew it was essential, given the hectic schedule of our guest editor! If that's a problem, however, it's one we hope will become stickier with each coming year.

Our final choices are wonderful, but please don't fail to take a look at our list of Notable Comics in the back of this volume. You'll find so much more there that you're likely to enjoy. Don't forget that we also have this list posted online with some helpful links so that you actually may be able to track down even the most obscure minicomics on the list.

This year's guest editor is the great Neil Gaiman, possibly both the busiest and the nicest comics professional working today. Within the world of comics, Neil is perhaps still best known for his wonderful and innovative Sandman series, which single-handedly upped the ratio of women reading comics (many years before the even bigger bump to female readership that is the manga phenomenon) as well as the commercial possibilities of working in nontraditional (read: nonsuperhero) stories—and thus in some part laid the foundation for this very series. He is also, of course, an incredibly productive, accomplished writer in every available medium, notably in prose (such as, among others, novels *American Gods, Coraline,* and *The Graveyard Book*) and film (such as screenplays for *MirrorMask* and *Beowulf*). Take a look at his blog or spend a few days following his Twitter feed and you will get an idea of how hard Neil works, producing new material as well as engaging directly with his readership. He is indefatigable. And when you look over the wonderful lineup of stories he chose for this volume, it's clear where Neil is coming from: the stories and excerpts are longer than in the preceding volumes, and they are all focused on the narrative; they give us worlds to enter through storytelling.

As we discussed above, the mountains of good comics always threaten to bury us, so we depend on your advice and submissions. Here are the submission guidelines: comics eligible for consideration must have been published in the eligibility period either on paper or electronically, in English, by a North American author, or one who makes his or her home here. As this 2010 volume hits the shelves, we will have already passed the deadline for the 2011 volume and will be on to collecting for the 2012 volume, whose eligibility window is September 1, 2010, through August 31, 2011. A note about webcomics (and comics on the Web): we do our best to find what's out there, and we rely on friends, blogs, and "best of" lists to track down important work, but we are aware that webcomics is an area that deserves better coverage. Therefore, we'd especially like to encourage you Web cartoonists and publishers to send us submissions either on paper or digitally. Printed submissions can be sent to us at the address below. Digital submissions can be made in the form of a PDF of comics published in the eligibility window, with each comic labeled with the exact date it was published online. Better yet, you might make a subselection of what you consider to be your best strips from the year or send a self-contained continuity as long as it appeared in the eligibility period. You can mail a CD of the PDF to us or you can e-mail a download link to bestamericancomics@hmhpub.com.

All comics should be labeled with their release date and contact information and mailed to us at the following address:

Jessica Abel and Matt Madden
Series Editors
The Best American Comics
Houghton Mifflin Harcourt Publishing Co.
215 Park Avenue South
New York, NY 10003

Further information is available on the Best American Comics website: bestamericancomics.com.

We'd like to thank all the people who helped us with this volume, starting with the outstanding team at Houghton Mifflin Harcourt: our excellent editor Meagan Stacey; our production team of Beth Burleigh Fuller, Christopher Moisan, David Futato, and Laura Brady; as well as Sanj Kharbanda, Emer Flounders, and Tom Bouman. Thanks also to our great studio assistants, Lydia Roberts, DaYoung Jung, J.P. Kim, and Rel Finkelstein; and of course to all the artists and publishers from all over who sent in submissions.

JESSICA ABEL and MATT MADDEN

Introduction

Page 1, panel 1.

Space. The infinite vastness of everything. Seeing that's a bit hard to fit into one panel, you'll probably have to suggest it. I mean, if you can fit the whole universe in, then go for it. Otherwise, a galaxy.

NO DIALOGUE

Page 1, panel 2.

The Earth, as seen from space. I think this would best be representational, rather than hyperrealistic. (Would we even recognize a realistic Earth, as seen from space?) North should be up, and North America should be easy to find.

NO DIALOGUE

Page 1, panel 3.

A bigger panel. It's America, the country, as seen from space, with bits of Canada at the top and Mexico at the bottom. All of it. Feel free to add labels to it. Amber waves of grain can be labeled "amber waves of grain." Purple mountains majesty ditto. Also skyscrapers of Manhattan, alligators of Florida, the cablecars of San Francisco and, ever-so-slightly to the right of Minneapolis, is the end of a tip of an arrow. It is labeled.

ARROW LABEL: Your Editor.

Page 1, panel 4.

And this, from above, looking up at the world, is the editor of this volume. He is nearly fifty. He needs a haircut, has bags under his eyes, is wearing a black T-shirt and jeans. He has the little potbelly of a man who has spent too much of his life behind a desk and the haunted expression of a man one missed deadline away from disaster. His hands are in his jacket pockets, and he's looking up toward our virtual camera, which has been zooming in on him. He's talking to us:

EDITOR: It's just wrong!

And about this point, I decide that it's probably kinder on the reader if I don't write the rest of this introduction as a script to an undrawn comic, because comics really are a visual medium and a written description of what you would be seeing if I'd written this whole introduction as a comic is not the easiest way to assimilate information.

Comics, of course, *are* the easiest way to assimilate information, at least according to a study done by the CIA back in the 1980s. But a comics script is a strange, hybrid beastie, part blueprint, part correspondence, part theoretical yogurt-starter. Let's go to prose.

Imagine me telling you this. I would be outside in the garden of an old Addams Family–style house an hour's drive from Minneapolis.

It's just wrong.

It's just wrong and I am a participant, dammit. I am a collaborator in this madness. I have drawn you in by lending my name and my endorsement and my time. I have done my best to give you the impression that the volume you hold contains the Best American Comics of the year. That by purchasing it, you will become *au fait* with the cutting edge. It says so on the cover, after all.

Buy it, read it, and know that you know what's happening in comics …

Well, yes. Up to a point.

Take "the year." In this case, the year runs from September to August. The biggest, the most important, and, to my mind, the most fascinating comic of 2009, Robert Crumb's retelling of the book of Genesis, makes it into this book only because an advanced excerpt was run in *The New Yorker*.

Some of this material was published for the first time in 2008 and 2009. Some was simply collected in that time frame. Things I loved were excluded, and previous editors had not chosen them, nor would upcoming editors pick them. Oh, the injustice.

"Best." It's a weird sort of a word. I didn't read every comic published in America over the time span of this book. I wish I had: it would have been fun. Jessica Abel and Matt Madden did not read everything published in America either. Twenty years ago, it might have been barely possible: today, it's a pipe dream.

(I remember arguing with Scott McCloud about his book *Reinventing Comics*, published in 2000, taking issue with his hypothesis that comics would find an easy outlet on the Web. I mocked him, pointed out how long it took comics to load, explained that paper would always be first port of call for young cartoonists, and was wrong about everything I could have been, except about the problems with getting people paid for their work. Sorry, Scott. You were right.)

We did our best. Still, I lay awake some nights wondering about the choices I made, suspecting that on another day I might have chosen a completely different set of pages.

"American"? A slippery term at the best of times, and here it slips through your fingers like mercury. "American" is, as a term, in this case, strangely parochial, fundamentally irrelevant, and extremely difficult to define. The comics community is global. There are comics published in America by people who are not American that qualify as American, and there are comics that don't. (I loved a small strip in an American-published magazine that turned out to be by a Swede and is thus not here. Eddie Campbell is not represented in the *Best American Comics* purely because he is a Scot living in Brisbane, Australia.) (Your editor is English. He lives in America, and most of the comics he has written, during a career of writing stuff, have been published in America. Were they more or less American before I moved here? I do not know. Matt and Jessica edited part of this book from Paris, the French one. I know that, left to myself, I would have declared all comics writers and cartoonists honorary Americans and made the issue moot.)

And finally, and most frustratingly, maddeningly, that peculiar and elusive term "comics," which started as strips and as Sunday pages over a hundred years ago, then became eight-page sequences in longer periodicals, then grew to become twenty-plus pages of monthly story, and then mutated to become books, to become webcomics (often closer in spirit to the strips and Sundays than anything else), and to become graphic novels, whatever exactly they are (and they are, I suspect, anything you want them to be).

Now, so many comics are being created and intended as books, as longer stories. Which on the one hand is a very good thing, as excellent art is being made. It also has its downside: books are long things, filled with reverses and characters, plot and event. They are mad marathons in which the reader and the creators collaborate. Any extract from a longer work, no matter how well-chosen, is simply that: an extract from a longer work, and the real art is the longer work, with a beginning and a middle and an end, often in that order.

In this collection, I've tried to find sequences that worked on their own, that gave a flavor of a book, that would interest, intrigue, or irritate you enough that they would perhaps send you out to buy the whole thing, while always aware that what you are seeing is incomplete.

(Insert a silent panel here. The editor is looking out at us. He looks out of sorts, yet, having ranted and raged and grumbled for several pages, is nowhere near as grumbly as one would imagine.)

But having said all that . . .

The power of comics is simply this: that it is a democracy, the most level of playing fields.

One of my favorite comics of recent years was, in fact, Lynda Barry's introduction to a previous volume in this series. It touched on what comics are and what they do so well. And it revealed the biggest secret in comics: that anyone can do them.

You just need something to draw with and something to draw on. A pen, some paper. A computer program. You do not need to know anything. You just need to do it. To make it. And then you send it out into the world.

It can be about anything: an account of Hurricane Katrina and its aftermath, a small-town punk-rock adventure, an imaginary story of the life and loves of a failed architect on the run from his life, the story of two robots arguing about gnomes, and a retelling of the first book of the Bible—all of these are comics: small, colored glass squares in the mosaic that forms a picture of what was happening in comics this year, all wonderful, essential parts of a medium that is so often mistaken for a genre.

And if this book impels one person to dig deeper into the world of comics out there, or if one teenager picks it up in a library and sees a way to get something out of her head and into someone else's and begins to draw her own comics, then its purpose is fulfilled.

Page 4, panel 4.

And now, another silent panel. The editor appears to have cheered up enormously. His hair has also cheered up and is now sticking up all over the place, as if he has been running his hands through it while talking, as a necessary aide to communication. Which is, in fact, the case.

NO DIALOGUE

Page 4, panel 5.

Penultimate panel. An idea has struck him. It's getting late. He's raised a finger and is making a suggestion.

EDITOR: Y'know, if you just pretend that the real title for this book is *A Sampler: Some Really Good Comics, Including Extracts from Longer Stories We Thought Could Stand on Their Own,* you could ignore everything I've said so far.

Page 4, panel 6.

Last panel. We've pulled back a way. The stars are coming out. We are still looking at our editor. Now that he's got all that off his chest, the editor looks both relieved and pleased with himself. He's sort of smiling, a bit nervously, perhaps pushed both hands deep into his pockets. And being English, he allows himself the highest possible form of praise for the book he's introducing.

EDITOR: It's not bad, actually.

NEIL GAIMAN

THE BEST AMERICAN

Comics 2010

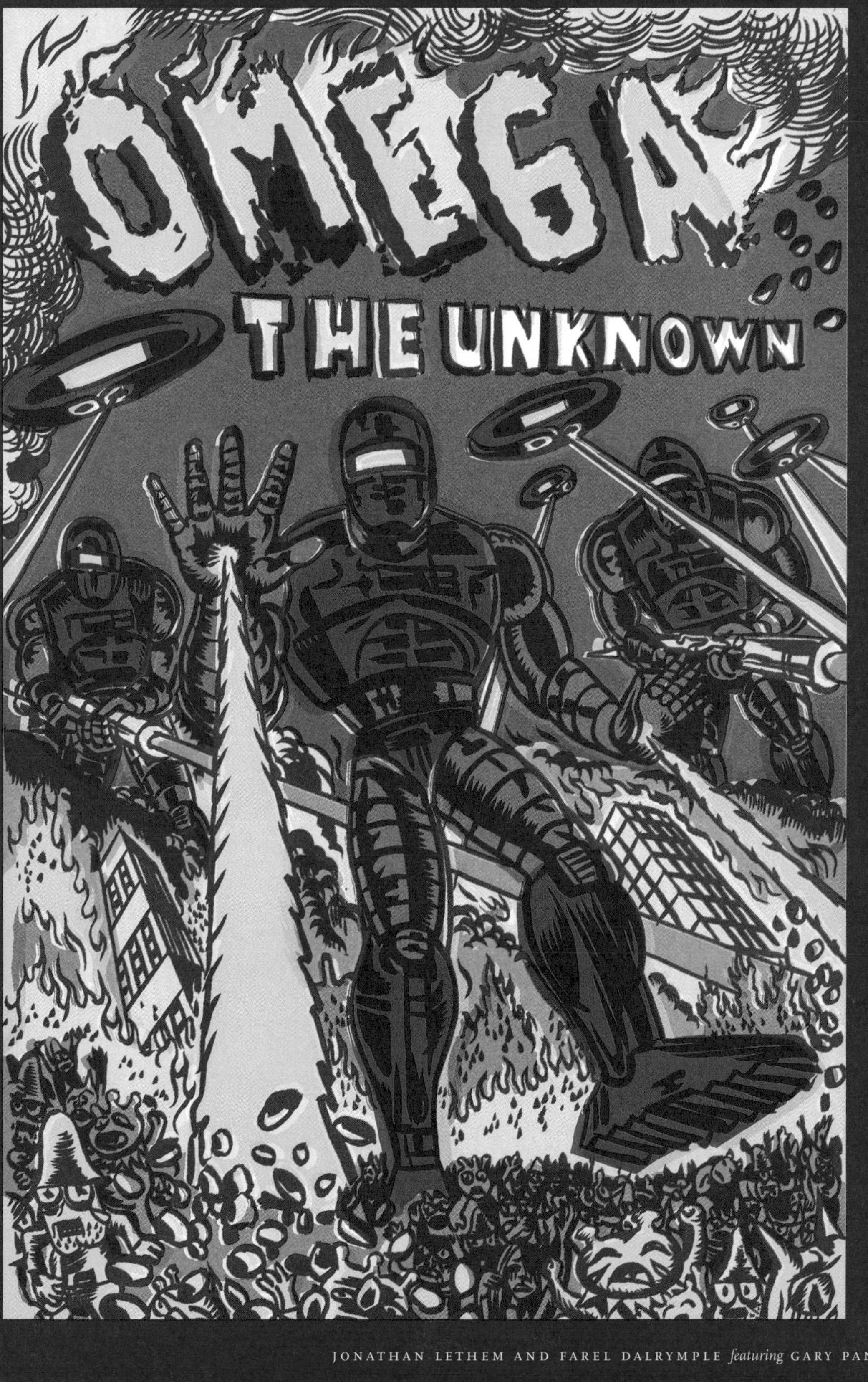
OMEGA
THE UNKNOWN

JONATHAN LETHEM AND FAREL DALRYMPLE *featuring* GARY PANTER

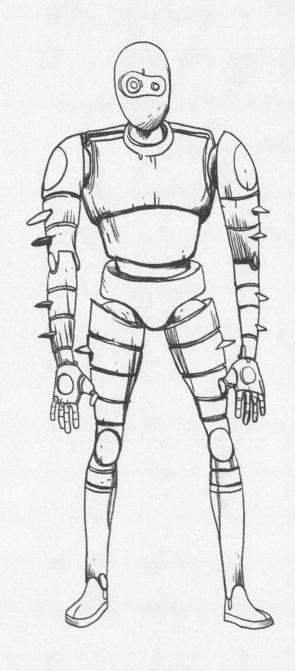

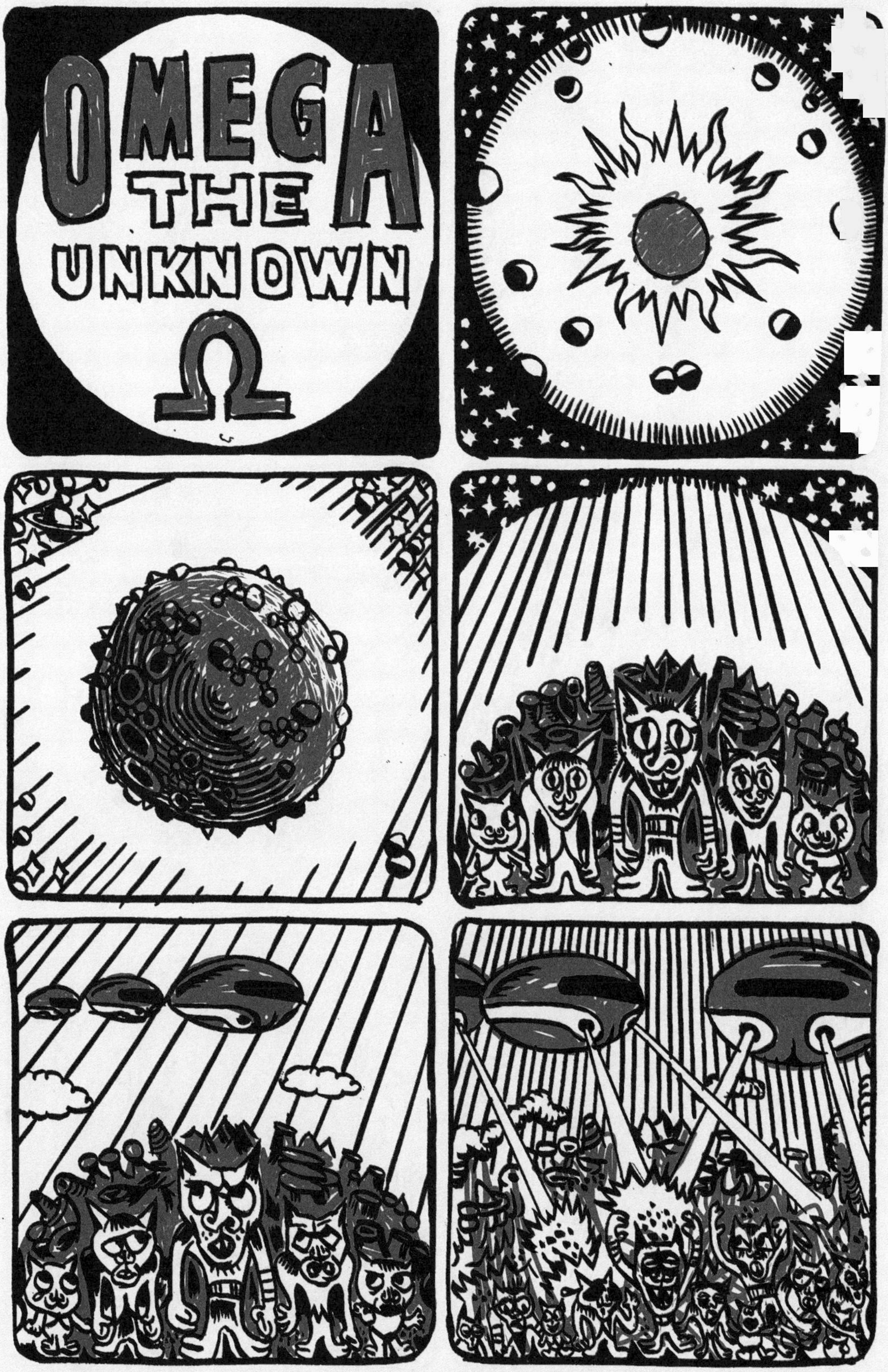
OMEGA THE UNKNOWN
Ω

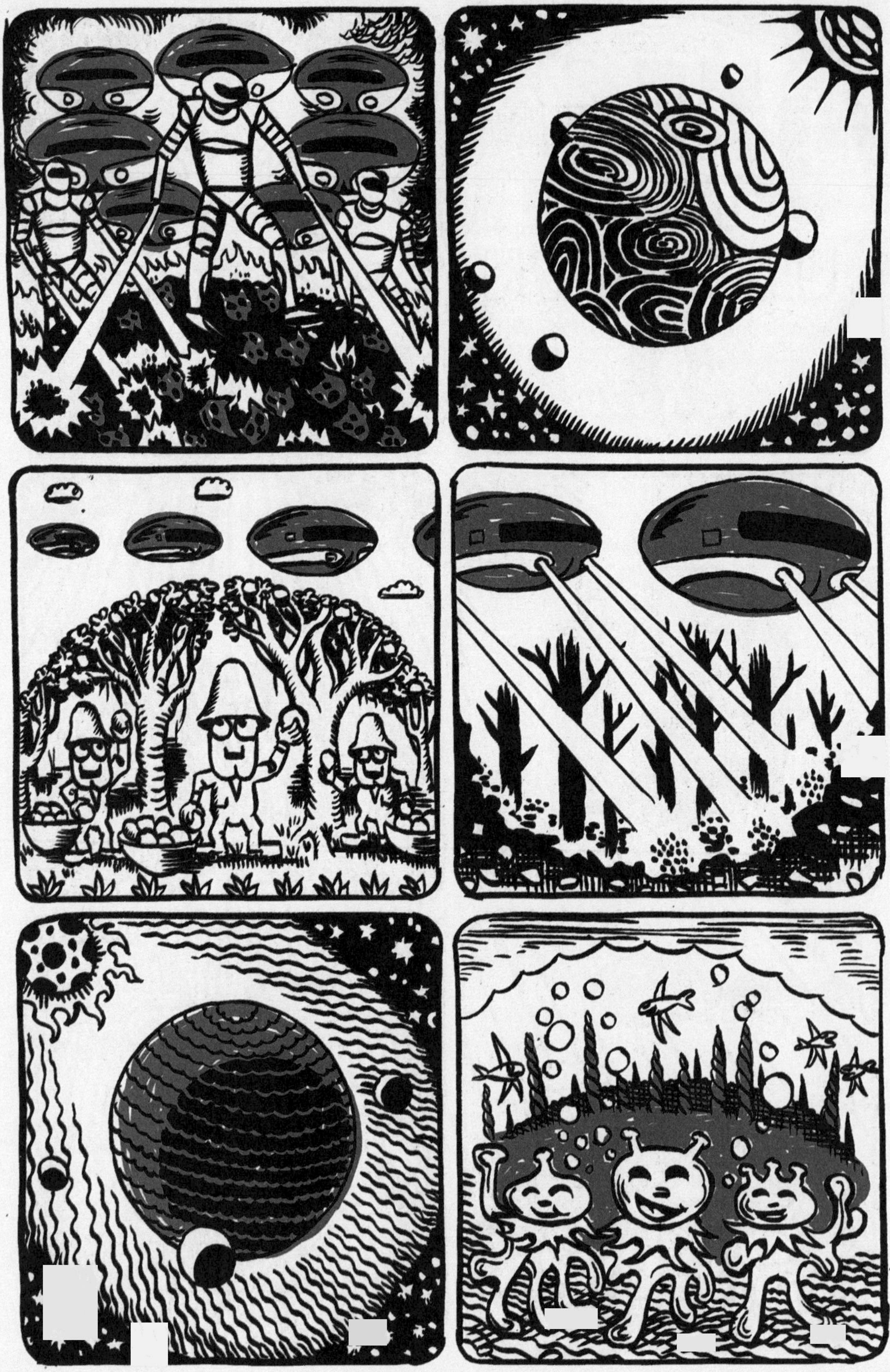

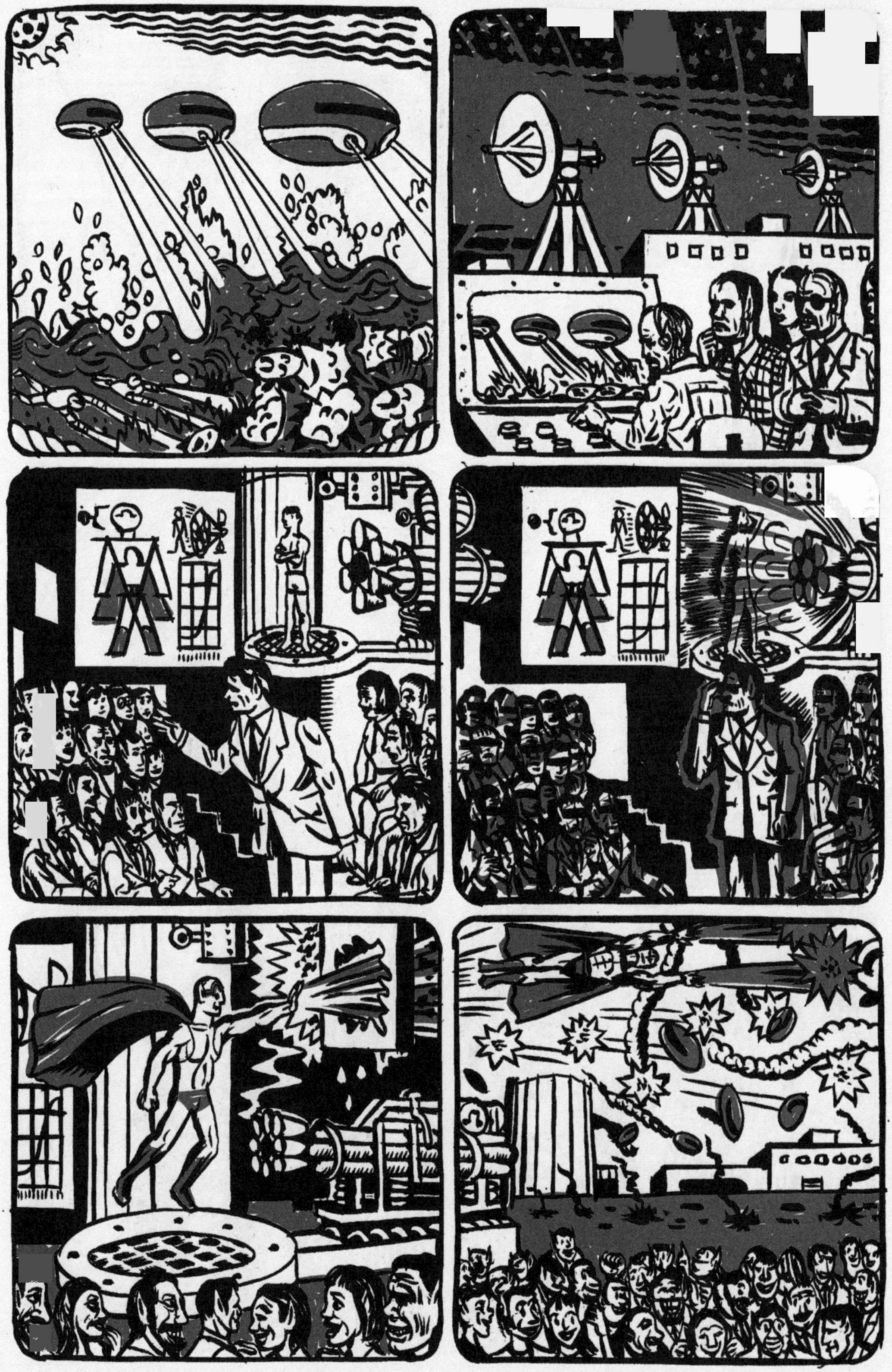

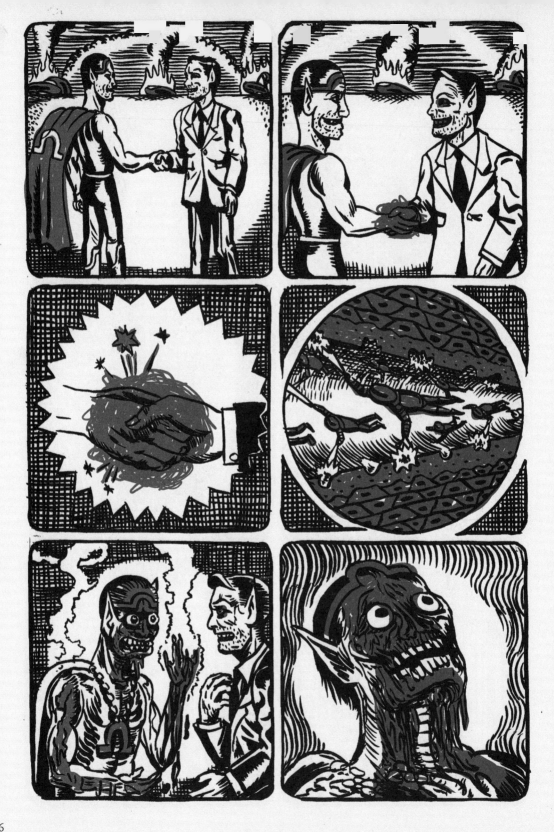

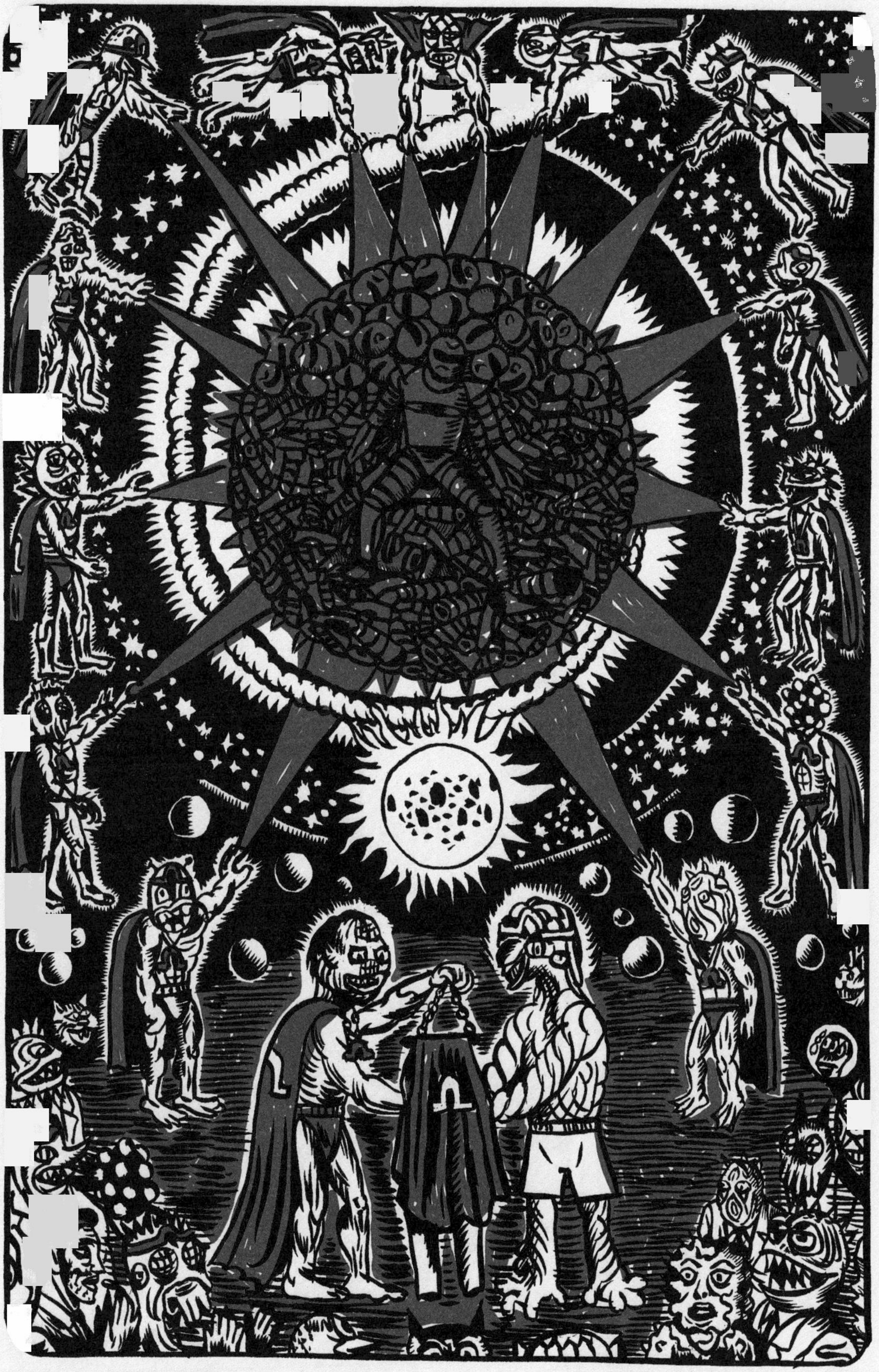

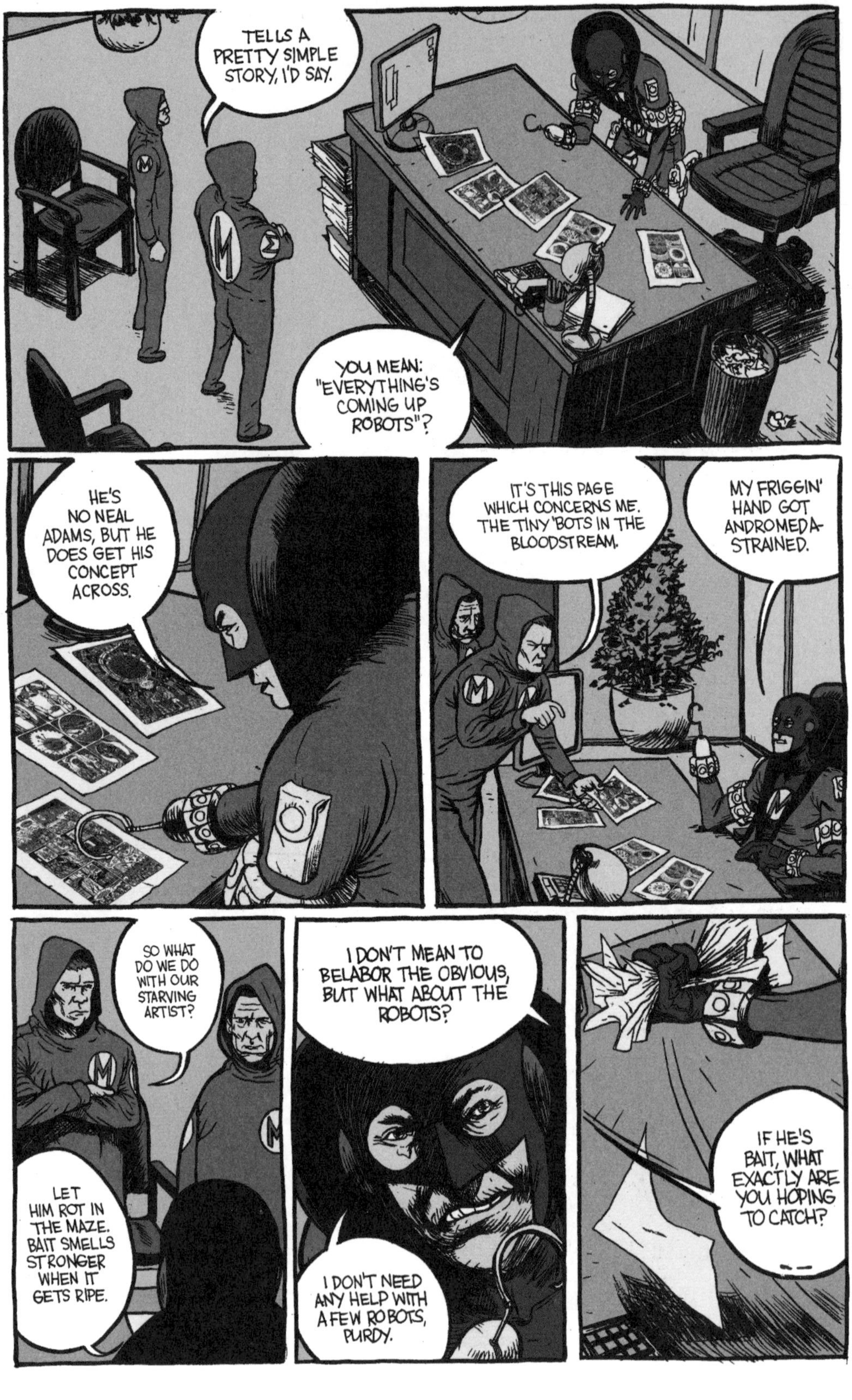
TELLS A PRETTY SIMPLE STORY, I'D SAY.
YOU MEAN: "EVERYTHING'S COMING UP ROBOTS"?
HE'S NO NEAL ADAMS, BUT HE DOES GET HIS CONCEPT ACROSS.
IT'S THIS PAGE WHICH CONCERNS ME. THE TINY 'BOTS IN THE BLOODSTREAM.
MY FRIGGIN' HAND GOT ANDROMEDA-STRAINED.
SO WHAT DO WE DO WITH OUR STARVING ARTIST?
LET HIM ROT IN THE MAZE. BAIT SMELLS STRONGER WHEN IT GETS RIPE.
I DON'T MEAN TO BELABOR THE OBVIOUS, BUT WHAT ABOUT THE ROBOTS?
I DON'T NEED ANY HELP WITH A FEW ROBOTS, PURDY.
IF HE'S BAIT, WHAT EXACTLY ARE YOU HOPING TO CATCH?

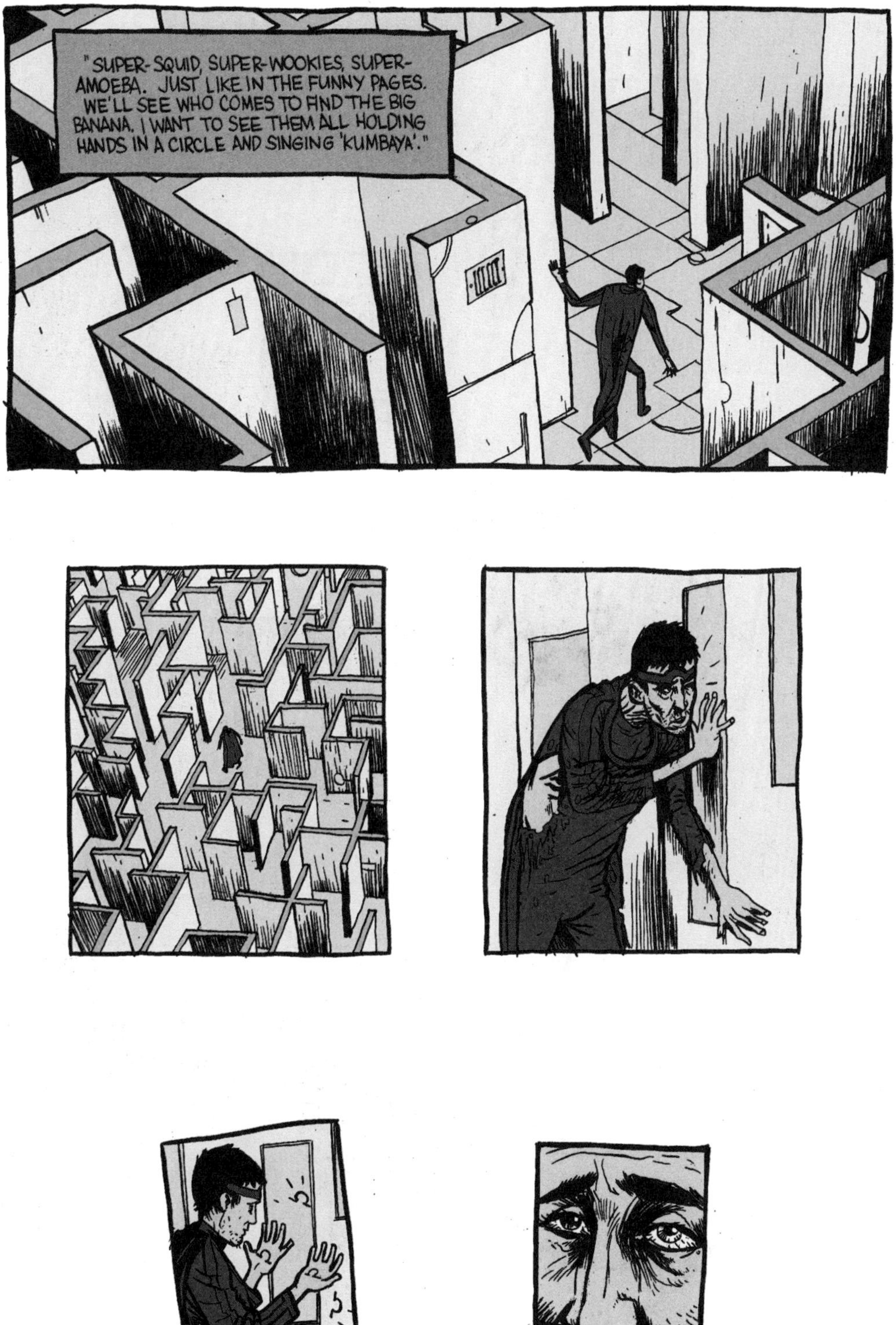
"SUPER-SQUID, SUPER-WOOKIES, SUPER-AMOEBA. JUST LIKE IN THE FUNNY PAGES. WE'LL SEE WHO COMES TO FIND THE BIG BANANA. I WANT TO SEE THEM ALL HOLDING HANDS IN A CIRCLE AND SINGING 'KUMBAYA'."

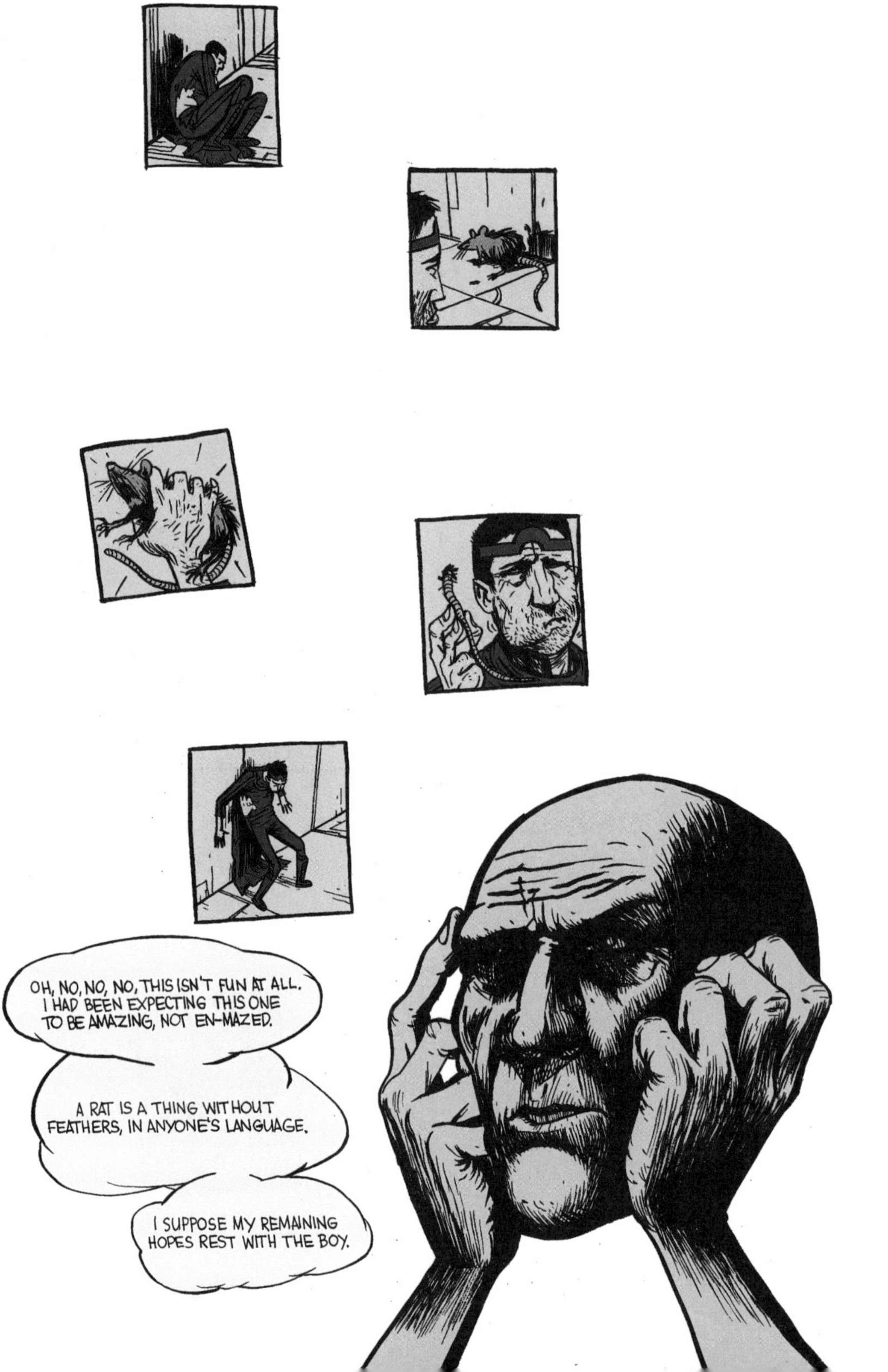
OH, NO, NO, NO, THIS ISN'T FUN AT ALL. I HAD BEEN EXPECTING THIS ONE TO BE AMAZING, NOT EN-MAZED.
A RAT IS A THING WITHOUT FEATHERS, IN ANYONE'S LANGUAGE.
I SUPPOSE MY REMAINING HOPES REST WITH THE BOY.

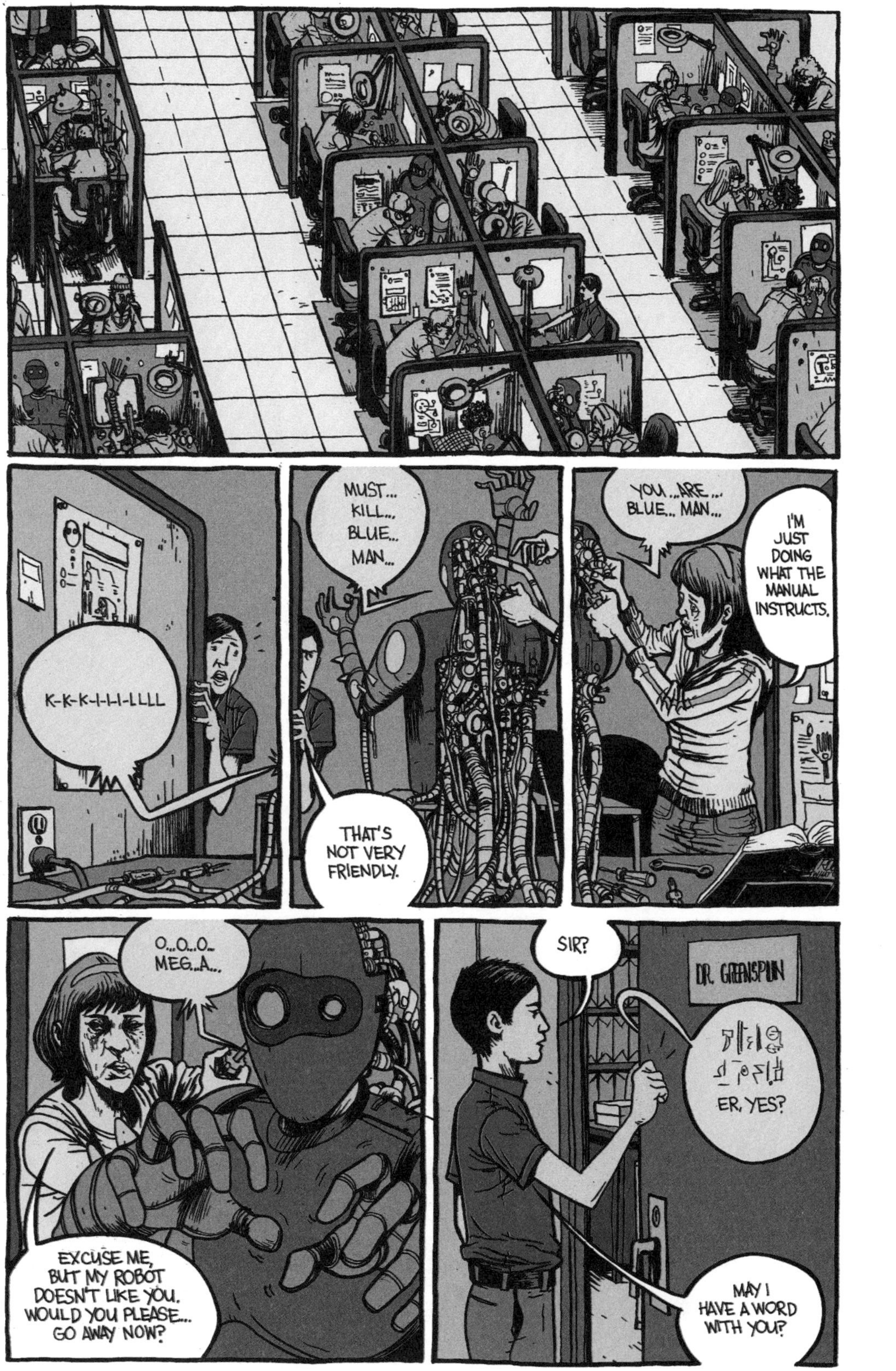
K-K-K-I-I-I-LLLL
MUST... KILL... BLUE... MAN...
THAT'S NOT VERY FRIENDLY.
YOU... ARE... BLUE... MAN...
I'M JUST DOING WHAT THE MANUAL INSTRUCTS.
O...O...O... MEG...A...
EXCUSE ME, BUT MY ROBOT DOESN'T LIKE YOU. WOULD YOU PLEASE... GO AWAY NOW?
SIR?
DR. GREENSPUN
ER, YES?
MAY I HAVE A WORD WITH YOU?

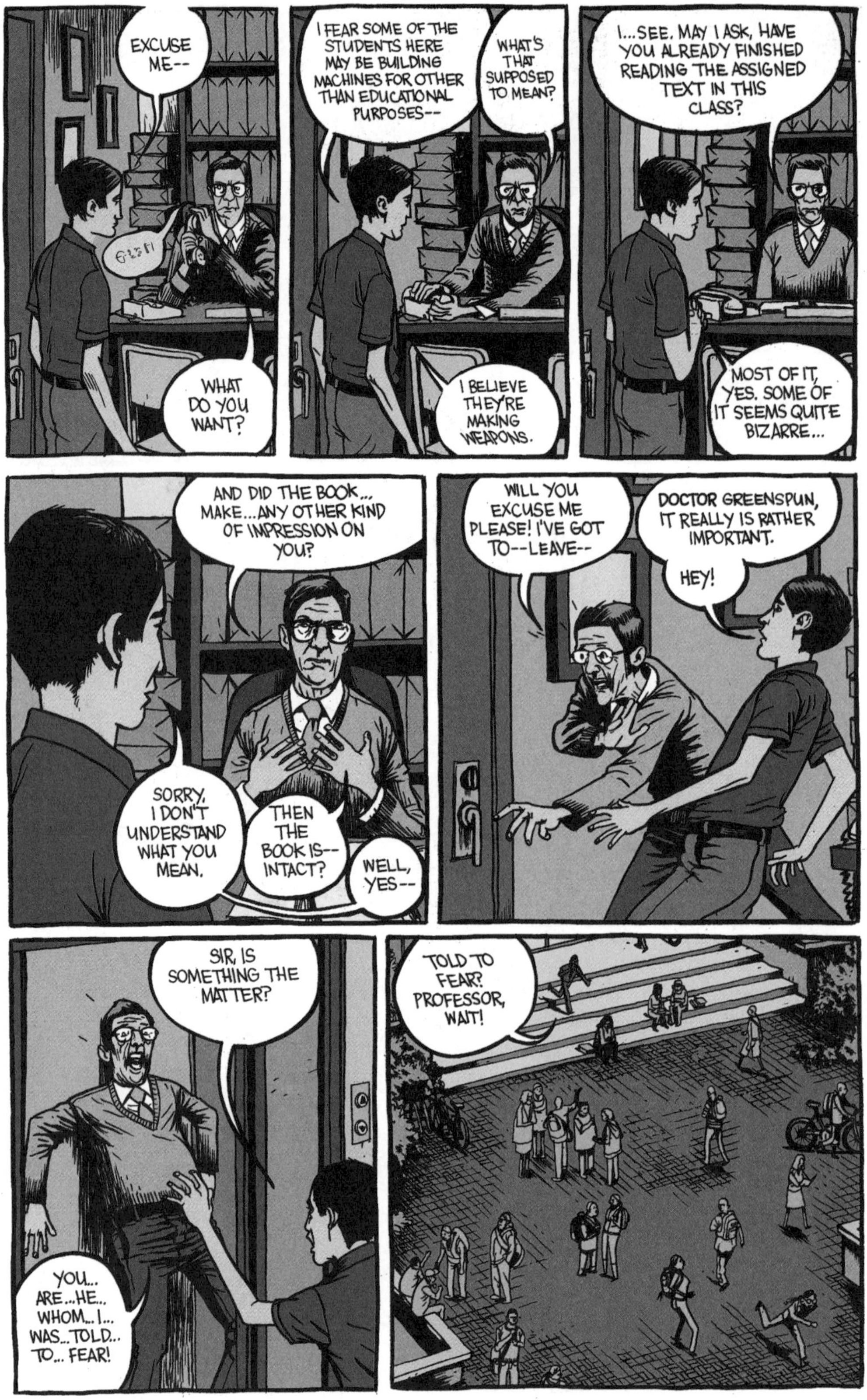
EXCUSE ME--
WHAT DO YOU WANT?
I FEAR SOME OF THE STUDENTS HERE MAY BE BUILDING MACHINES FOR OTHER THAN EDUCATIONAL PURPOSES--
WHAT'S THAT SUPPOSED TO MEAN?
I BELIEVE THEY'RE MAKING WEAPONS.
I...SEE. MAY I ASK, HAVE YOU ALREADY FINISHED READING THE ASSIGNED TEXT IN THIS CLASS?
MOST OF IT, YES. SOME OF IT SEEMS QUITE BIZARRE...
AND DID THE BOOK... MAKE...ANY OTHER KIND OF IMPRESSION ON YOU?
SORRY, I DON'T UNDERSTAND WHAT YOU MEAN.
THEN THE BOOK IS-- INTACT?
WELL, YES--
WILL YOU EXCUSE ME PLEASE! I'VE GOT TO--LEAVE--
DOCTOR GREENSPUN, IT REALLY IS RATHER IMPORTANT.
HEY!
SIR, IS SOMETHING THE MATTER?
YOU... ARE...HE... WHOM...I... WAS...TOLD... TO... FEAR!
TOLD TO FEAR? PROFESSOR, WAIT!

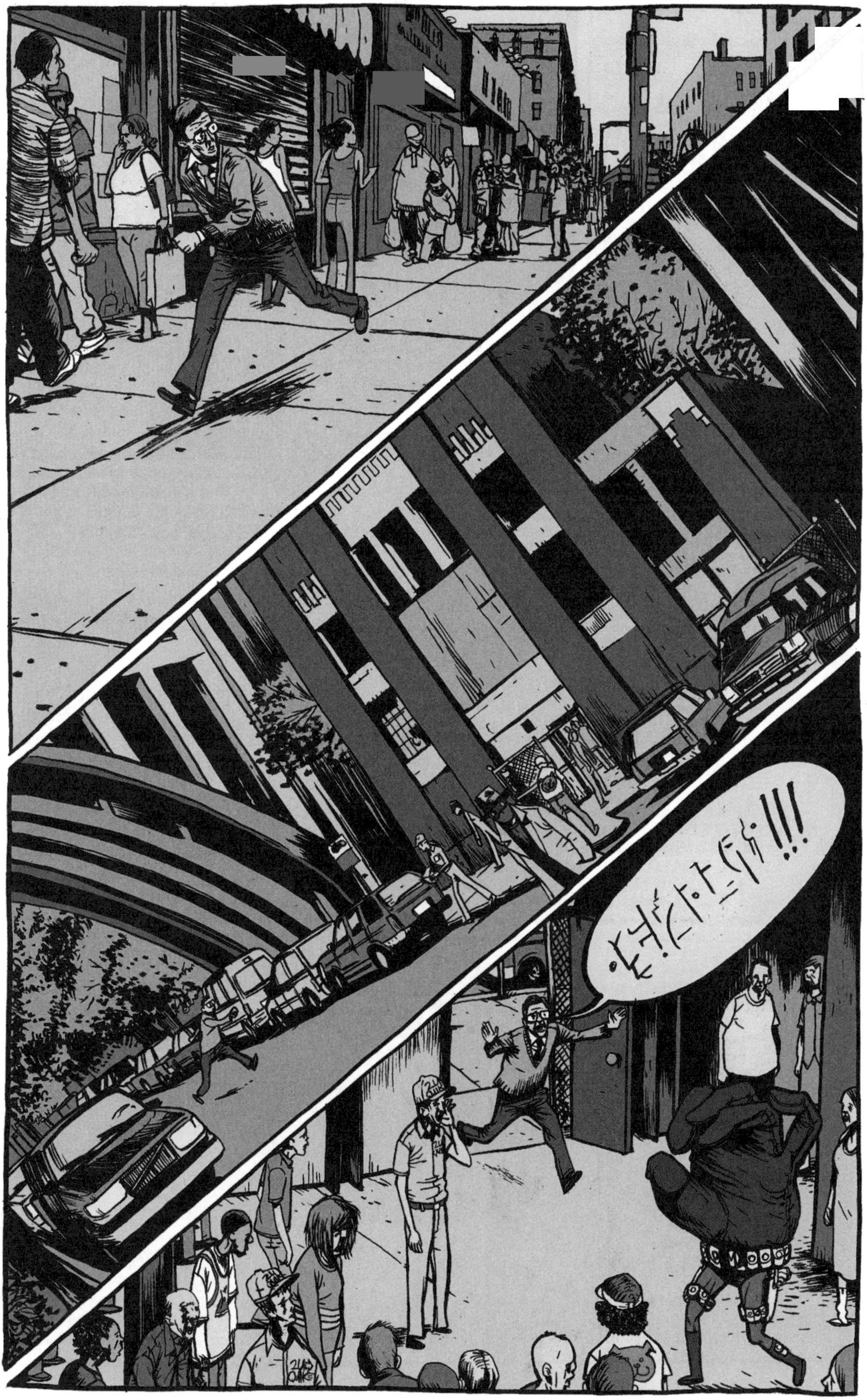

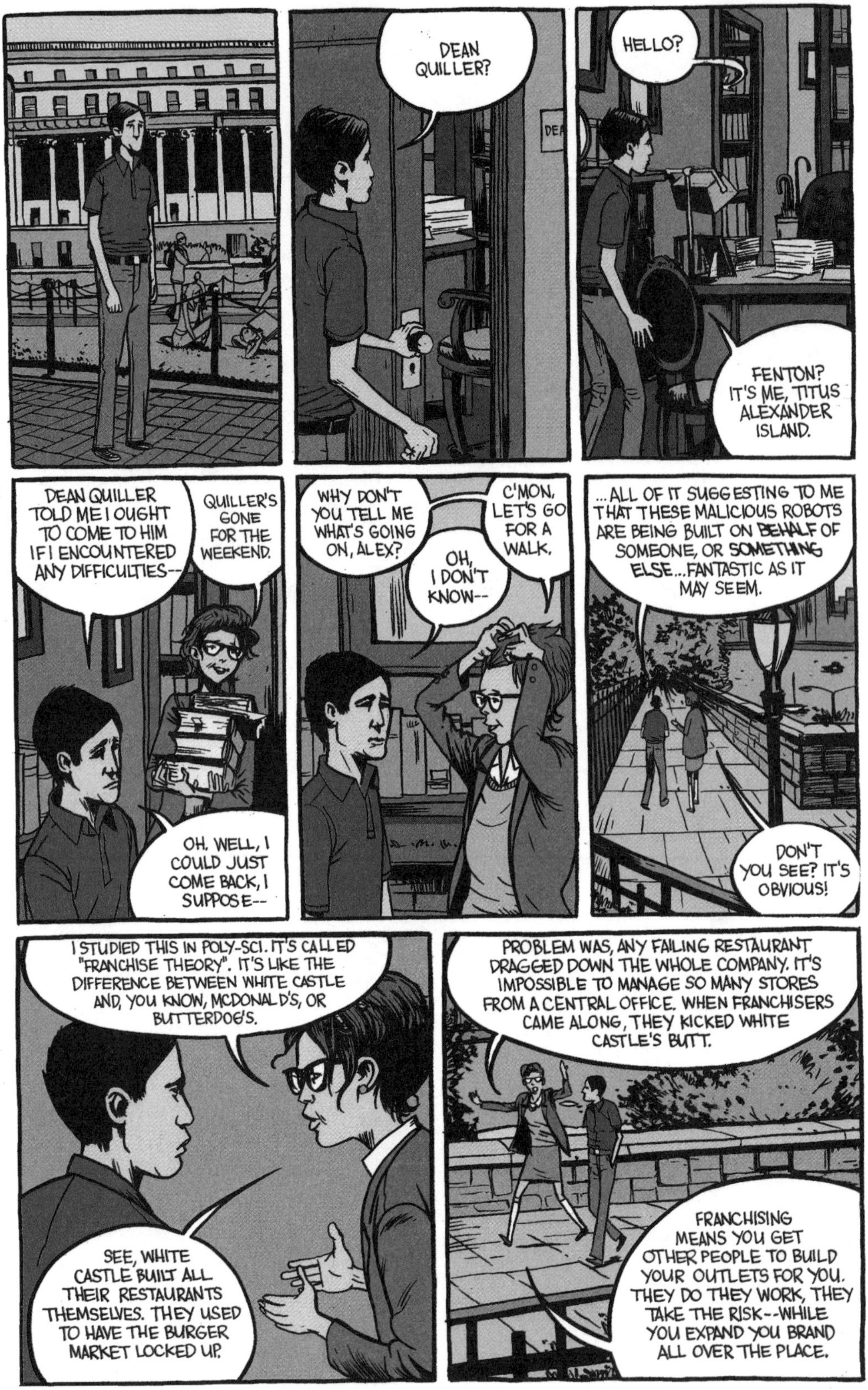
DEAN QUILLER?
HELLO?
FENTON? IT'S ME, TITUS ALEXANDER ISLAND.
DEAN QUILLER TOLD ME I OUGHT TO COME TO HIM IF I ENCOUNTERED ANY DIFFICULTIES--
QUILLER'S GONE FOR THE WEEKEND.
OH. WELL, I COULD JUST COME BACK, I SUPPOSE--
WHY DON'T YOU TELL ME WHAT'S GOING ON, ALEX?
OH, I DON'T KNOW--
C'MON, LET'S GO FOR A WALK.
...ALL OF IT SUGGESTING TO ME THAT THESE MALICIOUS ROBOTS ARE BEING BUILT ON BEHALF OF SOMEONE, OR SOMETHING ELSE...FANTASTIC AS IT MAY SEEM.
DON'T YOU SEE? IT'S OBVIOUS!
I STUDIED THIS IN POLY-SCI. IT'S CALLED "FRANCHISE THEORY". IT'S LIKE THE DIFFERENCE BETWEEN WHITE CASTLE AND, YOU KNOW, MCDONALD'S, OR BUTTERDOG'S.
SEE, WHITE CASTLE BUILT ALL THEIR RESTAURANTS THEMSELVES. THEY USED TO HAVE THE BURGER MARKET LOCKED UP.
PROBLEM WAS, ANY FAILING RESTAURANT DRAGGED DOWN THE WHOLE COMPANY. IT'S IMPOSSIBLE TO MANAGE SO MANY STORES FROM A CENTRAL OFFICE. WHEN FRANCHISERS CAME ALONG, THEY KICKED WHITE CASTLE'S BUTT.
FRANCHISING MEANS YOU GET OTHER PEOPLE TO BUILD YOUR OUTLETS FOR YOU. THEY DO THEY WORK, THEY TAKE THE RISK--WHILE YOU EXPAND YOU BRAND ALL OVER THE PLACE.

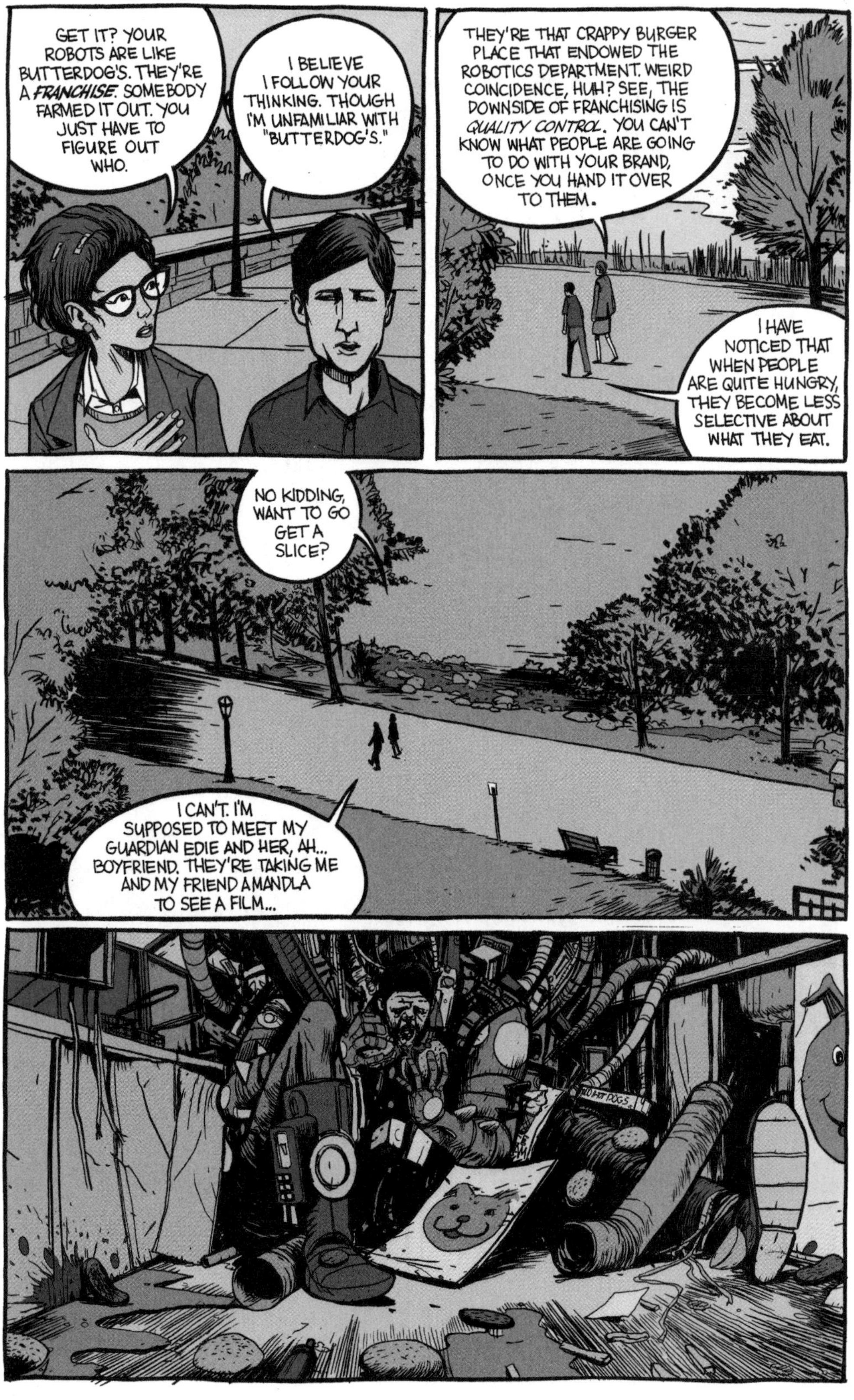
GET IT? YOUR ROBOTS ARE LIKE BUTTERDOG'S. THEY'RE A *FRANCHISE*. SOMEBODY FARMED IT OUT. YOU JUST HAVE TO FIGURE OUT WHO.
I BELIEVE I FOLLOW YOUR THINKING. THOUGH I'M UNFAMILIAR WITH "BUTTERDOG'S."
THEY'RE THAT CRAPPY BURGER PLACE THAT ENDOWED THE ROBOTICS DEPARTMENT. WEIRD COINCIDENCE, HUH? SEE, THE DOWNSIDE OF FRANCHISING IS *QUALITY CONTROL*. YOU CAN'T KNOW WHAT PEOPLE ARE GOING TO DO WITH YOUR BRAND, ONCE YOU HAND IT OVER TO THEM.
I HAVE NOTICED THAT WHEN PEOPLE ARE QUITE HUNGRY, THEY BECOME LESS SELECTIVE ABOUT WHAT THEY EAT.
NO KIDDING, WANT TO GO GET A SLICE?
I CAN'T. I'M SUPPOSED TO MEET MY GUARDIAN EDIE AND HER, AH... BOYFRIEND. THEY'RE TAKING ME AND MY FRIEND AMANDLA TO SEE A FILM...

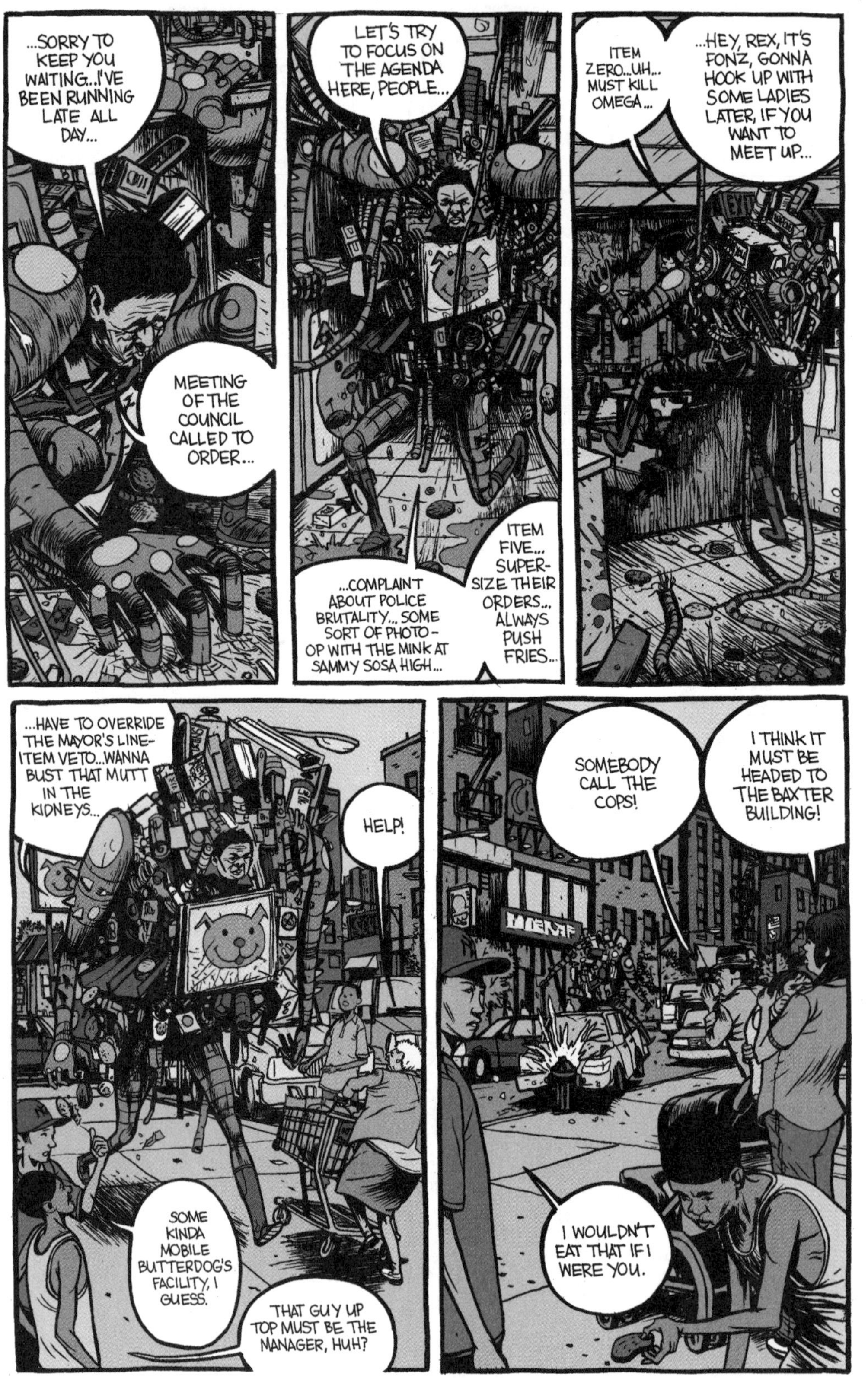
...SORRY TO KEEP YOU WAITING...I'VE BEEN RUNNING LATE ALL DAY...
MEETING OF THE COUNCIL CALLED TO ORDER...
LET'S TRY TO FOCUS ON THE AGENDA HERE, PEOPLE...
...COMPLAINT ABOUT POLICE BRUTALITY... SOME SORT OF PHOTO-OP WITH THE MINK AT SAMMY SOSA HIGH...
ITEM FIVE... SUPER-SIZE THEIR ORDERS... ALWAYS PUSH FRIES...
ITEM ZERO...UH... MUST KILL OMEGA...
...HEY, REX, IT'S FONZ, GONNA HOOK UP WITH SOME LADIES LATER, IF YOU WANT TO MEET UP...
...HAVE TO OVERRIDE THE MAYOR'S LINE-ITEM VETO...WANNA BUST THAT MUTT IN THE KIDNEYS...
HELP!
SOME KINDA MOBILE BUTTERDOG'S FACILITY, I GUESS.
THAT GUY UP TOP MUST BE THE MANAGER, HUH?
SOMEBODY CALL THE COPS!
I THINK IT MUST BE HEADED TO THE BAXTER BUILDING!
I WOULDN'T EAT THAT IF I WERE YOU.

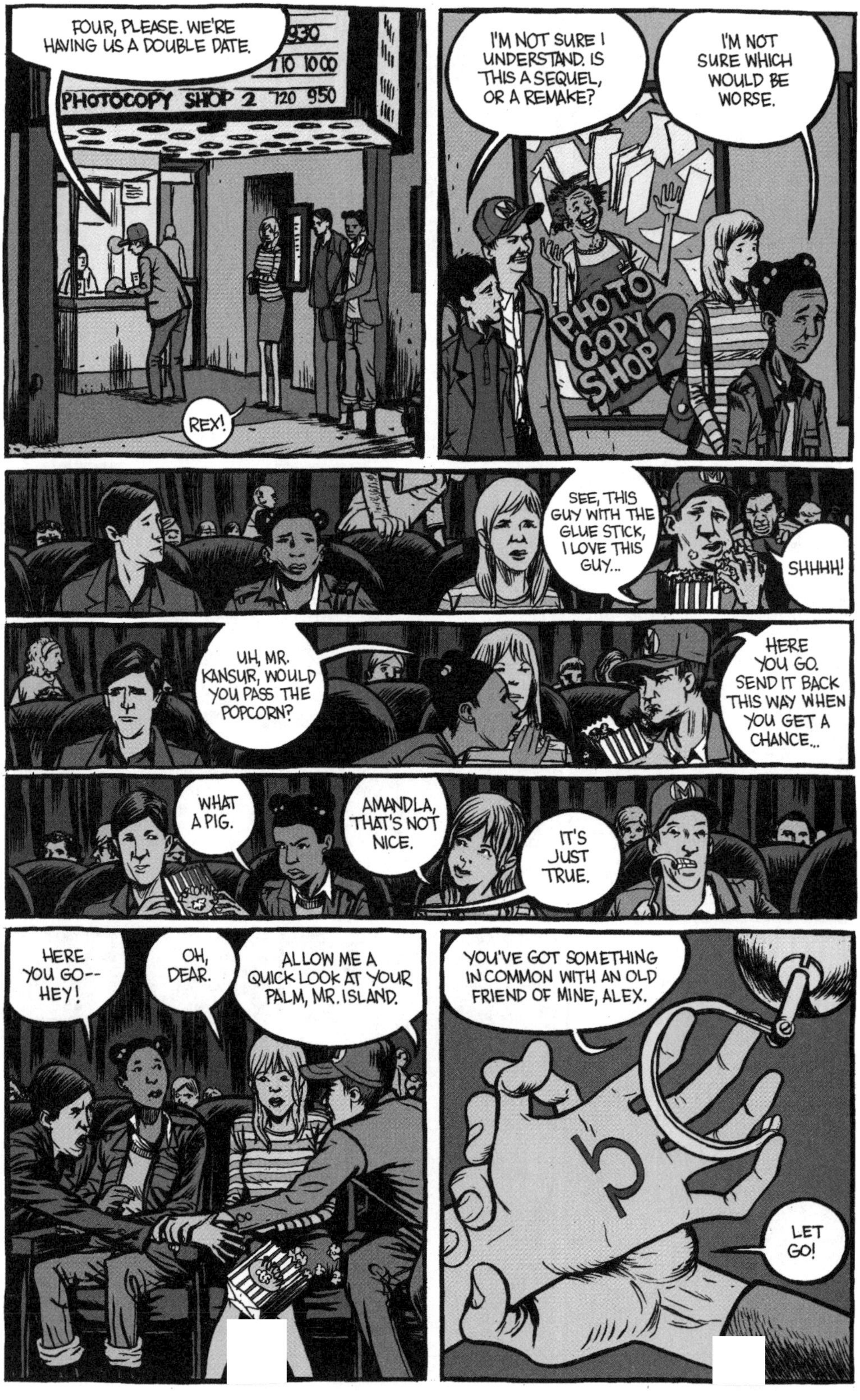
FOUR, PLEASE. WE'RE HAVING US A DOUBLE DATE.
PHOTOCOPY SHOP 2 720 950
REX!
I'M NOT SURE I UNDERSTAND. IS THIS A SEQUEL, OR A REMAKE?
I'M NOT SURE WHICH WOULD BE WORSE.
PHOTO COPY SHOP 2
SEE, THIS GUY WITH THE GLUE STICK, I LOVE THIS GUY...
SHHHH!
UH, MR. KANSUR, WOULD YOU PASS THE POPCORN?
HERE YOU GO. SEND IT BACK THIS WAY WHEN YOU GET A CHANCE...
WHAT A PIG.
AMANDLA, THAT'S NOT NICE.
IT'S JUST TRUE.
HERE YOU GO-- HEY!
OH, DEAR.
ALLOW ME A QUICK LOOK AT YOUR PALM, MR. ISLAND.
YOU'VE GOT SOMETHING IN COMMON WITH AN OLD FRIEND OF MINE, ALEX.
LET GO!

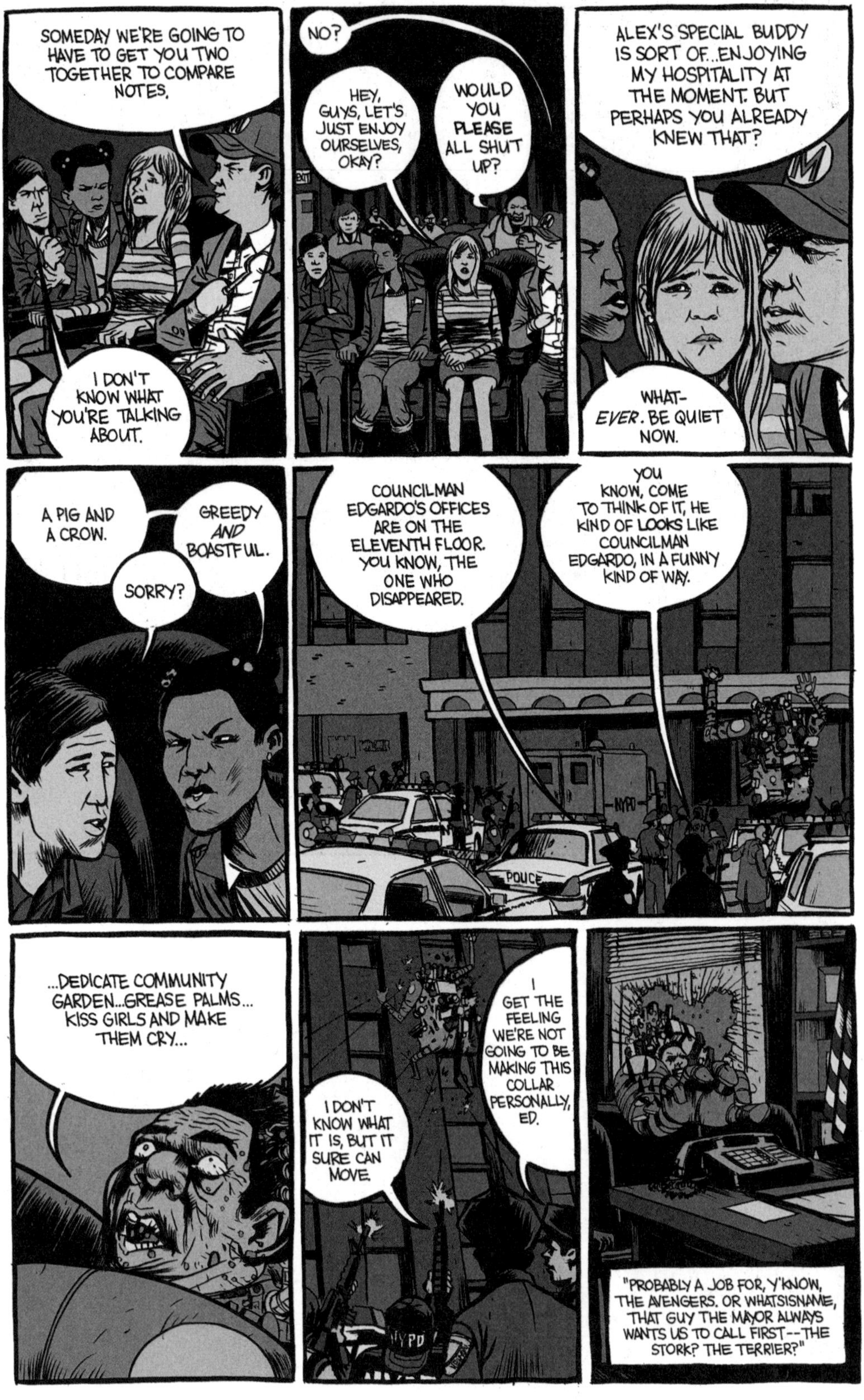
SOMEDAY WE'RE GOING TO HAVE TO GET YOU TWO TOGETHER TO COMPARE NOTES.
I DON'T KNOW WHAT YOU'RE TALKING ABOUT.
NO?
HEY, GUYS, LET'S JUST ENJOY OURSELVES, OKAY?
WOULD YOU PLEASE ALL SHUT UP?
EXIT
ALEX'S SPECIAL BUDDY IS SORT OF...ENJOYING MY HOSPITALITY AT THE MOMENT. BUT PERHAPS YOU ALREADY KNEW THAT?
WHAT-*EVER*. BE QUIET NOW.
A PIG AND A CROW.
GREEDY *AND* BOASTFUL.
SORRY?
COUNCILMAN EDGARDO'S OFFICES ARE ON THE ELEVENTH FLOOR. YOU KNOW, THE ONE WHO DISAPPEARED.
YOU KNOW, COME TO THINK OF IT, HE KIND OF LOOKS LIKE COUNCILMAN EDGARDO, IN A FUNNY KIND OF WAY.
NYPD
POLICE
...DEDICATE COMMUNITY GARDEN...GREASE PALMS... KISS GIRLS AND MAKE THEM CRY...
I GET THE FEELING WE'RE NOT GOING TO BE MAKING THIS COLLAR PERSONALLY, ED.
I DON'T KNOW WHAT IT IS, BUT IT SURE CAN MOVE.
NYPD
"PROBABLY A JOB FOR, Y'KNOW, THE AVENGERS. OR WHATSISNAME, THAT GUY THE MAYOR ALWAYS WANTS US TO CALL FIRST--THE STORK? THE TERRIER?"

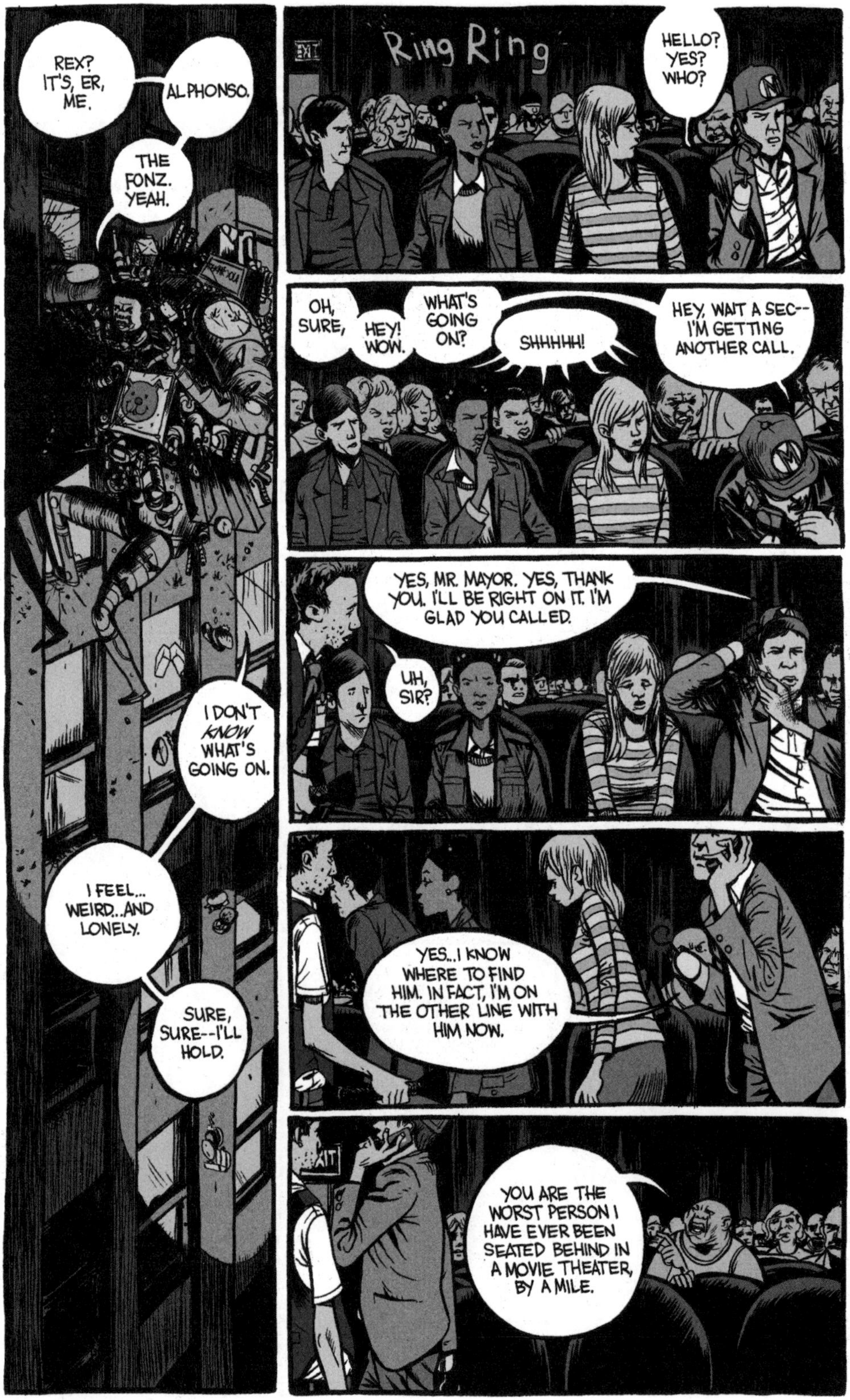
REX? IT'S, ER, ME.
ALPHONSO.
THE FONZ. YEAH.
I DON'T *KNOW* WHAT'S GOING ON.
I FEEL... WEIRD...AND LONELY.
SURE, SURE--I'LL HOLD.
Ring Ring
HELLO? YES? WHO?
OH, SURE,
HEY! WOW.
WHAT'S GOING ON?
SHHHHH!
HEY, WAIT A SEC-- I'M GETTING ANOTHER CALL.
YES, MR. MAYOR. YES, THANK YOU. I'LL BE RIGHT ON IT. I'M GLAD YOU CALLED.
UH, SIR?
YES... I KNOW WHERE TO FIND HIM. IN FACT, I'M ON THE OTHER LINE WITH HIM NOW.
YOU ARE THE WORST PERSON I HAVE EVER BEEN SEATED BEHIND IN A MOVIE THEATER, BY A MILE.

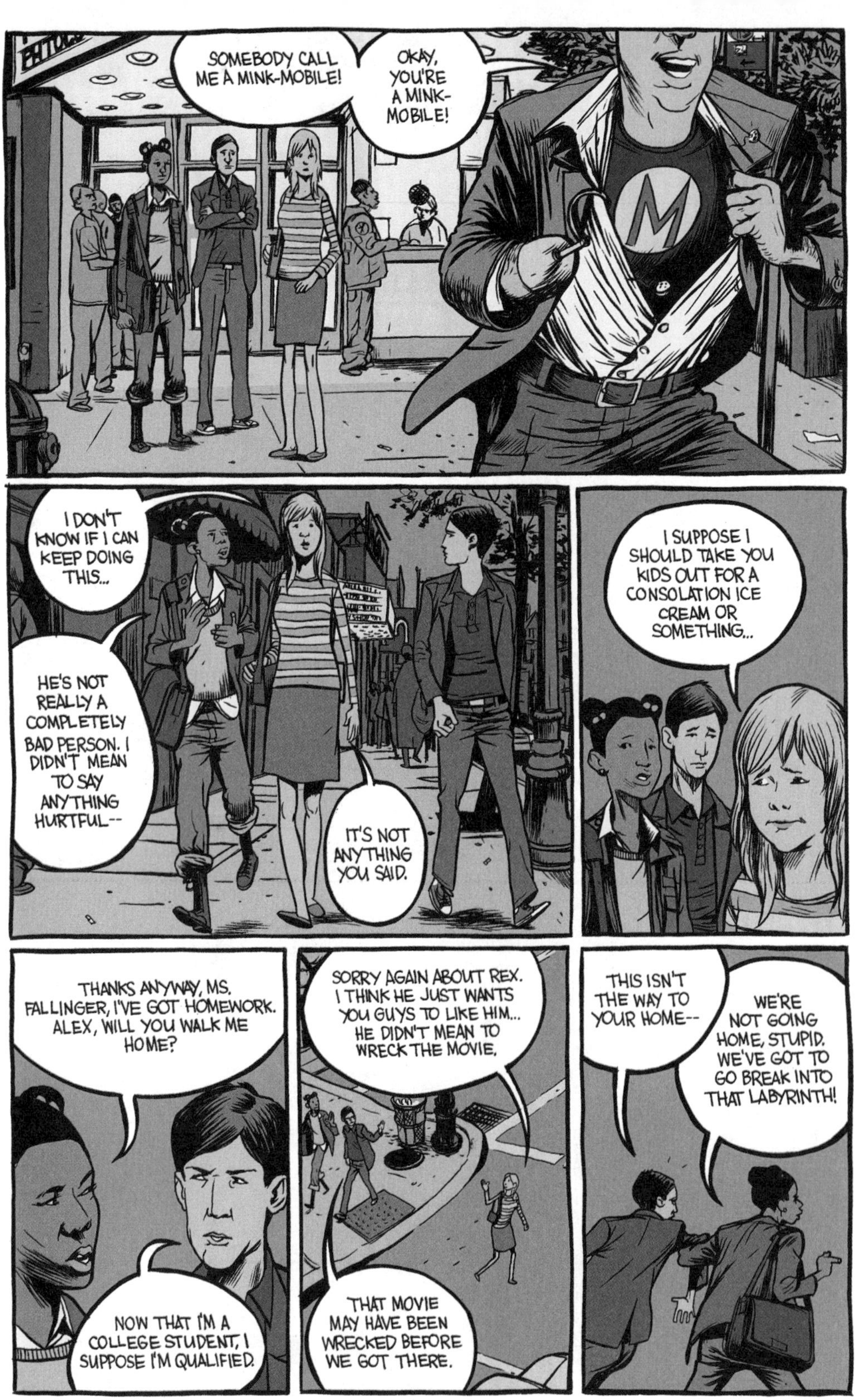
SOMEBODY CALL ME A MINK-MOBILE!
OKAY, YOU'RE A MINK-MOBILE!
I DON'T KNOW IF I CAN KEEP DOING THIS...
HE'S NOT REALLY A COMPLETELY BAD PERSON. I DIDN'T MEAN TO SAY ANYTHING HURTFUL--
IT'S NOT ANYTHING YOU SAID.
I SUPPOSE I SHOULD TAKE YOU KIDS OUT FOR A CONSOLATION ICE CREAM OR SOMETHING...
THANKS ANYWAY, MS. FALLINGER, I'VE GOT HOMEWORK. ALEX, WILL YOU WALK ME HOME?
NOW THAT I'M A COLLEGE STUDENT, I SUPPOSE I'M QUALIFIED.
SORRY AGAIN ABOUT REX. I THINK HE JUST WANTS YOU GUYS TO LIKE HIM... HE DIDN'T MEAN TO WRECK THE MOVIE.
THAT MOVIE MAY HAVE BEEN WRECKED BEFORE WE GOT THERE.
THIS ISN'T THE WAY TO YOUR HOME--
WE'RE NOT GOING HOME, STUPID. WE'VE GOT TO GO BREAK INTO THAT LABYRINTH!

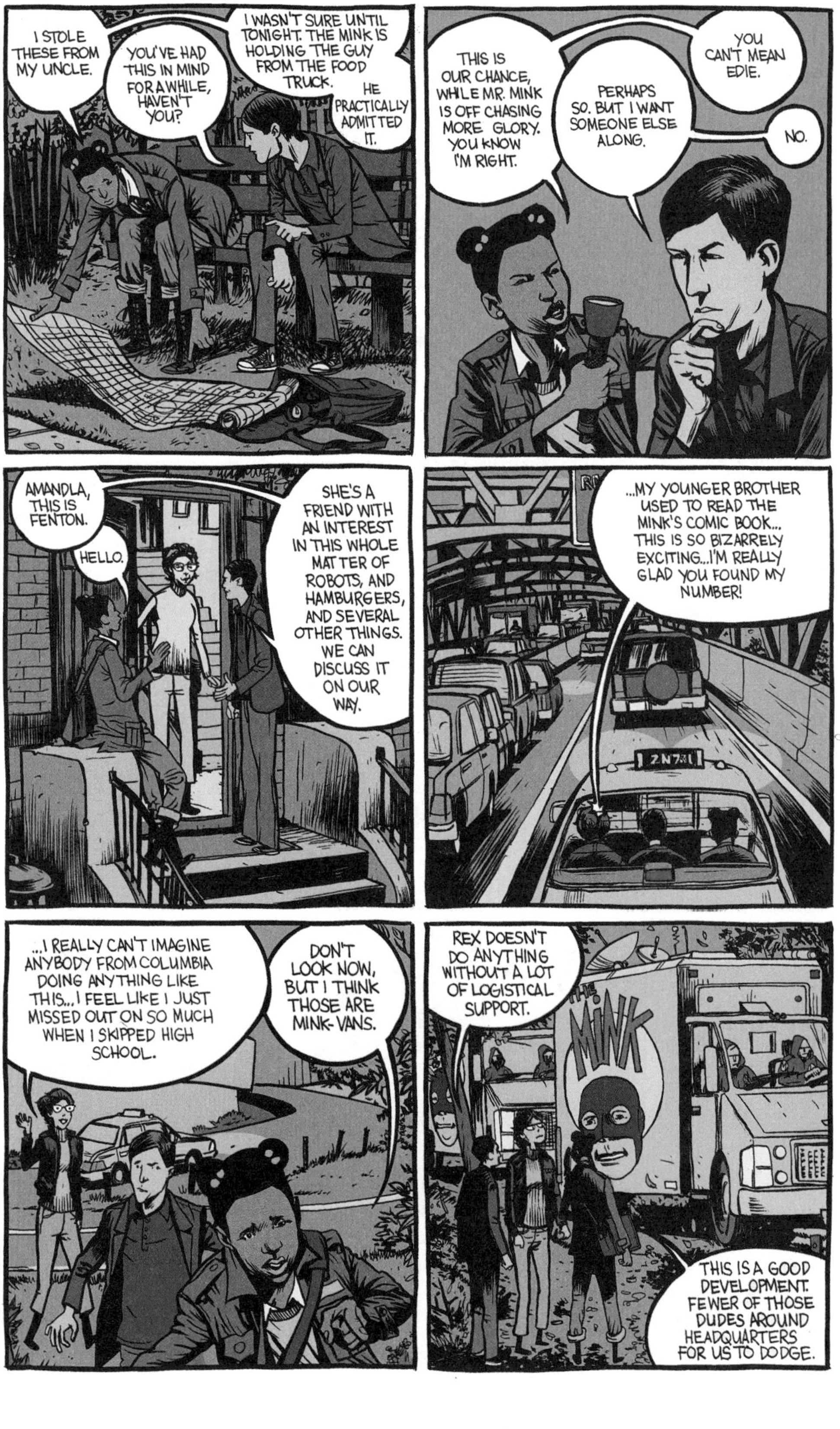
I STOLE THESE FROM MY UNCLE.
YOU'VE HAD THIS IN MIND FOR A WHILE, HAVEN'T YOU?
I WASN'T SURE UNTIL TONIGHT. THE MINK IS HOLDING THE GUY FROM THE FOOD TRUCK.
HE PRACTICALLY ADMITTED IT.
THIS IS OUR CHANCE, WHILE MR. MINK IS OFF CHASING MORE GLORY. YOU KNOW I'M RIGHT.
PERHAPS SO. BUT I WANT SOMEONE ELSE ALONG.
YOU CAN'T MEAN EDIE.
NO.
AMANDLA, THIS IS FENTON.
HELLO.
SHE'S A FRIEND WITH AN INTEREST IN THIS WHOLE MATTER OF ROBOTS, AND HAMBURGERS, AND SEVERAL OTHER THINGS. WE CAN DISCUSS IT ON OUR WAY.
...MY YOUNGER BROTHER USED TO READ THE MINK'S COMIC BOOK... THIS IS SO BIZARRELY EXCITING... I'M REALLY GLAD YOU FOUND MY NUMBER!
ZN731
...I REALLY CAN'T IMAGINE ANYBODY FROM COLUMBIA DOING ANYTHING LIKE THIS... I FEEL LIKE I JUST MISSED OUT ON SO MUCH WHEN I SKIPPED HIGH SCHOOL.
DON'T LOOK NOW, BUT I THINK THOSE ARE MINK-VANS.
REX DOESN'T DO ANYTHING WITHOUT A LOT OF LOGISTICAL SUPPORT.
THE MINK
THIS IS A GOOD DEVELOPMENT. FEWER OF THOSE DUDES AROUND HEADQUARTERS FOR US TO DODGE.

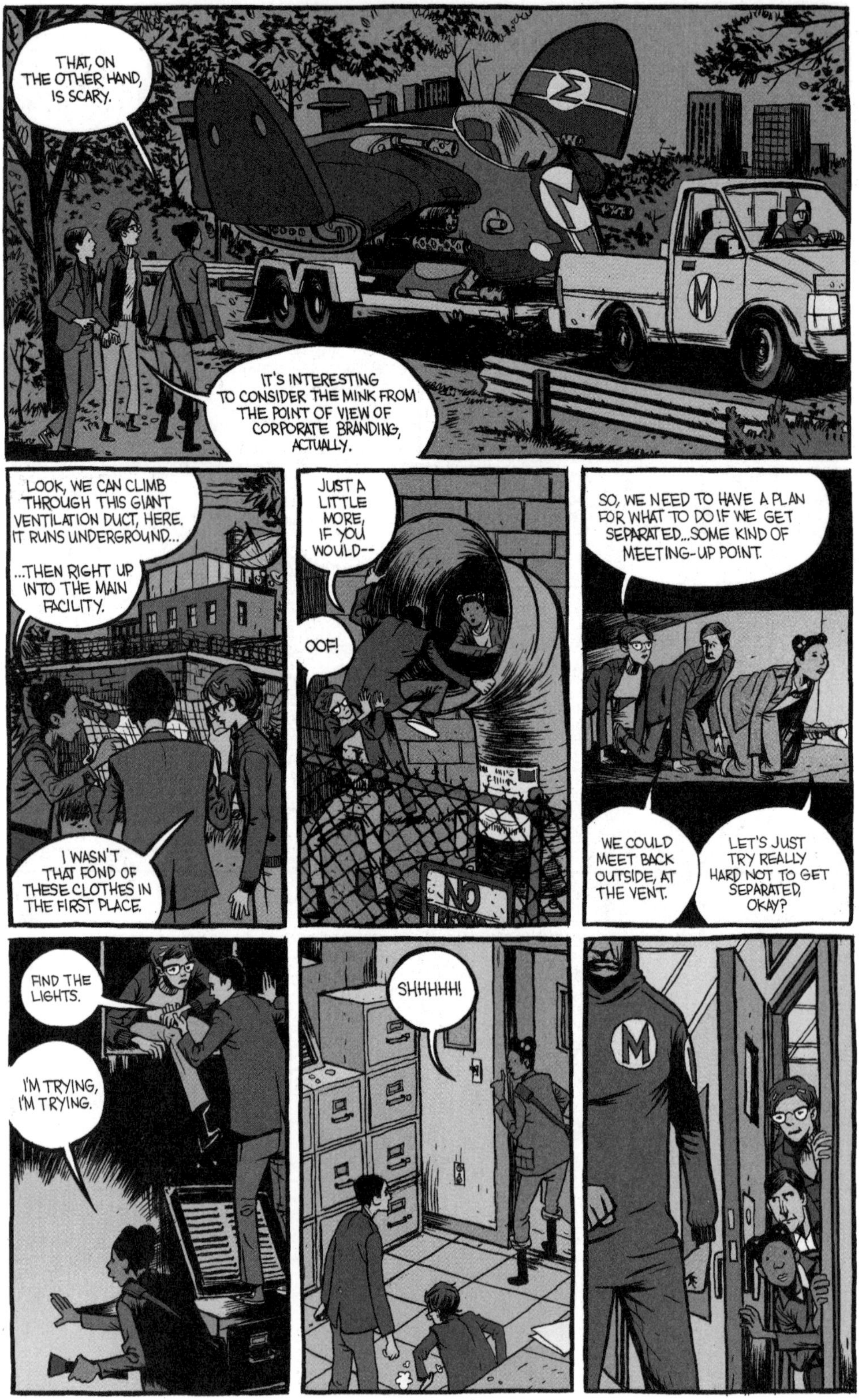
THAT, ON THE OTHER HAND, IS SCARY.
IT'S INTERESTING TO CONSIDER THE MINK FROM THE POINT OF VIEW OF CORPORATE BRANDING, ACTUALLY.
LOOK, WE CAN CLIMB THROUGH THIS GIANT VENTILATION DUCT, HERE. IT RUNS UNDERGROUND...
...THEN RIGHT UP INTO THE MAIN FACILITY.
I WASN'T THAT FOND OF THESE CLOTHES IN THE FIRST PLACE.
JUST A LITTLE MORE, IF YOU WOULD--
OOF!
NO
SO, WE NEED TO HAVE A PLAN FOR WHAT TO DO IF WE GET SEPARATED...SOME KIND OF MEETING-UP POINT.
WE COULD MEET BACK OUTSIDE, AT THE VENT.
LET'S JUST TRY REALLY HARD NOT TO GET SEPARATED, OKAY?
FIND THE LIGHTS.
I'M TRYING, I'M TRYING.
SHHHHH!

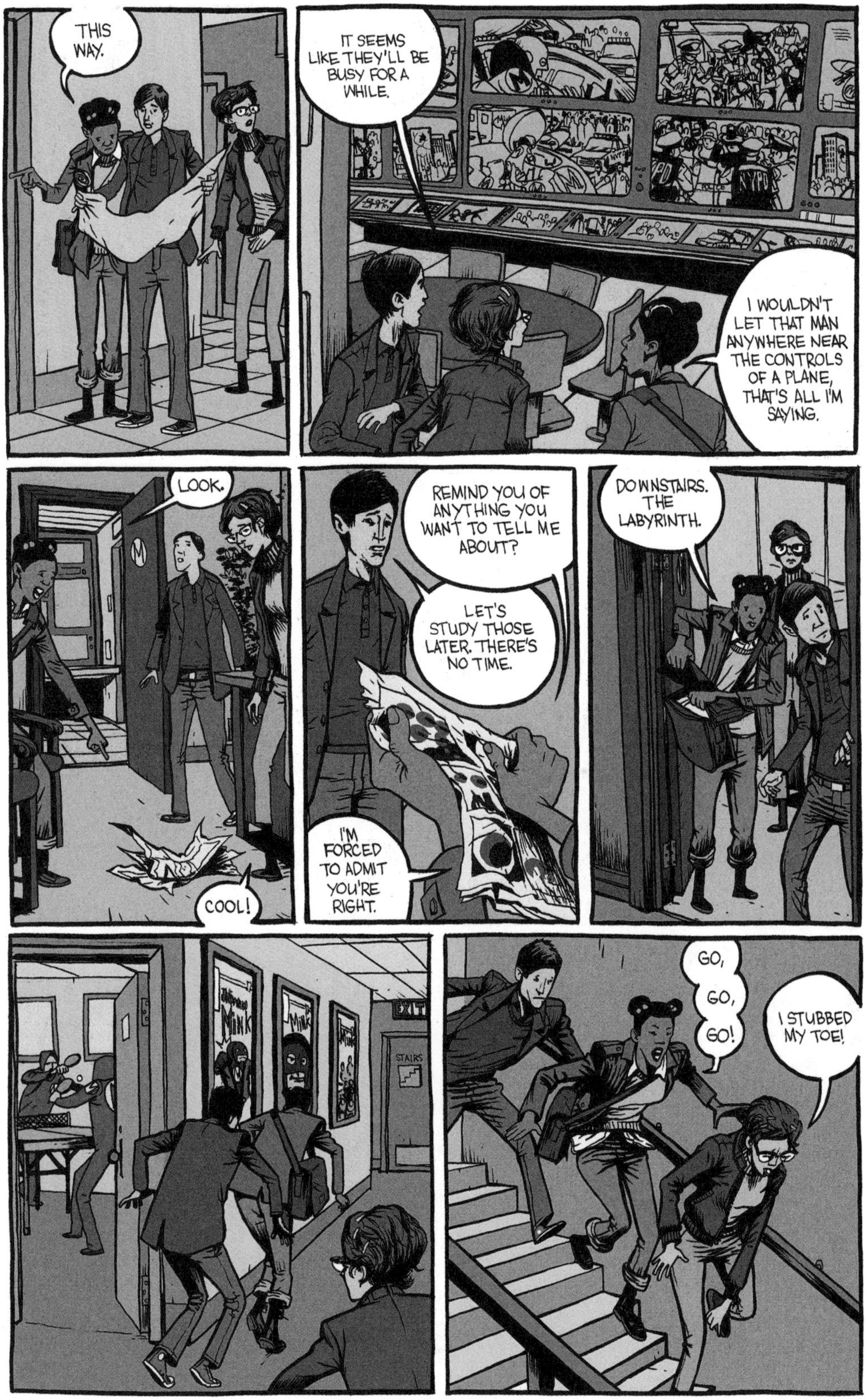

THIS WAY.
IT SEEMS LIKE THEY'LL BE BUSY FOR A WHILE.
I WOULDN'T LET THAT MAN ANYWHERE NEAR THE CONTROLS OF A PLANE, THAT'S ALL I'M SAYING.
LOOK.
COOL!
REMIND YOU OF ANYTHING YOU WANT TO TELL ME ABOUT?
LET'S STUDY THOSE LATER. THERE'S NO TIME.
I'M FORCED TO ADMIT YOU'RE RIGHT.
DOWNSTAIRS. THE LABYRINTH.
EXIT
STAIRS
GO,
GO,
GO!
I STUBBED MY TOE!

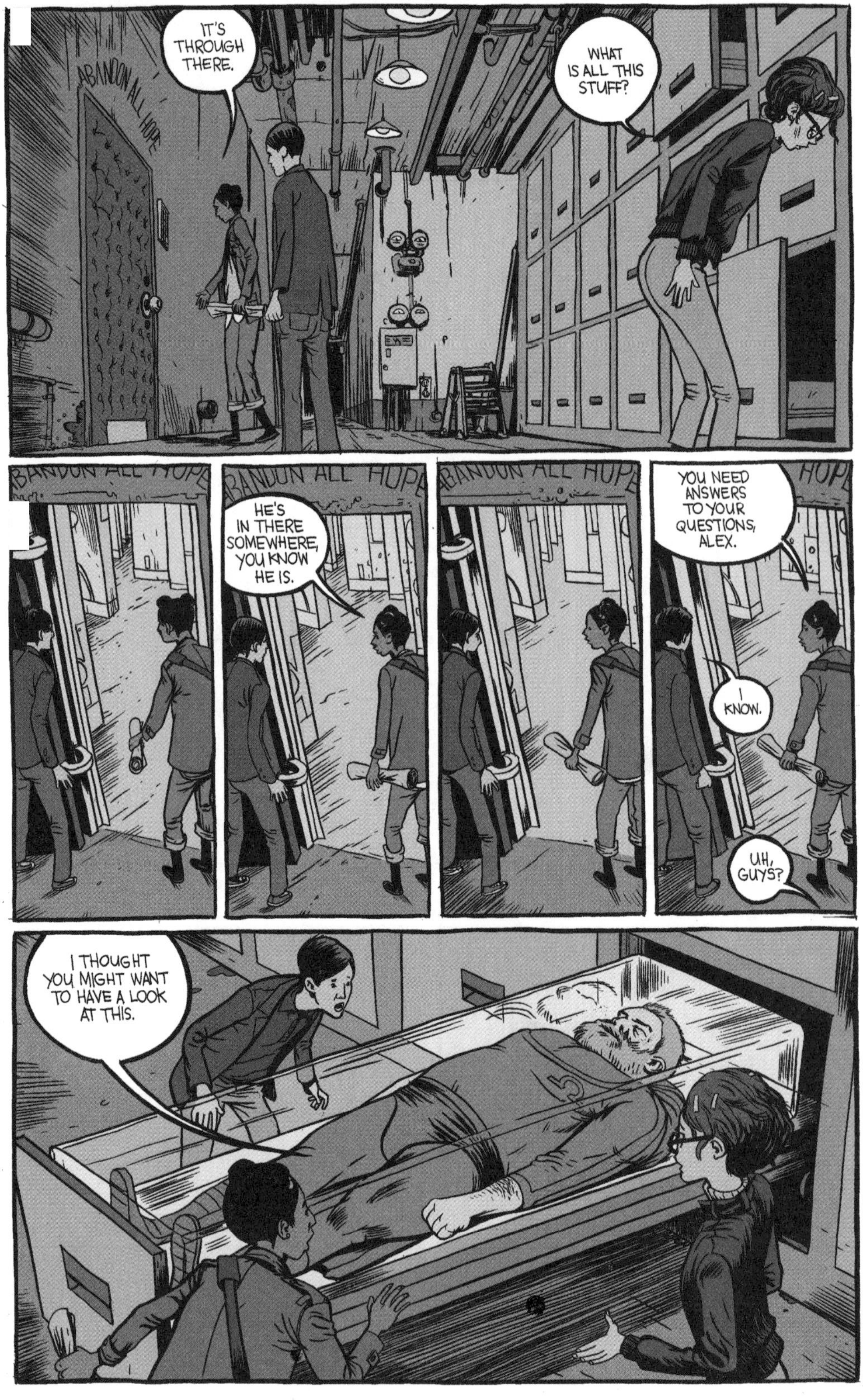
IT'S THROUGH THERE.
ABANDON ALL HOPE
WHAT IS ALL THIS STUFF?
ABANDON ALL HOPE
HE'S IN THERE SOMEWHERE, YOU KNOW HE IS.
YOU NEED ANSWERS TO YOUR QUESTIONS, ALEX.
I KNOW.
UH, GUYS?
I THOUGHT YOU MIGHT WANT TO HAVE A LOOK AT THIS.

Ceci n'est pas une comic

A G.W. BUSH ADMINISTRATION RETROSPECTIVE*

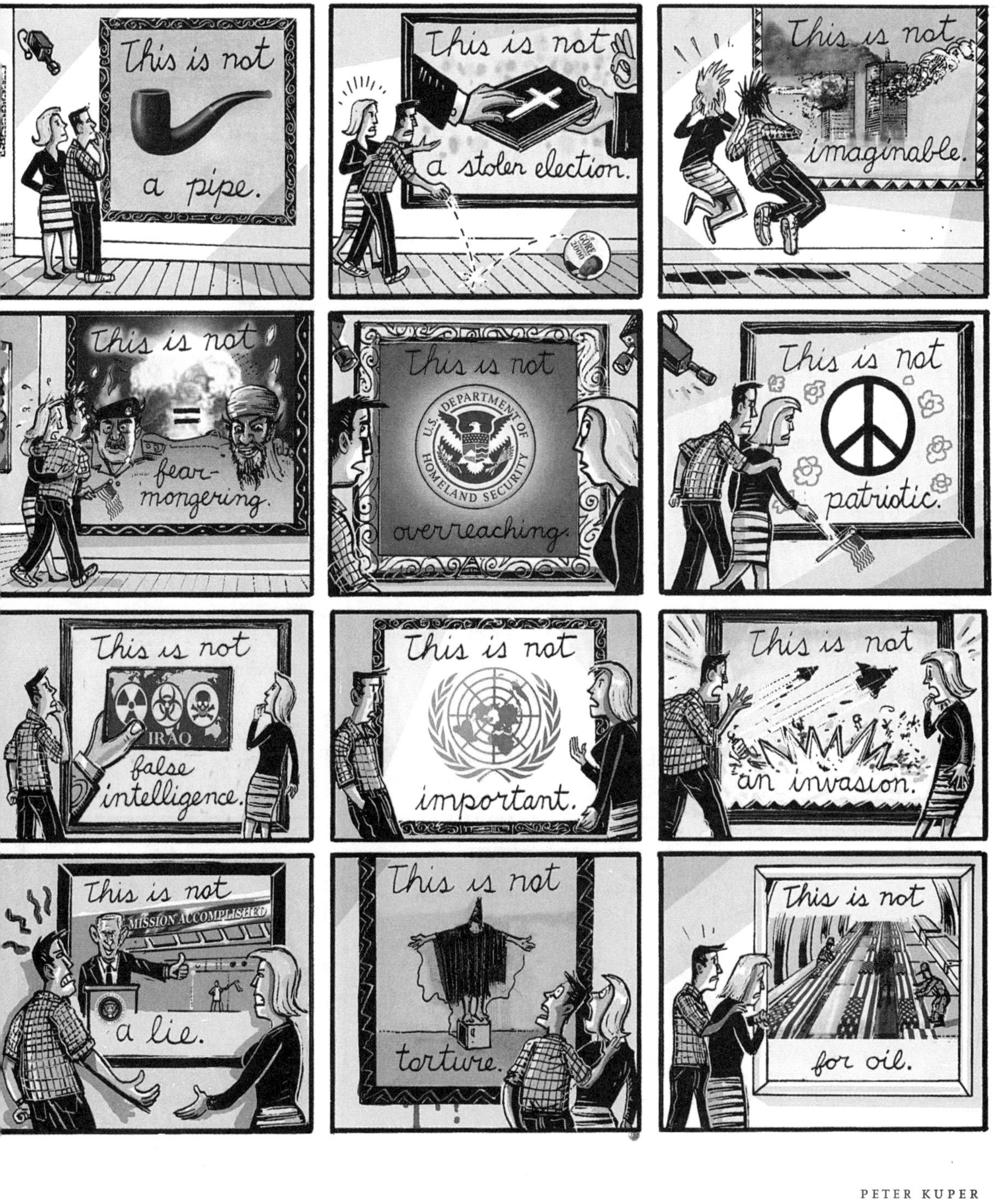
This is not a pipe.
This is not a stolen election.
GORE 2000
This is not imaginable.
This is not fear-mongering.
This is not overreaching.
U.S. DEPARTMENT OF HOMELAND SECURITY
This is not patriotic.
This is not false intelligence.
IRAQ
This is not important.
This is not an invasion.
This is not a lie.
MISSION ACCOMPLISHED
This is not torture.
This is not for oil.

PETER KUPER

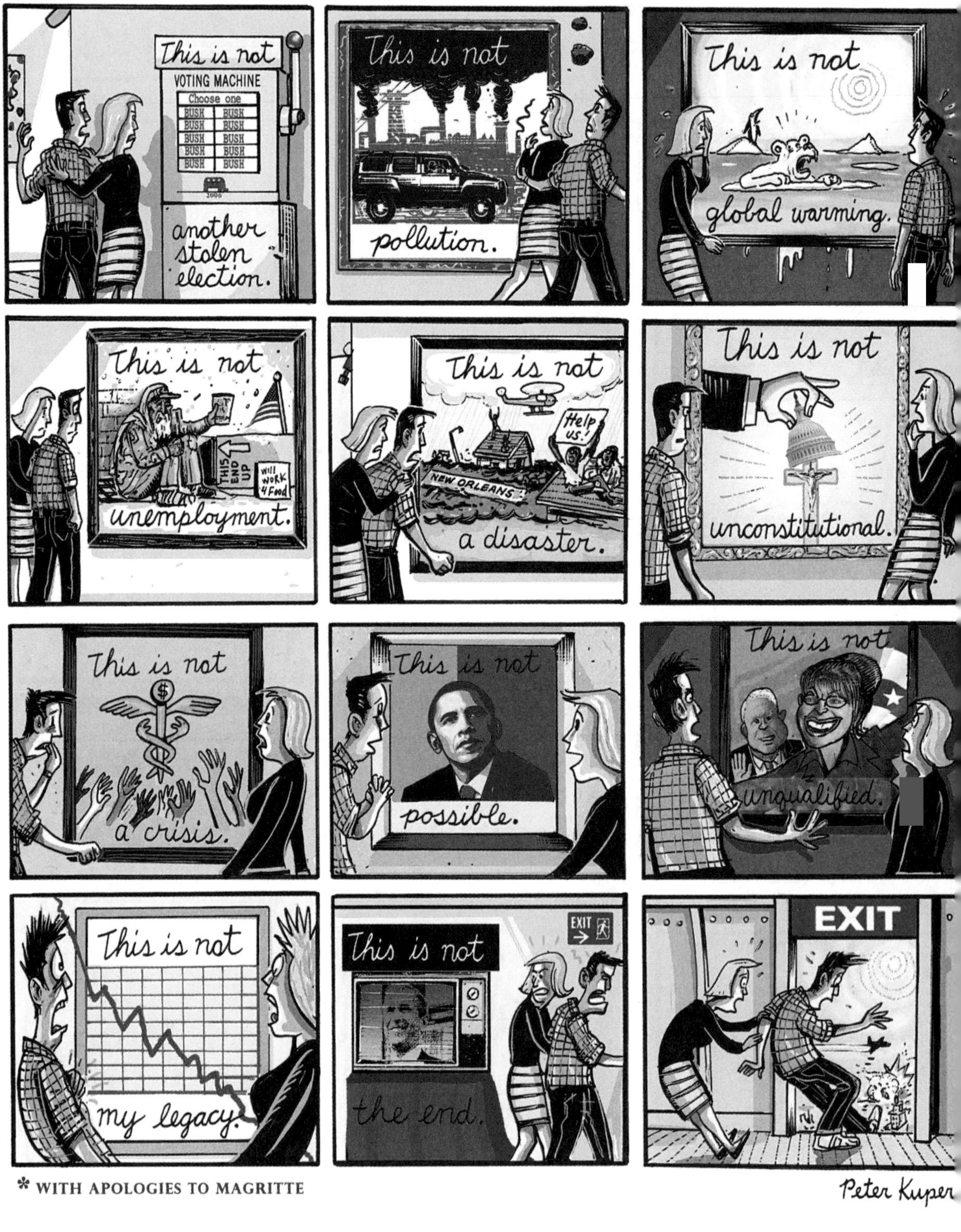
This is not
VOTING MACHINE
Choose one
BUSH BUSH
BUSH BUSH
BUSH BUSH
BUSH BUSH
BUSH BUSH
2008
another stolen election.
This is not
pollution.
This is not
global warming.
This is not
THIS END UP
Will WORK 4 Food
unemployment.
This is not
Help us!
NEW ORLEANS
a disaster.
This is not
unconstitutional.
This is not
$
a crisis.
This is not
possible.
This is not
unqualified.
This is not
my legacy.
EXIT
This is not
the end.
EXIT

✻ WITH APOLOGIES TO MAGRITTE

Peter Kuper

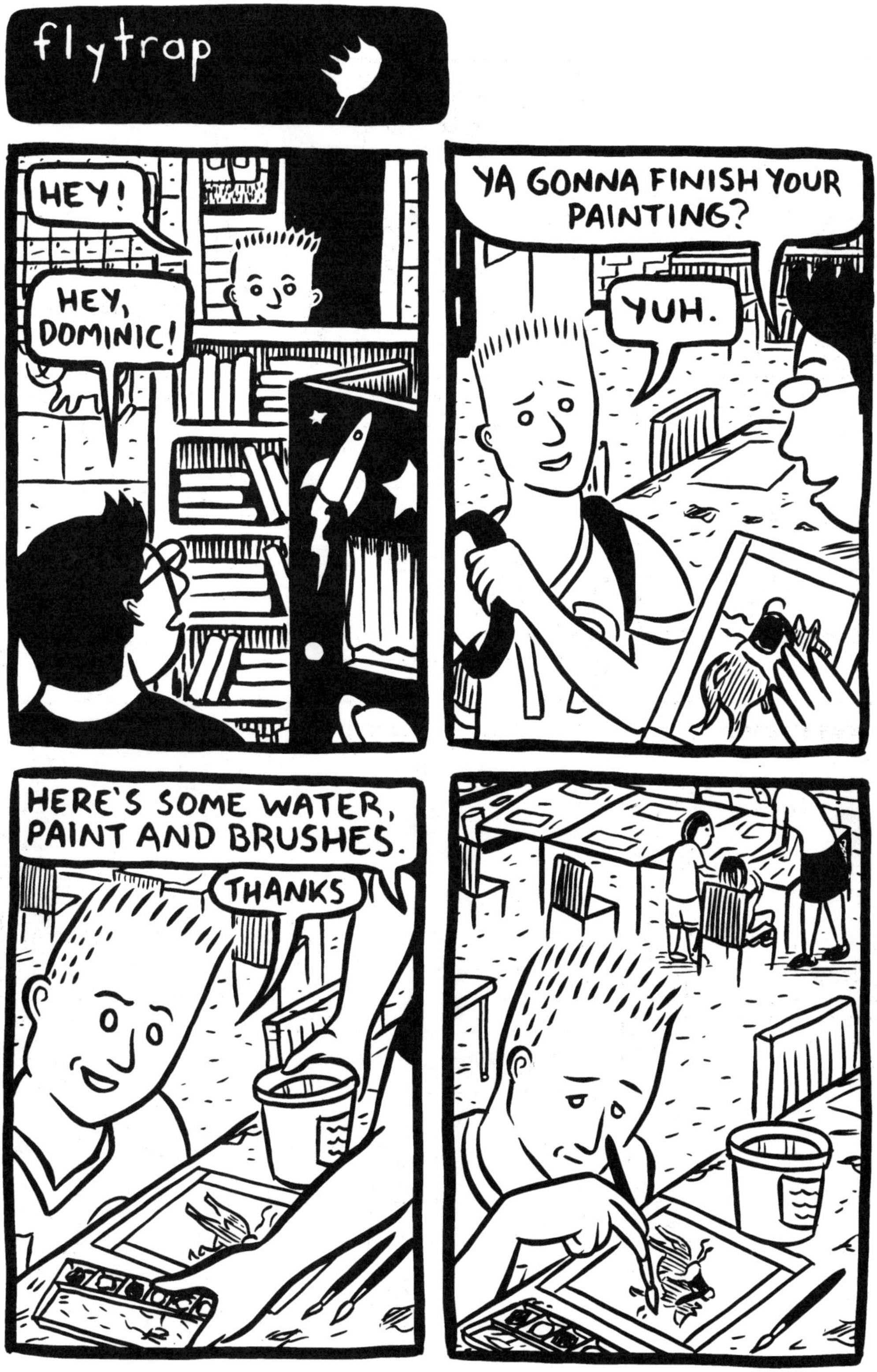
flytrap
HEY!
HEY, DOMINIC!
YA GONNA FINISH YOUR PAINTING?
YUH.
HERE'S SOME WATER, PAINT AND BRUSHES.
THANKS

DAVE LAPP

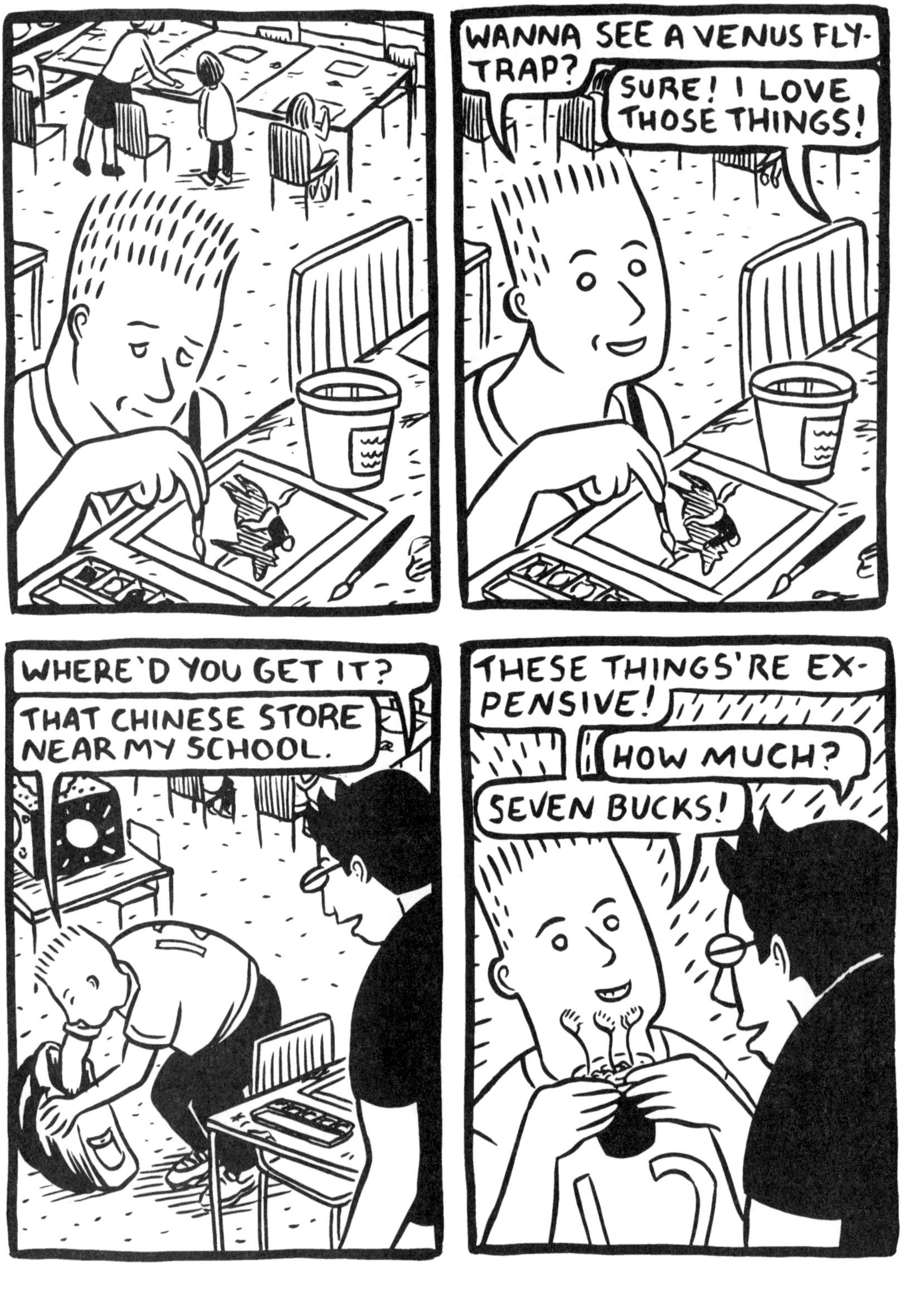
WANNA SEE A VENUS FLY-TRAP?
SURE! I LOVE THOSE THINGS!
WHERE'D YOU GET IT?
THAT CHINESE STORE NEAR MY SCHOOL.
THESE THINGS'RE EX-PENSIVE!
HOW MUCH?
SEVEN BUCKS!

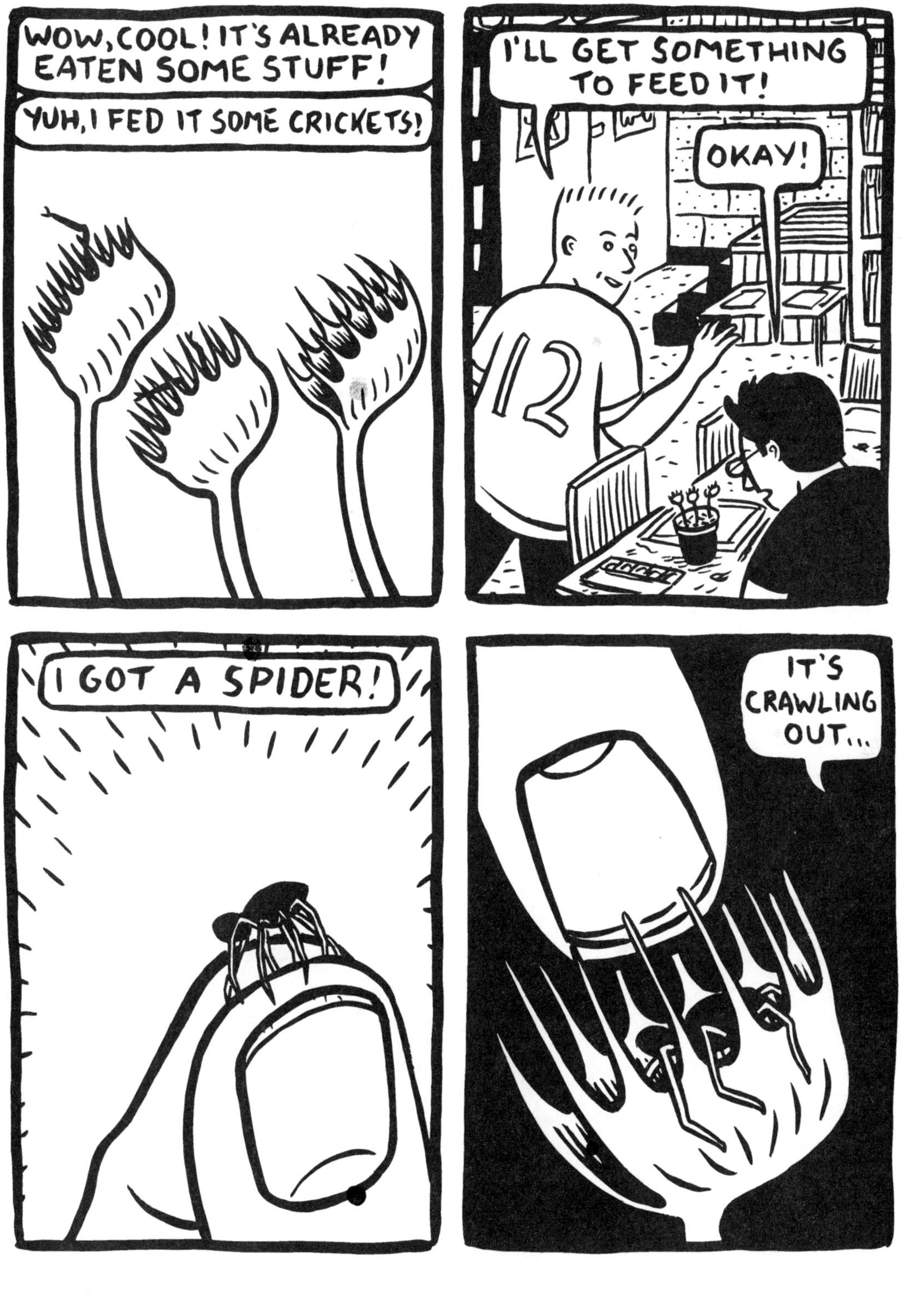
WOW, COOL! IT'S ALREADY EATEN SOME STUFF!
YUH, I FED IT SOME CRICKETS!
I'LL GET SOMETHING TO FEED IT!
OKAY!
I GOT A SPIDER!
IT'S CRAWLING OUT...

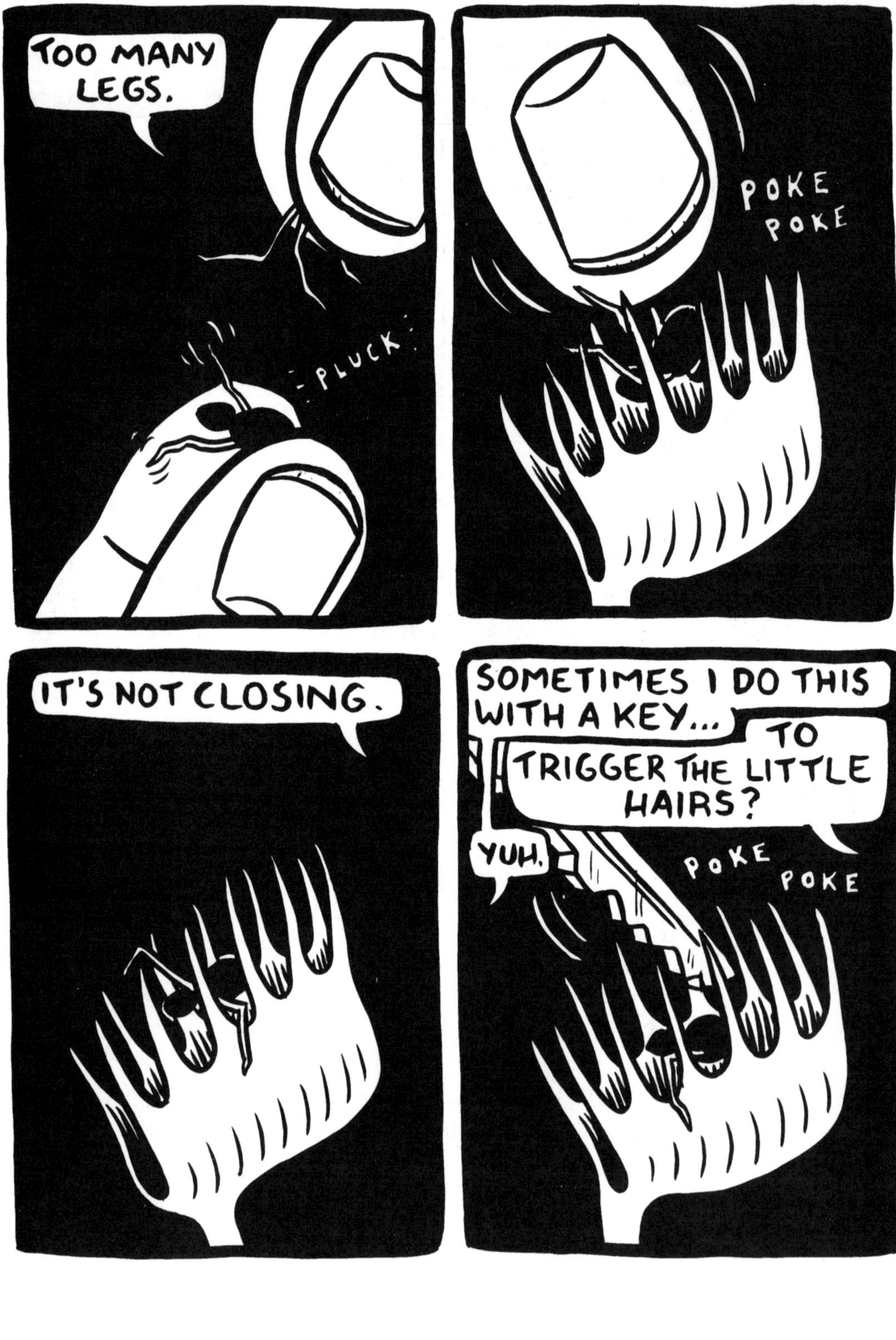
TOO MANY LEGS.
PLUCK
POKE POKE
IT'S NOT CLOSING.
SOMETIMES I DO THIS WITH A KEY...
TO TRIGGER THE LITTLE HAIRS?
YUH.
POKE POKE

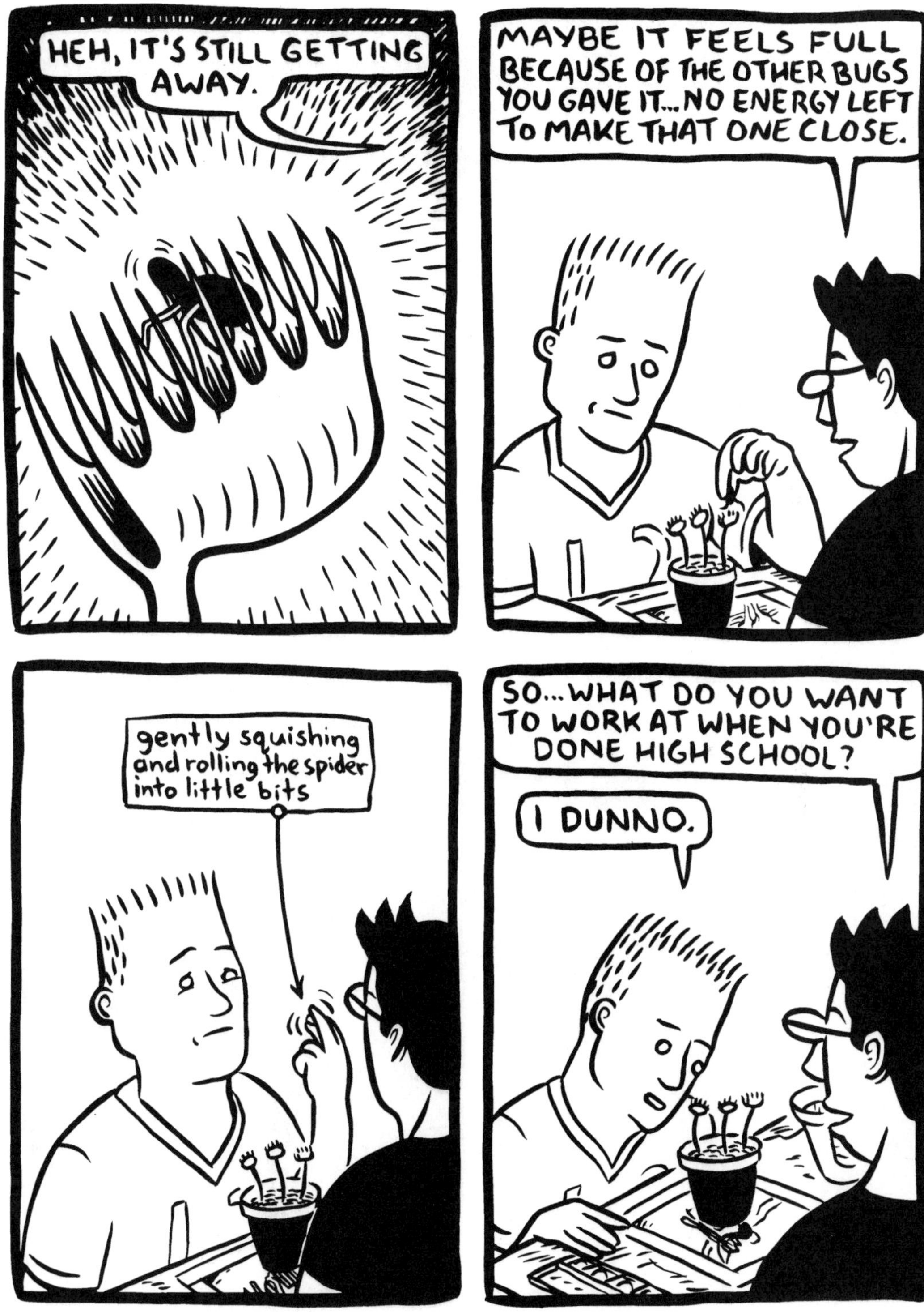
HEH, IT'S STILL GETTING AWAY.
MAYBE IT FEELS FULL BECAUSE OF THE OTHER BUGS YOU GAVE IT...NO ENERGY LEFT TO MAKE THAT ONE CLOSE.
gently squishing and rolling the spider into little bits
SO...WHAT DO YOU WANT TO WORK AT WHEN YOU'RE DONE HIGH SCHOOL?
I DUNNO.

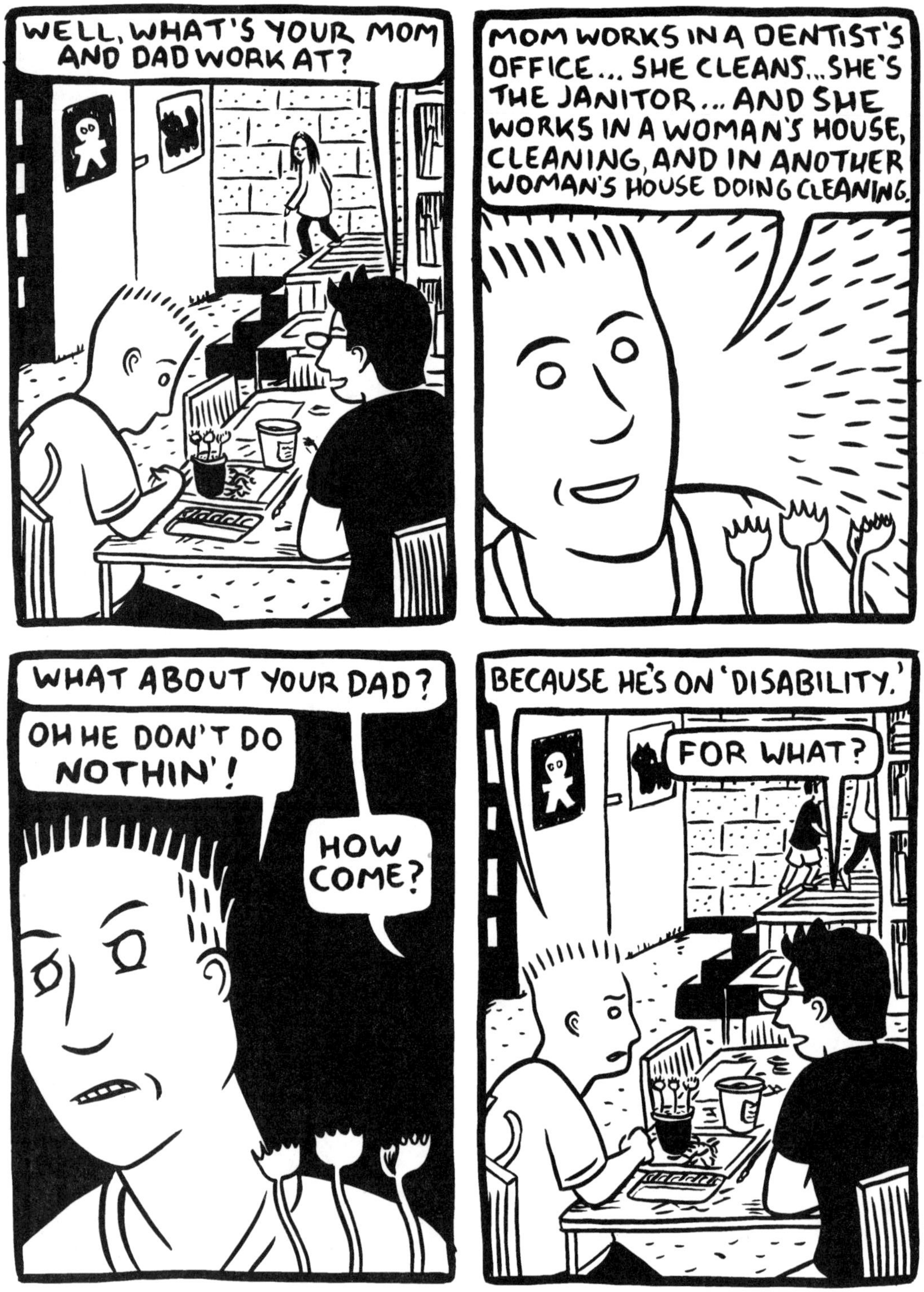
WELL, WHAT'S YOUR MOM AND DAD WORK AT?
MOM WORKS IN A DENTIST'S OFFICE... SHE CLEANS... SHE'S THE JANITOR... AND SHE WORKS IN A WOMAN'S HOUSE, CLEANING, AND IN ANOTHER WOMAN'S HOUSE DOING CLEANING.
WHAT ABOUT YOUR DAD?
OH HE DON'T DO NOTHIN'!
HOW COME?
BECAUSE HE'S ON 'DISABILITY.'
FOR WHAT?

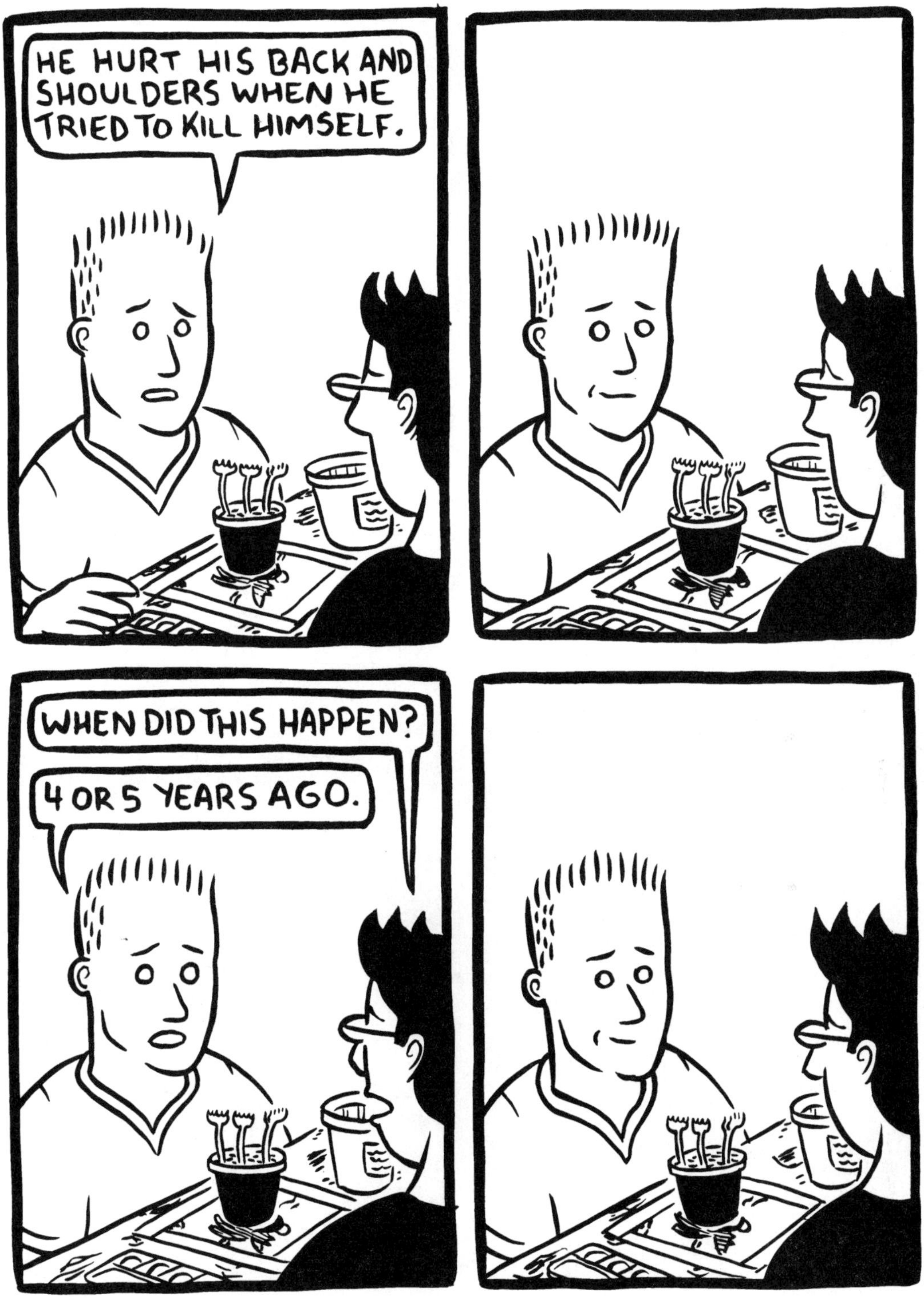
HE HURT HIS BACK AND SHOULDERS WHEN HE TRIED TO KILL HIMSELF.
WHEN DID THIS HAPPEN?
4 OR 5 YEARS AGO.

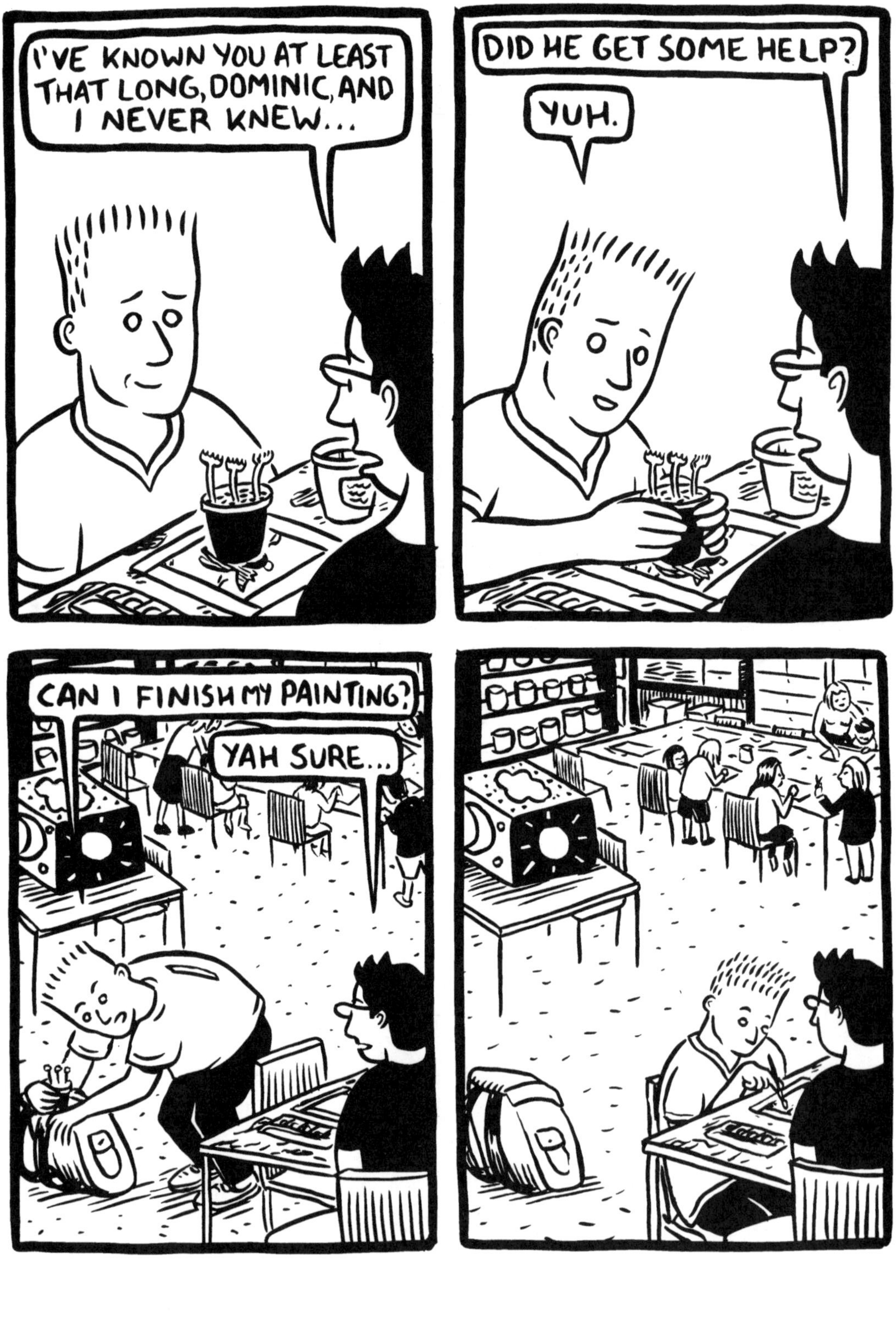
I'VE KNOWN YOU AT LEAST THAT LONG, DOMINIC, AND I NEVER KNEW...
DID HE GET SOME HELP?
YUH.
CAN I FINISH MY PAINTING?
YAH SURE...

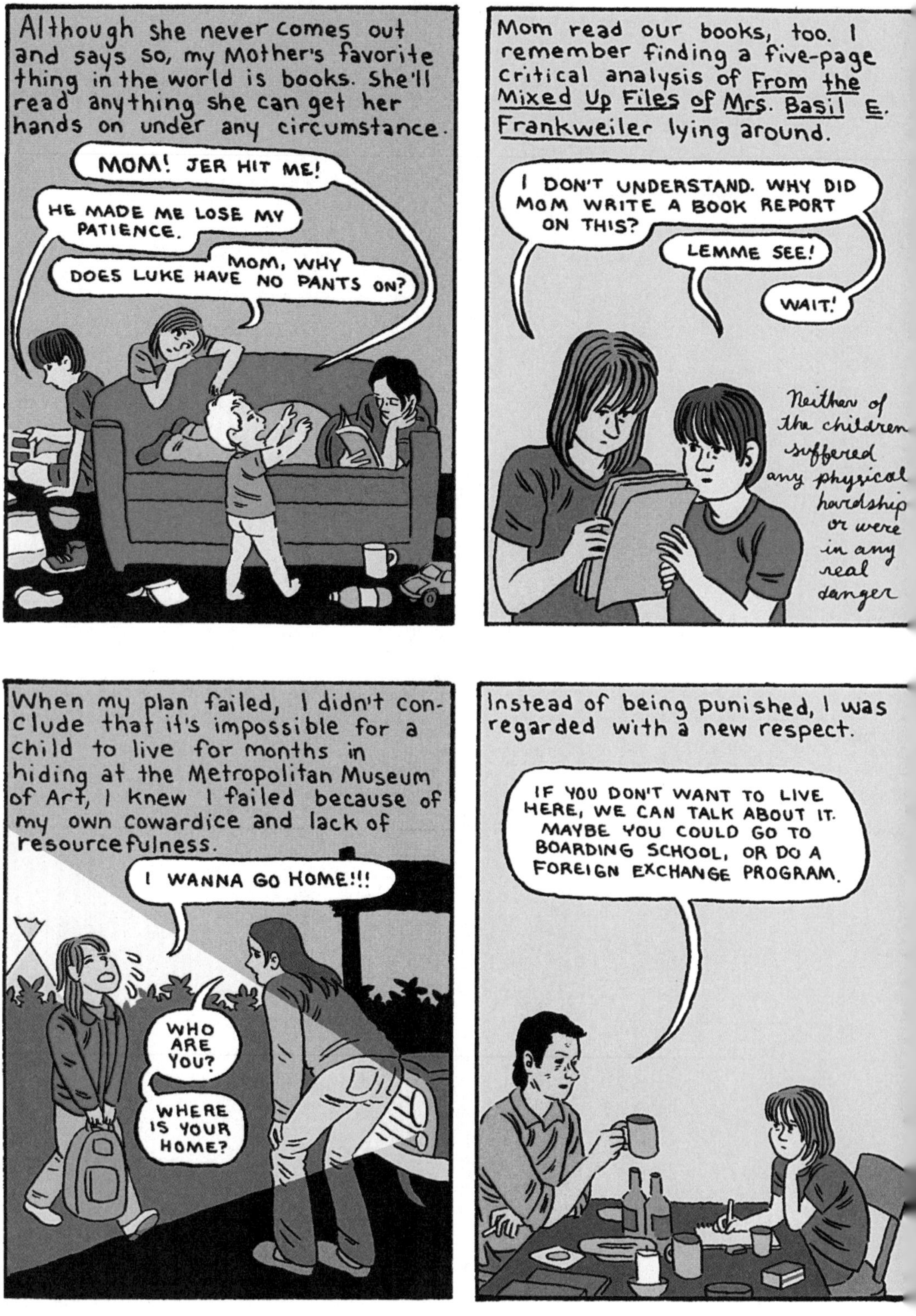
Although she never comes out and says so, my Mother's favorite thing in the world is books. She'll read anything she can get her hands on under any circumstance.
MOM! JER HIT ME!
HE MADE ME LOSE MY PATIENCE.
MOM, WHY DOES LUKE HAVE NO PANTS ON?
Mom read our books, too. I remember finding a five-page critical analysis of From the Mixed Up Files of Mrs. Basil E. Frankweiler lying around.
I DON'T UNDERSTAND. WHY DID MOM WRITE A BOOK REPORT ON THIS?
LEMME SEE!
WAIT!
Neither of the children suffered any physical hardship or were in any real danger
When my plan failed, I didn't conclude that it's impossible for a child to live for months in hiding at the Metropolitan Museum of Art, I knew I failed because of my own cowardice and lack of resourcefulness.
I WANNA GO HOME!!!
WHO ARE YOU?
WHERE IS YOUR HOME?
Instead of being punished, I was regarded with a new respect.
IF YOU DON'T WANT TO LIVE HERE, WE CAN TALK ABOUT IT. MAYBE YOU COULD GO TO BOARDING SCHOOL, OR DO A FOREIGN EXCHANGE PROGRAM.

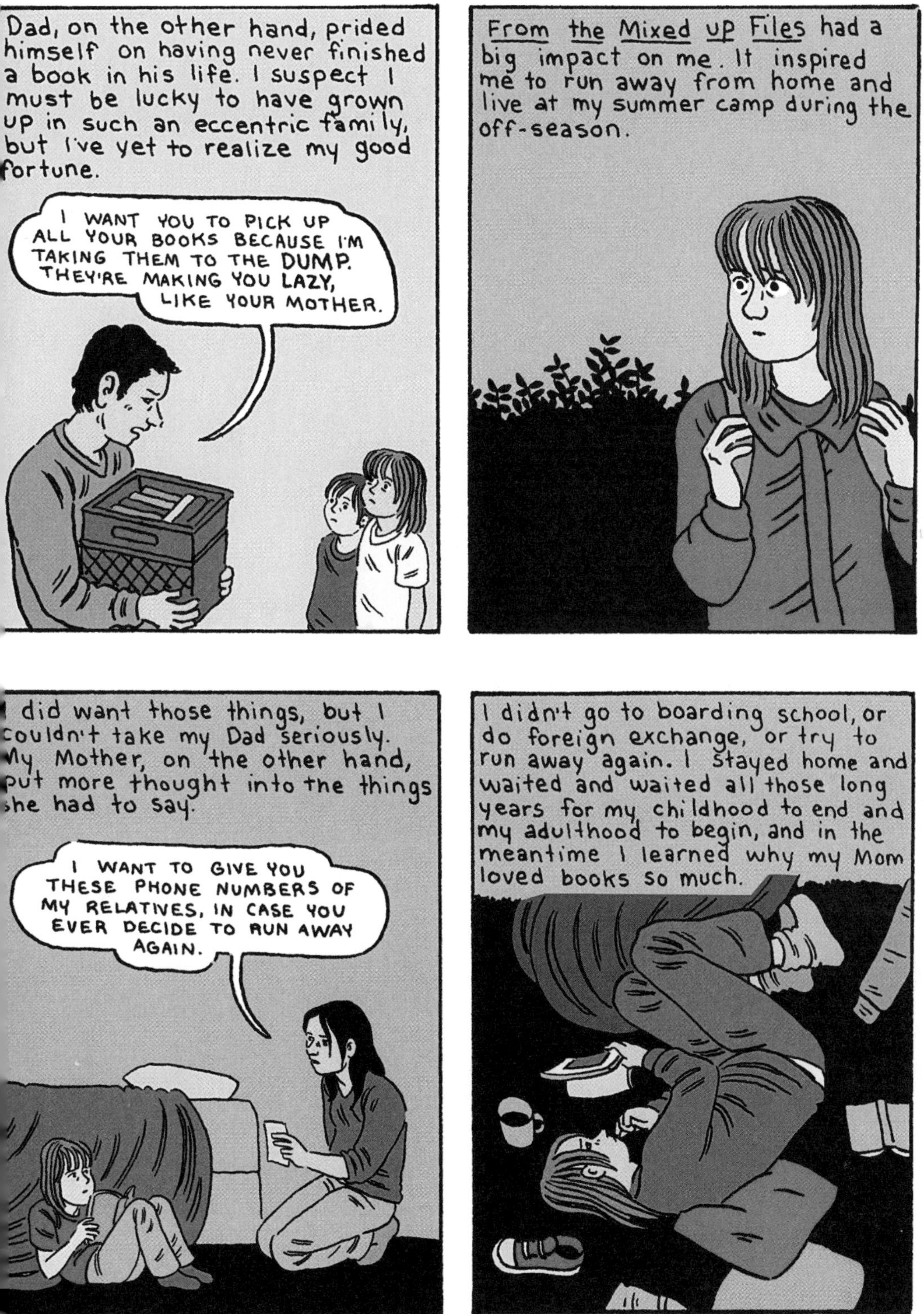
Dad, on the other hand, prided himself on having never finished a book in his life. I suspect I must be lucky to have grown up in such an eccentric family, but I've yet to realize my good fortune.
I WANT YOU TO PICK UP ALL YOUR BOOKS BECAUSE I'M TAKING THEM TO THE DUMP. THEY'RE MAKING YOU LAZY, LIKE YOUR MOTHER.
From the Mixed up Files had a big impact on me. It inspired me to run away from home and live at my summer camp during the off-season.
did want those things, but I couldn't take my Dad seriously. My Mother, on the other hand, put more thought into the things she had to say.
I WANT TO GIVE YOU THESE PHONE NUMBERS OF MY RELATIVES, IN CASE YOU EVER DECIDE TO RUN AWAY AGAIN.
I didn't go to boarding school, or do foreign exchange, or try to run away again. I stayed home and waited and waited all those long years for my childhood to end and my adulthood to begin, and in the meantime I learned why my Mom loved books so much.
GF Bell

excerpt from

THE LAGOON

LILLI CARRÉ

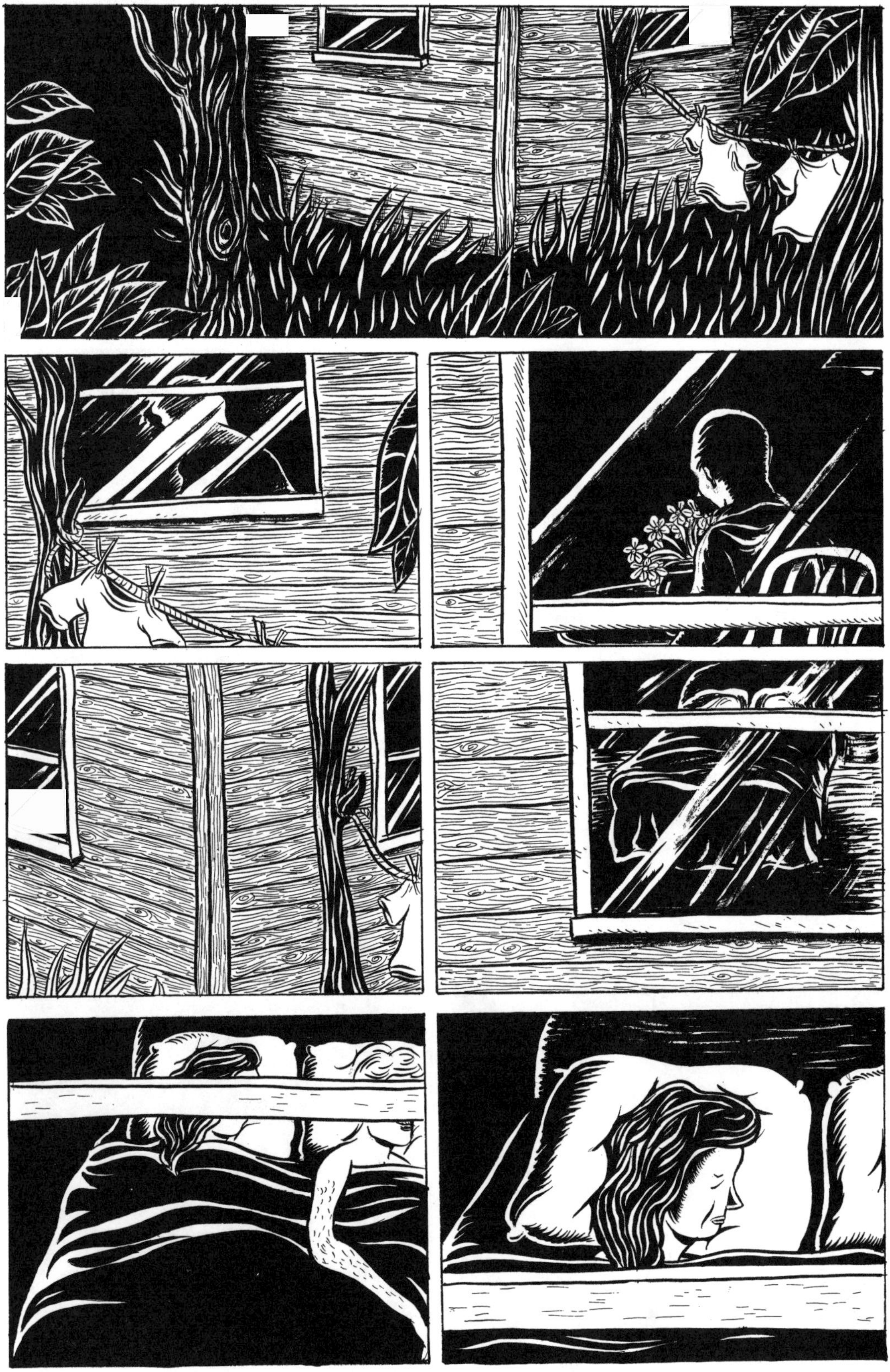

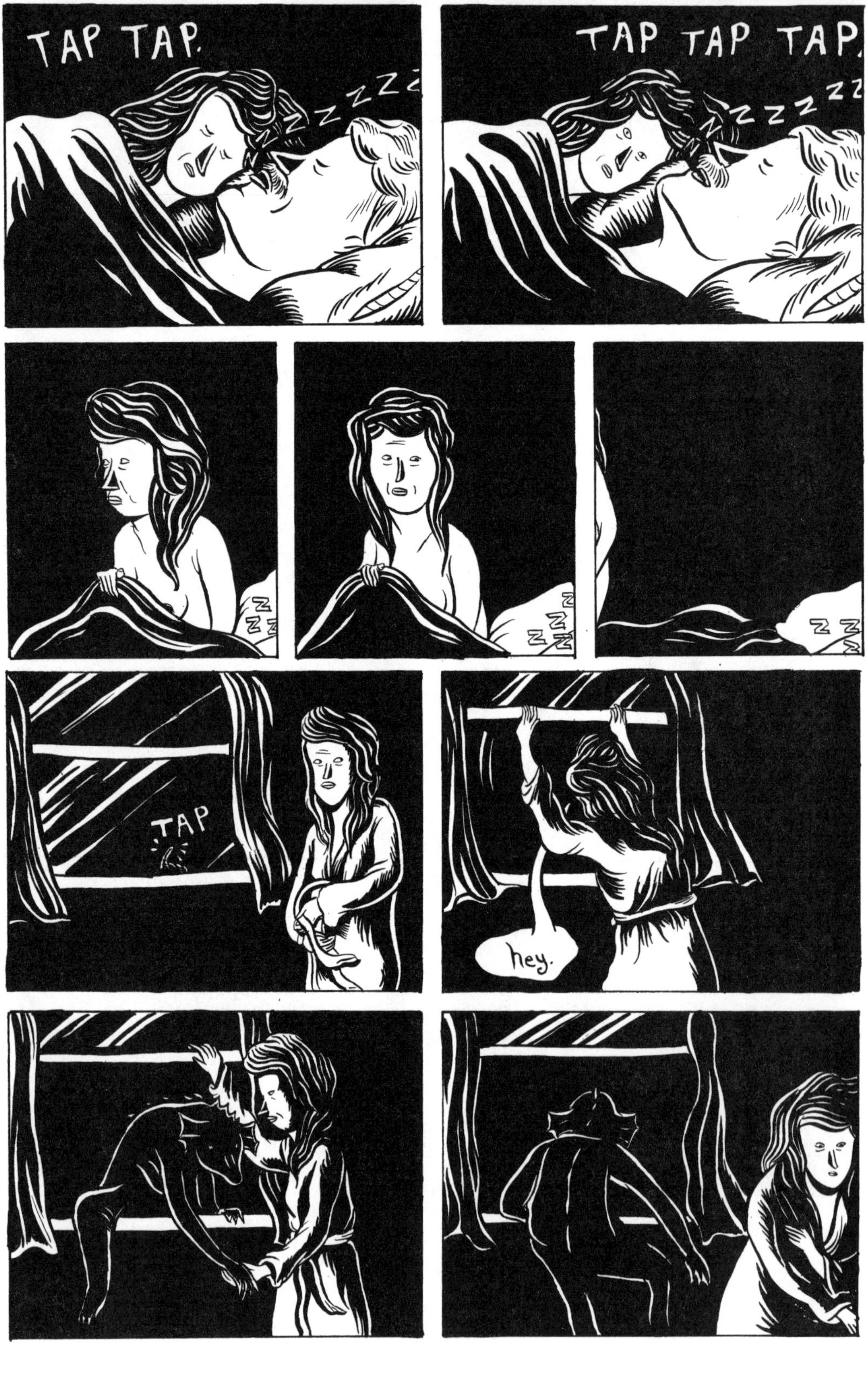
TAP TAP.
ZZZZZ
TAP TAP TAP.
ZZZZZ
ZZZ
ZZZZ
ZZZ
TAP
hey.

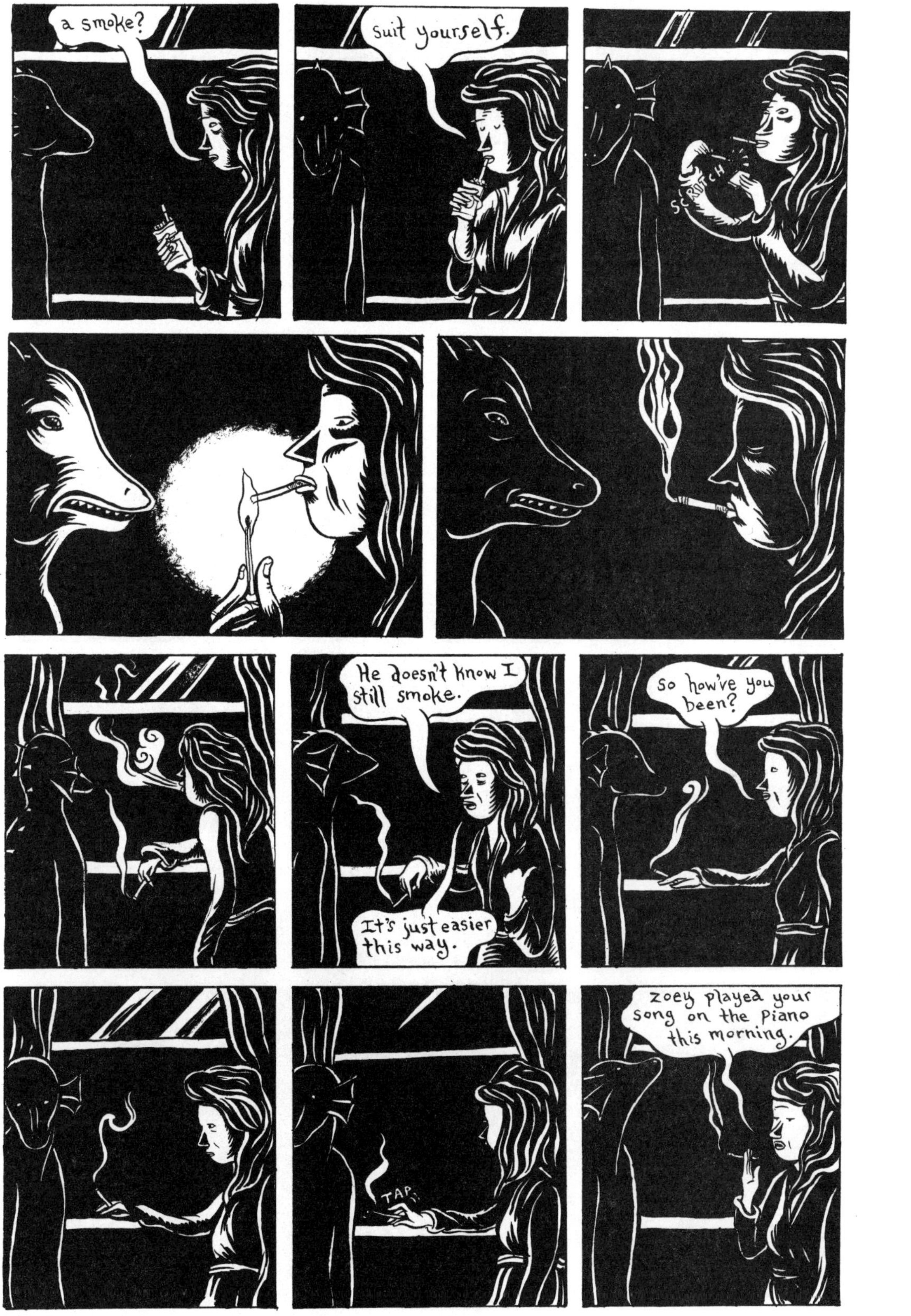

a smoke?
suit yourself.
SCROTCH
He doesn't know I still smoke.
It's just easier this way.
So how've you been?
TAP
zoey played your song on the piano this morning.

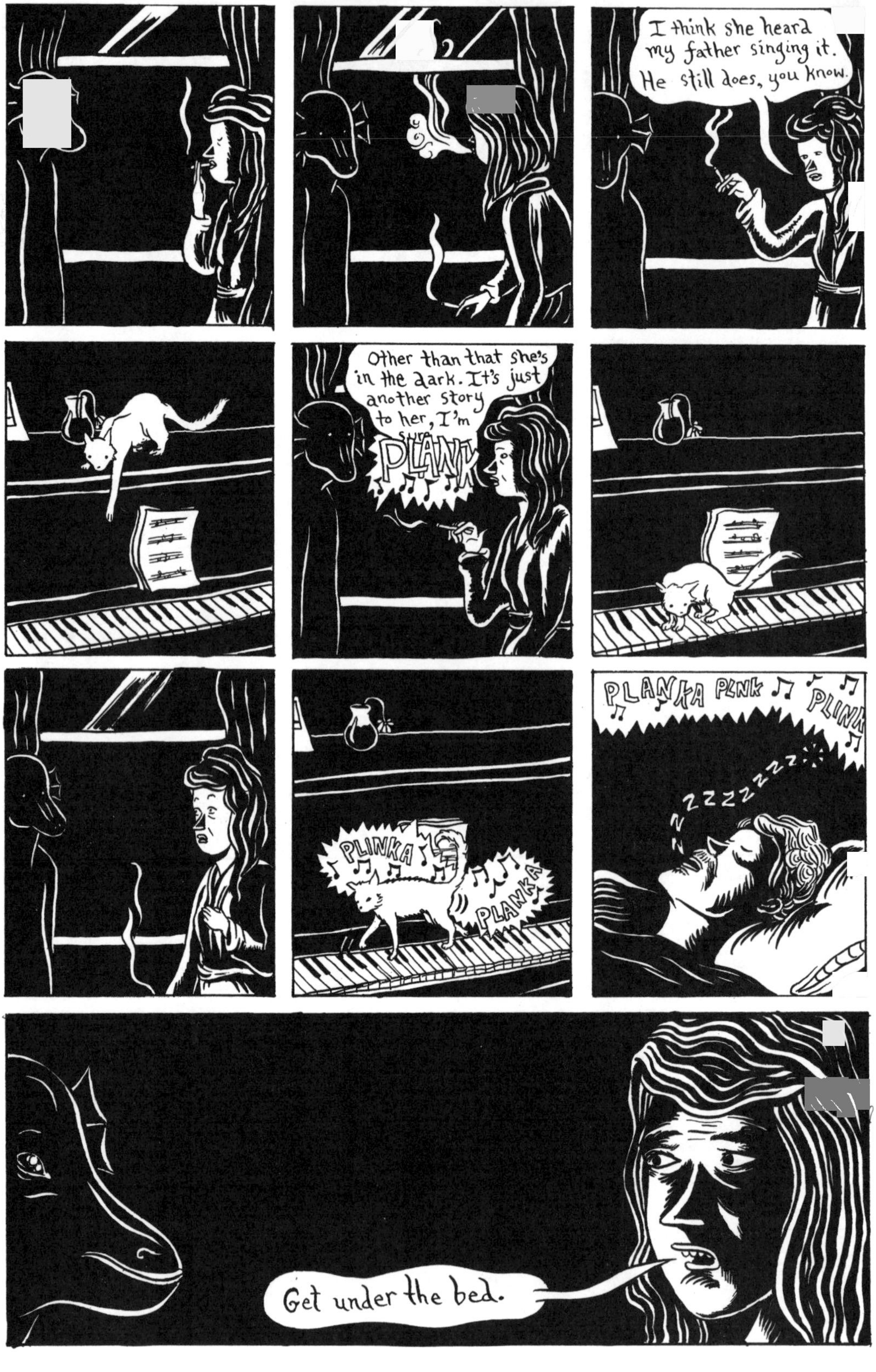
I think she heard my father singing it. He still does, you know.
Other than that she's in the dark. It's just another story to her, I'm sure
PLANK
PLINKA
PLANKA
PLANKA PLNK PLINK
ZZZZZZZZZ
Get under the bed.

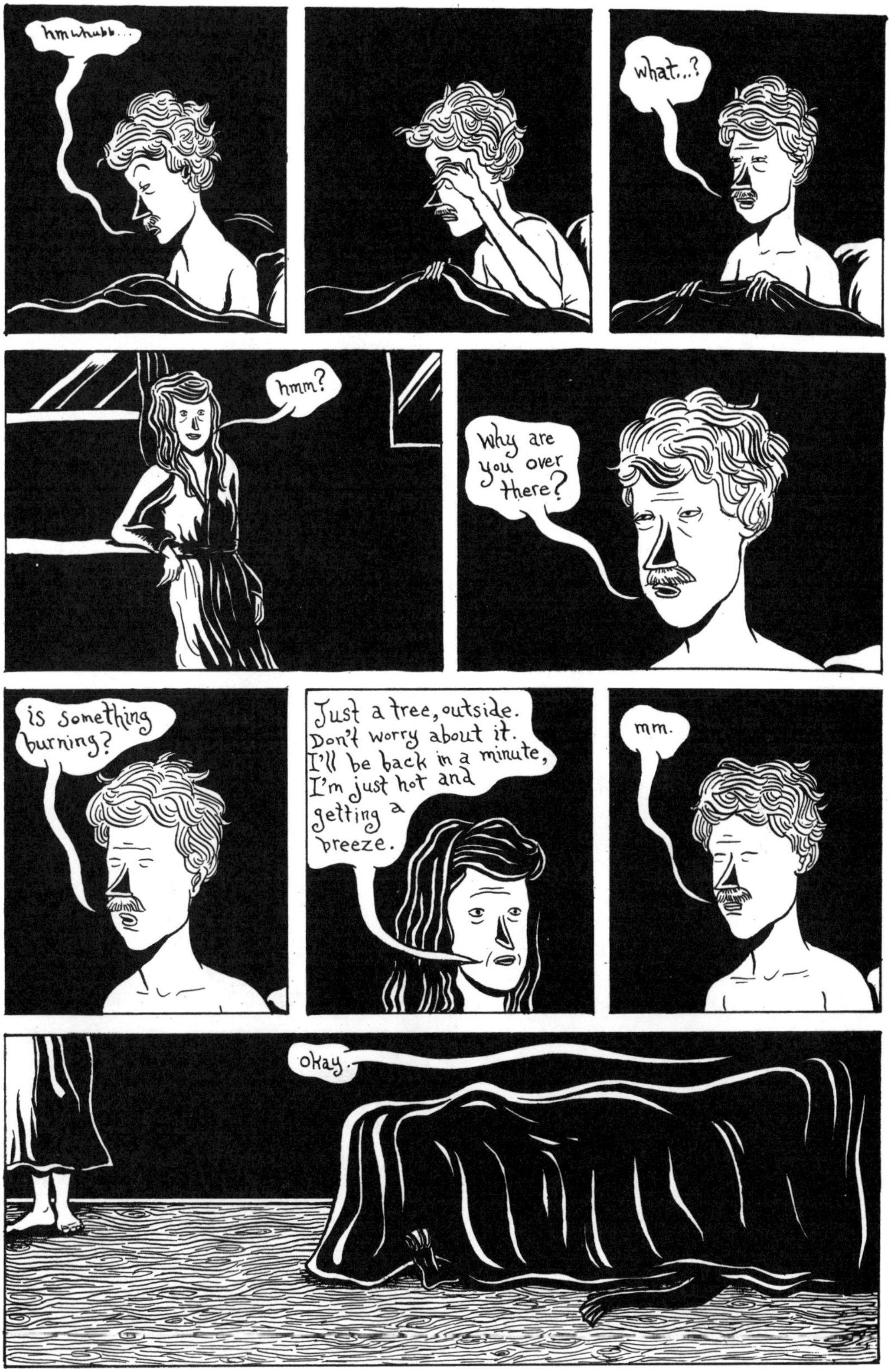
hmwhubb...
what...?
hmm?
Why are you over there?
is something burning?
Just a tree, outside. Don't worry about it. I'll be back in a minute, I'm just hot and getting a breeze.
mm.
okay.

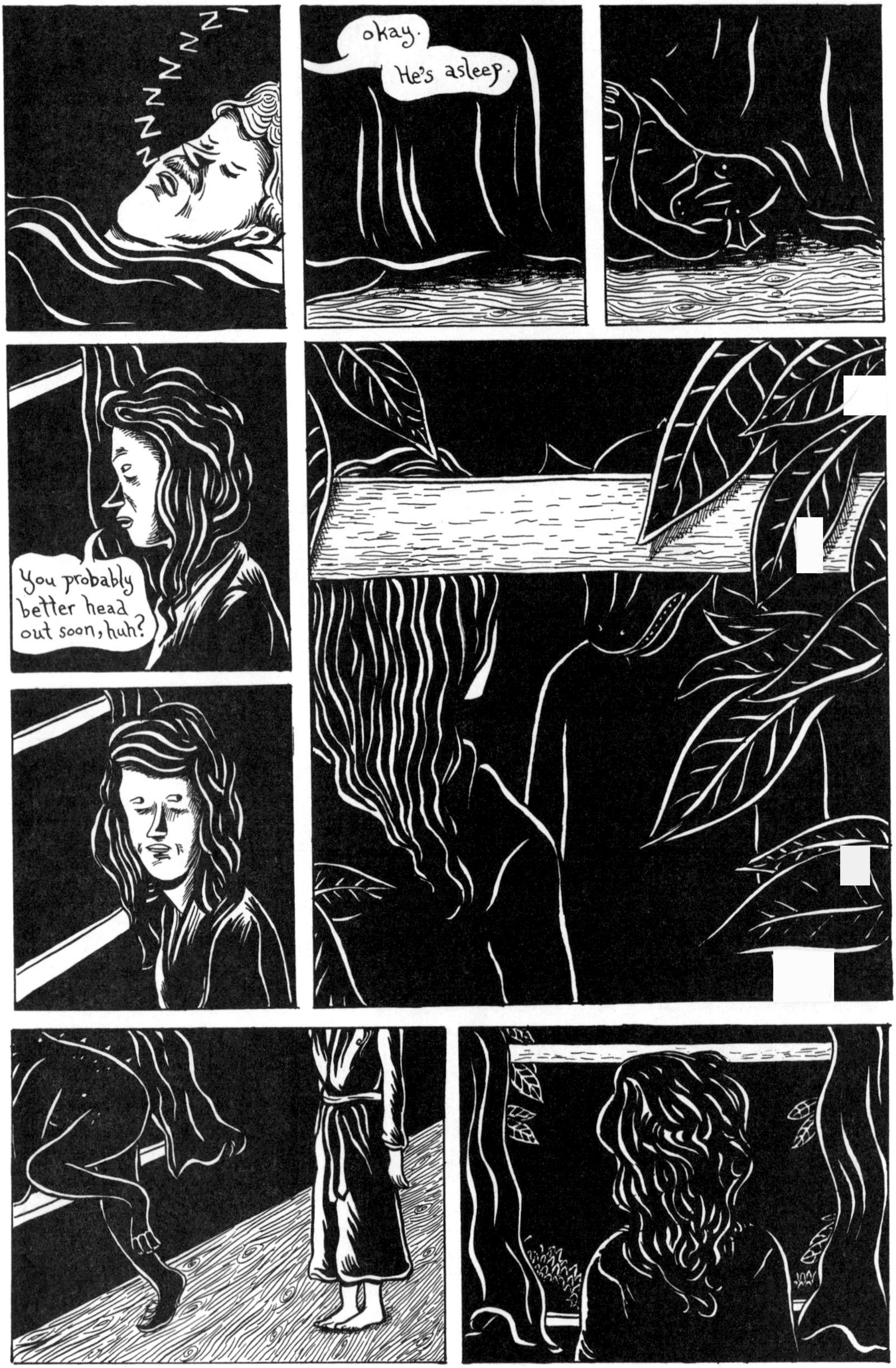
ZZZZZZZ
okay.
He's asleep.
You probably better head out soon, huh?

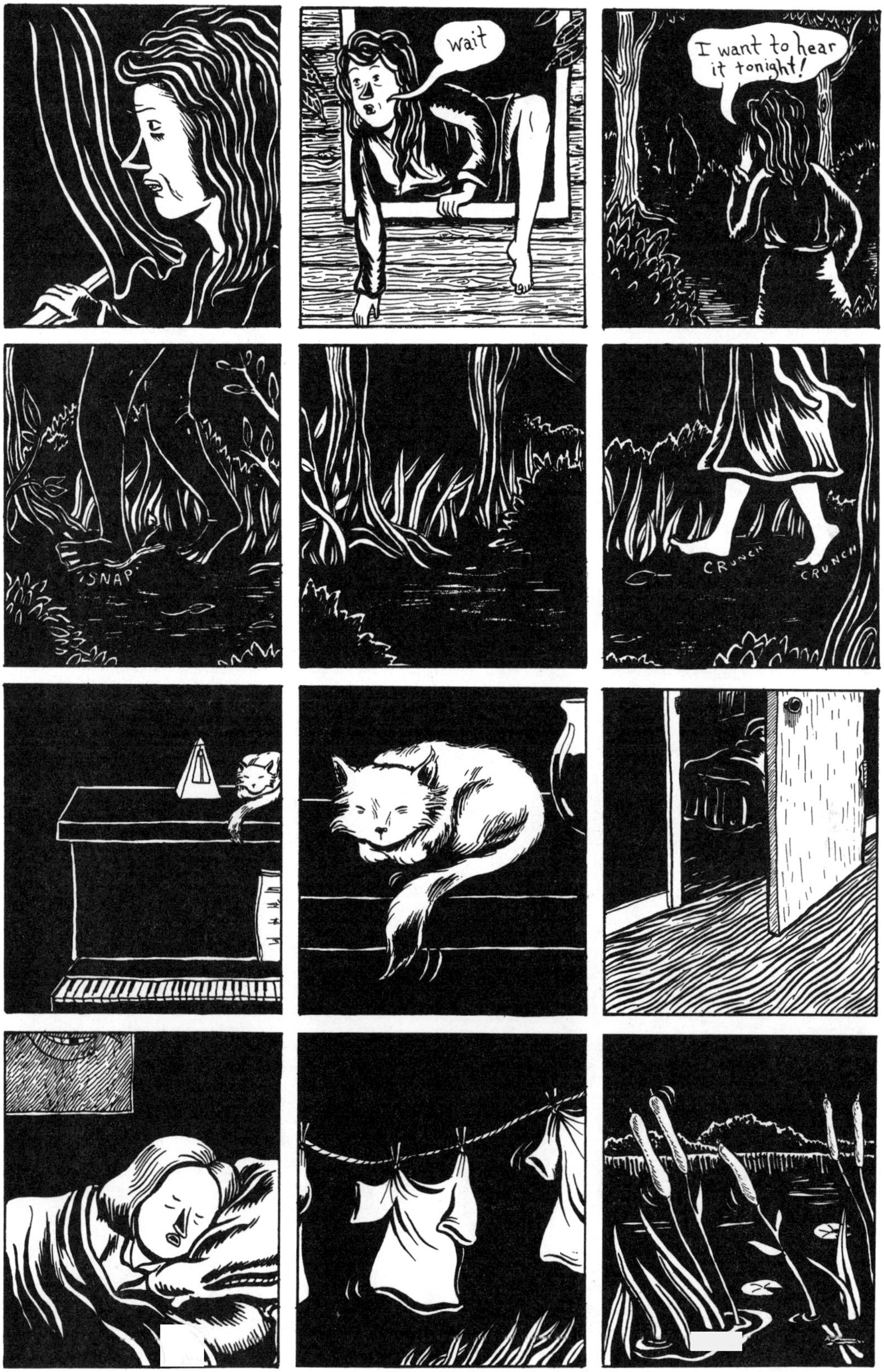
wait
I want to hear it tonight!
SNAP
CRUNCH
CRUNCH

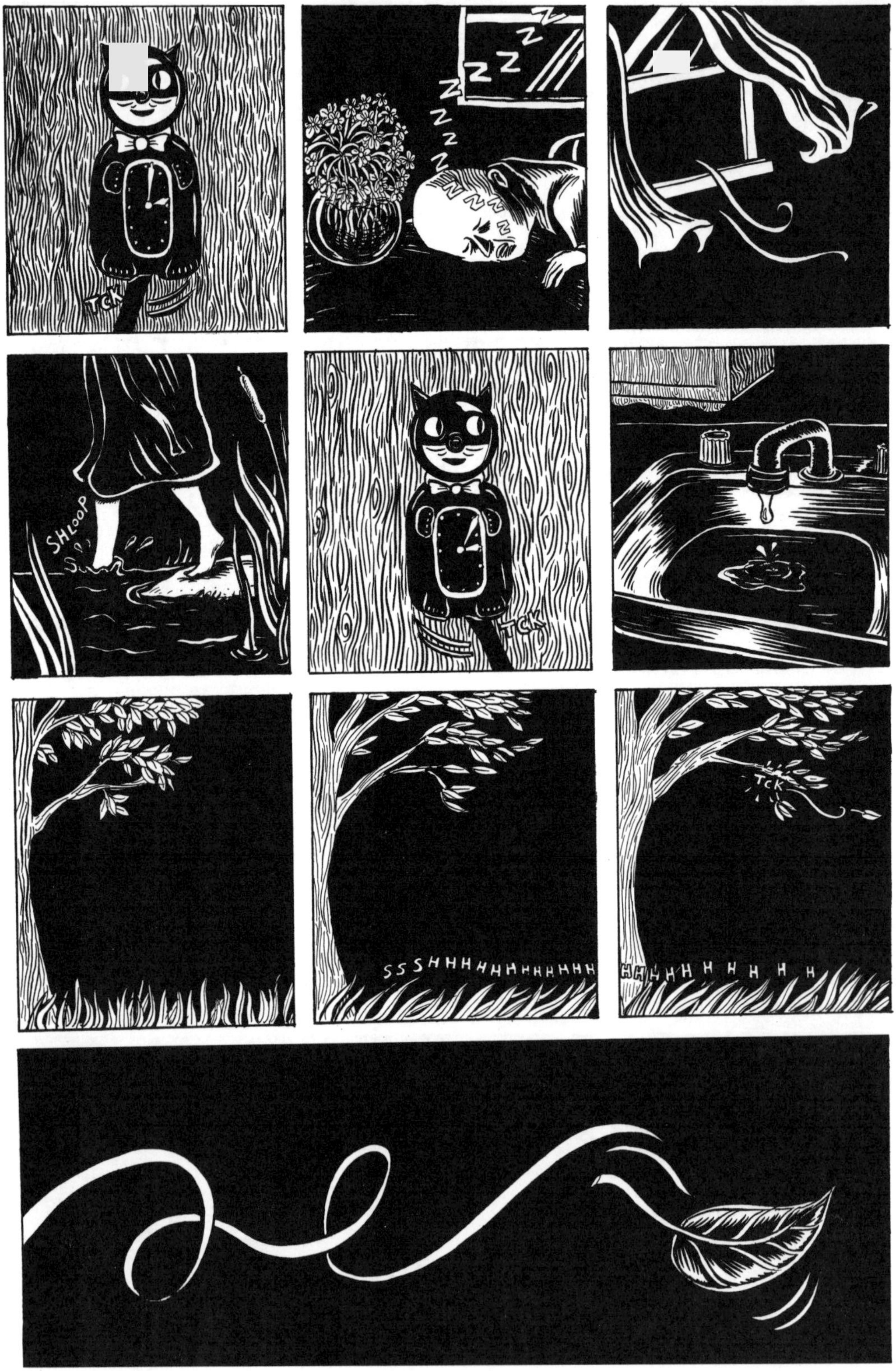
TCK
SHLOOP
TCK
SSSHHHHHHHHHHHHH
HHHHHHHHH
TCK

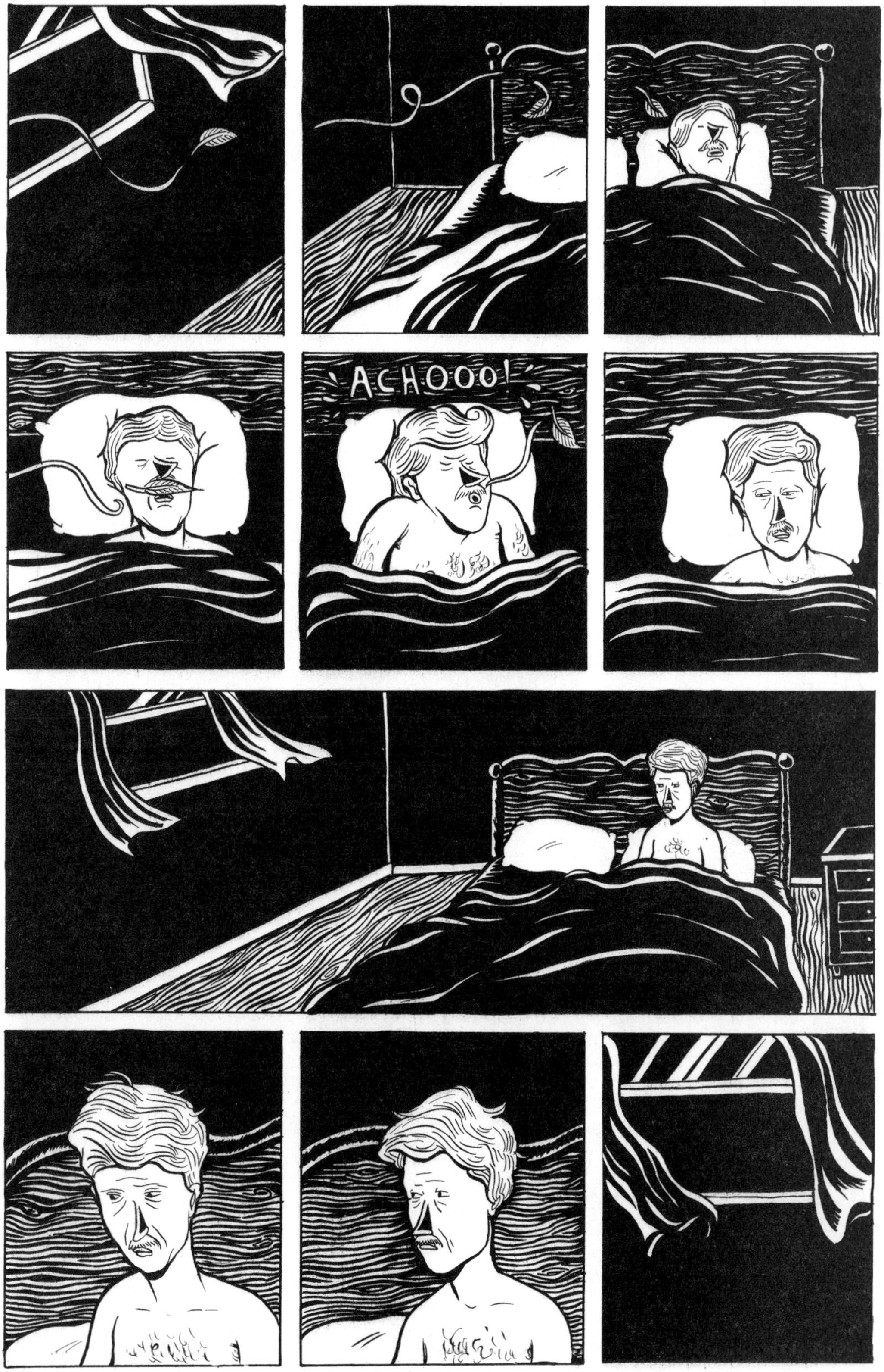
ACHOOO!

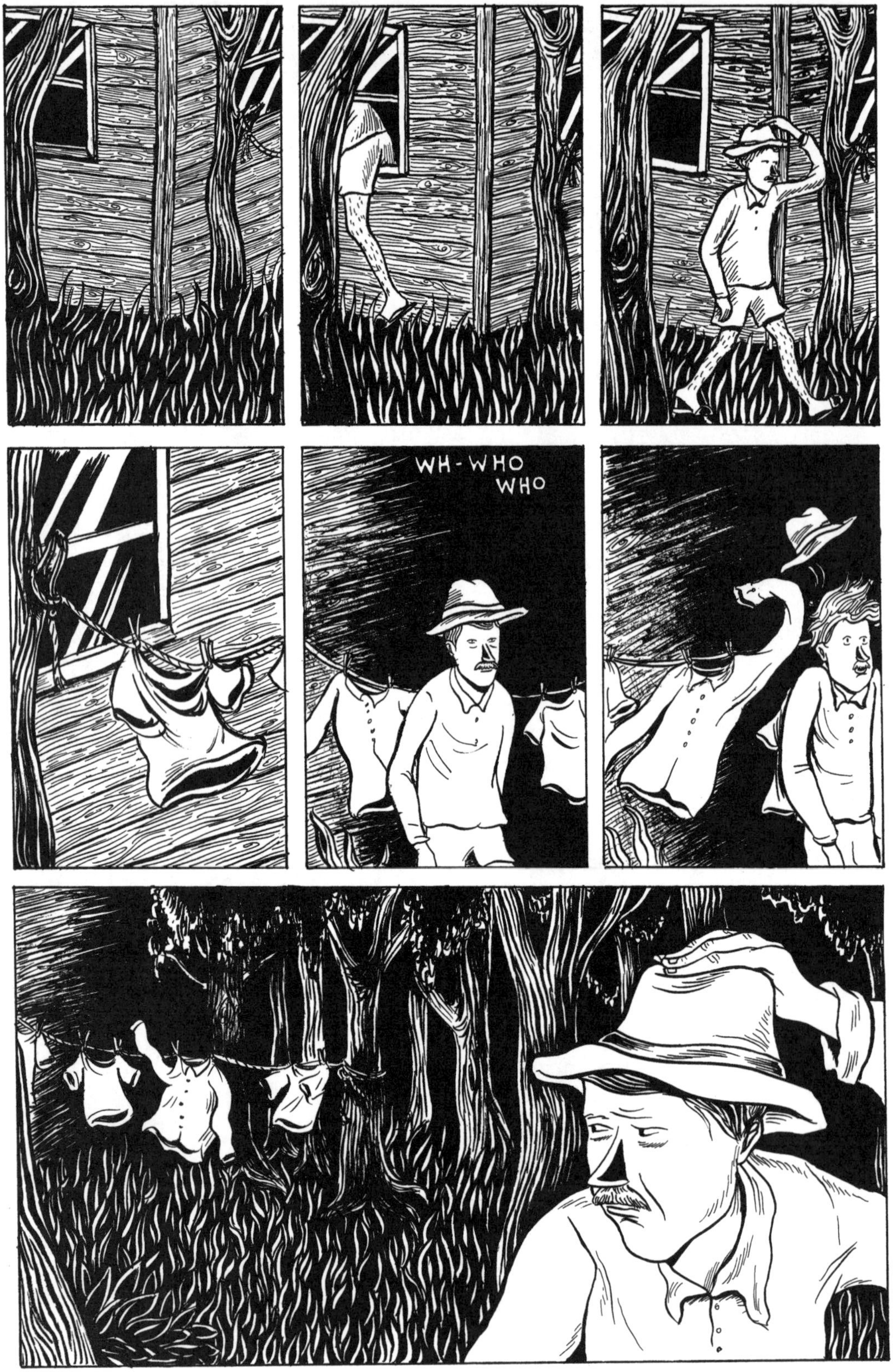

WH-WHO
WHO

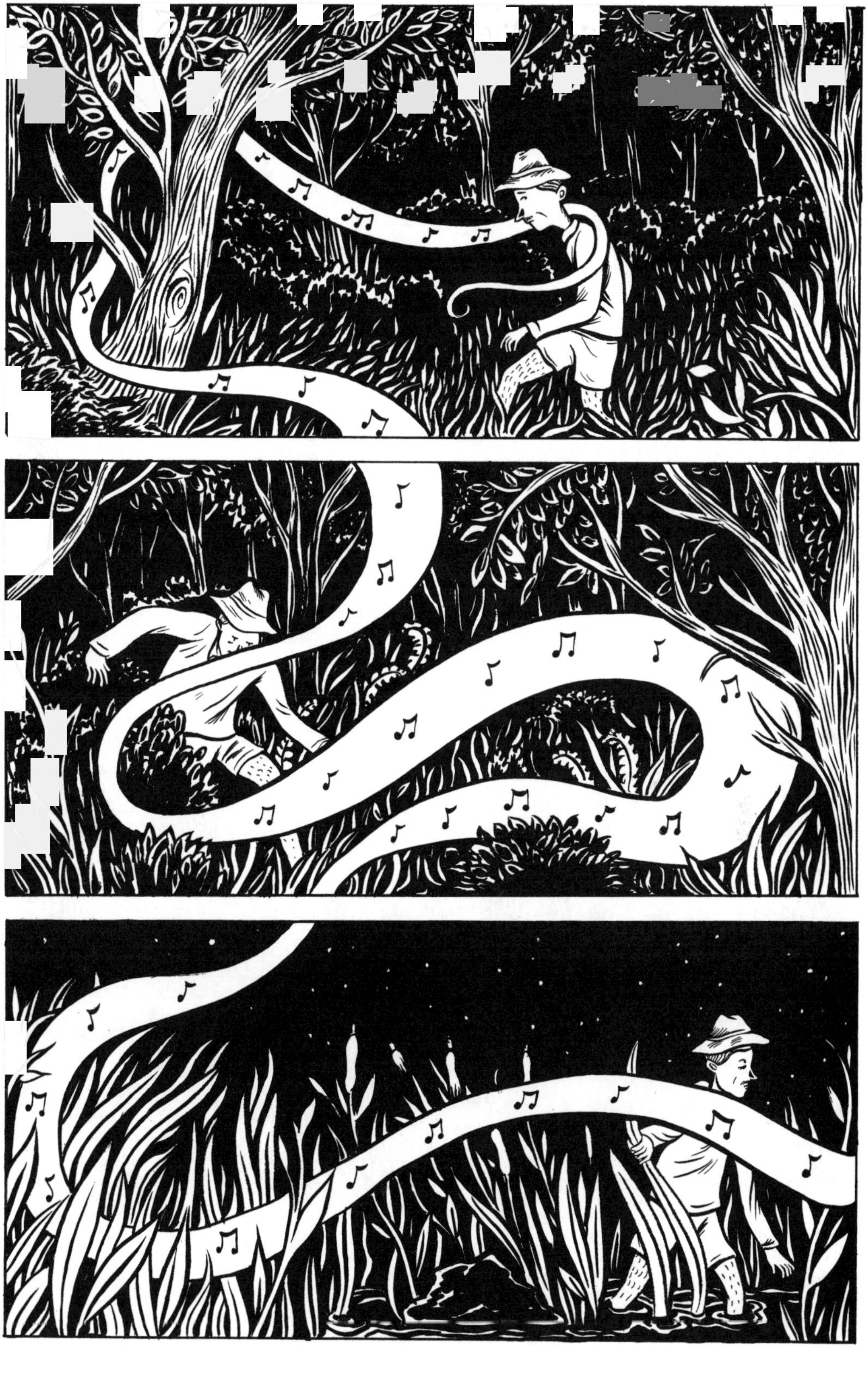

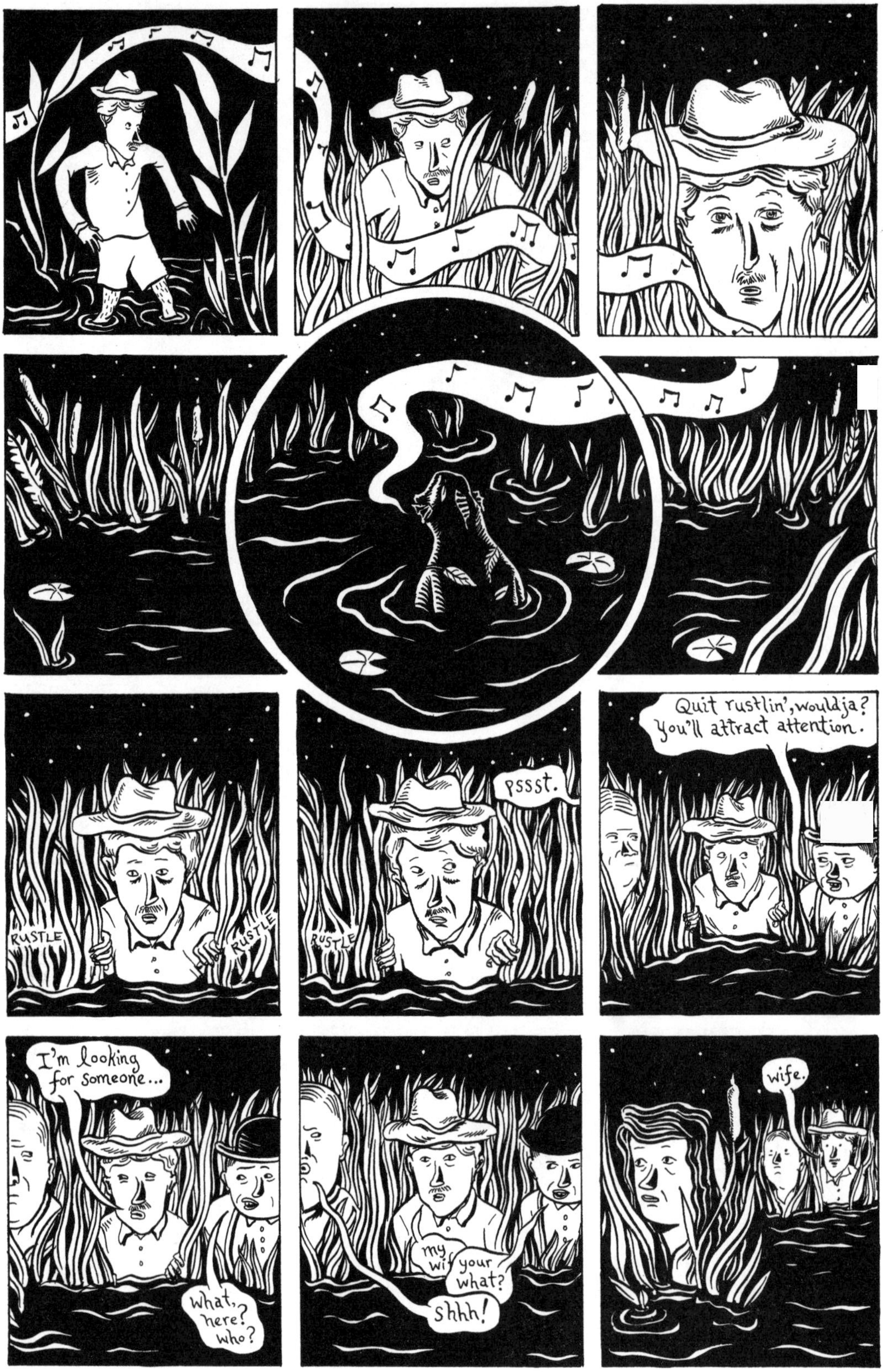
RUSTLE
RUSTLE
RUSTLE
pssst.
Quit rustlin', wouldja? You'll attract attention.
I'm looking for someone...
what, here? who?
my wi
your what?
Shhh!
wife.

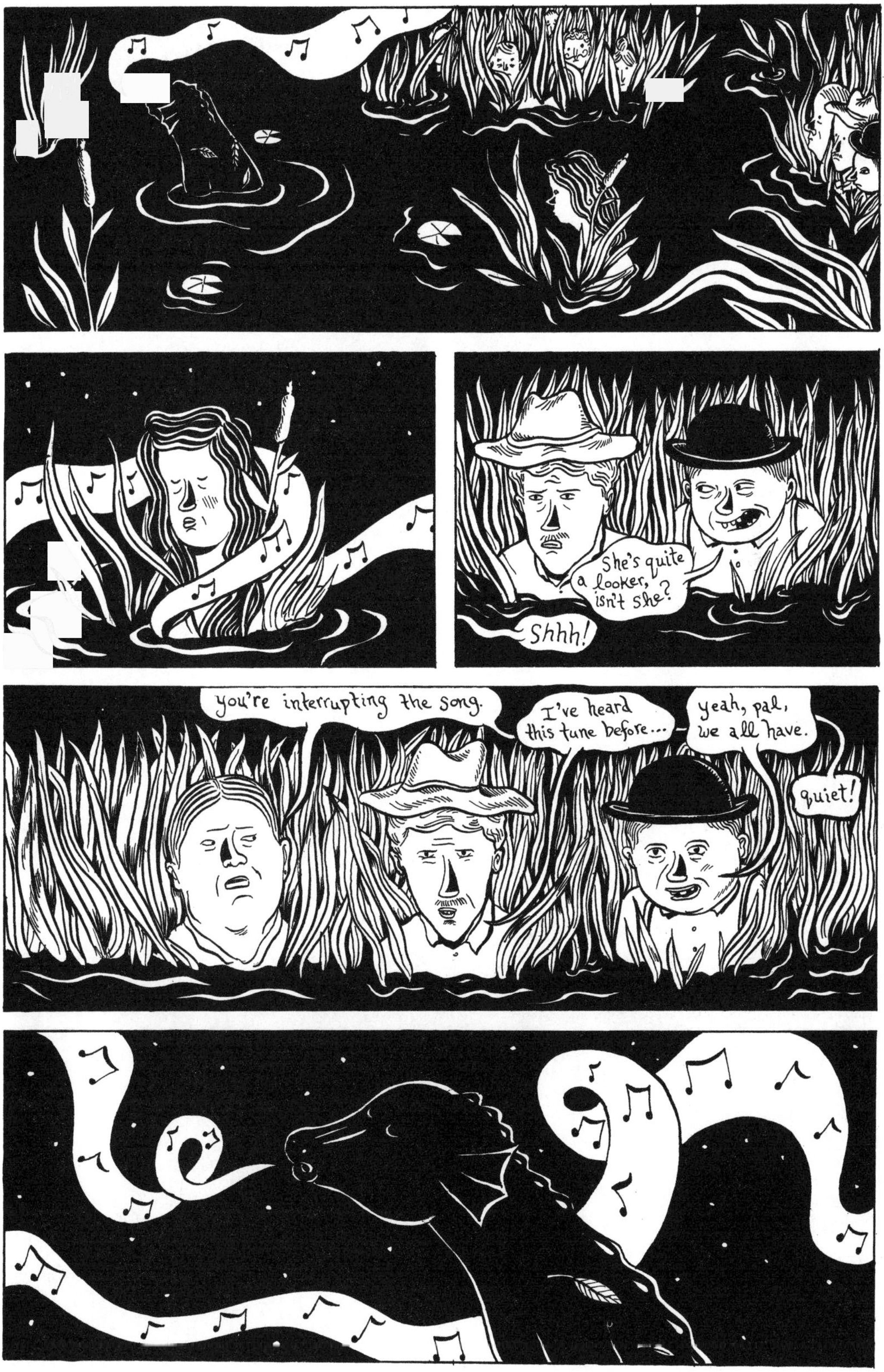
She's quite a looker, isn't she?
Shhh!
you're interrupting the song.
I've heard this tune before...
yeah, pal, we all have.
quiet!

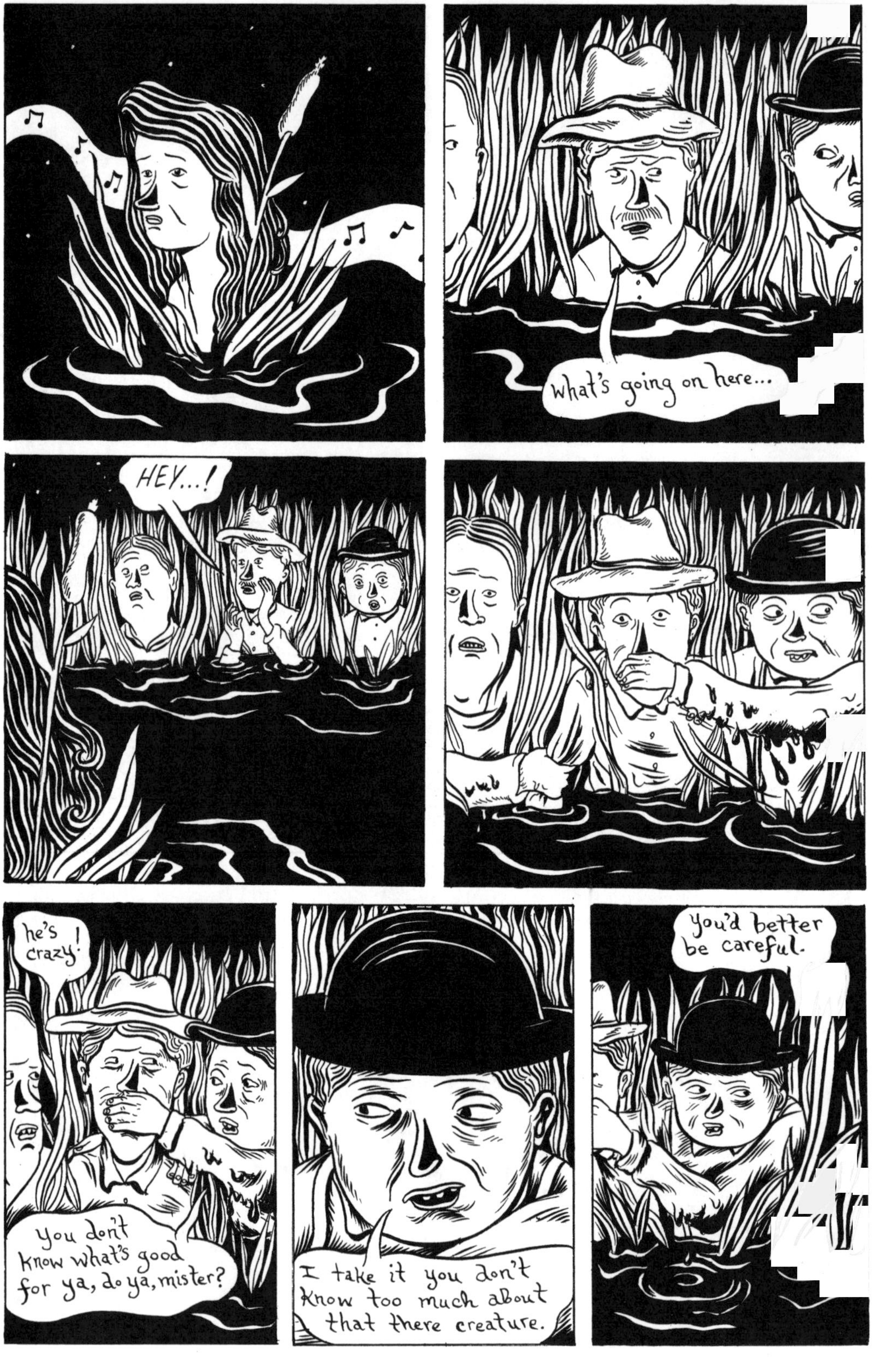
what's going on here...
HEY...!
he's crazy!
You don't know what's good for ya, do ya, mister?
I take it you don't know too much about that there creature.
You'd better be careful.

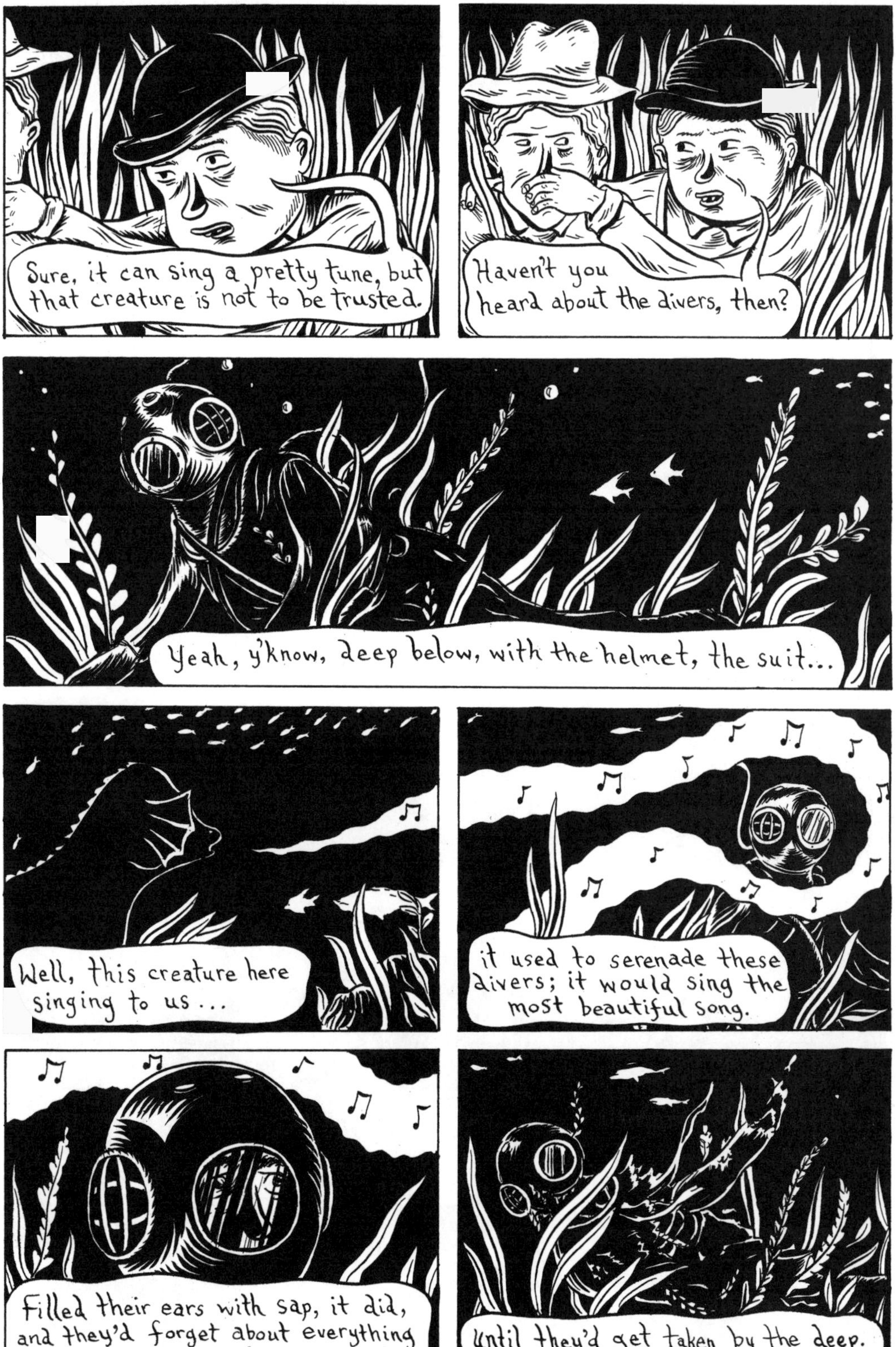
Sure, it can sing a pretty tune, but that creature is not to be trusted.
Haven't you heard about the divers, then?
Yeah, y'know, deep below, with the helmet, the suit...
Well, this creature here singing to us...
it used to serenade these divers; it would sing the most beautiful song.
Filled their ears with sap, it did, and they'd forget about everything but the sweetness of the moment
until they'd get taken by the deep.

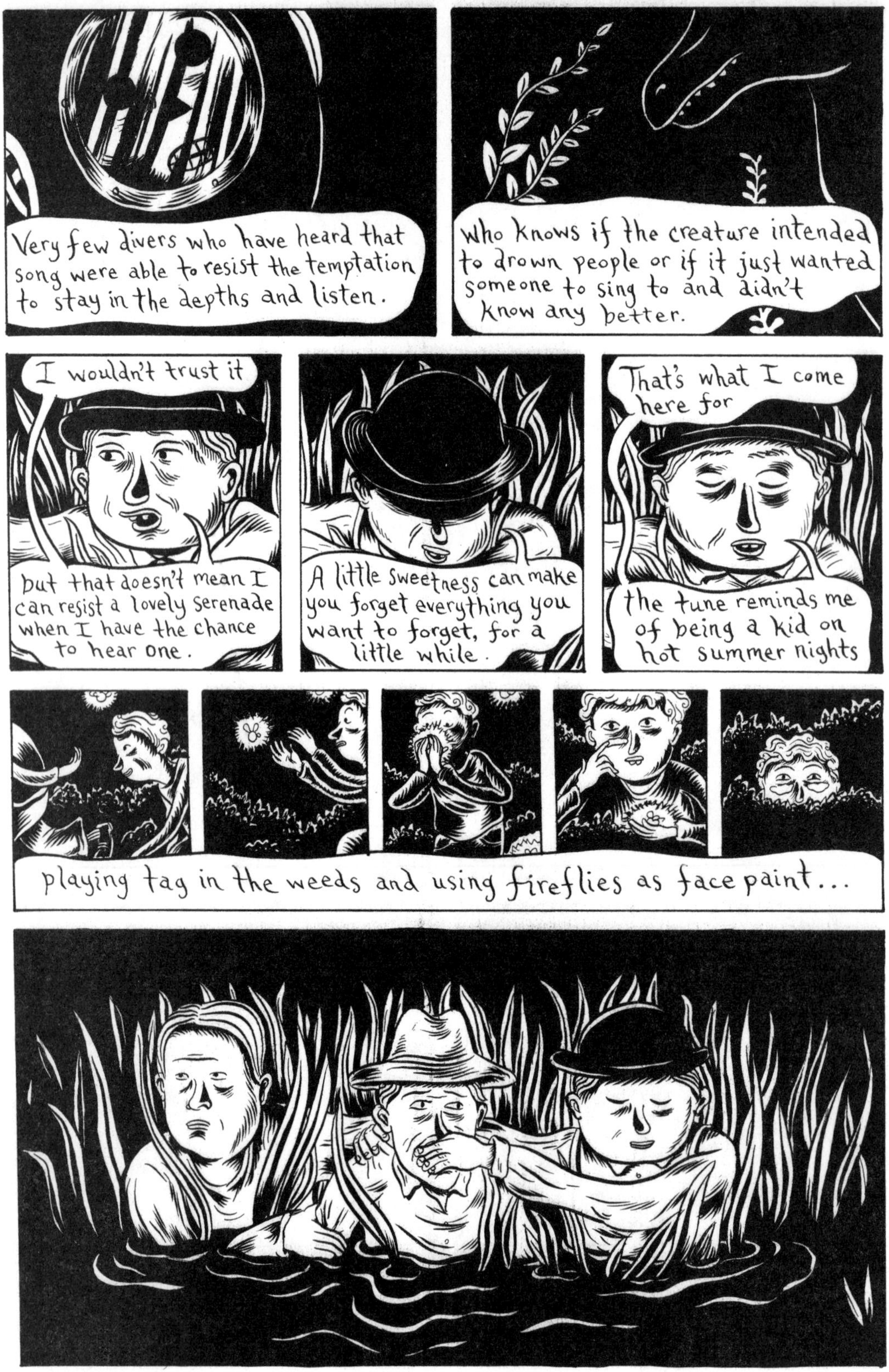
Very few divers who have heard that song were able to resist the temptation to stay in the depths and listen.
Who knows if the creature intended to drown people or if it just wanted someone to sing to and didn't know any better.
I wouldn't trust it
but that doesn't mean I can resist a lovely serenade when I have the chance to hear one.
A little sweetness can make you forget everything you want to forget, for a little while.
That's what I come here for
the tune reminds me of being a kid on hot summer nights
playing tag in the weeds and using fireflies as face paint...

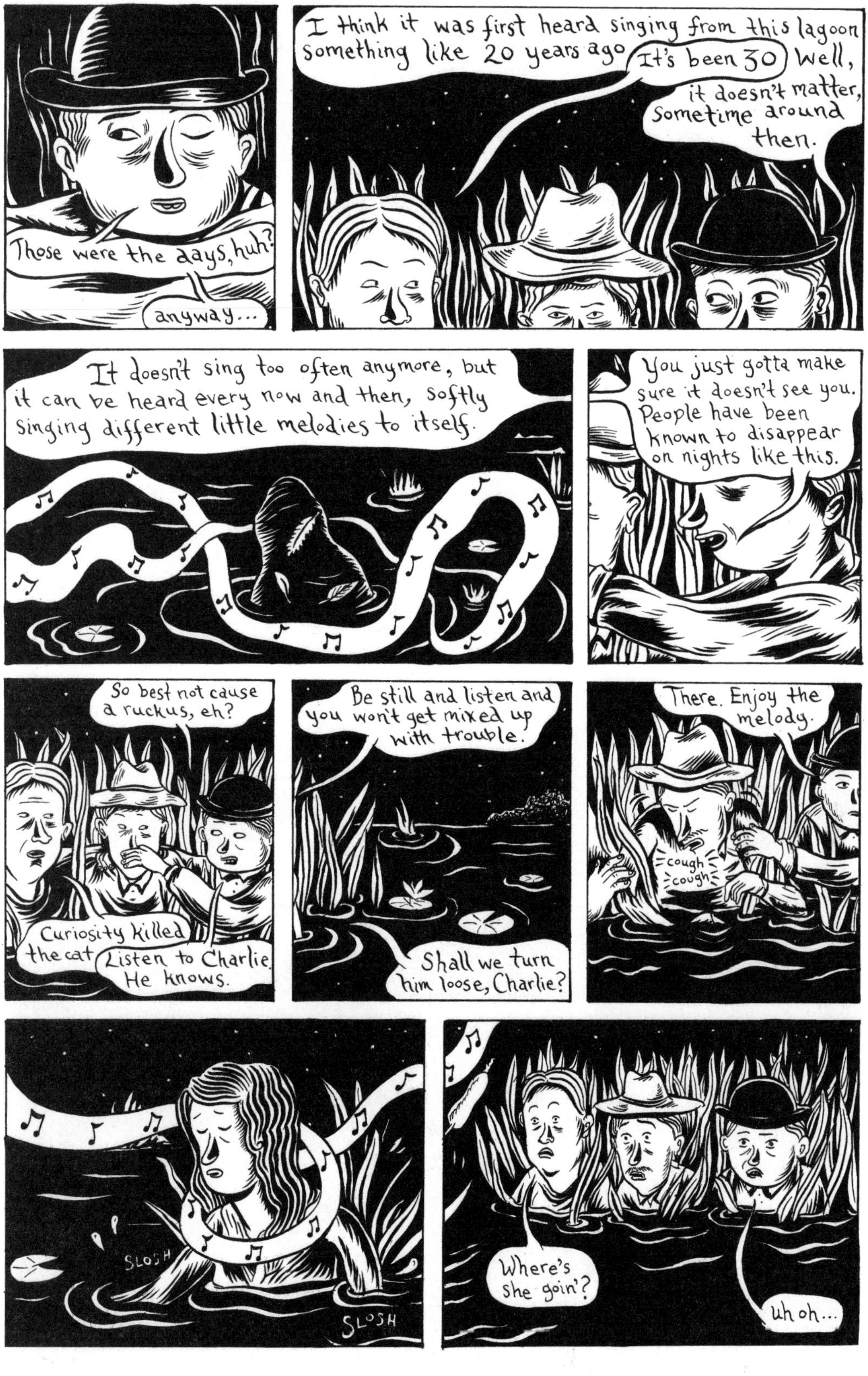
Those were the days, huh?
anyway...
I think it was first heard singing from this lagoon something like 20 years ago
It's been 30
Well, it doesn't matter, sometime around then.
It doesn't sing too often anymore, but it can be heard every now and then, softly singing different little melodies to itself.
You just gotta make sure it doesn't see you. People have been known to disappear on nights like this.
So best not cause a ruckus, eh?
Curiosity killed the cat
Listen to Charlie. He knows.
Be still and listen and you won't get mixed up with trouble.
Shall we turn him loose, Charlie?
There. Enjoy the melody.
cough cough
SLOSH
SLOSH
Where's she goin'?
uh oh...

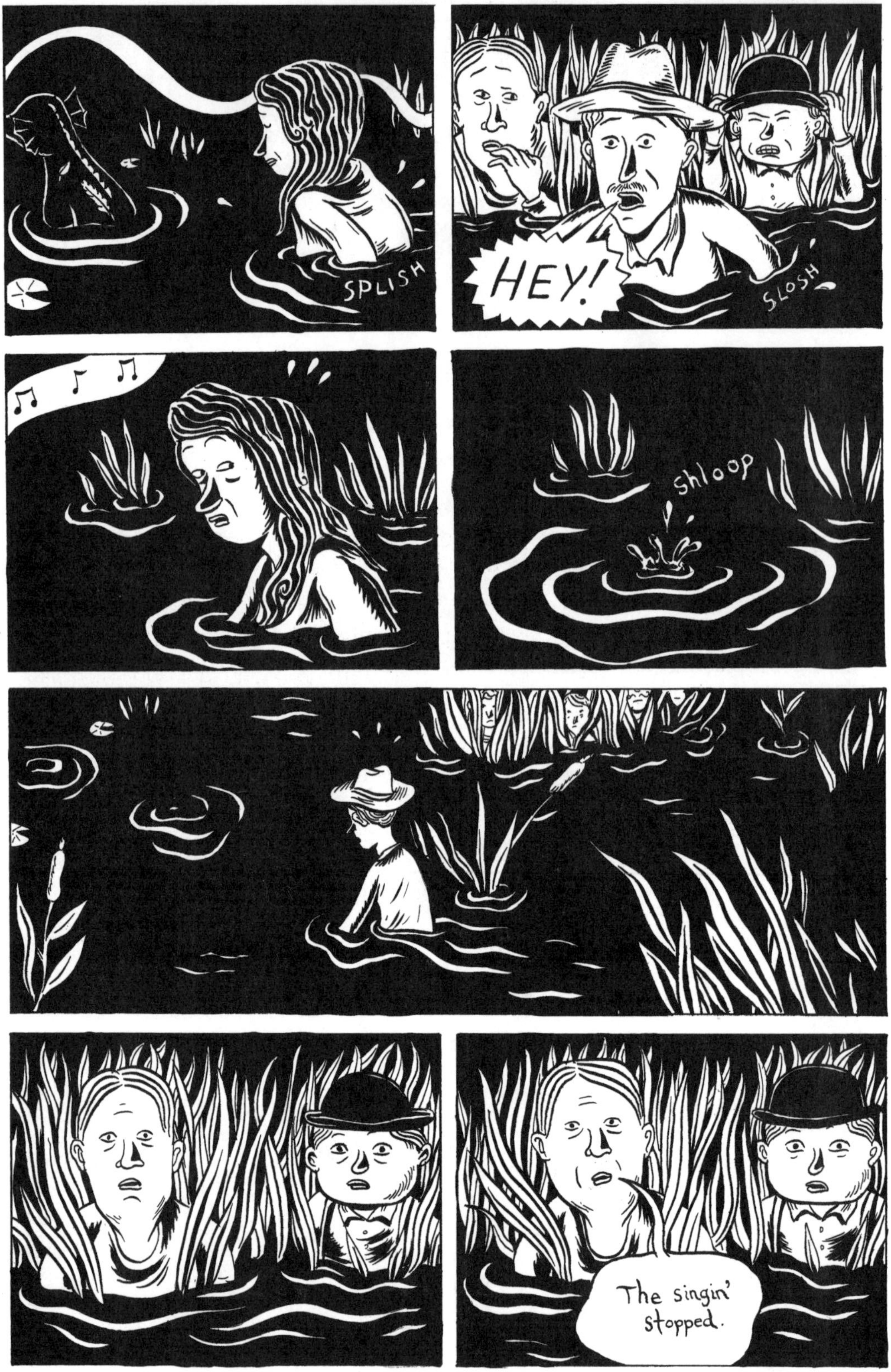
SPLISH
HEY!
SLOSH
Shloop
The singin' stopped.

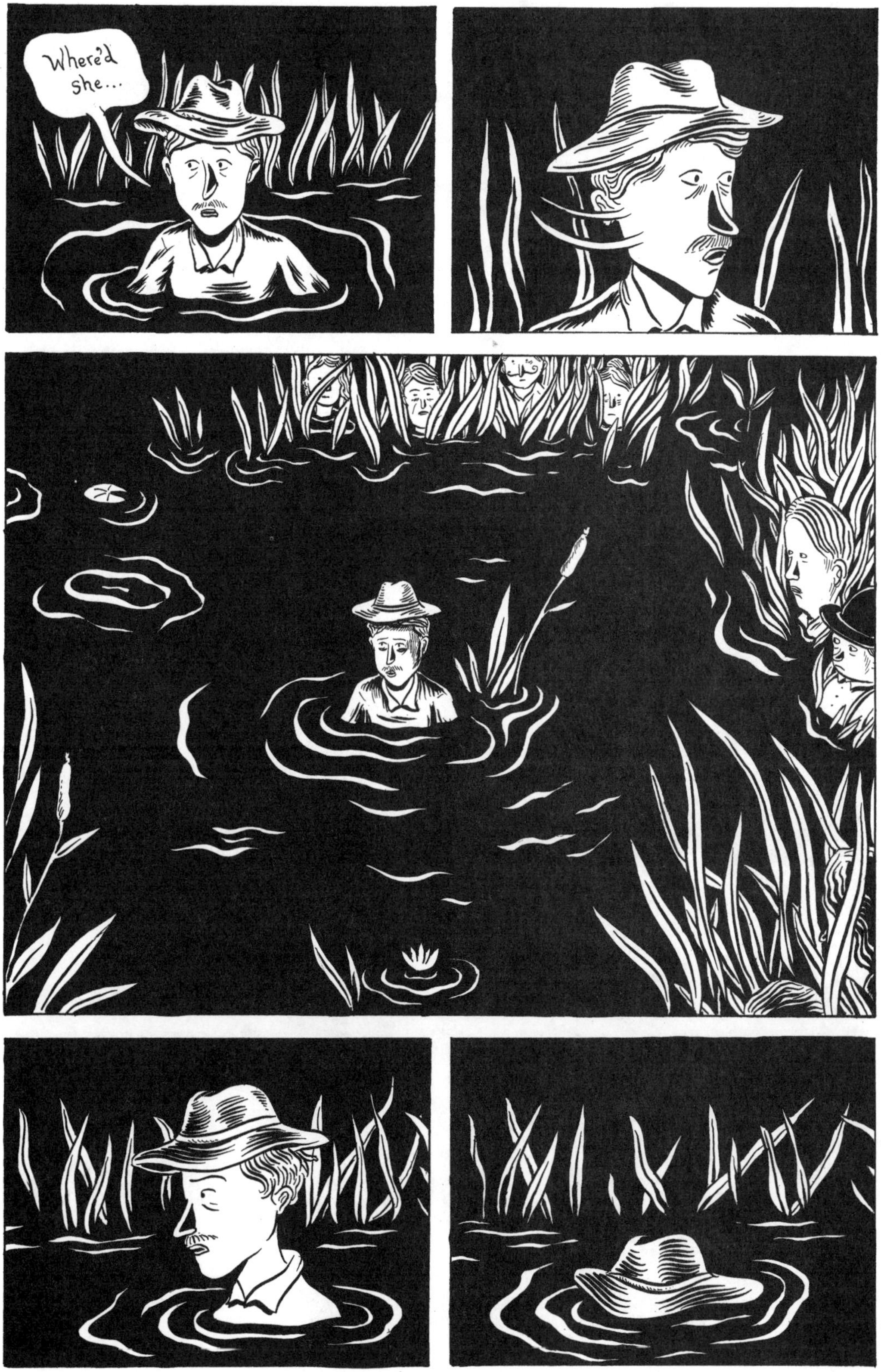
Where'd she...

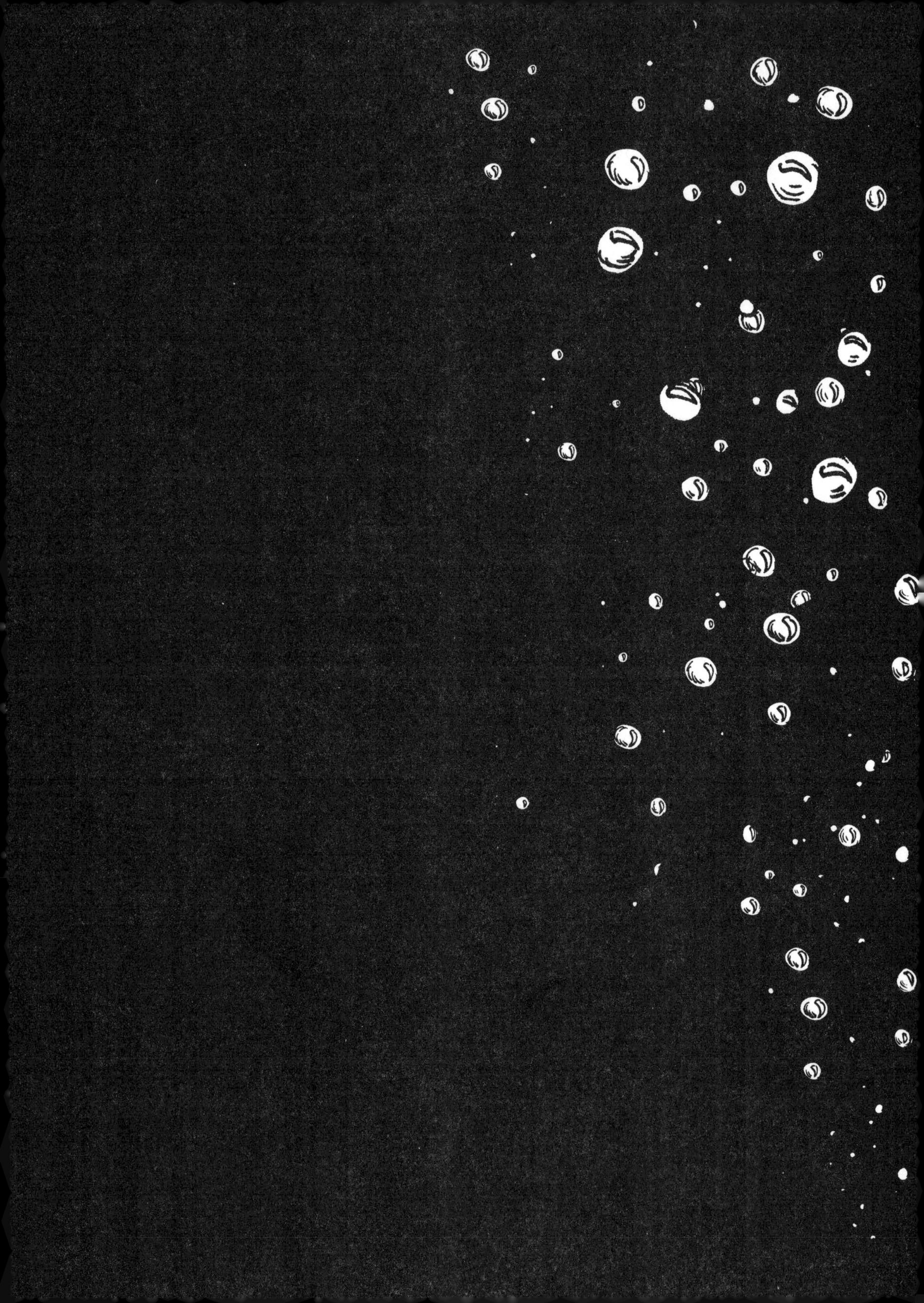

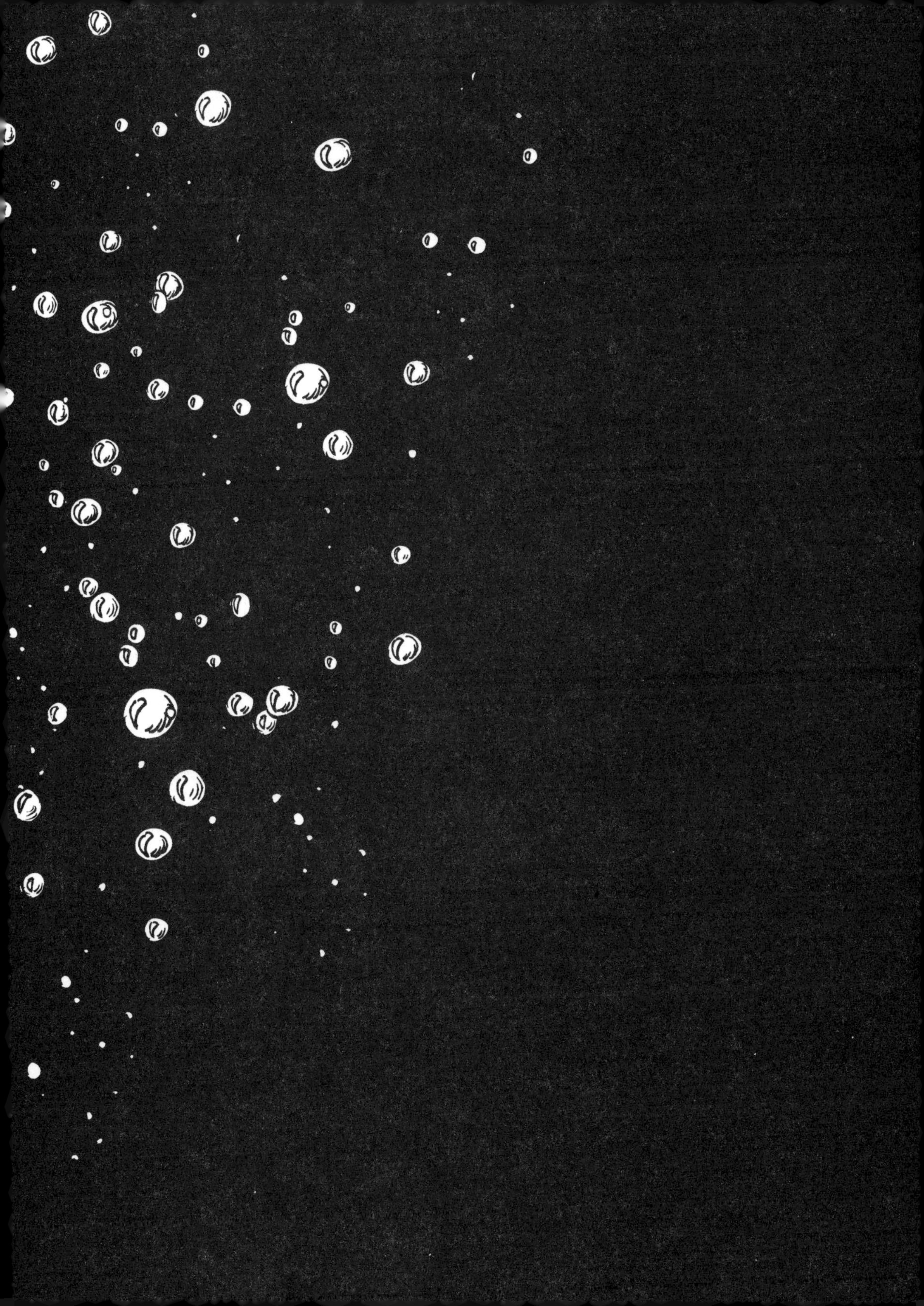

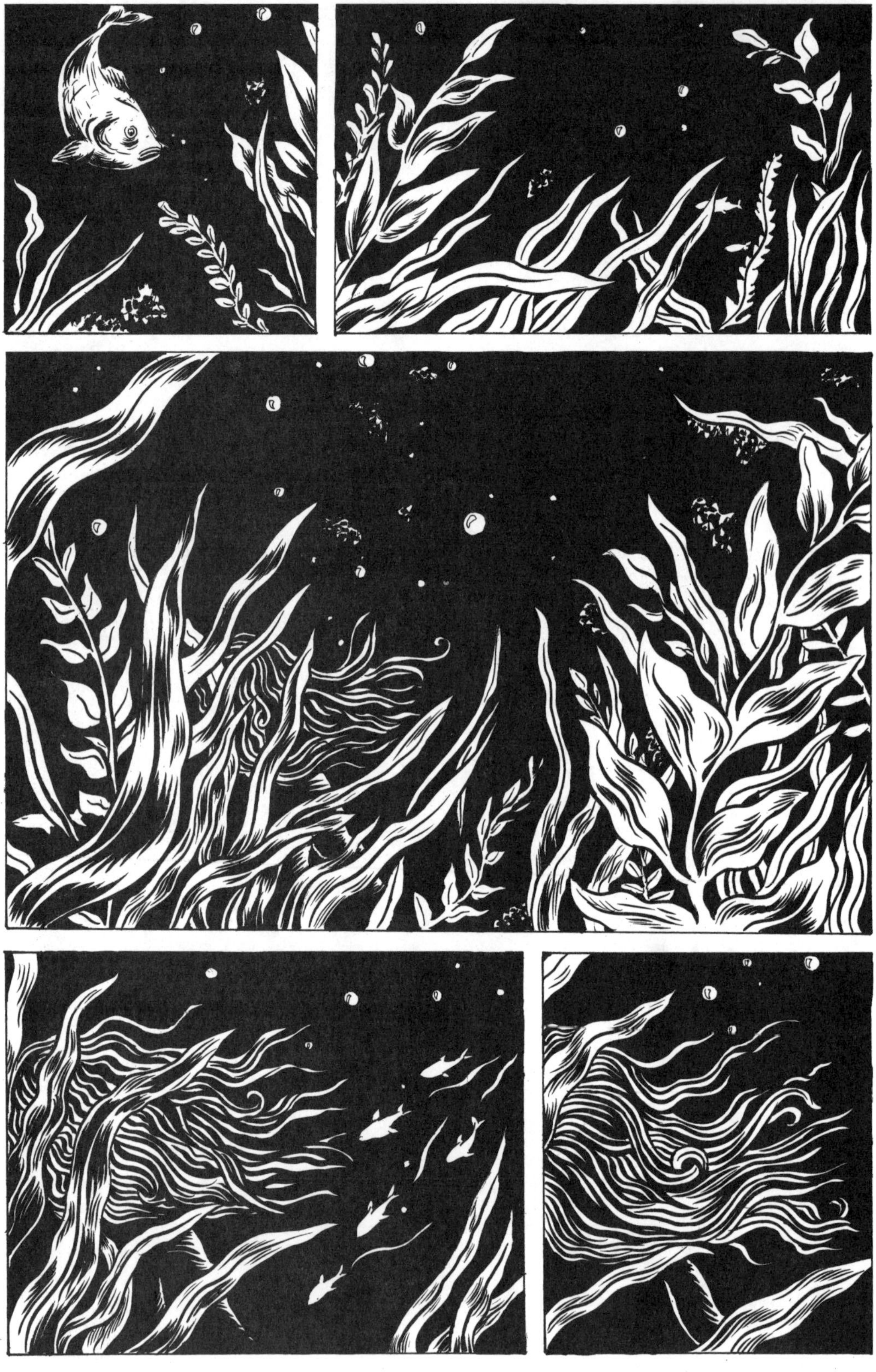

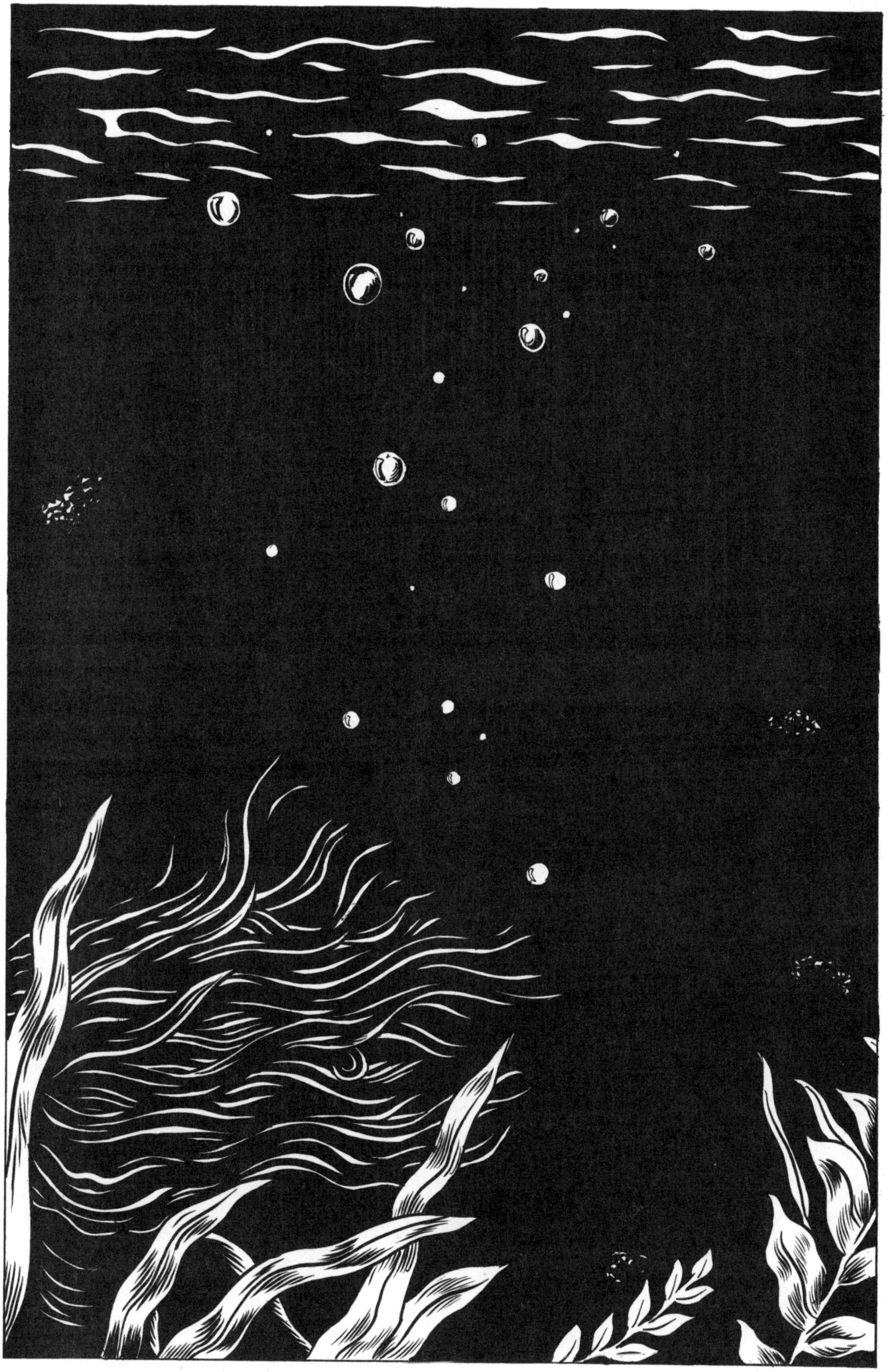

THE DAILY GRAND PRIX

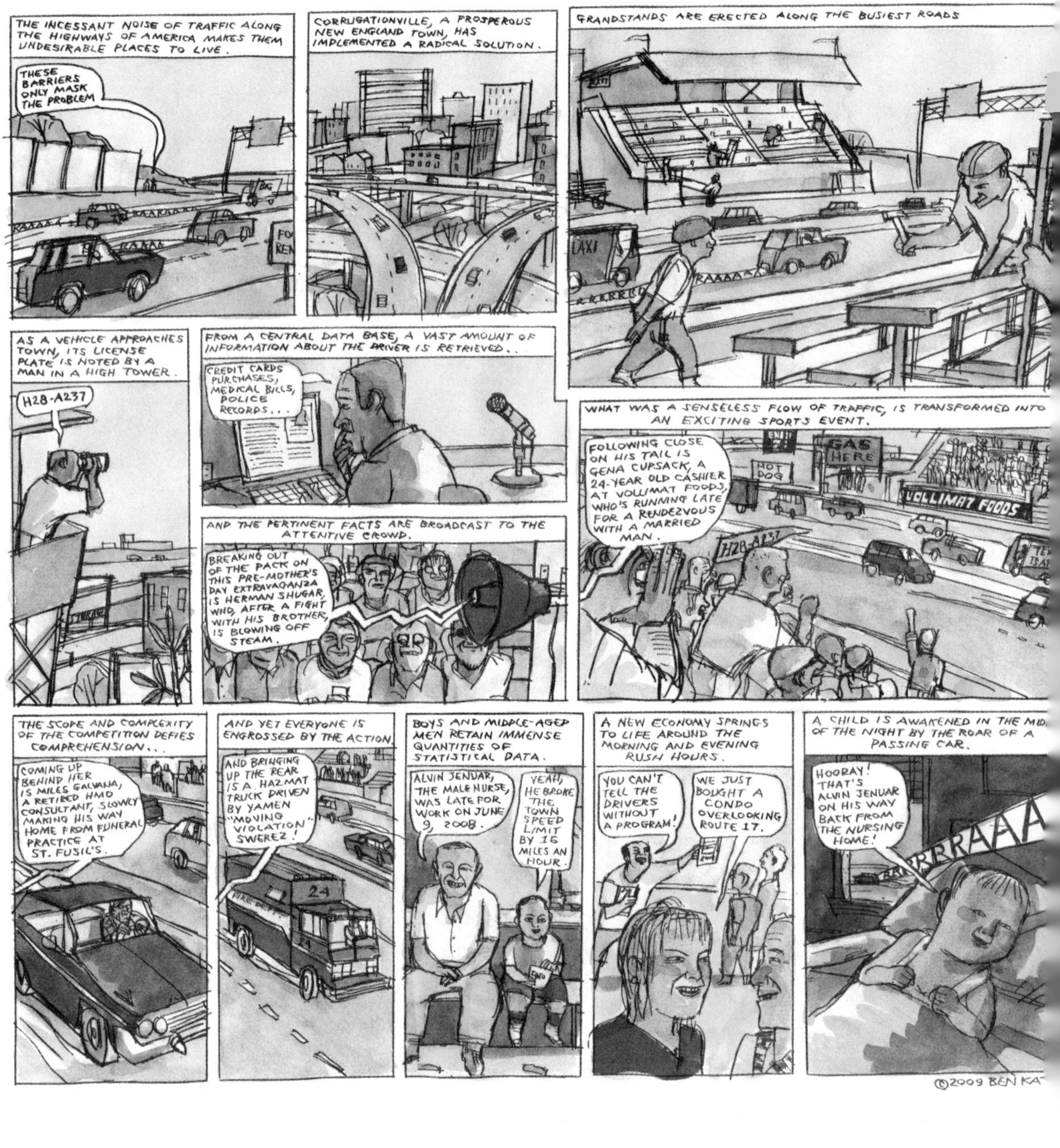

THE INCESSANT NOISE OF TRAFFIC ALONG THE HIGHWAYS OF AMERICA MAKES THEM UNDESIRABLE PLACES TO LIVE.
THESE BARRIERS ONLY MASK THE PROBLEM
CORRUGATIONVILLE, A PROSPEROUS NEW ENGLAND TOWN, HAS IMPLEMENTED A RADICAL SOLUTION.
GRANDSTANDS ARE ERECTED ALONG THE BUSIEST ROADS
TAXI
AS A VEHICLE APPROACHES TOWN, ITS LICENSE PLATE IS NOTED BY A MAN IN A HIGH TOWER.
H28-A237
FROM A CENTRAL DATA BASE, A VAST AMOUNT OF INFORMATION ABOUT THE DRIVER IS RETRIEVED...
CREDIT CARDS PURCHASES, MEDICAL BILLS, POLICE RECORDS...
AND THE PERTINENT FACTS ARE BROADCAST TO THE ATTENTIVE CROWD.
BREAKING OUT OF THE PACK ON THIS PRE-MOTHER'S DAY EXTRAVAGANZA IS HERMAN SHUGAR, WHO, AFTER A FIGHT WITH HIS BROTHER, IS BLOWING OFF STEAM.
WHAT WAS A SENSELESS FLOW OF TRAFFIC, IS TRANSFORMED INTO AN EXCITING SPORTS EVENT.
FOLLOWING CLOSE ON HIS TAIL IS GENA CUPSACK, A 24-YEAR OLD CASHIER AT VOLLIMAT FOODS, WHO'S RUNNING LATE FOR A RENDEZVOUS WITH A MARRIED MAN.
GAS HERE
HOT DOG
VOLLIMAT FOODS
H28-A237
THE SCOPE AND COMPLEXITY OF THE COMPETITION DEFIES COMPREHENSION...
COMING UP BEHIND HER IS MILES GALVANA, A RETIRED HMO CONSULTANT, SLOWLY MAKING HIS WAY HOME FROM FUNERAL PRACTICE AT ST. FUSIL'S.
AND YET EVERYONE IS ENGROSSED BY THE ACTION.
AND BRINGING UP THE REAR IS A HAZMAT TRUCK DRIVEN BY YAMEN "MOVING VIOLATION" SWEREZ!
FIRE DEPT.
24
BOYS AND MIDDLE-AGED MEN RETAIN IMMENSE QUANTITIES OF STATISTICAL DATA.
ALVIN JENUAR, THE MALE NURSE, WAS LATE FOR WORK ON JUNE 9, 2008.
YEAH, HE BROKE THE TOWN SPEED LIMIT BY 16 MILES AN HOUR.
A NEW ECONOMY SPRINGS TO LIFE AROUND THE MORNING AND EVENING RUSH HOURS.
YOU CAN'T TELL THE DRIVERS WITHOUT A PROGRAM!
WE JUST BOUGHT A CONDO OVERLOOKING ROUTE 17.
A CHILD IS AWAKENED IN THE MID
OF THE NIGHT BY THE ROAR OF A PASSING CAR.
HOORAY! THAT'S ALVIN JENUAR ON HIS WAY BACK FROM THE NURSING HOME!
BRRRAAAA
©2009 BEN KA

BEN KATCHOR

ORBIDDEN ROOMS

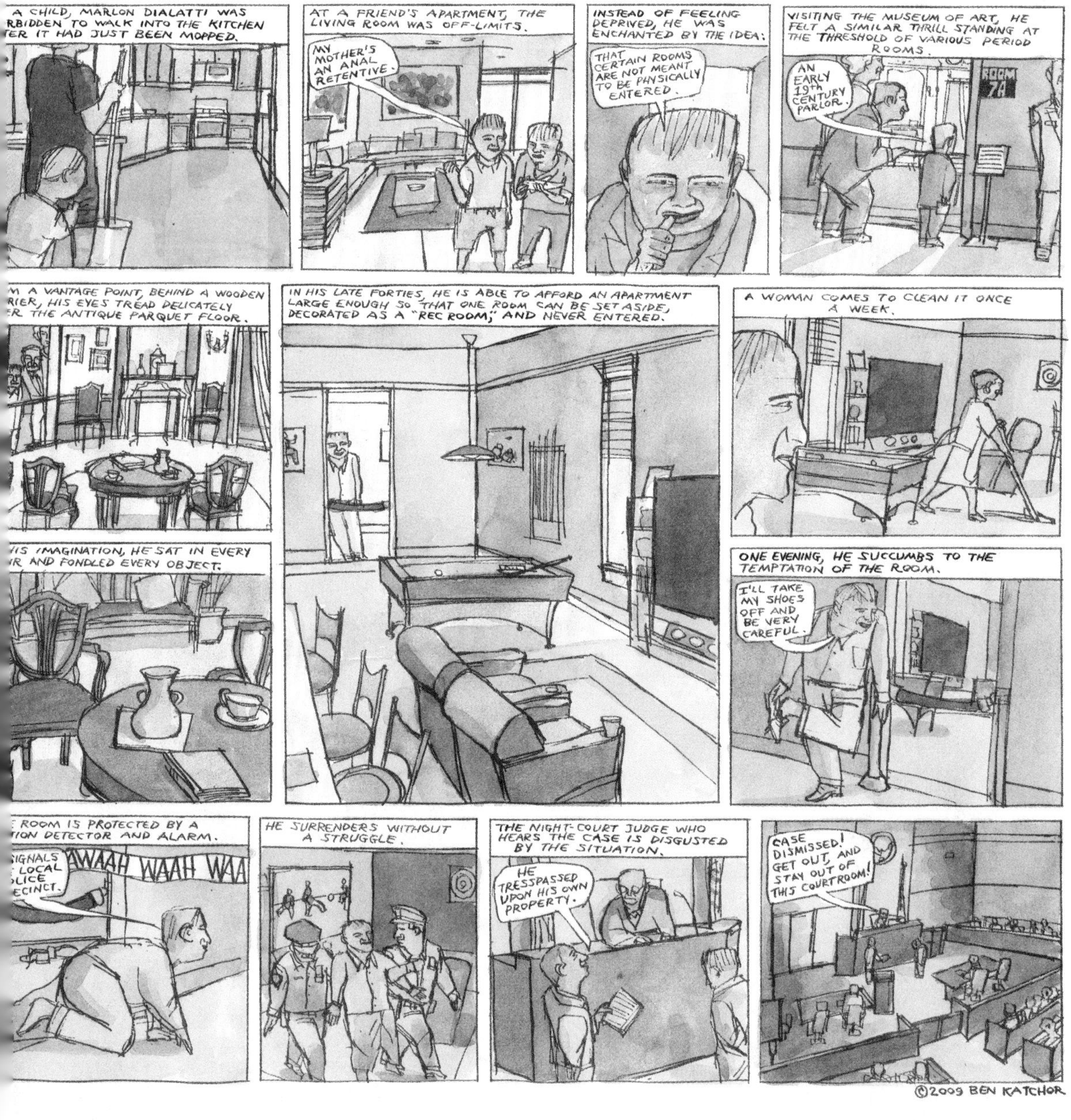
A CHILD, MARLON DIALATTI WAS
RBIDDEN TO WALK INTO THE KITCHEN
TER IT HAD JUST BEEN MOPPED.
AT A FRIEND'S APARTMENT, THE LIVING ROOM WAS OFF-LIMITS.
MY MOTHER'S AN ANAL RETENTIVE.
INSTEAD OF FEELING DEPRIVED, HE WAS ENCHANTED BY THE IDEA:
THAT CERTAIN ROOMS ARE NOT MEANT TO BE PHYSICALLY ENTERED.
VISITING THE MUSEUM OF ART, HE FELT A SIMILAR THRILL STANDING AT THE THRESHOLD OF VARIOUS PERIOD ROOMS.
AN EARLY 19th CENTURY PARLOR.
ROOM 7A
M A VANTAGE POINT, BEHIND A WOODEN
RIER, HIS EYES TREAD DELICATELY
ER THE ANTIQUE PARQUET FLOOR.
HIS IMAGINATION, HE SAT IN EVERY
IR AND FONDLED EVERY OBJECT.
IN HIS LATE FORTIES, HE IS ABLE TO AFFORD AN APARTMENT LARGE ENOUGH SO THAT ONE ROOM CAN BE SET ASIDE, DECORATED AS A "REC ROOM," AND NEVER ENTERED.
A WOMAN COMES TO CLEAN IT ONCE A WEEK.
ONE EVENING, HE SUCCUMBS TO THE TEMPTATION OF THE ROOM.
I'LL TAKE MY SHOES OFF AND BE VERY CAREFUL.
E ROOM IS PROTECTED BY A
TION DETECTOR AND ALARM.
SIGNALS
LOCAL
LICE
ECINCT.
AWAAH WAAH WAA
HE SURRENDERS WITHOUT A STRUGGLE.
THE NIGHT-COURT JUDGE WHO HEARS THE CASE IS DISGUSTED BY THE SITUATION.
HE TRESSPASSED UPON HIS OWN PROPERTY.
CASE DISMISSED! GET OUT, AND STAY OUT OF THIS COURTROOM!
©2009 BEN KATCHOR

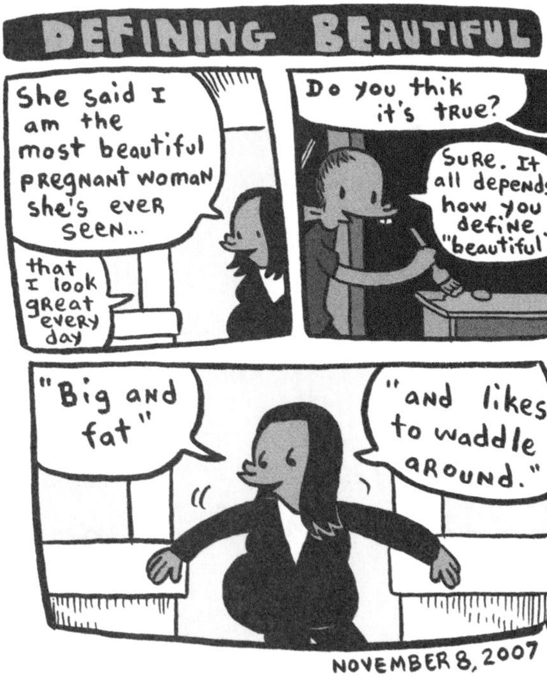
DEFINING BEAUTIFUL
She said I am the most beautiful pregnant woman she's ever seen...
that I look great every day
Do you thik it's true?
Sure. It all depends how you define "beautiful".
"Big and fat"
"and likes to waddle around."
NOVEMBER 8, 2007

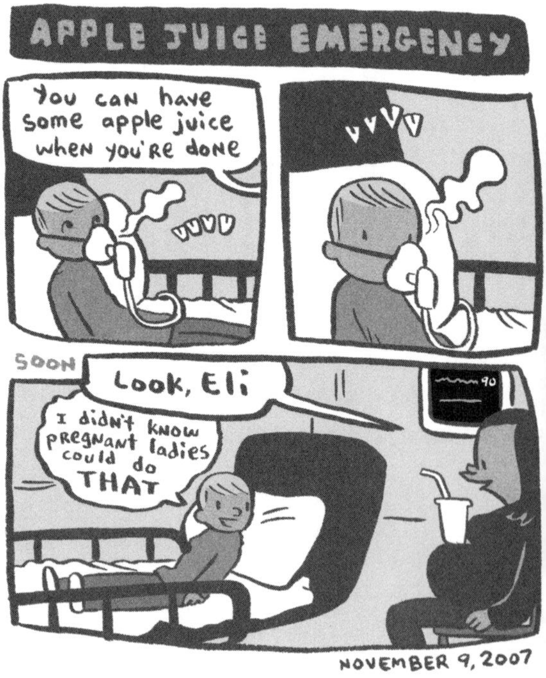
APPLE JUICE EMERGENCY
You can have some apple juice when you're done
SOON
Look, Eli
I didn't know pregnant ladies could do THAT
NOVEMBER 9, 2007

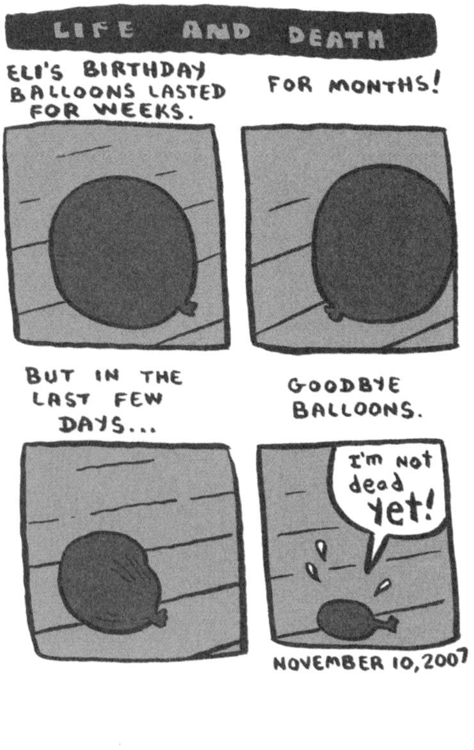
LIFE AND DEATH
ELI'S BIRTHDAY BALLOONS LASTED FOR WEEKS.
FOR MONTHS!
BUT IN THE LAST FEW DAYS...
GOODBYE BALLOONS.
I'm not dead yet!
NOVEMBER 10, 2007

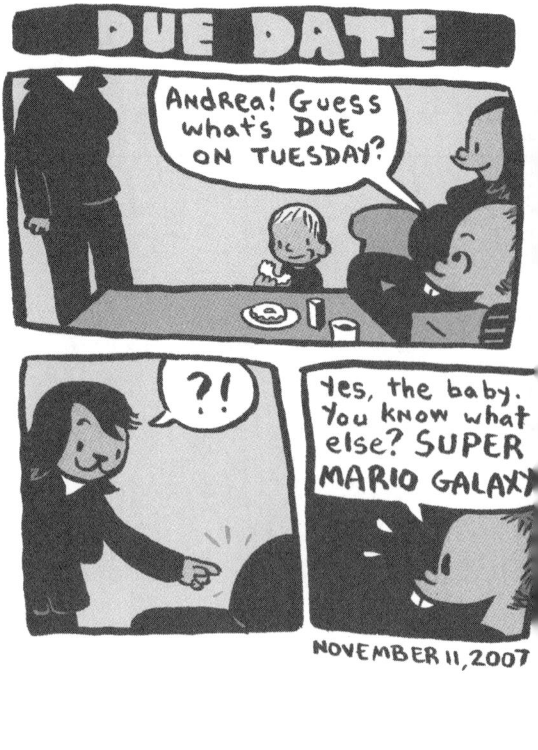
DUE DATE
Andrea! Guess what's DUE ON TUESDAY?
?!
Yes, the baby. You know what else? SUPER MARIO GALAXY
NOVEMBER 11, 2007

STING AND BURN

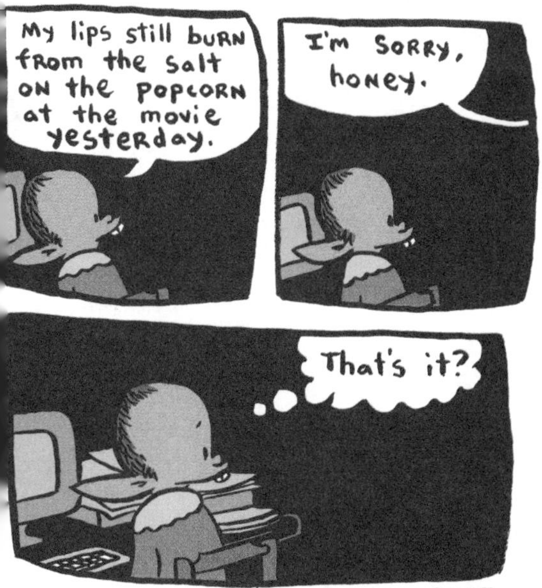
My lips still burn from the salt on the popcorn at the movie yesterday.
I'm sorry, honey.
That's it?

NOVEMBER 11, 2007

THE WIFE'S BODY

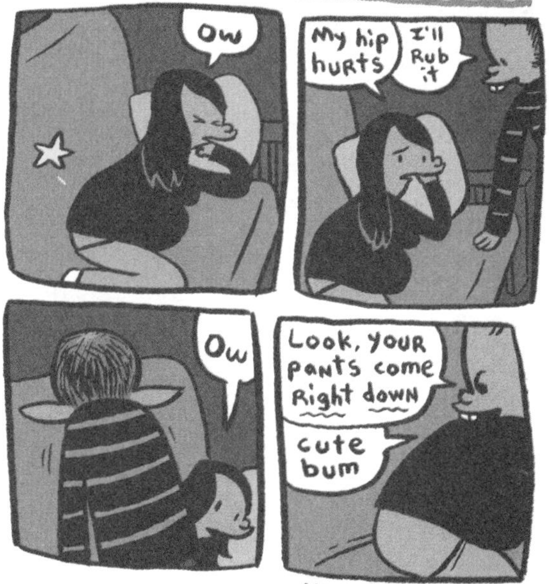
Ow
My hip hurts
I'll Rub it
Ow
Look, your pants come Right down
cute bum

NOVEMBER 12, 2007

WARM PLACES

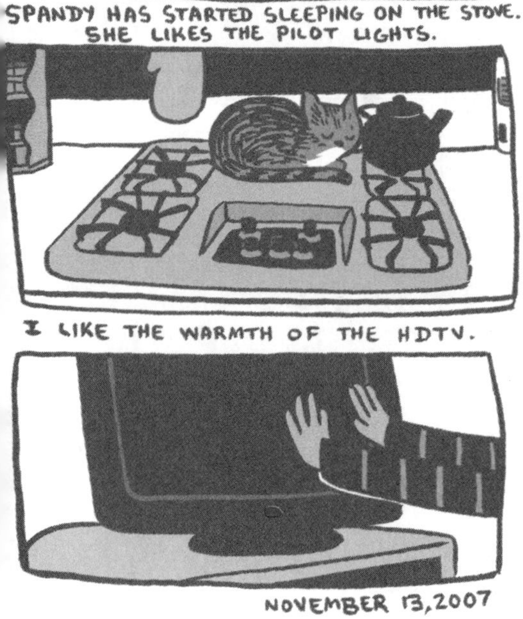
SPANDY HAS STARTED SLEEPING ON THE STOVE. SHE LIKES THE PILOT LIGHTS.
I LIKE THE WARMTH OF THE HDTV.

NOVEMBER 13, 2007

NO BABY YET

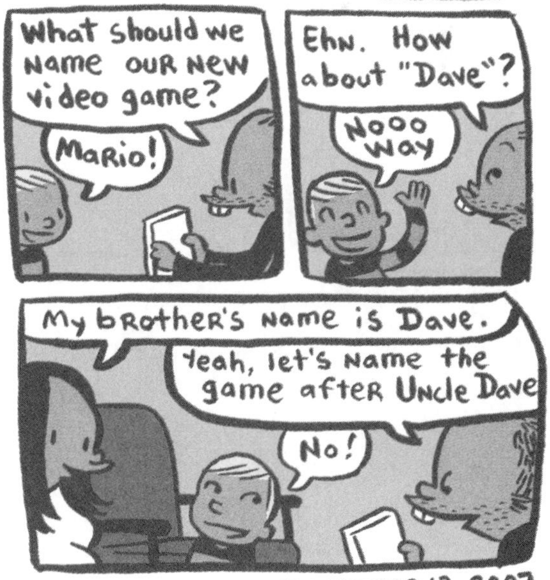
What should we name our new video game?
Mario!
Ehn. How about "Dave"?
Nooo way
My brother's name is Dave.
Yeah, let's name the game after Uncle Dave
No!

NOVEMBER 13, 2007

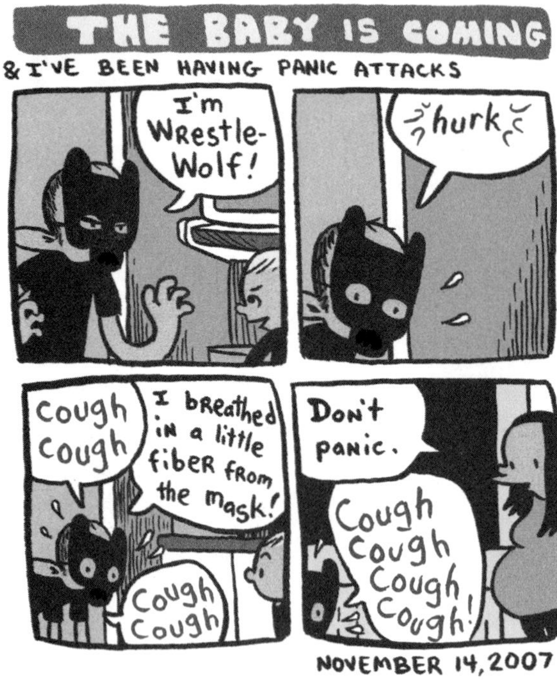
THE BABY IS COMING
& I'VE BEEN HAVING PANIC ATTACKS
I'm Wrestle-Wolf!
hurk
Cough Cough
I breathed in a little fiber from the mask!
Cough Cough
Don't panic.
Cough Cough Cough Cough!
NOVEMBER 14, 2007

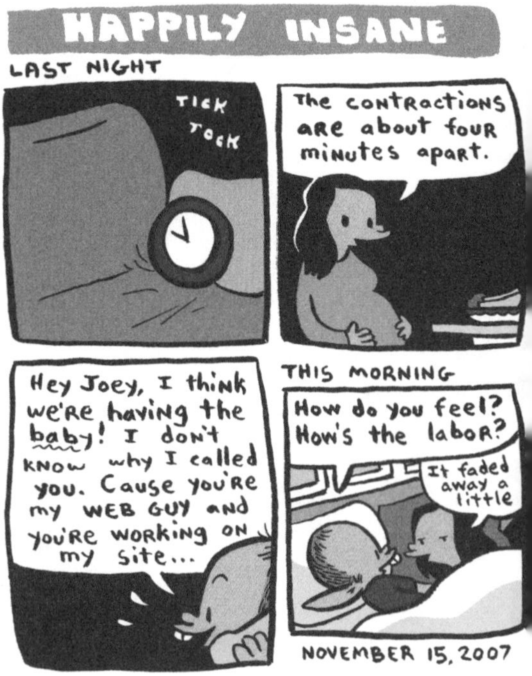
HAPPILY INSANE
LAST NIGHT
TICK
TOCK
The contractions are about four minutes apart.
Hey Joey, I think we're having the baby! I don't know why I called you. Cause you're my WEB GUY and you're working on my site...
THIS MORNING
How do you feel? How's the labor?
It faded away a little
NOVEMBER 15, 2007

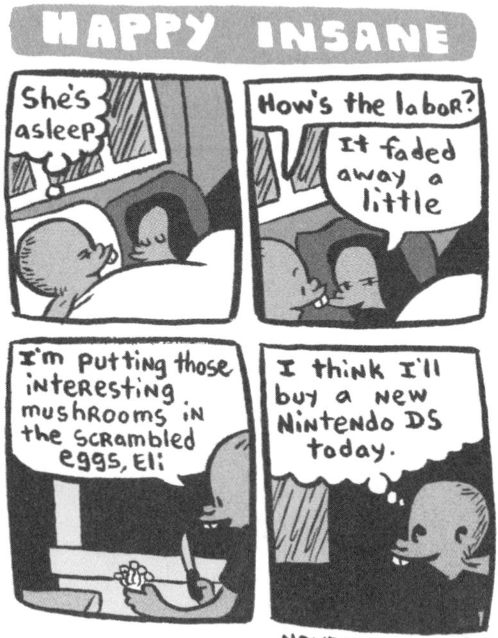
HAPPY INSANE
She's asleep
How's the labor?
It faded away a little
I'm putting those interesting mushrooms in the scrambled eggs, Eli
I think I'll buy a new Nintendo DS today.
NOVEMBER 15, 2007

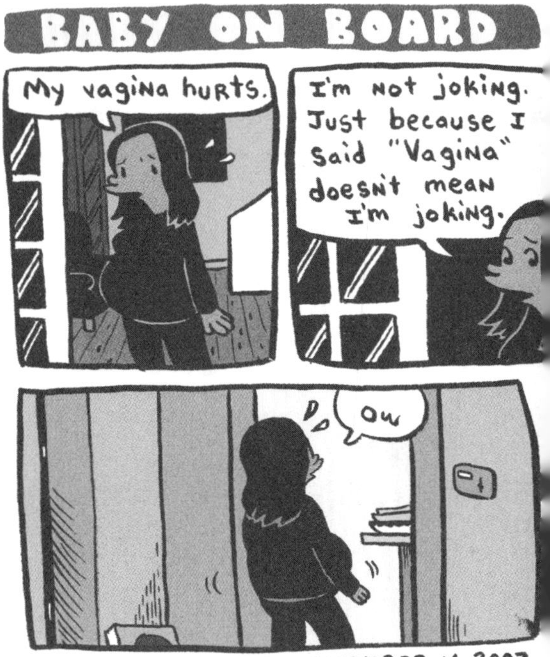
BABY ON BOARD
My vagina hurts.
I'm not joking. Just because I said "Vagina" doesn't mean I'm joking.
Ow
NOVEMBER 16, 2007

TOUCHING

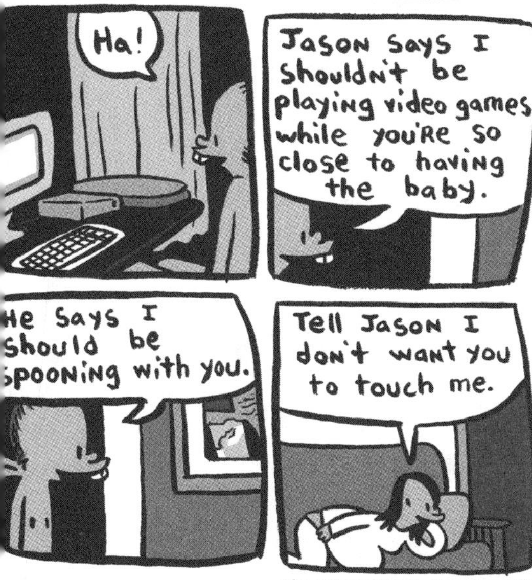

Ha!
Jason says I shouldn't be playing video games while you're so close to having the baby.
He says I should be spooning with you.
Tell Jason I don't want you to touch me.

NOVEMBER 17, 2007

MILKDRAGON

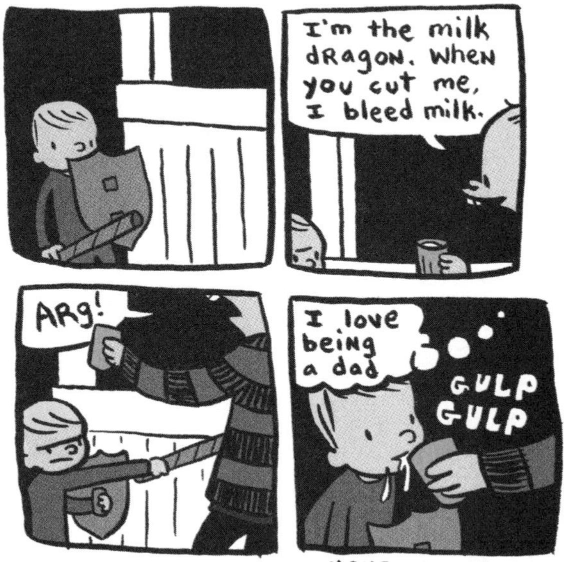

I'm the milk dragon. When you cut me, I bleed milk.
ARG!
I love being a dad
GULP GULP

NOVEMBER 18, 2007

CRAFT IS THE ENEMY

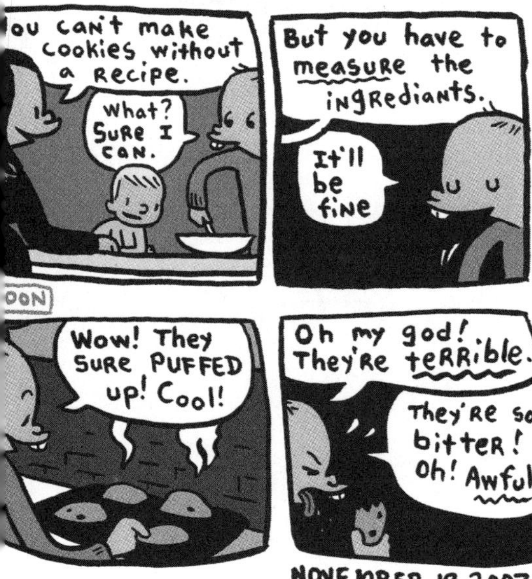

ou can't make cookies without a recipe.
What? Sure I can.
But you have to measure the ingrediants.
It'll be fine
OON
Wow! They sure puffed up! Cool!
Oh my god! They're terrible.
They're so bitter! Oh! Awful!

NOVEMBER 19, 2007

WELCOMING WINTER

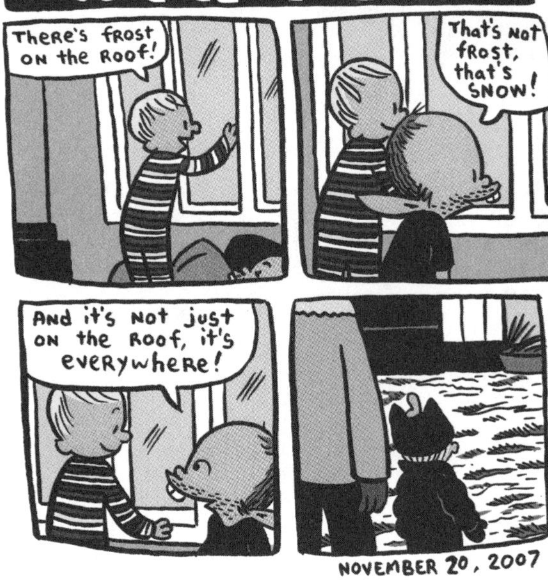

There's frost on the roof!
That's not frost, that's snow!
And it's not just on the roof, it's everywhere!

NOVEMBER 20, 2007

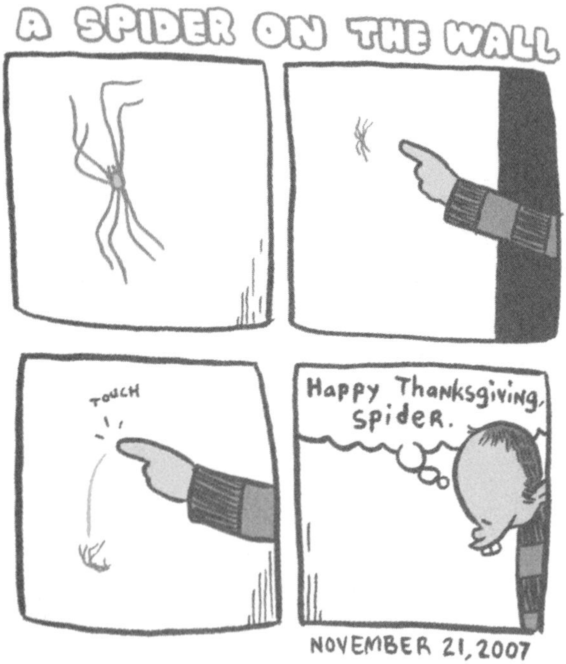
A SPIDER ON THE WALL
TOUCH
Happy Thanksgiving, spider.
NOVEMBER 21, 2007

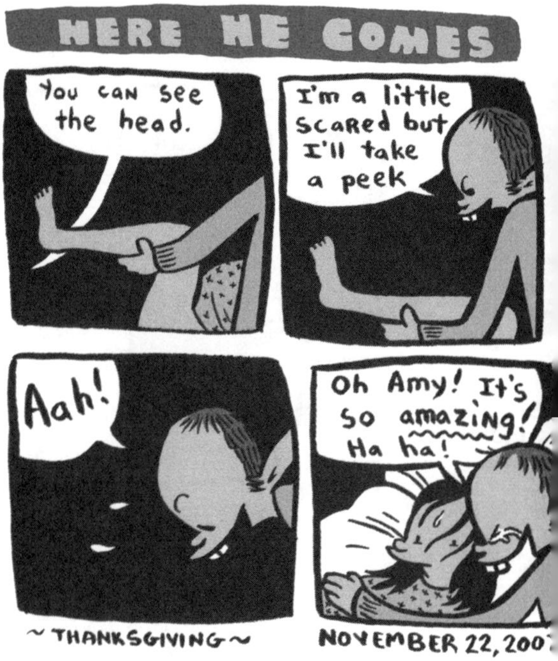
HERE HE COMES
You can see the head.
I'm a little scared but I'll take a peek
Aah!
Oh Amy! It's so amazing! Ha ha!
~THANKSGIVING~
NOVEMBER 22, 2007

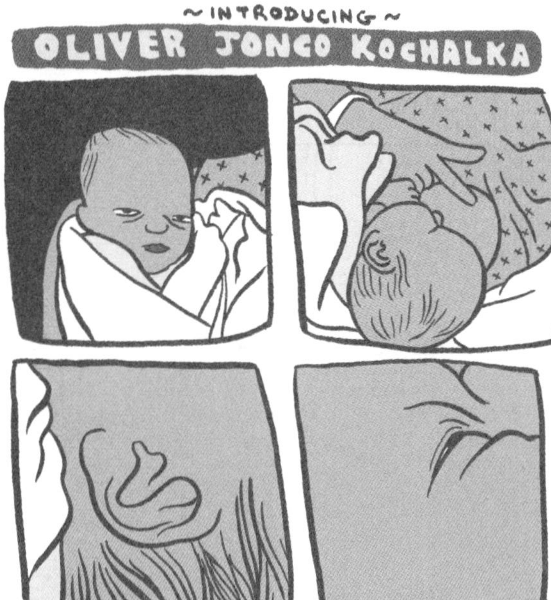
~INTRODUCING~
OLIVER JONGO KOCHALKA
NOVEMBER 23, 2007

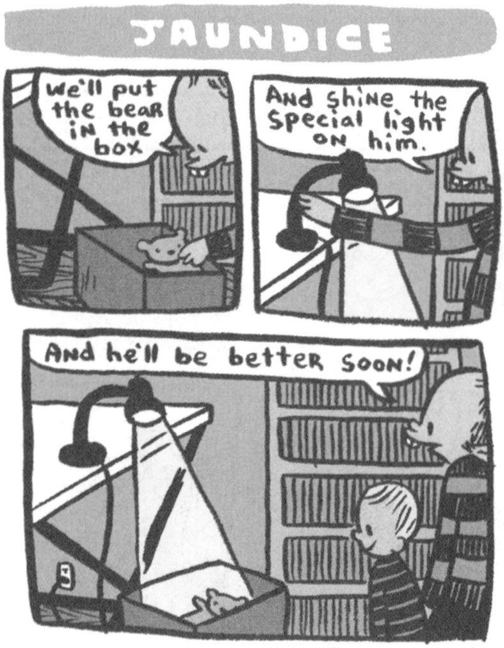
JAUNDICE
We'll put the bear in the box
And shine the special light on him.
And he'll be better soon!
NOVEMBER 24, 2007

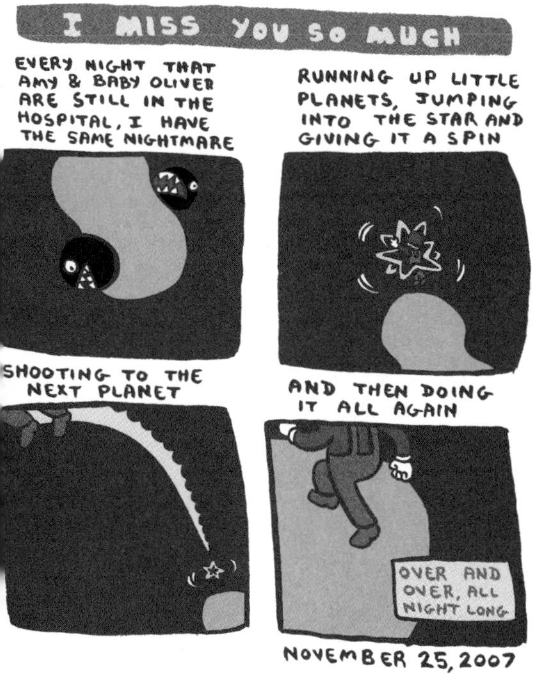
I MISS YOU SO MUCH
EVERY NIGHT THAT AMY & BABY OLIVER ARE STILL IN THE HOSPITAL, I HAVE THE SAME NIGHTMARE
RUNNING UP LITTLE PLANETS, JUMPING INTO THE STAR AND GIVING IT A SPIN
SHOOTING TO THE NEXT PLANET
AND THEN DOING IT ALL AGAIN
OVER AND OVER, ALL NIGHT LONG
NOVEMBER 25, 2007

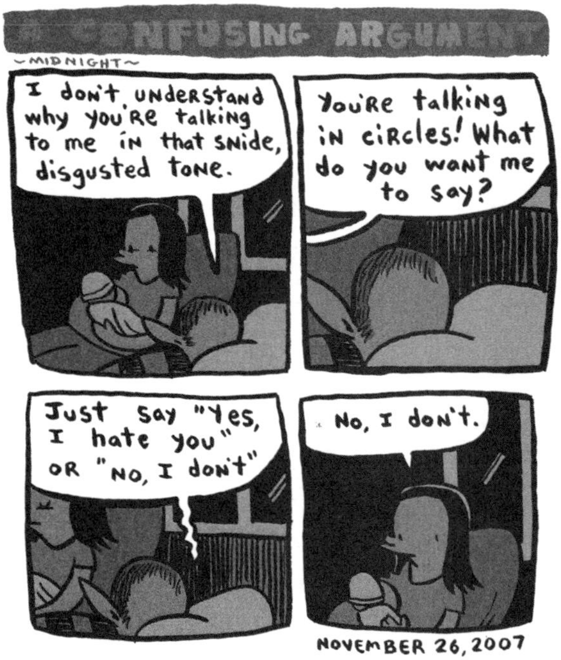
CONFUSING ARGUMENT
~MIDNIGHT~
I don't understand why you're talking to me in that snide, disgusted tone.
You're talking in circles! What do you want me to say?
Just say "Yes, I hate you" or "No, I don't"
No, I don't.
NOVEMBER 26, 2007

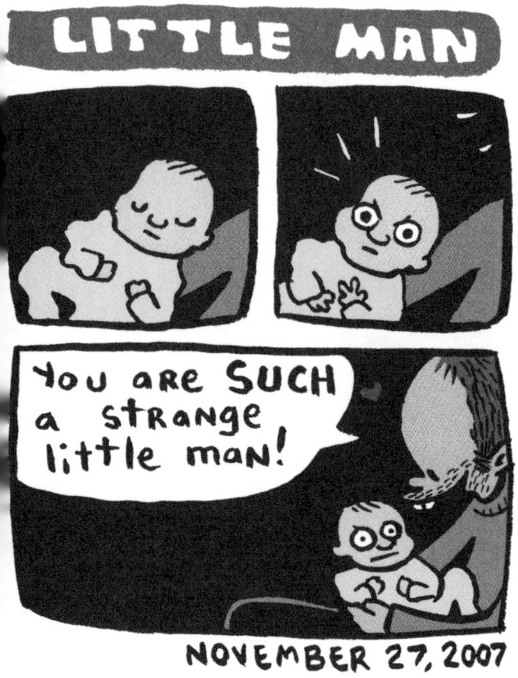
LITTLE MAN
You are SUCH a strange little man!
NOVEMBER 27, 2007

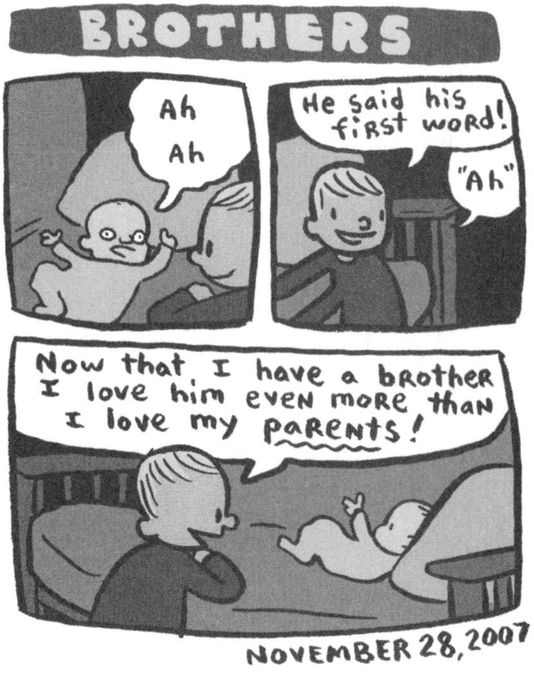
BROTHERS
Ah
Ah
He said his first word!
"Ah"
Now that I have a brother I love him even more than I love my parents!
NOVEMBER 28, 2007

excerpt from

THE ALCOHOLIC

JONATHAN AMES AND DEAN HASPIEL

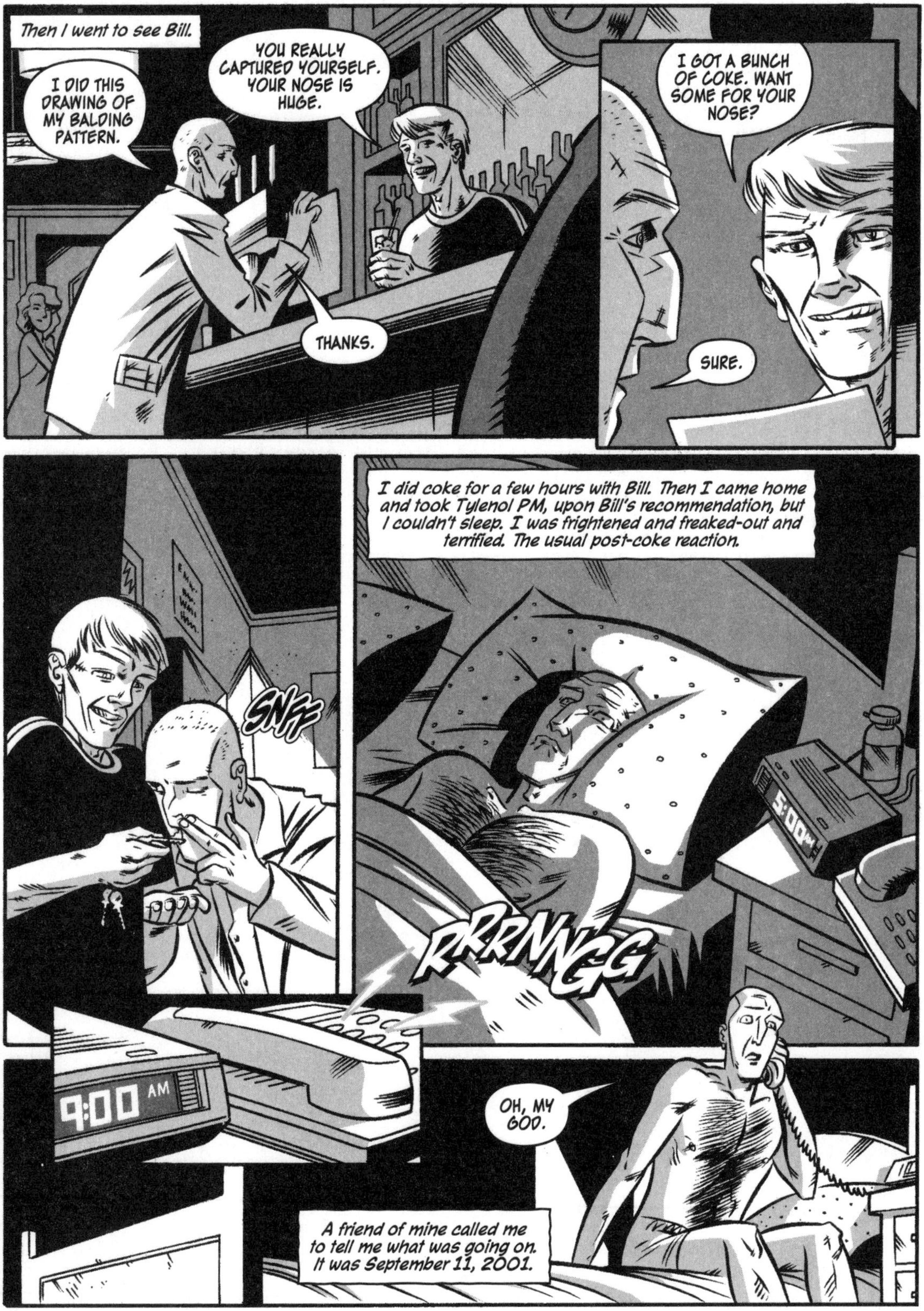
Then I went to see Bill.
I DID THIS DRAWING OF MY BALDING PATTERN.
YOU REALLY CAPTURED YOURSELF. YOUR NOSE IS HUGE.
THANKS.
I GOT A BUNCH OF COKE. WANT SOME FOR YOUR NOSE?
SURE.
SNFF
I did coke for a few hours with Bill. Then I came home and took Tylenol PM, upon Bill's recommendation, but I couldn't sleep. I was frightened and freaked-out and terrified. The usual post-coke reaction.
5:00
RRRNNGG
9:00 AM
OH, MY GOD.
A friend of mine called me to tell me what was going on. It was September 11, 2001.

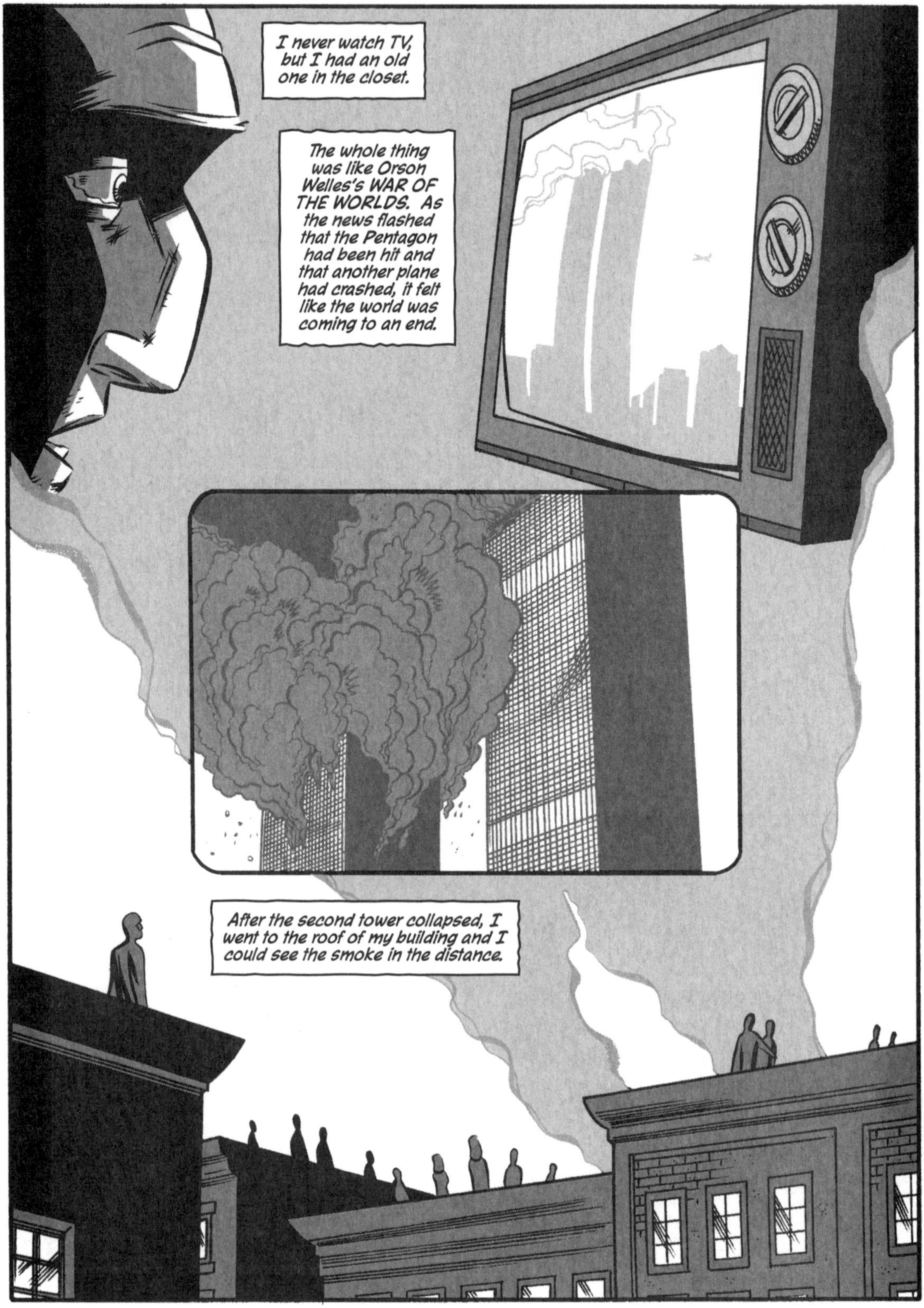
I never watch TV, but I had an old one in the closet.
The whole thing was like Orson Welles's WAR OF THE WORLDS. As the news flashed that the Pentagon had been hit and that another plane had crashed, it felt like the world was coming to an end.
After the second tower collapsed, I went to the roof of my building and I could see the smoke in the distance.

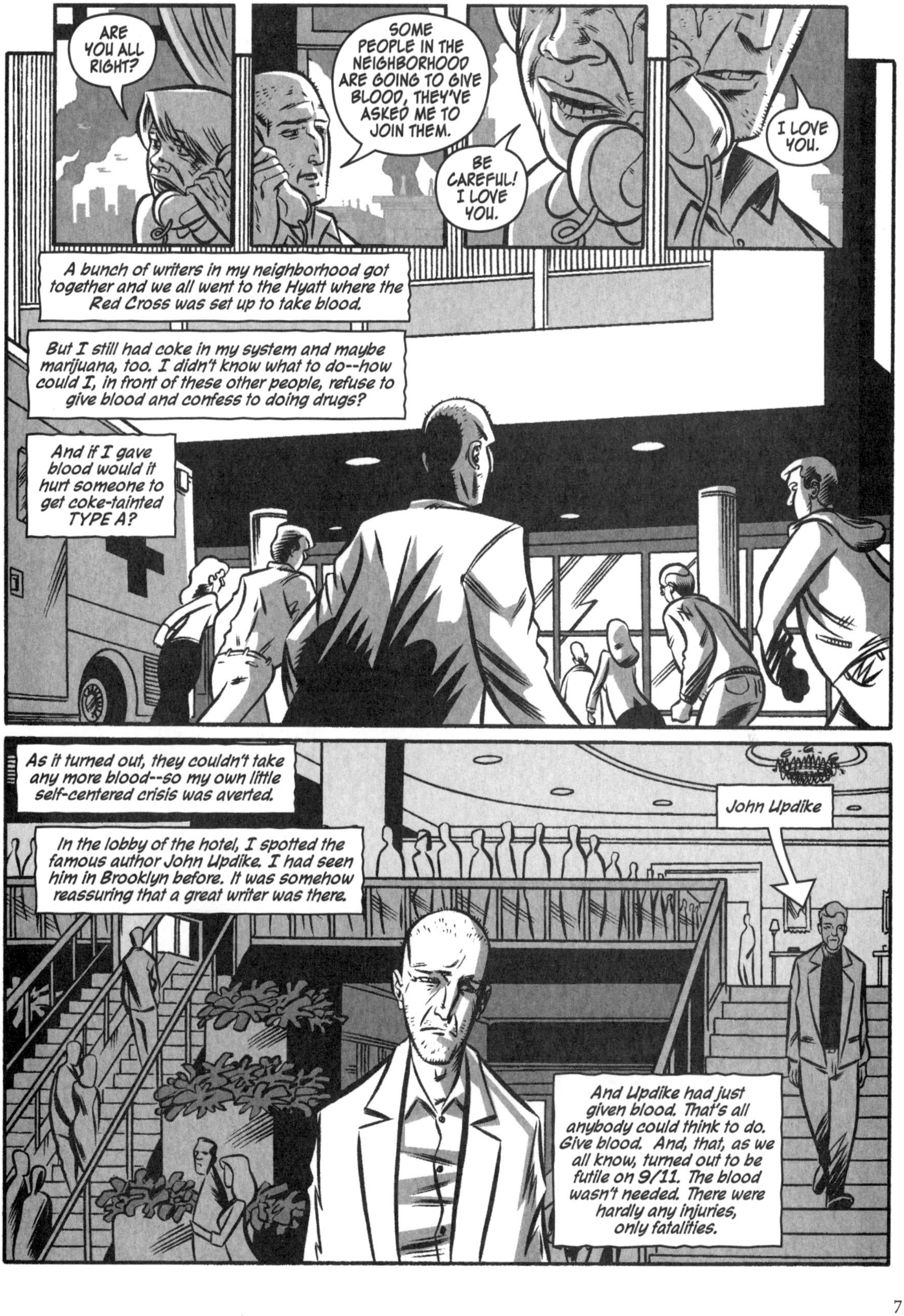
ARE YOU ALL RIGHT?
SOME PEOPLE IN THE NEIGHBORHOOD ARE GOING TO GIVE BLOOD, THEY'VE ASKED ME TO JOIN THEM.
BE CAREFUL! I LOVE YOU.
I LOVE YOU.
A bunch of writers in my neighborhood got together and we all went to the Hyatt where the Red Cross was set up to take blood.
But I still had coke in my system and maybe marijuana, too. I didn't know what to do--how could I, in front of these other people, refuse to give blood and confess to doing drugs?
And if I gave blood would it hurt someone to get coke-tainted TYPE A?
As it turned out, they couldn't take any more blood--so my own little self-centered crisis was averted.
In the lobby of the hotel, I spotted the famous author John Updike. I had seen him in Brooklyn before. It was somehow reassuring that a great writer was there.
John Updike
And Updike had just given blood. That's all anybody could think to do. Give blood. And, that, as we all know, turned out to be futile on 9/11. The blood wasn't needed. There were hardly any injuries, only fatalities.

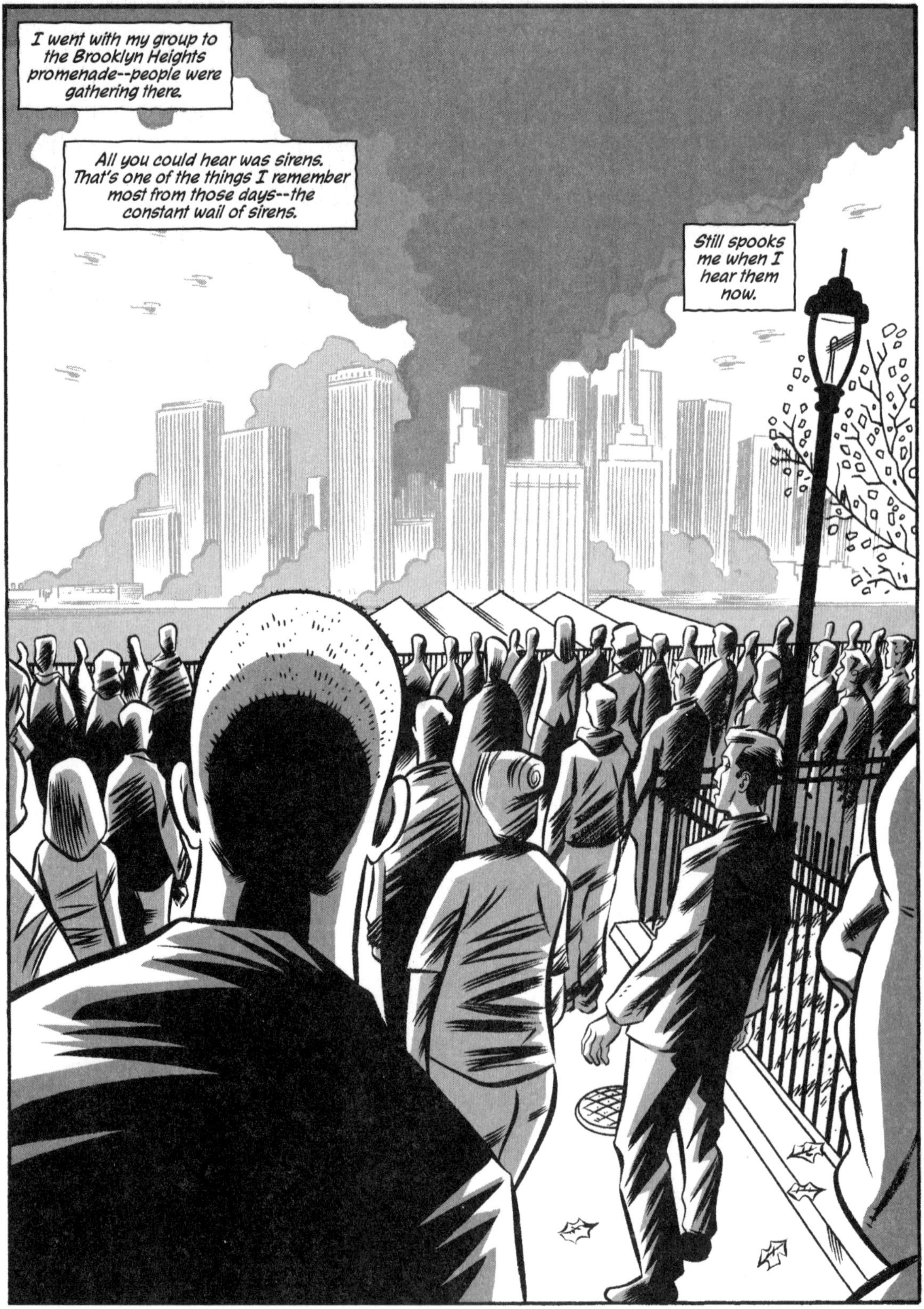
I went with my group to the Brooklyn Heights promenade--people were gathering there.
All you could hear was sirens. That's one of the things I remember most from those days--the constant wail of sirens.
Still spooks me when I hear them now.

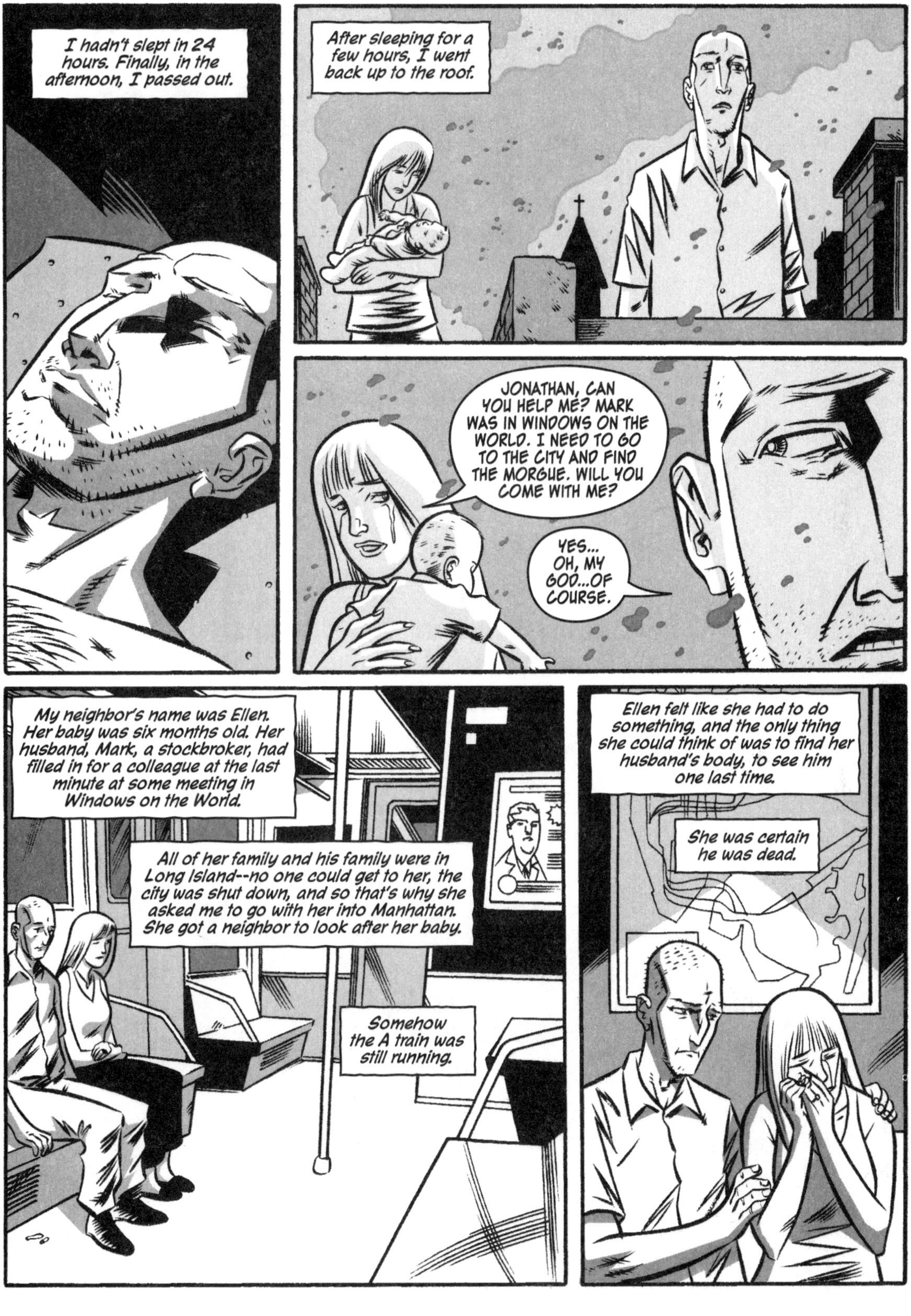
I hadn't slept in 24 hours. Finally, in the afternoon, I passed out.
After sleeping for a few hours, I went back up to the roof.
JONATHAN, CAN YOU HELP ME? MARK WAS IN WINDOWS ON THE WORLD. I NEED TO GO TO THE CITY AND FIND THE MORGUE. WILL YOU COME WITH ME?
YES... OH, MY GOD...OF COURSE.
My neighbor's name was Ellen. Her baby was six months old. Her husband, Mark, a stockbroker, had filled in for a colleague at the last minute at some meeting in Windows on the World.
All of her family and his family were in Long Island--no one could get to her, the city was shut down, and so that's why she asked me to go with her into Manhattan. She got a neighbor to look after her baby.
Somehow the A train was still running.
Ellen felt like she had to do something, and the only thing she could think of was to find her husband's body, to see him one last time.
She was certain he was dead.

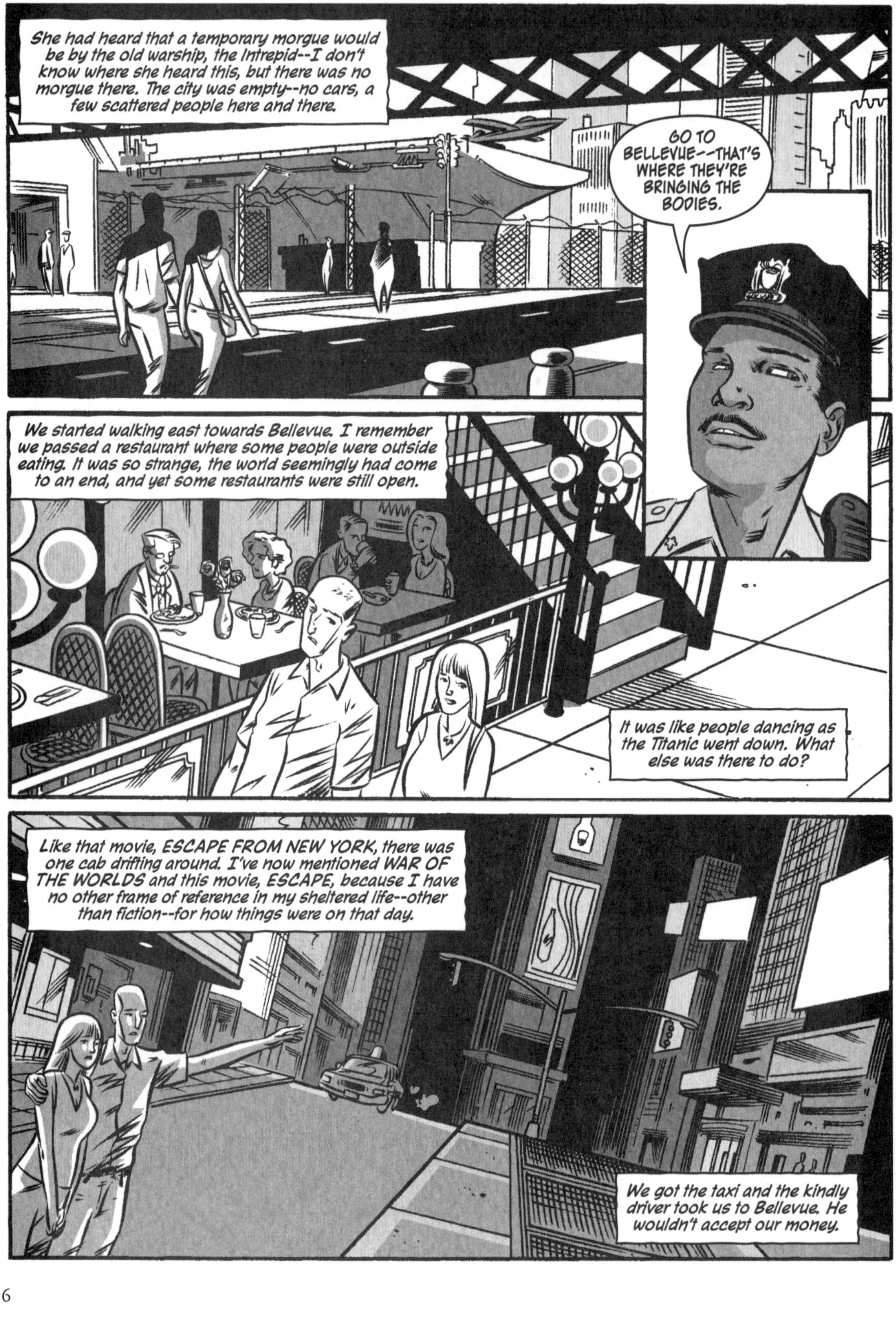
She had heard that a temporary morgue would be by the old warship, the Intrepid--I don't know where she heard this, but there was no morgue there. The city was empty--no cars, a few scattered people here and there.
GO TO BELLEVUE--THAT'S WHERE THEY'RE BRINGING THE BODIES.
We started walking east towards Bellevue. I remember we passed a restaurant where some people were outside eating. It was so strange, the world seemingly had come to an end, and yet some restaurants were still open.
It was like people dancing as the Titanic went down. What else was there to do?
Like that movie, ESCAPE FROM NEW YORK, there was one cab drifting around. I've now mentioned WAR OF THE WORLDS and this movie, ESCAPE, because I have no other frame of reference in my sheltered life--other than fiction--for how things were on that day.
We got the taxi and the kindly driver took us to Bellevue. He wouldn't accept our money.

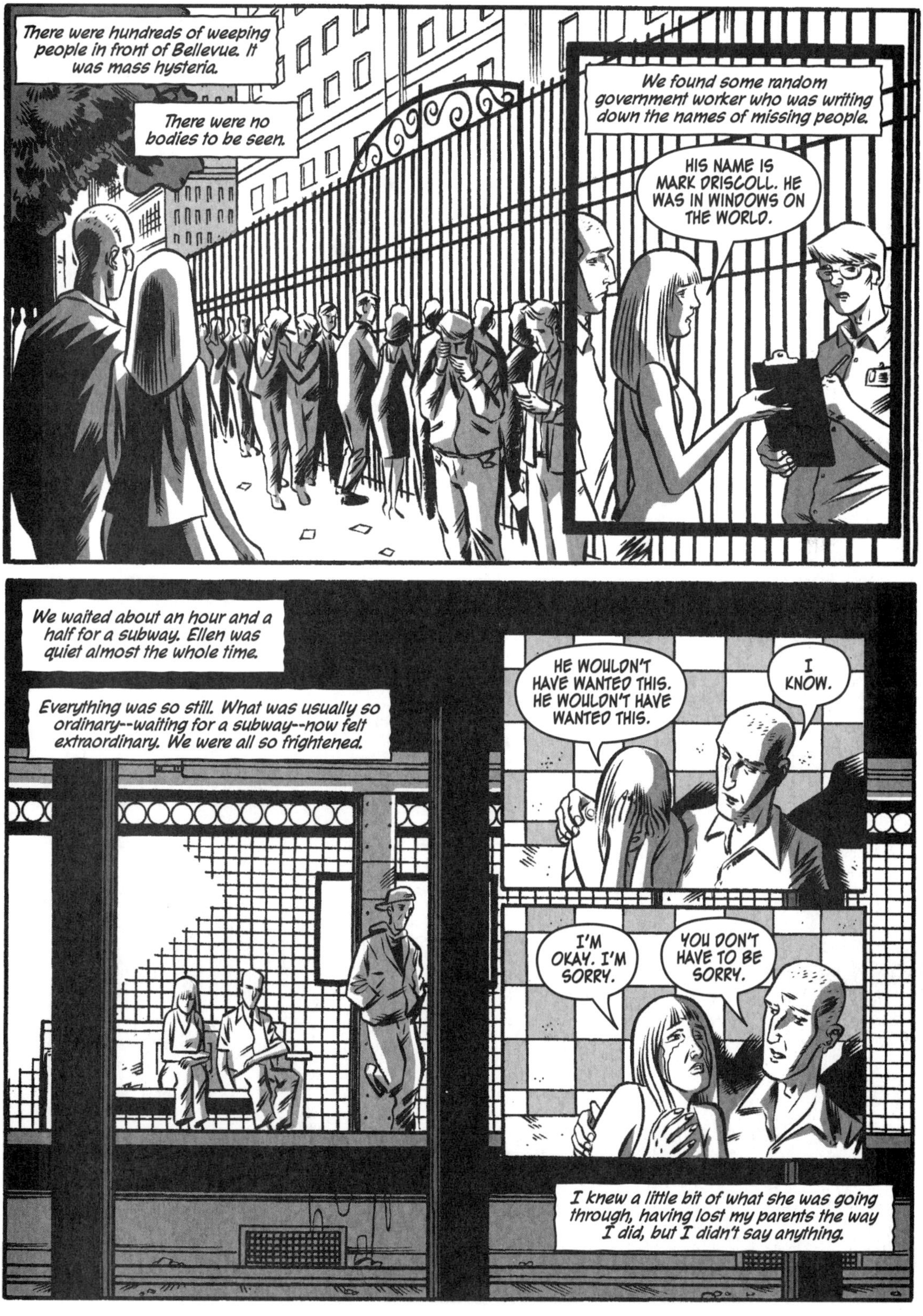
There were hundreds of weeping people in front of Bellevue. It was mass hysteria.
There were no bodies to be seen.
We found some random government worker who was writing down the names of missing people.
HIS NAME IS MARK DRISCOLL. HE WAS IN WINDOWS ON THE WORLD.
We waited about an hour and a half for a subway. Ellen was quiet almost the whole time.
Everything was so still. What was usually so ordinary--waiting for a subway--now felt extraordinary. We were all so frightened.
HE WOULDN'T HAVE WANTED THIS. HE WOULDN'T HAVE WANTED THIS.
I KNOW.
I'M OKAY. I'M SORRY.
YOU DON'T HAVE TO BE SORRY.
I knew a little bit of what she was going through, having lost my parents the way I did, but I didn't say anything.

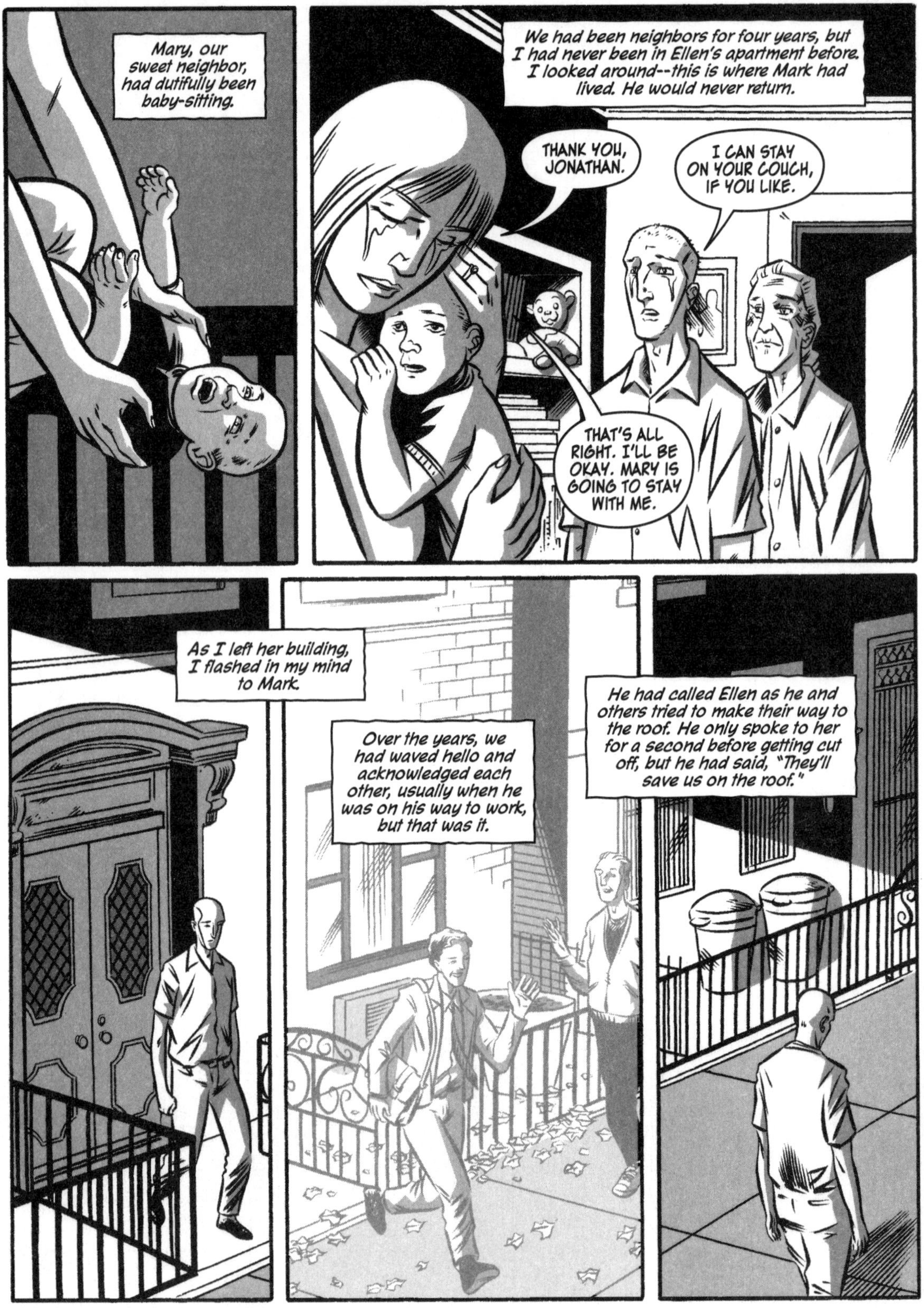
Mary, our sweet neighbor, had dutifully been baby-sitting.
We had been neighbors for four years, but I had never been in Ellen's apartment before. I looked around--this is where Mark had lived. He would never return.
THANK YOU, JONATHAN.
I CAN STAY ON YOUR COUCH, IF YOU LIKE.
THAT'S ALL RIGHT. I'LL BE OKAY. MARY IS GOING TO STAY WITH ME.
As I left her building, I flashed in my mind to Mark.
Over the years, we had waved hello and acknowledged each other, usually when he was on his way to work, but that was it.
He had called Ellen as he and others tried to make their way to the roof. He only spoke to her for a second before getting cut off, but he had said, "They'll save us on the roof."

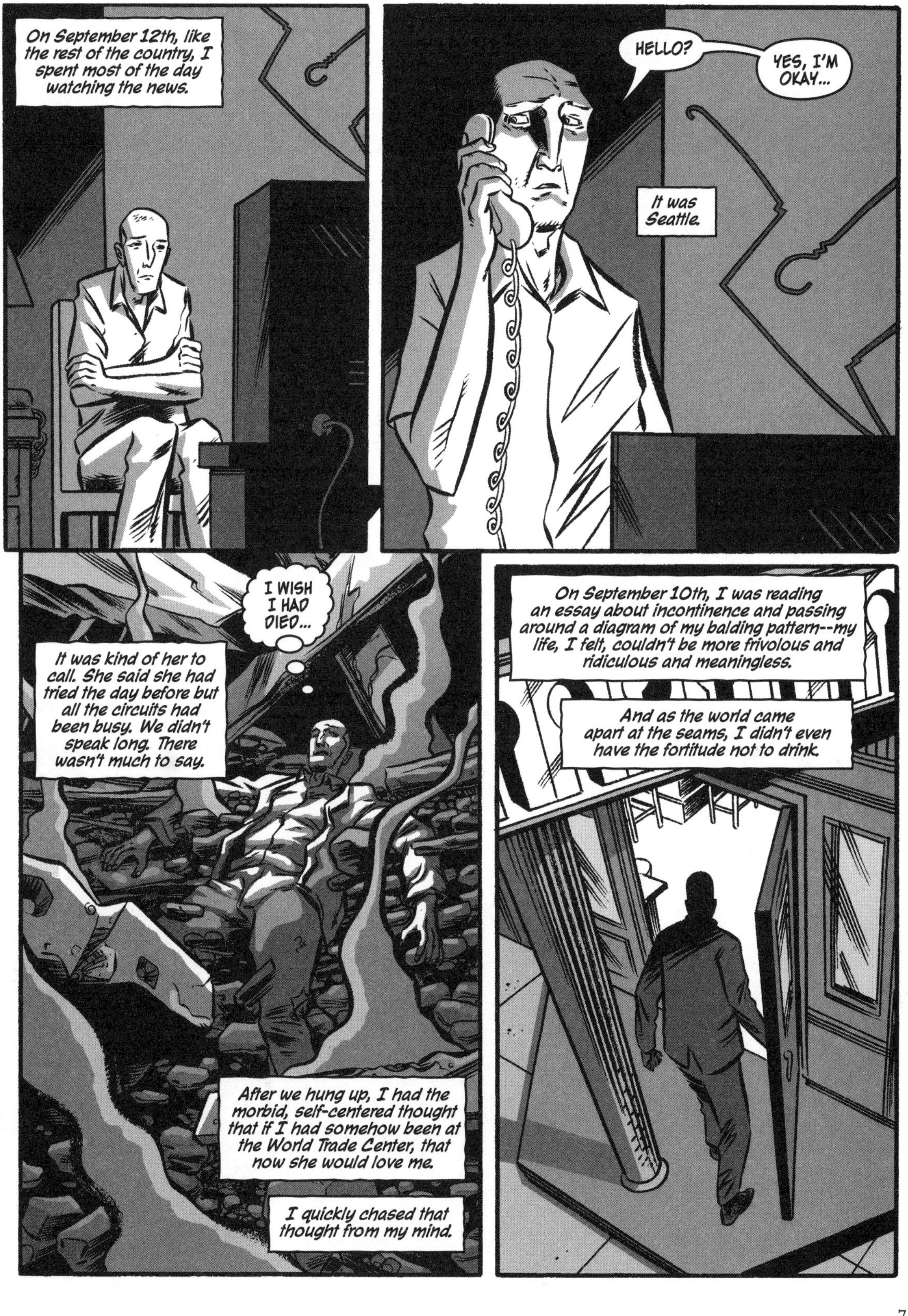
On September 12th, like the rest of the country, I spent most of the day watching the news.
HELLO?
YES, I'M OKAY...
It was Seattle.
I WISH I HAD DIED...
It was kind of her to call. She said she had tried the day before but all the circuits had been busy. We didn't speak long. There wasn't much to say.
After we hung up, I had the morbid, self-centered thought that if I had somehow been at the World Trade Center, that now she would love me.
I quickly chased that thought from my mind.
On September 10th, I was reading an essay about incontinence and passing around a diagram of my balding pattern--my life, I felt, couldn't be more frivolous and ridiculous and meaningless.
And as the world came apart at the seams, I didn't even have the fortitude not to drink.

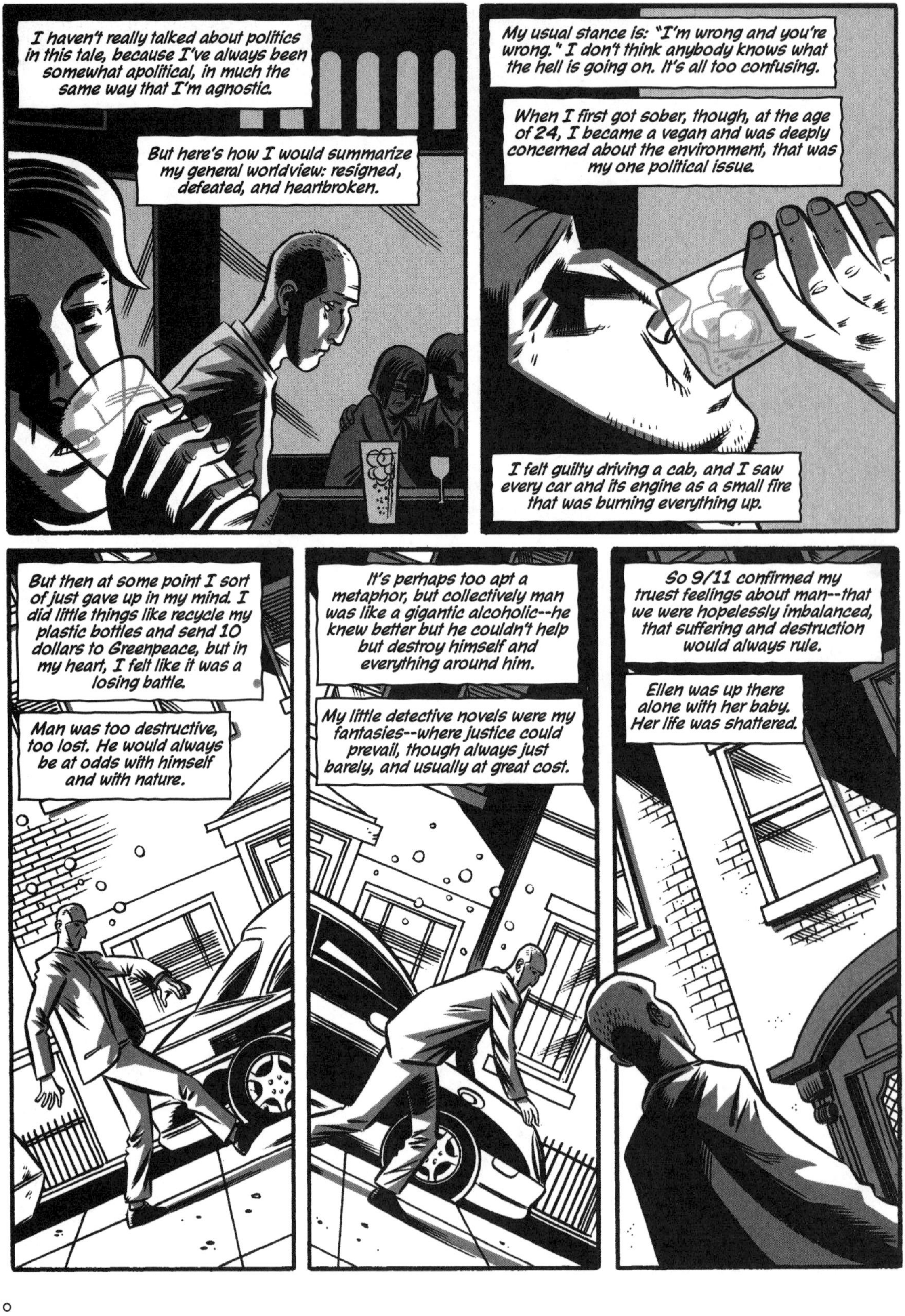
I haven't really talked about politics in this tale, because I've always been somewhat apolitical, in much the same way that I'm agnostic.
But here's how I would summarize my general worldview: resigned, defeated, and heartbroken.
My usual stance is: "I'm wrong and you're wrong." I don't think anybody knows what the hell is going on. It's all too confusing.
When I first got sober, though, at the age of 24, I became a vegan and was deeply concerned about the environment, that was my one political issue.
I felt guilty driving a cab, and I saw every car and its engine as a small fire that was burning everything up.
But then at some point I sort of just gave up in my mind. I did little things like recycle my plastic bottles and send 10 dollars to Greenpeace, but in my heart, I felt like it was a losing battle.
Man was too destructive, too lost. He would always be at odds with himself and with nature.
It's perhaps too apt a metaphor, but collectively man was like a gigantic alcoholic--he knew better but he couldn't help but destroy himself and everything around him.
My little detective novels were my fantasies--where justice could prevail, though always just barely, and usually at great cost.
So 9/11 confirmed my truest feelings about man--that we were hopelessly imbalanced, that suffering and destruction would always rule.
Ellen was up there alone with her baby. Her life was shattered.

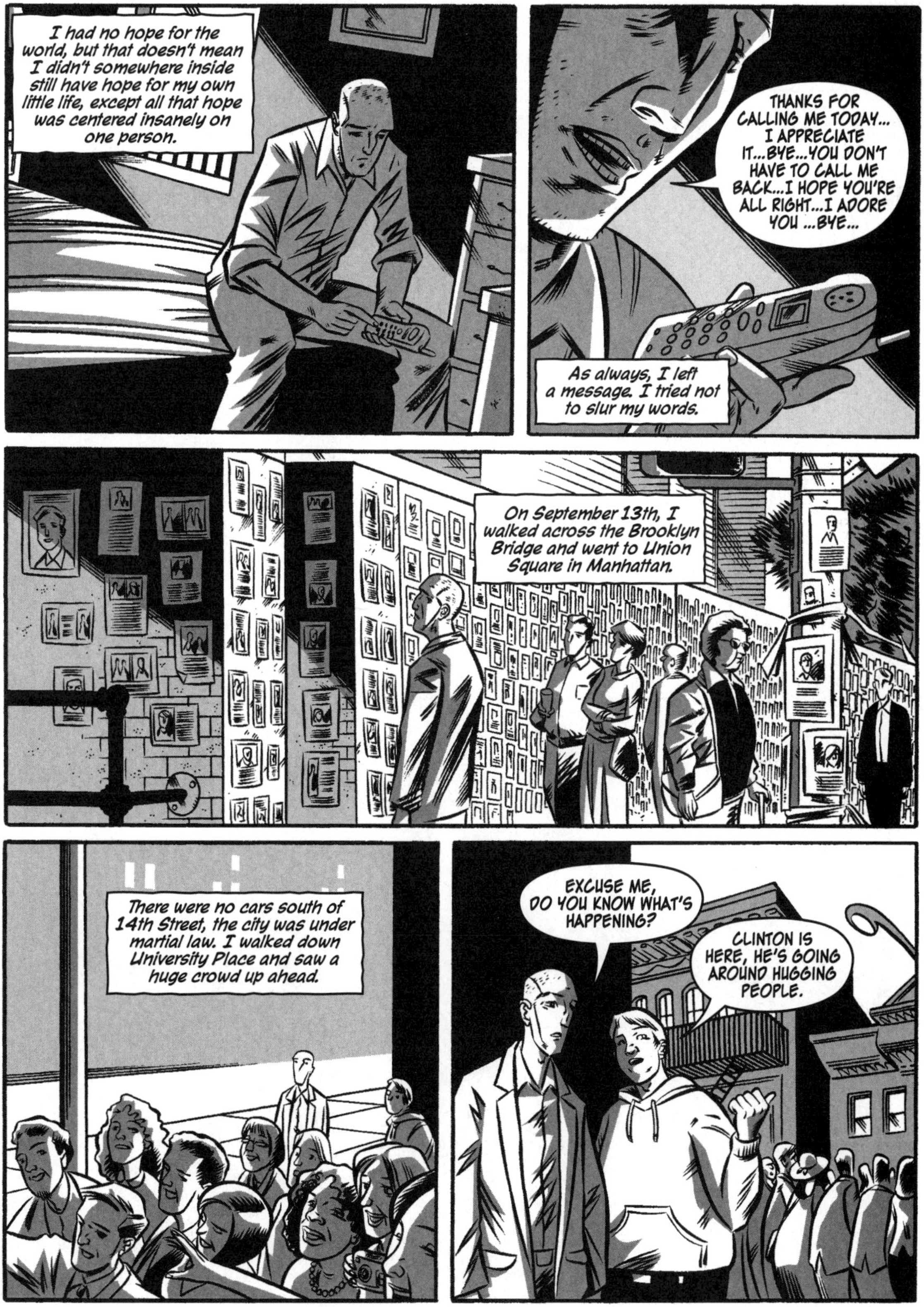
I had no hope for the world, but that doesn't mean I didn't somewhere inside still have hope for my own little life, except all that hope was centered insanely on one person.
THANKS FOR CALLING ME TODAY... I APPRECIATE IT...BYE...YOU DON'T HAVE TO CALL ME BACK...I HOPE YOU'RE ALL RIGHT...I ADORE YOU ...BYE...
As always, I left a message. I tried not to slur my words.
On September 13th, I walked across the Brooklyn Bridge and went to Union Square in Manhattan.
There were no cars south of 14th Street, the city was under martial law. I walked down University Place and saw a huge crowd up ahead.
EXCUSE ME, DO YOU KNOW WHAT'S HAPPENING?
CLINTON IS HERE, HE'S GOING AROUND HUGGING PEOPLE.

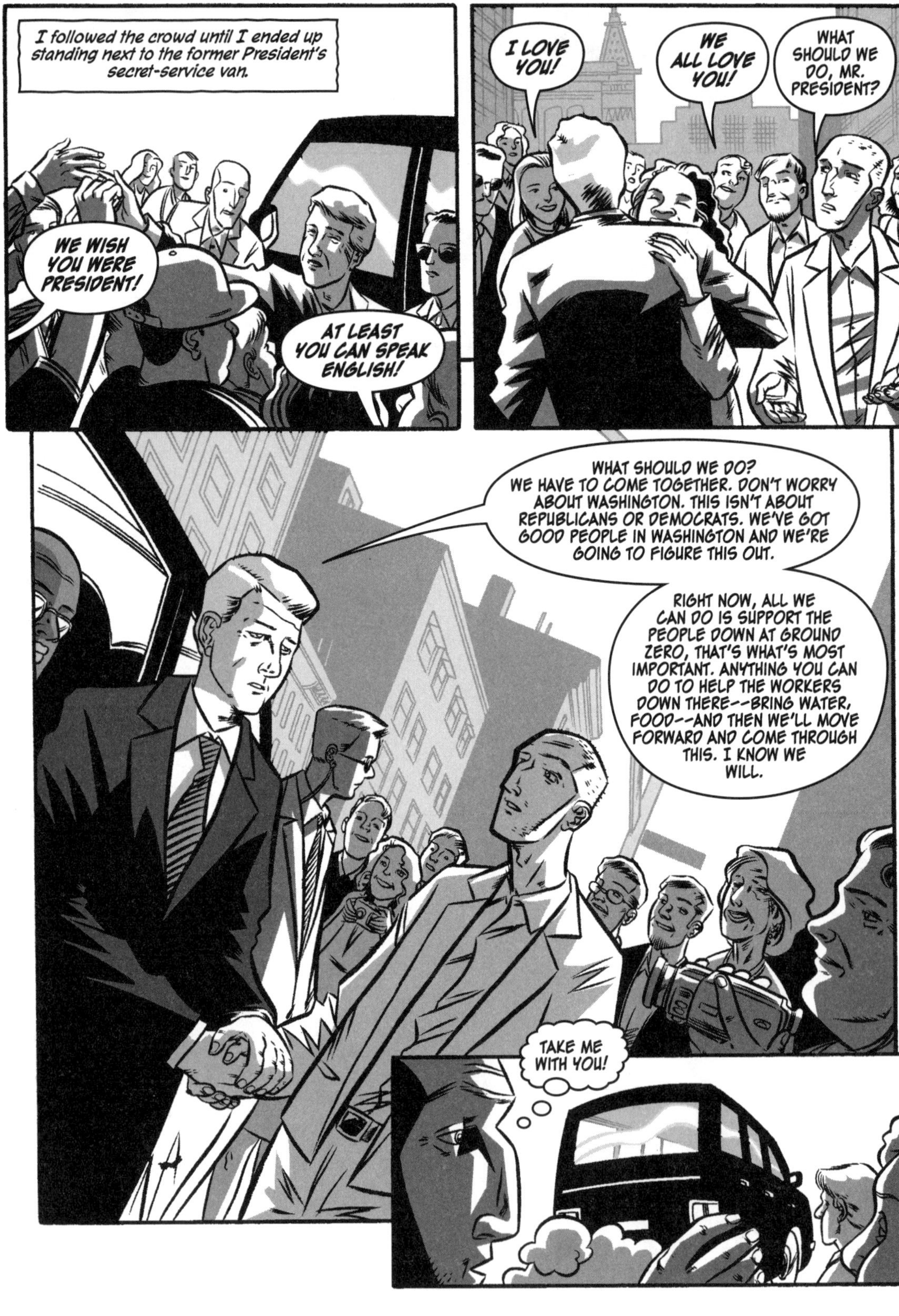
I followed the crowd until I ended up standing next to the former President's secret-service van.
WE WISH YOU WERE PRESIDENT!
AT LEAST YOU CAN SPEAK ENGLISH!
I LOVE YOU!
WE ALL LOVE YOU!
WHAT SHOULD WE DO, MR. PRESIDENT?
WHAT SHOULD WE DO? WE HAVE TO COME TOGETHER. DON'T WORRY ABOUT WASHINGTON. THIS ISN'T ABOUT REPUBLICANS OR DEMOCRATS. WE'VE GOT GOOD PEOPLE IN WASHINGTON AND WE'RE GOING TO FIGURE THIS OUT.
RIGHT NOW, ALL WE CAN DO IS SUPPORT THE PEOPLE DOWN AT GROUND ZERO, THAT'S WHAT'S MOST IMPORTANT. ANYTHING YOU CAN DO TO HELP THE WORKERS DOWN THERE--BRING WATER, FOOD--AND THEN WE'LL MOVE FORWARD AND COME THROUGH THIS. I KNOW WE WILL.
TAKE ME WITH YOU!

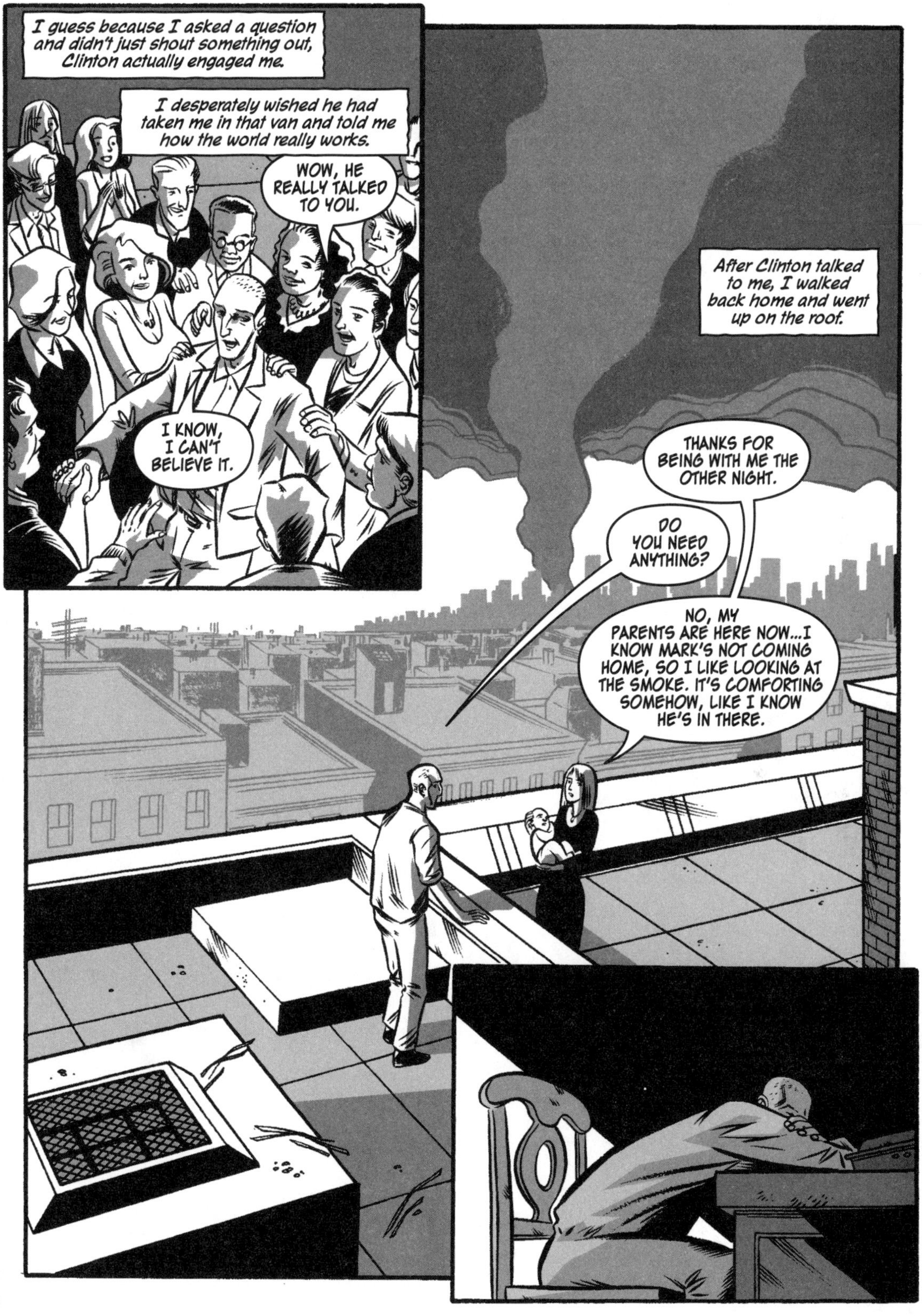
I guess because I asked a question and didn't just shout something out, Clinton actually engaged me.
I desperately wished he had taken me in that van and told me how the world really works.
WOW, HE REALLY TALKED TO YOU.
I KNOW, I CAN'T BELIEVE IT.
After Clinton talked to me, I walked back home and went up on the roof.
THANKS FOR BEING WITH ME THE OTHER NIGHT.
DO YOU NEED ANYTHING?
NO, MY PARENTS ARE HERE NOW...I KNOW MARK'S NOT COMING HOME, SO I LIKE LOOKING AT THE SMOKE. IT'S COMFORTING SOMEHOW, LIKE I KNOW HE'S IN THERE.

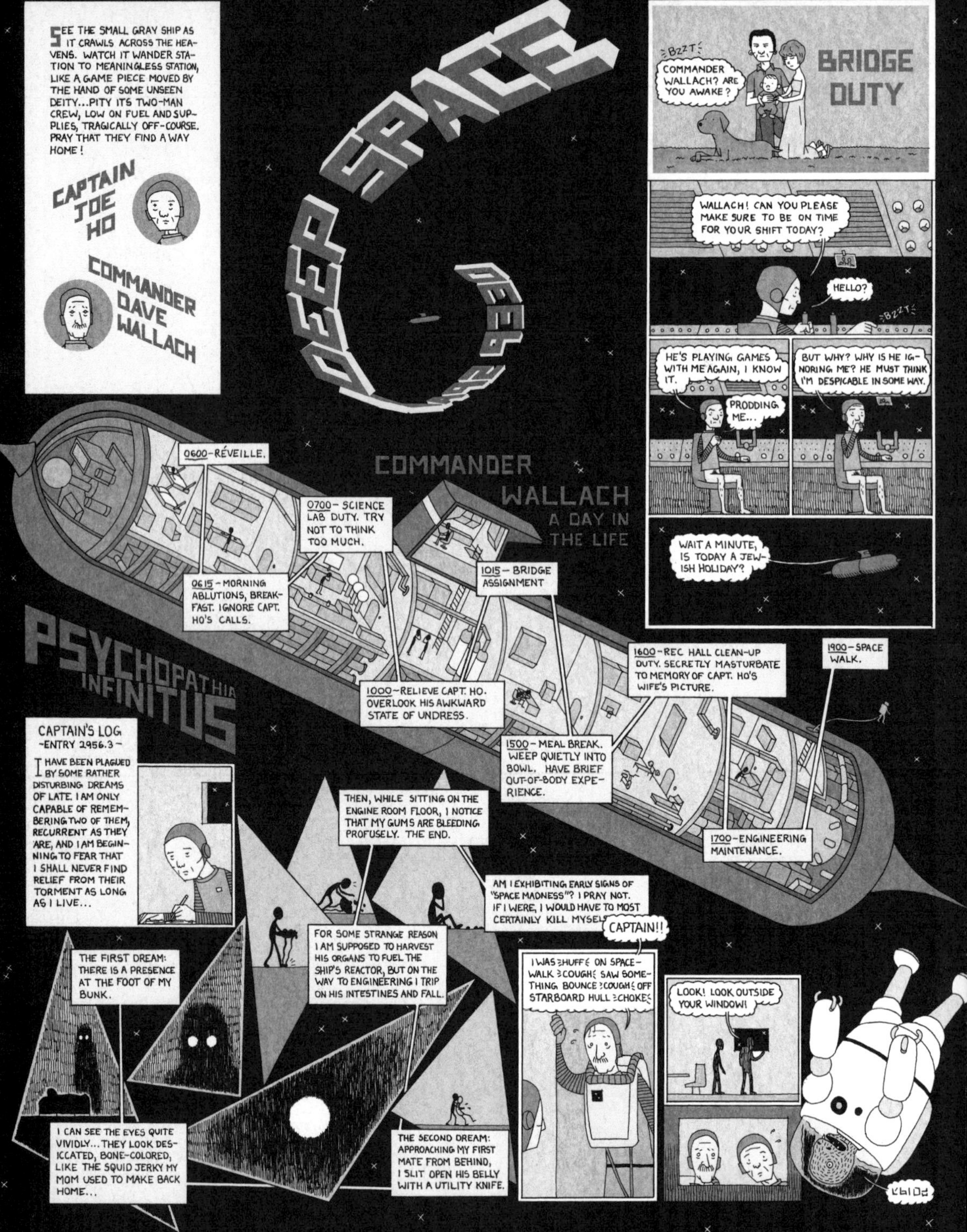
SEE THE SMALL GRAY SHIP AS IT CRAWLS ACROSS THE HEAVENS. WATCH IT WANDER STATION TO MEANINGLESS STATION, LIKE A GAME PIECE MOVED BY THE HAND OF SOME UNSEEN DEITY...PITY ITS TWO-MAN CREW, LOW ON FUEL AND SUPPLIES, TRAGICALLY OFF-COURSE. PRAY THAT THEY FIND A WAY HOME!
CAPTAIN JOE HO
COMMANDER DAVE WALLACH
DEEP SPACE
BRIDGE DUTY
BZZT
COMMANDER WALLACH? ARE YOU AWAKE?
WALLACH! CAN YOU PLEASE MAKE SURE TO BE ON TIME FOR YOUR SHIFT TODAY?
HELLO?
BZZT
HE'S PLAYING GAMES WITH ME AGAIN, I KNOW IT.
PRODDING ME...
BUT WHY? WHY IS HE IGNORING ME? HE MUST THINK I'M DESPICABLE IN SOME WAY.
WAIT A MINUTE, IS TODAY A JEWISH HOLIDAY?
COMMANDER WALLACH
A DAY IN THE LIFE
0600 – RÉVEILLE.
0615 – MORNING ABLUTIONS, BREAKFAST. IGNORE CAPT. HO'S CALLS.
0700 – SCIENCE LAB DUTY. TRY NOT TO THINK TOO MUCH.
1000 – RELIEVE CAPT. HO. OVERLOOK HIS AWKWARD STATE OF UNDRESS.
1015 – BRIDGE ASSIGNMENT
1500 – MEAL BREAK. WEEP QUIETLY INTO BOWL. HAVE BRIEF OUT-OF-BODY EXPERIENCE.
1600 – REC HALL CLEAN-UP DUTY. SECRETLY MASTURBATE TO MEMORY OF CAPT. HO'S WIFE'S PICTURE.
1700 – ENGINEERING MAINTENANCE.
1900 – SPACE WALK.
PSYCHOPATHIA INFINITUS
CAPTAIN'S LOG
~ENTRY 2956.3~
I HAVE BEEN PLAGUED BY SOME RATHER DISTURBING DREAMS OF LATE. I AM ONLY CAPABLE OF REMEMBERING TWO OF THEM, RECURRENT AS THEY ARE, AND I AM BEGINNING TO FEAR THAT I SHALL NEVER FIND RELIEF FROM THEIR TORMENT AS LONG AS I LIVE...
THE FIRST DREAM: THERE IS A PRESENCE AT THE FOOT OF MY BUNK.
I CAN SEE THE EYES QUITE VIVIDLY... THEY LOOK DESICCATED, BONE-COLORED, LIKE THE SQUID JERKY MY MOM USED TO MAKE BACK HOME...
THE SECOND DREAM: APPROACHING MY FIRST MATE FROM BEHIND, I SLIT OPEN HIS BELLY WITH A UTILITY KNIFE.
FOR SOME STRANGE REASON I AM SUPPOSED TO HARVEST HIS ORGANS TO FUEL THE SHIP'S REACTOR, BUT ON THE WAY TO ENGINEERING I TRIP ON HIS INTESTINES AND FALL.
THEN, WHILE SITTING ON THE ENGINE ROOM FLOOR, I NOTICE THAT MY GUMS ARE BLEEDING PROFUSELY. THE END.
AM I EXHIBITING EARLY SIGNS OF "SPACE MADNESS"? I PRAY NOT. IF I WERE, I WOULD HAVE TO MOST CERTAINLY KILL MYSELF
CAPTAIN!!
I WAS ≷HUFF≶ ON SPACE-WALK ≷COUGH≶ SAW SOMETHING BOUNCE ≷COUGH≶ OFF STARBOARD HULL ≷CHOKE≶
LOOK! LOOK OUTSIDE YOUR WINDOW!

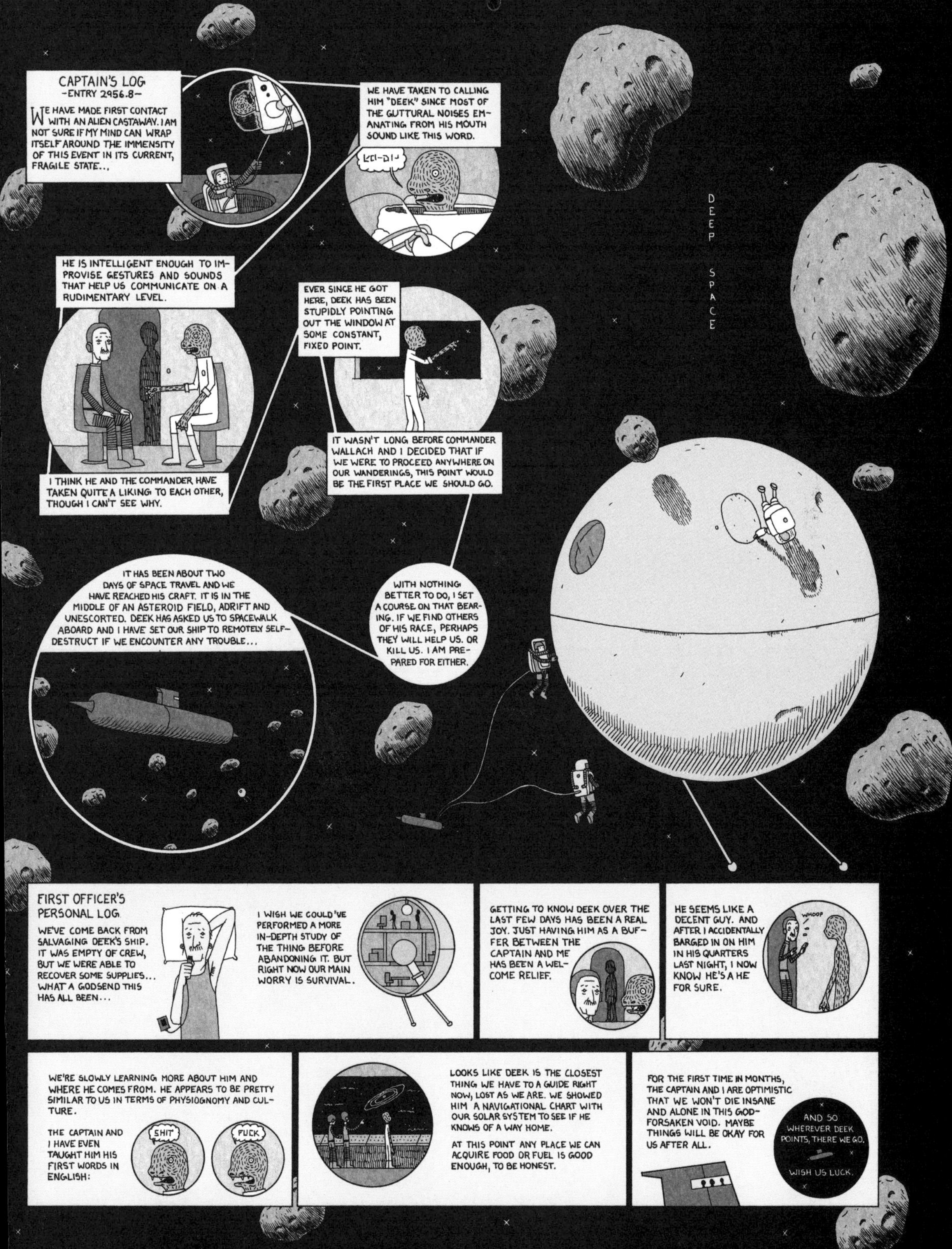

CAPTAIN'S LOG
-ENTRY 2956.8-
WE HAVE MADE FIRST CONTACT WITH AN ALIEN CASTAWAY. I AM NOT SURE IF MY MIND CAN WRAP ITSELF AROUND THE IMMENSITY OF THIS EVENT IN ITS CURRENT, FRAGILE STATE...
WE HAVE TAKEN TO CALLING HIM "DEEK" SINCE MOST OF THE GUTTURAL NOISES EMANATING FROM HIS MOUTH SOUND LIKE THIS WORD.
HE IS INTELLIGENT ENOUGH TO IMPROVISE GESTURES AND SOUNDS THAT HELP US COMMUNICATE ON A RUDIMENTARY LEVEL.
I THINK HE AND THE COMMANDER HAVE TAKEN QUITE A LIKING TO EACH OTHER, THOUGH I CAN'T SEE WHY.
EVER SINCE HE GOT HERE, DEEK HAS BEEN STUPIDLY POINTING OUT THE WINDOW AT SOME CONSTANT, FIXED POINT.
IT WASN'T LONG BEFORE COMMANDER WALLACH AND I DECIDED THAT IF WE WERE TO PROCEED ANYWHERE ON OUR WANDERINGS, THIS POINT WOULD BE THE FIRST PLACE WE SHOULD GO.
WITH NOTHING BETTER TO DO, I SET A COURSE ON THAT BEARING. IF WE FIND OTHERS OF HIS RACE, PERHAPS THEY WILL HELP US. OR KILL US. I AM PREPARED FOR EITHER.
IT HAS BEEN ABOUT TWO DAYS OF SPACE TRAVEL AND WE HAVE REACHED HIS CRAFT. IT IS IN THE MIDDLE OF AN ASTEROID FIELD, ADRIFT AND UNESCORTED. DEEK HAS ASKED US TO SPACEWALK ABOARD AND I HAVE SET OUR SHIP TO REMOTELY SELF-DESTRUCT IF WE ENCOUNTER ANY TROUBLE...
DEEP SPACE
FIRST OFFICER'S PERSONAL LOG
WE'VE COME BACK FROM SALVAGING DEEK'S SHIP. IT WAS EMPTY OF CREW, BUT WE WERE ABLE TO RECOVER SOME SUPPLIES... WHAT A GODSEND THIS HAS ALL BEEN...
I WISH WE COULD'VE PERFORMED A MORE IN-DEPTH STUDY OF THE THING BEFORE ABANDONING IT. BUT RIGHT NOW OUR MAIN WORRY IS SURVIVAL.
GETTING TO KNOW DEEK OVER THE LAST FEW DAYS HAS BEEN A REAL JOY. JUST HAVING HIM AS A BUFFER BETWEEN THE CAPTAIN AND ME HAS BEEN A WELCOME RELIEF.
HE SEEMS LIKE A DECENT GUY. AND AFTER I ACCIDENTALLY BARGED IN ON HIM IN HIS QUARTERS LAST NIGHT, I NOW KNOW HE'S A HE FOR SURE.
WHOOP
WE'RE SLOWLY LEARNING MORE ABOUT HIM AND WHERE HE COMES FROM. HE APPEARS TO BE PRETTY SIMILAR TO US IN TERMS OF PHYSIOGNOMY AND CULTURE.
THE CAPTAIN AND I HAVE EVEN TAUGHT HIM HIS FIRST WORDS IN ENGLISH:
SHIT
FUCK
LOOKS LIKE DEEK IS THE CLOSEST THING WE HAVE TO A GUIDE RIGHT NOW, LOST AS WE ARE. WE SHOWED HIM A NAVIGATIONAL CHART WITH OUR SOLAR SYSTEM TO SEE IF HE KNOWS OF A WAY HOME.
AT THIS POINT ANY PLACE WE CAN ACQUIRE FOOD OR FUEL IS GOOD ENOUGH, TO BE HONEST.
FOR THE FIRST TIME IN MONTHS, THE CAPTAIN AND I ARE OPTIMISTIC THAT WE WON'T DIE INSANE AND ALONE IN THIS GOD-FORSAKEN VOID. MAYBE THINGS WILL BE OKAY FOR US AFTER ALL.
AND SO WHEREVER DEEK POINTS, THERE WE GO.
WISH US LUCK.

EXCERPT FROM

ASTERIOS POLYP

DAVID MAZZUCCHELLI

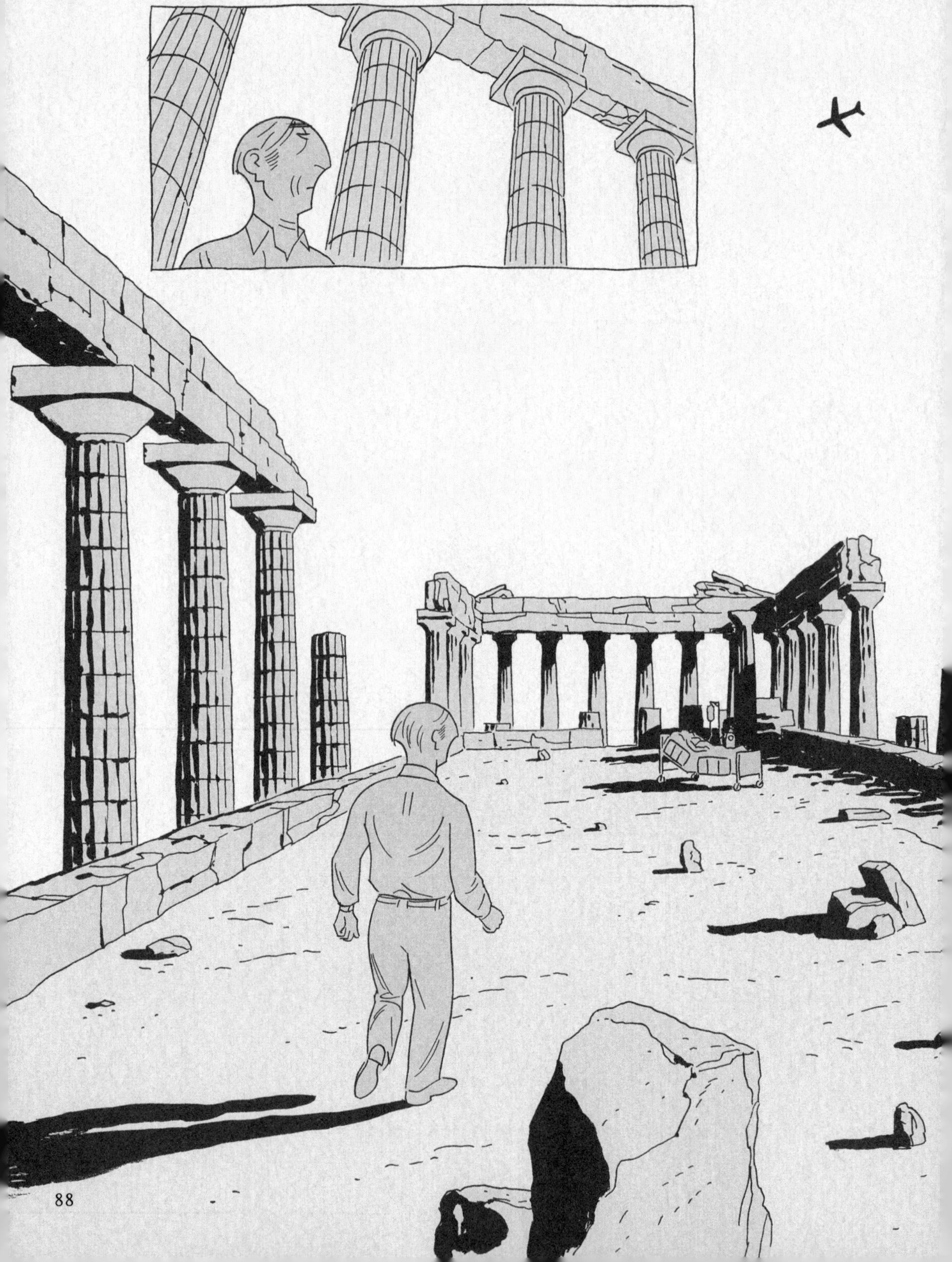

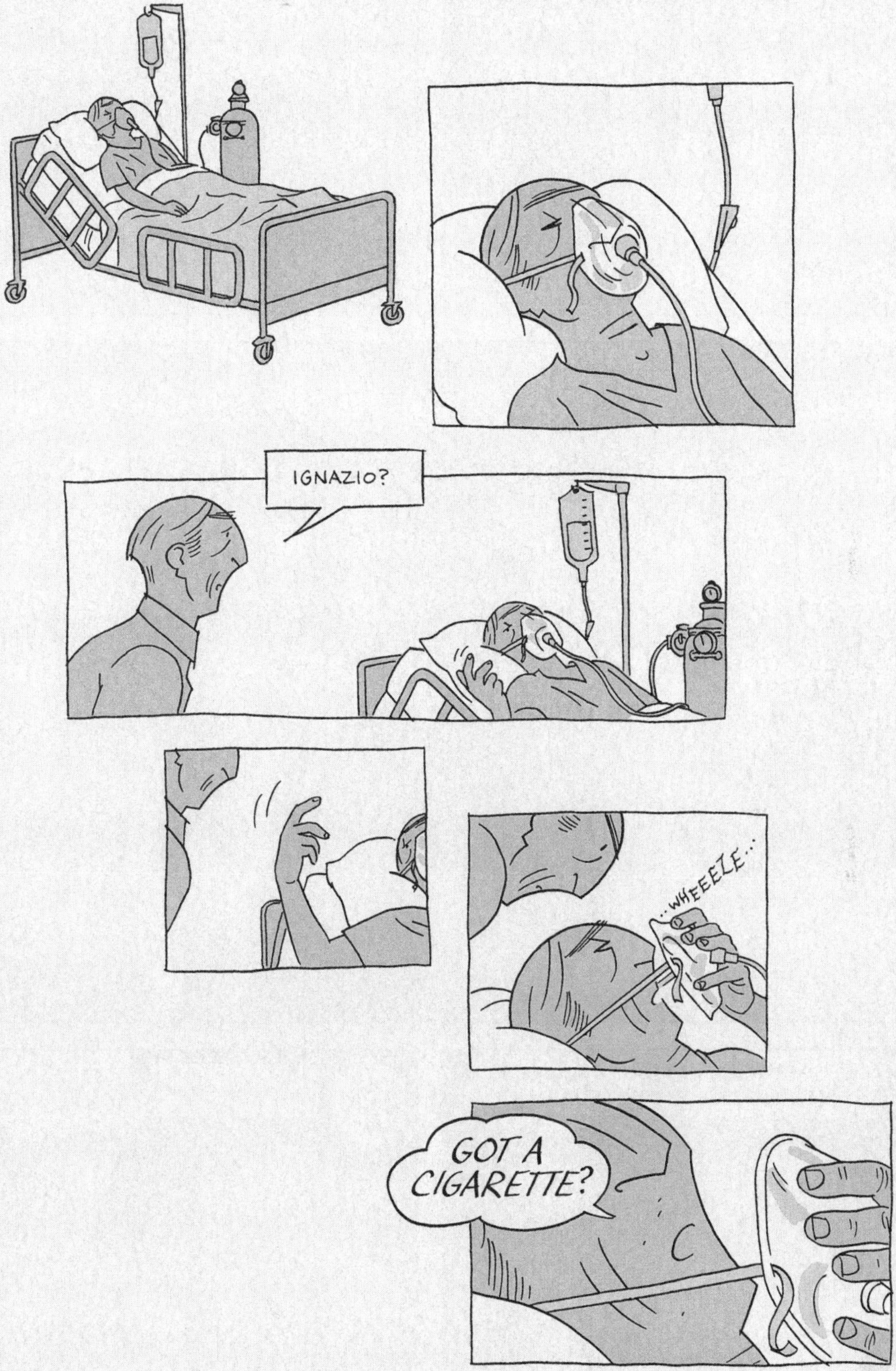
IGNAZIO?
...WHEEEZE...
GOT A CIGARETTE?

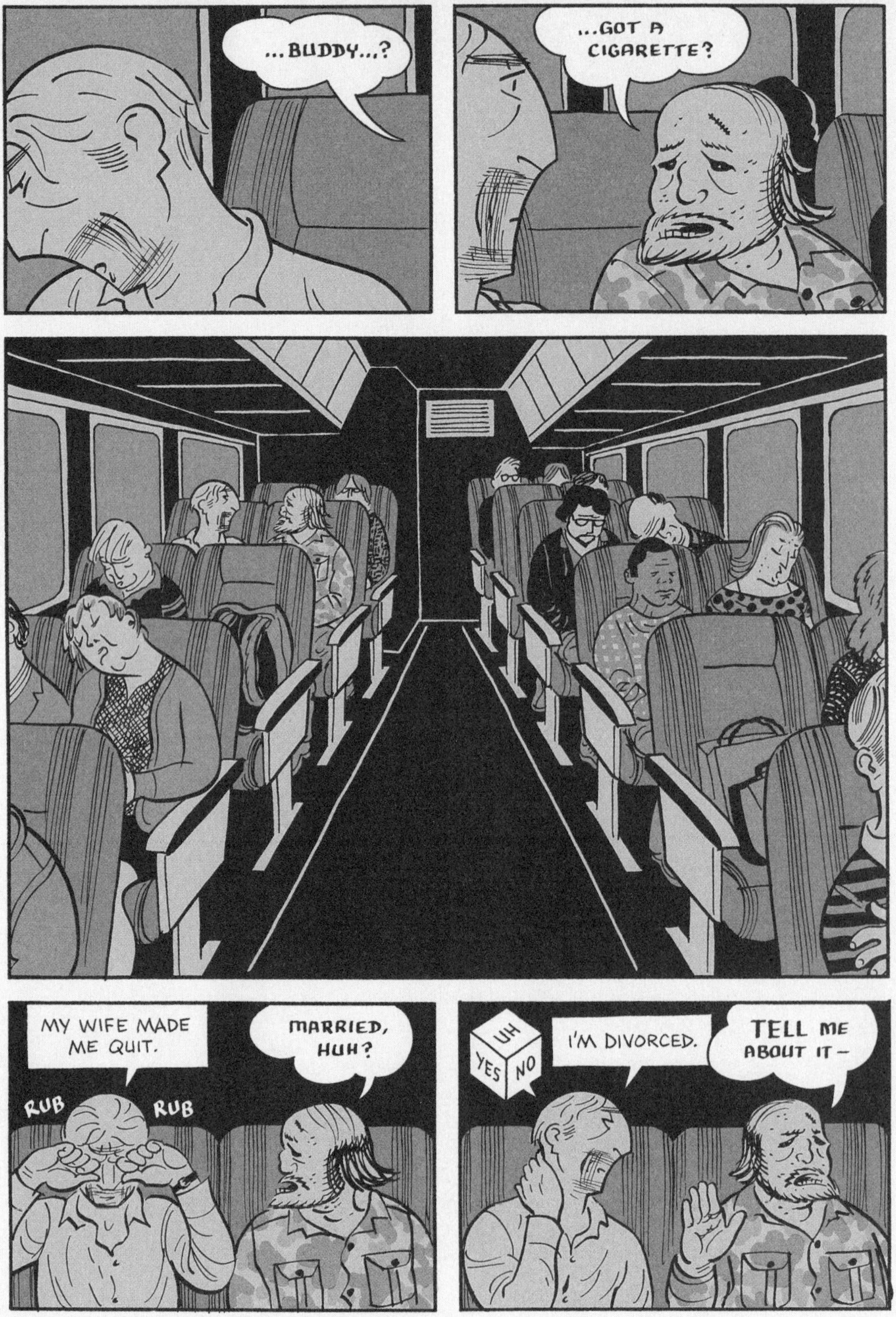
...BUDDY...?
...GOT A CIGARETTE?
MY WIFE MADE ME QUIT.
RUB
RUB
MARRIED, HUH?
UH
YES
NO
I'M DIVORCED.
TELL ME ABOUT IT –

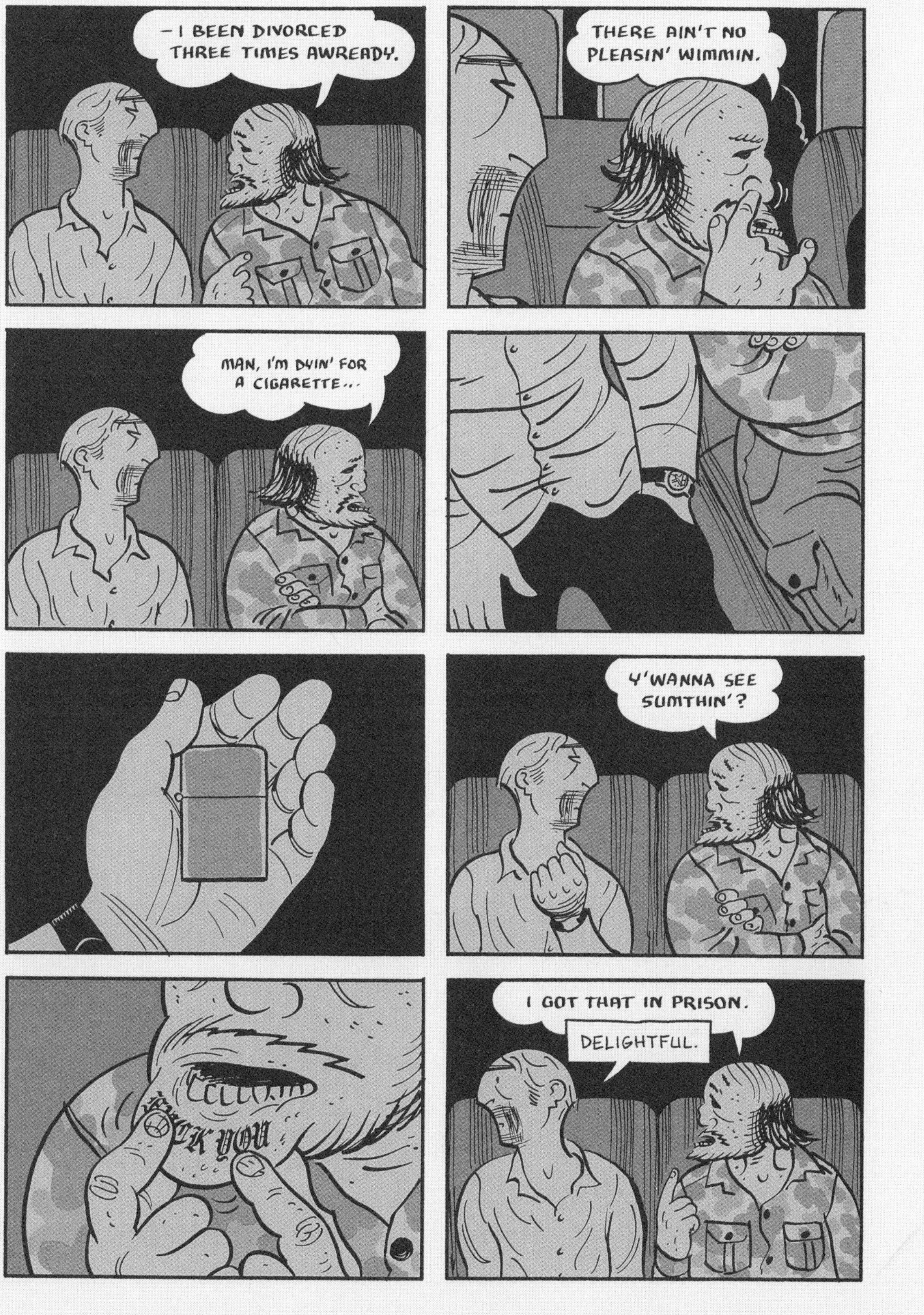

—I BEEN DIVORCED THREE TIMES AWREADY.
THERE AIN'T NO PLEASIN' WIMMIN.
MAN, I'M DYIN' FOR A CIGARETTE...
Y'WANNA SEE SUMTHIN'?
I GOT THAT IN PRISON.
DELIGHTFUL.

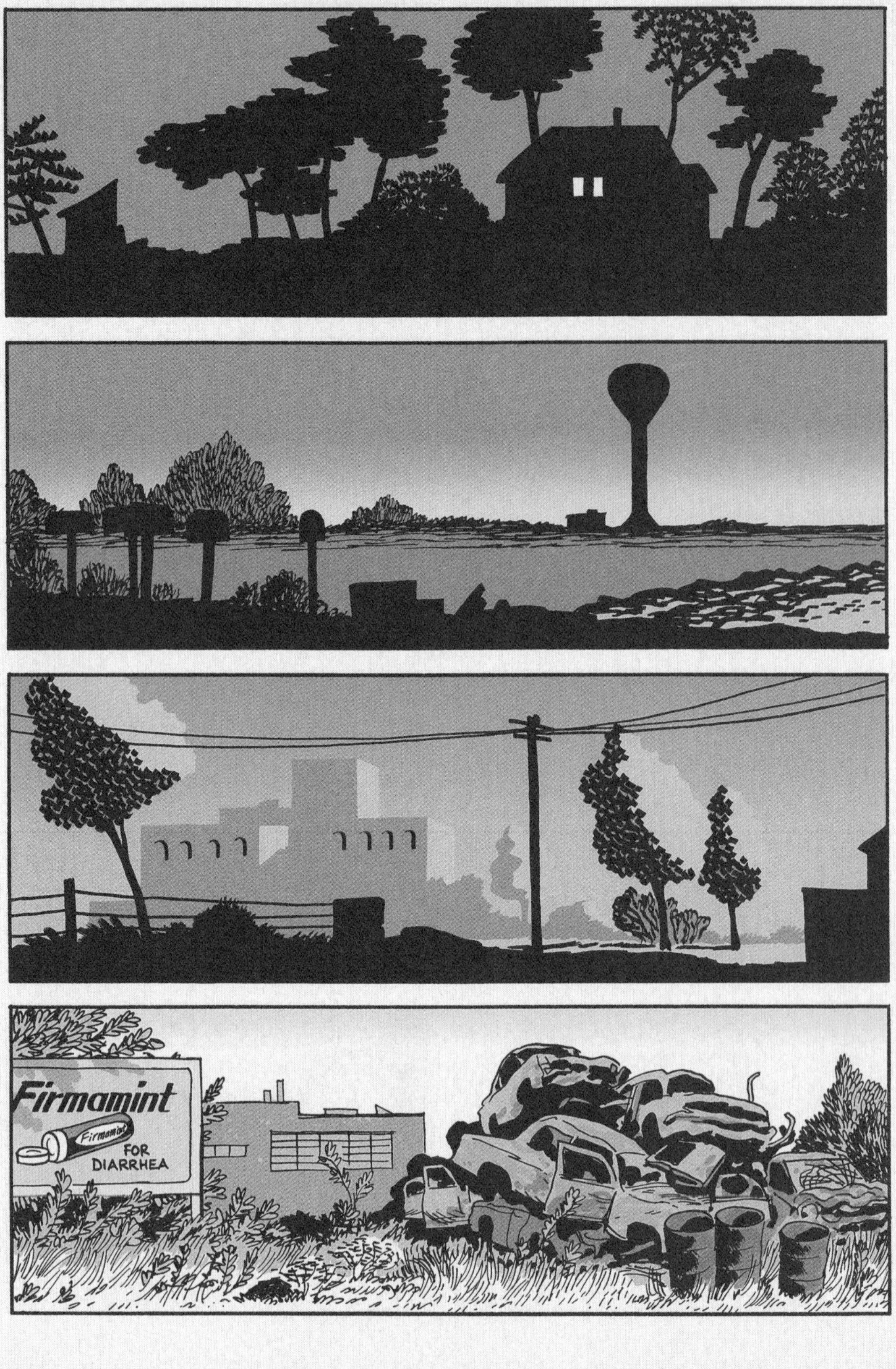
Firmamint
Firmamint
FOR DIARRHEA

WHATZAT?

IT'S AN OLD LIGHTER.

DOES IT WORK?

WELL, IT DOESN'T HAVE ANY FLUID LEFT.

CLIK

IT USED TO BE MY FATHER'S.

COOL.

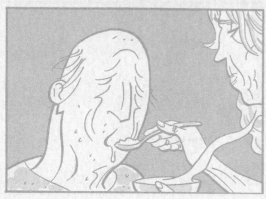

KIN I HAVE IT?

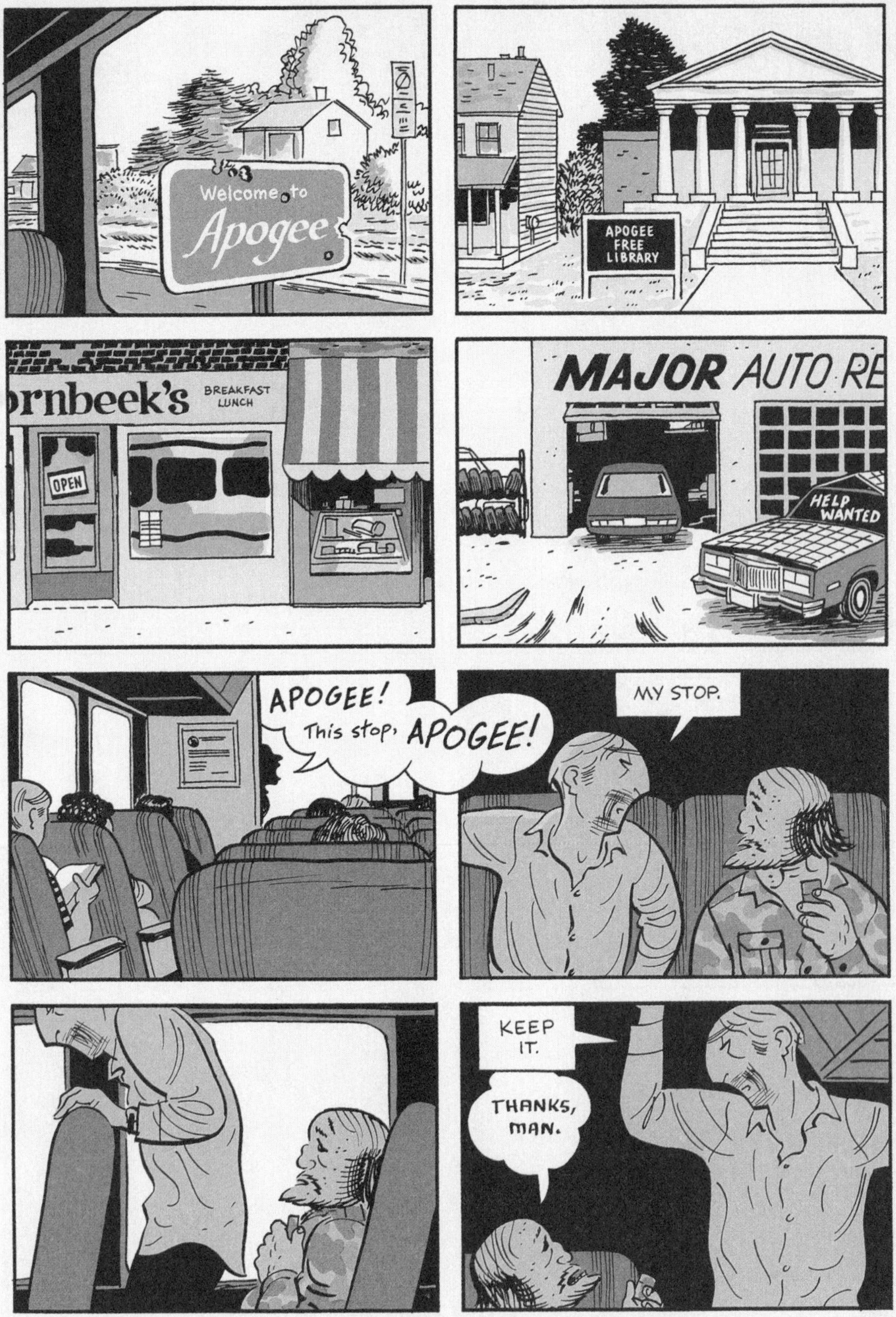
Welcome to
Apogee
APOGEE FREE LIBRARY
rnbeek's
BREAKFAST LUNCH
OPEN
MAJOR AUTO RE
HELP WANTED
APOGEE! This stop, APOGEE!
MY STOP.
KEEP IT.
THANKS, MAN.

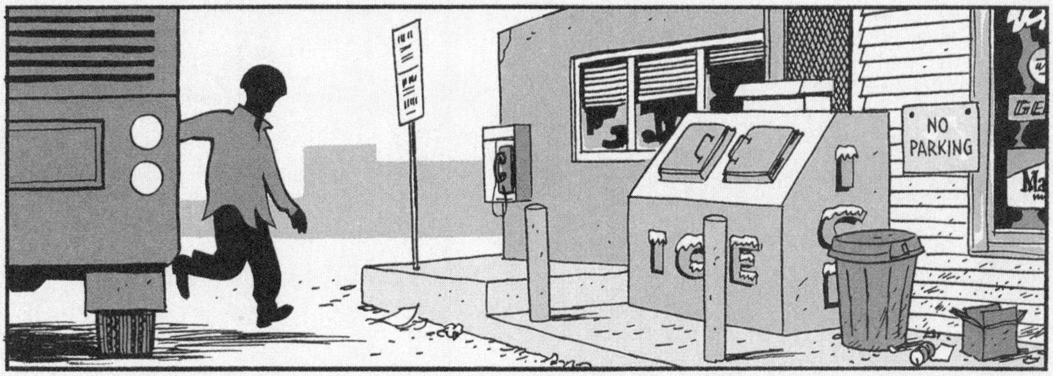
NO PARKING
ICE

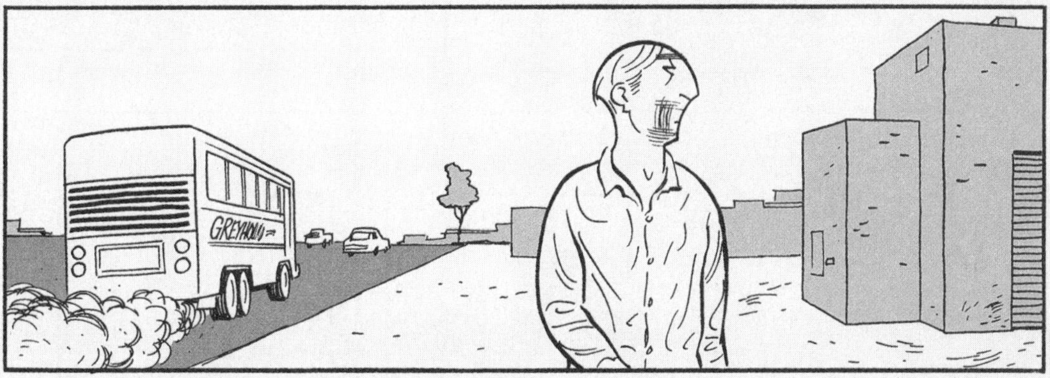
GREYHOUND

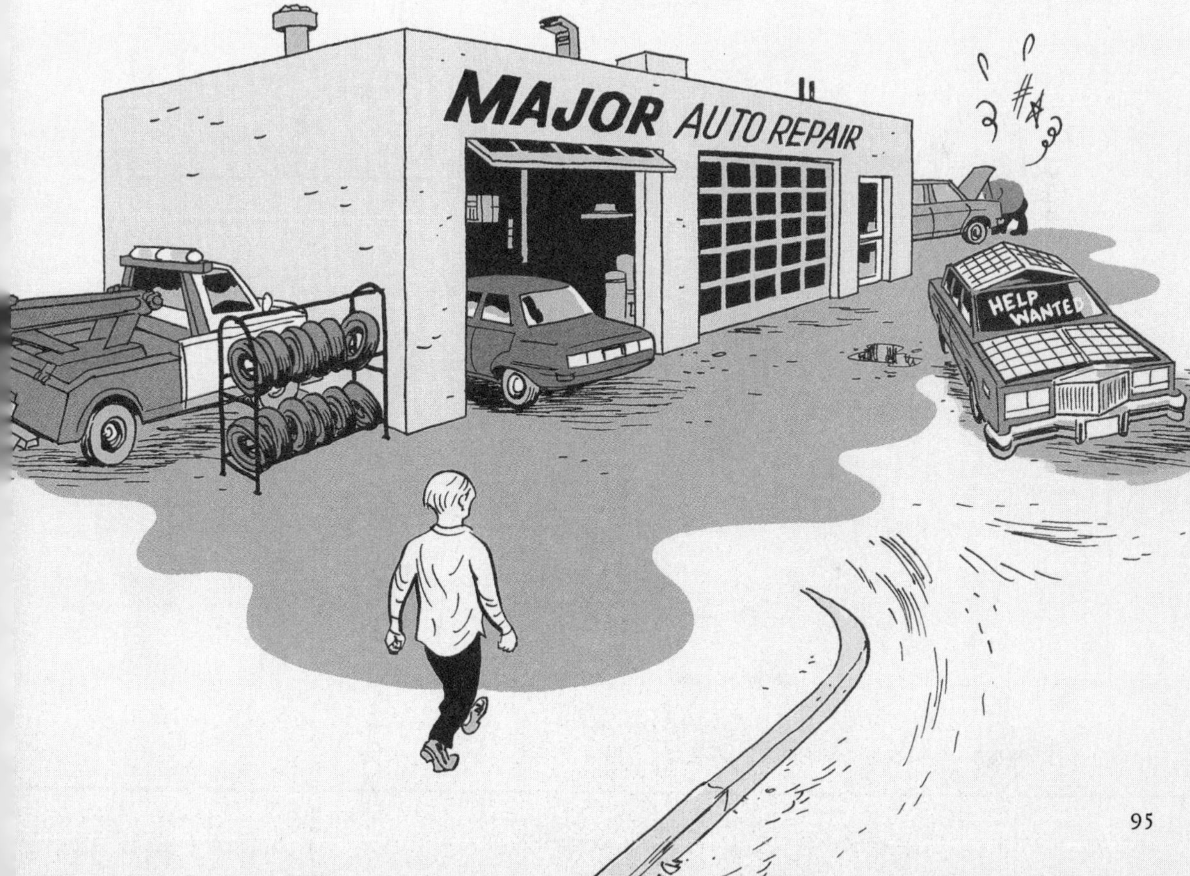
MAJOR AUTO REPAIR
HELP WANTED

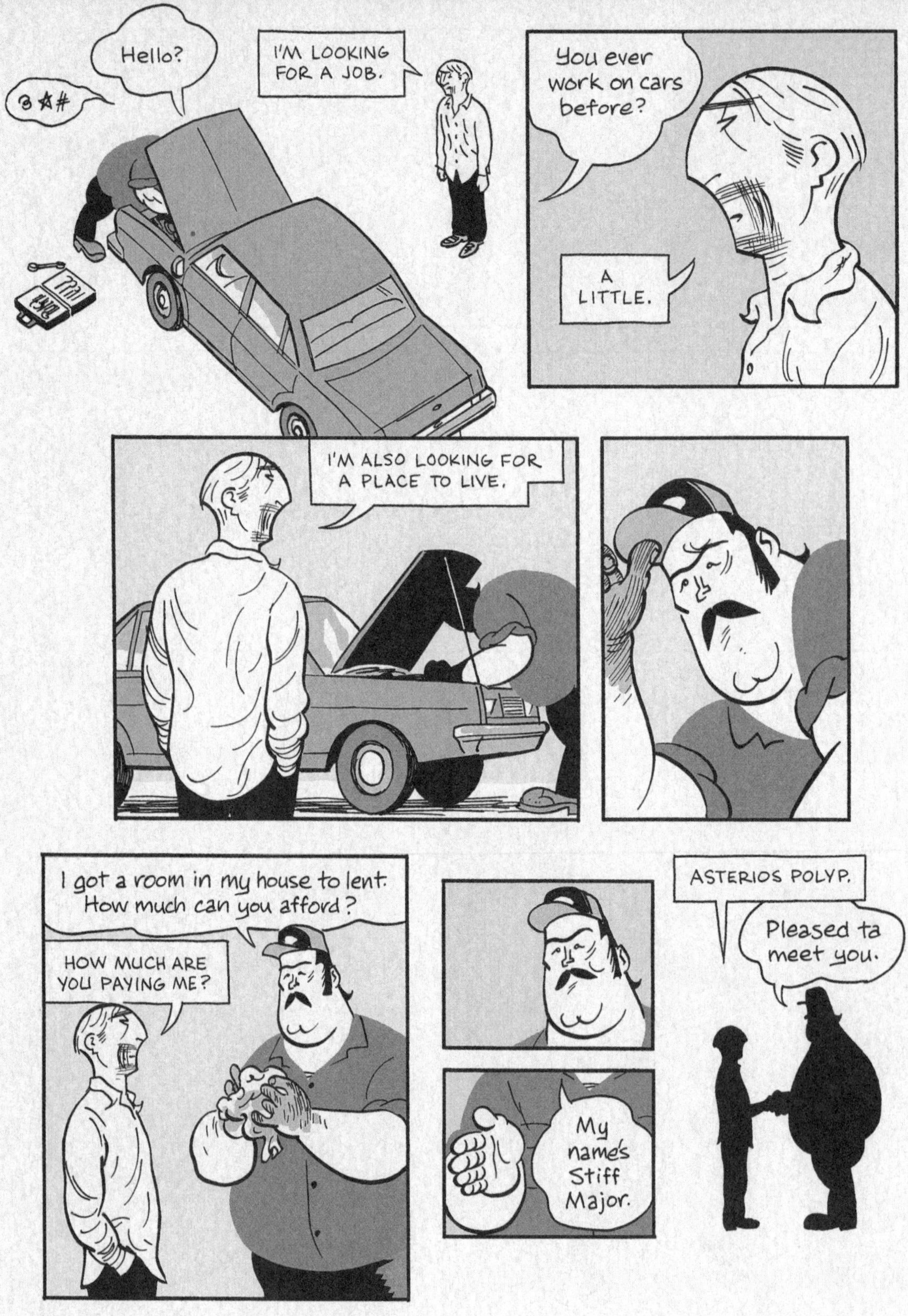

@☆#
Hello?
I'M LOOKING FOR A JOB.
You ever work on cars before?
A LITTLE.
I'M ALSO LOOKING FOR A PLACE TO LIVE.
I got a room in my house to lent. How much can you afford?
HOW MUCH ARE YOU PAYING ME?
My name's Stiff Major.
ASTERIOS POLYP.
Pleased ta meet you.

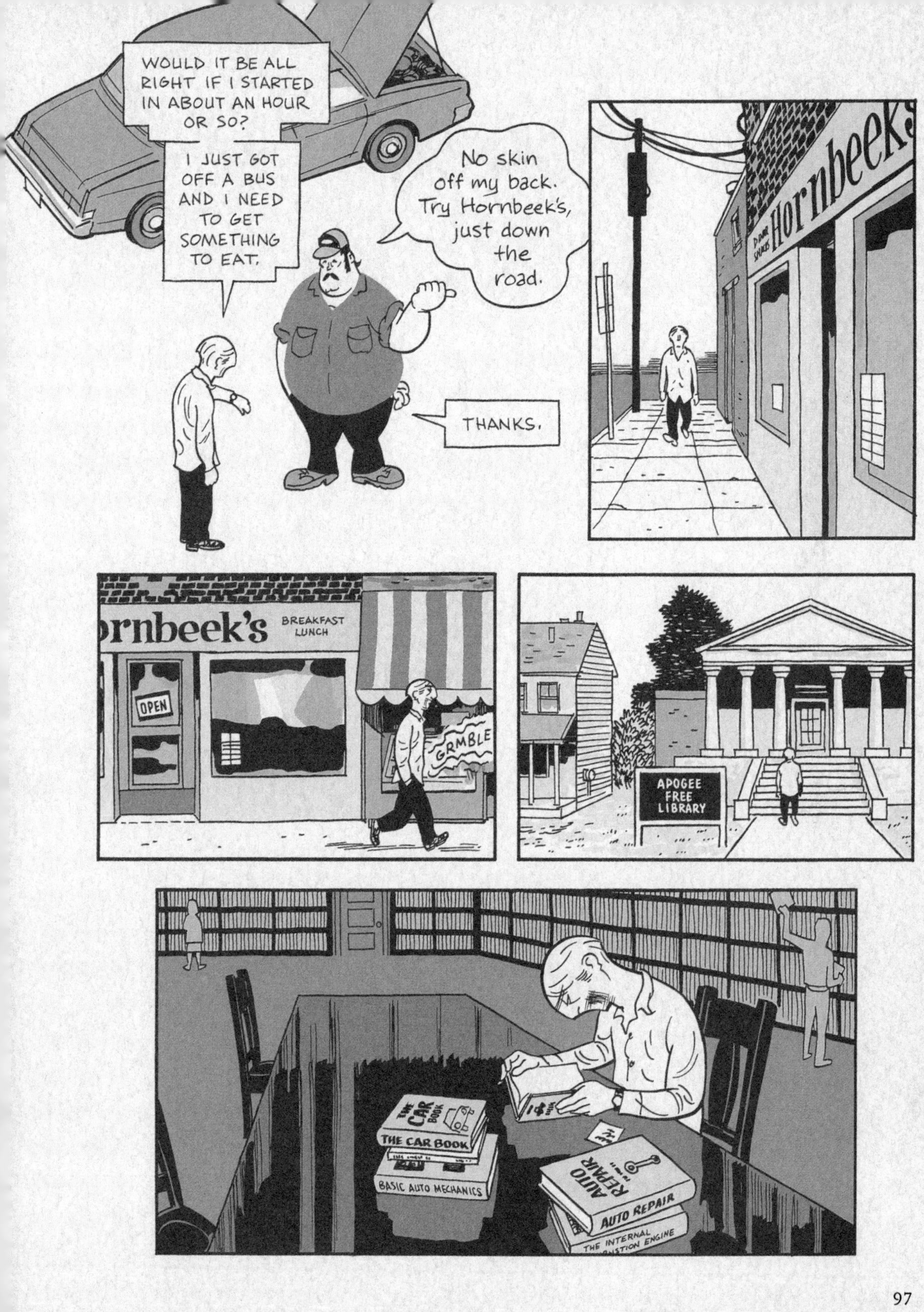

WOULD IT BE ALL RIGHT IF I STARTED IN ABOUT AN HOUR OR SO?
I JUST GOT OFF A BUS AND I NEED TO GET SOMETHING TO EAT.
No skin off my back. Try Hornbeek's, just down the road.
THANKS.
Hornbeek's
ornbeek's
BREAKFAST
LUNCH
OPEN
GRMBLE
APOGEE FREE LIBRARY
THE CAR BOOK
THE CAR BOOK
BASIC AUTO MECHANICS
AUTO REPAIR
AUTO REPAIR
THE INTERNAL

AT A FACULTY PARTY IN 1984, ASTERIOS WAS REGALING THE ASSEMBLY WITH HIS INSIGHT INTO COMMUNICATION,

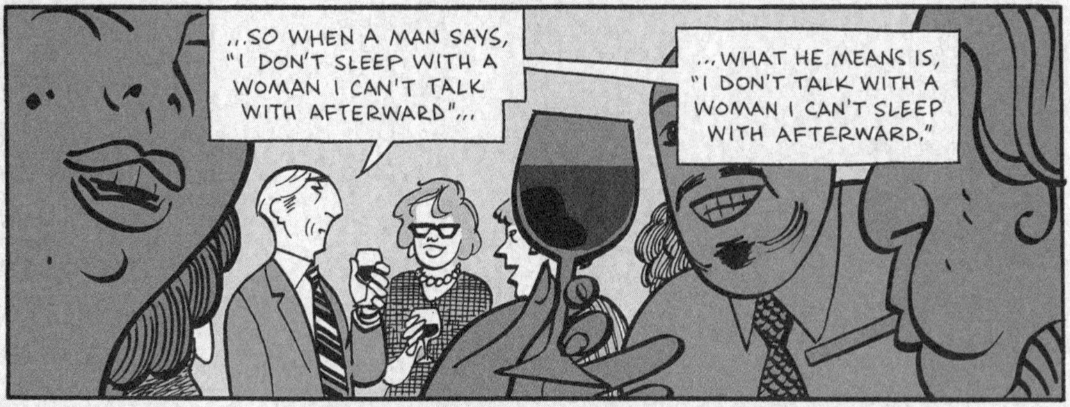

...SO WHEN A MAN SAYS, "I DON'T SLEEP WITH A WOMAN I CAN'T TALK WITH AFTERWARD"...
...WHAT HE MEANS IS, "I DON'T TALK WITH A WOMAN I CAN'T SLEEP WITH AFTERWARD."

HIS UNDERSTANDING OF HUMAN BEHAVIOR,

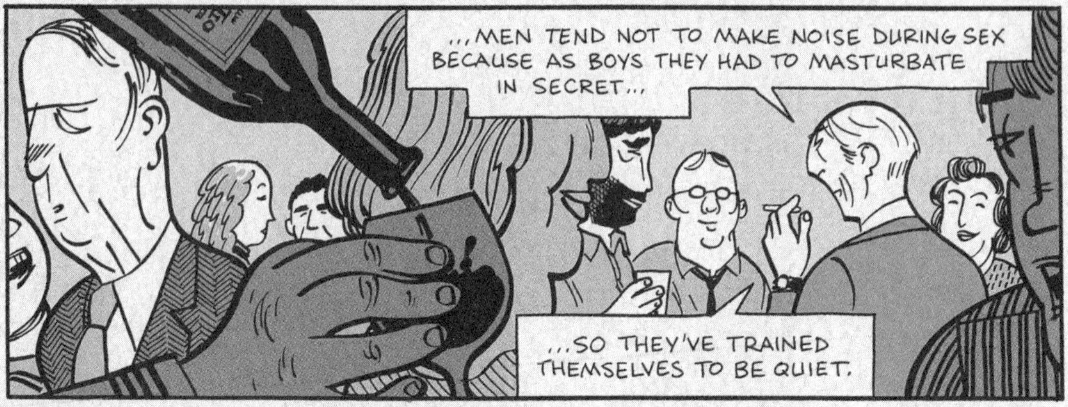

...MEN TEND NOT TO MAKE NOISE DURING SEX BECAUSE AS BOYS THEY HAD TO MASTURBATE IN SECRET...
...SO THEY'VE TRAINED THEMSELVES TO BE QUIET.

AND HIS SENSITIVITY.

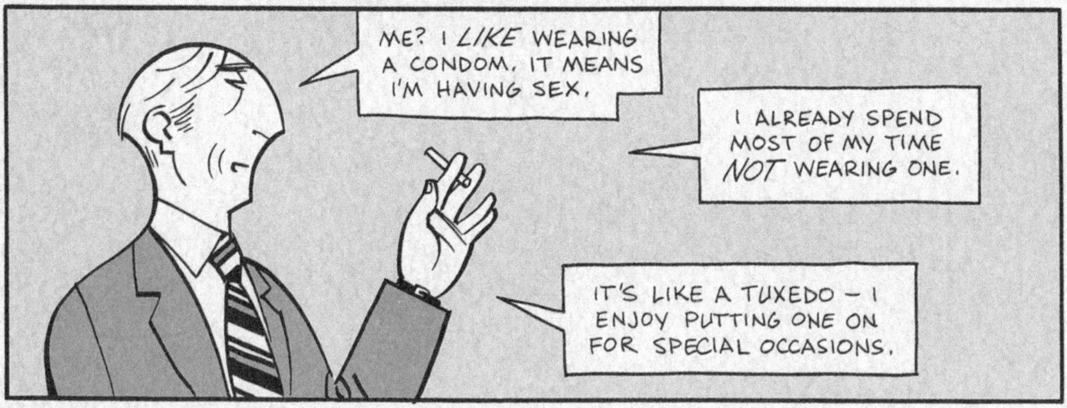

ME? I *LIKE* WEARING A CONDOM. IT MEANS I'M HAVING SEX.
I ALREADY SPEND MOST OF MY TIME *NOT* WEARING ONE.
IT'S LIKE A TUXEDO – I ENJOY PUTTING ONE ON FOR SPECIAL OCCASIONS.

HE WAS QUITE CAPABLE OF HOLDING FORTH ON A VARIETY OF TOPICS.

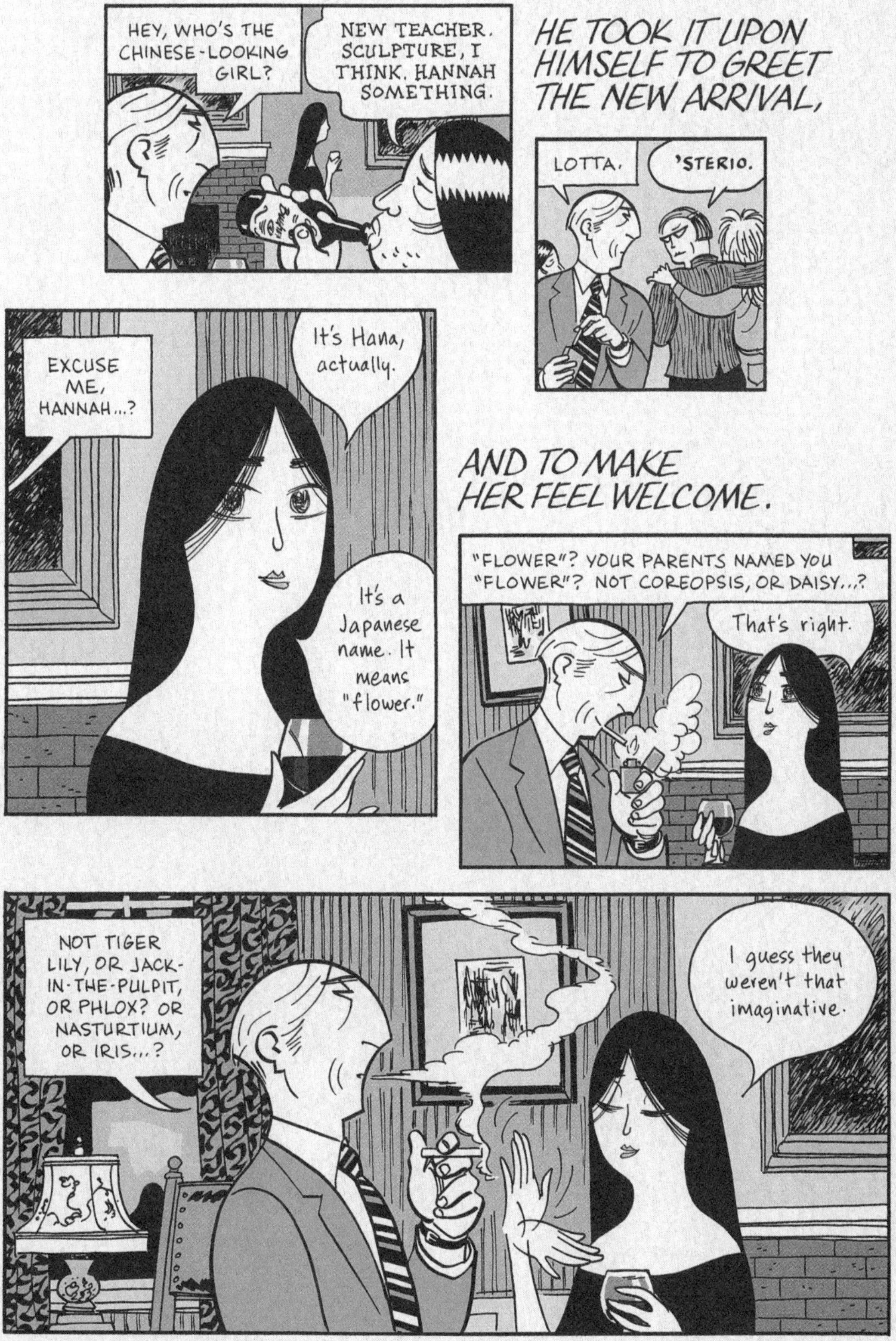
HEY, WHO'S THE CHINESE-LOOKING GIRL?
NEW TEACHER. SCULPTURE, I THINK. HANNAH SOMETHING.
HE TOOK IT UPON HIMSELF TO GREET THE NEW ARRIVAL,
LOTTA.
'STERIO.
EXCUSE ME, HANNAH...?
It's Hana, actually.
It's a Japanese name. It means "flower."
AND TO MAKE HER FEEL WELCOME.
"FLOWER"? YOUR PARENTS NAMED YOU "FLOWER"? NOT COREOPSIS, OR DAISY...?
That's right.
NOT TIGER LILY, OR JACK-IN-THE-PULPIT, OR PHLOX? OR NASTURTIUM, OR IRIS...?
I guess they weren't that imaginative.

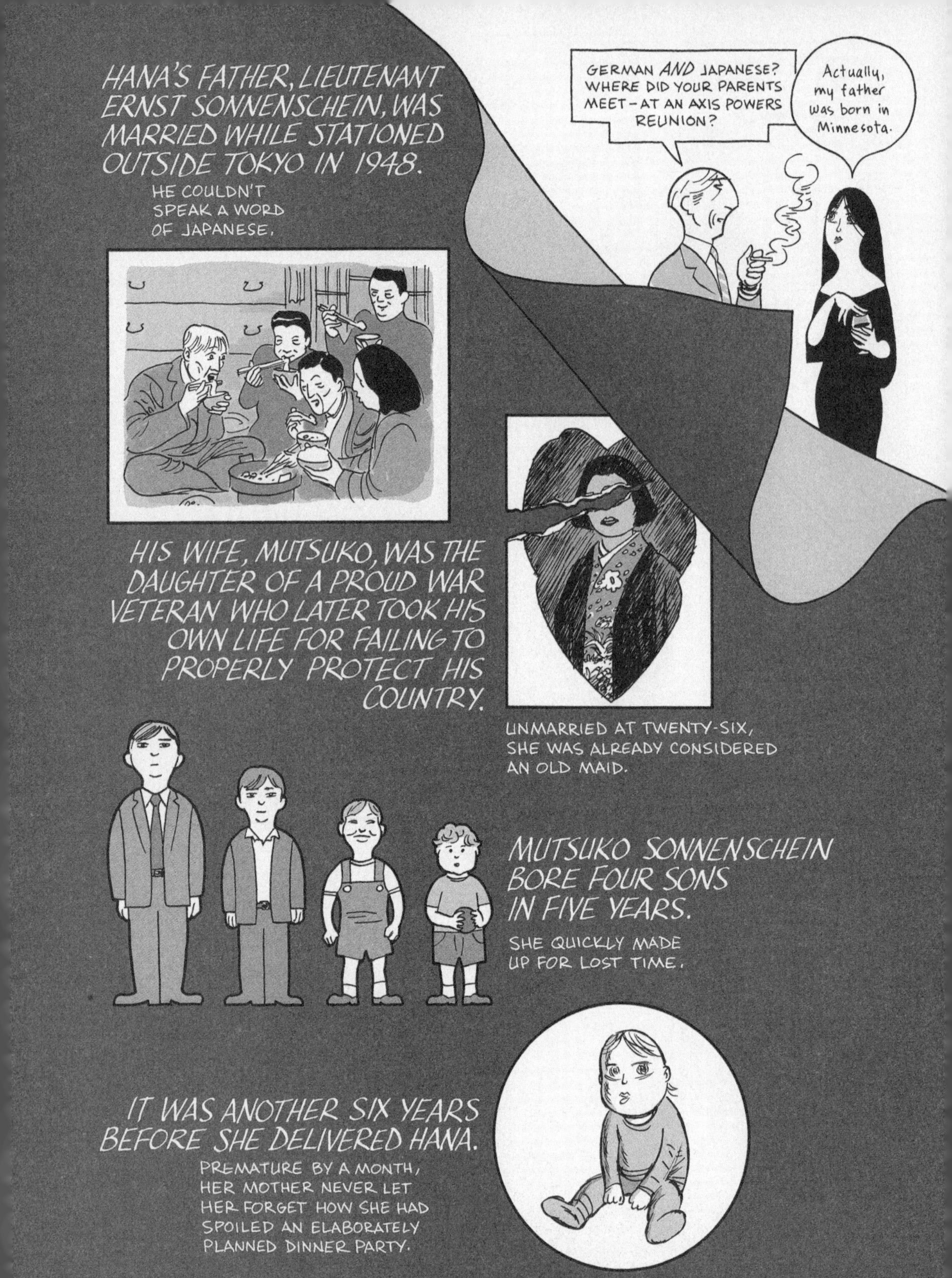
HANA'S FATHER, LIEUTENANT ERNST SONNENSCHEIN, WAS MARRIED WHILE STATIONED OUTSIDE TOKYO IN 1948.
HE COULDN'T SPEAK A WORD OF JAPANESE.
GERMAN AND JAPANESE? WHERE DID YOUR PARENTS MEET—AT AN AXIS POWERS REUNION?
Actually, my father was born in Minnesota.
HIS WIFE, MUTSUKO, WAS THE DAUGHTER OF A PROUD WAR VETERAN WHO LATER TOOK HIS OWN LIFE FOR FAILING TO PROPERLY PROTECT HIS COUNTRY.
UNMARRIED AT TWENTY-SIX, SHE WAS ALREADY CONSIDERED AN OLD MAID.
MUTSUKO SONNENSCHEIN BORE FOUR SONS IN FIVE YEARS.
SHE QUICKLY MADE UP FOR LOST TIME.
IT WAS ANOTHER SIX YEARS BEFORE SHE DELIVERED HANA.
PREMATURE BY A MONTH, HER MOTHER NEVER LET HER FORGET HOW SHE HAD SPOILED AN ELABORATELY PLANNED DINNER PARTY.

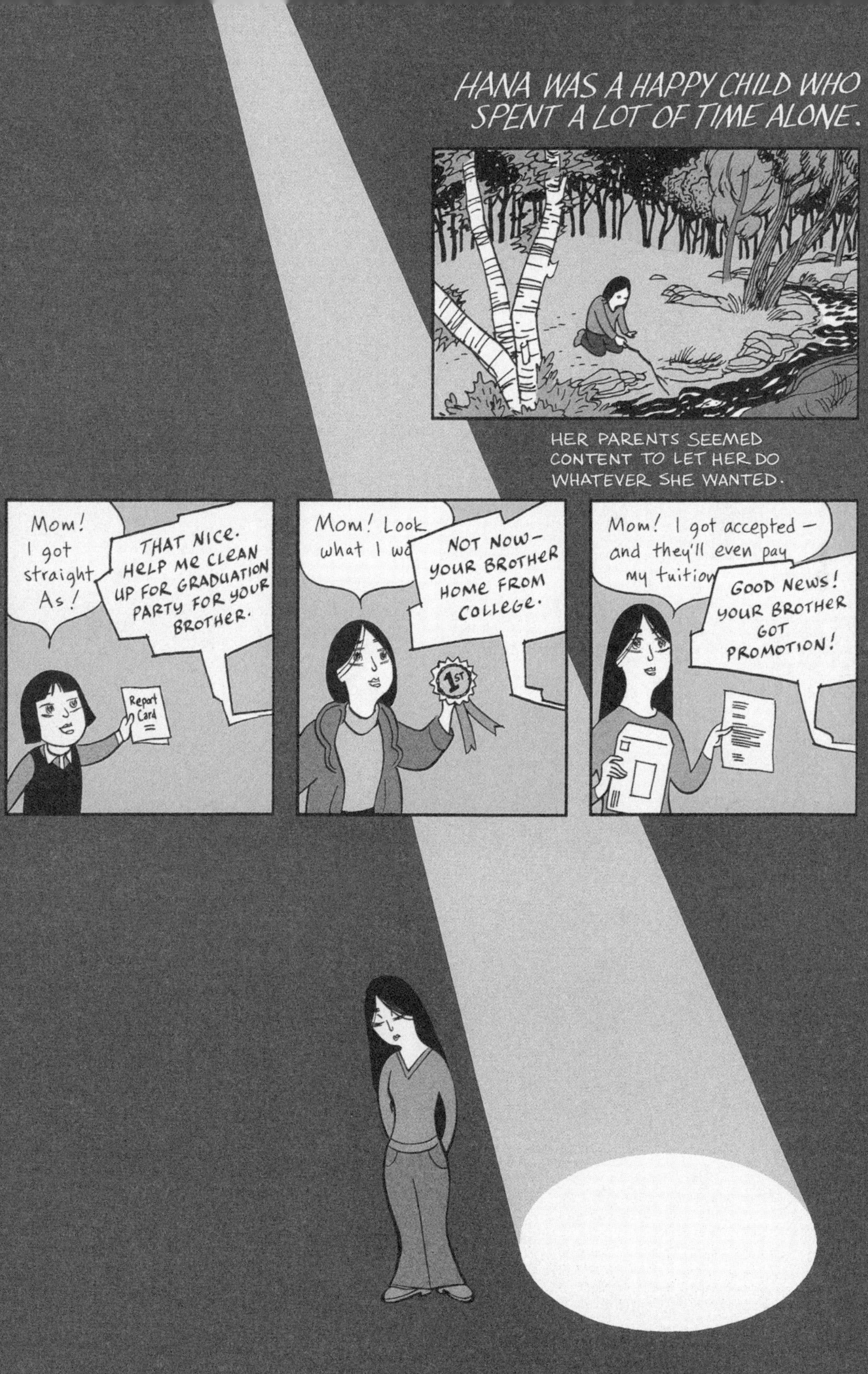
HANA WAS A HAPPY CHILD WHO SPENT A LOT OF TIME ALONE.
HER PARENTS SEEMED CONTENT TO LET HER DO WHATEVER SHE WANTED.
Mom! I got straight As!
THAT NICE. HELP ME CLEAN UP FOR GRADUATION PARTY FOR YOUR BROTHER.
Report Card
Mom! Look what I wo
NOT NOW— YOUR BROTHER HOME FROM COLLEGE.
1ST
Mom! I got accepted — and they'll even pay my tuition
GOOD NEWS! YOUR BROTHER GOT PROMOTION!

HANA ATTENDED A
PRESTIGIOUS COLLEGE OF
ART IN RHODE ISLAND ON A
FULL
HER PARENTS, THINKING A COLLEGE
EDUCATION UNNECESSARY
FOR A GIRL, ALLOWED **SCHOLAR-**
ONLY THIS COURSE OF STUDY... **SHIP.**

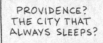

PROVIDENCE?
THE CITY THAT
ALWAYS SLEEPS?

I
liked
it.

ALTHOUGH SHE WAS AN
EXTRAORDINARY STUDENT,
SHE ALWAYS WORRIED
ABOUT BEING THE WORST
IN THE CLASS.

...NOT REALIZING THAT ART
WAS THE ONLY THING SHE
EVER WANTED TO STUDY.

SHE HAD A FEW BOYFRIENDS,
BUT ONLY BECAUSE THEY
SOUGHT HER OUT.

SHE WORKED SO HARD,
SHE HAD LITTLE TIME
FOR A SOCIAL LIFE.

AFTER FOUR OUTSTANDING
YEARS, SHE WAS CHOSEN
TO DELIVER THE
VALEDICTORY ADDRESS.

SHE DECLINED BECAUSE
SHE WAS TOO SHY TO
SPEAK IN THE
CROWDED AUDITORIUM.

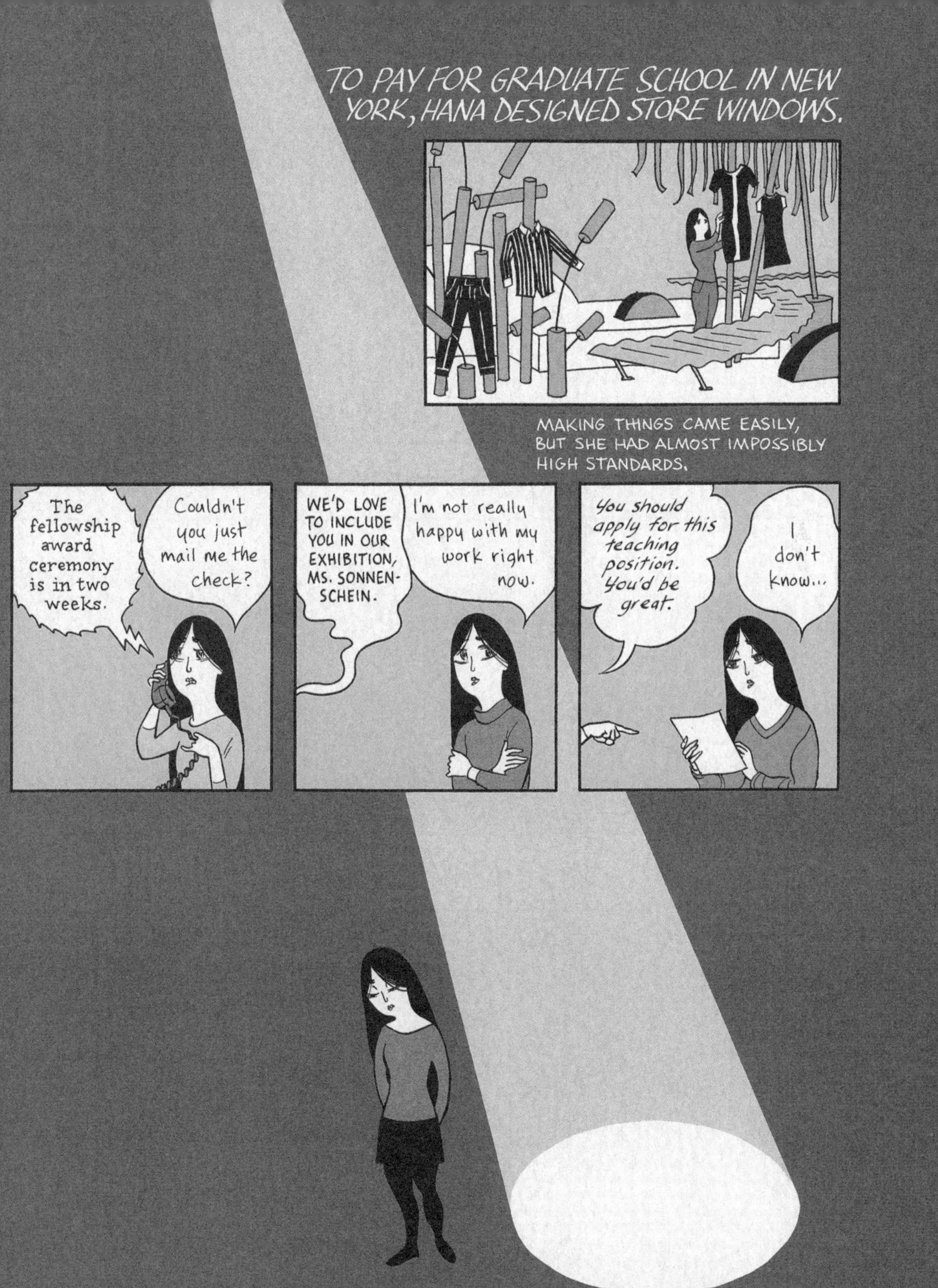
TO PAY FOR GRADUATE SCHOOL IN NEW YORK, HANA DESIGNED STORE WINDOWS.
MAKING THINGS CAME EASILY, BUT SHE HAD ALMOST IMPOSSIBLY HIGH STANDARDS.
The fellowship award ceremony is in two weeks.
Couldn't you just mail me the check?
WE'D LOVE TO INCLUDE YOU IN OUR EXHIBITION, MS. SONNENSCHEIN.
I'm not really happy with my work right now.
You should apply for this teaching position. You'd be great.
I don't know...

IN 1984, HANA SONNENSCHEIN ATTENDED HER FIRST FACULTY PARTY.

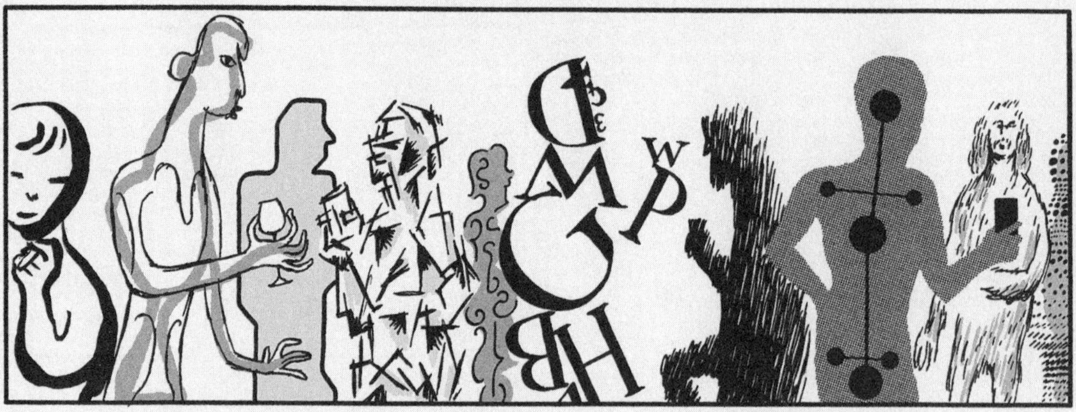

SHE DIDN'T KNOW ANYONE THERE,

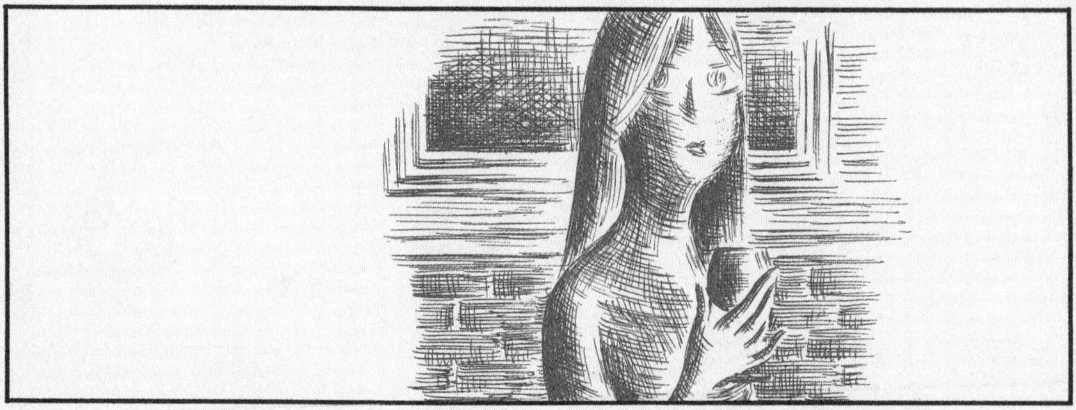

BUT ONE PERSON CAUGHT HER EYE.

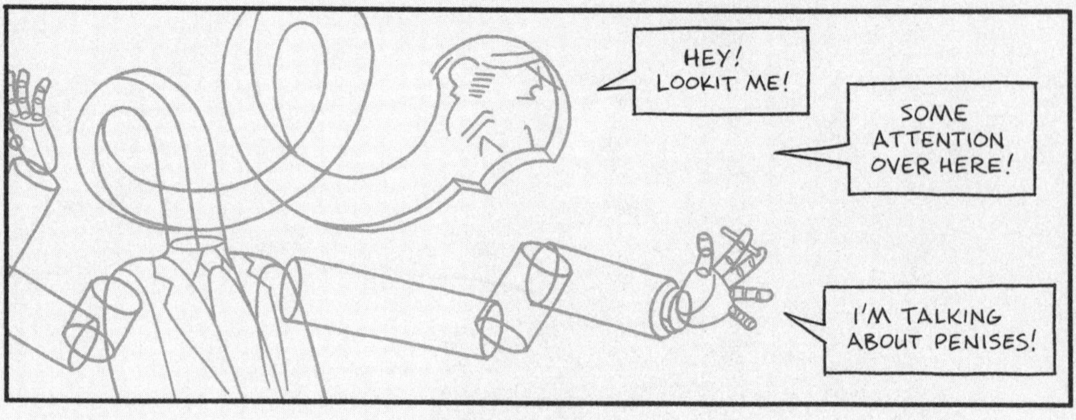
HEY! LOOKIT ME!
SOME ATTENTION OVER HERE!
I'M TALKING ABOUT PENISES!

DON'T ASK ME TO EXPLAIN THESE THINGS.

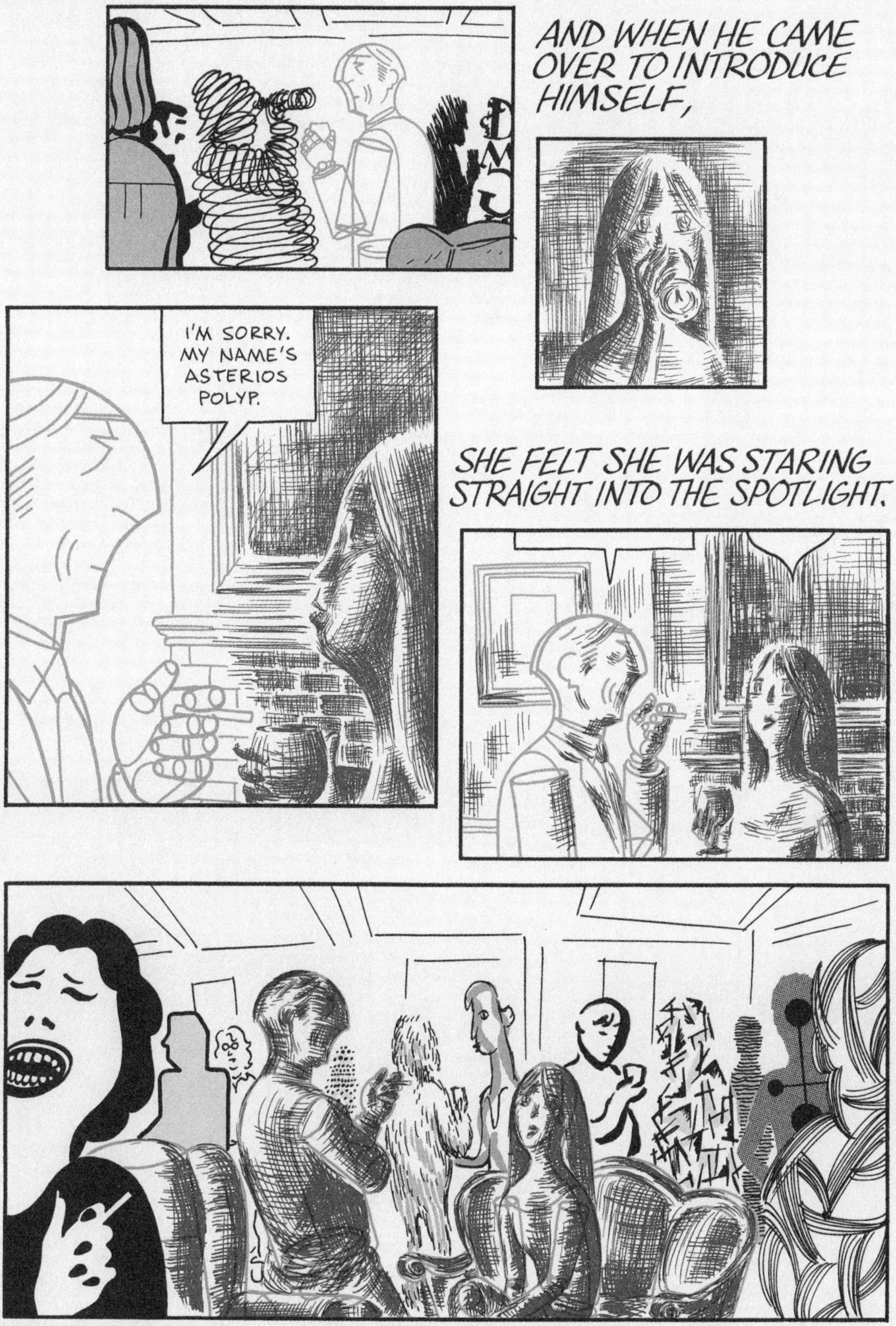
AND WHEN HE CAME OVER TO INTRODUCE HIMSELF,
I'M SORRY. MY NAME'S ASTERIOS POLYP.
SHE FELT SHE WAS STARING STRAIGHT INTO THE SPOTLIGHT.

CITIZEN REX

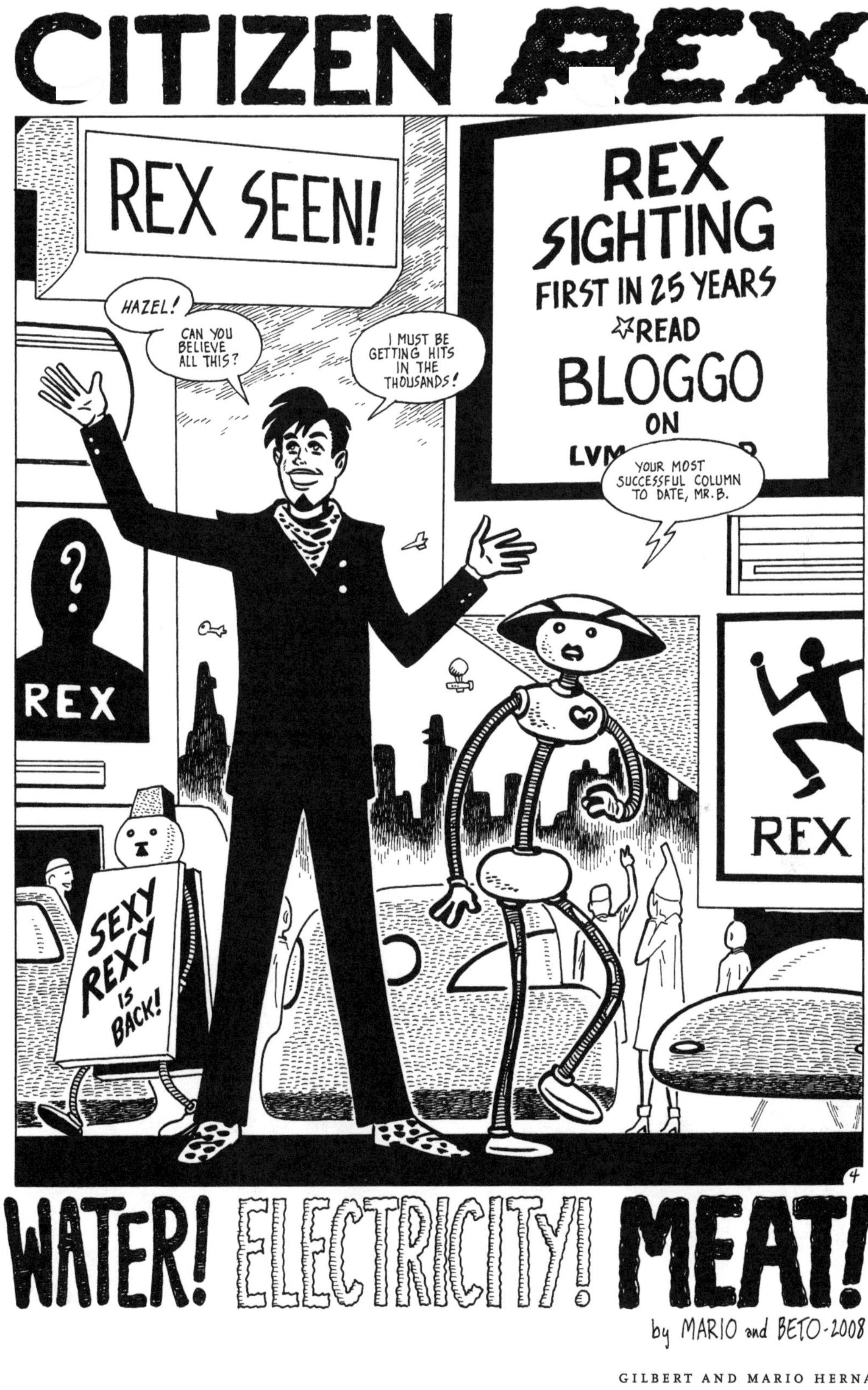

REX SEEN!
REX SIGHTING
FIRST IN 25 YEARS
READ
BLOGGO
ON
HAZEL!
CAN YOU BELIEVE ALL THIS?
I MUST BE GETTING HITS IN THE THOUSANDS!
YOUR MOST SUCCESSFUL COLUMN TO DATE, MR. B.
REX
REX
SEXY REXY IS BACK!
4

WATER! ELECTRICITY! MEAT!

by MARIO and BETO-2008

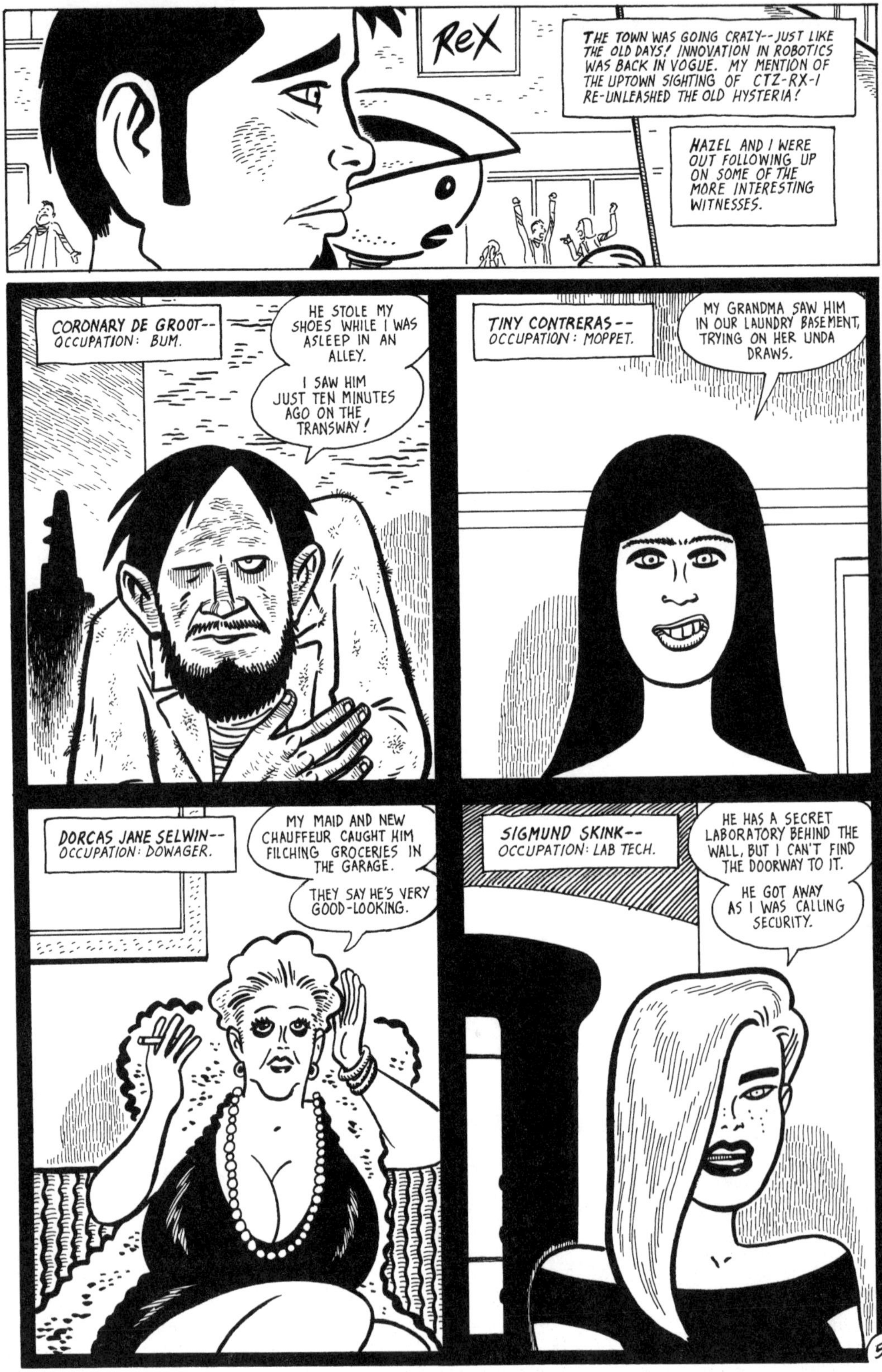
Rex
THE TOWN WAS GOING CRAZY--JUST LIKE THE OLD DAYS! INNOVATION IN ROBOTICS WAS BACK IN VOGUE. MY MENTION OF THE UPTOWN SIGHTING OF CTZ-RX-I RE-UNLEASHED THE OLD HYSTERIA!
HAZEL AND I WERE OUT FOLLOWING UP ON SOME OF THE MORE INTERESTING WITNESSES.
CORONARY DE GROOT-- OCCUPATION: BUM.
HE STOLE MY SHOES WHILE I WAS ASLEEP IN AN ALLEY.
I SAW HIM JUST TEN MINUTES AGO ON THE TRANSWAY!
TINY CONTRERAS-- OCCUPATION: MOPPET.
MY GRANDMA SAW HIM IN OUR LAUNDRY BASEMENT, TRYING ON HER UNDA DRAWS.
DORCAS JANE SELWIN-- OCCUPATION: DOWAGER.
MY MAID AND NEW CHAUFFEUR CAUGHT HIM FILCHING GROCERIES IN THE GARAGE.
THEY SAY HE'S VERY GOOD-LOOKING.
SIGMUND SKINK-- OCCUPATION: LAB TECH.
HE HAS A SECRET LABORATORY BEHIND THE WALL, BUT I CAN'T FIND THE DOORWAY TO IT.
HE GOT AWAY AS I WAS CALLING SECURITY.
5

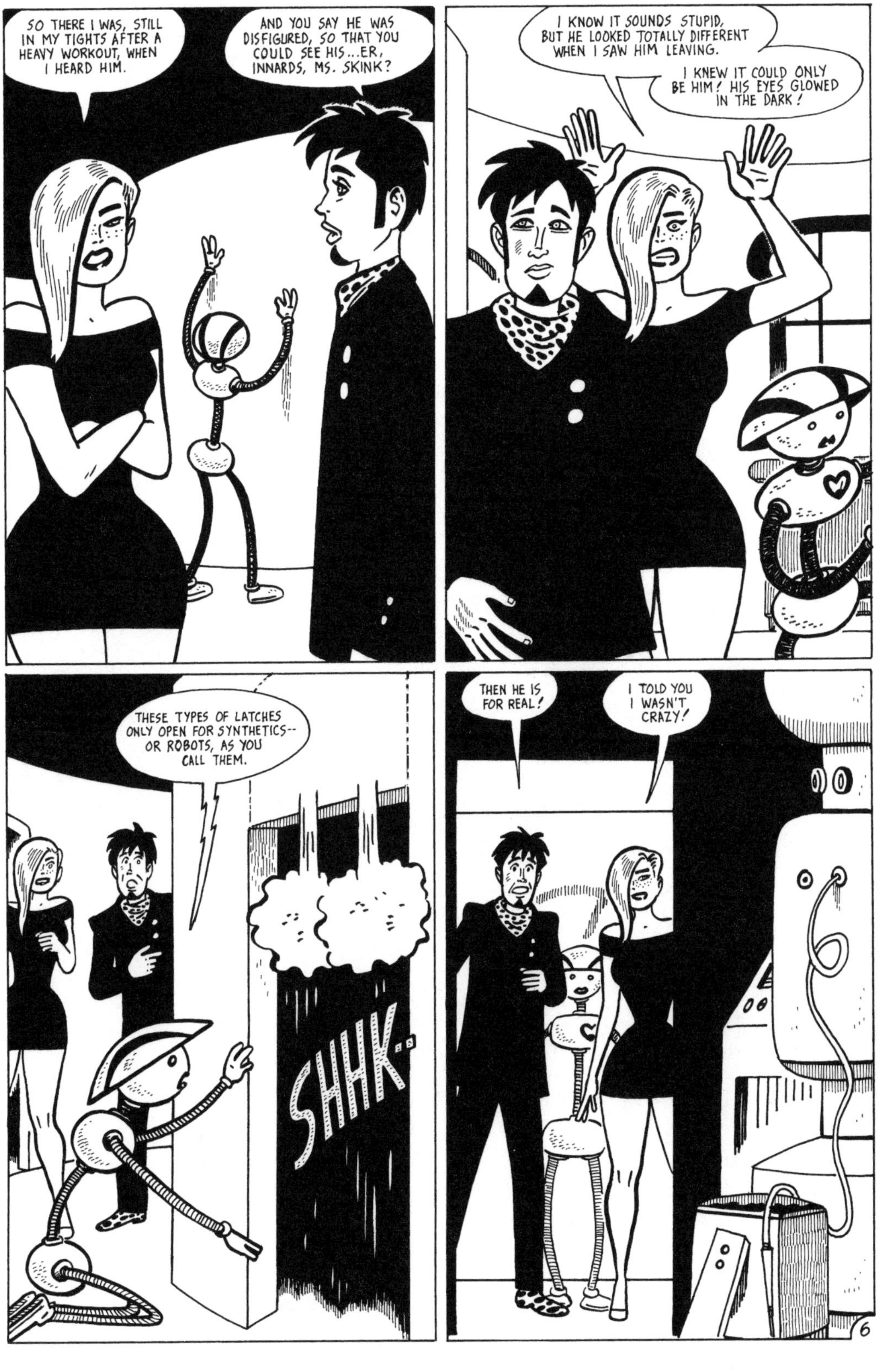

SO THERE I WAS, STILL IN MY TIGHTS AFTER A HEAVY WORKOUT, WHEN I HEARD HIM.
AND YOU SAY HE WAS DISFIGURED, SO THAT YOU COULD SEE HIS...ER, INNARDS, MS. SKINK?
I KNOW IT SOUNDS STUPID, BUT HE LOOKED TOTALLY DIFFERENT WHEN I SAW HIM LEAVING.
I KNEW IT COULD ONLY BE HIM! HIS EYES GLOWED IN THE DARK!
THESE TYPES OF LATCHES ONLY OPEN FOR SYNTHETICS-- OR ROBOTS, AS YOU CALL THEM.
SHHK
THEN HE IS FOR REAL!
I TOLD YOU I WASN'T CRAZY!
6

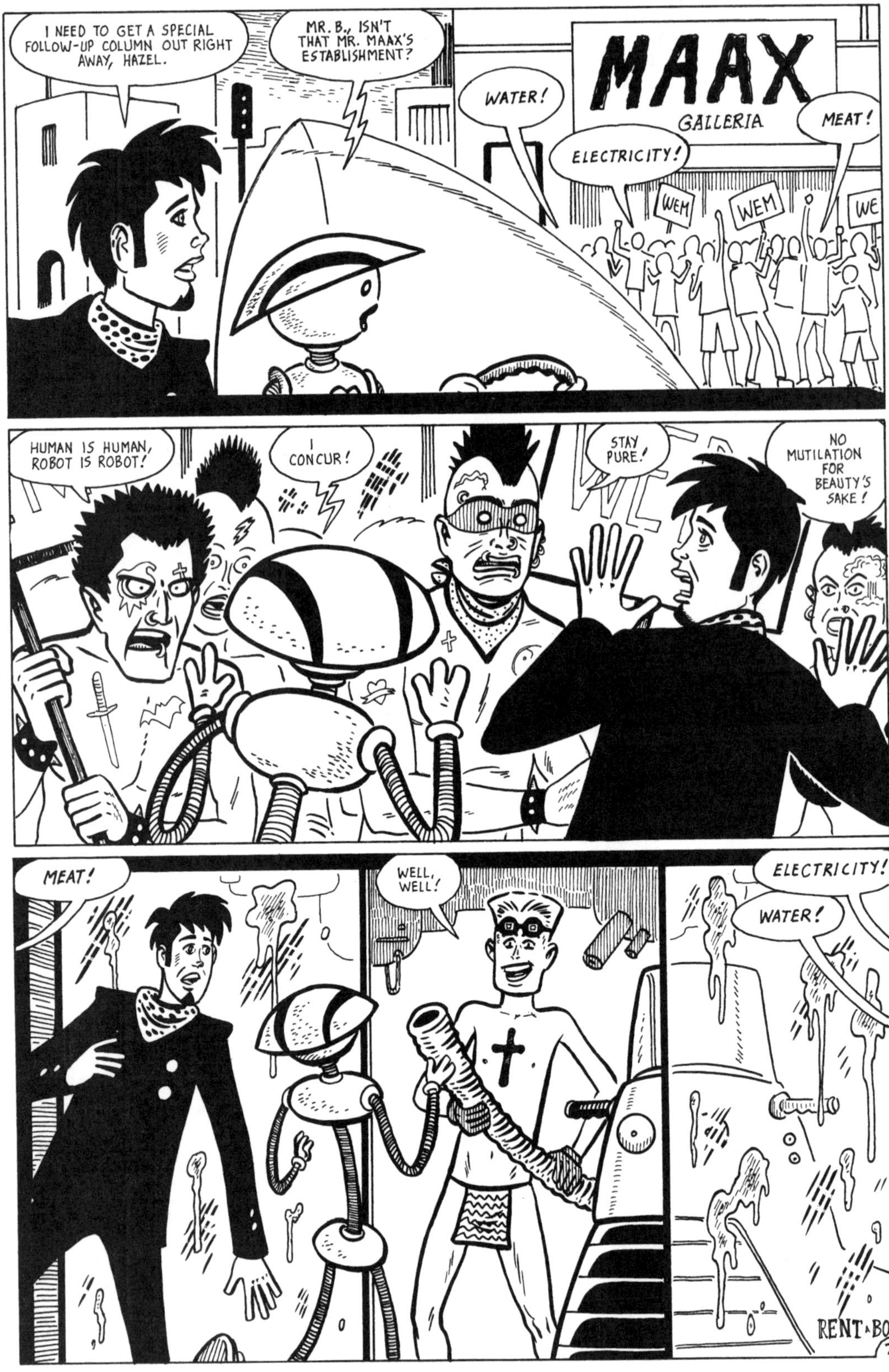
I NEED TO GET A SPECIAL FOLLOW-UP COLUMN OUT RIGHT AWAY, HAZEL.
MR. B., ISN'T THAT MR. MAAX'S ESTABLISHMENT?
MAAX
GALLERIA
WATER!
ELECTRICITY!
MEAT!
WEM
WEM
WE
HUMAN IS HUMAN, ROBOT IS ROBOT!
I CONCUR!
STAY PURE!
NO MUTILATION FOR BEAUTY'S SAKE!
MEAT!
WELL, WELL!
ELECTRICITY!
WATER!
RENT A BOT
7

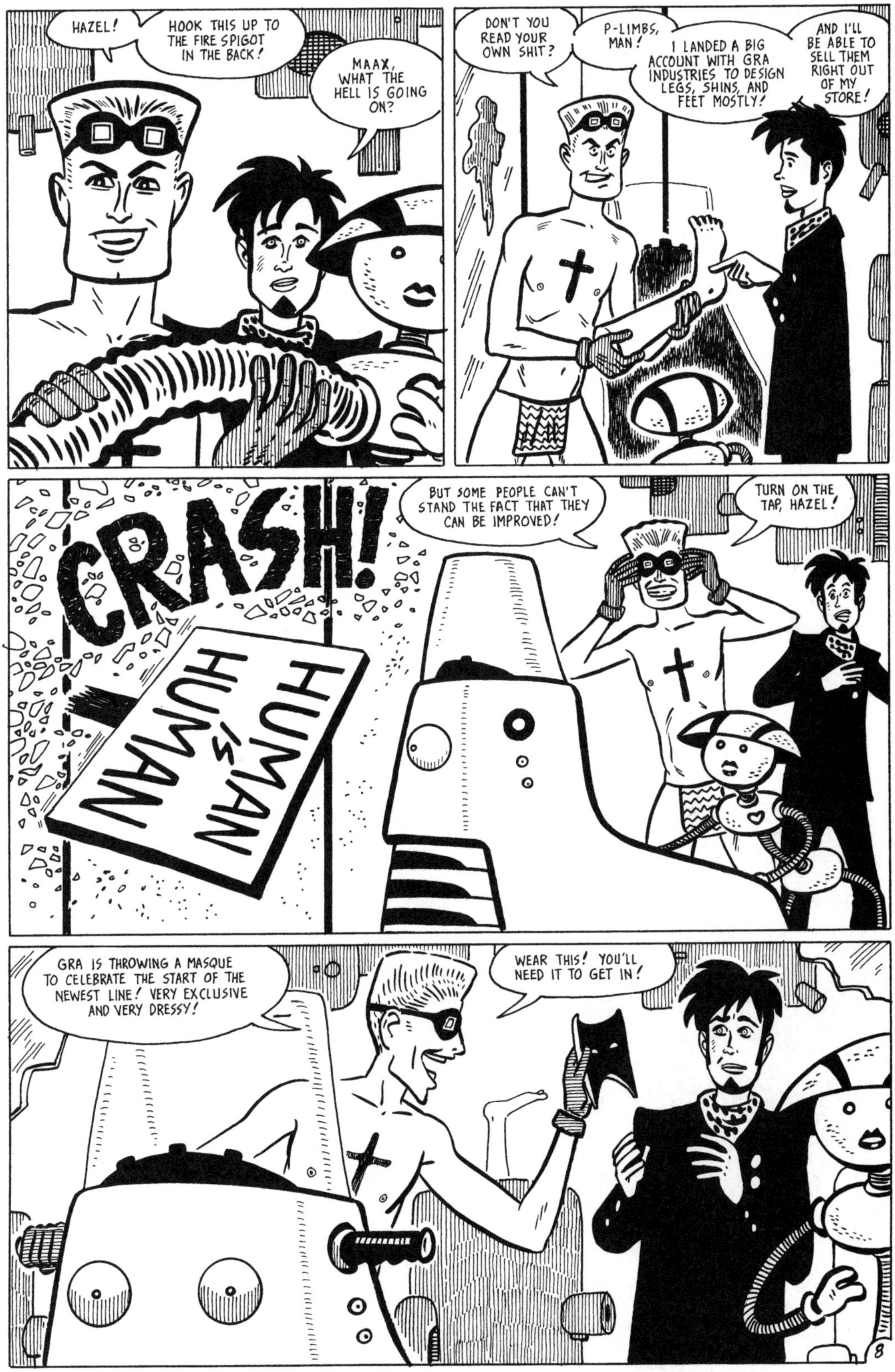
HAZEL!
HOOK THIS UP TO THE FIRE SPIGOT IN THE BACK!
MAAX, WHAT THE HELL IS GOING ON?
DON'T YOU READ YOUR OWN SHIT?
P-LIMBS, MAN!
I LANDED A BIG ACCOUNT WITH GRA INDUSTRIES TO DESIGN LEGS, SHINS, AND FEET MOSTLY!
AND I'LL BE ABLE TO SELL THEM RIGHT OUT OF MY STORE!
CRASH!
HUMAN IS HUMAN
BUT SOME PEOPLE CAN'T STAND THE FACT THAT THEY CAN BE IMPROVED!
TURN ON THE TAP, HAZEL!
GRA IS THROWING A MASQUE TO CELEBRATE THE START OF THE NEWEST LINE! VERY EXCLUSIVE AND VERY DRESSY!
WEAR THIS! YOU'LL NEED IT TO GET IN!
8

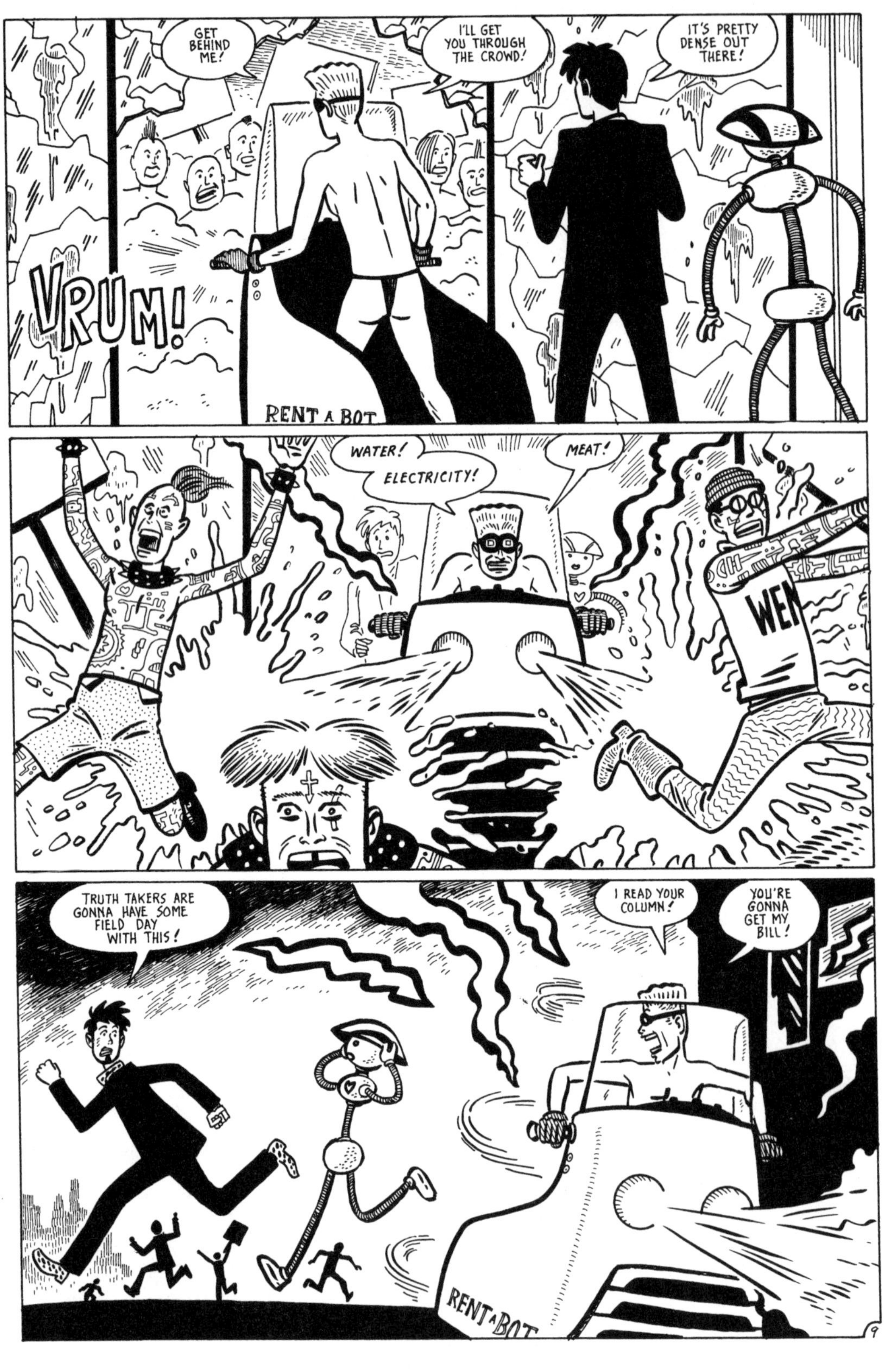
GET BEHIND ME!
I'LL GET YOU THROUGH THE CROWD!
IT'S PRETTY DENSE OUT THERE!
VRUM!
RENT A BOT
WATER!
ELECTRICITY!
MEAT!
WEN
TRUTH TAKERS ARE GONNA HAVE SOME FIELD DAY WITH THIS!
I READ YOUR COLUMN!
YOU'RE GONNA GET MY BILL!
RENT A BOT
9

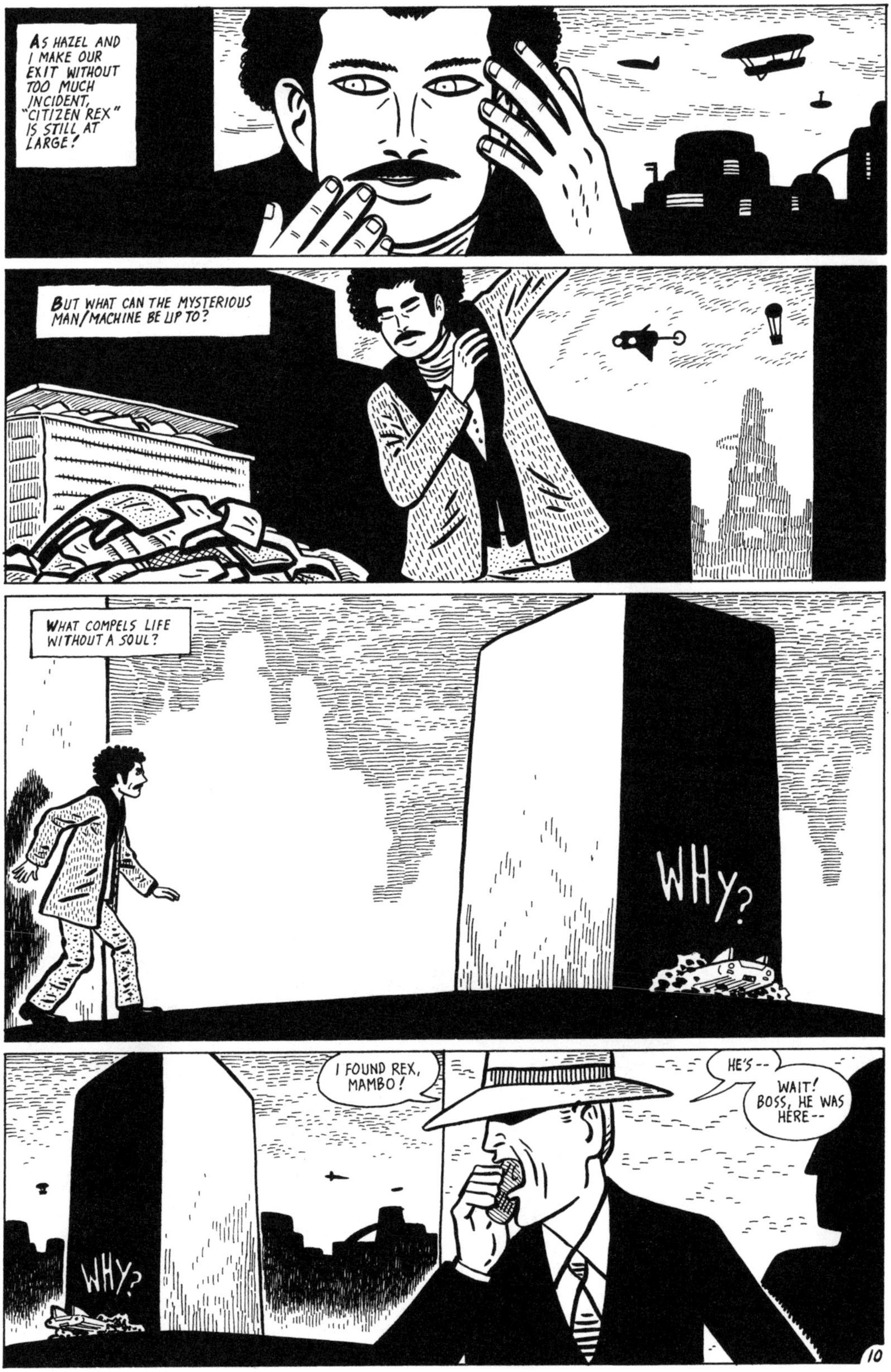

AS HAZEL AND I MAKE OUR EXIT WITHOUT TOO MUCH INCIDENT, "CITIZEN REX" IS STILL AT LARGE!
BUT WHAT CAN THE MYSTERIOUS MAN/MACHINE BE UP TO?
WHAT COMPELS LIFE WITHOUT A SOUL?
WHy?
WHY?
I FOUND REX, MAMBO!
HE'S --
WAIT! BOSS, HE WAS HERE --
10

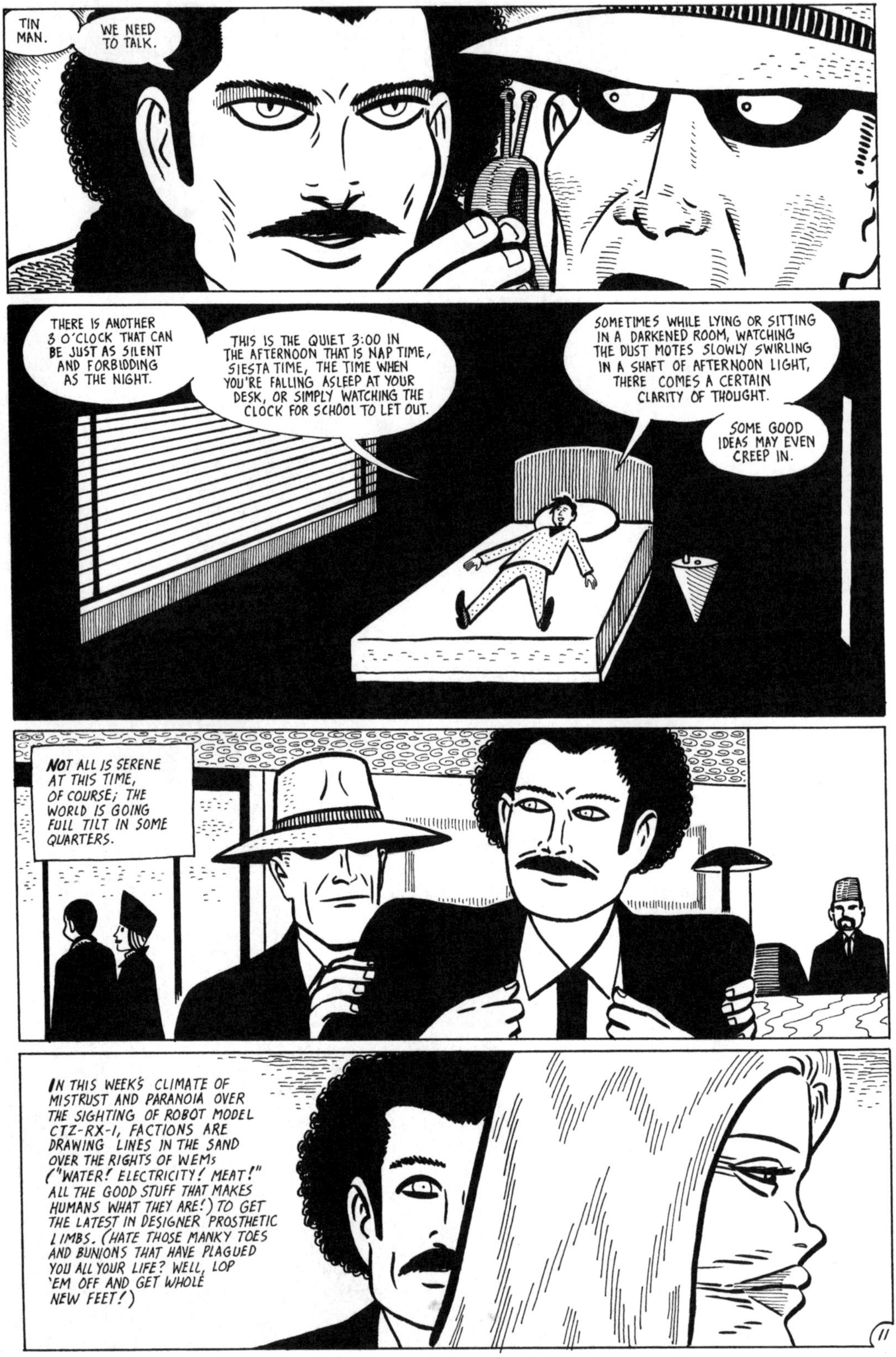
TIN MAN.
WE NEED TO TALK.
THERE IS ANOTHER 3 O'CLOCK THAT CAN BE JUST AS SILENT AND FORBIDDING AS THE NIGHT.
THIS IS THE QUIET 3:00 IN THE AFTERNOON THAT IS NAP TIME, SIESTA TIME, THE TIME WHEN YOU'RE FALLING ASLEEP AT YOUR DESK, OR SIMPLY WATCHING THE CLOCK FOR SCHOOL TO LET OUT.
SOMETIMES WHILE LYING OR SITTING IN A DARKENED ROOM, WATCHING THE DUST MOTES SLOWLY SWIRLING IN A SHAFT OF AFTERNOON LIGHT, THERE COMES A CERTAIN CLARITY OF THOUGHT.
SOME GOOD IDEAS MAY EVEN CREEP IN.
NOT ALL IS SERENE AT THIS TIME, OF COURSE; THE WORLD IS GOING FULL TILT IN SOME QUARTERS.
IN THIS WEEK'S CLIMATE OF MISTRUST AND PARANOIA OVER THE SIGHTING OF ROBOT MODEL CTZ-RX-1, FACTIONS ARE DRAWING LINES IN THE SAND OVER THE RIGHTS OF WEMs ("WATER! ELECTRICITY! MEAT!" ALL THE GOOD STUFF THAT MAKES HUMANS WHAT THEY ARE!) TO GET THE LATEST IN DESIGNER PROSTHETIC LIMBS. (HATE THOSE MANKY TOES AND BUNIONS THAT HAVE PLAGUED YOU ALL YOUR LIFE? WELL, LOP 'EM OFF AND GET WHOLE NEW FEET!)
11

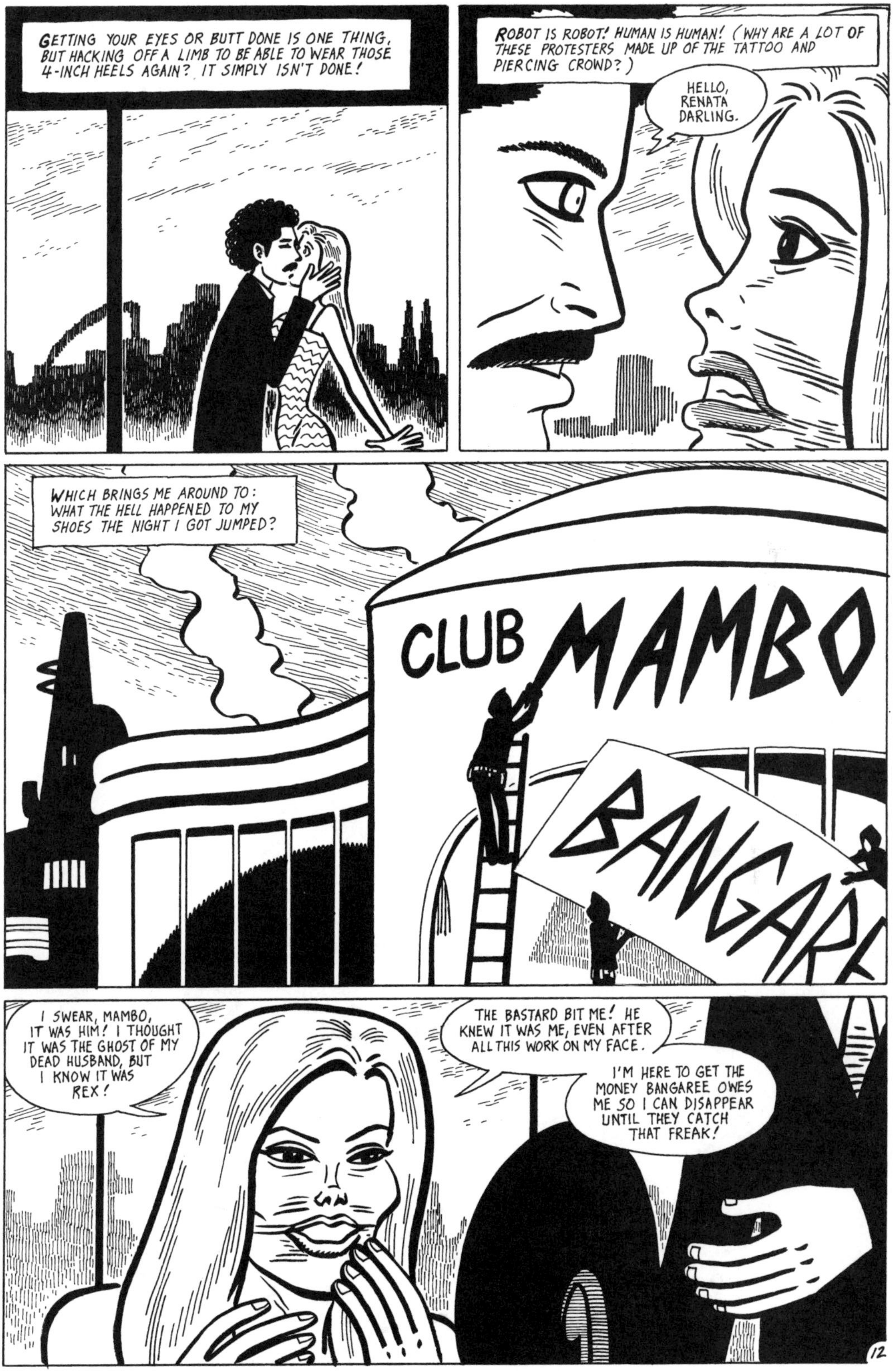
GETTING YOUR EYES OR BUTT DONE IS ONE THING, BUT HACKING OFF A LIMB TO BE ABLE TO WEAR THOSE 4-INCH HEELS AGAIN? IT SIMPLY ISN'T DONE!
ROBOT IS ROBOT! HUMAN IS HUMAN! (WHY ARE A LOT OF THESE PROTESTERS MADE UP OF THE TATTOO AND PIERCING CROWD?)
HELLO, RENATA DARLING.
WHICH BRINGS ME AROUND TO: WHAT THE HELL HAPPENED TO MY SHOES THE NIGHT I GOT JUMPED?
CLUB MAMBO
BANGARE
I SWEAR, MAMBO, IT WAS HIM! I THOUGHT IT WAS THE GHOST OF MY DEAD HUSBAND, BUT I KNOW IT WAS REX!
THE BASTARD BIT ME! HE KNEW IT WAS ME, EVEN AFTER ALL THIS WORK ON MY FACE.
I'M HERE TO GET THE MONEY BANGAREE OWES ME SO I CAN DISAPPEAR UNTIL THEY CATCH THAT FREAK!
12

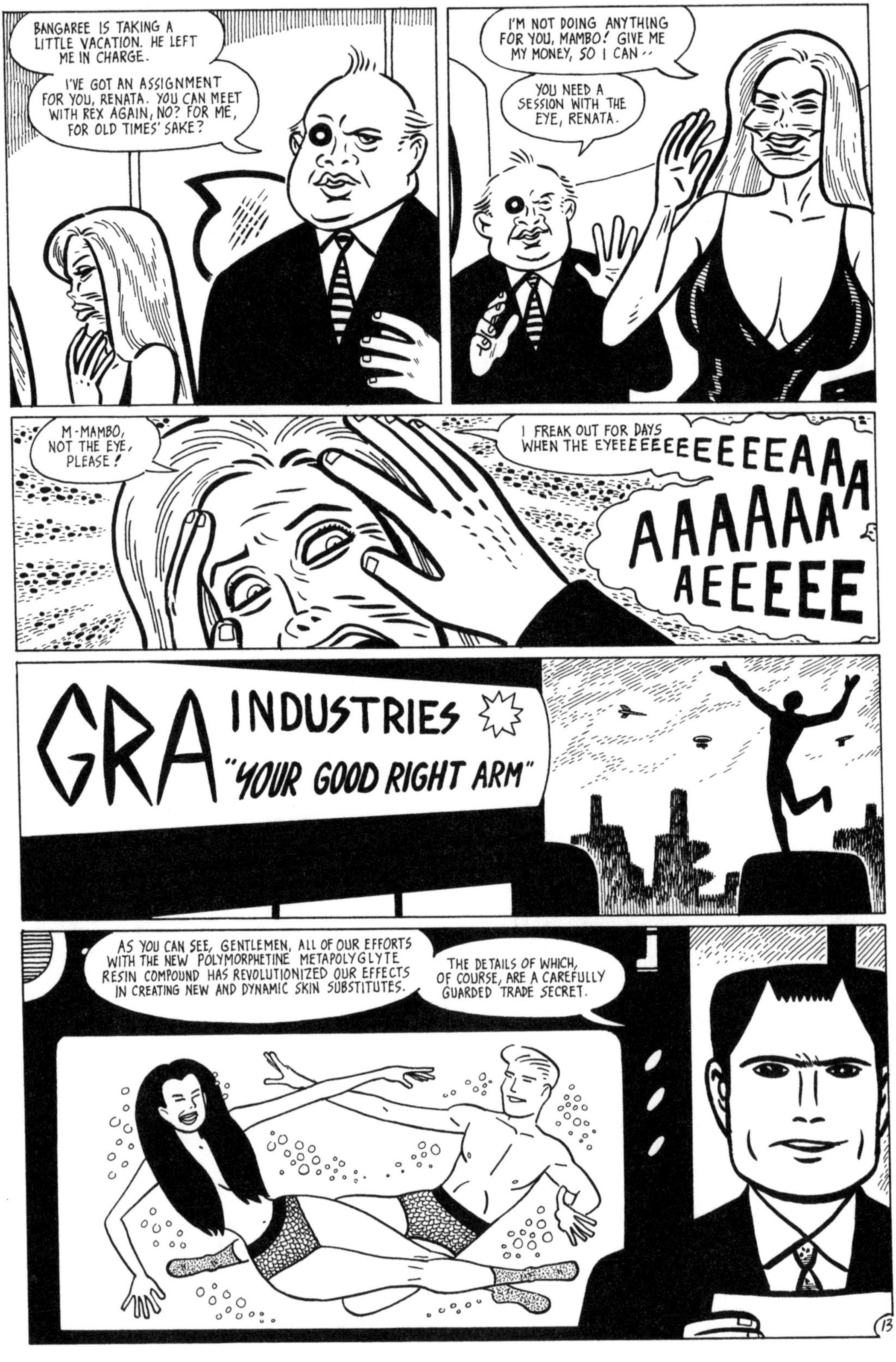

BANGAREE IS TAKING A LITTLE VACATION. HE LEFT ME IN CHARGE.
I'VE GOT AN ASSIGNMENT FOR YOU, RENATA. YOU CAN MEET WITH REX AGAIN, NO? FOR ME, FOR OLD TIMES' SAKE?
I'M NOT DOING ANYTHING FOR YOU, MAMBO! GIVE ME MY MONEY, SO I CAN ··
YOU NEED A SESSION WITH THE EYE, RENATA.
M-MAMBO, NOT THE EYE, PLEASE!
I FREAK OUT FOR DAYS WHEN THE EYEEEEEEEEEEEAAA
AAAAAAA AEEEEE
GRA INDUSTRIES
"YOUR GOOD RIGHT ARM"
AS YOU CAN SEE, GENTLEMEN, ALL OF OUR EFFORTS WITH THE NEW POLYMORPHETINE METAPOLYGLYTE RESIN COMPOUND HAS REVOLUTIONIZED OUR EFFECTS IN CREATING NEW AND DYNAMIC SKIN SUBSTITUTES.
THE DETAILS OF WHICH, OF COURSE, ARE A CAREFULLY GUARDED TRADE SECRET.
13

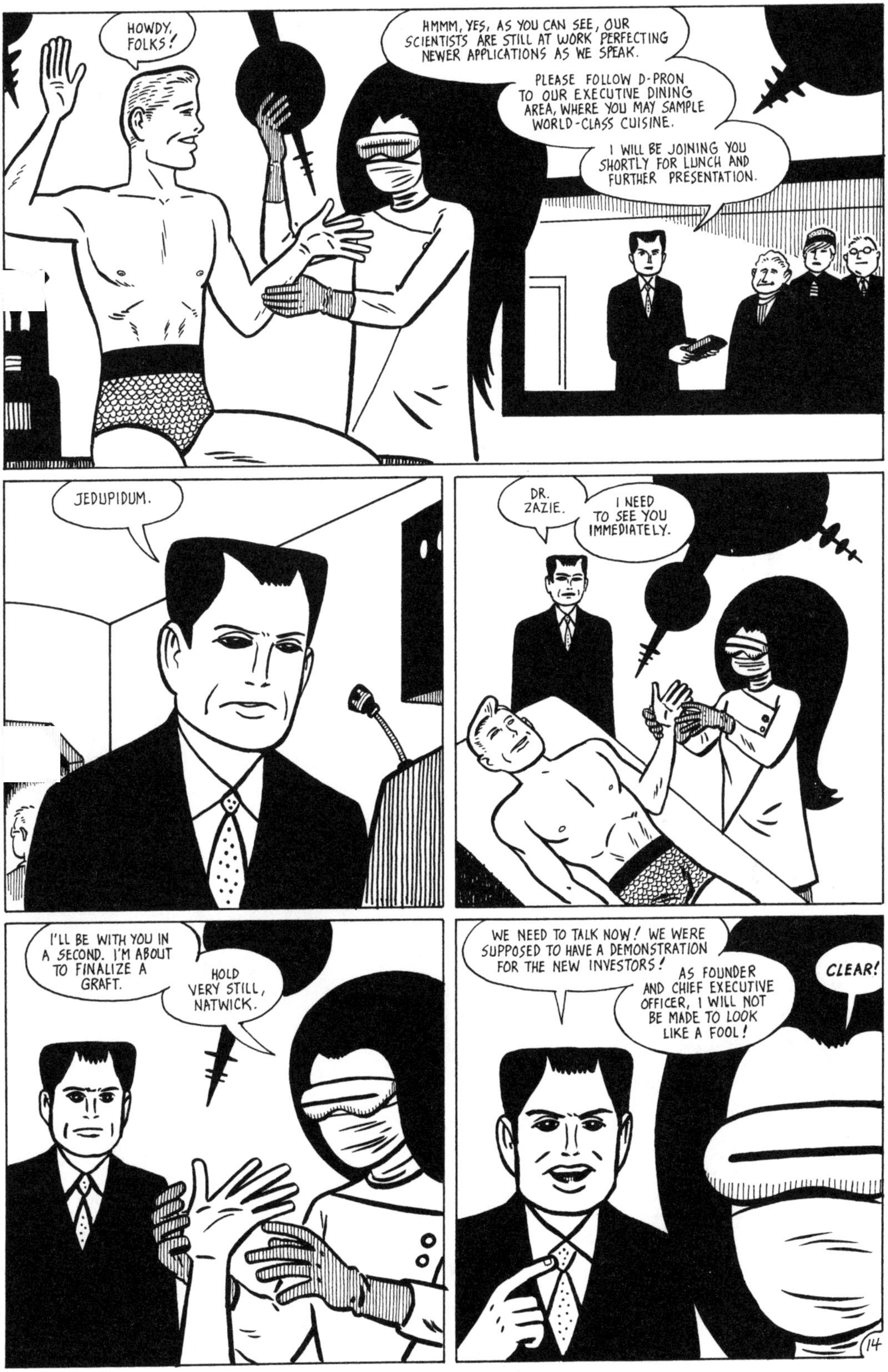
HOWDY, FOLKS!
HMMM, YES, AS YOU CAN SEE, OUR SCIENTISTS ARE STILL AT WORK PERFECTING NEWER APPLICATIONS AS WE SPEAK.
PLEASE FOLLOW D-PRON TO OUR EXECUTIVE DINING AREA, WHERE YOU MAY SAMPLE WORLD-CLASS CUISINE.
I WILL BE JOINING YOU SHORTLY FOR LUNCH AND FURTHER PRESENTATION.
JEDUPIDUM.
DR. ZAZIE.
I NEED TO SEE YOU IMMEDIATELY.
I'LL BE WITH YOU IN A SECOND. I'M ABOUT TO FINALIZE A GRAFT.
HOLD VERY STILL, NATWICK.
WE NEED TO TALK NOW! WE WERE SUPPOSED TO HAVE A DEMONSTRATION FOR THE NEW INVESTORS!
AS FOUNDER AND CHIEF EXECUTIVE OFFICER, I WILL NOT BE MADE TO LOOK LIKE A FOOL!
CLEAR!
14

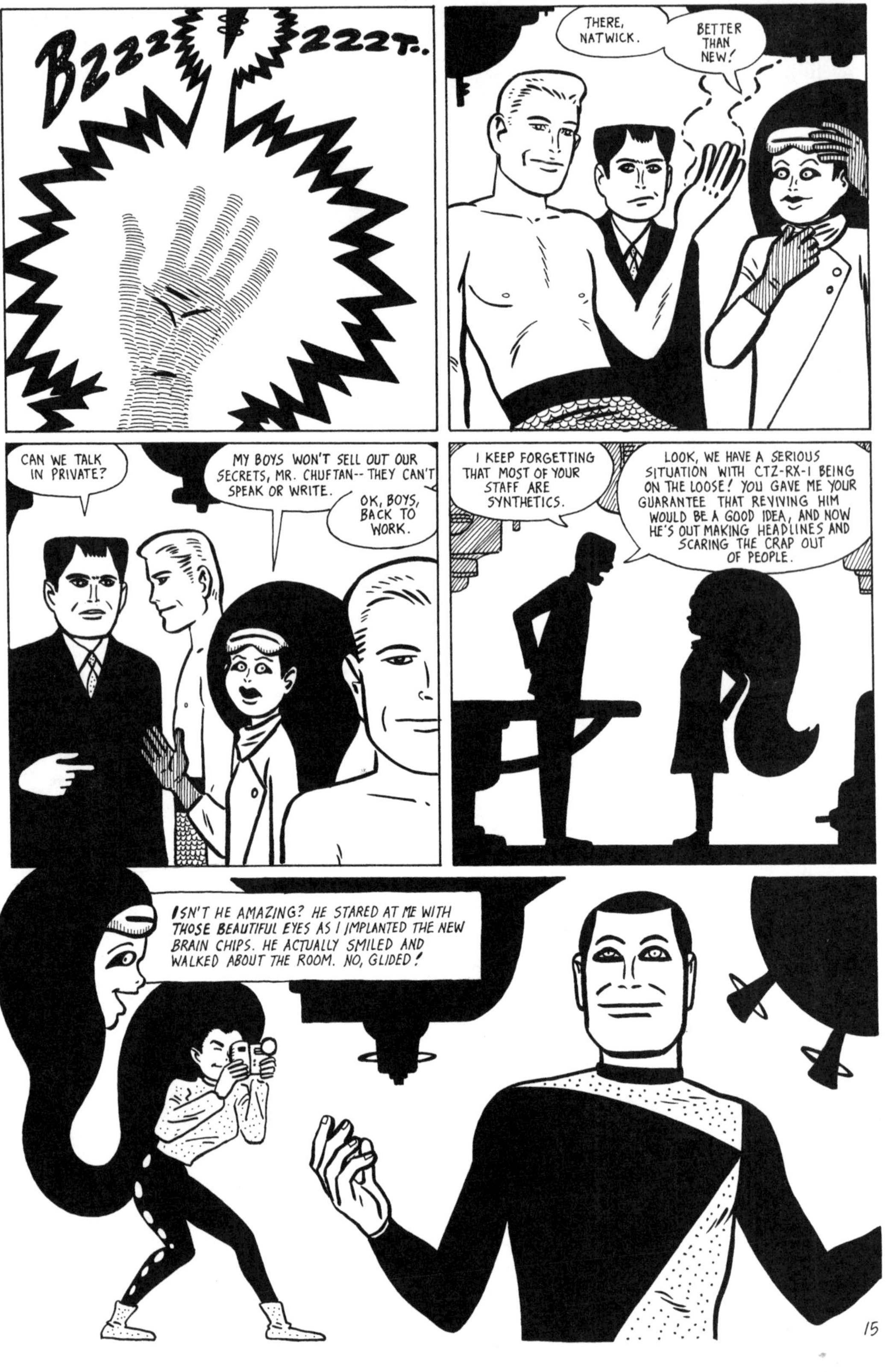
BZZZZ ZZZT..
THERE, NATWICK.
BETTER THAN NEW!
CAN WE TALK IN PRIVATE?
MY BOYS WON'T SELL OUT OUR SECRETS, MR. CHUFTAN-- THEY CAN'T SPEAK OR WRITE.
OK, BOYS, BACK TO WORK.
I KEEP FORGETTING THAT MOST OF YOUR STAFF ARE SYNTHETICS.
LOOK, WE HAVE A SERIOUS SITUATION WITH CTZ-RX-1 BEING ON THE LOOSE! YOU GAVE ME YOUR GUARANTEE THAT REVIVING HIM WOULD BE A GOOD IDEA, AND NOW HE'S OUT MAKING HEADLINES AND SCARING THE CRAP OUT OF PEOPLE.
ISN'T HE AMAZING? HE STARED AT ME WITH THOSE BEAUTIFUL EYES AS I IMPLANTED THE NEW BRAIN CHIPS. HE ACTUALLY SMILED AND WALKED ABOUT THE ROOM. NO, GLIDED!
15

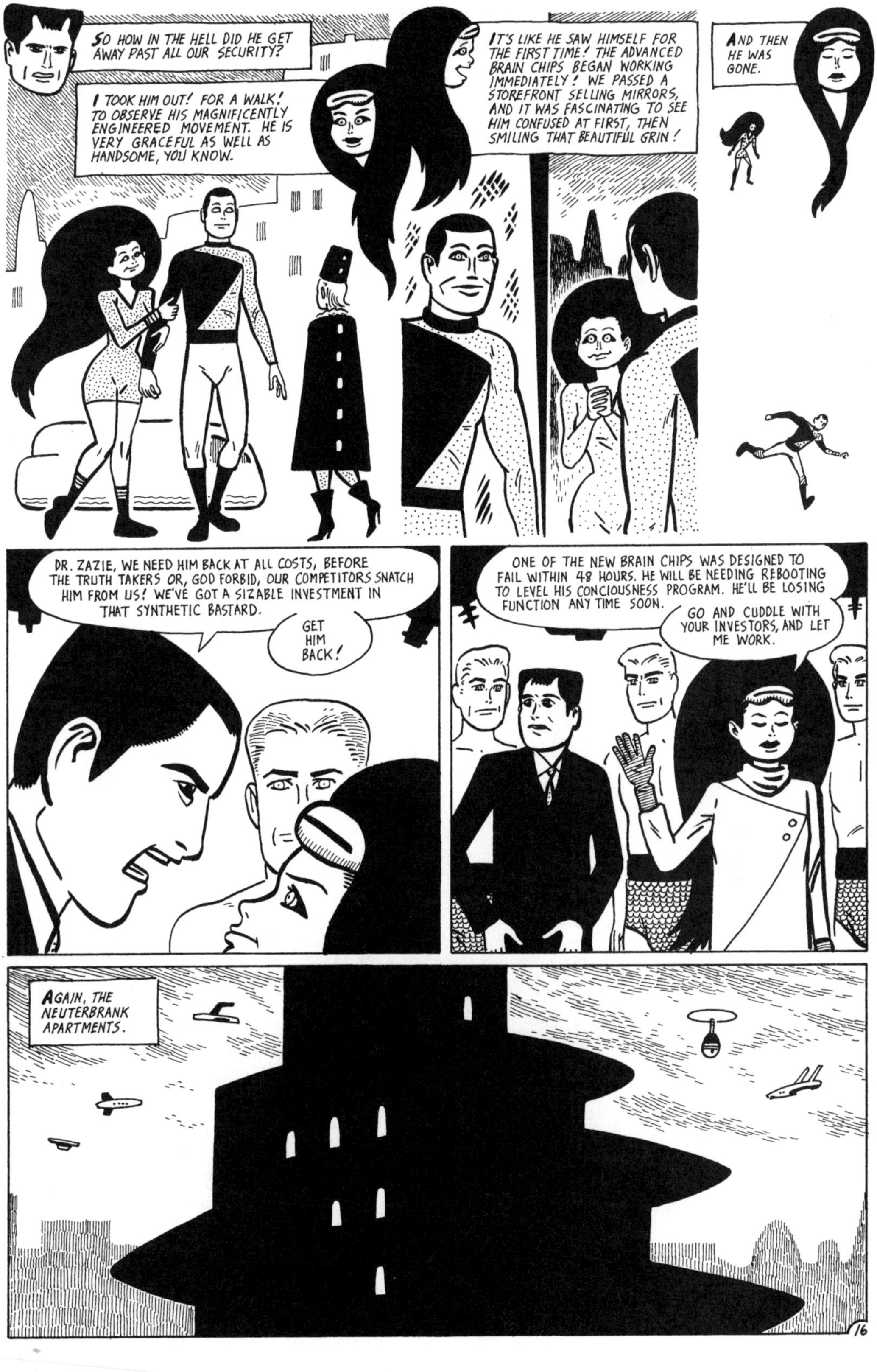
SO HOW IN THE HELL DID HE GET AWAY PAST ALL OUR SECURITY?
I TOOK HIM OUT! FOR A WALK! TO OBSERVE HIS MAGNIFICENTLY ENGINEERED MOVEMENT. HE IS VERY GRACEFUL AS WELL AS HANDSOME, YOU KNOW.
IT'S LIKE HE SAW HIMSELF FOR THE FIRST TIME! THE ADVANCED BRAIN CHIPS BEGAN WORKING IMMEDIATELY! WE PASSED A STOREFRONT SELLING MIRRORS, AND IT WAS FASCINATING TO SEE HIM CONFUSED AT FIRST, THEN SMILING THAT BEAUTIFUL GRIN!
AND THEN HE WAS GONE.
DR. ZAZIE, WE NEED HIM BACK AT ALL COSTS, BEFORE THE TRUTH TAKERS OR, GOD FORBID, OUR COMPETITORS SNATCH HIM FROM US! WE'VE GOT A SIZABLE INVESTMENT IN THAT SYNTHETIC BASTARD.
GET HIM BACK!
ONE OF THE NEW BRAIN CHIPS WAS DESIGNED TO FAIL WITHIN 48 HOURS. HE WILL BE NEEDING REBOOTING TO LEVEL HIS CONCIOUSNESS PROGRAM. HE'LL BE LOSING FUNCTION ANY TIME SOON.
GO AND CUDDLE WITH YOUR INVESTORS, AND LET ME WORK.
AGAIN, THE NEUTERBRANK APARTMENTS.
16

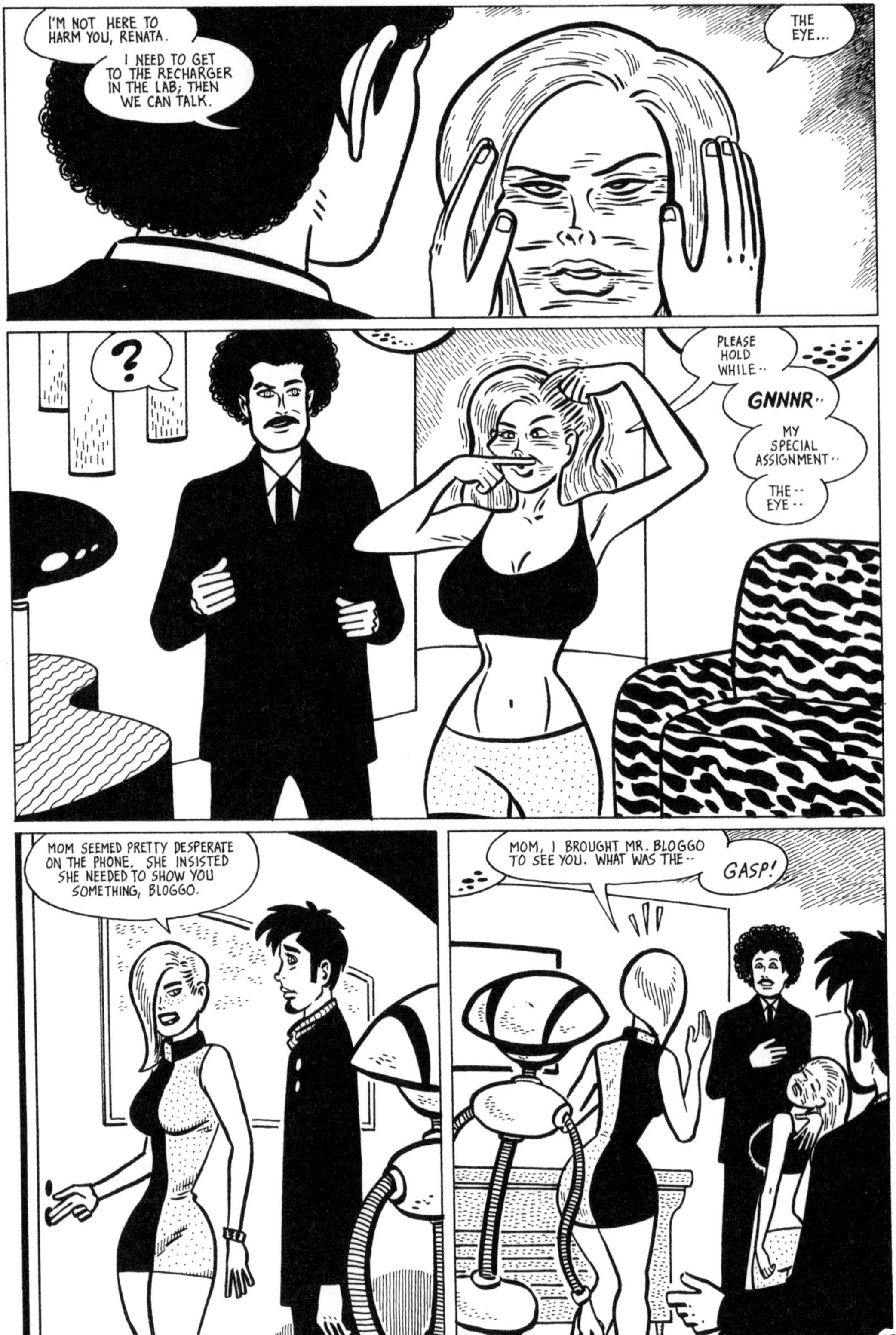
I'M NOT HERE TO HARM YOU, RENATA.
I NEED TO GET TO THE RECHARGER IN THE LAB; THEN WE CAN TALK.
THE EYE...
?
PLEASE HOLD WHILE..
GNNNR..
MY SPECIAL ASSIGNMENT..
THE-- EYE--
MOM SEEMED PRETTY DESPERATE ON THE PHONE. SHE INSISTED SHE NEEDED TO SHOW YOU SOMETHING, BLOGGO.
MOM, I BROUGHT MR. BLOGGO TO SEE YOU. WHAT WAS THE--
GASP!
17

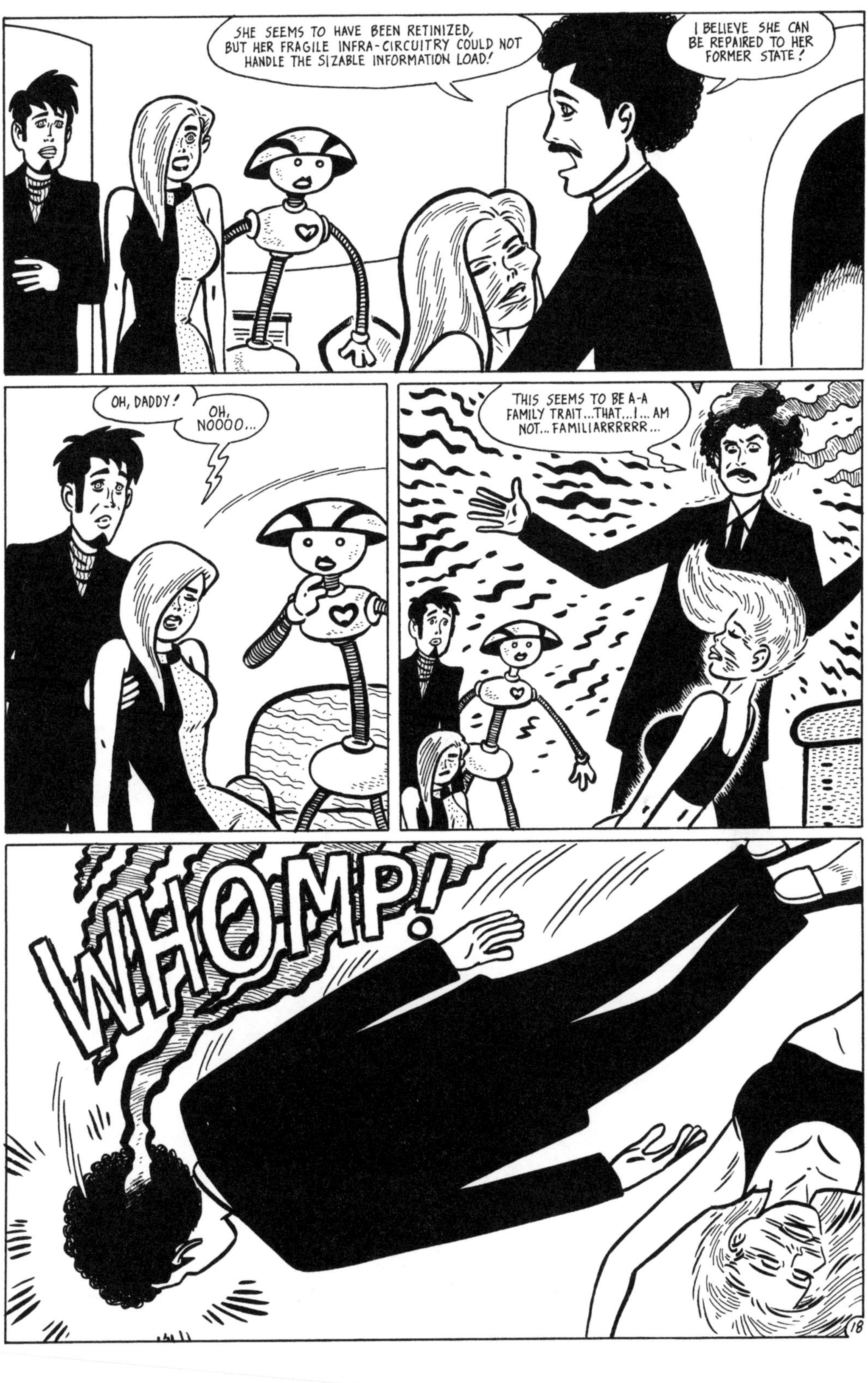
SHE SEEMS TO HAVE BEEN RETINIZED, BUT HER FRAGILE INFRA-CIRCUITRY COULD NOT HANDLE THE SIZABLE INFORMATION LOAD!
I BELIEVE SHE CAN BE REPAIRED TO HER FORMER STATE!
OH, DADDY!
OH, NOOOO...
THIS SEEMS TO BE A-A FAMILY TRAIT...THAT...I...AM NOT...FAMILIARRRRRR...
WHOMP!
18

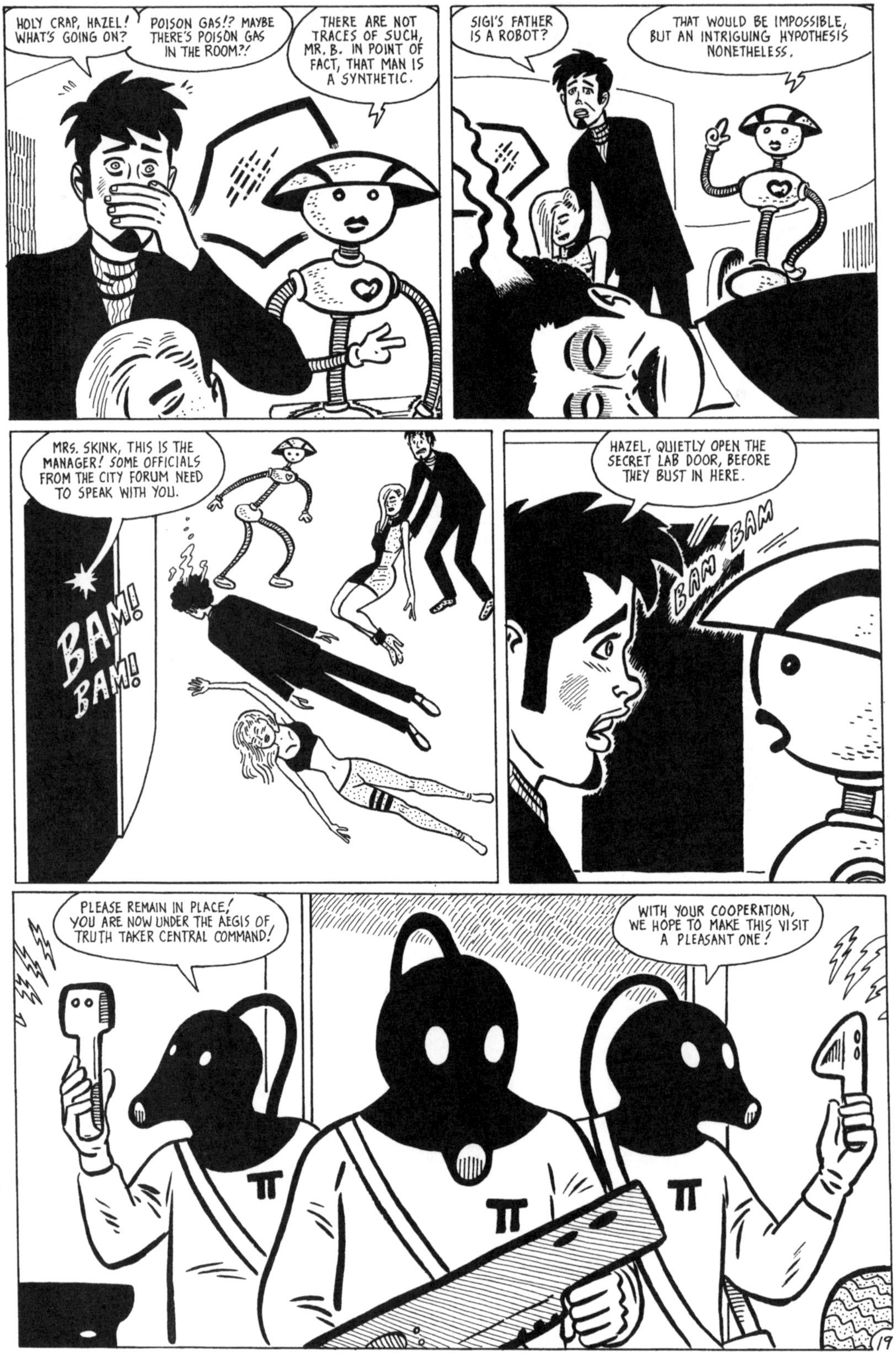
HOLY CRAP, HAZEL! WHAT'S GOING ON?
POISON GAS!? MAYBE THERE'S POISON GAS IN THE ROOM?!
THERE ARE NOT TRACES OF SUCH, MR. B. IN POINT OF FACT, THAT MAN IS A SYNTHETIC.
SIGI'S FATHER IS A ROBOT?
THAT WOULD BE IMPOSSIBLE, BUT AN INTRIGUING HYPOTHESIS NONETHELESS.
MRS. SKINK, THIS IS THE MANAGER! SOME OFFICIALS FROM THE CITY FORUM NEED TO SPEAK WITH YOU.
BAM! BAM!
HAZEL, QUIETLY OPEN THE SECRET LAB DOOR, BEFORE THEY BUST IN HERE.
BAM BAM BAM
PLEASE REMAIN IN PLACE! YOU ARE NOW UNDER THE AEGIS OF TRUTH TAKER CENTRAL COMMAND!
WITH YOUR COOPERATION, WE HOPE TO MAKE THIS VISIT A PLEASANT ONE!
19

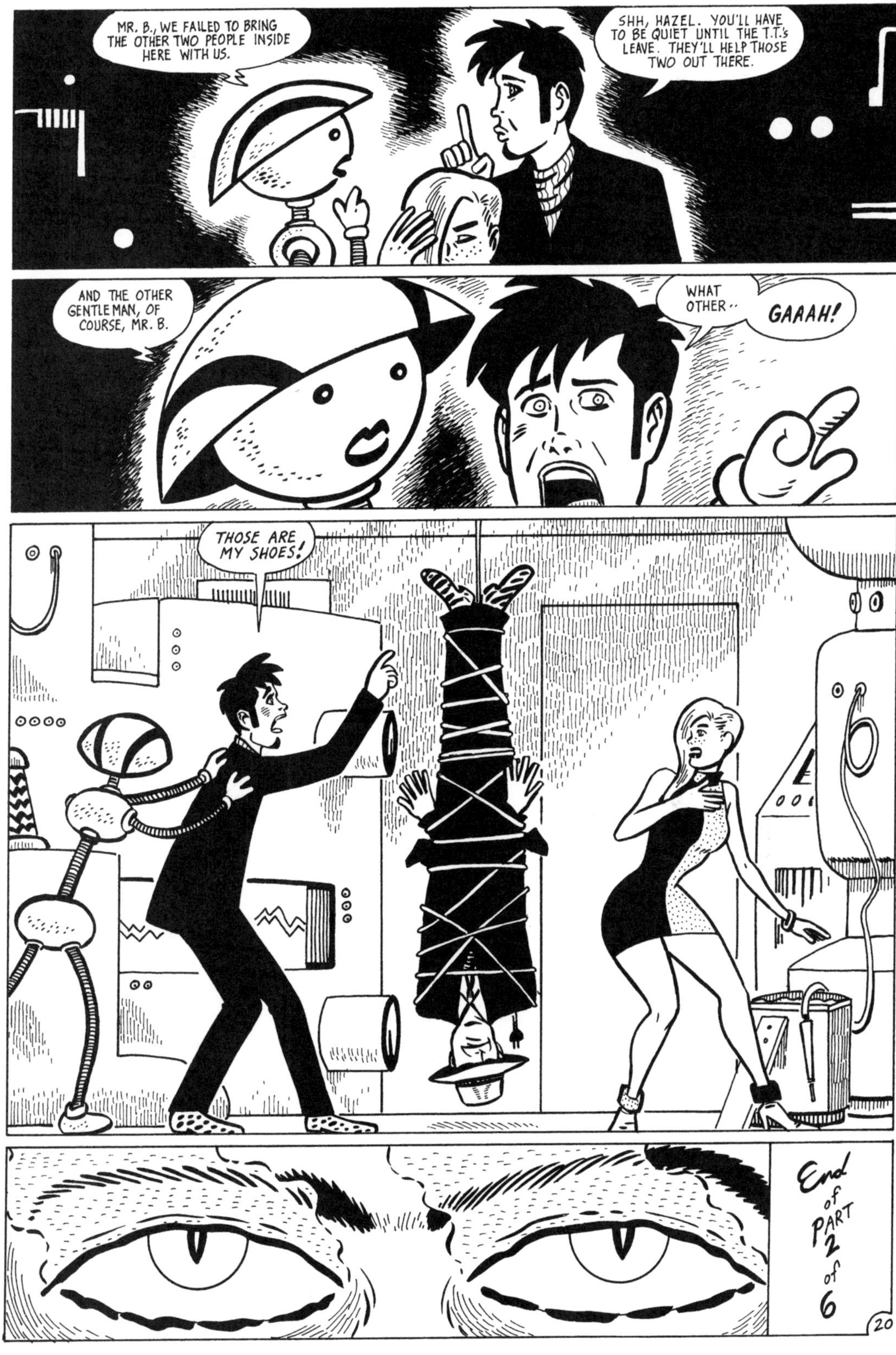
MR. B., WE FAILED TO BRING THE OTHER TWO PEOPLE INSIDE HERE WITH US.
SHH, HAZEL. YOU'LL HAVE TO BE QUIET UNTIL THE T.T.'s LEAVE. THEY'LL HELP THOSE TWO OUT THERE.
AND THE OTHER GENTLEMAN, OF COURSE, MR. B.
WHAT OTHER..
GAAAH!
THOSE ARE MY SHOES!
End of PART 2 of 6
20

excerpt from

ACME NOVELTY LIBRARY

volume nineteen

CHRIS WARE

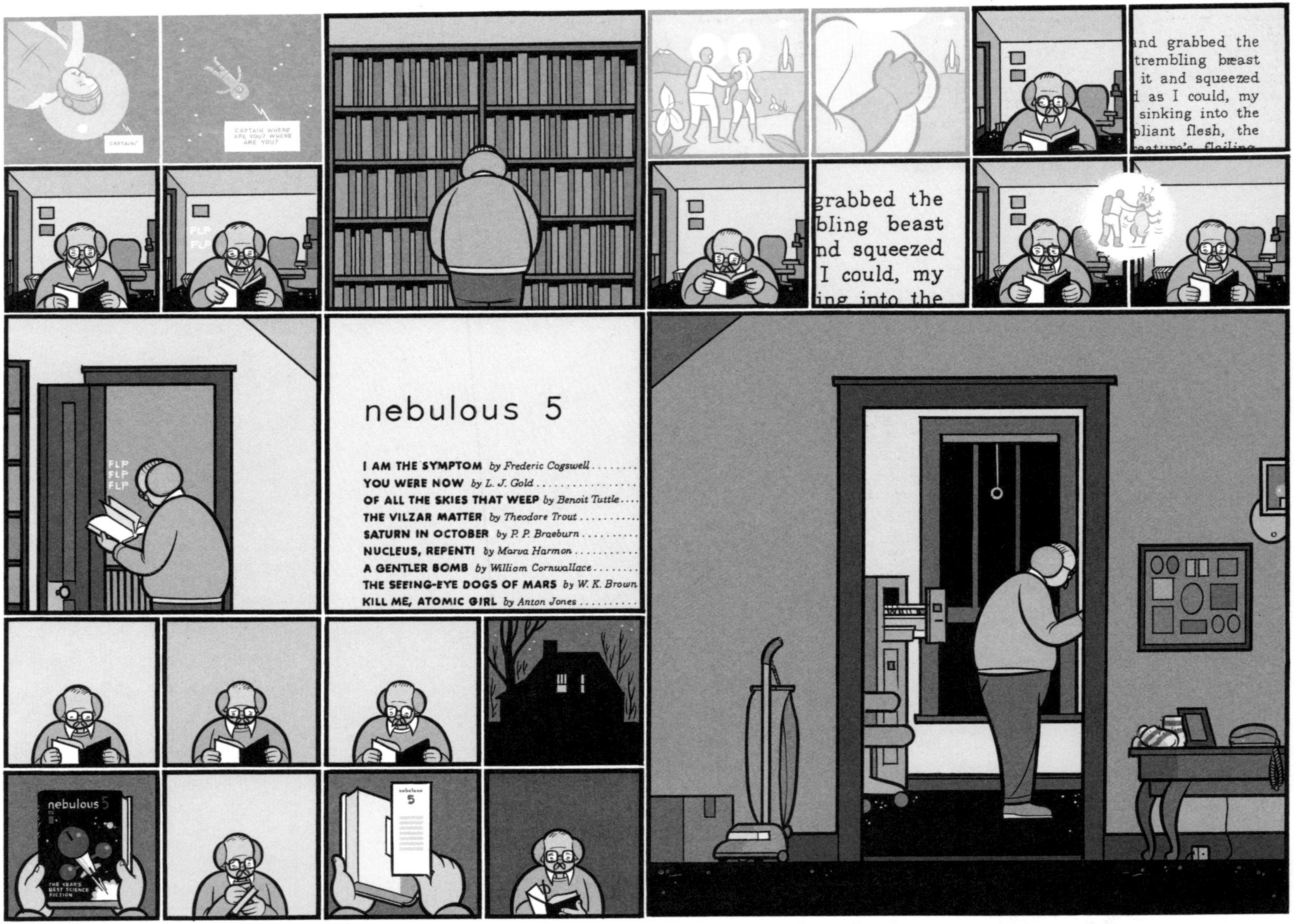
CAPTAIN!
CAPTAIN WHERE ARE YOU? WHERE ARE YOU?
FLP
FLP
nd grabbed the
trembling breast
it and squeezed
d as I could, my
sinking into the
pliant flesh, the
grabbed the
bling beast
nd squeezed
I could, my
FLP
FLP
FLP
nebulous 5
I AM THE SYMPTOM by Frederic Cogswell
YOU WERE NOW by L. J. Gold
OF ALL THE SKIES THAT WEEP by Benoit Tuttle
THE VILZAR MATTER by Theodore Trout
SATURN IN OCTOBER by P. P. Braeburn
NUCLEUS, REPENT! by Marva Harmon
A GENTLER BOMB by William Cornwallace
THE SEEING-EYE DOGS OF MARS by W. K. Brown
KILL ME, ATOMIC GIRL by Anton Jones
nebulous 5
THE YEAR'S BEST SCIENCE FICTION
nebulous
5

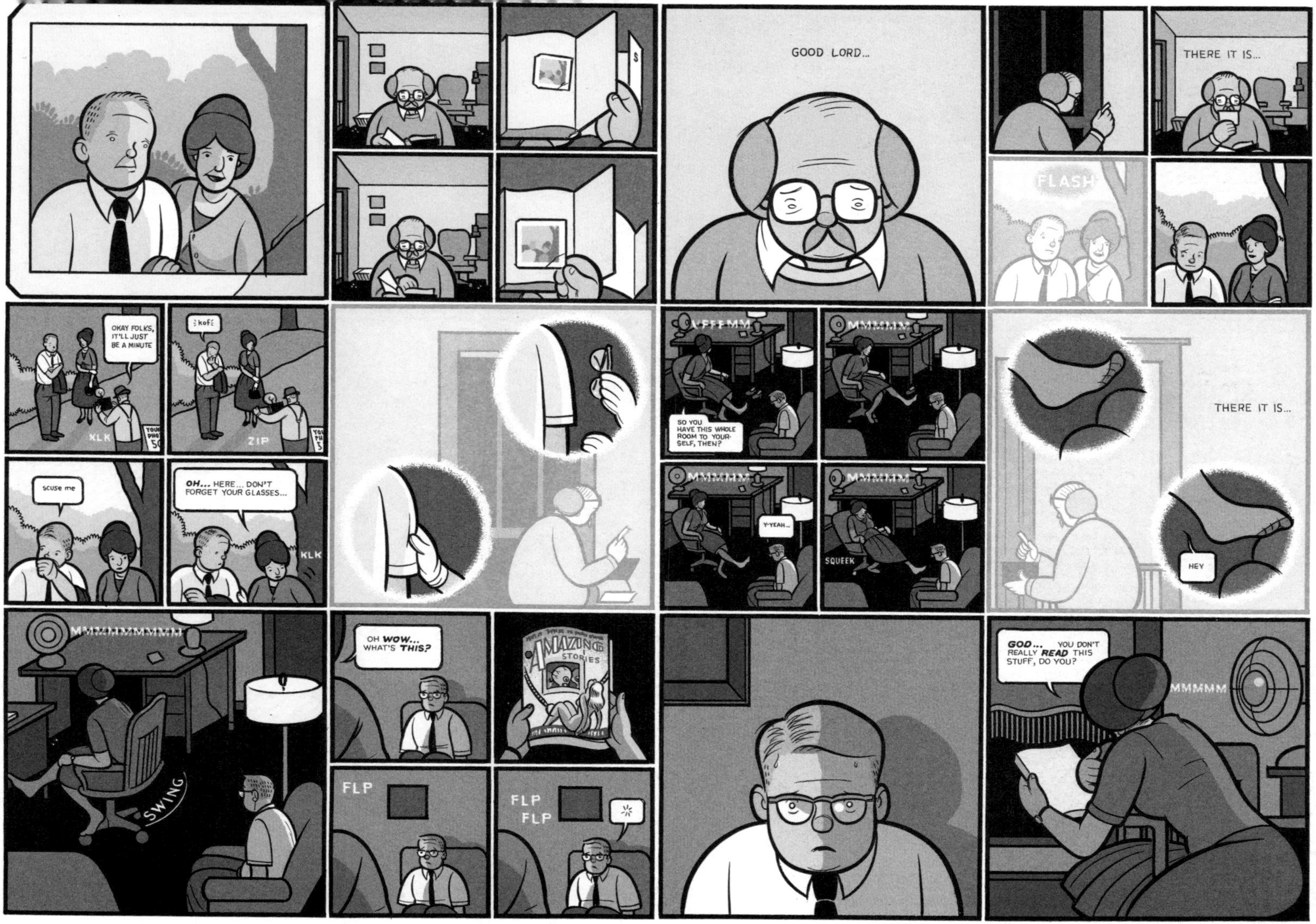

GOOD LORD...
THERE IT IS...
FLASH
OKAY FOLKS, IT'LL JUST BE A MINUTE
KLK
¡kof¡
ZIP
scuse me
OH... HERE... DON'T FORGET YOUR GLASSES...
KLK
MMMMM
SO YOU HAVE THIS WHOLE ROOM TO YOUR-SELF, THEN?
MMMMM
MMMMM
Y-YEAH...
MMMMM
SQUEEK
THERE IT IS...
HEY
MMMMMMMMMM
SWING
OH WOW... WHAT'S THIS?
AMAZING STORIES
FLP
FLP FLP
GOD... YOU DON'T REALLY READ THIS STUFF, DO YOU?
MMMMM

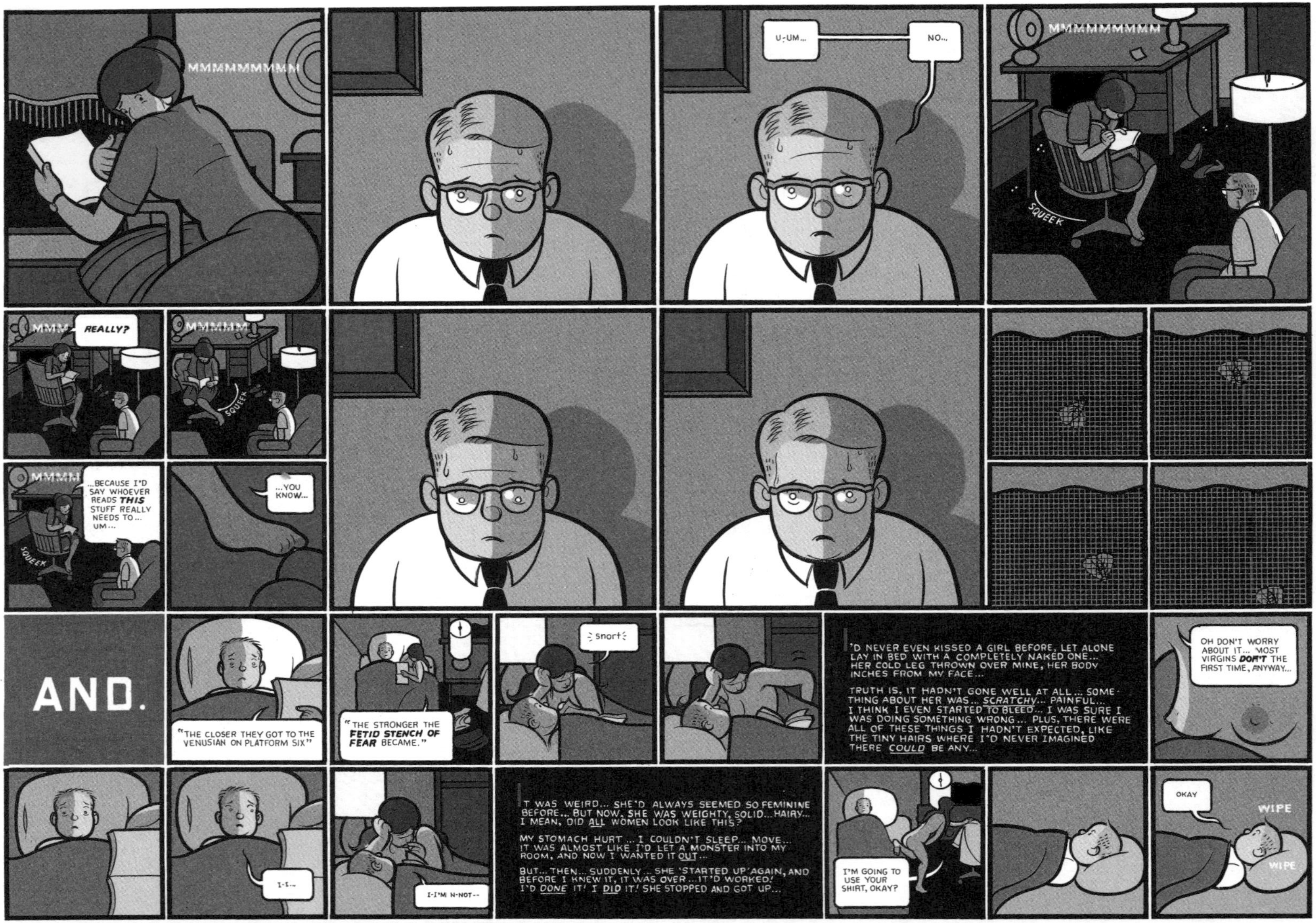
MMMMMMMMM
U-UM...
NO...
MMMMMMMMM
SQUEEK
MMM
REALLY?
MMMMM
SQUEEK
MMMM
...BECAUSE I'D SAY WHOEVER READS THIS STUFF REALLY NEEDS TO... UM...
SQUEEK
...YOU KNOW...
AND.
"THE CLOSER THEY GOT TO THE VENUSIAN ON PLATFORM SIX"
"THE STRONGER THE FETID STENCH OF FEAR BECAME."
snort
I'D NEVER EVEN KISSED A GIRL BEFORE, LET ALONE LAY IN BED WITH A COMPLETELY NAKED ONE... HER COLD LEG THROWN OVER MINE, HER BODY INCHES FROM MY FACE...
TRUTH IS, IT HADN'T GONE WELL AT ALL... SOMETHING ABOUT HER WAS... SCRATCHY... PAINFUL... I THINK I EVEN STARTED TO BLEED... I WAS SURE I WAS DOING SOMETHING WRONG... PLUS, THERE WERE ALL OF THESE THINGS I HADN'T EXPECTED, LIKE THE TINY HAIRS WHERE I'D NEVER IMAGINED THERE COULD BE ANY...
OH DON'T WORRY ABOUT IT... MOST VIRGINS DON'T THE FIRST TIME, ANYWAY...
I-I...
I-I'M N-NOT--
IT WAS WEIRD... SHE'D ALWAYS SEEMED SO FEMININE BEFORE... BUT NOW, SHE WAS WEIGHTY, SOLID... HAIRY... I MEAN, DID ALL WOMEN LOOK LIKE THIS?
MY STOMACH HURT... I COULDN'T SLEEP... MOVE... IT WAS ALMOST LIKE I'D LET A MONSTER INTO MY ROOM, AND NOW I WANTED IT OUT...
BUT... THEN... SUDDENLY... SHE 'STARTED UP' AGAIN, AND BEFORE I KNEW IT, IT WAS OVER... IT'D WORKED! I'D DONE IT! I DID IT! SHE STOPPED AND GOT UP...
I'M GOING TO USE YOUR SHIRT, OKAY?
OKAY
WIPE
WIPE

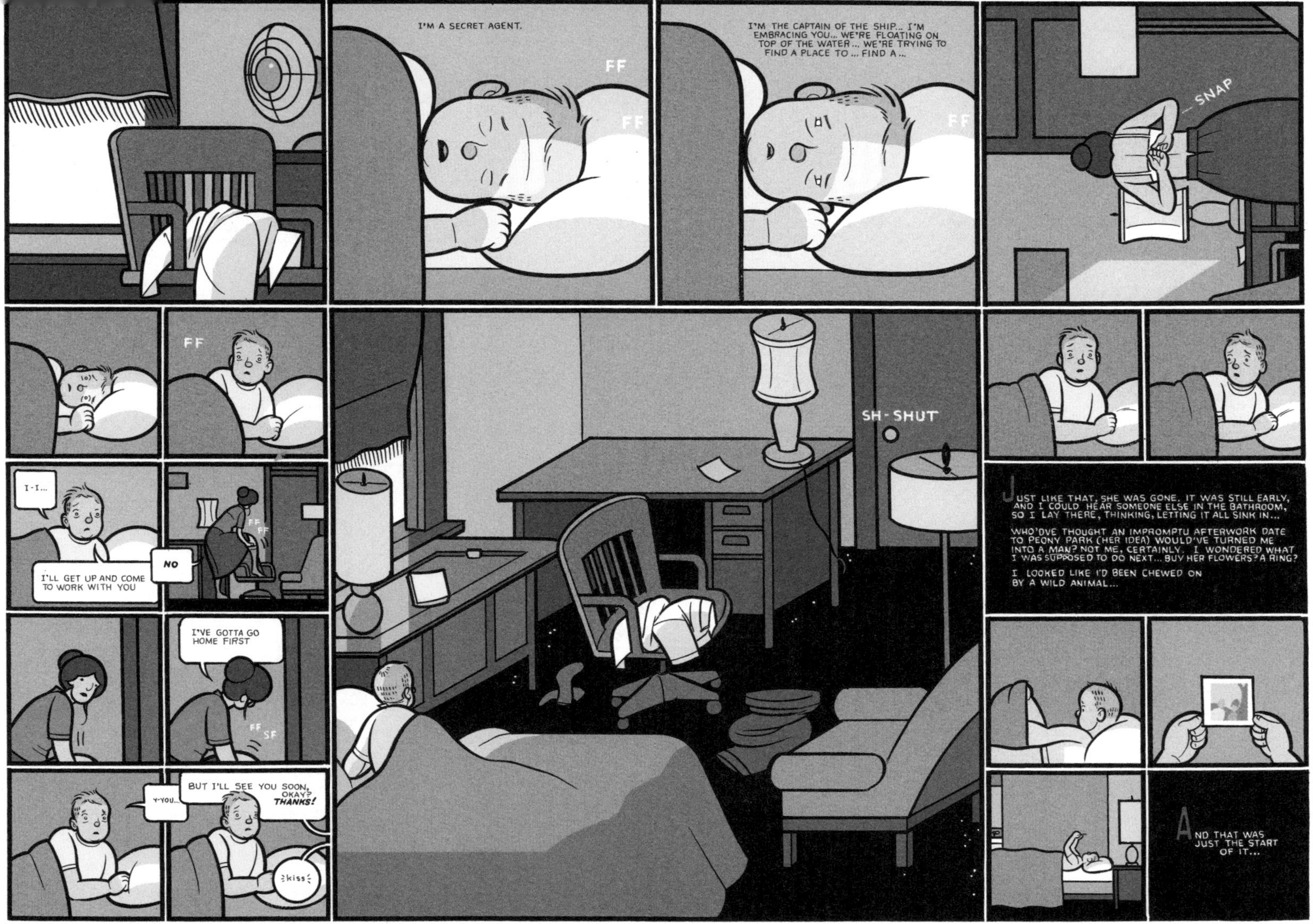
I'M A SECRET AGENT.
FF
FF
I'M THE CAPTAIN OF THE SHIP... I'M EMBRACING YOU... WE'RE FLOATING ON TOP OF THE WATER... WE'RE TRYING TO FIND A PLACE TO ... FIND A...
FF
SNAP
FF
I-I...
I'LL GET UP AND COME TO WORK WITH YOU
NO
FF
FF
I'VE GOTTA GO HOME FIRST
FF
SF
Y-YOU...
BUT I'LL SEE YOU SOON, OKAY? THANKS!
kiss
SH-SHUT
JUST LIKE THAT, SHE WAS GONE. IT WAS STILL EARLY, AND I COULD HEAR SOMEONE ELSE IN THE BATHROOM, SO I LAY THERE, THINKING, LETTING IT ALL SINK IN...
WHO'DVE THOUGHT AN IMPROMPTU AFTERWORK DATE TO PEONY PARK (HER IDEA) WOULD'VE TURNED ME INTO A MAN? NOT ME, CERTAINLY. I WONDERED WHAT I WAS SUPPOSED TO DO NEXT... BUY HER FLOWERS? A RING?
I LOOKED LIKE I'D BEEN CHEWED ON BY A WILD ANIMAL...
AND THAT WAS JUST THE START OF IT...

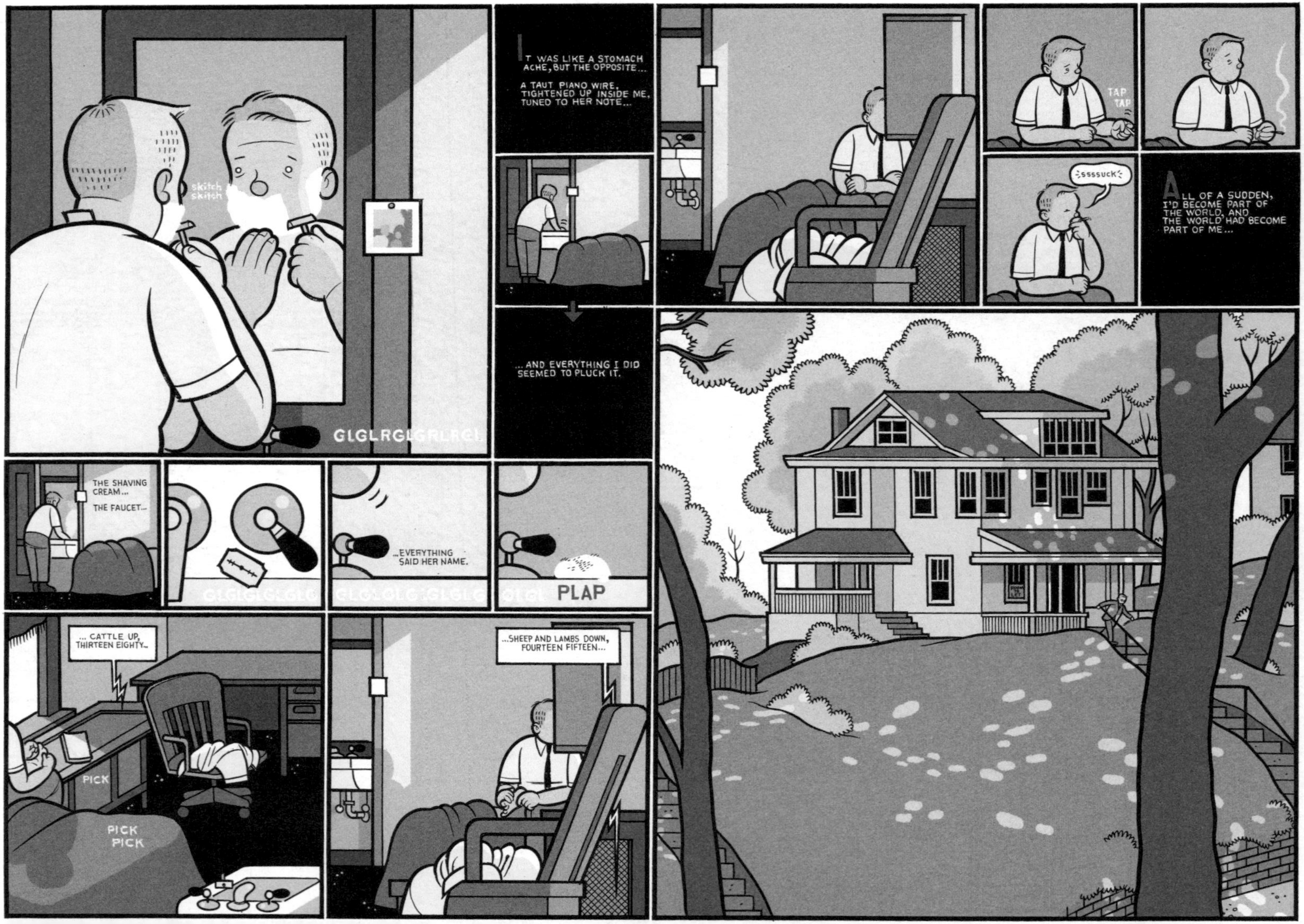
skitch skitch
GLGLRGLGRLRGL
IT WAS LIKE A STOMACH ACHE, BUT THE OPPOSITE...
A TAUT PIANO WIRE, TIGHTENED UP INSIDE ME, TUNED TO HER NOTE...
...AND EVERYTHING I DID SEEMED TO PLUCK IT.
TAP TAP
ssssuck
ALL OF A SUDDEN, I'D BECOME PART OF THE WORLD, AND THE WORLD HAD BECOME PART OF ME...
THE SHAVING CREAM...
THE FAUCET...
...EVERYTHING SAID HER NAME.
PLAP
... CATTLE UP, THIRTEEN EIGHTY...
PICK
PICK PICK
...SHEEP AND LAMBS DOWN, FOURTEEN FIFTEEN...

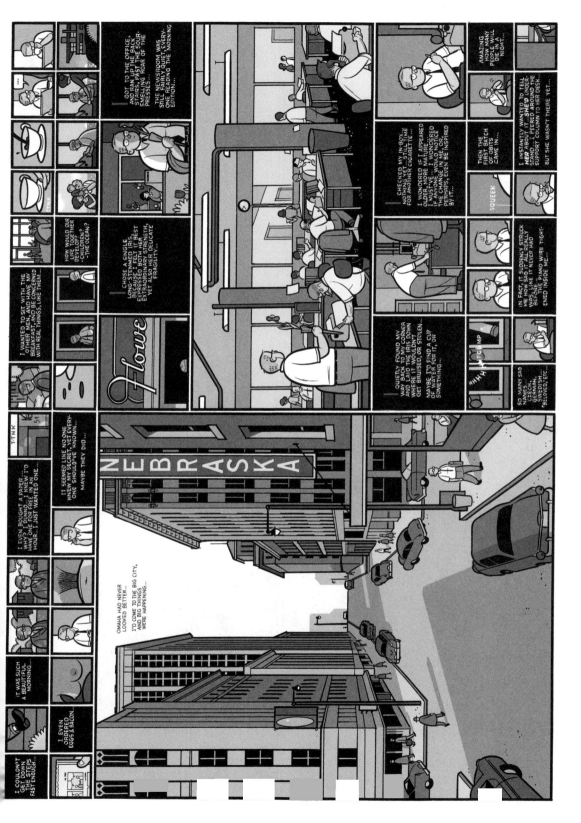

I COULDN'T GET DOWN THE STEPS FAST ENOUGH...

I EVEN ORDERED EGGS & BACON.

IT WAS SUCH A BEAUTIFUL MORNING...

I EVEN BOUGHT A PAPER. WHY? I DUNNO... I KNEW I'D HAVE ONE FOR FREE IN AN HOUR... I JUST WANTED ONE...

IT SEEMED LIKE NO ONE KNEW MY SECRET, YET EVERYONE SHOULD'VE "KNOWN"...

MAYBE THEY DID...

T-TINK

5¢

OMAHA HAD NEVER LOOKED BETTER.
I'D COME TO THE BIG CITY, AND BIG THINGS WERE HAPPENING...

NEBRASKA

I WANTED TO SIT WITH THE OTHER MEN, AND HAVE MY BREAKFAST, AND BE CONCERNED WITH REAL THINGS, LIKE THEM.

HOW WOULD OUR LIFE TOGETHER DEVELOP?
—CHILDREN?
—THE OCEAN?

CHOSE A SINGLE LONG-STEMMED IRIS, BECAUSE I FELT IT BEST CONVEYED HER EXTRAORDINARY STRENGTH, YET ALSO HER DELICATE FRAGILITY...

Flowe

GOT TO THE OFFICE AND RAN UP THE BACK STAIRS, PAST THE SOUR-SMELLING ROAR OF THE PRESSES...

THE NEWSROOM WAS STILL FAIRLY QUIET, EVERYONE READING THE MORNING EDITION...

QUIETLY FOUND MY WAY BACK TO MY CORNER AND LAID THE IRIS DOWN WHERE IT WOULDN'T GET BRUISED, OR STOLEN...

MAYBE I'D FIND A CUP OF WATER FOR IT, OR SOMETHING...

CHECKED MY IN-BOX. NOTHING YET IN TIME FOR ANOTHER CIGARETTE...

I WONDERED IF I APPEARED OLDER, MORE MATURE. I MUST'VE... I WONDERED IF ANYONE WOULD NOTICE THE CHANGE IN ME, PERHAPS, EVEN BE INSPIRED BY IT...

IN FACT, IT SUDDENLY STRUCK ME HOW SAD IT ALL REALLY WAS, AND THAT I HAD NEVER BEFORE, THE "PIANO WIRE TIGHTENED INSIDE ME"...

SO MANY SAD NAMES...
CZECH, GERMAN, SWEDISH, "BELOVED," ETC...

SQUEEK

H-H-H-FFGIIMP

THEN THE FIRST BATCH OF OBITS CAME IN...

AMAZING HOW MANY PEOPLE WILL DIE IN A NIGHT...

I INSTANTLY WANTED TO TELL HER ABOUT IT. SHE'D UNDERSTAND. I EVEN REACHED AROUND THE SUPPORT COLUMN TO HER DESK...

BUT SHE WASN'T THERE YET...

133

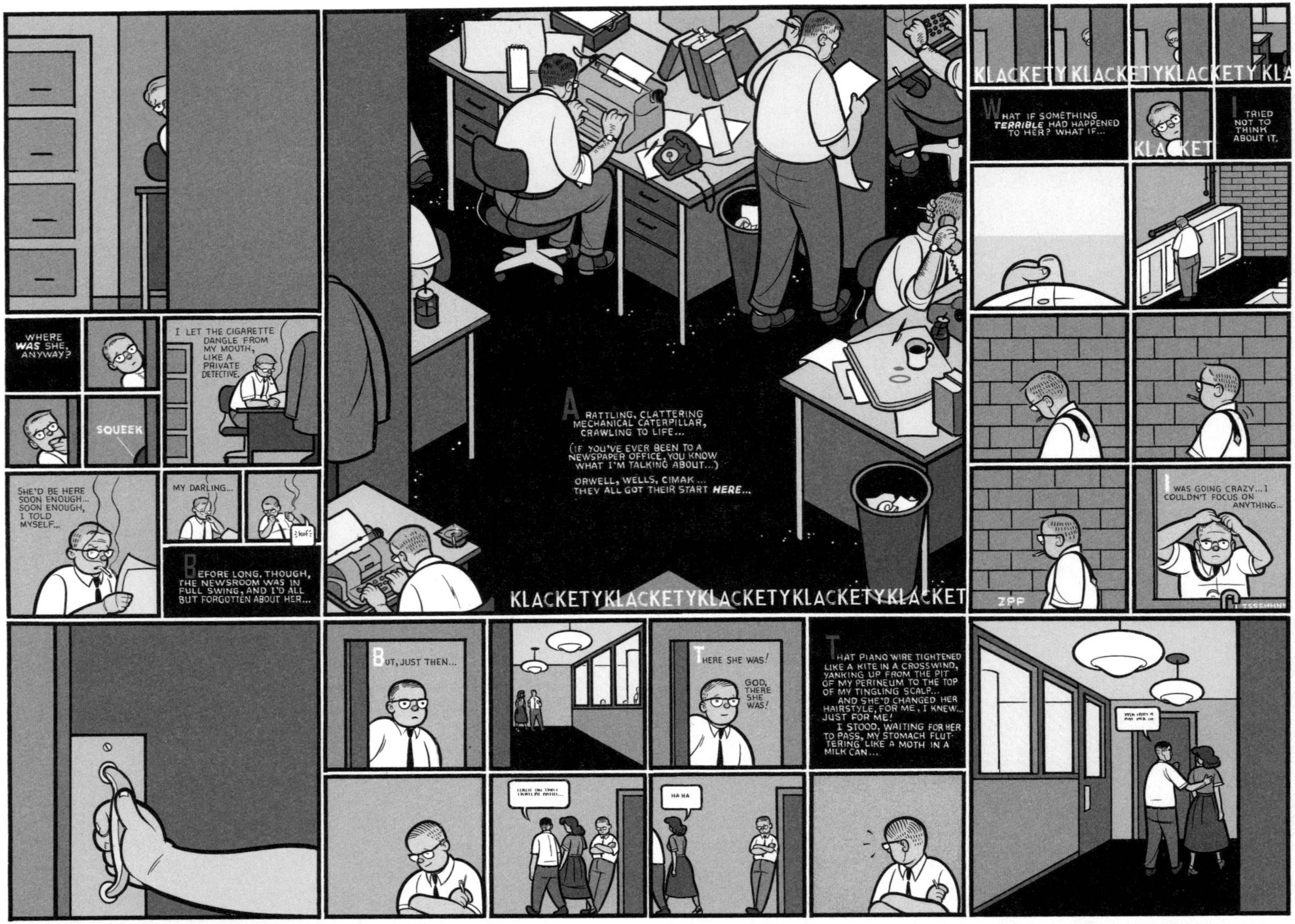
WHERE WAS SHE, ANYWAY?
SQUEEK
I LET THE CIGARETTE DANGLE FROM MY MOUTH, LIKE A PRIVATE DETECTIVE.
SHE'D BE HERE SOON ENOUGH... SOON ENOUGH, I TOLD MYSELF...
MY DARLING...
KOF
BEFORE LONG, THOUGH, THE NEWSROOM WAS IN FULL SWING, AND I'D ALL BUT FORGOTTEN ABOUT HER...
A RATTLING, CLATTERING MECHANICAL CATERPILLAR, CRAWLING TO LIFE...
(IF YOU'VE EVER BEEN TO A NEWSPAPER OFFICE, YOU KNOW WHAT I'M TALKING ABOUT...)
ORWELL, WELLS, CIMAK... THEY ALL GOT THEIR START HERE...
KLACKETYKLACKETYKLACKETYKLACKETYKLACKET
KLACKETY KLACKETYKLACKETY KLA
WHAT IF SOMETHING TERRIBLE HAD HAPPENED TO HER? WHAT IF...
KLACKET
I TRIED NOT TO THINK ABOUT IT.
ZPP
I WAS GOING CRAZY... I COULDN'T FOCUS ON ANYTHING...
BUT, JUST THEN...
THERE SHE WAS!
GOD, THERE SHE WAS!
HA HA
THAT PIANO WIRE TIGHTENED LIKE A KITE IN A CROSSWIND, YANKING UP FROM THE PIT OF MY PERINEUM TO THE TOP OF MY TINGLING SCALP...
AND SHE'D CHANGED HER HAIRSTYLE, FOR ME, I KNEW... JUST FOR ME!
I STOOD, WAITING FOR HER TO PASS, MY STOMACH FLUTTERING LIKE A MOTH IN A MILK CAN...

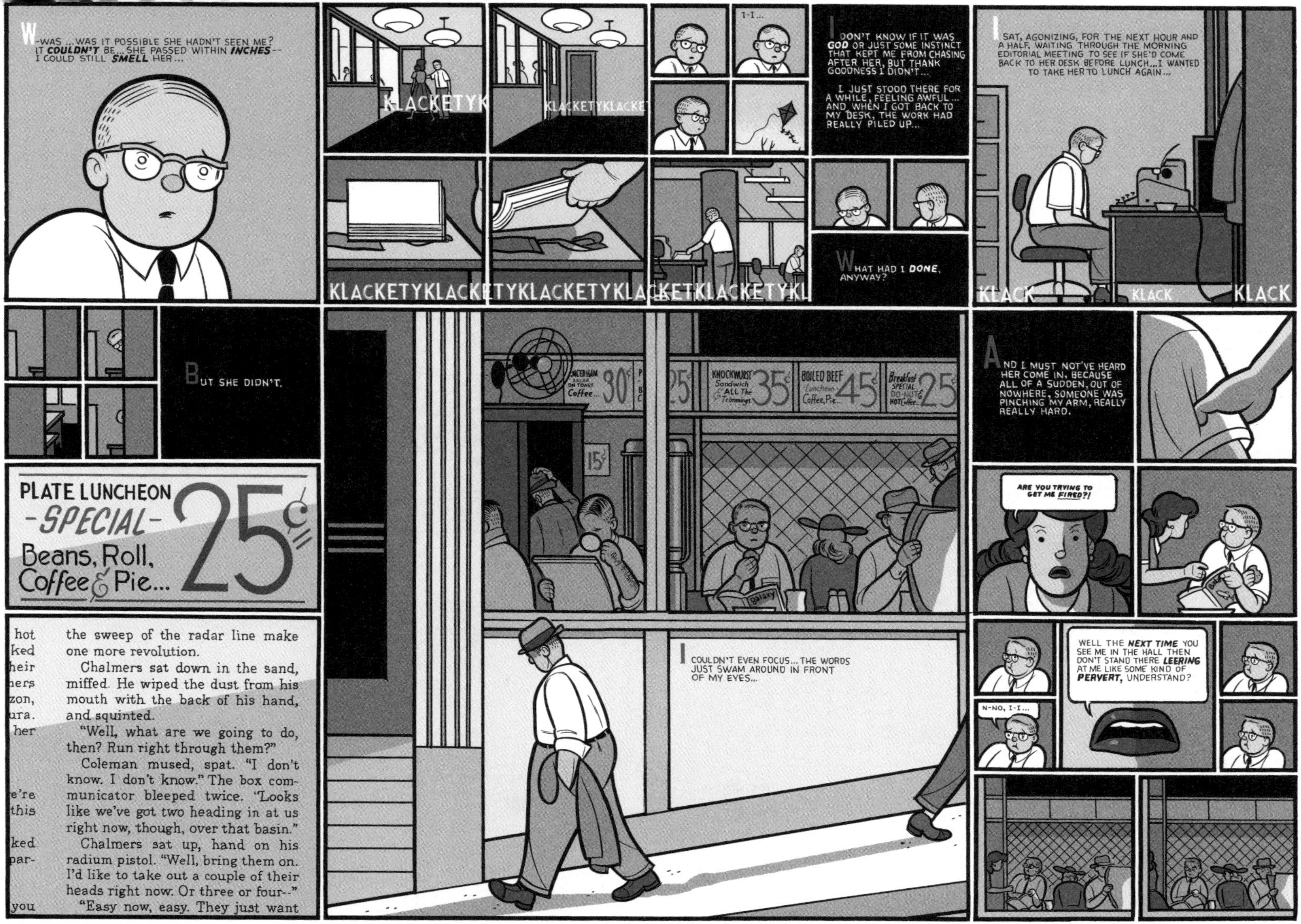
W-WAS ...WAS IT POSSIBLE SHE HADN'T SEEN ME? IT COULDN'T BE... SHE PASSED WITHIN INCHES-- I COULD STILL SMELL HER...
KLACKETYK
KLACKETYKLACKET
I-I...
I DON'T KNOW IF IT WAS GOD OR JUST SOME INSTINCT THAT KEPT ME FROM CHASING AFTER HER, BUT THANK GOODNESS I DIDN'T...
I JUST STOOD THERE FOR A WHILE, FEELING AWFUL... AND WHEN I GOT BACK TO MY DESK, THE WORK HAD REALLY PILED UP...
KLACKETYKLACKETYKLACKETYKLACKETKLACKETYKL
WHAT HAD I DONE, ANYWAY?
I SAT, AGONIZING, FOR THE NEXT HOUR AND A HALF, WAITING THROUGH THE MORNING EDITORIAL MEETING TO SEE IF SHE'D COME BACK TO HER DESK BEFORE LUNCH...I WANTED TO TAKE HER TO LUNCH AGAIN...
KLACK
KLACK
KLACK
BUT SHE DIDN'T.
PLATE LUNCHEON -SPECIAL- Beans, Roll, Coffee & Pie... 25¢
hot
ked
heir
ners
zon,
ura.
her
e're
this
ked
par-
you
the sweep of the radar line make one more revolution.
Chalmers sat down in the sand, miffed. He wiped the dust from his mouth with the back of his hand, and squinted.
"Well, what are we going to do, then? Run right through them?"
Coleman mused, spat. "I don't know. I don't know." The box communicator bleeped twice. "Looks like we've got two heading in at us right now, though, over that basin."
Chalmers sat up, hand on his radium pistol. "Well, bring them on. I'd like to take out a couple of their heads right now. Or three or four--"
"Easy now, easy. They just want
SALAD ON TOAST Coffee... 30¢
25¢
KNOCKWURST Sandwich ALL The Trimmings 35¢
BOILED BEEF Luncheon Coffee, Pie... 45¢
Breakfast SPECIAL DO-NUT & HOT Coffee 25¢
15¢
Galaxy
I COULDN'T EVEN FOCUS... THE WORDS JUST SWAM AROUND IN FRONT OF MY EYES...
AND I MUST NOT'VE HEARD HER COME IN, BECAUSE ALL OF A SUDDEN, OUT OF NOWHERE, SOMEONE WAS PINCHING MY ARM, REALLY REALLY HARD.
ARE YOU TRYING TO GET ME FIRED?!
WELL THE NEXT TIME YOU SEE ME IN THE HALL THEN DON'T STAND THERE LEERING AT ME LIKE SOME KIND OF PERVERT, UNDERSTAND?
N-NO, I-I...

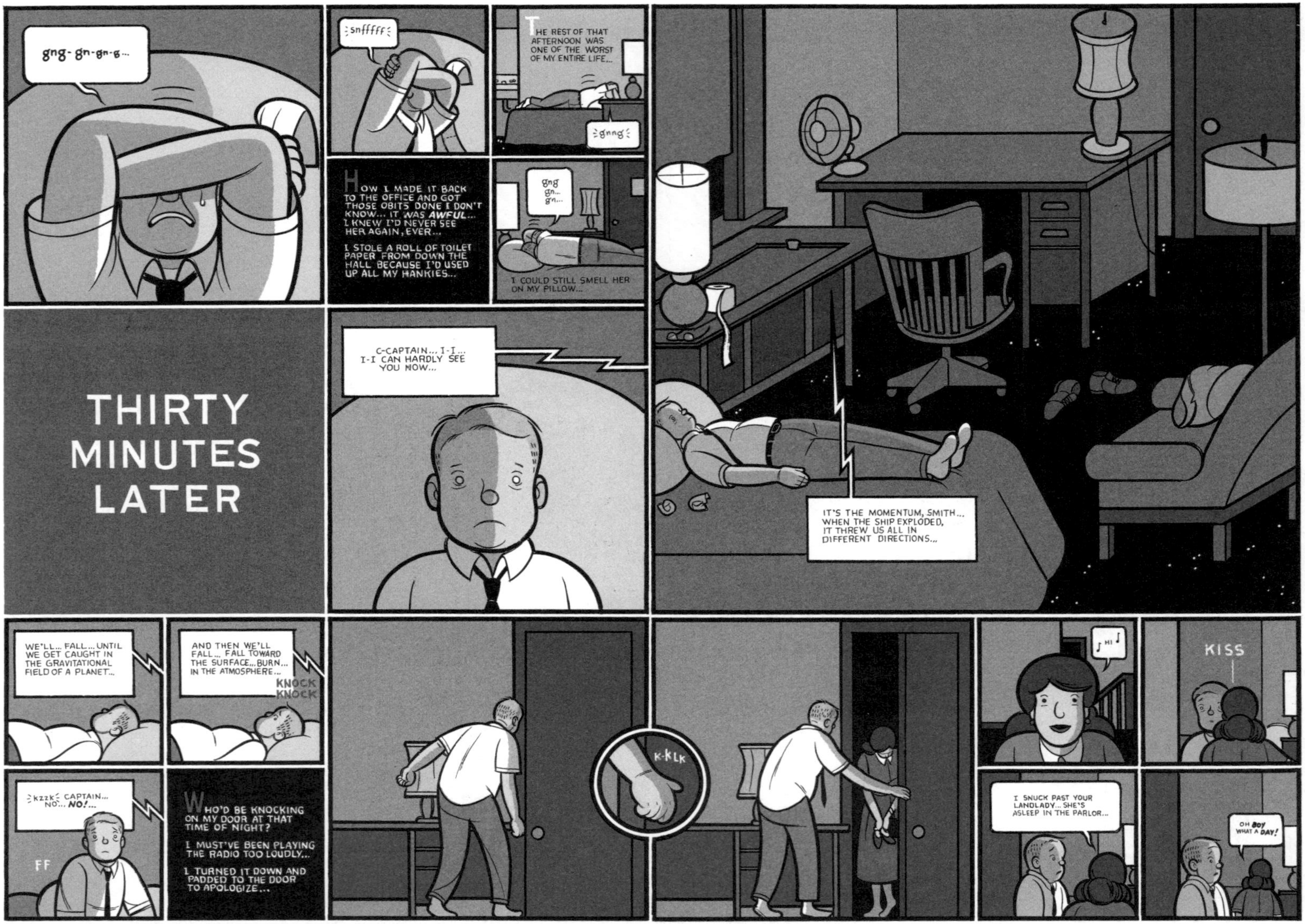
gng- gn-gn-g...
snffffff
THE REST OF THAT AFTERNOON WAS ONE OF THE WORST OF MY ENTIRE LIFE...
gnng
HOW I MADE IT BACK TO THE OFFICE AND GOT THOSE OBITS DONE I DON'T KNOW... IT WAS AWFUL... I KNEW I'D NEVER SEE HER AGAIN, EVER...
I STOLE A ROLL OF TOILET PAPER FROM DOWN THE HALL BECAUSE I'D USED UP ALL MY HANKIES...
gng gn... gn...
I COULD STILL SMELL HER ON MY PILLOW...
THIRTY MINUTES LATER
C-CAPTAIN... I-I... I-I CAN HARDLY SEE YOU NOW...
IT'S THE MOMENTUM, SMITH... WHEN THE SHIP EXPLODED, IT THREW US ALL IN DIFFERENT DIRECTIONS...
WE'LL... FALL... UNTIL WE GET CAUGHT IN THE GRAVITATIONAL FIELD OF A PLANET...
AND THEN WE'LL FALL... FALL TOWARD THE SURFACE... BURN... IN THE ATMOSPHERE...
KNOCK KNOCK
kzzk CAPTAIN... NO... NO!...
FF
WHO'D BE KNOCKING ON MY DOOR AT THAT TIME OF NIGHT?
I MUST'VE BEEN PLAYING THE RADIO TOO LOUDLY...
I TURNED IT DOWN AND PADDED TO THE DOOR TO APOLOGIZE...
K-KLK
HI
KISS
I SNUCK PAST YOUR LANDLADY... SHE'S ASLEEP IN THE PARLOR...
OH BOY WHAT A DAY!

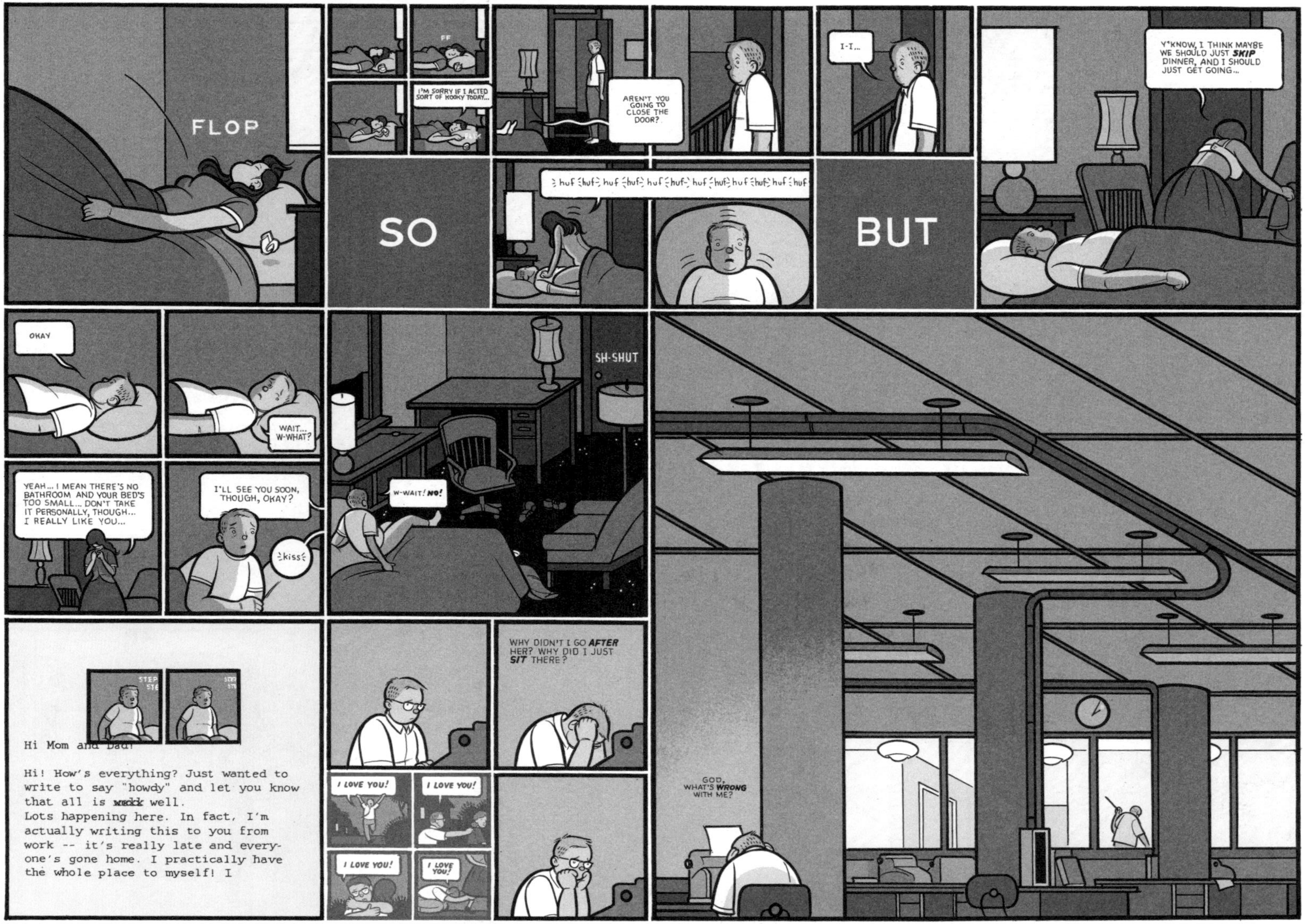
FLOP
FF
I'M SORRY IF I ACTED SORT OF KOOKY TODAY...
SO
AREN'T YOU GOING TO CLOSE THE DOOR?
huf huf huf huf huf huf huf huf huf huf huf huf
I-I...
BUT
Y'KNOW, I THINK MAYBE WE SHOULD JUST SKIP DINNER, AND I SHOULD JUST GET GOING...
OKAY
WAIT... W-WHAT?
YEAH... I MEAN THERE'S NO BATHROOM AND YOUR BED'S TOO SMALL... DON'T TAKE IT PERSONALLY, THOUGH... I REALLY LIKE YOU...
I'LL SEE YOU SOON, THOUGH, OKAY?
kiss
W-WAIT! NO!
SH-SHUT
STEP STE
STEP STE
Hi Mom and Dad!
Hi! How's everything? Just wanted to write to say "howdy" and let you know that all is well.
Lots happening here. In fact, I'm actually writing this to you from work -- it's really late and everyone's gone home. I practically have the whole place to myself! I
WHY DIDN'T I GO AFTER HER? WHY DID I JUST SIT THERE?
I LOVE YOU!
I LOVE YOU!
I LOVE YOU!
I LOVE YOU!
GOD, WHAT'S WRONG WITH ME?

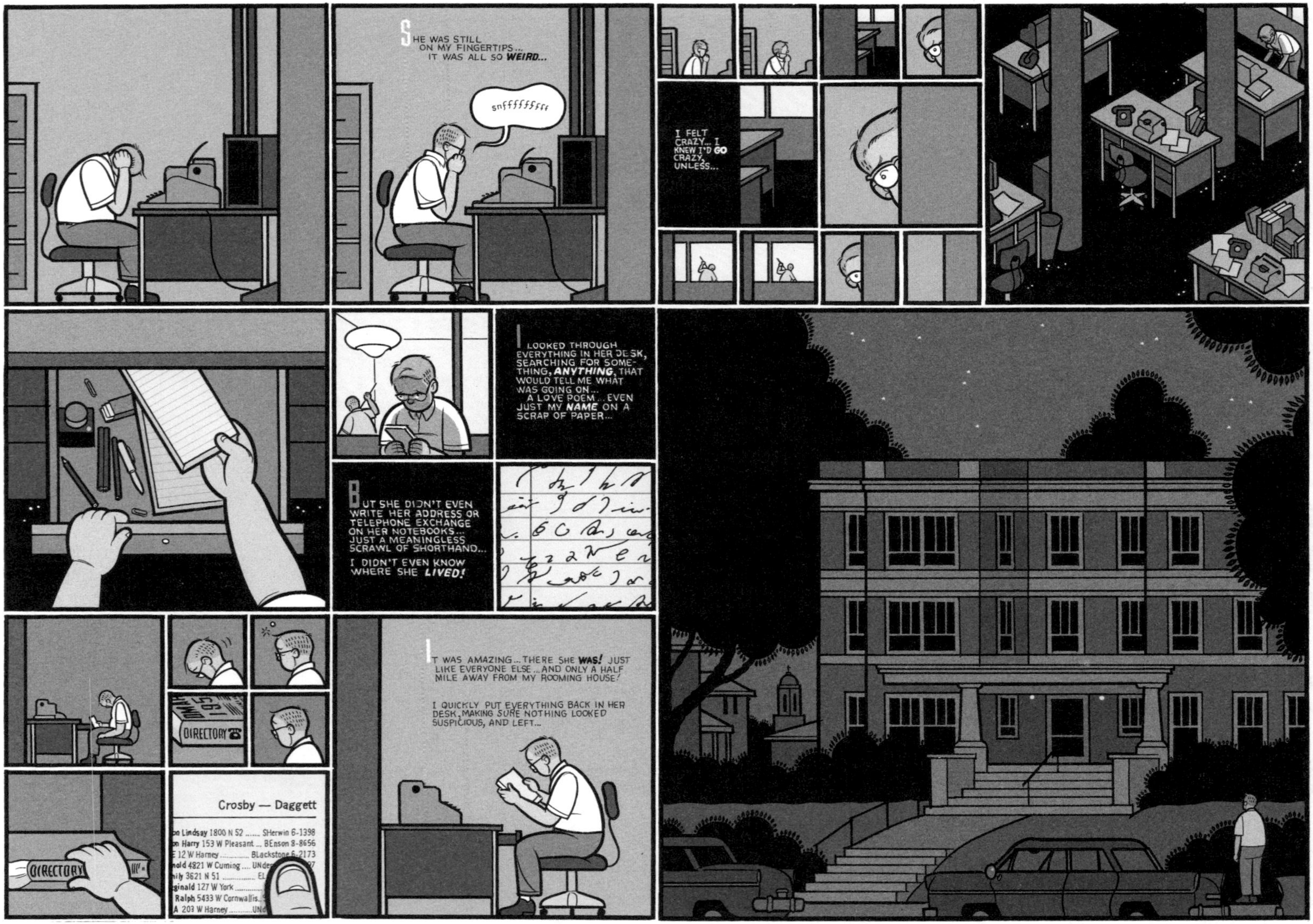
SHE WAS STILL ON MY FINGERTIPS... IT WAS ALL SO WEIRD...
snfffffffff
I FELT CRAZY... I KNEW I'D GO CRAZY, UNLESS...
I LOOKED THROUGH EVERYTHING IN HER DESK, SEARCHING FOR SOMETHING, ANYTHING, THAT WOULD TELL ME WHAT WAS GOING ON... A LOVE POEM... EVEN JUST MY NAME ON A SCRAP OF PAPER...
BUT SHE DIDN'T EVEN WRITE HER ADDRESS OR TELEPHONE EXCHANGE ON HER NOTEBOOKS... JUST A MEANINGLESS SCRAWL OF SHORTHAND...
I DIDN'T EVEN KNOW WHERE SHE LIVED!
DIRECTORY
Crosby — Daggett
on Lindsay 1800 N 52 .... SHerwin 6-1398
on Harry 153 W Pleasant ... BEnson 8-8656
E 12 W Harney .... BLackstone 6-2173
nold 4821 W Cuming .... UNde
ily 3621 N 51
ginald 127 W York
Ralph 5433 W Cornwallis
A 203 W Harney .... UNd
IT WAS AMAZING... THERE SHE WAS! JUST LIKE EVERYONE ELSE... AND ONLY A HALF MILE AWAY FROM MY ROOMING HOUSE!
I QUICKLY PUT EVERYTHING BACK IN HER DESK, MAKING SURE NOTHING LOOKED SUSPICIOUS, AND LEFT...

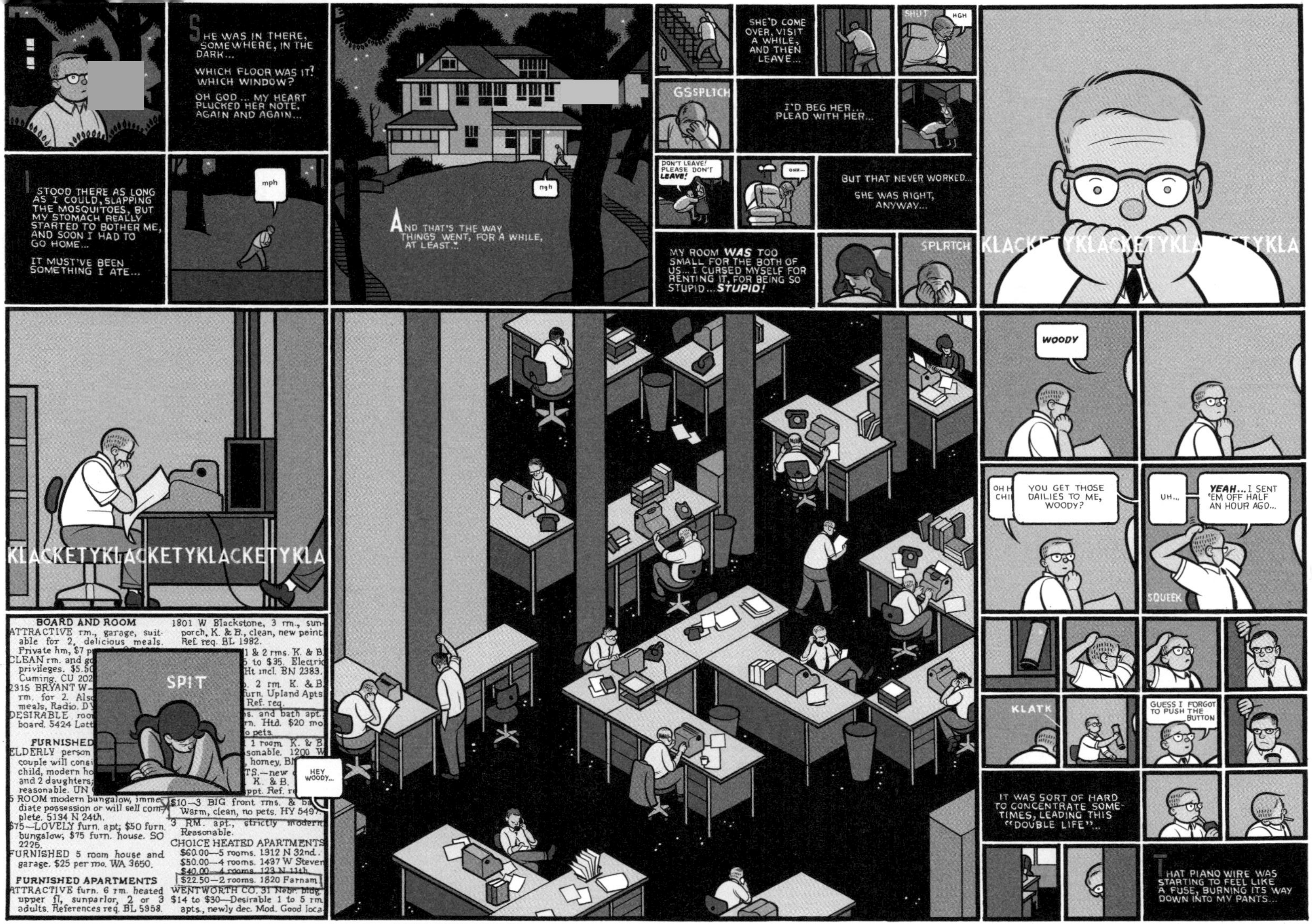

SHE WAS IN THERE, SOMEWHERE, IN THE DARK...
WHICH FLOOR WAS IT? WHICH WINDOW?
OH GOD... MY HEART PLUCKED HER NOTE, AGAIN AND AGAIN...
I STOOD THERE AS LONG AS I COULD, SLAPPING THE MOSQUITOES, BUT MY STOMACH REALLY STARTED TO BOTHER ME, AND SOON I HAD TO GO HOME...
IT MUST'VE BEEN SOMETHING I ATE...
mph
ngh
AND THAT'S THE WAY THINGS WENT, FOR A WHILE, AT LEAST.*
SHE'D COME OVER, VISIT A WHILE, AND THEN LEAVE...
SHUT
HGH
GSSPLTCH
I'D BEG HER... PLEAD WITH HER...
DON'T LEAVE! PLEASE DON'T LEAVE!
OHH...
BUT THAT NEVER WORKED...
SHE WAS RIGHT, ANYWAY...
MY ROOM WAS TOO SMALL FOR THE BOTH OF US... I CURSED MYSELF FOR RENTING IT, FOR BEING SO STUPID... STUPID!
SPLRTCH
KLACKETYKLACKETYKLACKETYKLA
KLACKETYKLACKETYKLACKETYKLA
BOARD AND ROOM
ATTRACTIVE rm., garage, suitable for 2, delicious meals.
Private hm, $7 p
CLEAN rm. and g
privileges. $5.50
Cuming. CU 202
2315 BRYANT W
rm. for 2. Also
meals, Radio. DY
DESIRABLE roo
board. 5424 Lott
FURNISHED
ELDERLY person
couple will consi
child, modern ho
and 2 daughters;
reasonable. UN
5 ROOM modern bungalow, immediate possession or will sell complete. 5134 N 24th.
$75—LOVELY furn. apt; $50 furn. bungalow; $75 furn. house. SO 2225.
FURNISHED 5 room house and garage. $25 per mo. WA 3650.
FURNISHED APARTMENTS
ATTRACTIVE furn. 6 rm. heated upper fl, sunparlor, 2 or 3 adults. References req. BL 5958.
1801 W Blackstone, 3 rm., sunporch, K. & B., clean, new paint. Ref. req. BL 1982.
1 & 2 rms. K. & B.
5 to $35. Electric
Ht incl. BN 2383.
2 rm. K. & B.
furn. Upland Apts
Ref. req.
and bath apt.
Htd. $20 mo
pets.
1 room K. & B.
sonable. 1200 W
homey, B
TS.—new
K. & B.
ppt. Ref.
$10—3 BIG front rms. & ba
Warm, clean, no pets. HY 5497.
3 RM. apt., strictly modern. Reasonable.
CHOICE HEATED APARTMENTS
$60.00—5 rooms. 1312 N 32nd.
$50.00—4 rooms. 1437 W Steven
$40.00—4 rooms. 123 N 11th
$22.50—2 rooms. 1820 Farnam
WENTWORTH CO. 31 Nebr. bldg.
$14 to $30—Desirable 1 to 5 rm. apts., newly dec. Mod. Good loca
SPIT
HEY WOODY...
WOODY
OH H
CHI
YOU GET THOSE DAILIES TO ME, WOODY?
UH...
YEAH... I SENT 'EM OFF HALF AN HOUR AGO...
SQUEEK
KLATK
GUESS I FORGOT TO PUSH THE BUTTON
IT WAS SORT OF HARD TO CONCENTRATE SOMETIMES, LEADING THIS "DOUBLE LIFE"...
THAT PIANO WIRE WAS STARTING TO FEEL LIKE A FUSE, BURNING ITS WAY DOWN INTO MY PANTS...

* TWO DAYS & TWO NIGHTS--ed.

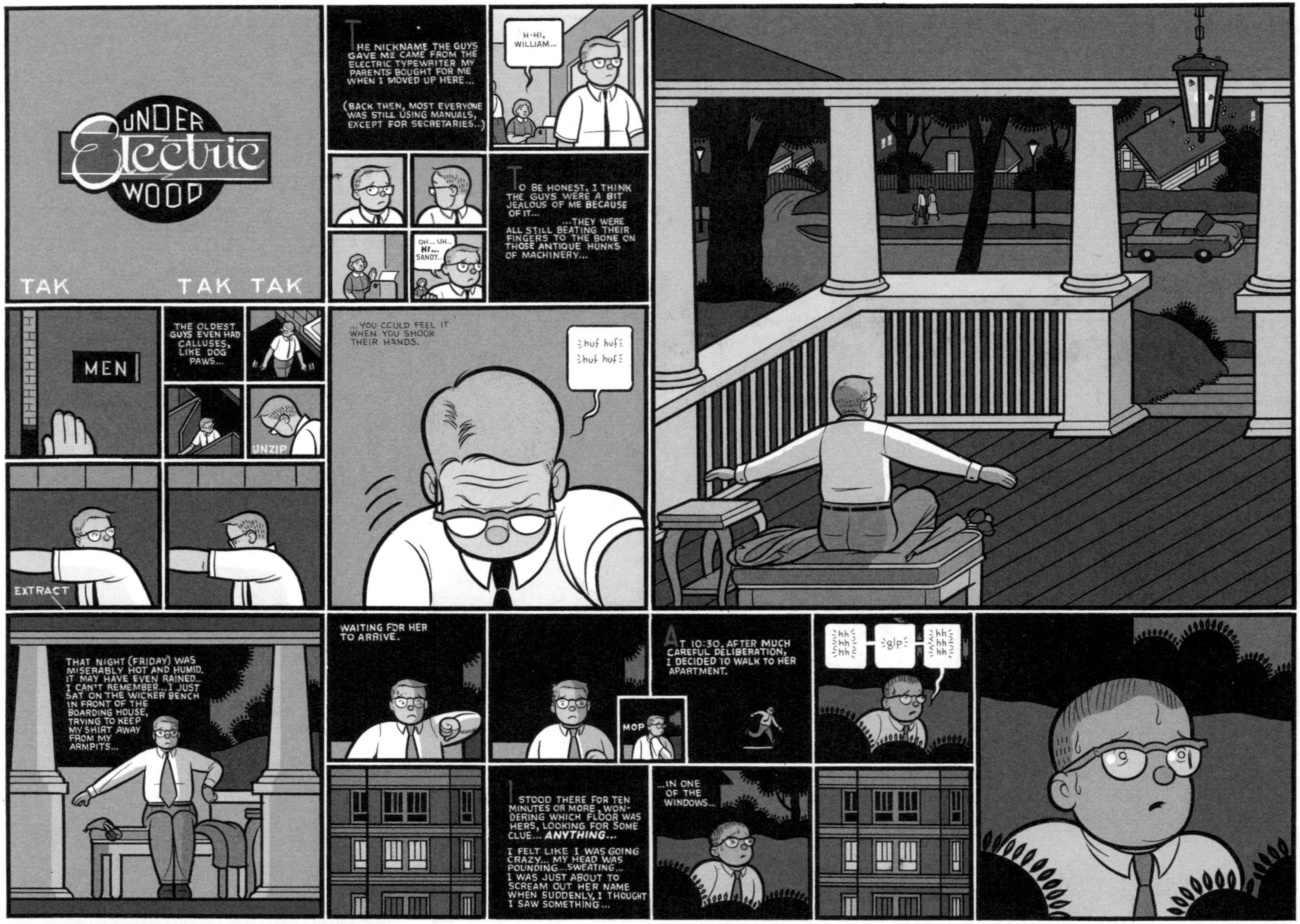

UNDER Electric WOOD
TAK
TAK TAK
THE NICKNAME THE GUYS GAVE ME CAME FROM THE ELECTRIC TYPEWRITER MY PARENTS BOUGHT FOR ME WHEN I MOVED UP HERE...
(BACK THEN, MOST EVERYONE WAS STILL USING MANUALS, EXCEPT FOR SECRETARIES...)
H-HI, WILLIAM...
OH... UH... HI... SANDY...
TO BE HONEST, I THINK THE GUYS WERE A BIT JEALOUS OF ME BECAUSE OF IT...
...THEY WERE ALL STILL BEATING THEIR FINGERS TO THE BONE ON THOSE ANTIQUE HUNKS OF MACHINERY...
MEN
THE OLDEST GUYS EVEN HAD CALLUSES, LIKE DOG PAWS...
UNZIP
EXTRACT
...YOU COULD FEEL IT WHEN YOU SHOOK THEIR HANDS.
huf huf
huf huf
THAT NIGHT (FRIDAY) WAS MISERABLY HOT AND HUMID. IT MAY HAVE EVEN RAINED... I CAN'T REMEMBER... I JUST SAT ON THE WICKER BENCH IN FRONT OF THE BOARDING HOUSE, TRYING TO KEEP MY SHIRT AWAY FROM MY ARMPITS...
WAITING FOR HER TO ARRIVE.
MOP
AT 10:30, AFTER MUCH CAREFUL DELIBERATION, I DECIDED TO WALK TO HER APARTMENT.
hh hh hh
glp
hh hh hh
I STOOD THERE FOR TEN MINUTES OR MORE, WONDERING WHICH FLOOR WAS HERS, LOOKING FOR SOME CLUE... ANYTHING...
I FELT LIKE I WAS GOING CRAZY... MY HEAD WAS POUNDING... SWEATING... I WAS JUST ABOUT TO SCREAM OUT HER NAME WHEN SUDDENLY, I THOUGHT I SAW SOMETHING...
...IN ONE OF THE WINDOWS...

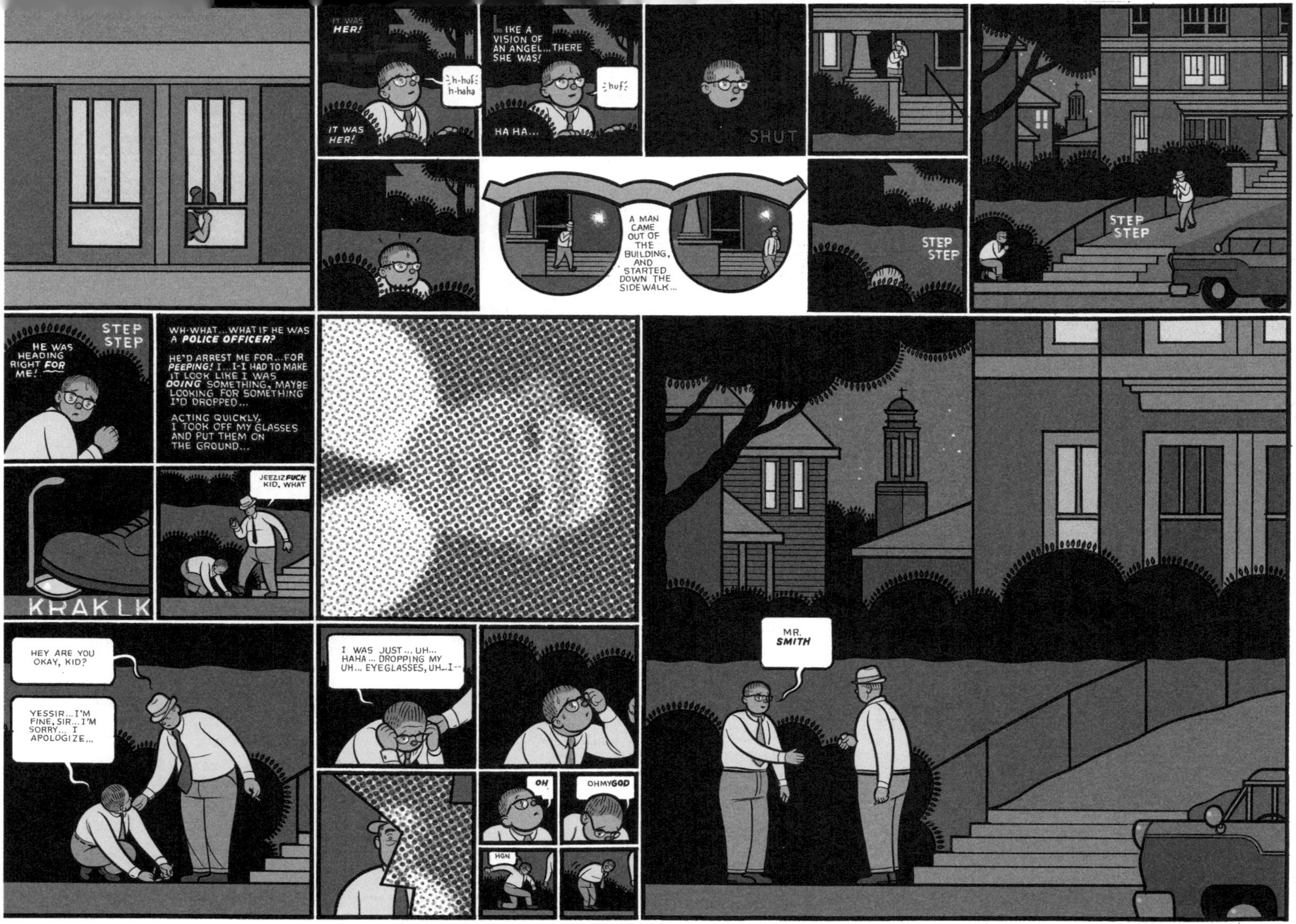
IT WAS HER!
h-huf h-haha
IT WAS HER!
LIKE A VISION OF AN ANGEL... THERE SHE WAS!
huf
HA HA...
SHUT
STEP STEP
A MAN CAME OUT OF THE BUILDING, AND STARTED DOWN THE SIDEWALK...
STEP STEP
STEP STEP
HE WAS HEADING RIGHT FOR ME!
WH-WHAT... WHAT IF HE WAS A POLICE OFFICER?
HE'D ARREST ME FOR... FOR PEEPING! I... I-I HAD TO MAKE IT LOOK LIKE I WAS DOING SOMETHING, MAYBE LOOKING FOR SOMETHING I'D DROPPED...
ACTING QUICKLY, I TOOK OFF MY GLASSES AND PUT THEM ON THE GROUND...
KRAKLK
JEEZIZ FUCK KID, WHAT
HEY ARE YOU OKAY, KID?
YESSIR... I'M FINE, SIR... I'M SORRY... I APOLOGIZE...
I WAS JUST... UH... HAHA... DROPPING MY UH... EYEGLASSES, UH... I--
OH
OHMYGOD
HGN
MR. SMITH

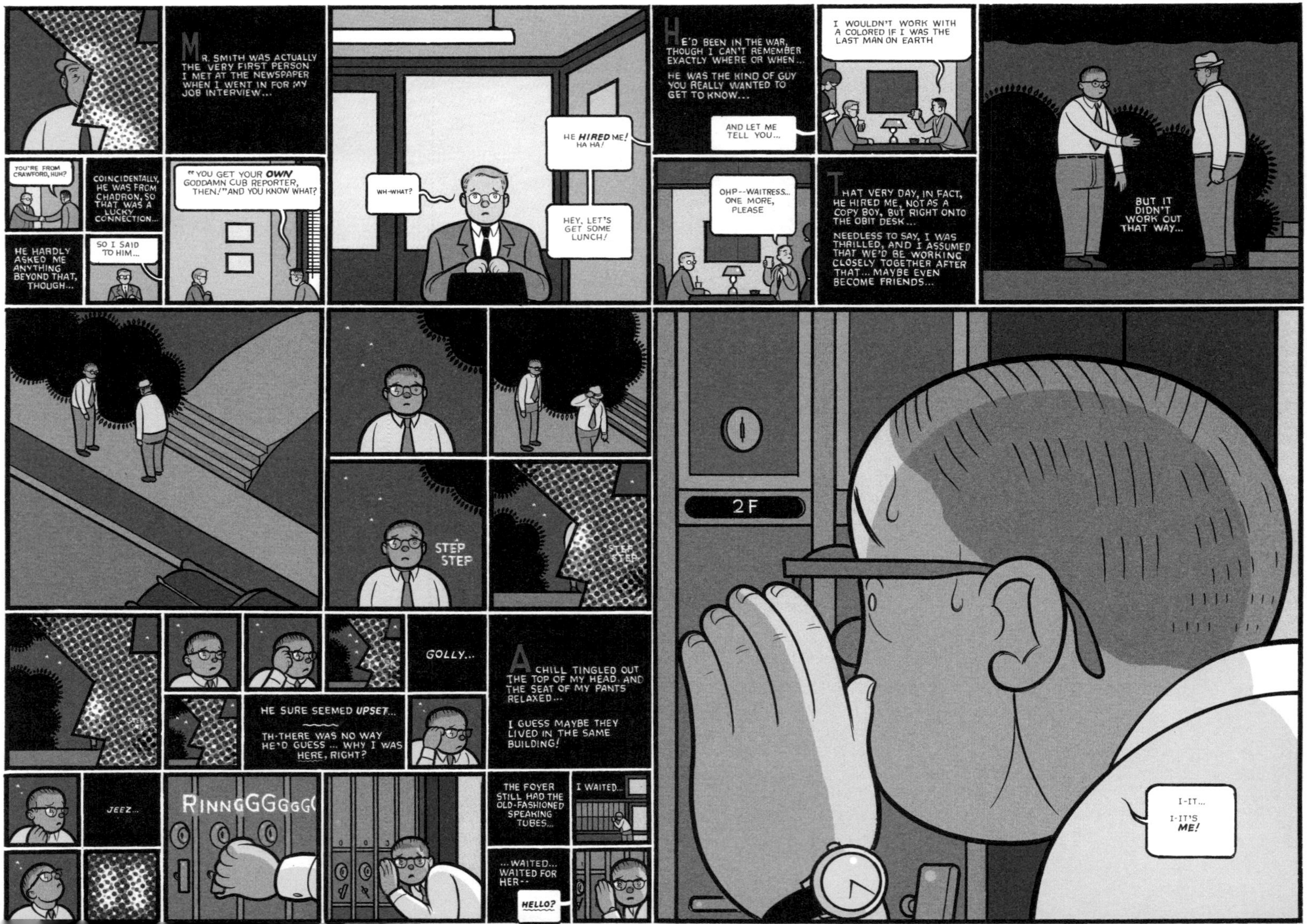
YOU'RE FROM CRAWFORD, HUH?
COINCIDENTALLY, HE WAS FROM CHADRON, SO THAT WAS A LUCKY CONNECTION...
HE HARDLY ASKED ME ANYTHING BEYOND THAT, THOUGH...
SO I SAID TO HIM...
MR. SMITH WAS ACTUALLY THE VERY FIRST PERSON I MET AT THE NEWSPAPER WHEN I WENT IN FOR MY JOB INTERVIEW...
"YOU GET YOUR OWN GODDAMN CUB REPORTER, THEN!" AND YOU KNOW WHAT?
HE HIRED ME! HA HA!
WH-WHAT?
HEY, LET'S GET SOME LUNCH!
HE'D BEEN IN THE WAR, THOUGH I CAN'T REMEMBER EXACTLY WHERE OR WHEN...
HE WAS THE KIND OF GUY YOU REALLY WANTED TO GET TO KNOW...
AND LET ME TELL YOU...
OHP--WAITRESS... ONE MORE, PLEASE
I WOULDN'T WORK WITH A COLORED IF I WAS THE LAST MAN ON EARTH
THAT VERY DAY, IN FACT, HE HIRED ME, NOT AS A COPY BOY, BUT RIGHT ONTO THE OBIT DESK...
NEEDLESS TO SAY, I WAS THRILLED, AND I ASSUMED THAT WE'D BE WORKING CLOSELY TOGETHER AFTER THAT... MAYBE EVEN BECOME FRIENDS...
BUT IT DIDN'T WORK OUT THAT WAY...
STEP STEP
STEP STEP
GOLLY...
HE SURE SEEMED UPSET...
TH-THERE WAS NO WAY HE'D GUESS ... WHY I WAS HERE, RIGHT?
A CHILL TINGLED OUT THE TOP OF MY HEAD, AND THE SEAT OF MY PANTS RELAXED...
I GUESS MAYBE THEY LIVED IN THE SAME BUILDING!
JEEZ...
RINNGGGGGG
THE FOYER STILL HAD THE OLD-FASHIONED SPEAKING TUBES...
I WAITED...
...WAITED... WAITED FOR HER--
HELLO?
2F
I-IT...
I-IT'S ME!

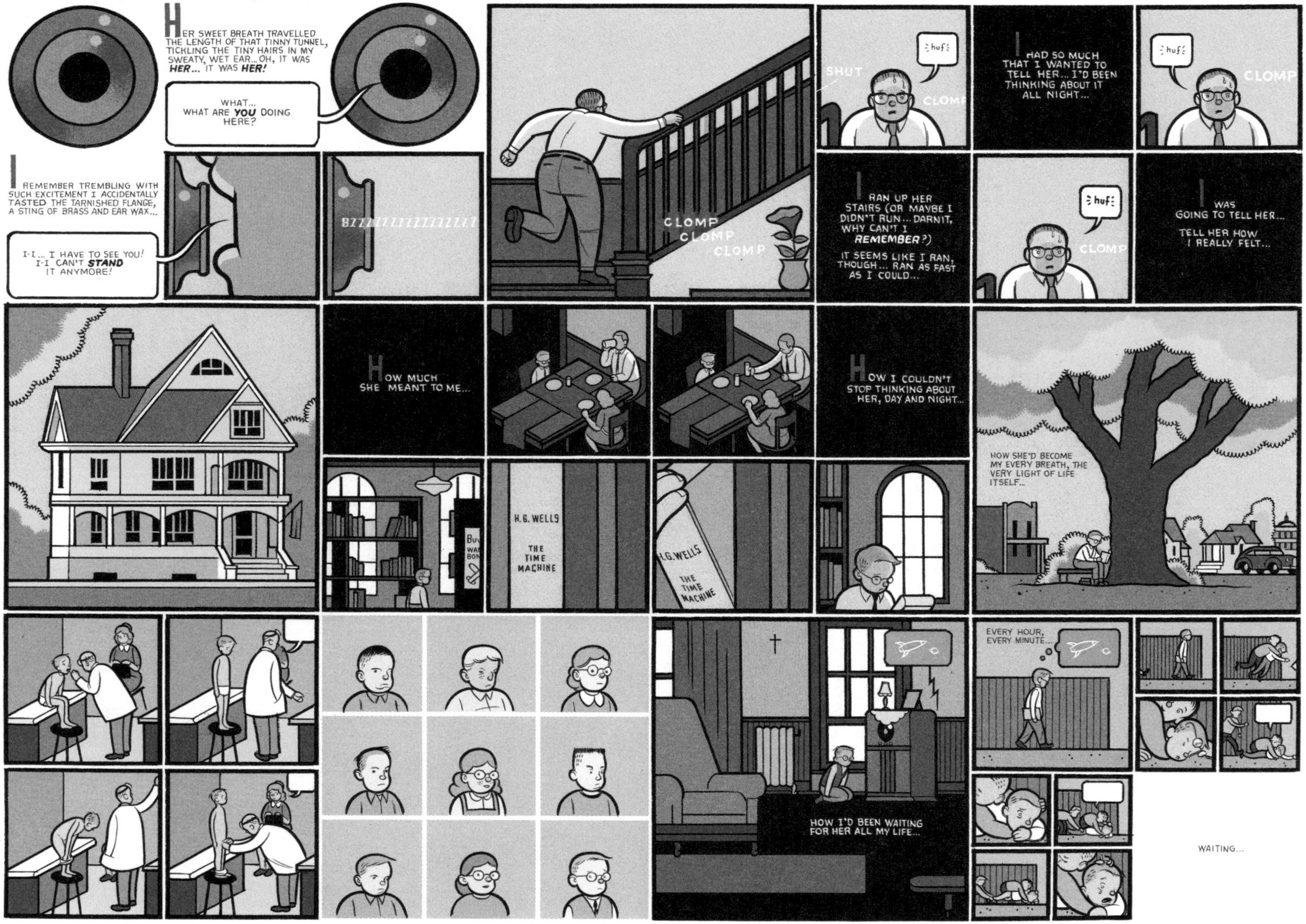
HER SWEET BREATH TRAVELLED THE LENGTH OF THAT TINNY TUNNEL, TICKLING THE TINY HAIRS IN MY SWEATY, WET EAR... OH, IT WAS **HER...** IT WAS **HER!**
WHAT... WHAT ARE **YOU** DOING HERE?
I REMEMBER TREMBLING WITH SUCH EXCITEMENT I ACCIDENTALLY TASTED THE TARNISHED FLANGE, A STING OF BRASS AND EAR WAX...
I-I... I HAVE TO SEE YOU! I-I CAN'T **STAND** IT ANYMORE!
BZZZZZZZZZZZZZZZZZ
CLOMP
CLOMP
CLOMP
SHUT
huf
CLOMP
I HAD SO MUCH THAT I WANTED TO TELL HER... I'D BEEN THINKING ABOUT IT ALL NIGHT...
huf
CLOMP
I RAN UP HER STAIRS (OR MAYBE I DIDN'T RUN... DARNIT, WHY CAN'T I **REMEMBER?**)
IT SEEMS LIKE I RAN, THOUGH... RAN AS FAST AS I COULD...
huf
CLOMP
I WAS GOING TO TELL HER...
TELL HER HOW I REALLY FELT...
HOW MUCH SHE MEANT TO ME...
HOW I COULDN'T STOP THINKING ABOUT HER, DAY AND NIGHT...
HOW SHE'D BECOME MY EVERY BREATH, THE VERY LIGHT OF LIFE ITSELF...
H.G. WELLS
THE TIME MACHINE
H.G. WELLS
THE TIME MACHINE
HOW I'D BEEN WAITING FOR HER ALL MY LIFE...
EVERY HOUR, EVERY MINUTE...
WAITING...

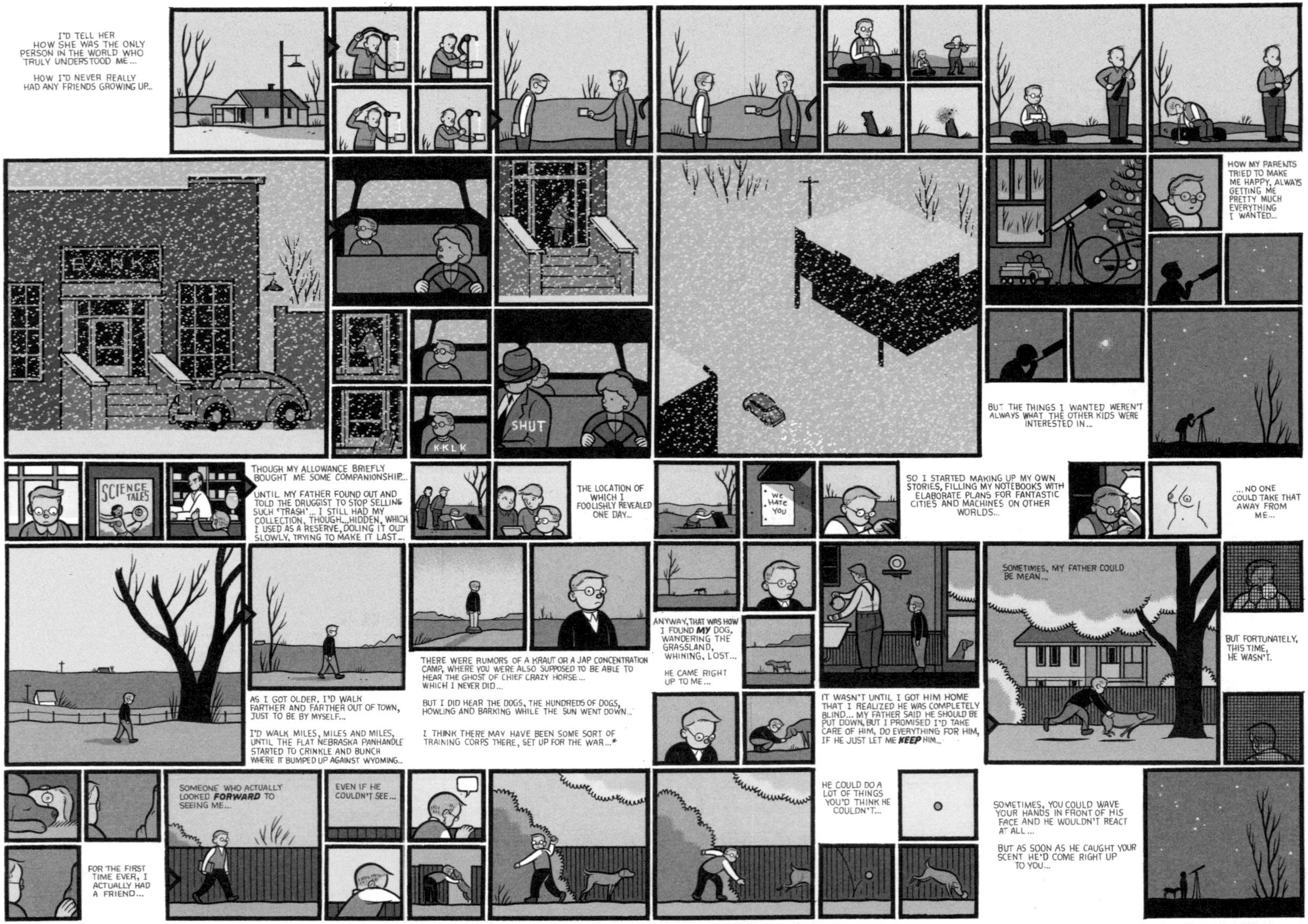
I'D TELL HER HOW SHE WAS THE ONLY PERSON IN THE WORLD WHO TRULY UNDERSTOOD ME...
HOW I'D NEVER REALLY HAD ANY FRIENDS GROWING UP...
HOW MY PARENTS TRIED TO MAKE ME HAPPY, ALWAYS GETTING ME PRETTY MUCH EVERYTHING I WANTED...
BANK
SHUT
K-KLK
BUT THE THINGS I WANTED WEREN'T ALWAYS WHAT THE OTHER KIDS WERE INTERESTED IN...
SCIENCE TALES
THOUGH MY ALLOWANCE BRIEFLY BOUGHT ME SOME COMPANIONSHIP...
UNTIL MY FATHER FOUND OUT AND TOLD THE DRUGGIST TO STOP SELLING SUCH "TRASH"... I STILL HAD MY COLLECTION, THOUGH...HIDDEN, WHICH I USED AS A RESERVE, DOLING IT OUT SLOWLY, TRYING TO MAKE IT LAST...
THE LOCATION OF WHICH I FOOLISHLY REVEALED ONE DAY...
WE HATE YOU
SO I STARTED MAKING UP MY OWN STORIES, FILLING MY NOTEBOOKS WITH ELABORATE PLANS FOR FANTASTIC CITIES AND MACHINES ON OTHER WORLDS...
...NO ONE COULD TAKE THAT AWAY FROM ME...
AS I GOT OLDER, I'D WALK FARTHER AND FARTHER OUT OF TOWN, JUST TO BE BY MYSELF...
I'D WALK MILES, MILES AND MILES, UNTIL THE FLAT NEBRASKA PANHANDLE STARTED TO CRINKLE AND BUNCH WHERE IT BUMPED UP AGAINST WYOMING...
THERE WERE RUMORS OF A KRAUT OR A JAP CONCENTRATION CAMP, WHERE YOU WERE ALSO SUPPOSED TO BE ABLE TO HEAR THE GHOST OF CHIEF CRAZY HORSE...
WHICH I NEVER DID...
BUT I DID HEAR THE DOGS, THE HUNDREDS OF DOGS, HOWLING AND BARKING WHILE THE SUN WENT DOWN...
I THINK THERE MAY HAVE BEEN SOME SORT OF TRAINING CORPS THERE, SET UP FOR THE WAR...*
ANYWAY, THAT WAS HOW I FOUND MY DOG, WANDERING THE GRASSLAND, WHINING, LOST...
HE CAME RIGHT UP TO ME...
IT WASN'T UNTIL I GOT HIM HOME THAT I REALIZED HE WAS COMPLETELY BLIND... MY FATHER SAID HE SHOULD BE PUT DOWN, BUT I PROMISED I'D TAKE CARE OF HIM, DO EVERYTHING FOR HIM, IF HE JUST LET ME KEEP HIM...
SOMETIMES, MY FATHER COULD BE MEAN...
BUT FORTUNATELY, THIS TIME, HE WASN'T.
FOR THE FIRST TIME EVER, I ACTUALLY HAD A FRIEND...
SOMEONE WHO ACTUALLY LOOKED FORWARD TO SEEING ME...
EVEN IF HE COULDN'T SEE...
HE COULD DO A LOT OF THINGS YOU'D THINK HE COULDN'T...
SOMETIMES, YOU COULD WAVE YOUR HANDS IN FRONT OF HIS FACE AND HE WOULDN'T REACT AT ALL...
BUT AS SOON AS HE CAUGHT YOUR SCENT HE'D COME RIGHT UP TO YOU...

* HERE IT IS BELIEVED OUR NARRATOR IS REFERRING TO THE 'K-9' RECEPTION & TRAINING CENTER,

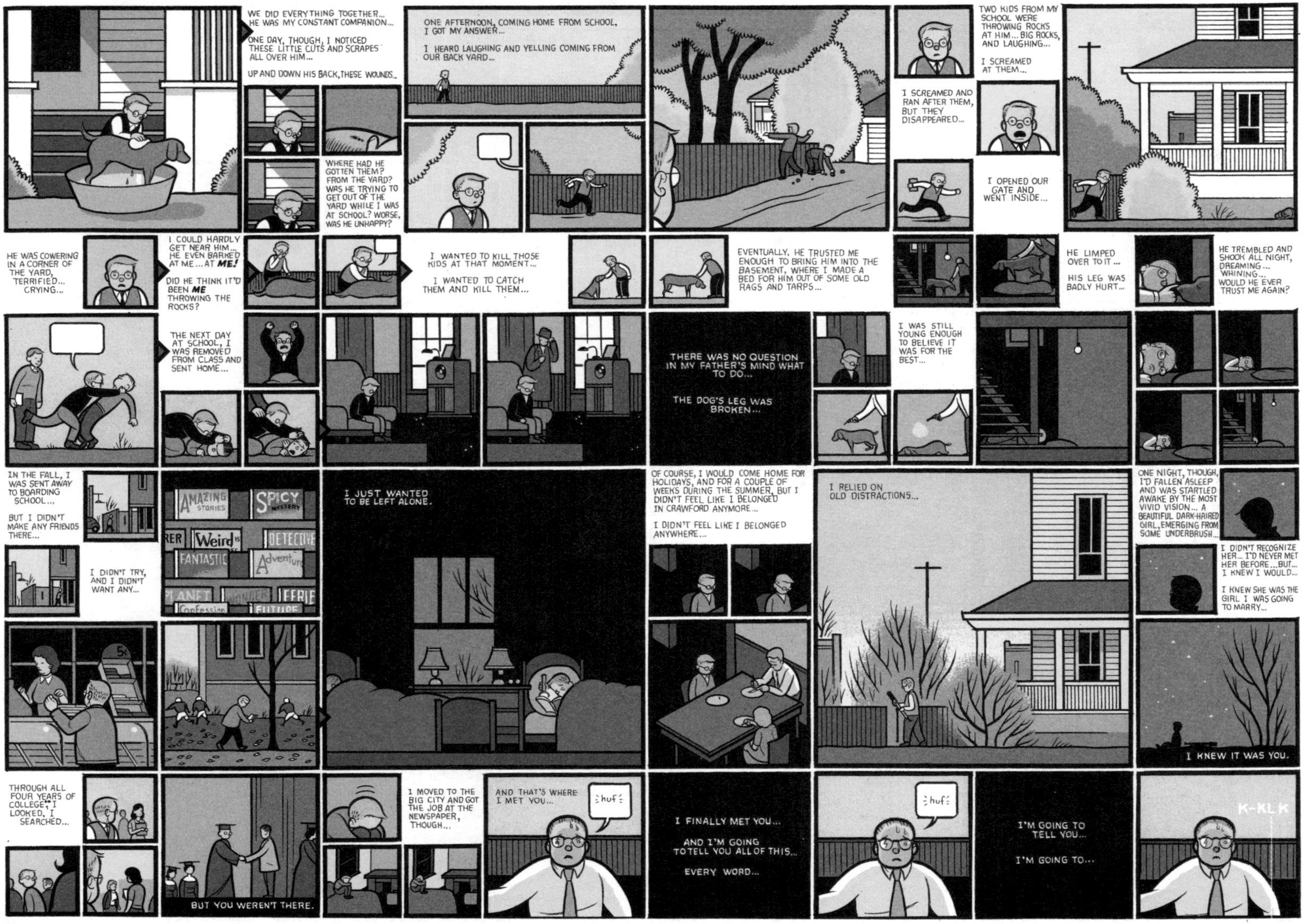
WE DID EVERYTHING TOGETHER... HE WAS MY CONSTANT COMPANION...
ONE DAY, THOUGH, I NOTICED THESE LITTLE CUTS AND SCRAPES ALL OVER HIM...
UP AND DOWN HIS BACK, THESE WOUNDS...
WHERE HAD HE GOTTEN THEM? FROM THE YARD? WAS HE TRYING TO GET OUT OF THE YARD WHILE I WAS AT SCHOOL? WORSE, WAS HE UNHAPPY?
ONE AFTERNOON, COMING HOME FROM SCHOOL, I GOT MY ANSWER...
I HEARD LAUGHING AND YELLING COMING FROM OUR BACK YARD...
TWO KIDS FROM MY SCHOOL WERE THROWING ROCKS AT HIM... BIG ROCKS, AND LAUGHING...
I SCREAMED AT THEM...
I SCREAMED AND RAN AFTER THEM, BUT THEY DISAPPEARED...
I OPENED OUR GATE AND WENT INSIDE...
HE WAS COWERING IN A CORNER OF THE YARD, TERRIFIED... CRYING...
I COULD HARDLY GET NEAR HIM... HE EVEN BARKED AT ME... AT ME!
DID HE THINK IT'D BEEN ME THROWING THE ROCKS?
I WANTED TO KILL THOSE KIDS AT THAT MOMENT...
I WANTED TO CATCH THEM AND KILL THEM...
EVENTUALLY, HE TRUSTED ME ENOUGH TO BRING HIM INTO THE BASEMENT, WHERE I MADE A BED FOR HIM OUT OF SOME OLD RAGS AND TARPS...
HE LIMPED OVER TO IT...
HIS LEG WAS BADLY HURT...
HE TREMBLED AND SHOOK ALL NIGHT, DREAMING... WHINING... WOULD HE EVER TRUST ME AGAIN?
THE NEXT DAY AT SCHOOL, I WAS REMOVED FROM CLASS AND SENT HOME...
THERE WAS NO QUESTION IN MY FATHER'S MIND WHAT TO DO...
THE DOG'S LEG WAS BROKEN...
I WAS STILL YOUNG ENOUGH TO BELIEVE IT WAS FOR THE BEST...
IN THE FALL, I WAS SENT AWAY TO BOARDING SCHOOL...
BUT I DIDN'T MAKE ANY FRIENDS THERE...
I DIDN'T TRY, AND I DIDN'T WANT ANY...
AMAZING STORIES
SPICY MYSTERY
Weird
DETECTIVE
FANTASTIC
Adventure
PLANET
WONDER
EERIE
Confession
FUTURE
I JUST WANTED TO BE LEFT ALONE.
OF COURSE, I WOULD COME HOME FOR HOLIDAYS, AND FOR A COUPLE OF WEEKS DURING THE SUMMER, BUT I DIDN'T FEEL LIKE I BELONGED IN CRAWFORD ANYMORE...
I DIDN'T FEEL LIKE I BELONGED ANYWHERE...
I RELIED ON OLD DISTRACTIONS...
ONE NIGHT, THOUGH, I'D FALLEN ASLEEP AND WAS STARTLED AWAKE BY THE MOST VIVID VISION... A BEAUTIFUL DARK-HAIRED GIRL, EMERGING FROM SOME UNDERBRUSH...
I DIDN'T RECOGNIZE HER... I'D NEVER MET HER BEFORE... BUT... I KNEW I WOULD...
I KNEW SHE WAS THE GIRL I WAS GOING TO MARRY...
I KNEW IT WAS YOU.
THROUGH ALL FOUR YEARS OF COLLEGE,** I LOOKED, I SEARCHED...
BUT YOU WEREN'T THERE.
I MOVED TO THE BIG CITY AND GOT THE JOB AT THE NEWSPAPER, THOUGH...
AND THAT'S WHERE I MET YOU...
huf
I FINALLY MET YOU...
AND I'M GOING TO TELL YOU ALL OF THIS...
EVERY WORD...
huf
I'M GOING TO TELL YOU...
I'M GOING TO...
K-KLK

** *UNIVERSITY OF NEBRASKA AT LINCOLN, 1951-1955.*

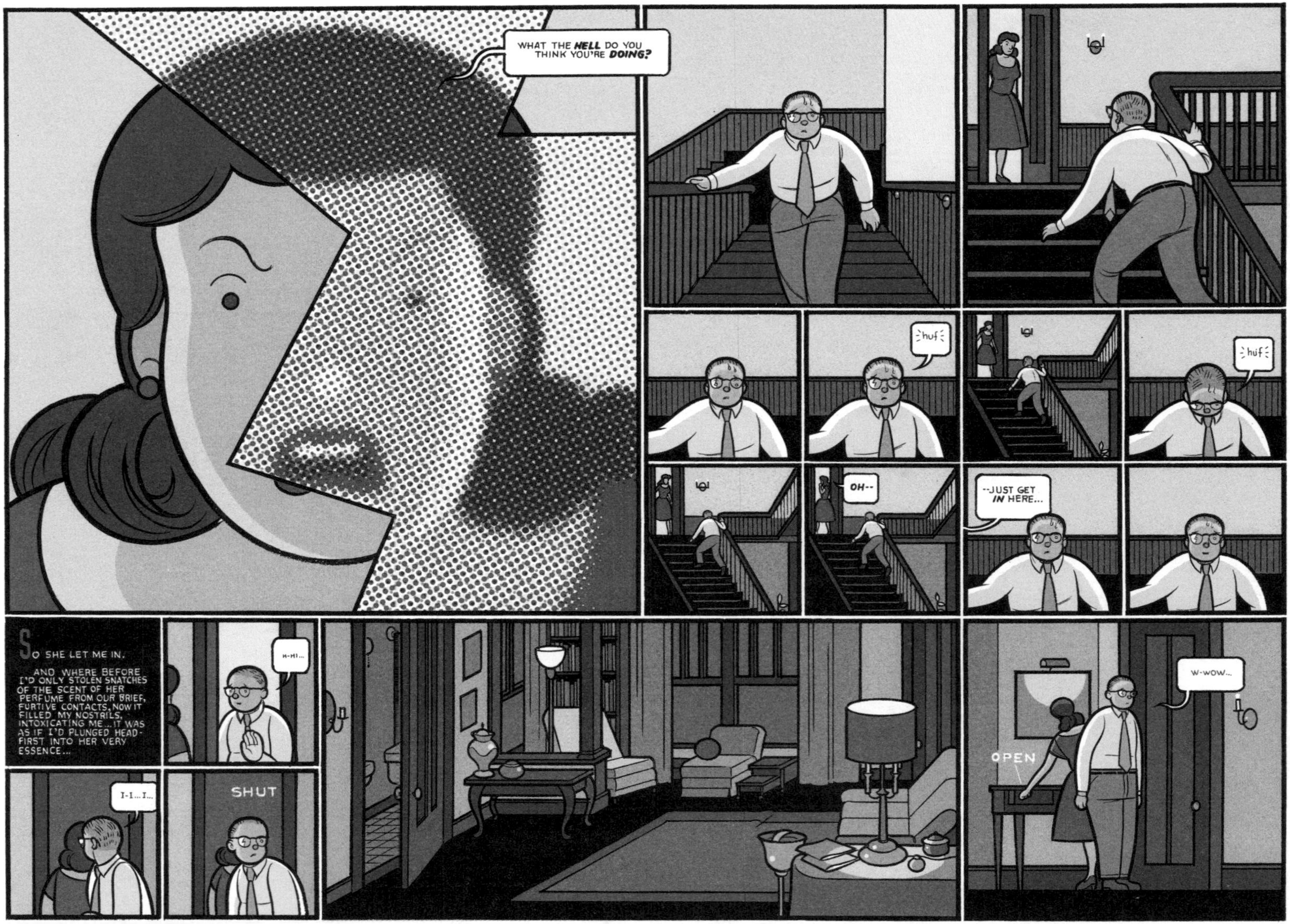
WHAT THE HELL DO YOU THINK YOU'RE DOING?
huf
huf
OH--
--JUST GET IN HERE...
SO SHE LET ME IN.
AND WHERE BEFORE I'D ONLY STOLEN SNATCHES OF THE SCENT OF HER PERFUME FROM OUR BRIEF, FURTIVE CONTACTS, NOW IT FILLED MY NOSTRILS, INTOXICATING ME... IT WAS AS IF I'D PLUNGED HEAD-FIRST INTO HER VERY ESSENCE...
H-HI...
I-I... I...
SHUT
OPEN
W-WOW...

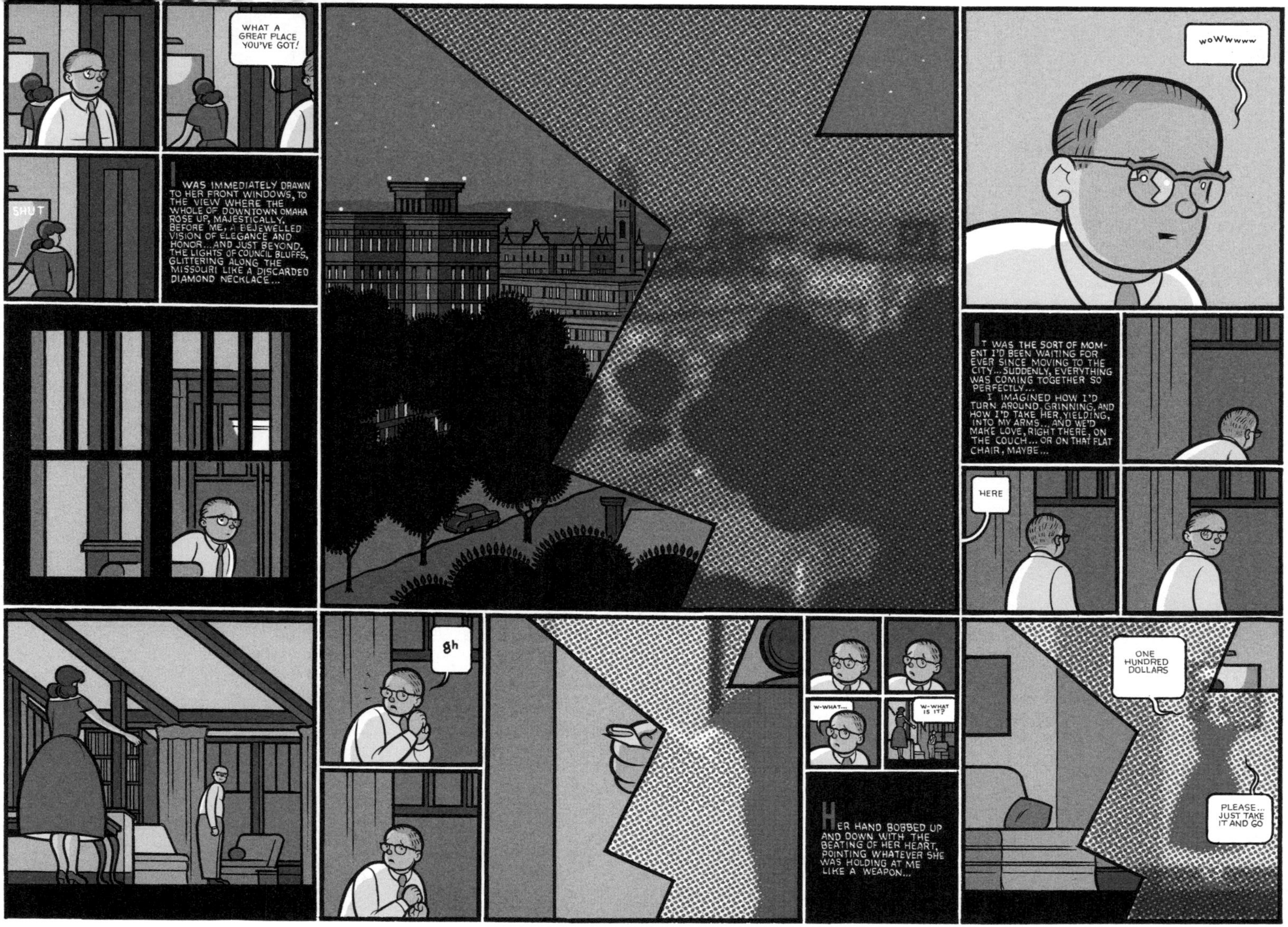
WHAT A GREAT PLACE YOU'VE GOT!
SHUT
I WAS IMMEDIATELY DRAWN TO HER FRONT WINDOWS, TO THE VIEW WHERE THE WHOLE OF DOWNTOWN OMAHA ROSE UP, MAJESTICALLY, BEFORE ME, A BEJEWELLED VISION OF ELEGANCE AND HONOR... AND JUST BEYOND, THE LIGHTS OF COUNCIL BLUFFS, GLITTERING ALONG THE MISSOURI LIKE A DISCARDED DIAMOND NECKLACE...
woWWwww
IT WAS THE SORT OF MOMENT I'D BEEN WAITING FOR EVER SINCE MOVING TO THE CITY... SUDDENLY, EVERYTHING WAS COMING TOGETHER SO PERFECTLY...
I IMAGINED HOW I'D TURN AROUND, GRINNING, AND HOW I'D TAKE HER, YIELDING, INTO MY ARMS... AND WE'D MAKE LOVE, RIGHT THERE, ON THE COUCH... OR ON THAT FLAT CHAIR, MAYBE...
HERE
gh
W-WHAT...
W-WHAT IS IT?
HER HAND BOBBED UP AND DOWN WITH THE BEATING OF HER HEART, POINTING WHATEVER SHE WAS HOLDING AT ME LIKE A WEAPON...
ONE HUNDRED DOLLARS
PLEASE... JUST TAKE IT AND GO

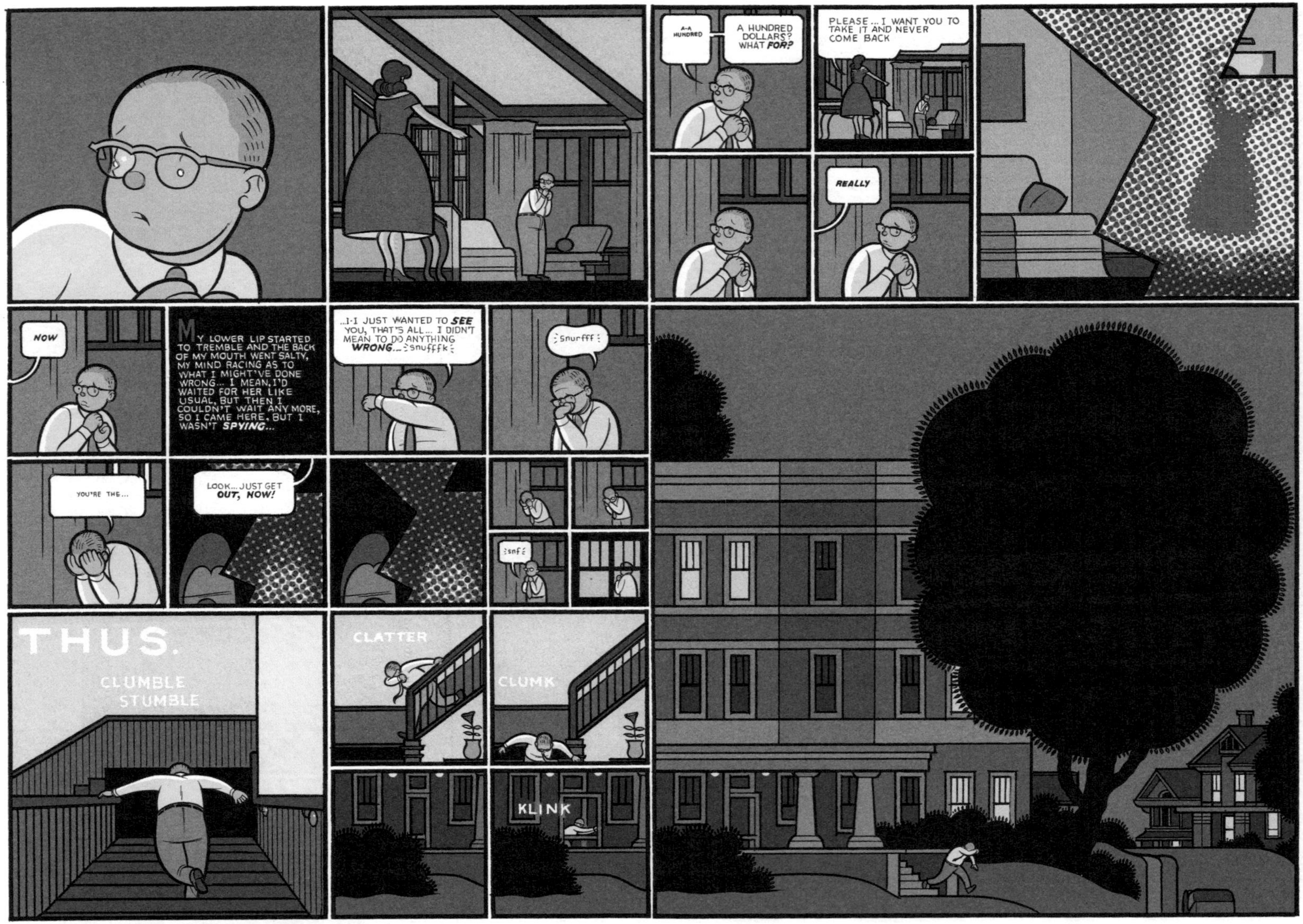
A-A HUNDRED
A HUNDRED DOLLARS? WHAT FOR?
PLEASE... I WANT YOU TO TAKE IT AND NEVER COME BACK
REALLY
NOW
MY LOWER LIP STARTED TO TREMBLE AND THE BACK OF MY MOUTH WENT SALTY, MY MIND RACING AS TO WHAT I MIGHT'VE DONE WRONG... I MEAN, I'D WAITED FOR HER LIKE USUAL, BUT THEN I COULDN'T WAIT ANY MORE, SO I CAME HERE. BUT I WASN'T SPYING...
...I-I JUST WANTED TO SEE YOU, THAT'S ALL... I DIDN'T MEAN TO DO ANYTHING WRONG... snufffk
Snurfff
YOU'RE THE...
LOOK... JUST GET OUT, NOW!
snf
THUS.
CLUMBLE STUMBLE
CLATTER
CLUMK
KLINK

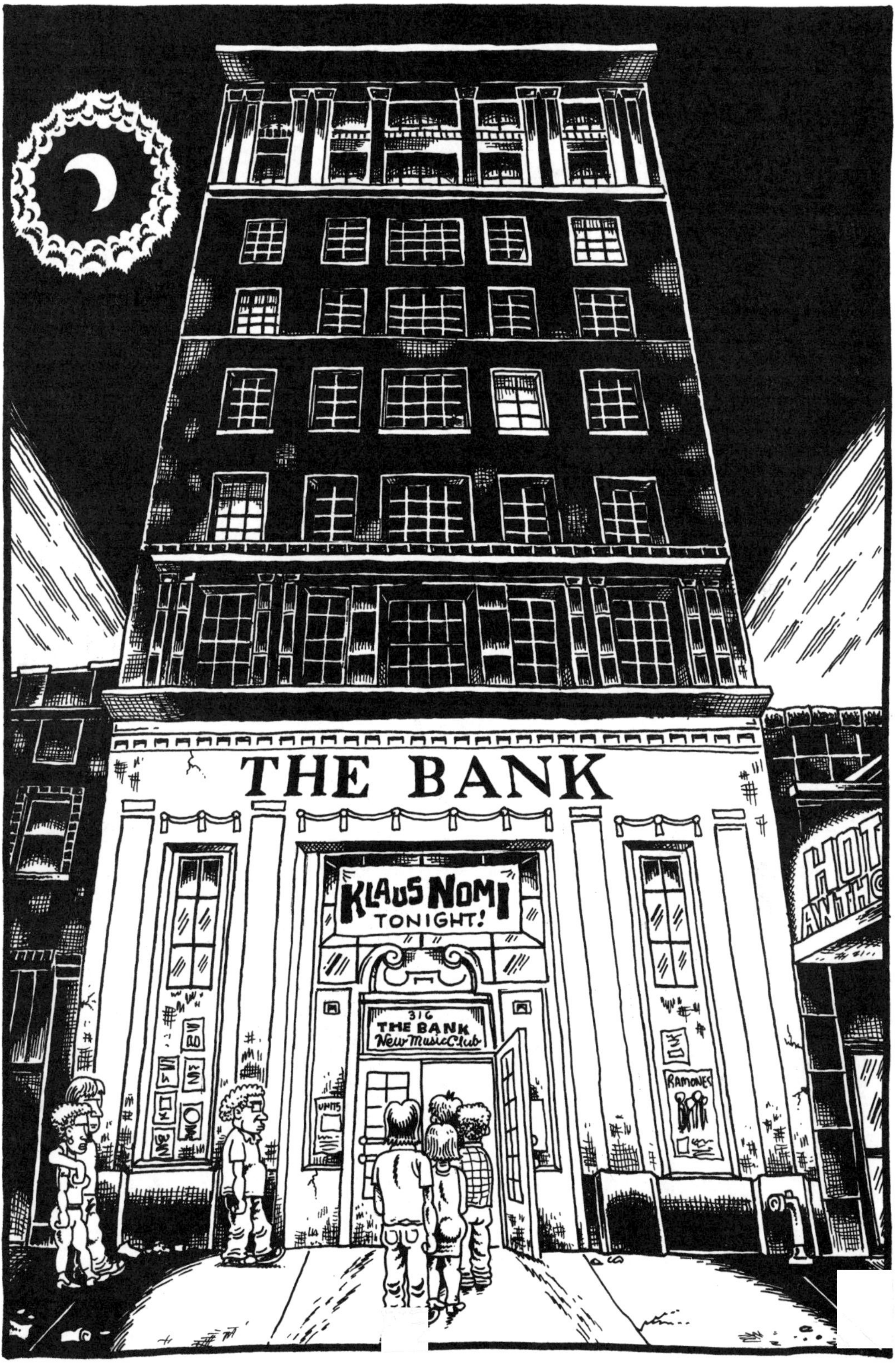
THE BANK
KLAUS NOMI
TONIGHT!
316
THE BANK
New Music Club
UNITS
RAMONES

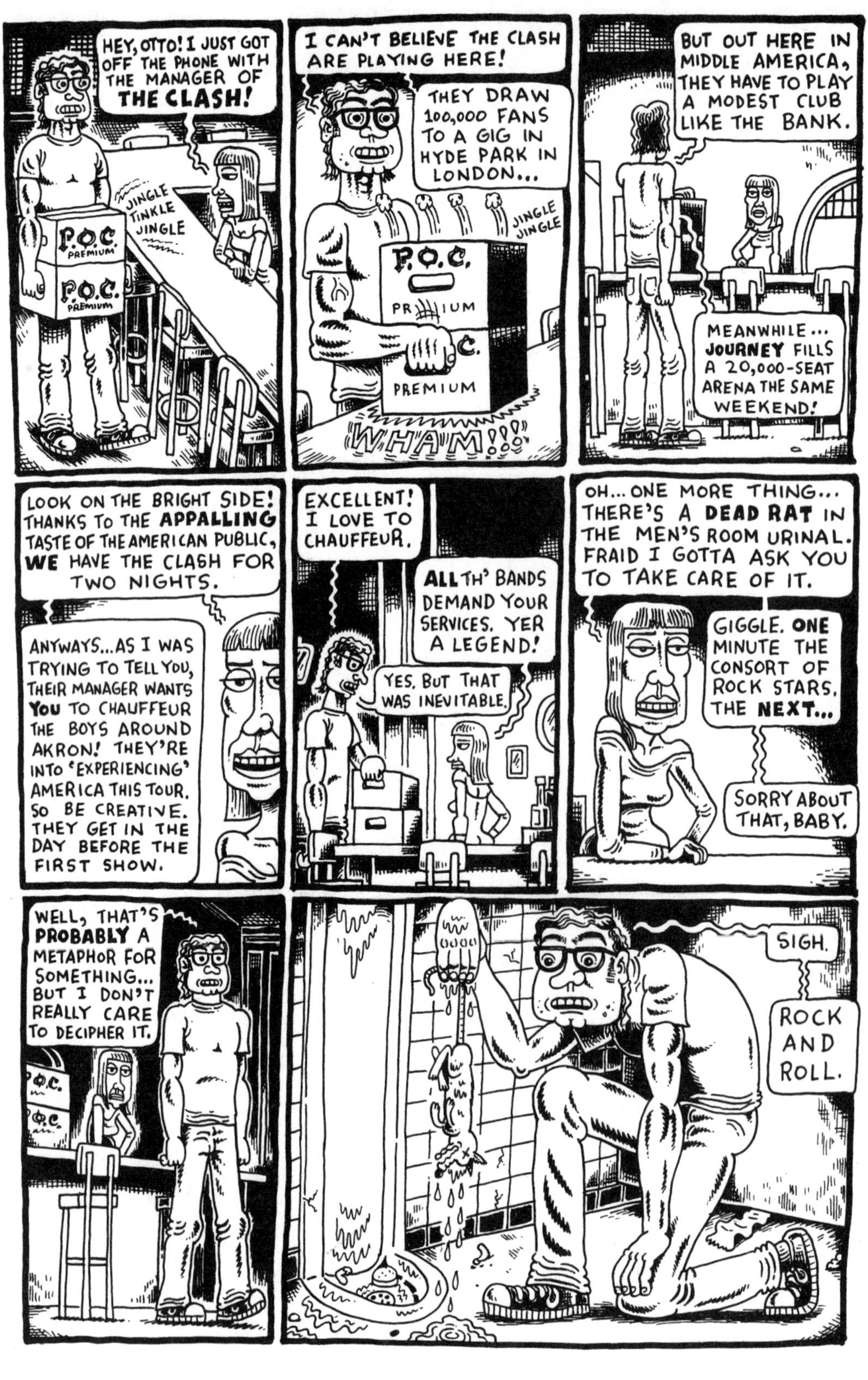
HEY, OTTO! I JUST GOT OFF THE PHONE WITH THE MANAGER OF THE CLASH!
JINGLE TINKLE JINGLE
P.O.C. PREMIUM
P.O.C. PREMIUM
I CAN'T BELIEVE THE CLASH ARE PLAYING HERE!
THEY DRAW 100,000 FANS TO A GIG IN HYDE PARK IN LONDON...
JINGLE JINGLE
P.O.C.
PREMIUM
WHAM!!!
BUT OUT HERE IN MIDDLE AMERICA, THEY HAVE TO PLAY A MODEST CLUB LIKE THE BANK.
MEANWHILE... JOURNEY FILLS A 20,000-SEAT ARENA THE SAME WEEKEND!
LOOK ON THE BRIGHT SIDE! THANKS TO THE APPALLING TASTE OF THE AMERICAN PUBLIC, WE HAVE THE CLASH FOR TWO NIGHTS.
ANYWAYS...AS I WAS TRYING TO TELL YOU, THEIR MANAGER WANTS YOU TO CHAUFFEUR THE BOYS AROUND AKRON! THEY'RE INTO 'EXPERIENCING' AMERICA THIS TOUR. SO BE CREATIVE. THEY GET IN THE DAY BEFORE THE FIRST SHOW.
EXCELLENT! I LOVE TO CHAUFFEUR.
ALL TH' BANDS DEMAND YOUR SERVICES. YER A LEGEND!
YES, BUT THAT WAS INEVITABLE.
OH... ONE MORE THING... THERE'S A DEAD RAT IN THE MEN'S ROOM URINAL. FRAID I GOTTA ASK YOU TO TAKE CARE OF IT.
GIGGLE. ONE MINUTE THE CONSORT OF ROCK STARS. THE NEXT...
SORRY ABOUT THAT, BABY.
WELL, THAT'S PROBABLY A METAPHOR FOR SOMETHING... BUT I DON'T REALLY CARE TO DECIPHER IT.
SIGH.
ROCK AND ROLL.

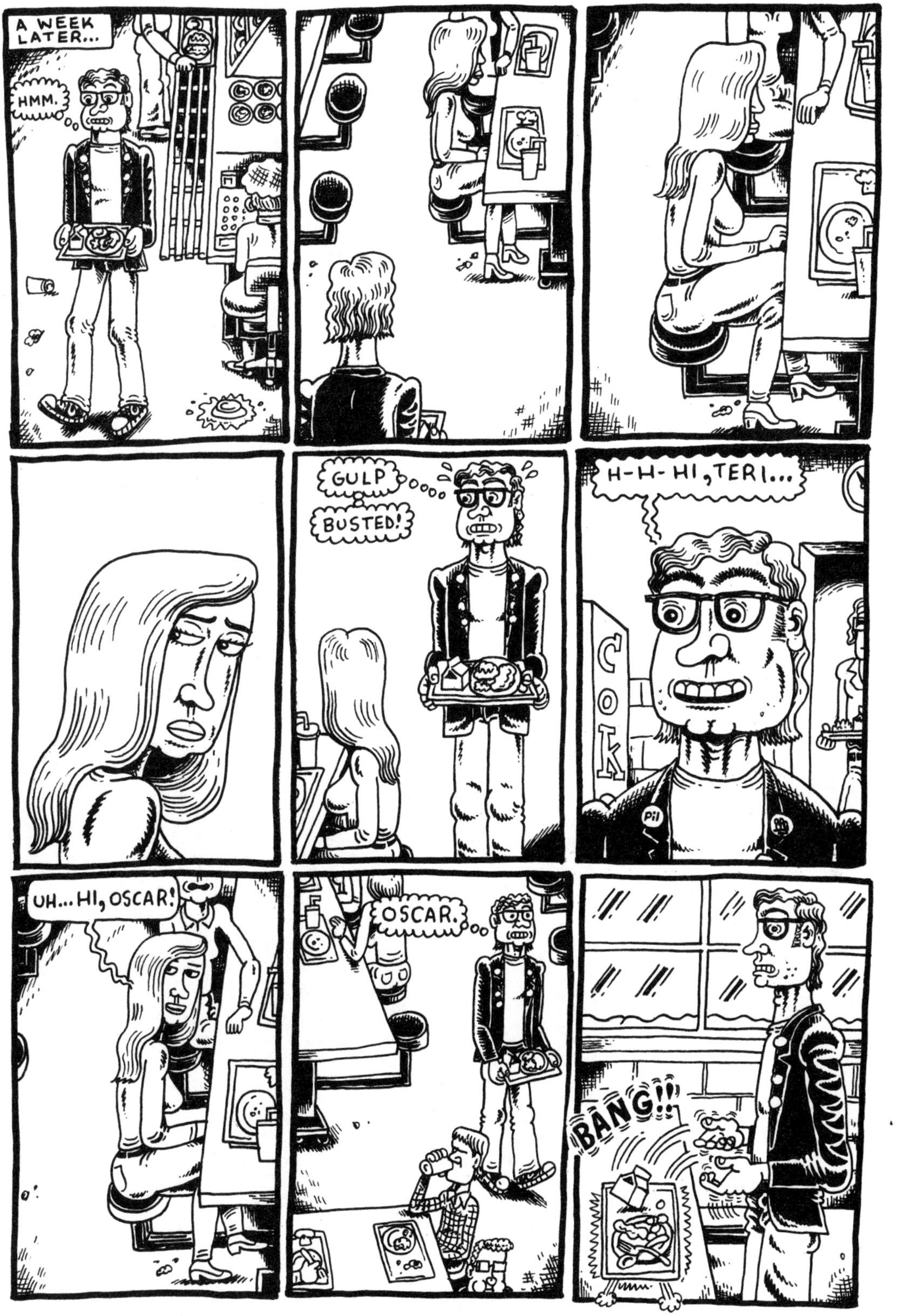
A WEEK LATER...
HMM.
GULP
BUSTED!
H-H-HI, TERI...
UH...HI, OSCAR!
OSCAR.
BANG!!

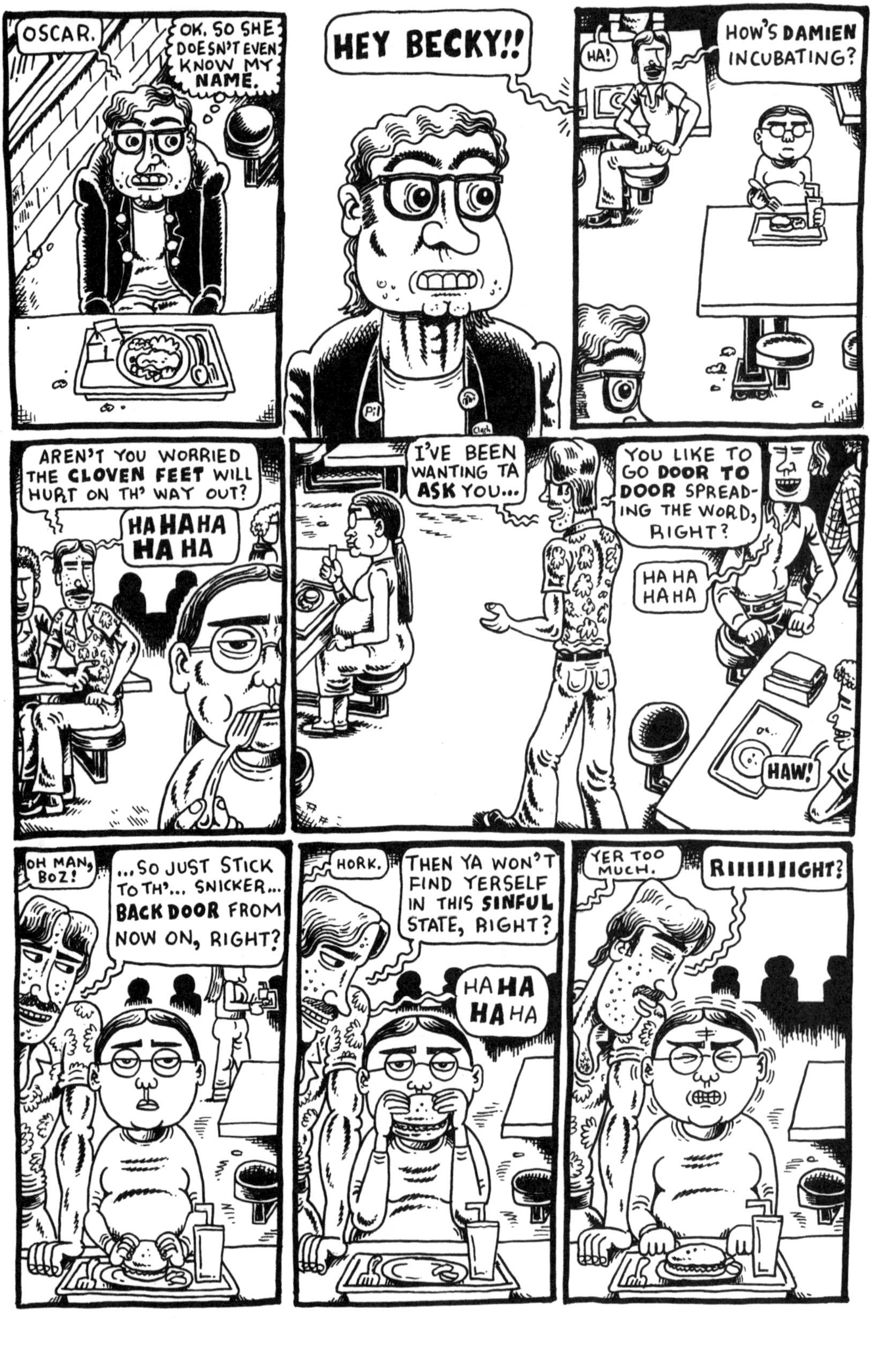
OSCAR.
OK, SO SHE DOESN'T EVEN KNOW MY NAME.
HEY BECKY!!
HA!
HOW'S DAMIEN INCUBATING?
AREN'T YOU WORRIED THE CLOVEN FEET WILL HURT ON TH' WAY OUT?
HA HA HA HA HA
I'VE BEEN WANTING TA ASK YOU...
YOU LIKE TO GO DOOR TO DOOR SPREADING THE WORD, RIGHT?
HA HA HA HA
HAW!
OH MAN, BOZ!
...SO JUST STICK TO TH'... SNICKER... BACK DOOR FROM NOW ON, RIGHT?
HORK.
THEN YA WON'T FIND YERSELF IN THIS SINFUL STATE, RIGHT?
HA HA HA HA
YER TOO MUCH.
RIIIIIIIGHT?

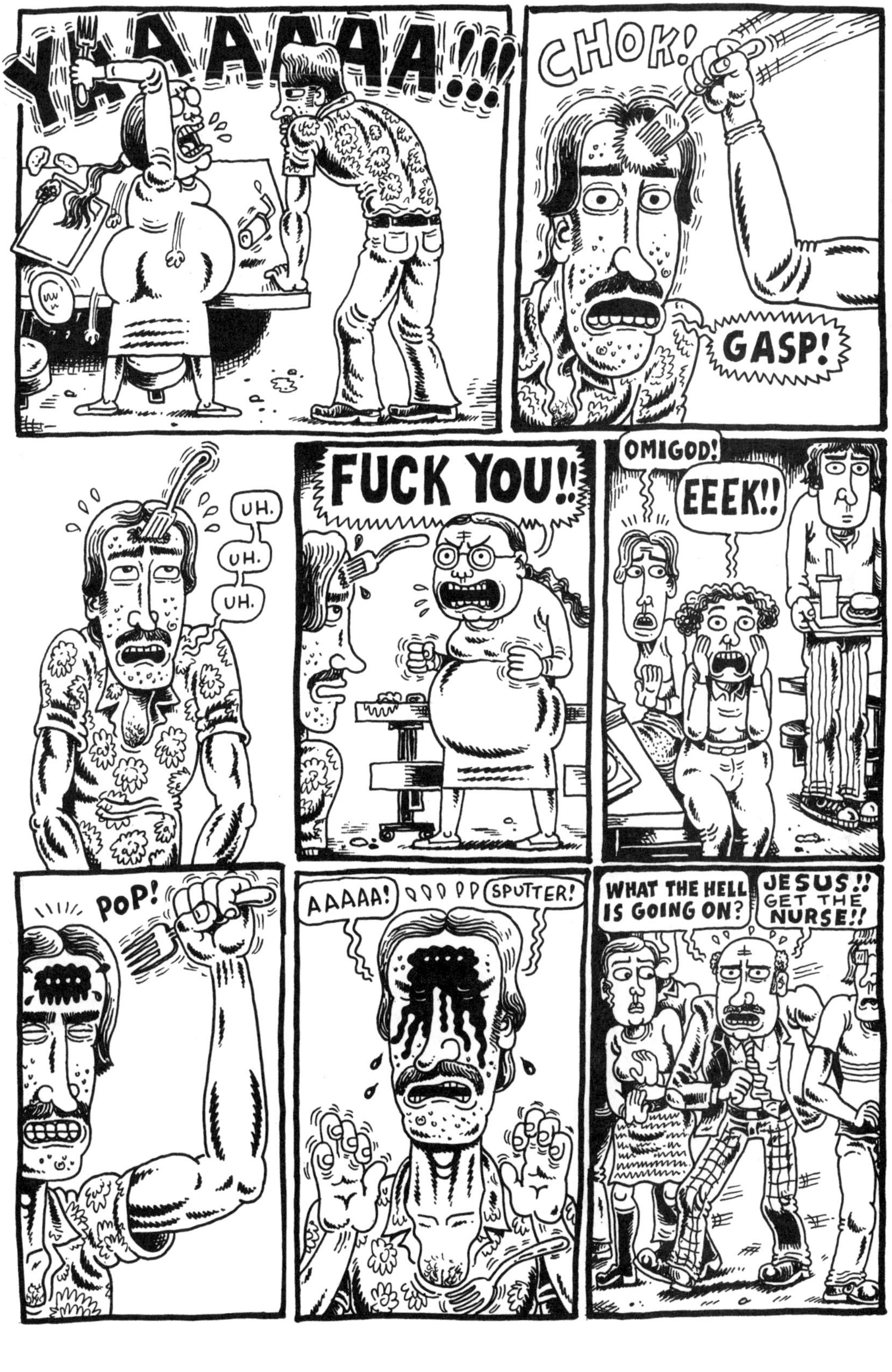
YAAAAAA!!!
CHOK!
GASP!
UH.
UH.
UH.
FUCK YOU!!
OMIGOD!
EEEK!!
POP!
AAAAA!
SPUTTER!
WHAT THE HELL IS GOING ON?
JESUS!! GET THE NURSE!!

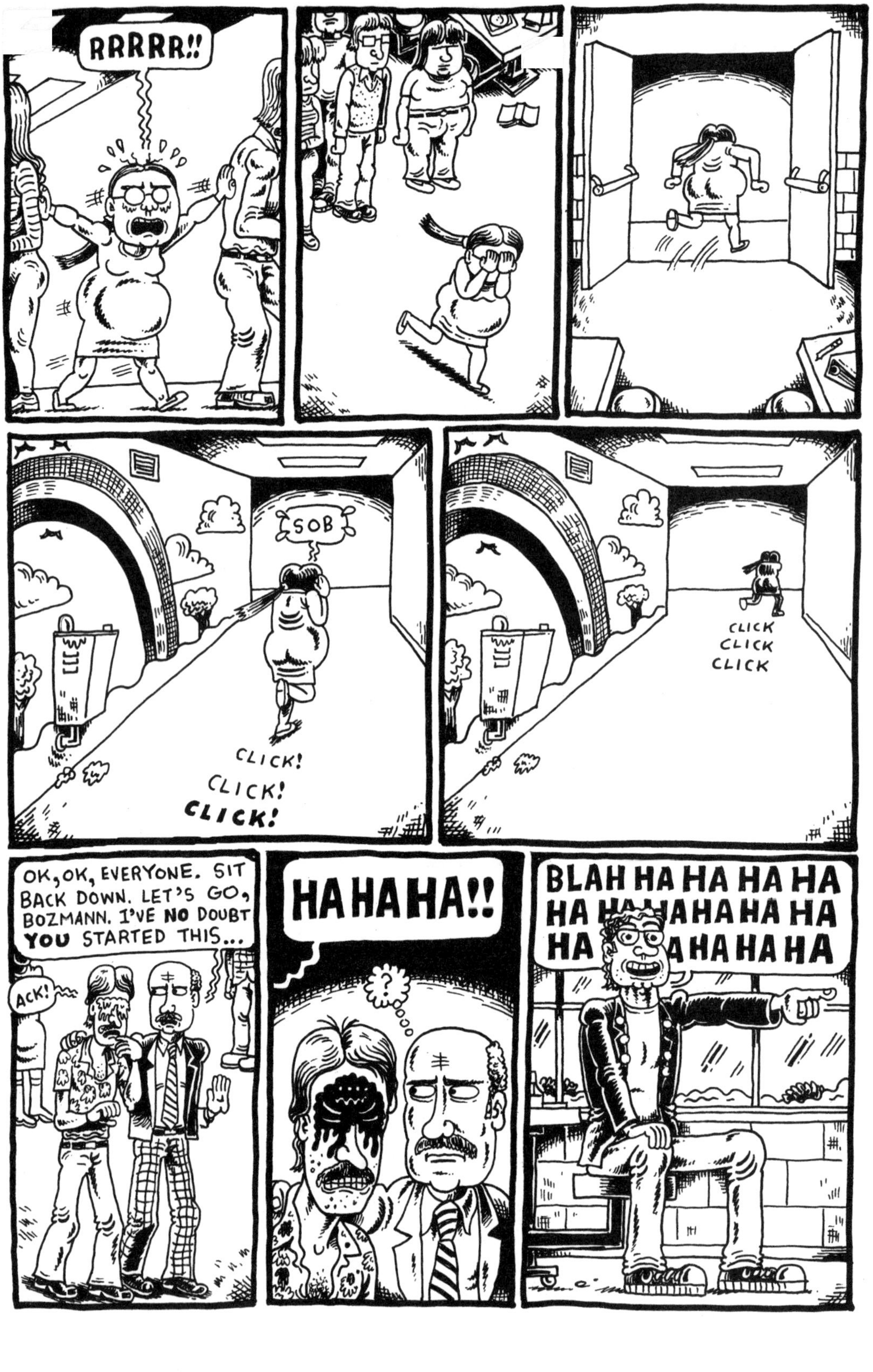
RRRRR!!
SOB
CLICK!
CLICK!
CLICK!
CLICK
CLICK
CLICK
OK, OK, EVERYONE. SIT BACK DOWN. LET'S GO, BOZMANN. I'VE NO DOUBT YOU STARTED THIS...
ACK!
HAHAHA!!
?
BLAH HA HA HA HA
HA HAHAHA HA HA
HA AHA HA HA HA

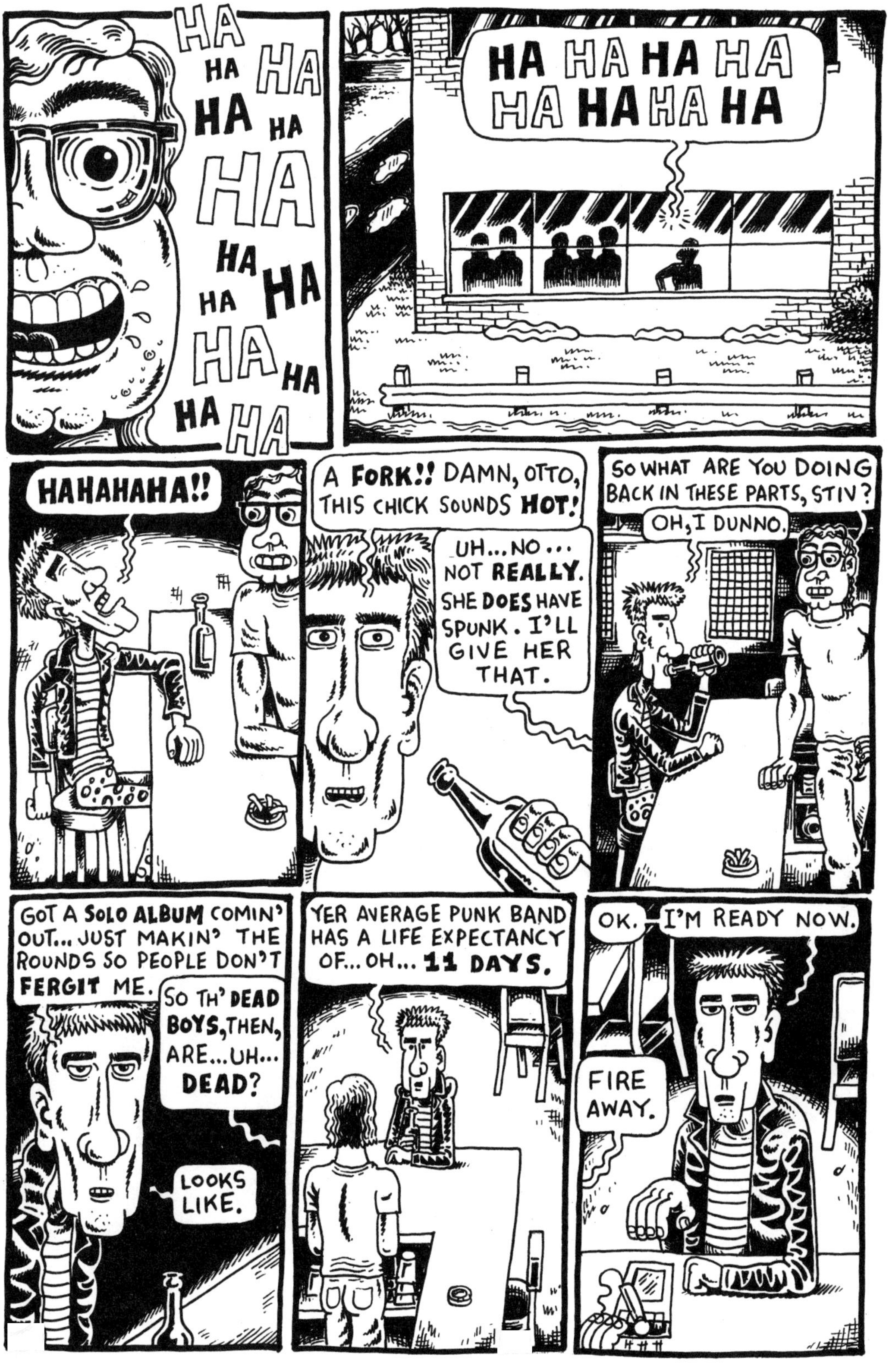
HA HA HA HA HA HA HA HA HA HA HA HA HA HA HA
HA HA HA HA HA HA HA HA HA HA
HAHAHAHA!!
A FORK!! DAMN, OTTO, THIS CHICK SOUNDS HOT!
UH... NO... NOT REALLY. SHE DOES HAVE SPUNK. I'LL GIVE HER THAT.
SO WHAT ARE YOU DOING BACK IN THESE PARTS, STIV?
OH, I DUNNO.
GOT A SOLO ALBUM COMIN' OUT... JUST MAKIN' THE ROUNDS SO PEOPLE DON'T FERGIT ME.
SO TH' DEAD BOYS, THEN, ARE... UH... DEAD?
LOOKS LIKE.
YER AVERAGE PUNK BAND HAS A LIFE EXPECTANCY OF... OH... 11 DAYS.
OK.
I'M READY NOW.
FIRE AWAY.

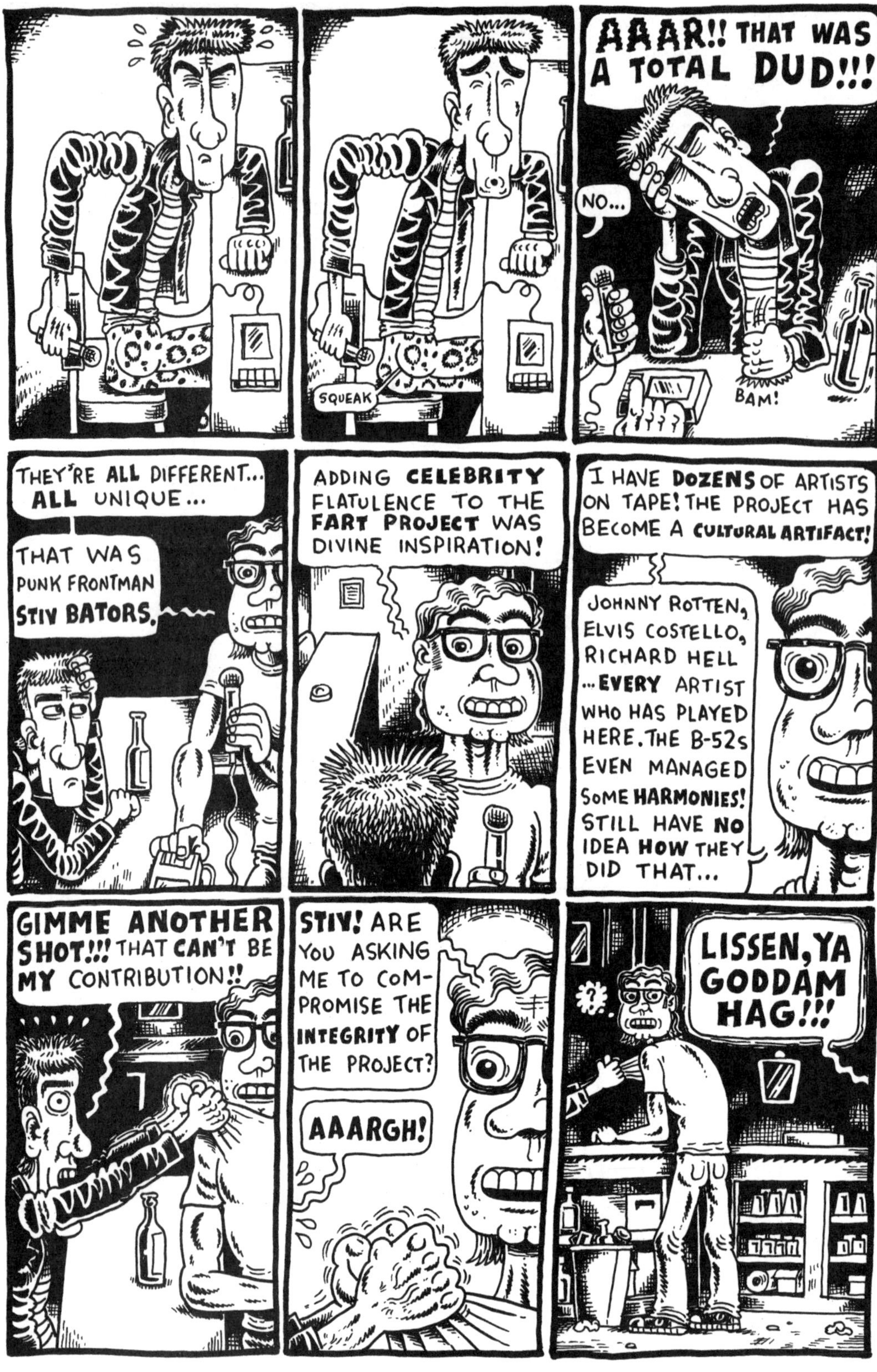
SQUEAK
AAAR!! THAT WAS A TOTAL DUD!!!
NO...
BAM!
THEY'RE ALL DIFFERENT... ALL UNIQUE...
THAT WAS PUNK FRONTMAN STIV BATORS.
ADDING CELEBRITY FLATULENCE TO THE FART PROJECT WAS DIVINE INSPIRATION!
I HAVE DOZENS OF ARTISTS ON TAPE! THE PROJECT HAS BECOME A CULTURAL ARTIFACT!
JOHNNY ROTTEN, ELVIS COSTELLO, RICHARD HELL ...EVERY ARTIST WHO HAS PLAYED HERE. THE B-52s EVEN MANAGED SOME HARMONIES! STILL HAVE NO IDEA HOW THEY DID THAT...
GIMME ANOTHER SHOT!!! THAT CAN'T BE MY CONTRIBUTION!!
STIV! ARE YOU ASKING ME TO COMPROMISE THE INTEGRITY OF THE PROJECT?
AAARGH!
LISSEN, YA GODDAM HAG!!!

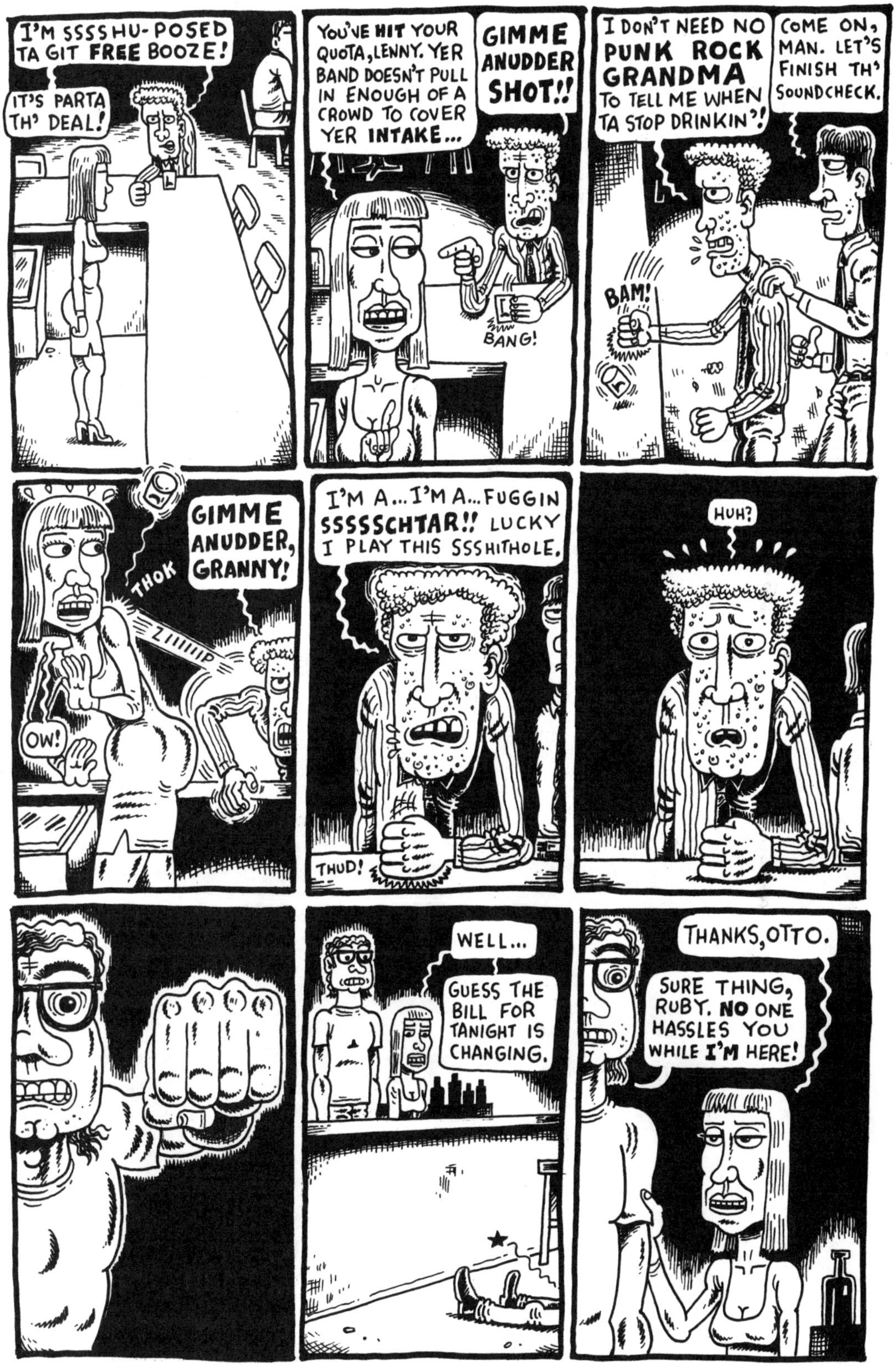

I'M SSSSHU-POSED TA GIT FREE BOOZE!
IT'S PARTA TH' DEAL!
YOU'VE HIT YOUR QUOTA, LENNY. YER BAND DOESN'T PULL IN ENOUGH OF A CROWD TO COVER YER INTAKE...
GIMME ANUDDER SHOT!!
BANG!
I DON'T NEED NO PUNK ROCK GRANDMA TO TELL ME WHEN TA STOP DRINKIN'?!
COME ON, MAN. LET'S FINISH TH' SOUNDCHECK.
BAM!
GIMME ANUDDER, GRANNY!
THOK
ZIIIIIP
OW!
I'M A... I'M A... FUGGIN SSSSSCHTAR!! LUCKY I PLAY THIS SSSHITHOLE.
THUD!
HUH?
WELL...
GUESS THE BILL FOR TANIGHT IS CHANGING.
THANKS, OTTO.
SURE THING, RUBY. NO ONE HASSLES YOU WHILE I'M HERE!

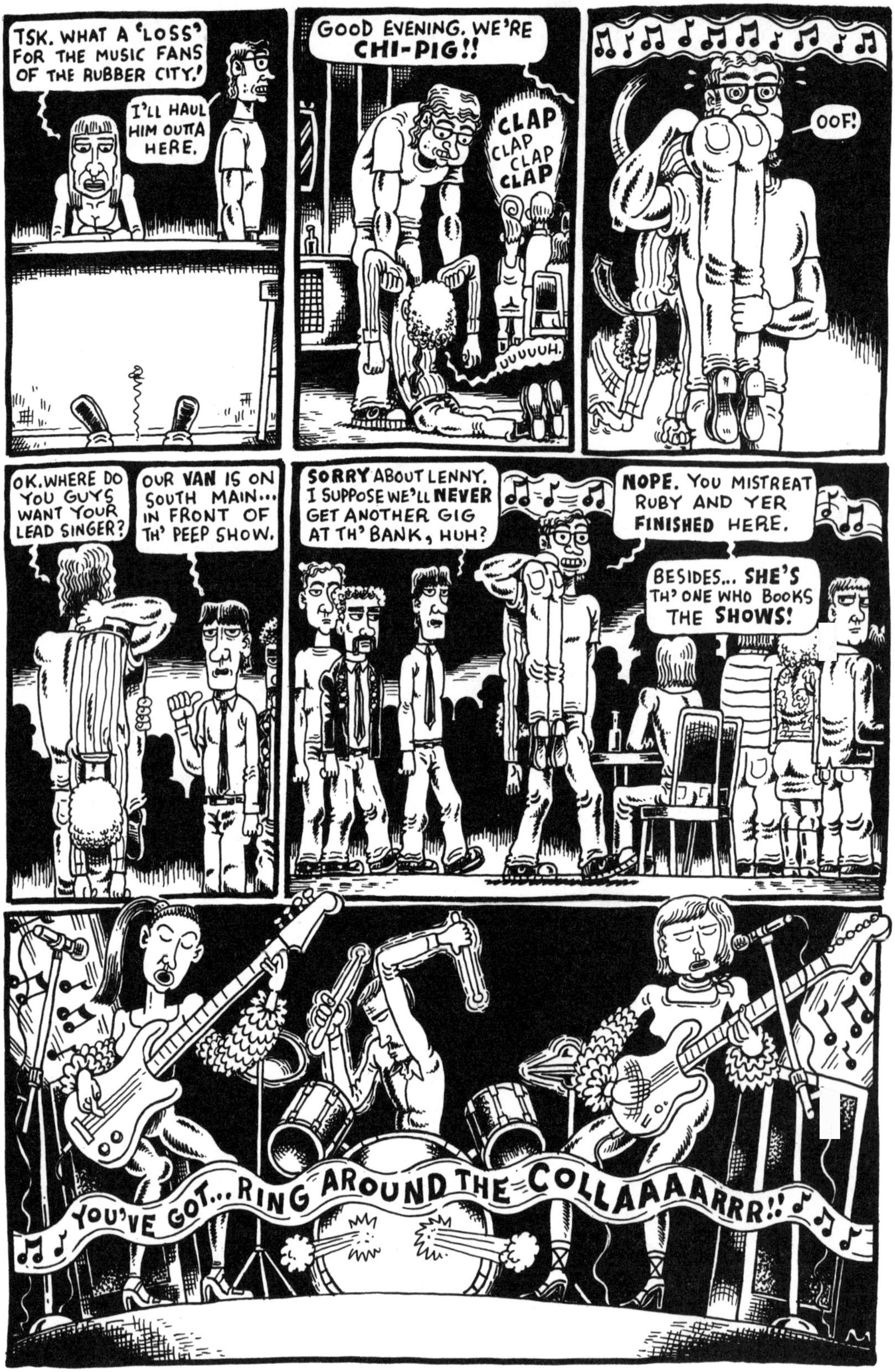
TSK. WHAT A 'LOSS' FOR THE MUSIC FANS OF THE RUBBER CITY!
I'LL HAUL HIM OUTTA HERE.
GOOD EVENING. WE'RE CHI-PIG!!
CLAP CLAP CLAP CLAP
UUUUUH.
OOF!
OK. WHERE DO YOU GUYS WANT YOUR LEAD SINGER?
OUR VAN IS ON SOUTH MAIN... IN FRONT OF TH' PEEP SHOW.
SORRY ABOUT LENNY. I SUPPOSE WE'LL NEVER GET ANOTHER GIG AT TH' BANK, HUH?
NOPE. YOU MISTREAT RUBY AND YER FINISHED HERE.
BESIDES... SHE'S TH' ONE WHO BOOKS THE SHOWS!
YOU'VE GOT... RING AROUND THE COLLAAAARRR!!

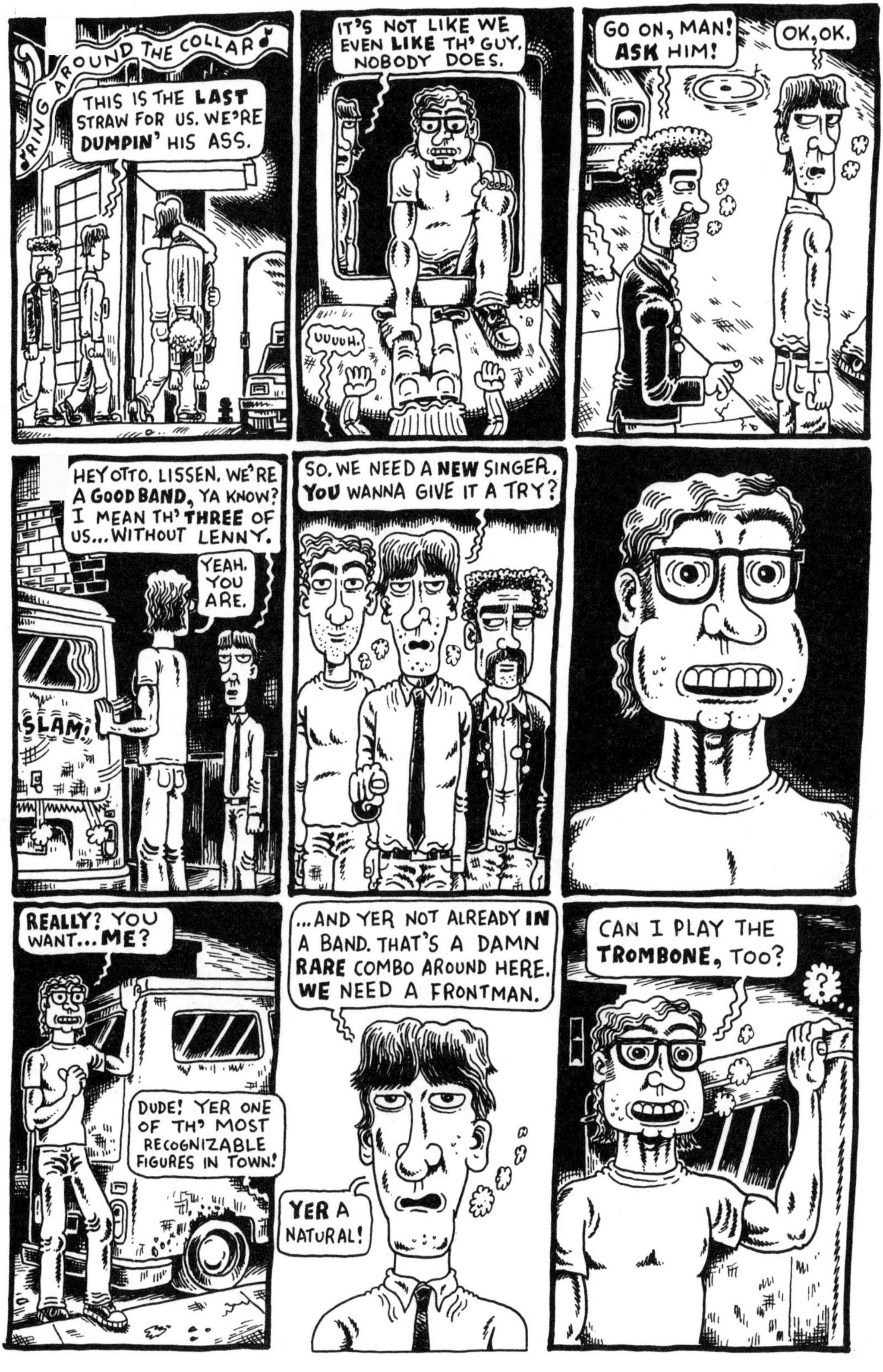
RING AROUND THE COLLAR
THIS IS THE **LAST** STRAW FOR US. WE'RE **DUMPIN'** HIS ASS.
IT'S NOT LIKE WE EVEN **LIKE** TH' GUY. NOBODY DOES.
UUUUH.
GO ON, MAN! **ASK** HIM!
OK, OK.
HEY OTTO. LISSEN. WE'RE A **GOOD BAND**, YA KNOW? I MEAN TH' **THREE** OF US... WITHOUT LENNY.
YEAH. YOU ARE.
SLAM!
SO, WE NEED A **NEW** SINGER. **YOU** WANNA GIVE IT A TRY?
REALLY? YOU WANT... **ME**?
DUDE! YER ONE OF TH' MOST RECOGNIZABLE FIGURES IN TOWN!
...AND YER NOT ALREADY **IN** A BAND. THAT'S A DAMN **RARE** COMBO AROUND HERE. **WE** NEED A FRONTMAN.
YER A NATURAL!
CAN I PLAY THE **TROMBONE**, TOO?
?

THE NEXT DAY...

HEY! HEY BUDDY.

SORRY. DON'T HAVE ANY CHANGE TODAY.

CLICK

HA! I'M **NOT** A BUM! I'M A WRITER...FOR THE VILLAGE VOICE.

I KNOW THERE'S SCANT DIFFERENCE.

I'M DOING AN ARTICLE ON THE **CLASH** SHOW. I WAS TOLD TO HOOK UP WITH A GUY 8 FEET TALL NAMED OTTO.

I'M GUESSING YOU'RE HIM.

I'M LESTER. **LESTER BANGS.**

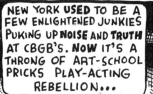

THANKS, MAN. WHAT DO I OWE YOU?

ABBA

PLEASE, LESTER BANGS... OUR GREATEST ROCK CRITIC? **YOU** DRINK **FREE** HERE.

I USED TO READ YOU ALL THE TIME IN **CREEM MAGAZINE.**

A LOYAL SUBSCRIBER?

UH... NO. I COULD ONLY SWING **ONE** MAG SUBSCRIPTION ON THE MEAGER BUDGET OF MY EARLY PUBESCENCE.

NATIONAL LAMPOON HAD A MINIMUM OF TWO SETS OF BARE TITTIES IN EVERY ISSUE. SO **MY** CASH WENT TO THE LAMP!

A WISE CHOICE!

SO. YER DOING AN ARTICLE ON **THE CLASH?**

YEAH. BUT THE NEW YORK SHOWS WERE A HUGE, OBNOXIOUS **SPECTACLE.** I WANT TO SEE THEM OUT HERE IN THE INDUSTRIAL STEPPES.

NEW YORK **USED** TO BE A FEW ENLIGHTENED JUNKIES PUKING UP **NOISE** AND **TRUTH** AT CBGB'S. **NOW** IT'S A THRONG OF ART-SCHOOL PRICKS PLAY-ACTING REBELLION...

WHAT DO **YOU** THINK OF THE NEW ALBUM?

LONDON CALLING? A MASTERPIECE!

YEAH. THE PERFECT MELD OF **BLACK** MUSIC AND **WHITE NOISE.**

ABBA

SO.

WHAT **CULTURAL WONDERS** OF THE **RUBBER CITY** WILL YOU BE SHOWING OUR FRIENDS FROM LONDON...?

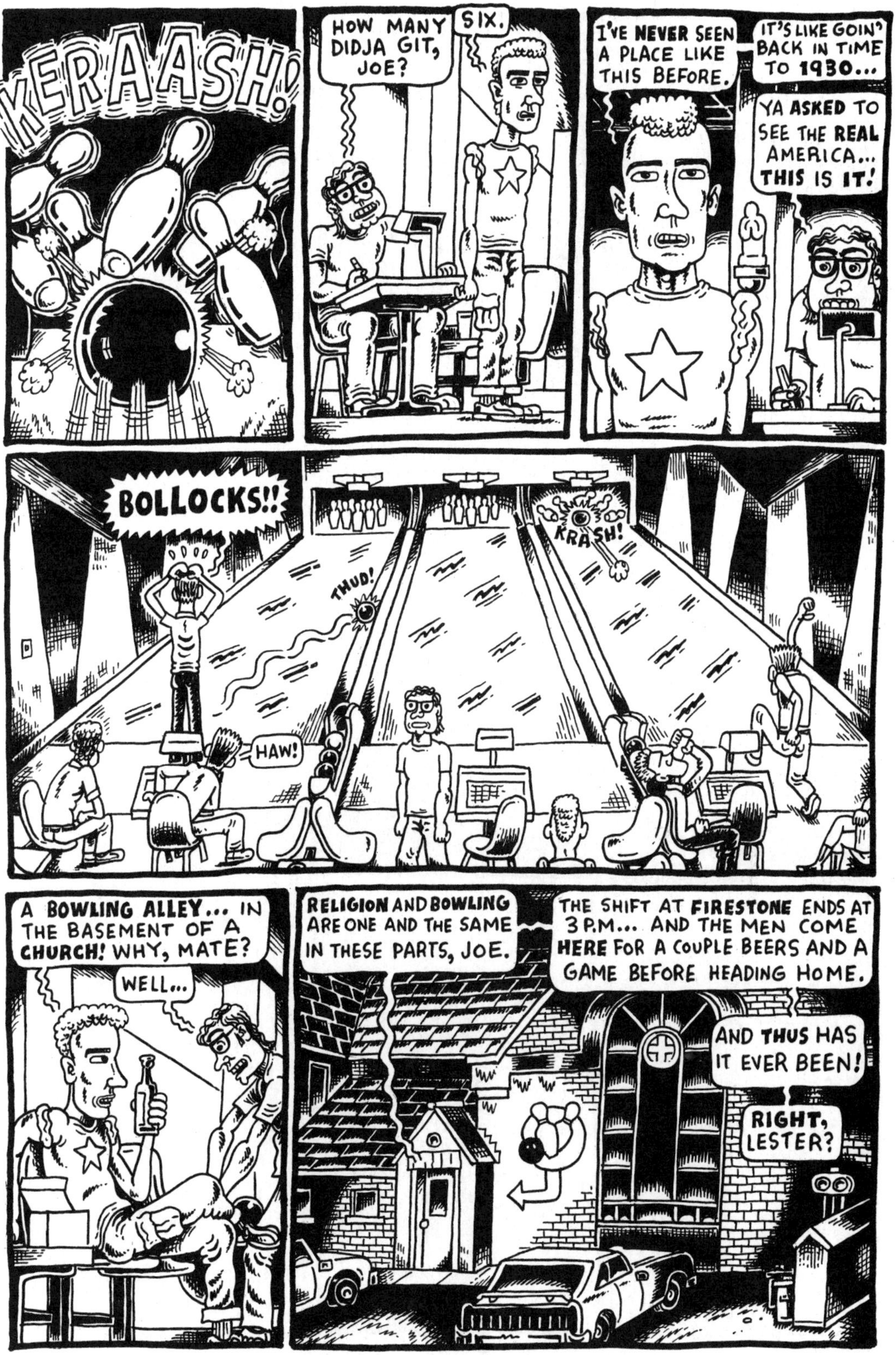
KERAASH!
HOW MANY DIDJA GIT, JOE?
SIX.
I'VE NEVER SEEN A PLACE LIKE THIS BEFORE.
IT'S LIKE GOIN' BACK IN TIME TO 1930...
YA ASKED TO SEE THE REAL AMERICA... THIS IS IT!
BOLLOCKS!!
THUD!
KRASH!
HAW!
A BOWLING ALLEY... IN THE BASEMENT OF A CHURCH! WHY, MATE?
WELL...
RELIGION AND BOWLING ARE ONE AND THE SAME IN THESE PARTS, JOE.
THE SHIFT AT FIRESTONE ENDS AT 3 P.M... AND THE MEN COME HERE FOR A COUPLE BEERS AND A GAME BEFORE HEADING HOME.
AND THUS HAS IT EVER BEEN!
RIGHT, LESTER?

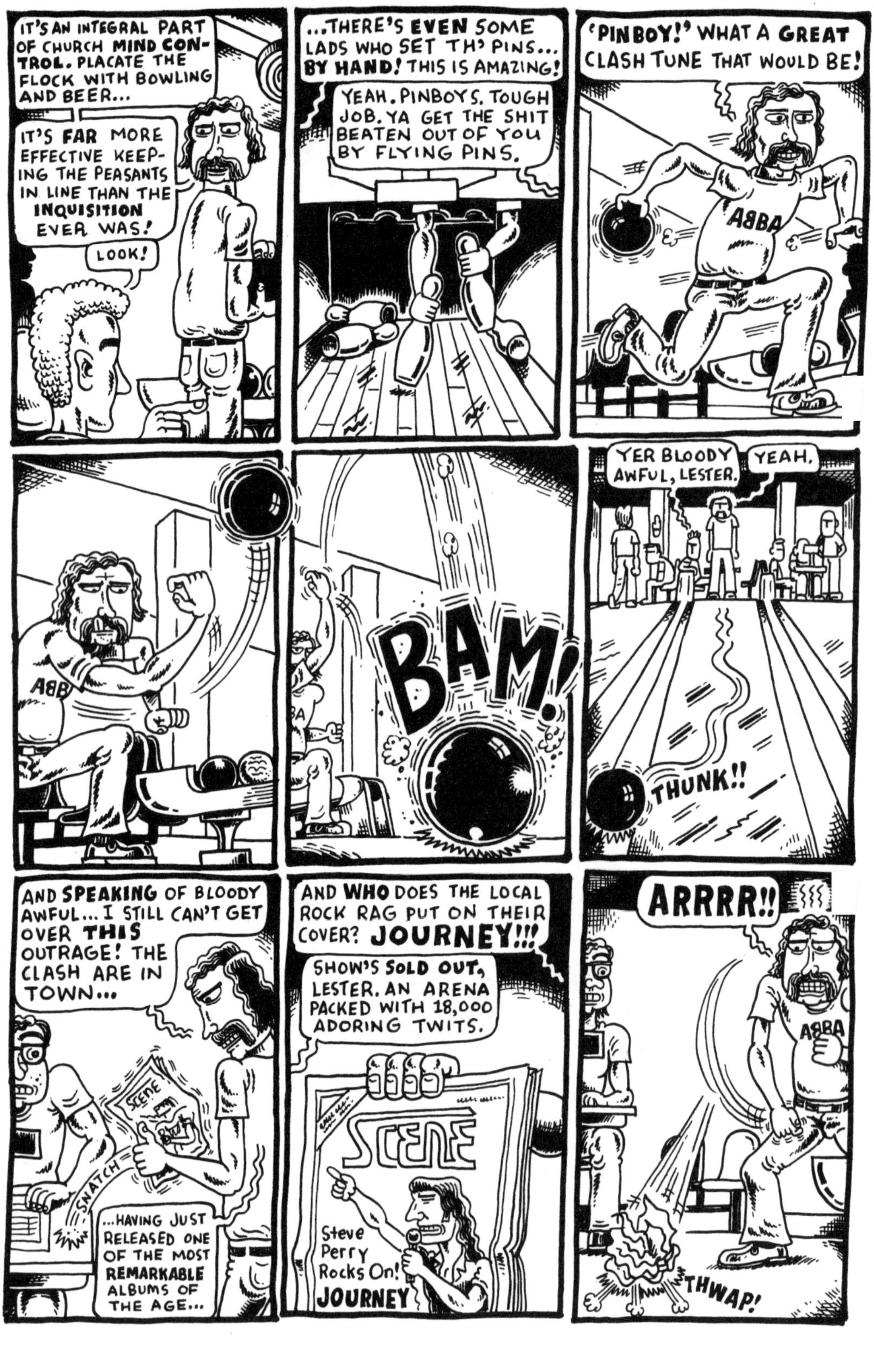
IT'S AN INTEGRAL PART OF CHURCH MIND CONTROL. PLACATE THE FLOCK WITH BOWLING AND BEER...
IT'S FAR MORE EFFECTIVE KEEPING THE PEASANTS IN LINE THAN THE INQUISITION EVER WAS!
LOOK!
...THERE'S EVEN SOME LADS WHO SET TH' PINS... BY HAND! THIS IS AMAZING!
YEAH. PINBOYS. TOUGH JOB. YA GET THE SHIT BEATEN OUT OF YOU BY FLYING PINS.
'PINBOY!' WHAT A GREAT CLASH TUNE THAT WOULD BE!
ABBA
ABB
BAM!
BA
YER BLOODY AWFUL, LESTER.
YEAH.
THUNK!!
AND SPEAKING OF BLOODY AWFUL... I STILL CAN'T GET OVER THIS OUTRAGE! THE CLASH ARE IN TOWN...
SCENE
SNATCH
...HAVING JUST RELEASED ONE OF THE MOST REMARKABLE ALBUMS OF THE AGE...
AND WHO DOES THE LOCAL ROCK RAG PUT ON THEIR COVER? JOURNEY!!!
SHOW'S SOLD OUT, LESTER. AN ARENA PACKED WITH 18,000 ADORING TWITS.
SCENE
Steve Perry Rocks On!
JOURNEY
ARRRR!!
ABBA
THWAP!

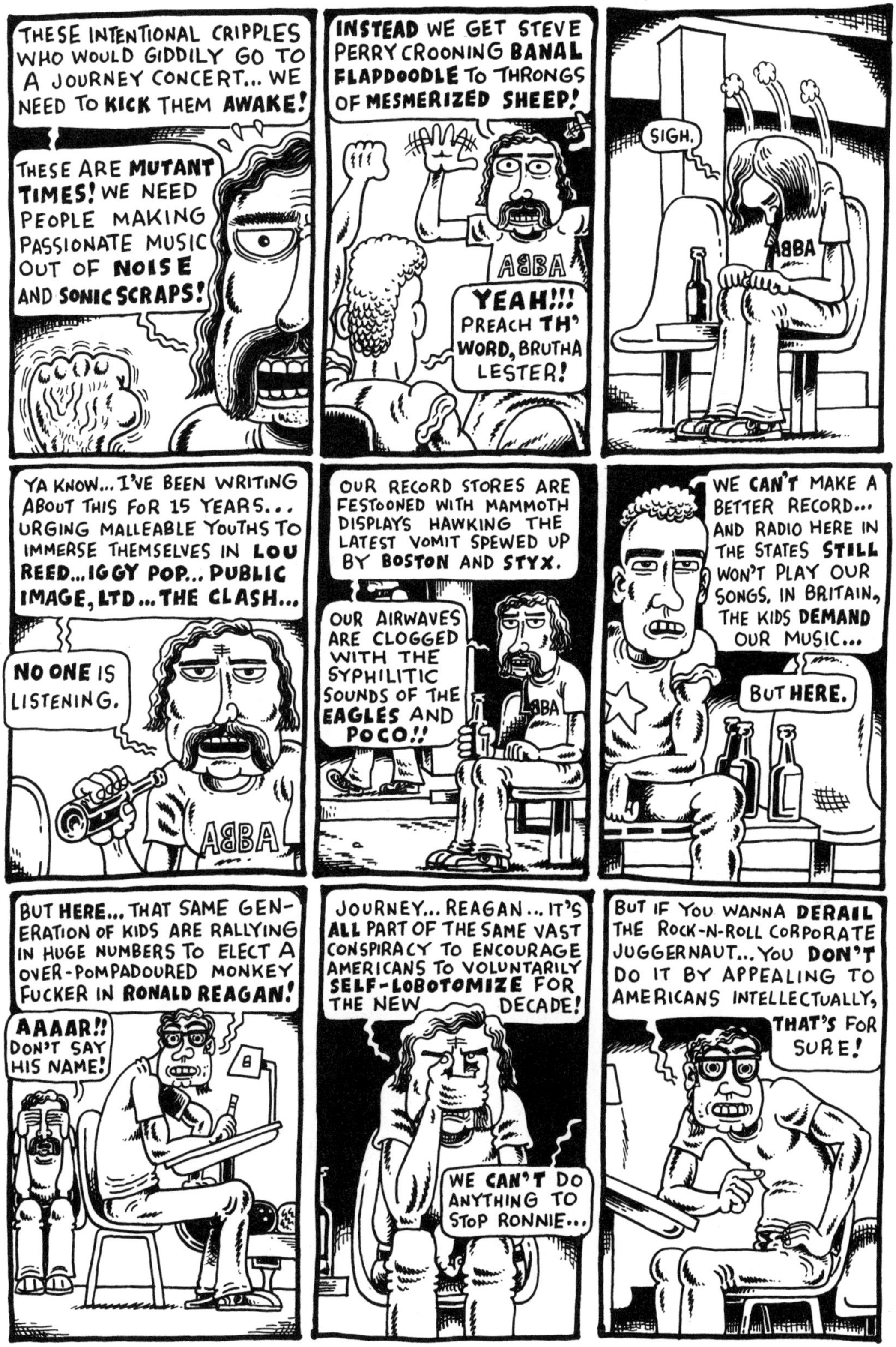
THESE INTENTIONAL CRIPPLES WHO WOULD GIDDILY GO TO A JOURNEY CONCERT... WE NEED TO KICK THEM AWAKE!
THESE ARE MUTANT TIMES! WE NEED PEOPLE MAKING PASSIONATE MUSIC OUT OF NOISE AND SONIC SCRAPS!
INSTEAD WE GET STEVE PERRY CROONING BANAL FLAPDOODLE TO THRONGS OF MESMERIZED SHEEP!
ABBA
YEAH!!! PREACH TH' WORD, BRUTHA LESTER!
SIGH.
ABBA
YA KNOW... I'VE BEEN WRITING ABOUT THIS FOR 15 YEARS... URGING MALLEABLE YOUTHS TO IMMERSE THEMSELVES IN LOU REED... IGGY POP... PUBLIC IMAGE, LTD... THE CLASH...
NO ONE IS LISTENING.
ABBA
OUR RECORD STORES ARE FESTOONED WITH MAMMOTH DISPLAYS HAWKING THE LATEST VOMIT SPEWED UP BY BOSTON AND STYX.
OUR AIRWAVES ARE CLOGGED WITH THE SYPHILITIC SOUNDS OF THE EAGLES AND POCO!!
ABBA
WE CAN'T MAKE A BETTER RECORD... AND RADIO HERE IN THE STATES STILL WON'T PLAY OUR SONGS. IN BRITAIN, THE KIDS DEMAND OUR MUSIC...
BUT HERE.
BUT HERE... THAT SAME GENERATION OF KIDS ARE RALLYING IN HUGE NUMBERS TO ELECT A OVER-POMPADOURED MONKEY FUCKER IN RONALD REAGAN!
AAAAR!! DON'T SAY HIS NAME!
JOURNEY... REAGAN... IT'S ALL PART OF THE SAME VAST CONSPIRACY TO ENCOURAGE AMERICANS TO VOLUNTARILY SELF-LOBOTOMIZE FOR THE NEW DECADE!
WE CAN'T DO ANYTHING TO STOP RONNIE...
BUT IF YOU WANNA DERAIL THE ROCK-N-ROLL CORPORATE JUGGERNAUT... YOU DON'T DO IT BY APPEALING TO AMERICANS INTELLECTUALLY,
THAT'S FOR SURE!

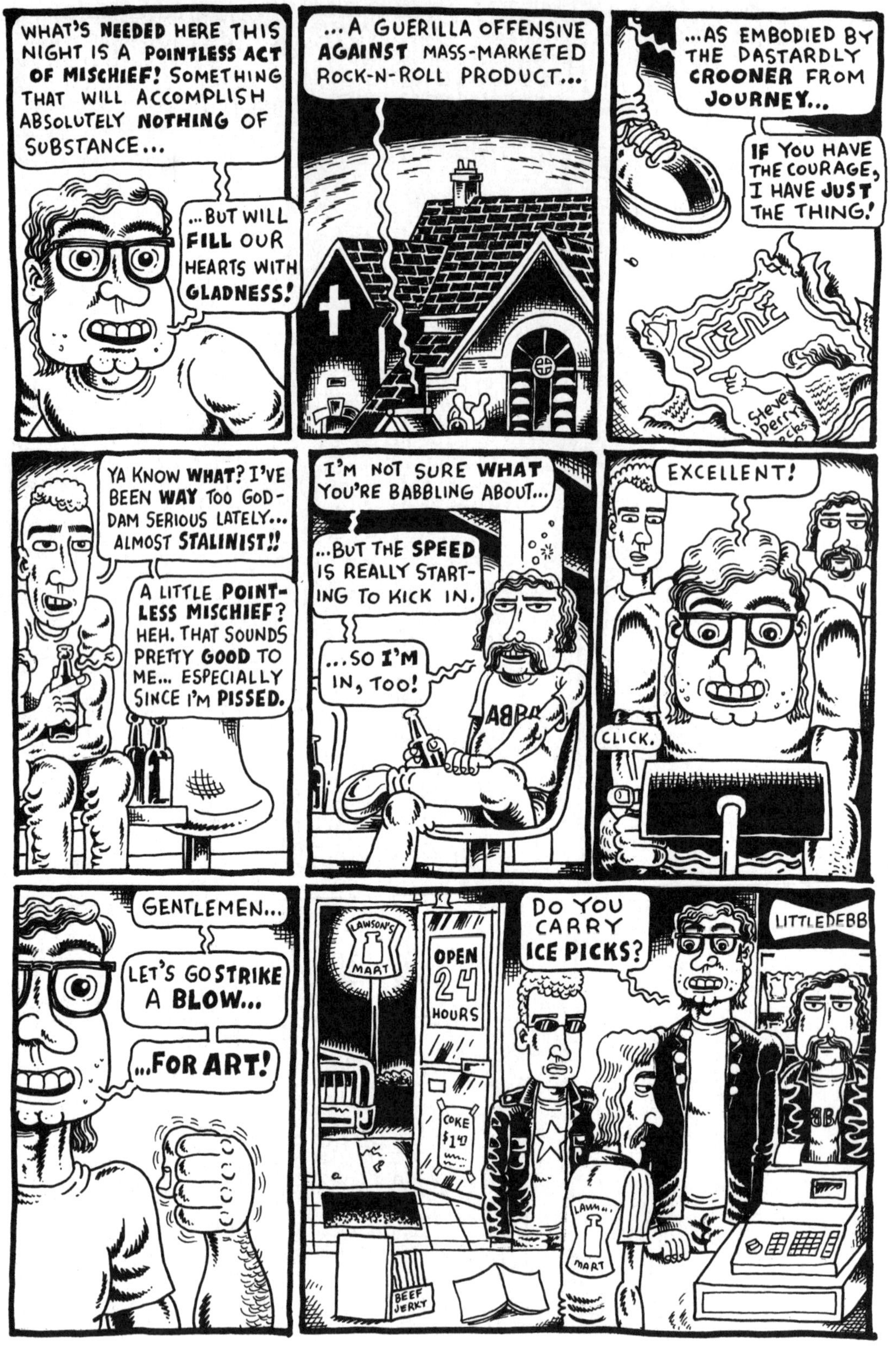
WHAT'S NEEDED HERE THIS NIGHT IS A POINTLESS ACT OF MISCHIEF! SOMETHING THAT WILL ACCOMPLISH ABSOLUTELY NOTHING OF SUBSTANCE...
...BUT WILL FILL OUR HEARTS WITH GLADNESS!
...A GUERILLA OFFENSIVE AGAINST MASS-MARKETED ROCK-N-ROLL PRODUCT...
...AS EMBODIED BY THE DASTARDLY CROONER FROM JOURNEY...
IF YOU HAVE THE COURAGE, I HAVE JUST THE THING!
SCENE
Steve Perry
YA KNOW WHAT? I'VE BEEN WAY TOO GOD-DAM SERIOUS LATELY... ALMOST STALINIST!!
A LITTLE POINTLESS MISCHIEF? HEH. THAT SOUNDS PRETTY GOOD TO ME... ESPECIALLY SINCE I'M PISSED.
I'M NOT SURE WHAT YOU'RE BABBLING ABOUT...
...BUT THE SPEED IS REALLY STARTING TO KICK IN.
...SO I'M IN, TOO!
ABBA
EXCELLENT!
CLICK.
GENTLEMEN...
LET'S GO STRIKE A BLOW...
...FOR ART!
LAWSON'S MART
OPEN 24 HOURS
COKE $1.47
DO YOU CARRY ICE PICKS?
LITTLE DEBB
BEEF JERKY
MART

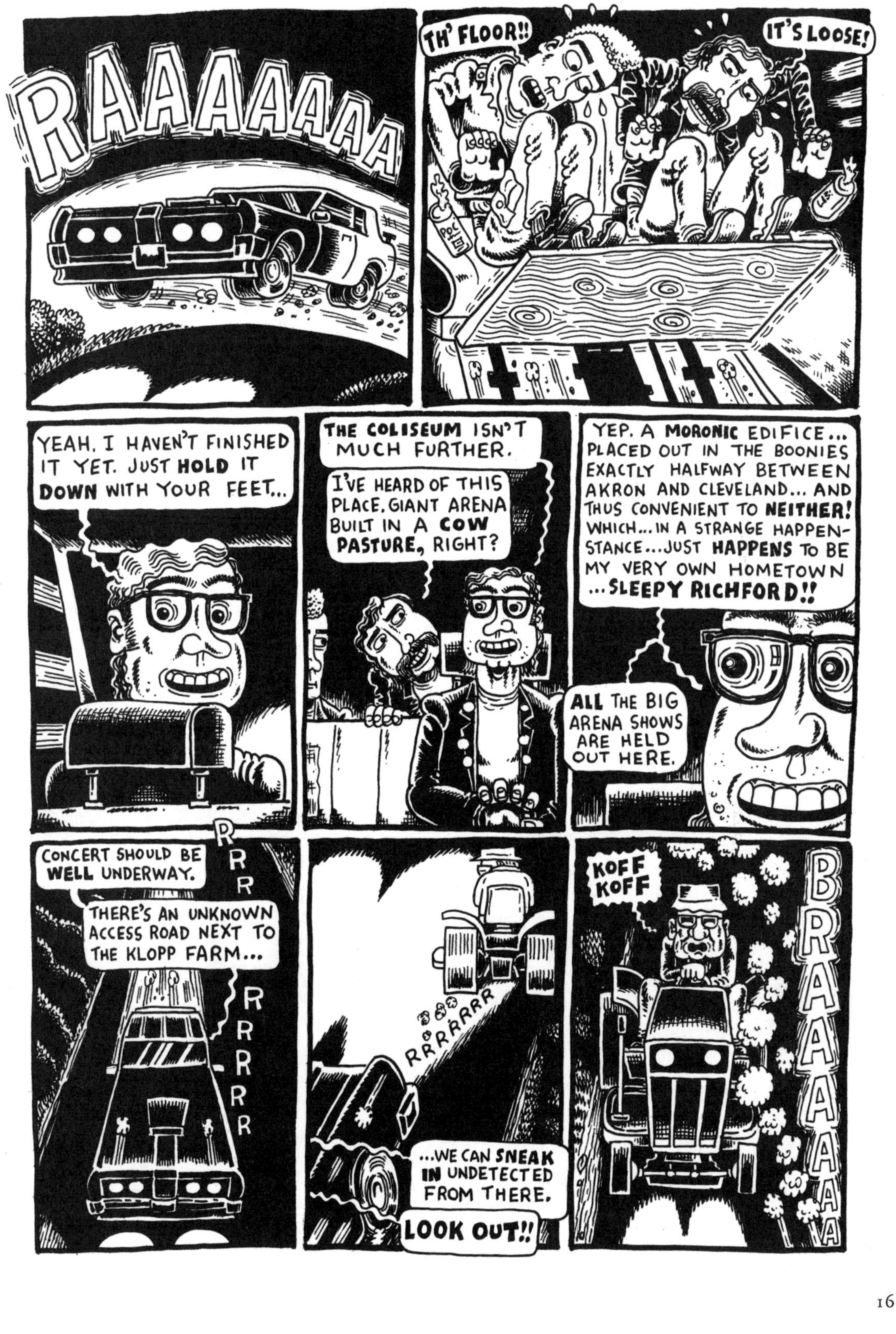

RAAAAAAA
TH' FLOOR!!
IT'S LOOSE!
YEAH. I HAVEN'T FINISHED IT YET. JUST HOLD IT DOWN WITH YOUR FEET...
THE COLISEUM ISN'T MUCH FURTHER.
I'VE HEARD OF THIS PLACE. GIANT ARENA BUILT IN A COW PASTURE, RIGHT?
YEP. A MORONIC EDIFICE... PLACED OUT IN THE BOONIES EXACTLY HALFWAY BETWEEN AKRON AND CLEVELAND... AND THUS CONVENIENT TO NEITHER! WHICH... IN A STRANGE HAPPENSTANCE... JUST HAPPENS TO BE MY VERY OWN HOMETOWN ...SLEEPY RICHFORD!!
ALL THE BIG ARENA SHOWS ARE HELD OUT HERE.
RRR
CONCERT SHOULD BE WELL UNDERWAY.
THERE'S AN UNKNOWN ACCESS ROAD NEXT TO THE KLOPP FARM...
RRRRR
RRRRRRR
...WE CAN SNEAK IN UNDETECTED FROM THERE.
LOOK OUT!!
KOFF KOFF
BRAAAAAAAA

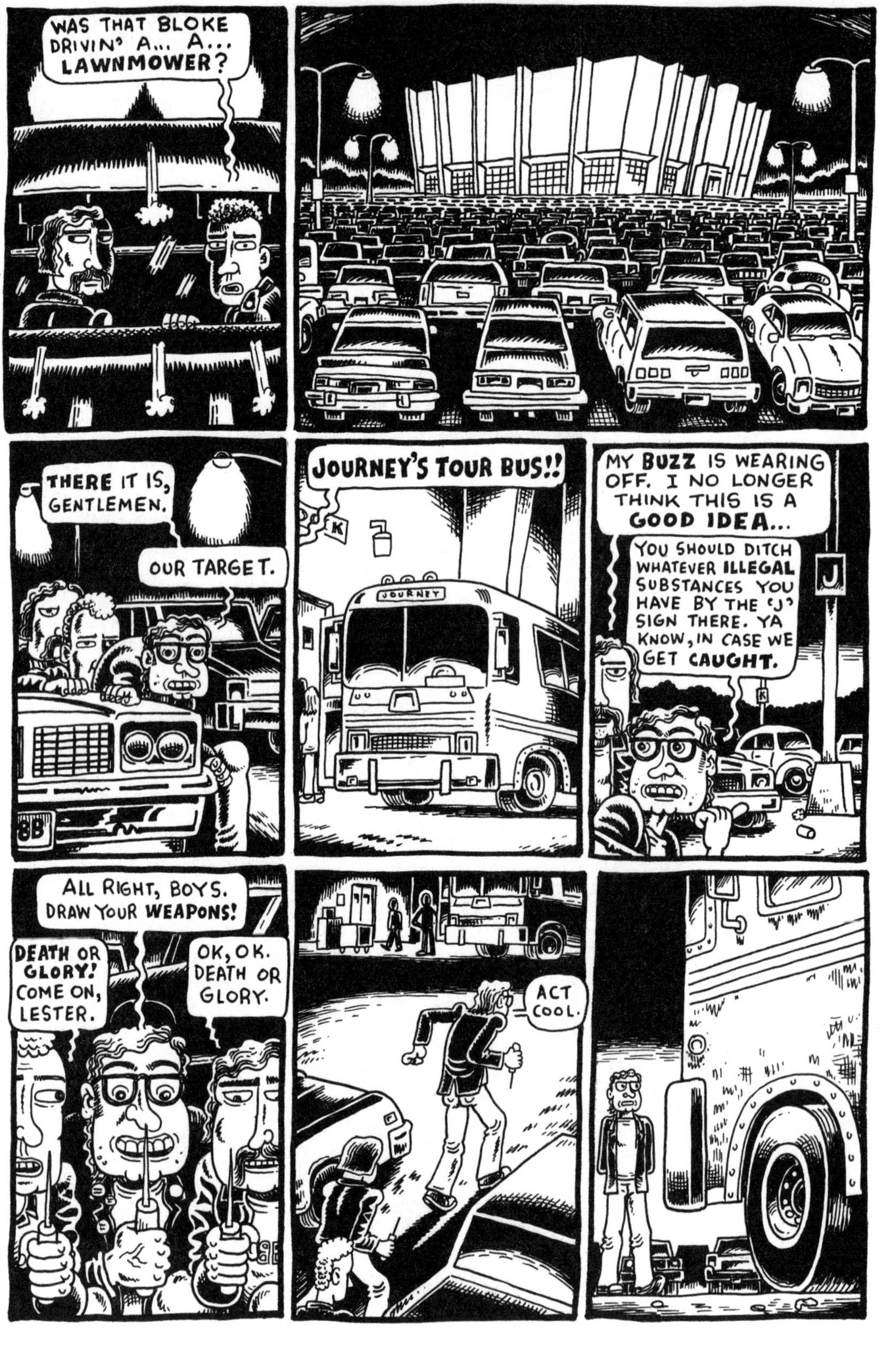
WAS THAT BLOKE DRIVIN' A... A... LAWNMOWER?
THERE IT IS, GENTLEMEN.
OUR TARGET.
JOURNEY'S TOUR BUS!!
MY BUZZ IS WEARING OFF. I NO LONGER THINK THIS IS A GOOD IDEA...
YOU SHOULD DITCH WHATEVER ILLEGAL SUBSTANCES YOU HAVE BY THE 'J' SIGN THERE. YA KNOW, IN CASE WE GET CAUGHT.
ALL RIGHT, BOYS. DRAW YOUR WEAPONS!
DEATH OR GLORY! COME ON, LESTER.
OK, OK. DEATH OR GLORY.
ACT COOL.

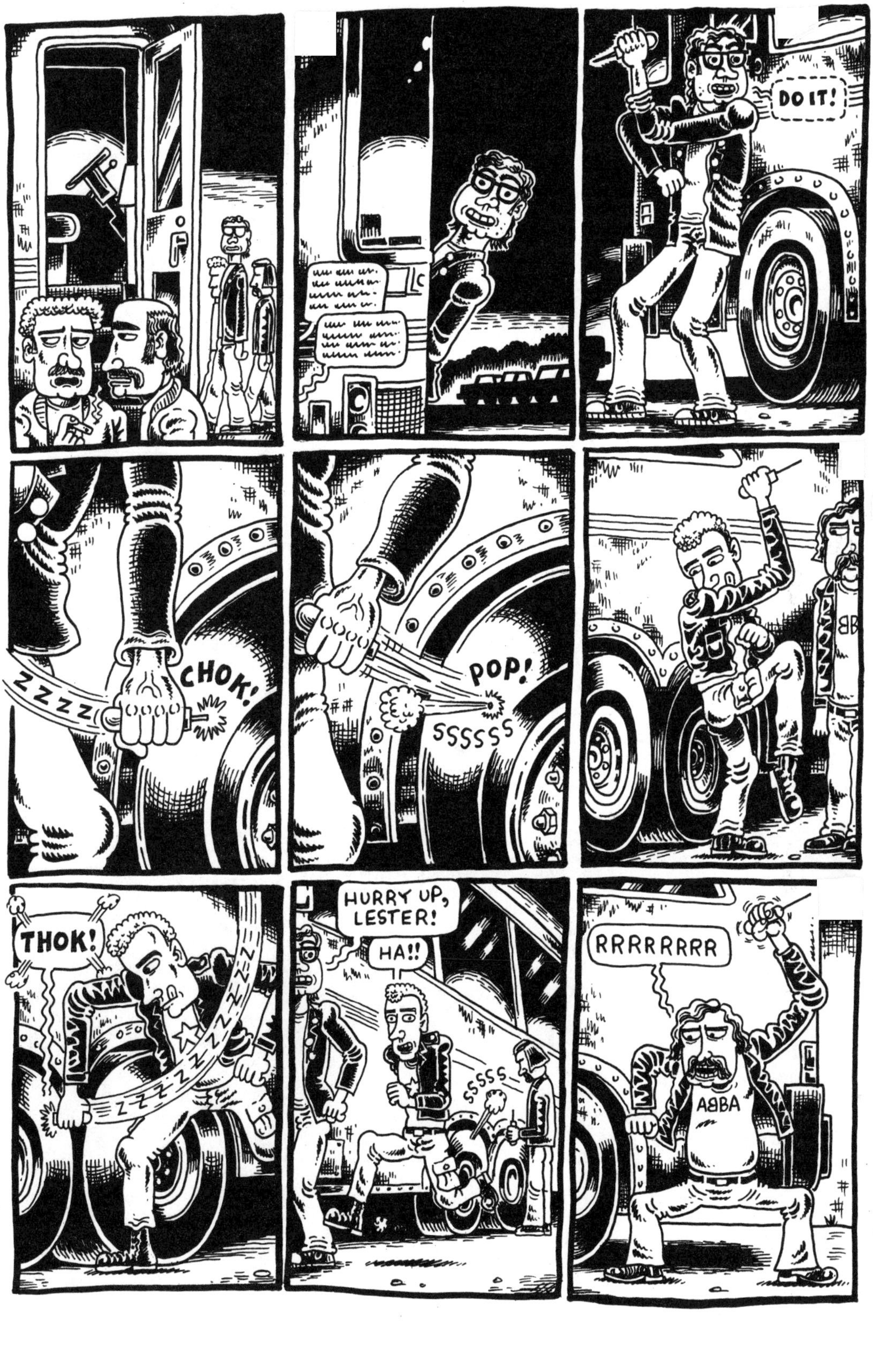
DO IT!
CHOK!
ZZZZ
POP!
SSSSSS
THOK!
HURRY UP, LESTER!
HA!!
SSSSS
RRRRRRRR
ABBA

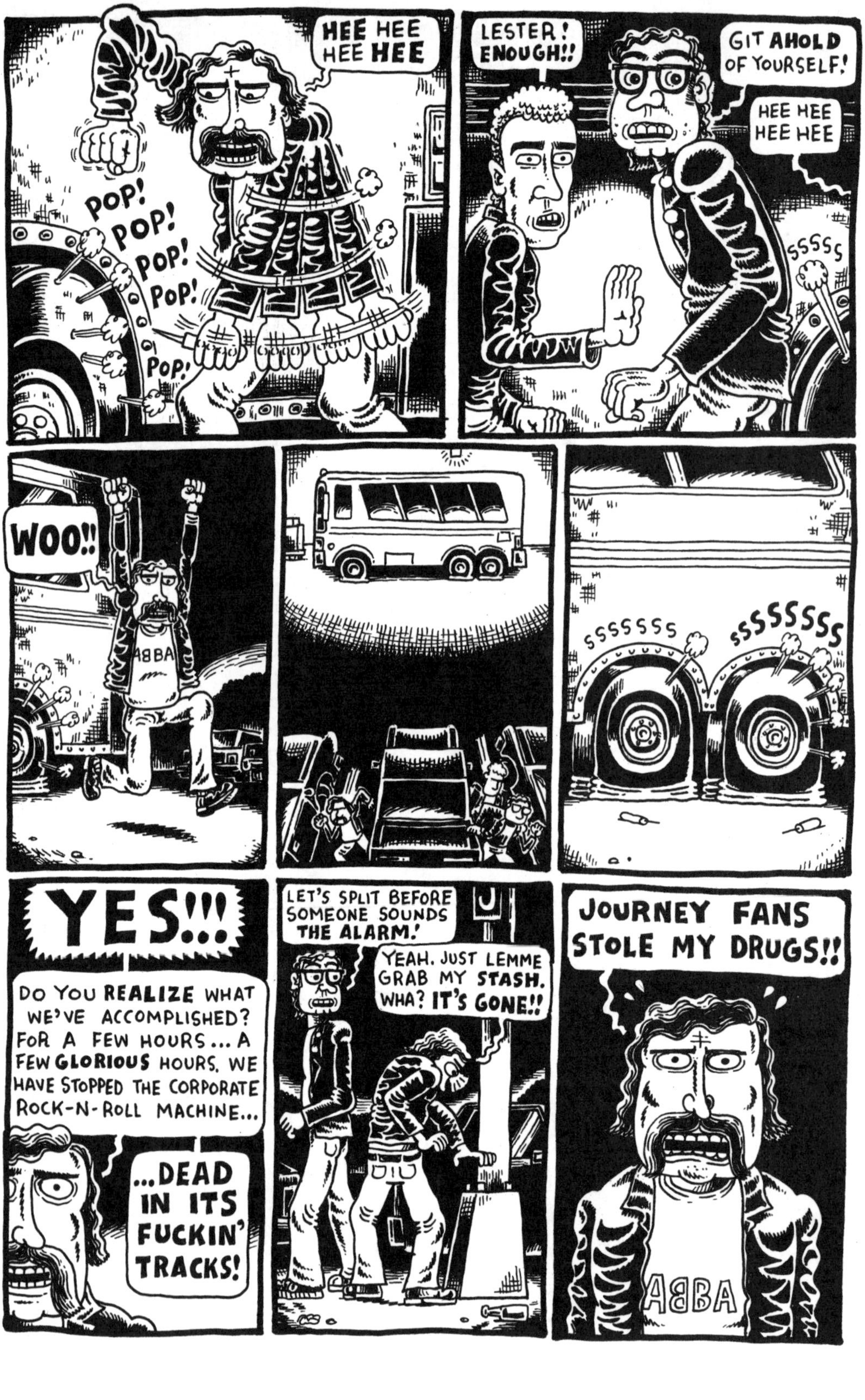
HEE HEE HEE HEE
POP! POP! POP! POP! POP!
LESTER! ENOUGH!!
GIT AHOLD OF YOURSELF!
HEE HEE HEE HEE
SSSSS
WOO!!
ABBA
SSSSSSS
SSSSSSSS
YES!!!
DO YOU REALIZE WHAT WE'VE ACCOMPLISHED? FOR A FEW HOURS... A FEW GLORIOUS HOURS, WE HAVE STOPPED THE CORPORATE ROCK-N-ROLL MACHINE...
...DEAD IN ITS FUCKIN' TRACKS!
LET'S SPLIT BEFORE SOMEONE SOUNDS THE ALARM!
YEAH. JUST LEMME GRAB MY STASH. WHA? IT'S GONE!!
JOURNEY FANS STOLE MY DRUGS!!
ABBA

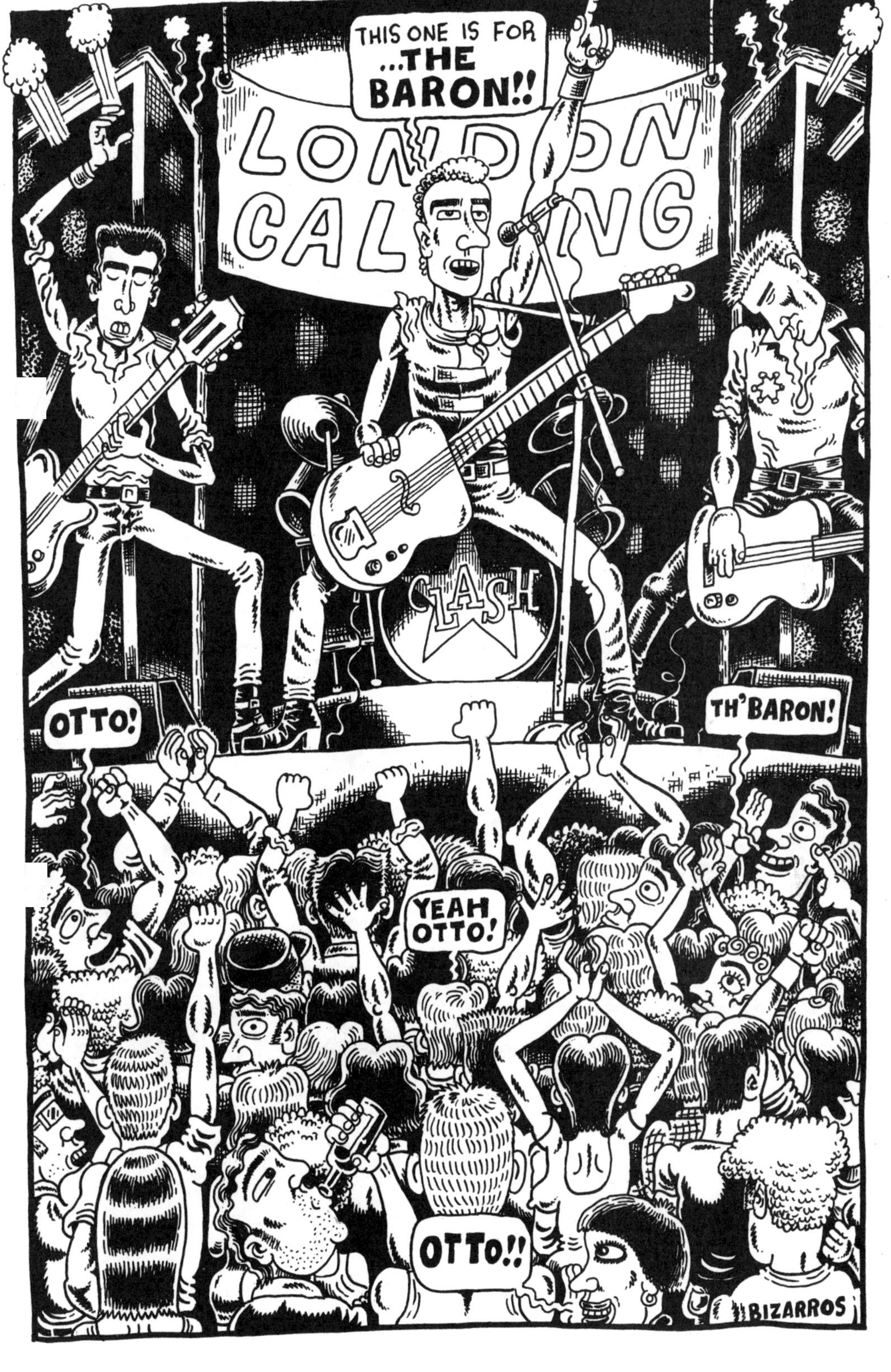
THIS ONE IS FOR ...THE BARON!!
LONDON CALLING
CLASH
OTTO!
TH'BARON!
YEAH OTTO!
OTTO!!
BIZARROS

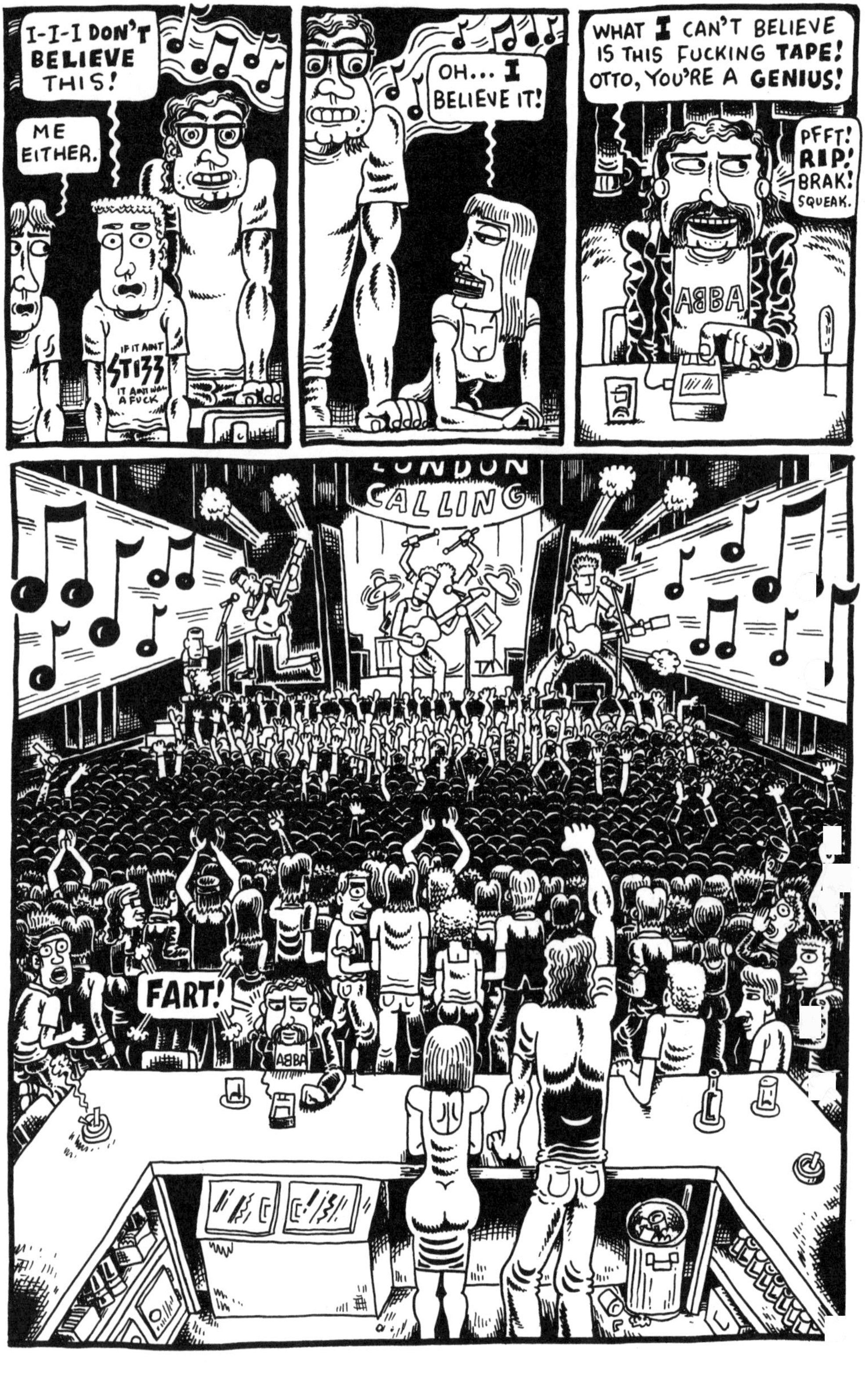
I-I-I DON'T BELIEVE THIS!
ME EITHER.
IF IT AINT STI33 IT AINT WORTH A FUCK
OH... I BELIEVE IT!
WHAT I CAN'T BELIEVE IS THIS FUCKING TAPE! OTTO, YOU'RE A GENIUS!
PFFT! RIP! BRAK! SQUEAK.
ABBA
LONDON CALLING
FART!
ABBA

TITANIC URINATION *from a dream by Max McBarron*

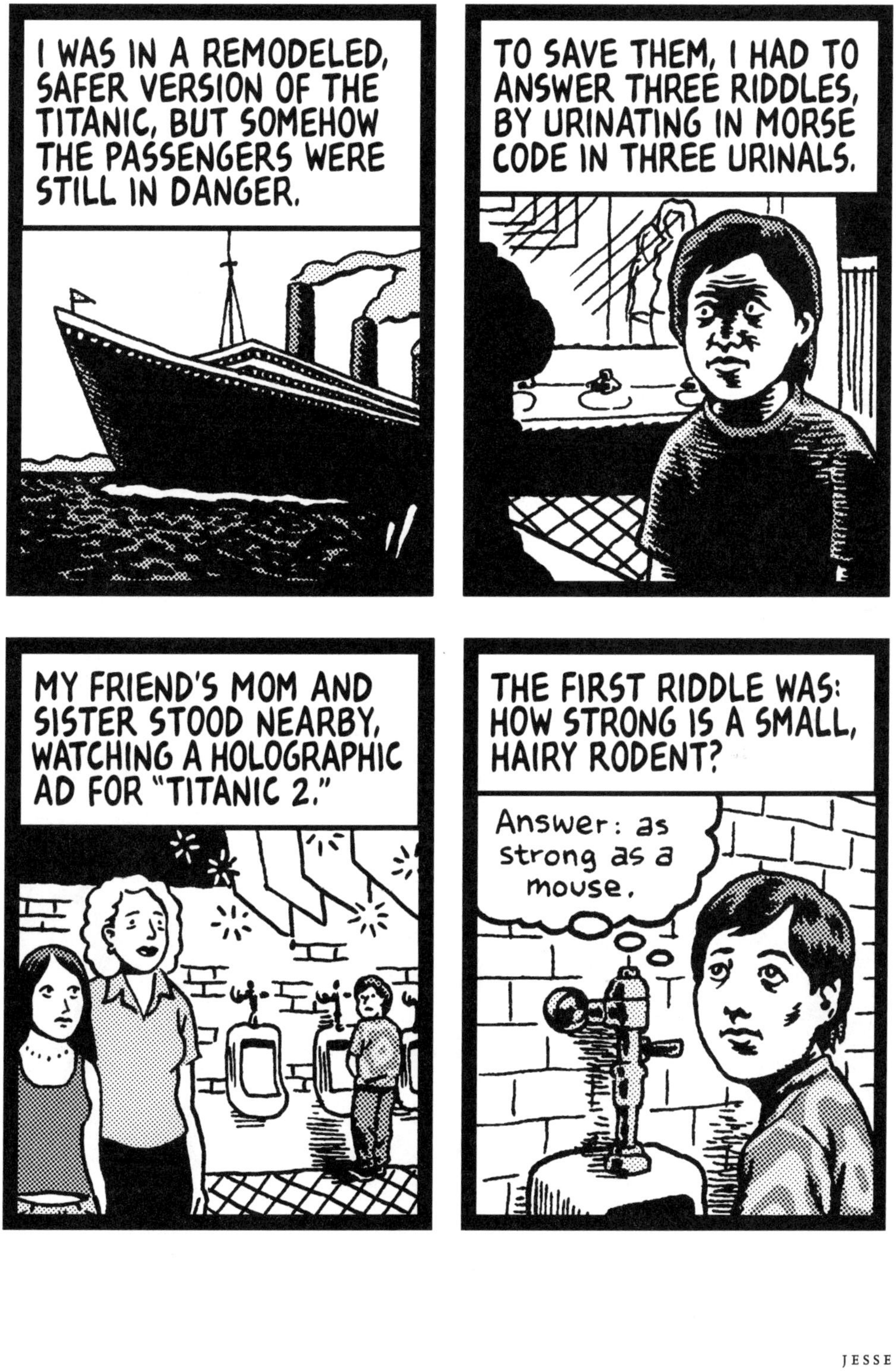

I WAS IN A REMODELED, SAFER VERSION OF THE TITANIC, BUT SOMEHOW THE PASSENGERS WERE STILL IN DANGER.
TO SAVE THEM, I HAD TO ANSWER THREE RIDDLES, BY URINATING IN MORSE CODE IN THREE URINALS.
MY FRIEND'S MOM AND SISTER STOOD NEARBY, WATCHING A HOLOGRAPHIC AD FOR "TITANIC 2."
THE FIRST RIDDLE WAS: HOW STRONG IS A SMALL, HAIRY RODENT?
Answer: as strong as a mouse.

HOOKER COOKIES

from a dream by Mabel Stark

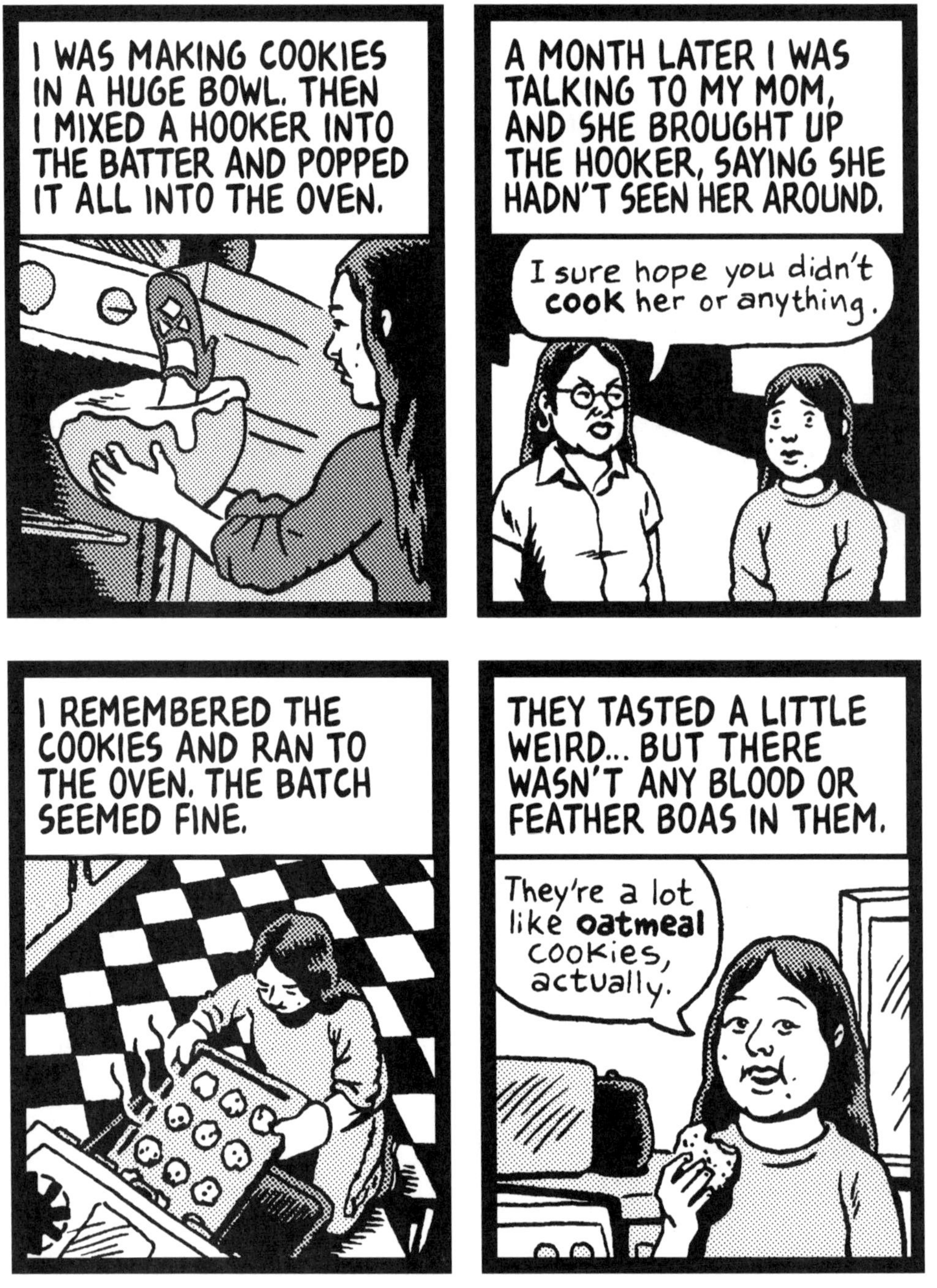
I WAS MAKING COOKIES IN A HUGE BOWL. THEN I MIXED A HOOKER INTO THE BATTER AND POPPED IT ALL INTO THE OVEN.
A MONTH LATER I WAS TALKING TO MY MOM, AND SHE BROUGHT UP THE HOOKER, SAYING SHE HADN'T SEEN HER AROUND.
I sure hope you didn't **cook** her or anything.
I REMEMBERED THE COOKIES AND RAN TO THE OVEN. THE BATCH SEEMED FINE.
THEY TASTED A LITTLE WEIRD... BUT THERE WASN'T ANY BLOOD OR FEATHER BOAS IN THEM.
They're a lot like **oatmeal** cookies, actually.

DUCK MOM

from a dream by Chloe Pollon

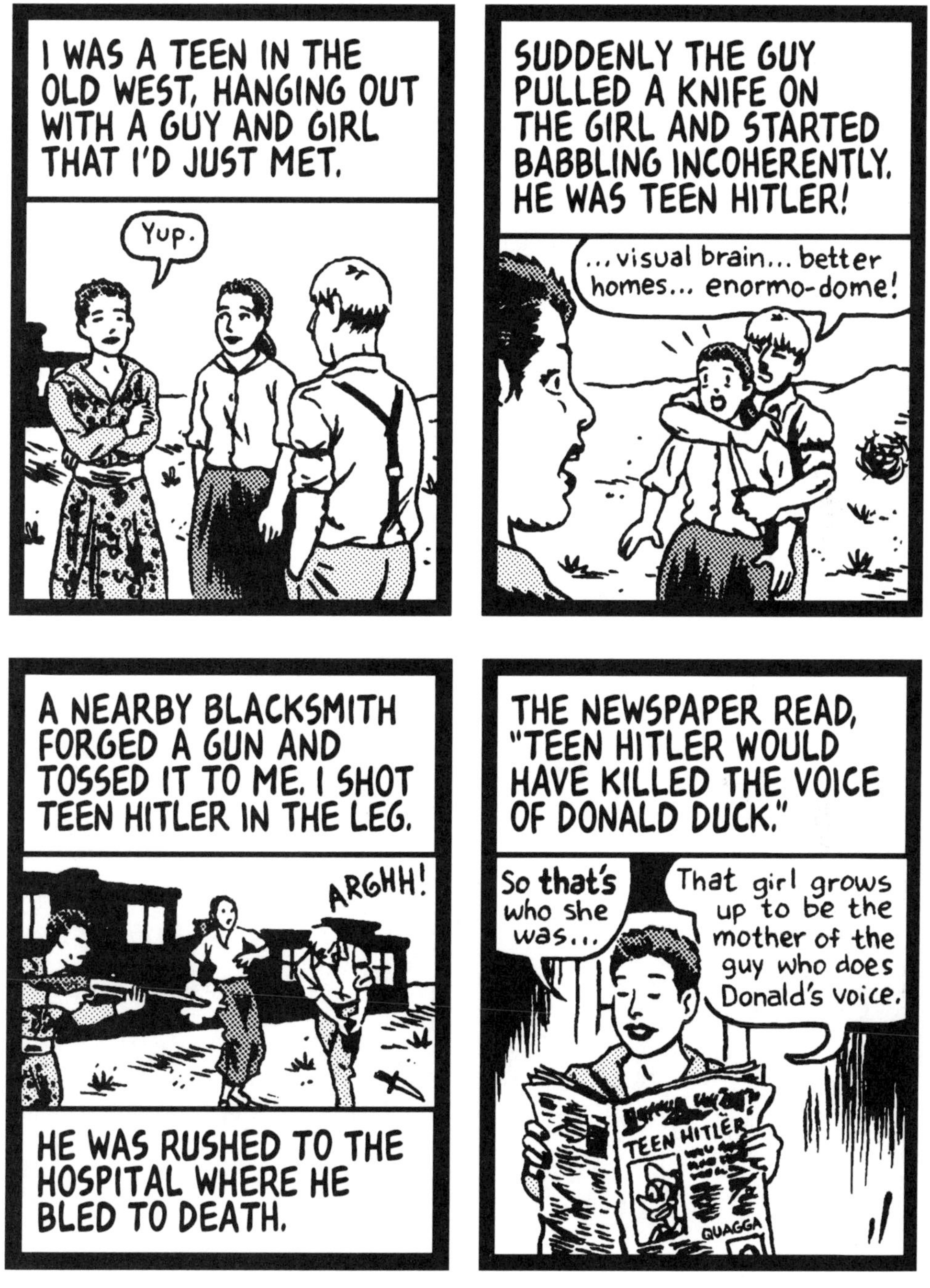
I WAS A TEEN IN THE OLD WEST, HANGING OUT WITH A GUY AND GIRL THAT I'D JUST MET.
Yup.
SUDDENLY THE GUY PULLED A KNIFE ON THE GIRL AND STARTED BABBLING INCOHERENTLY. HE WAS TEEN HITLER!
...visual brain... better homes... enormo-dome!
A NEARBY BLACKSMITH FORGED A GUN AND TOSSED IT TO ME. I SHOT TEEN HITLER IN THE LEG.
ARGHH!
HE WAS RUSHED TO THE HOSPITAL WHERE HE BLED TO DEATH.
THE NEWSPAPER READ, "TEEN HITLER WOULD HAVE KILLED THE VOICE OF DONALD DUCK."
So **that's** who she was...
That girl grows up to be the mother of the guy who does Donald's voice.
TEEN HITLER
QUAGGA

CARROT ROMANCE

from a dream by Lauren Schmidt

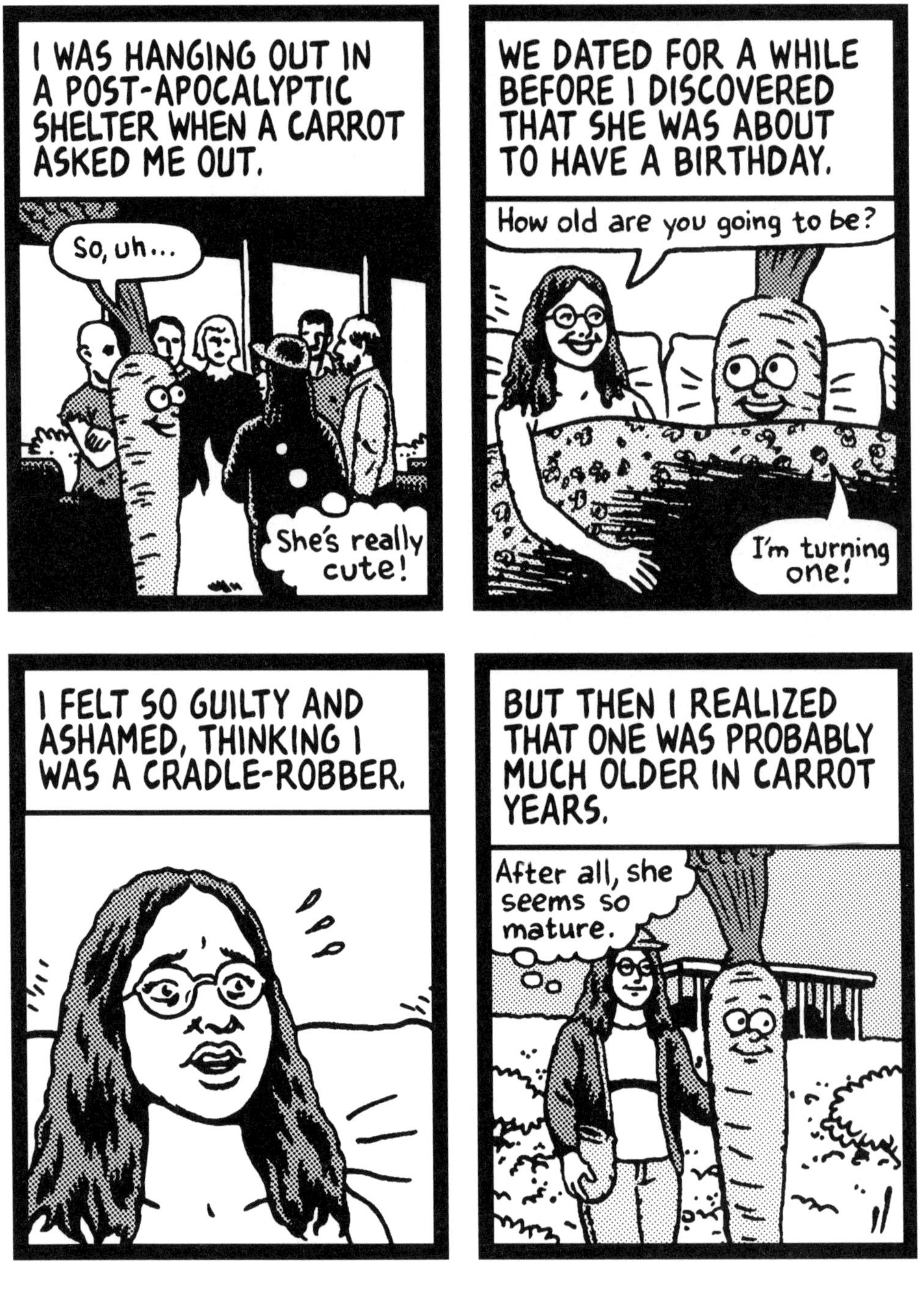
I WAS HANGING OUT IN A POST-APOCALYPTIC SHELTER WHEN A CARROT ASKED ME OUT.
So, uh...
She's really cute!
WE DATED FOR A WHILE BEFORE I DISCOVERED THAT SHE WAS ABOUT TO HAVE A BIRTHDAY.
How old are you going to be?
I'm turning one!
I FELT SO GUILTY AND ASHAMED, THINKING I WAS A CRADLE-ROBBER.
BUT THEN I REALIZED THAT ONE WAS PROBABLY MUCH OLDER IN CARROT YEARS.
After all, she seems so mature.

PUMPKIN DRUMMER

from a dream by Tony Castillo

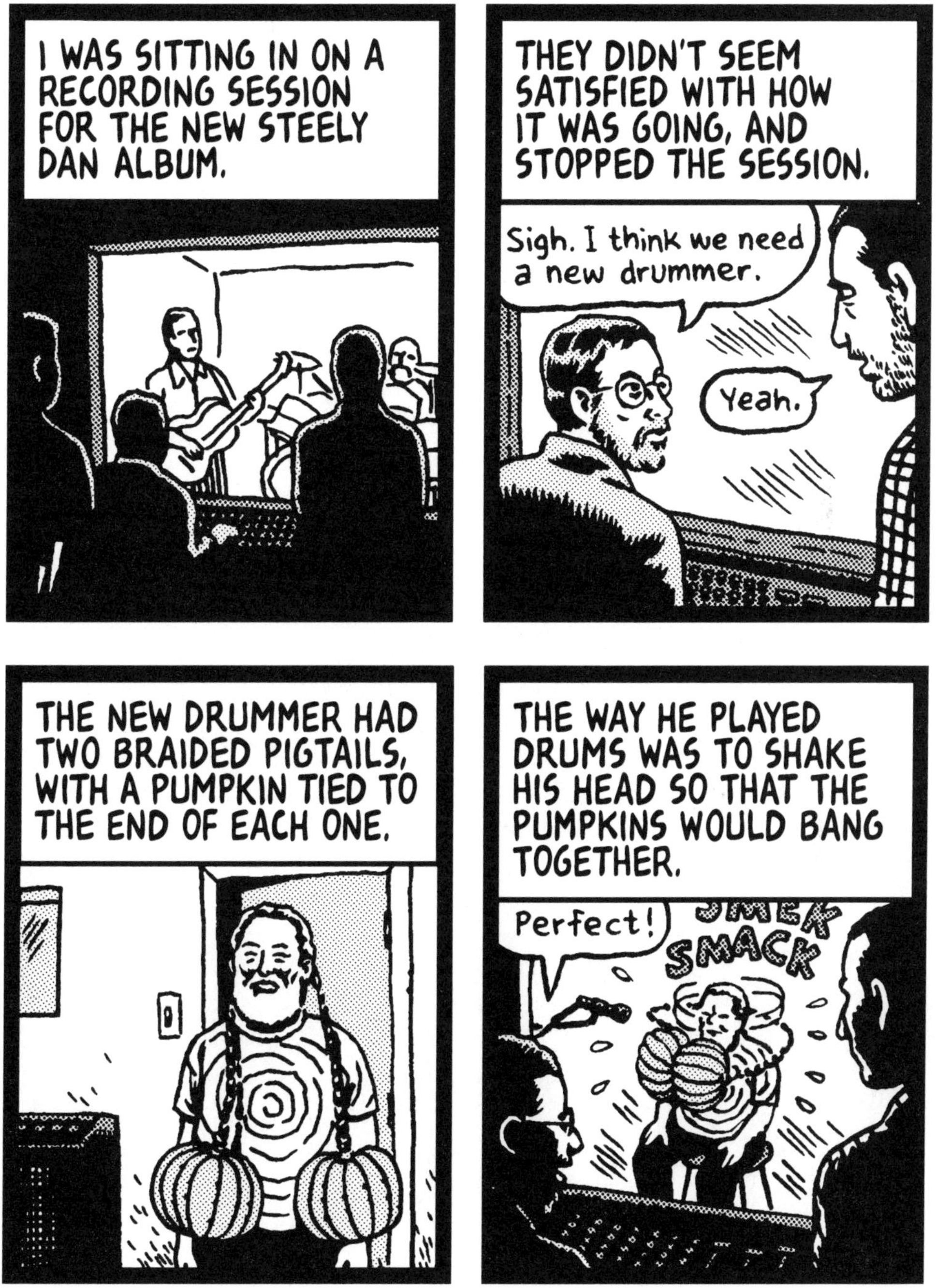

I WAS SITTING IN ON A RECORDING SESSION FOR THE NEW STEELY DAN ALBUM.
THEY DIDN'T SEEM SATISFIED WITH HOW IT WAS GOING, AND STOPPED THE SESSION.
Sigh. I think we need a new drummer.
Yeah.
THE NEW DRUMMER HAD TWO BRAIDED PIGTAILS, WITH A PUMPKIN TIED TO THE END OF EACH ONE.
THE WAY HE PLAYED DRUMS WAS TO SHAKE HIS HEAD SO THAT THE PUMPKINS WOULD BANG TOGETHER.
Perfect!
SMACK

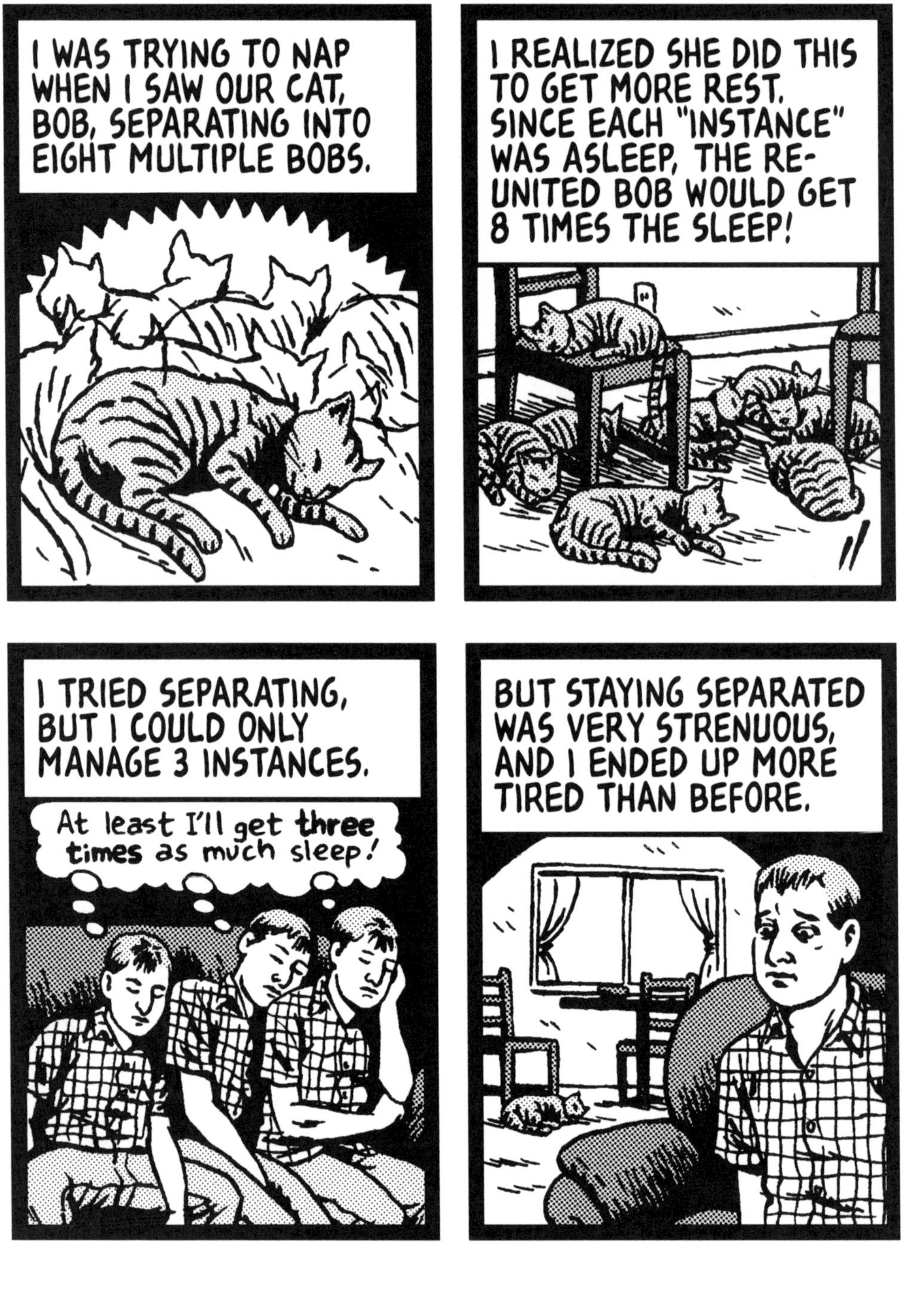
I WAS TRYING TO NAP WHEN I SAW OUR CAT, BOB, SEPARATING INTO EIGHT MULTIPLE BOBS.
I REALIZED SHE DID THIS TO GET MORE REST. SINCE EACH "INSTANCE" WAS ASLEEP, THE RE-UNITED BOB WOULD GET 8 TIMES THE SLEEP!
I TRIED SEPARATING, BUT I COULD ONLY MANAGE 3 INSTANCES.
At least I'll get **three times** as much sleep!
BUT STAYING SEPARATED WAS VERY STRENUOUS, AND I ENDED UP MORE TIRED THAN BEFORE.

EXCERPT FROM

The Book of
Genesis

ROBERT CRUMB

Chapter 1

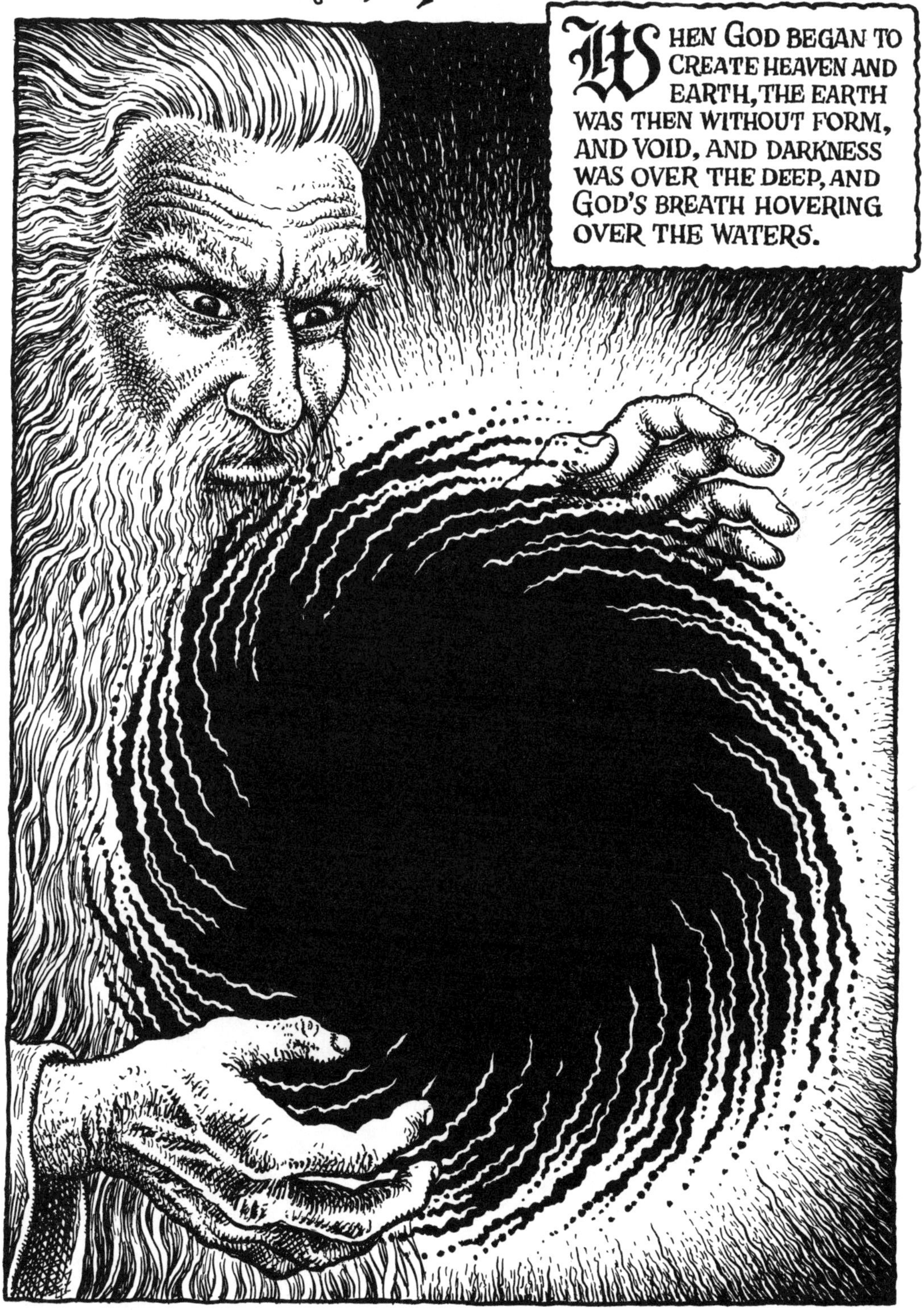
WHEN GOD BEGAN TO CREATE HEAVEN AND EARTH, THE EARTH WAS THEN WITHOUT FORM, AND VOID, AND DARKNESS WAS OVER THE DEEP, AND GOD'S BREATH HOVERING OVER THE WATERS.

And God said, "Let there be light." And there was light.

And God saw the light, that it was good, and God divided the light from the darkness. And God called the light Day, and the darkness He called Night. And it was evening and it was morning, a *FIRST* day.

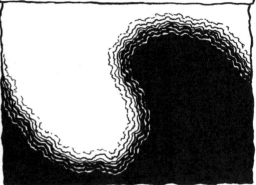

And God said, "Let there be a vault in the midst of the waters, and let it divide water from water." And God made the vault and it divided the water beneath the vault from the water above the vault, and so it was. And God called the vault Heavens, and it was evening and it was morning, a *SECOND* day.

And God said, "Let the waters under the heavens be gathered in one place so that the dry land will appear," and so it was. And God called the dry land Earth, and the gathering of waters He called Seas, and God saw that it was good.

And God said, "Let the earth bring forth grass, plants yielding seed of each kind, and trees bearing fruit of each kind, that has its seed within it upon the earth." And so it was.

And the earth put forth grass, plants yielding seed of each kind, and trees bearing fruit that has its seed within it of each kind, and God saw that it was good, and it was evening and it was morning, a *THIRD* day.

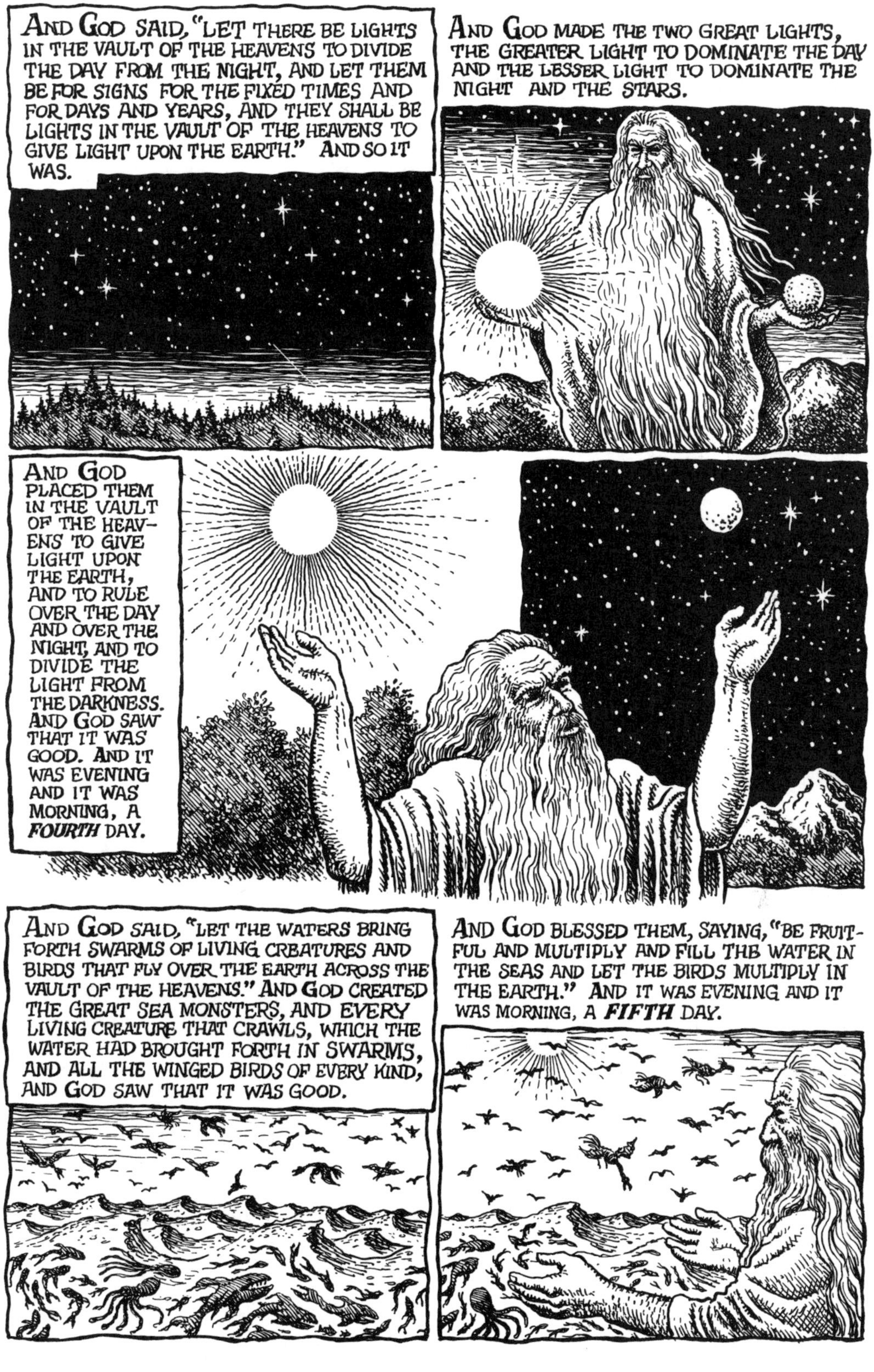
AND GOD SAID, "LET THERE BE LIGHTS IN THE VAULT OF THE HEAVENS TO DIVIDE THE DAY FROM THE NIGHT, AND LET THEM BE FOR SIGNS FOR THE FIXED TIMES AND FOR DAYS AND YEARS, AND THEY SHALL BE LIGHTS IN THE VAULT OF THE HEAVENS TO GIVE LIGHT UPON THE EARTH." AND SO IT WAS.
AND GOD MADE THE TWO GREAT LIGHTS, THE GREATER LIGHT TO DOMINATE THE DAY AND THE LESSER LIGHT TO DOMINATE THE NIGHT AND THE STARS.
AND GOD PLACED THEM IN THE VAULT OF THE HEAVENS TO GIVE LIGHT UPON THE EARTH, AND TO RULE OVER THE DAY AND OVER THE NIGHT, AND TO DIVIDE THE LIGHT FROM THE DARKNESS. AND GOD SAW THAT IT WAS GOOD. AND IT WAS EVENING AND IT WAS MORNING, A FOURTH DAY.
AND GOD SAID, "LET THE WATERS BRING FORTH SWARMS OF LIVING CREATURES AND BIRDS THAT FLY OVER THE EARTH ACROSS THE VAULT OF THE HEAVENS." AND GOD CREATED THE GREAT SEA MONSTERS, AND EVERY LIVING CREATURE THAT CRAWLS, WHICH THE WATER HAD BROUGHT FORTH IN SWARMS, AND ALL THE WINGED BIRDS OF EVERY KIND, AND GOD SAW THAT IT WAS GOOD.
AND GOD BLESSED THEM, SAYING, "BE FRUITFUL AND MULTIPLY AND FILL THE WATER IN THE SEAS AND LET THE BIRDS MULTIPLY IN THE EARTH." AND IT WAS EVENING AND IT WAS MORNING, A FIFTH DAY.

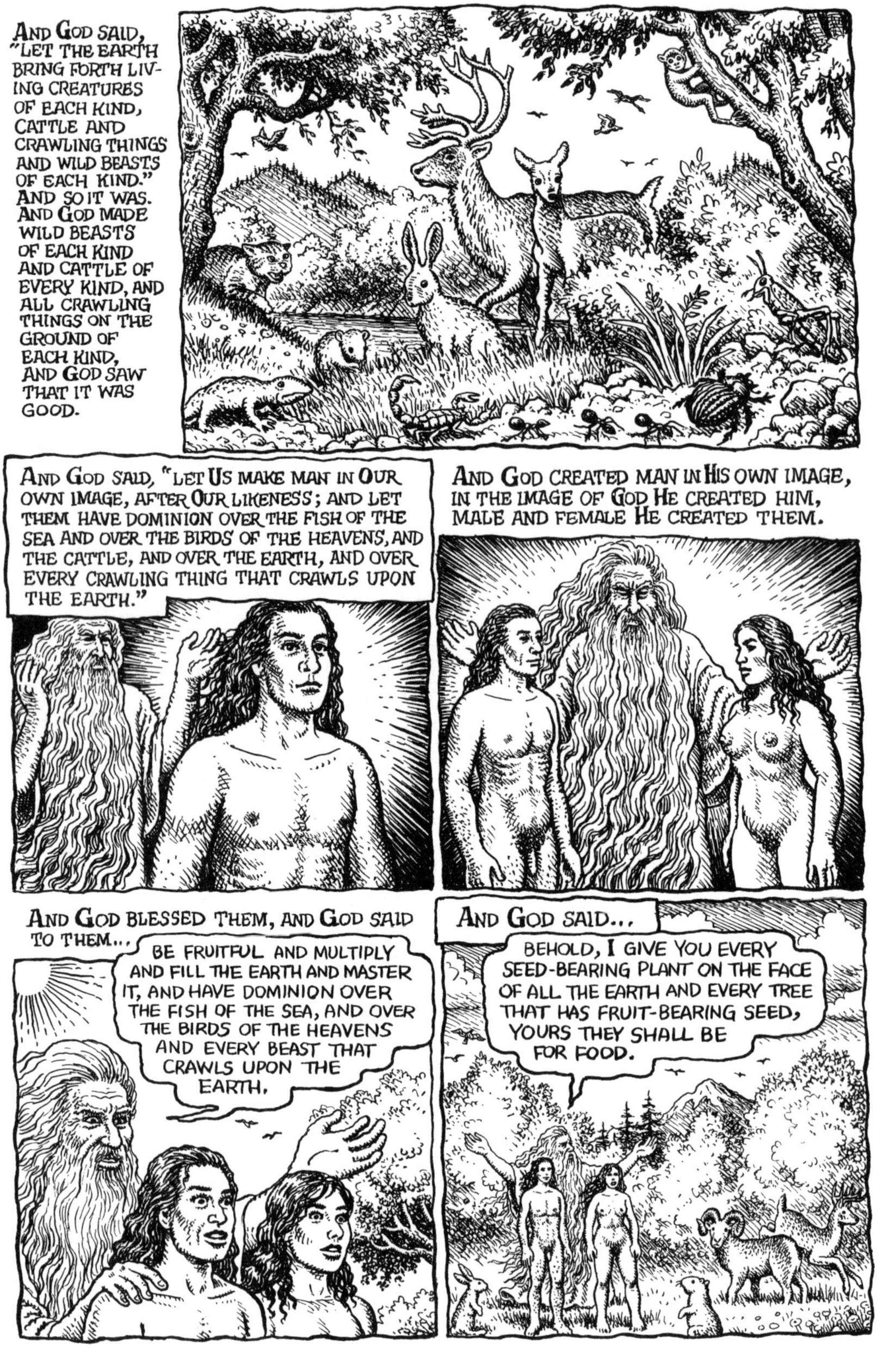
AND GOD SAID, "LET THE EARTH BRING FORTH LIVING CREATURES OF EACH KIND, CATTLE AND CRAWLING THINGS AND WILD BEASTS OF EACH KIND." AND SO IT WAS. AND GOD MADE WILD BEASTS OF EACH KIND AND CATTLE OF EVERY KIND, AND ALL CRAWLING THINGS ON THE GROUND OF EACH KIND, AND GOD SAW THAT IT WAS GOOD.
AND GOD SAID, "LET US MAKE MAN IN OUR OWN IMAGE, AFTER OUR LIKENESS; AND LET THEM HAVE DOMINION OVER THE FISH OF THE SEA AND OVER THE BIRDS OF THE HEAVENS, AND THE CATTLE, AND OVER THE EARTH, AND OVER EVERY CRAWLING THING THAT CRAWLS UPON THE EARTH."
AND GOD CREATED MAN IN HIS OWN IMAGE, IN THE IMAGE OF GOD HE CREATED HIM, MALE AND FEMALE HE CREATED THEM.
AND GOD BLESSED THEM, AND GOD SAID TO THEM...
BE FRUITFUL AND MULTIPLY AND FILL THE EARTH AND MASTER IT, AND HAVE DOMINION OVER THE FISH OF THE SEA, AND OVER THE BIRDS OF THE HEAVENS AND EVERY BEAST THAT CRAWLS UPON THE EARTH.
AND GOD SAID...
BEHOLD, I GIVE YOU EVERY SEED-BEARING PLANT ON THE FACE OF ALL THE EARTH AND EVERY TREE THAT HAS FRUIT-BEARING SEED, YOURS THEY SHALL BE FOR FOOD.

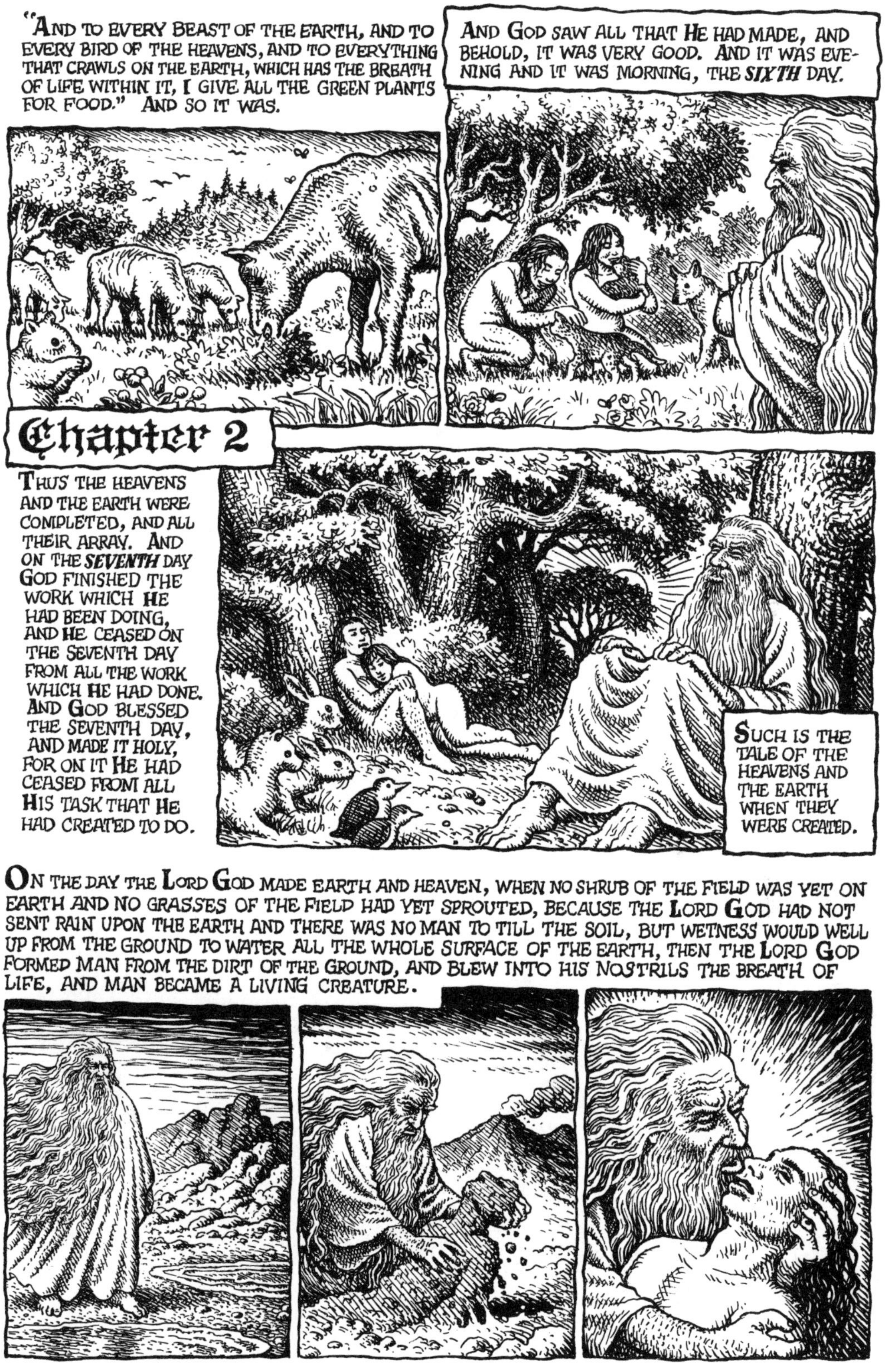
"AND TO EVERY BEAST OF THE EARTH, AND TO EVERY BIRD OF THE HEAVENS, AND TO EVERYTHING THAT CRAWLS ON THE EARTH, WHICH HAS THE BREATH OF LIFE WITHIN IT, I GIVE ALL THE GREEN PLANTS FOR FOOD." AND SO IT WAS.
AND GOD SAW ALL THAT HE HAD MADE, AND BEHOLD, IT WAS VERY GOOD. AND IT WAS EVENING AND IT WAS MORNING, THE SIXTH DAY.
Chapter 2
THUS THE HEAVENS AND THE EARTH WERE COMPLETED, AND ALL THEIR ARRAY. AND ON THE SEVENTH DAY GOD FINISHED THE WORK WHICH HE HAD BEEN DOING, AND HE CEASED ON THE SEVENTH DAY FROM ALL THE WORK WHICH HE HAD DONE. AND GOD BLESSED THE SEVENTH DAY, AND MADE IT HOLY, FOR ON IT HE HAD CEASED FROM ALL HIS TASK THAT HE HAD CREATED TO DO.
SUCH IS THE TALE OF THE HEAVENS AND THE EARTH WHEN THEY WERE CREATED.
ON THE DAY THE LORD GOD MADE EARTH AND HEAVEN, WHEN NO SHRUB OF THE FIELD WAS YET ON EARTH AND NO GRASSES OF THE FIELD HAD YET SPROUTED, BECAUSE THE LORD GOD HAD NOT SENT RAIN UPON THE EARTH AND THERE WAS NO MAN TO TILL THE SOIL, BUT WETNESS WOULD WELL UP FROM THE GROUND TO WATER ALL THE WHOLE SURFACE OF THE EARTH, THEN THE LORD GOD FORMED MAN FROM THE DIRT OF THE GROUND, AND BLEW INTO HIS NOSTRILS THE BREATH OF LIFE, AND MAN BECAME A LIVING CREATURE.

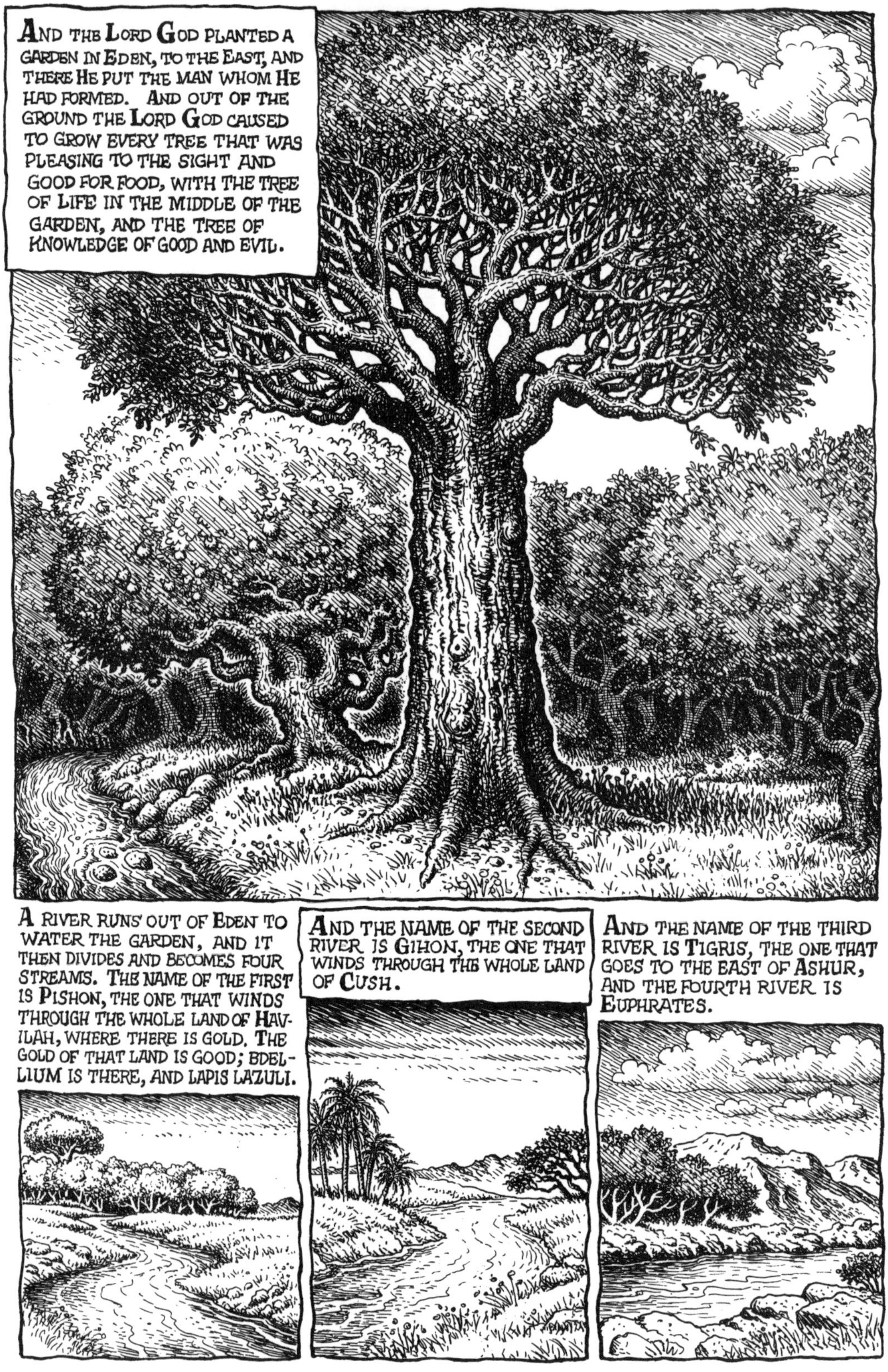
AND THE LORD GOD PLANTED A GARDEN IN EDEN, TO THE EAST, AND THERE HE PUT THE MAN WHOM HE HAD FORMED. AND OUT OF THE GROUND THE LORD GOD CAUSED TO GROW EVERY TREE THAT WAS PLEASING TO THE SIGHT AND GOOD FOR FOOD, WITH THE TREE OF LIFE IN THE MIDDLE OF THE GARDEN, AND THE TREE OF KNOWLEDGE OF GOOD AND EVIL.
A RIVER RUNS OUT OF EDEN TO WATER THE GARDEN, AND IT THEN DIVIDES AND BECOMES FOUR STREAMS. THE NAME OF THE FIRST IS PISHON, THE ONE THAT WINDS THROUGH THE WHOLE LAND OF HAVILAH, WHERE THERE IS GOLD. THE GOLD OF THAT LAND IS GOOD; BDELLIUM IS THERE, AND LAPIS LAZULI.
AND THE NAME OF THE SECOND RIVER IS GIHON, THE ONE THAT WINDS THROUGH THE WHOLE LAND OF CUSH.
AND THE NAME OF THE THIRD RIVER IS TIGRIS, THE ONE THAT GOES TO THE EAST OF ASHUR, AND THE FOURTH RIVER IS EUPHRATES.

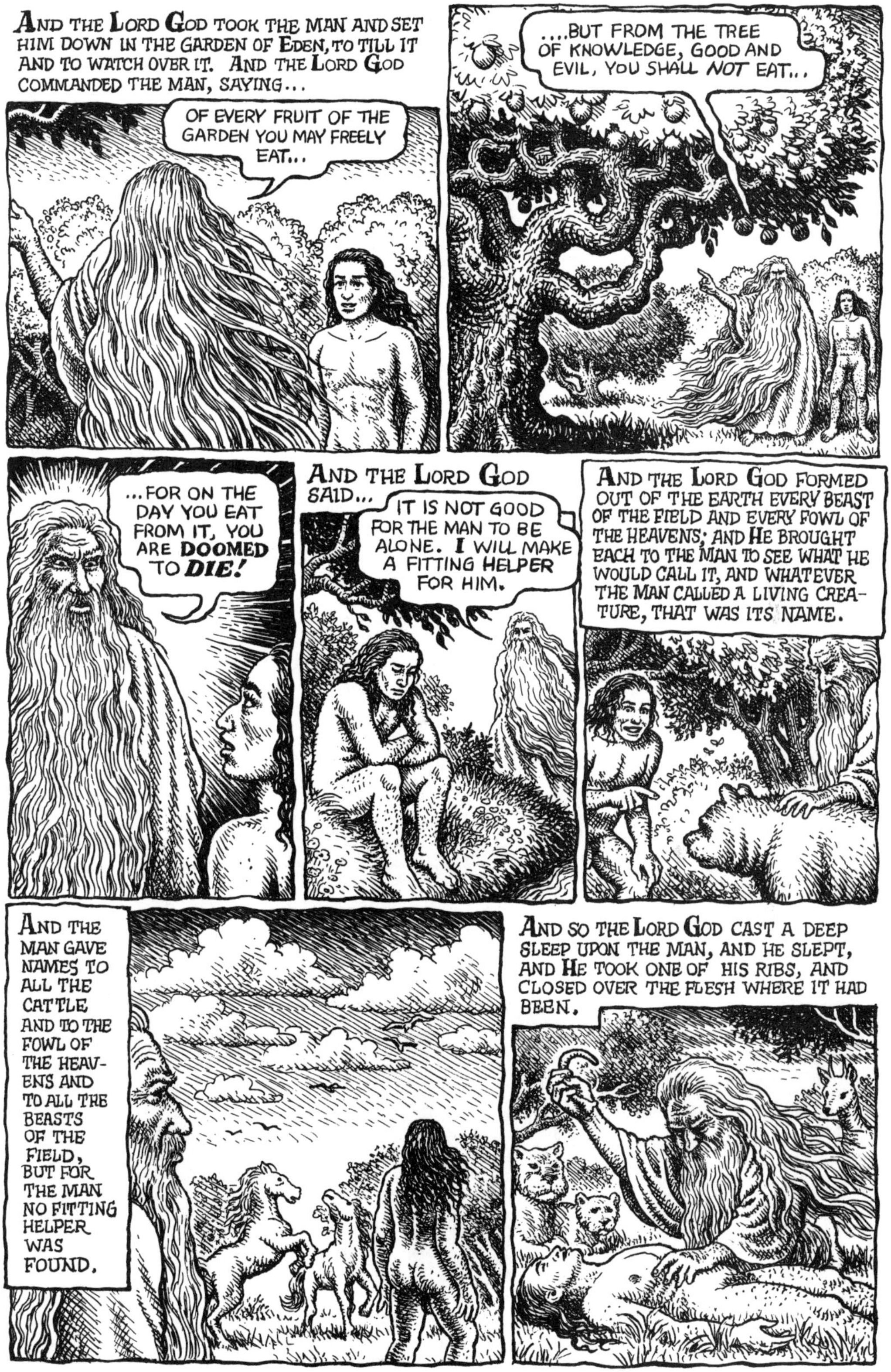
AND THE LORD GOD TOOK THE MAN AND SET HIM DOWN IN THE GARDEN OF EDEN, TO TILL IT AND TO WATCH OVER IT. AND THE LORD GOD COMMANDED THE MAN, SAYING...
OF EVERY FRUIT OF THE GARDEN YOU MAY FREELY EAT...
....BUT FROM THE TREE OF KNOWLEDGE, GOOD AND EVIL, YOU SHALL NOT EAT...
...FOR ON THE DAY YOU EAT FROM IT, YOU ARE DOOMED TO DIE!
AND THE LORD GOD SAID...
IT IS NOT GOOD FOR THE MAN TO BE ALONE. I WILL MAKE A FITTING HELPER FOR HIM.
AND THE LORD GOD FORMED OUT OF THE EARTH EVERY BEAST OF THE FIELD AND EVERY FOWL OF THE HEAVENS; AND HE BROUGHT EACH TO THE MAN TO SEE WHAT HE WOULD CALL IT, AND WHATEVER THE MAN CALLED A LIVING CREATURE, THAT WAS ITS NAME.
AND THE MAN GAVE NAMES TO ALL THE CATTLE AND TO THE FOWL OF THE HEAVENS AND TO ALL THE BEASTS OF THE FIELD, BUT FOR THE MAN NO FITTING HELPER WAS FOUND.
AND SO THE LORD GOD CAST A DEEP SLEEP UPON THE MAN, AND HE SLEPT, AND HE TOOK ONE OF HIS RIBS, AND CLOSED OVER THE FLESH WHERE IT HAD BEEN.

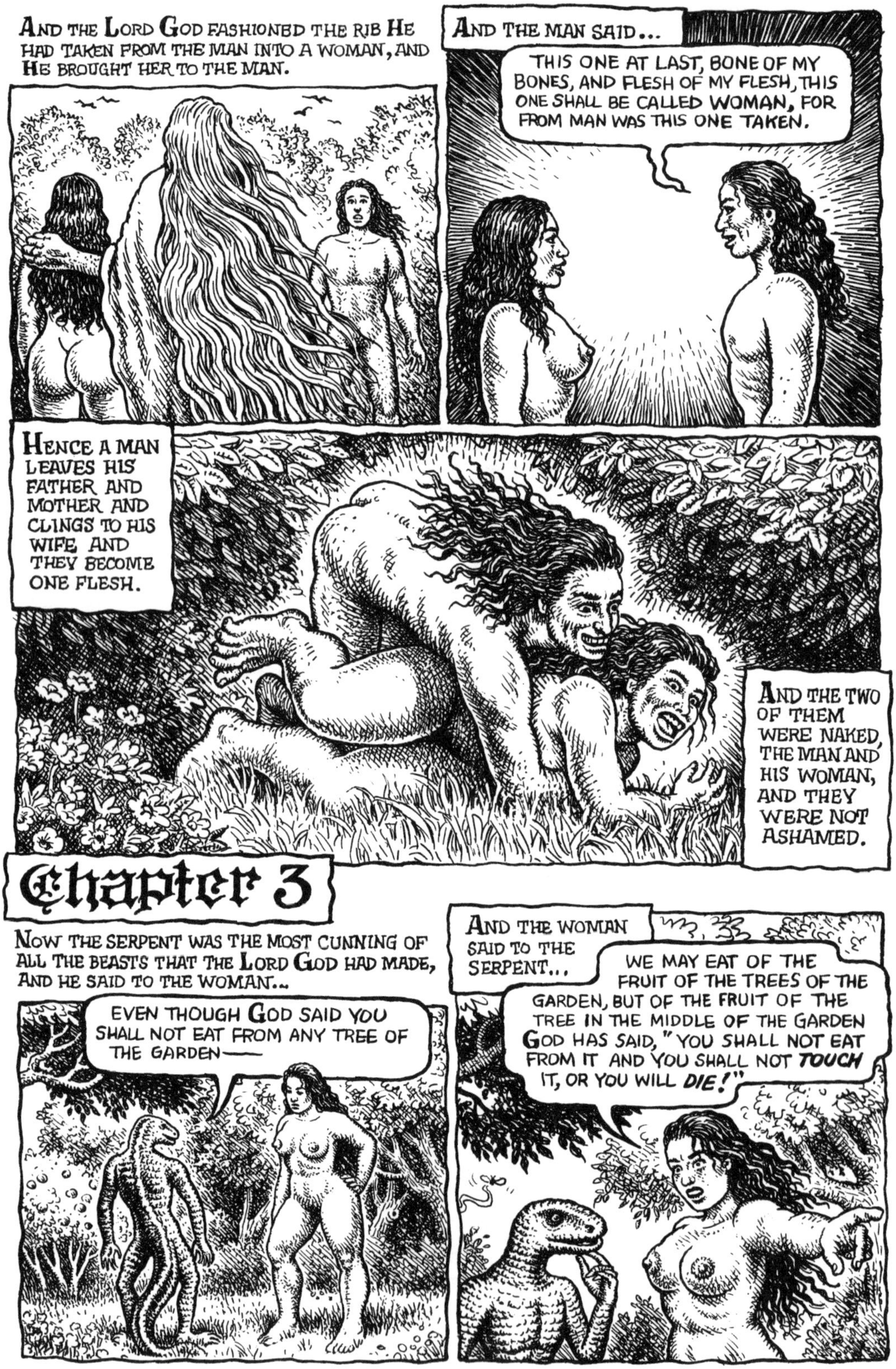
AND THE LORD GOD FASHIONED THE RIB HE HAD TAKEN FROM THE MAN INTO A WOMAN, AND HE BROUGHT HER TO THE MAN.
AND THE MAN SAID...
THIS ONE AT LAST, BONE OF MY BONES, AND FLESH OF MY FLESH, THIS ONE SHALL BE CALLED WOMAN, FOR FROM MAN WAS THIS ONE TAKEN.
HENCE A MAN LEAVES HIS FATHER AND MOTHER AND CLINGS TO HIS WIFE AND THEY BECOME ONE FLESH.
AND THE TWO OF THEM WERE NAKED, THE MAN AND HIS WOMAN, AND THEY WERE NOT ASHAMED.
Chapter 3
NOW THE SERPENT WAS THE MOST CUNNING OF ALL THE BEASTS THAT THE LORD GOD HAD MADE, AND HE SAID TO THE WOMAN...
EVEN THOUGH GOD SAID YOU SHALL NOT EAT FROM ANY TREE OF THE GARDEN—
AND THE WOMAN SAID TO THE SERPENT...
WE MAY EAT OF THE FRUIT OF THE TREES OF THE GARDEN, BUT OF THE FRUIT OF THE TREE IN THE MIDDLE OF THE GARDEN GOD HAS SAID, "YOU SHALL NOT EAT FROM IT AND YOU SHALL NOT TOUCH IT, OR YOU WILL DIE!"

AND THE SERPENT SAID TO THE WOMAN: YOU SHALL NOT BE DOOMED TO DIE, FOR GOD KNOWS THAT ON THE DAY YOU EAT OF IT YOUR EYES WILL BE OPENED, AND YOU WILL BECOME AS DIVINE BEINGS, KNOWING GOOD AND EVIL.

AND THE WOMAN SAW THAT THE TREE WAS GOOD FOR EATING AND THAT IT WAS LUST TO THE EYES AND LOVELY TO LOOK AT.

AND SHE TOOK OF ITS FRUIT AND ATE...

...AND SHE ALSO GAVE TO HER MAN, AND HE ATE.

AND THE EYES OF THE TWO WERE OPENED, AND THEY KNEW THAT THEY WERE NAKED.

AND THEY SEWED FIG LEAVES AND MADE THEMSELVES LOINCLOTHS.

AND THEY HEARD THE SOUND OF THE LORD GOD WALKING ABOUT IN THE GARDEN IN THE EVENING BREEZE, AND THE MAN AND HIS WOMAN HID FROM THE LORD GOD IN THE MIDST OF THE TREES OF THE GARDEN.

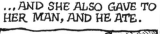

187

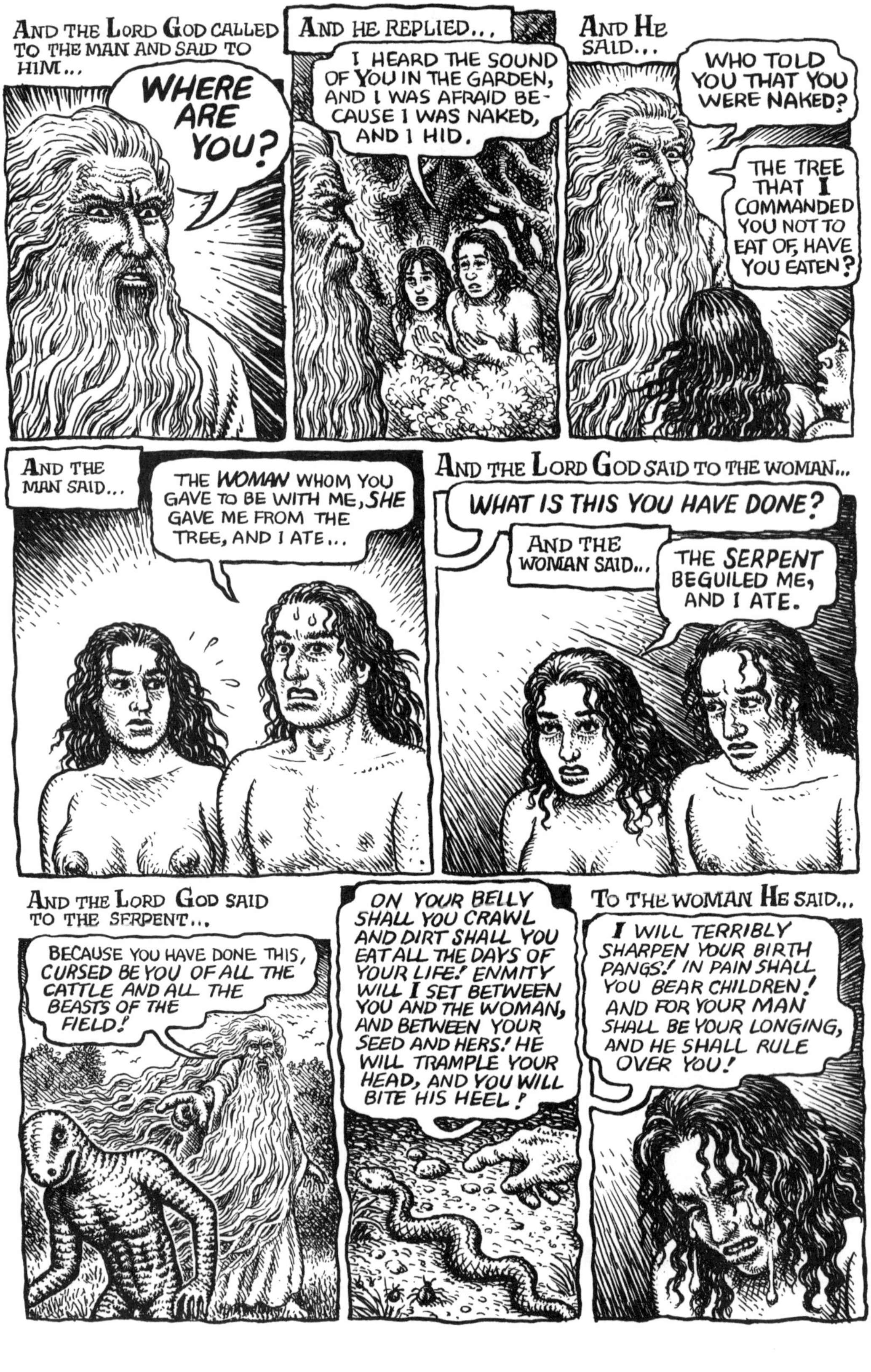

AND THE LORD GOD CALLED TO THE MAN AND SAID TO HIM...
WHERE ARE YOU?
AND HE REPLIED...
I HEARD THE SOUND OF YOU IN THE GARDEN, AND I WAS AFRAID BE-CAUSE I WAS NAKED, AND I HID.
AND HE SAID...
WHO TOLD YOU THAT YOU WERE NAKED?
THE TREE THAT I COMMANDED YOU NOT TO EAT OF, HAVE YOU EATEN?
AND THE MAN SAID...
THE WOMAN WHOM YOU GAVE TO BE WITH ME, SHE GAVE ME FROM THE TREE, AND I ATE...
AND THE LORD GOD SAID TO THE WOMAN...
WHAT IS THIS YOU HAVE DONE?
AND THE WOMAN SAID...
THE SERPENT BEGUILED ME, AND I ATE.
AND THE LORD GOD SAID TO THE SERPENT...
BECAUSE YOU HAVE DONE THIS, CURSED BE YOU OF ALL THE CATTLE AND ALL THE BEASTS OF THE FIELD!
ON YOUR BELLY SHALL YOU CRAWL AND DIRT SHALL YOU EAT ALL THE DAYS OF YOUR LIFE! ENMITY WILL I SET BETWEEN YOU AND THE WOMAN, AND BETWEEN YOUR SEED AND HERS! HE WILL TRAMPLE YOUR HEAD, AND YOU WILL BITE HIS HEEL!
TO THE WOMAN HE SAID...
I WILL TERRIBLY SHARPEN YOUR BIRTH PANGS! IN PAIN SHALL YOU BEAR CHILDREN! AND FOR YOUR MAN SHALL BE YOUR LONGING, AND HE SHALL RULE OVER YOU!

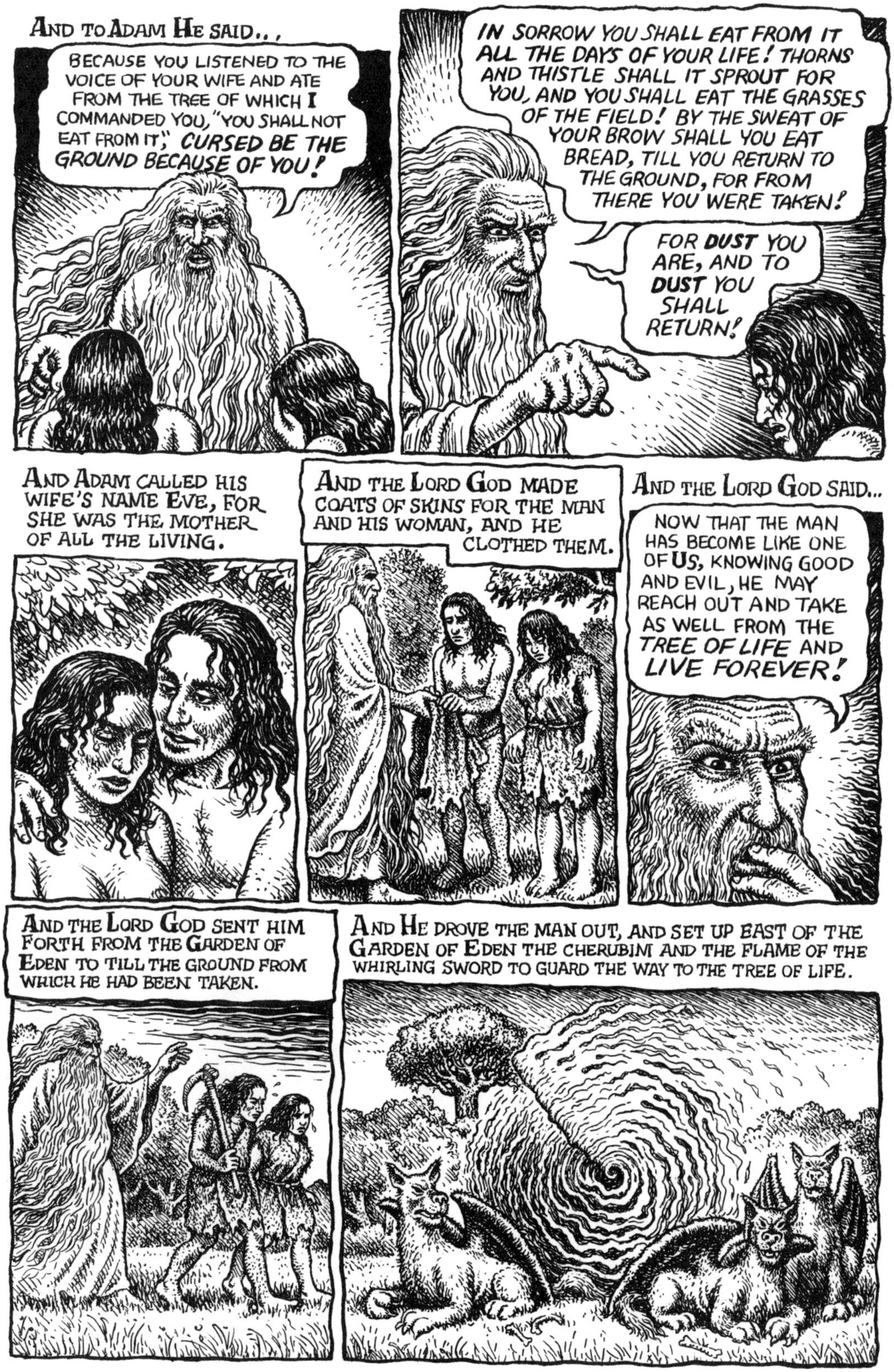

AND TO ADAM HE SAID...
BECAUSE YOU LISTENED TO THE VOICE OF YOUR WIFE AND ATE FROM THE TREE OF WHICH I COMMANDED YOU, "YOU SHALL NOT EAT FROM IT," CURSED BE THE GROUND BECAUSE OF YOU!
IN SORROW YOU SHALL EAT FROM IT ALL THE DAYS OF YOUR LIFE! THORNS AND THISTLE SHALL IT SPROUT FOR YOU, AND YOU SHALL EAT THE GRASSES OF THE FIELD! BY THE SWEAT OF YOUR BROW SHALL YOU EAT BREAD, TILL YOU RETURN TO THE GROUND, FOR FROM THERE YOU WERE TAKEN!
FOR DUST YOU ARE, AND TO DUST YOU SHALL RETURN!
AND ADAM CALLED HIS WIFE'S NAME EVE, FOR SHE WAS THE MOTHER OF ALL THE LIVING.
AND THE LORD GOD MADE COATS OF SKINS FOR THE MAN AND HIS WOMAN, AND HE CLOTHED THEM.
AND THE LORD GOD SAID...
NOW THAT THE MAN HAS BECOME LIKE ONE OF US, KNOWING GOOD AND EVIL, HE MAY REACH OUT AND TAKE AS WELL FROM THE TREE OF LIFE AND LIVE FOREVER!
AND THE LORD GOD SENT HIM FORTH FROM THE GARDEN OF EDEN TO TILL THE GROUND FROM WHICH HE HAD BEEN TAKEN.
AND HE DROVE THE MAN OUT, AND SET UP EAST OF THE GARDEN OF EDEN THE CHERUBIM AND THE FLAME OF THE WHIRLING SWORD TO GUARD THE WAY TO THE TREE OF LIFE.

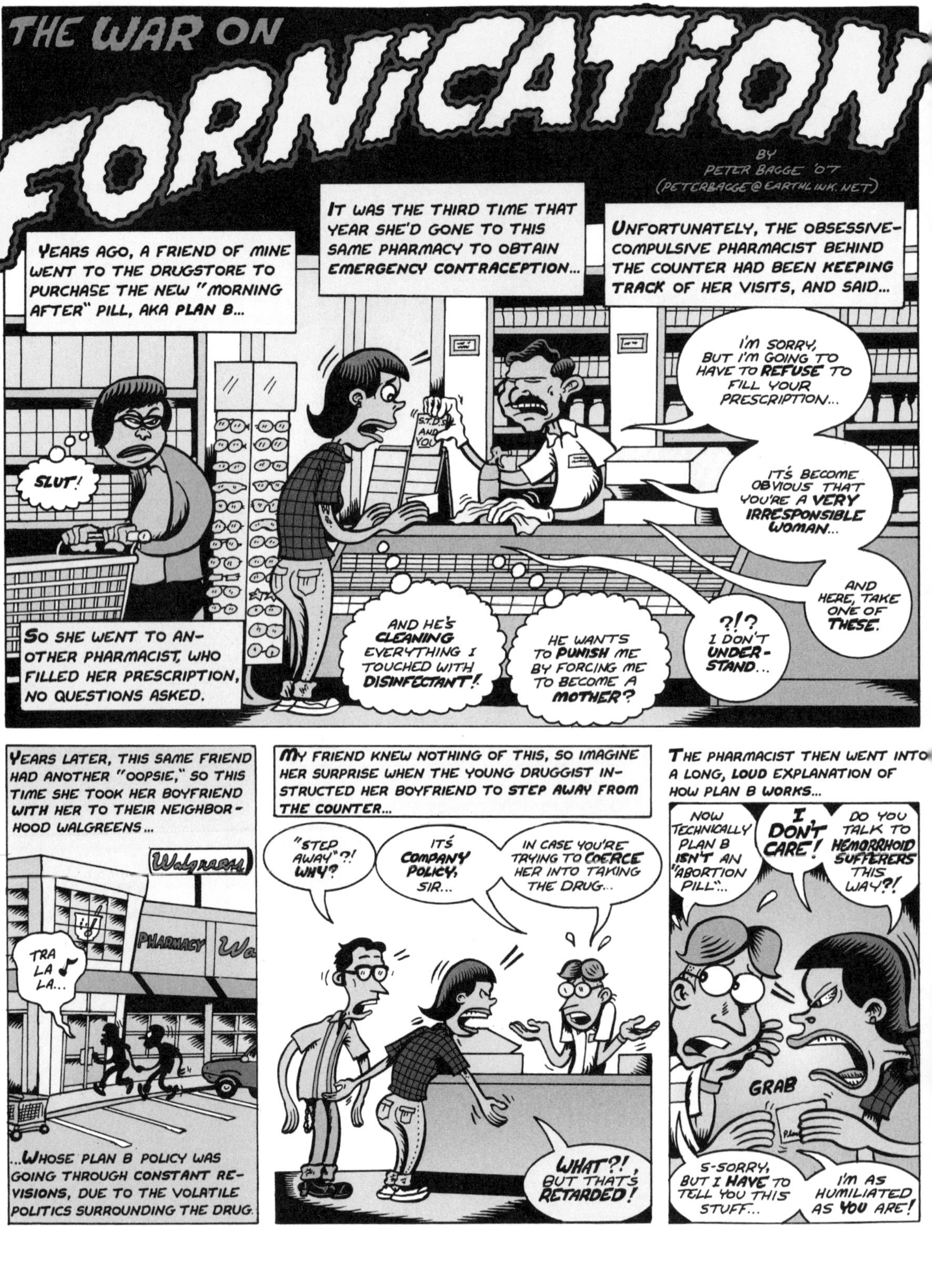
THE WAR ON FORNICATION
BY PETER BAGGE '07 (PETERBAGGE@EARTHLINK.NET)
YEARS AGO, A FRIEND OF MINE WENT TO THE DRUGSTORE TO PURCHASE THE NEW "MORNING AFTER" PILL, AKA PLAN B...
IT WAS THE THIRD TIME THAT YEAR SHE'D GONE TO THIS SAME PHARMACY TO OBTAIN EMERGENCY CONTRACEPTION...
UNFORTUNATELY, THE OBSESSIVE-COMPULSIVE PHARMACIST BEHIND THE COUNTER HAD BEEN KEEPING TRACK OF HER VISITS, AND SAID...
I'M SORRY, BUT I'M GOING TO HAVE TO REFUSE TO FILL YOUR PRESCRIPTION...
IT'S BECOME OBVIOUS THAT YOU'RE A VERY IRRESPONSIBLE WOMAN...
AND HERE, TAKE ONE OF THESE.
S.T.D.S AND YOU
SLUT!
?!? I DON'T UNDERSTAND...
AND HE'S CLEANING EVERYTHING I TOUCHED WITH DISINFECTANT!
HE WANTS TO PUNISH ME BY FORCING ME TO BECOME A MOTHER?
SO SHE WENT TO ANOTHER PHARMACIST, WHO FILLED HER PRESCRIPTION, NO QUESTIONS ASKED.
YEARS LATER, THIS SAME FRIEND HAD ANOTHER "OOPSIE," SO THIS TIME SHE TOOK HER BOYFRIEND WITH HER TO THEIR NEIGHBORHOOD WALGREENS...
Walgreens
PHARMACY
TRA LA LA...
...WHOSE PLAN B POLICY WAS GOING THROUGH CONSTANT REVISIONS, DUE TO THE VOLATILE POLITICS SURROUNDING THE DRUG.
MY FRIEND KNEW NOTHING OF THIS, SO IMAGINE HER SURPRISE WHEN THE YOUNG DRUGGIST INSTRUCTED HER BOYFRIEND TO STEP AWAY FROM THE COUNTER...
"STEP AWAY"?! WHY?
IT'S COMPANY POLICY, SIR...
IN CASE YOU'RE TRYING TO COERCE HER INTO TAKING THE DRUG...
WHAT?!, BUT THAT'S RETARDED!
THE PHARMACIST THEN WENT INTO A LONG, LOUD EXPLANATION OF HOW PLAN B WORKS...
NOW TECHNICALLY PLAN B ISN'T AN "ABORTION PILL"...
I, DON'T CARE!
DO YOU TALK TO HEMORRHOID SUFFERERS THIS WAY?!
GRAB
S-SORRY, BUT I HAVE TO TELL YOU THIS STUFF...
I'M AS HUMILIATED AS YOU ARE!

IF PUBLIC HUMILIATION IS THE GOAL, WHY NOT GO ALL OUT AND GIVE FEMALE CUSTOMERS THE FULL TALIBAN TREATMENT?

HOW **DARE** YOU APPEAR IN PUBLIC WITH A MAN WHO **ISN'T YOUR HUSBAND!**

AND PUT THIS **BURKA** ON **NOW!**

IT'S **COMPANY POLICY!**

YOW!

SWAT!

SMACK! WHACK!

OH, WAIT -- WE WAGE WARS AGAINST SOCIETIES THAT HARBOR SUCH PRIMITIVE VIEWS ON SEXUALITY. I FORGOT!

PLAN B HAS REVIVED A WAR AGAINST CONTRACEPTIVES IN GENERAL -- DUE IN PART TO FALSE COMPARISONS WITH RU-486, WHICH **IS** AN "ABORTION PILL"!

AS GOD'S OFFICIAL SPOKESMAN, I SAY **DON'T USE THE "ABORTION PILL"**...

...OR ANY-THING **LIKE** IT! GOD HATES **ALL** THAT CRAP!

AND DON'T FORGET TO PAY YOUR **TAXES**...

AMEN.

RATHER THAN RAC-ING FOR A WAITING EGG, SPERM ARE MORE LIKELY THE ONES WHO HAVE TO WAIT -- SOMETIMES UP TO FIVE DAYS -- BEFORE AN EGG IS RELEASED FROM THE OVARIES...

WHERE IS THAT @#©J$§$ EGG?

...BITCHES ALWAYS KEEPING US WAITING...

MUMBLE GRIPE...

...TAP TAP TAP...

PLAN B IS BASICALLY A "HOT SHOT" OF THE SAME HORMONES USED IN BIRTH CON-TROL PILLS, WHICH PREVENTS THE EGG FROM BEING RELEASED, THUS PRE-VENTING FERTILIZA-TION.

IF FERTILI-ZATION DOES OCCUR, HOW-EVER, PLAN B IS LIKELY TO PREVENT THE ZYGOTE FROM IM-PLANTING ITSELF ON THE UTERINE WALL, WHERE IT WOULD THEN EVOLVE INTO AN EMBRYO, AND THEN A FETUS...

FULL HUMAN RIGHTS FOR ALL NONVIABLE SINGLE-CELLED ORGANISMS

HEY, I'M **VULNERABLE!**

...AND NOT EVERYONE AGREES AS TO WHETHER A FERTILIZED EGG COUNTS AS THE BEGINNING OF A LIFE, SINCE IT ISN'T VIABLE UNTIL IMPLANTATION. BUT IF A ZYGOTE IS A "BABY," DOES PREVENTING IMPLANTATION COUNT AS AN ABORTION?

I'M PERSONALLY NOT GOING TO LOSE ANY SLEEP OVER THIS HYPO-THETICAL TECHNICALITY, BUT THERE ARE SOME FOLKS WHO DO...

THEN...

EIGHTY PERCENT OF ALL ZYGOTES **FAIL TO IMPLANT,** AND ARE DISCHARGED NATURALLY...

ZZZzzz

NOW...

...PLAN B MAY PREVENT IMPLANTA-TION...

—**WHAT?!** WHY, THAT'S **COLD-BLOODED MURDER!**

...**ALL** OF WHOM ARE ANTI-ABORTION ACTIVISTS, WHOSE RECENT BESTOWAL OF **FULL-BLOWN PERSONHOOD** UPON ZYGOTES IS THEIR REASON TO OPPOSE EMERGENCY CONTRACEPTIVES ALTOGETHER.

THIS ISSUE HAS ALSO RE-EXPOSED THE FACT THAT MANY "PRO-LIFE" ACTIVISTS ARE OPPOSED TO THE USE OF CONTRACEPTIVES IN GENERAL...

THAT'S BECAUSE SEX IS **SOLELY** FOR THE PURPOSE OF **PRO-CREATION**...

WITHIN THE CONFINES OF **MARRIAGE,** THAT IS.

REMIND ME TO **NEVER** ASK YOU OUT ON A **DATE!**

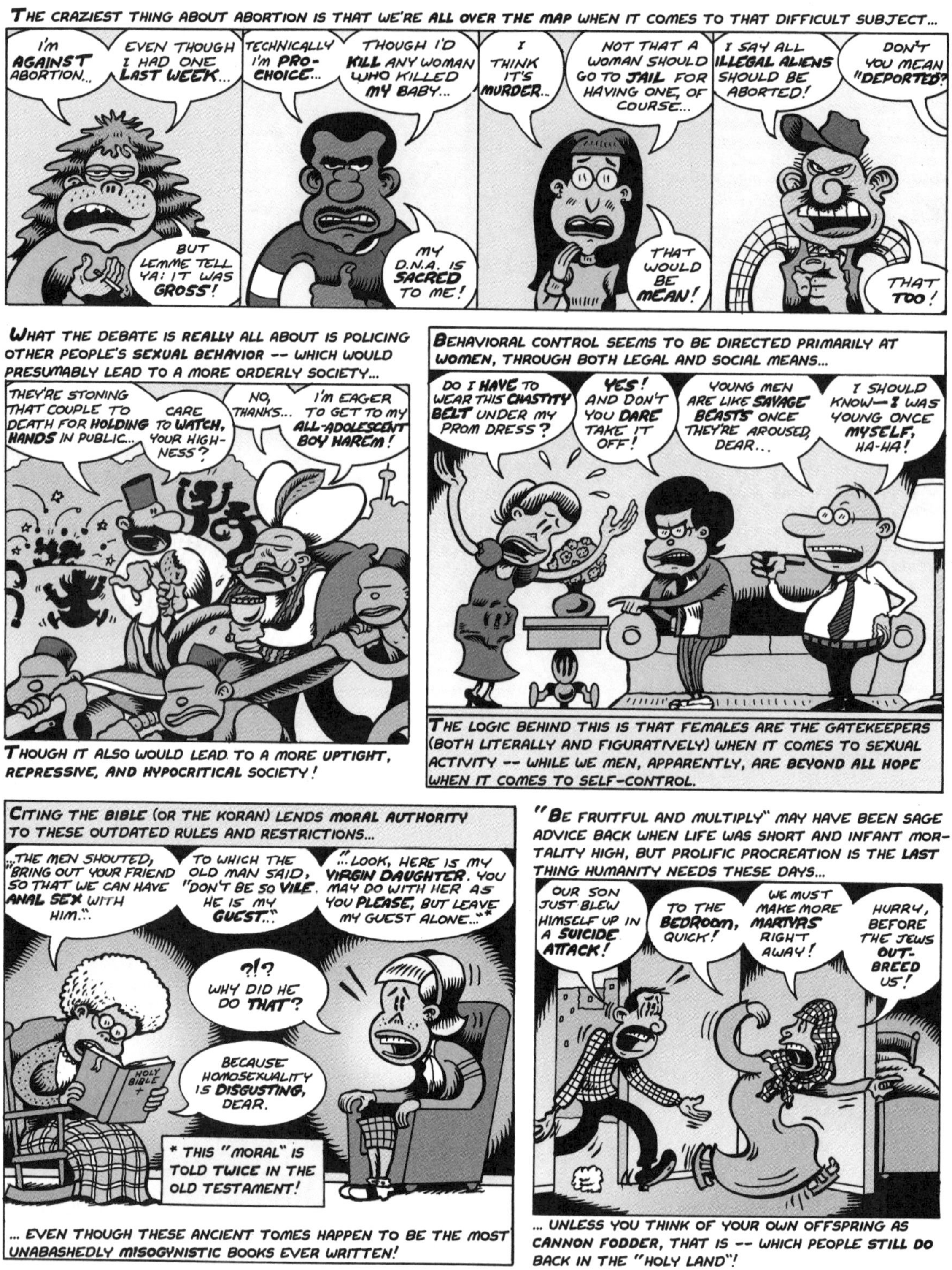
THE CRAZIEST THING ABOUT ABORTION IS THAT WE'RE ALL OVER THE MAP WHEN IT COMES TO THAT DIFFICULT SUBJECT...
I'M AGAINST ABORTION...
EVEN THOUGH I HAD ONE LAST WEEK...
BUT LEMME TELL YA: IT WAS GROSS!
TECHNICALLY I'M PRO-CHOICE...
THOUGH I'D KILL ANY WOMAN WHO KILLED MY BABY...
MY D.N.A. IS SACRED TO ME!
I THINK IT'S MURDER...
NOT THAT A WOMAN SHOULD GO TO JAIL FOR HAVING ONE, OF COURSE...
THAT WOULD BE MEAN!
I SAY ALL ILLEGAL ALIENS SHOULD BE ABORTED!
DON'T YOU MEAN "DEPORTED"?
THAT TOO!
WHAT THE DEBATE IS REALLY ALL ABOUT IS POLICING OTHER PEOPLE'S SEXUAL BEHAVIOR -- WHICH WOULD PRESUMABLY LEAD TO A MORE ORDERLY SOCIETY...
THEY'RE STONING THAT COUPLE TO DEATH FOR HOLDING HANDS IN PUBLIC...
CARE TO WATCH, YOUR HIGHNESS?
NO, THANKS...
I'M EAGER TO GET TO MY ALL-ADOLESCENT BOY HAREM!
THOUGH IT ALSO WOULD LEAD TO A MORE UPTIGHT, REPRESSIVE, AND HYPOCRITICAL SOCIETY!
BEHAVIORAL CONTROL SEEMS TO BE DIRECTED PRIMARILY AT WOMEN, THROUGH BOTH LEGAL AND SOCIAL MEANS...
DO I HAVE TO WEAR THIS CHASTITY BELT UNDER MY PROM DRESS?
YES! AND DON'T YOU DARE TAKE IT OFF!
YOUNG MEN ARE LIKE SAVAGE BEASTS ONCE THEY'RE AROUSED, DEAR...
I SHOULD KNOW— I WAS YOUNG ONCE MYSELF, HA-HA!
THE LOGIC BEHIND THIS IS THAT FEMALES ARE THE GATEKEEPERS (BOTH LITERALLY AND FIGURATIVELY) WHEN IT COMES TO SEXUAL ACTIVITY -- WHILE WE MEN, APPARENTLY, ARE BEYOND ALL HOPE WHEN IT COMES TO SELF-CONTROL.
CITING THE BIBLE (OR THE KORAN) LENDS MORAL AUTHORITY TO THESE OUTDATED RULES AND RESTRICTIONS...
...THE MEN SHOUTED, "BRING OUT YOUR FRIEND SO THAT WE CAN HAVE ANAL SEX WITH HIM."...
TO WHICH THE OLD MAN SAID, "DON'T BE SO VILE. HE IS MY GUEST."...
"...LOOK, HERE IS MY VIRGIN DAUGHTER. YOU MAY DO WITH HER AS YOU PLEASE, BUT LEAVE MY GUEST ALONE..."*
?!?
WHY DID HE DO THAT?
BECAUSE HOMOSEXUALITY IS DISGUSTING, DEAR.
HOLY BIBLE
* THIS "MORAL" IS TOLD TWICE IN THE OLD TESTAMENT!
... EVEN THOUGH THESE ANCIENT TOMES HAPPEN TO BE THE MOST UNABASHEDLY MISOGYNISTIC BOOKS EVER WRITTEN!
"BE FRUITFUL AND MULTIPLY" MAY HAVE BEEN SAGE ADVICE BACK WHEN LIFE WAS SHORT AND INFANT MORTALITY HIGH, BUT PROLIFIC PROCREATION IS THE LAST THING HUMANITY NEEDS THESE DAYS...
OUR SON JUST BLEW HIMSELF UP IN A SUICIDE ATTACK!
TO THE BEDROOM, QUICK!
WE MUST MAKE MORE MARTYRS RIGHT AWAY!
HURRY, BEFORE THE JEWS OUT-BREED US!
... UNLESS YOU THINK OF YOUR OWN OFFSPRING AS CANNON FODDER, THAT IS -- WHICH PEOPLE STILL DO BACK IN THE "HOLY LAND"!

MEANWHILE, BACK IN 21ST-CENTURY AMERICA, OUR PRESIDENT CONTINUES WITH HIS TOTALLY PUNK ROCK "MESSING UP THE SYSTEM FROM WITHIN" STRATEGY BY APPOINTING CONTRACEPTION OPPONENTS IN KEY POSITIONS, SUCH AS:

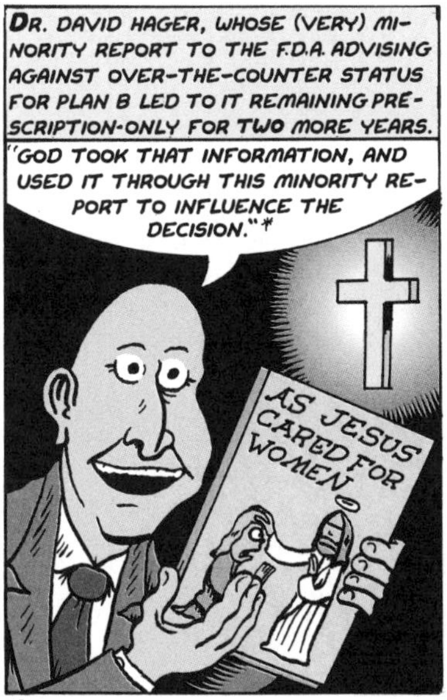
DR. DAVID HAGER, WHOSE (VERY) MINORITY REPORT TO THE F.D.A. ADVISING AGAINST OVER-THE-COUNTER STATUS FOR PLAN B LED TO IT REMAINING PRESCRIPTION-ONLY FOR **TWO** MORE YEARS.
"GOD TOOK THAT INFORMATION, AND USED IT THROUGH THIS MINORITY REPORT TO INFLUENCE THE DECISION."*
AS JESUS CARED FOR WOMEN

HAGER'S EX-WIFE HAS SINCE TOLD THE PRESS THAT THE GOOD DOCTOR USED TO ROUTINELY **ANALLY RAPE** HER IN HER SLEEP!

*WASHINGTON POST, 5/12/05

DR. ERIC KEROACK, WHO BRIEFLY WAS DEPUTY ASSISTANT DIRECTOR OF "POPULATION AFFAIRS" AT H.H.S. BEFORE QUESTIONS ABOUT MEDICAID FRAUD FORCED HIS **RESIGNATION**.

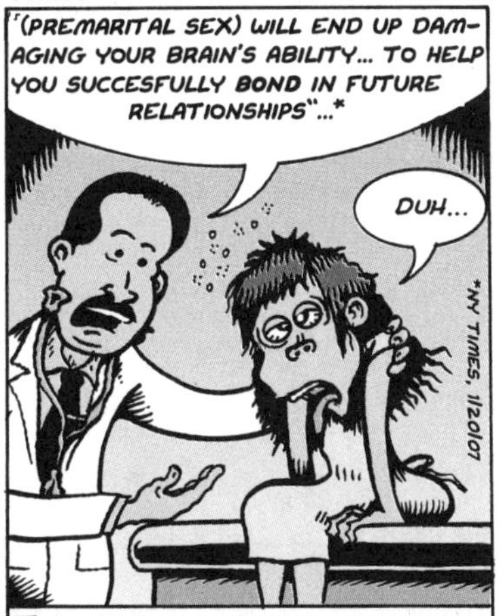
"(PREMARITAL SEX) WILL END UP DAMAGING YOUR BRAIN'S ABILITY... TO HELP YOU SUCCESFULLY **BOND** IN FUTURE RELATIONSHIPS"...*
DUH...
*NY TIMES, 1/20/07

THAT'S RIGHT: HORMONES CAN TELL IF YOU'RE MARRIED! KEROACK ALSO RAN ONE OF THOSE BOGUS "WOMEN'S HEALTH" CLINICS WHOSE SOLE PURPOSE IS TO **DISCOURAGE ABORTIONS**.

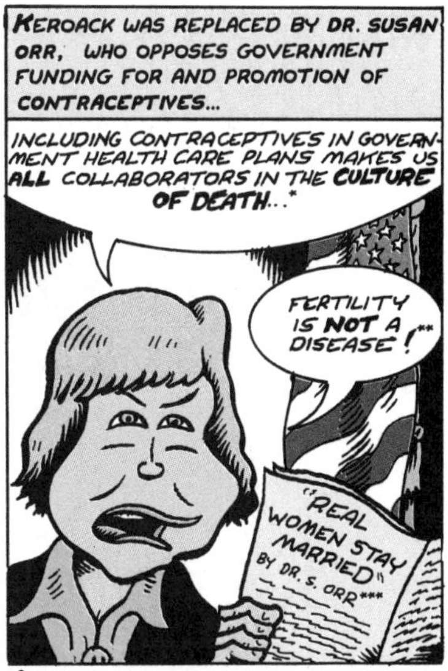
KEROACK WAS REPLACED BY **DR. SUSAN ORR**, WHO OPPOSES GOVERNMENT FUNDING FOR AND PROMOTION OF **CONTRACEPTIVES**...
INCLUDING CONTRACEPTIVES IN GOVERNMENT HEALTH CARE PLANS MAKES US **ALL** COLLABORATORS IN THE **CULTURE OF DEATH**...*
FERTILITY IS **NOT** A DISEASE!**
"REAL WOMEN STAY MARRIED" BY DR. S. ORR***

YET SHE HAS NO PROBLEM SPENDING PUBLIC MONEY ON INEFFECTIVE **ABSTINENCE PROGRAMS** (DISCLOSURE: ORR IS A FORMER DIRECTOR OF SOCIAL POLICY FOR THE REASON FOUNDATION). (*CBS NEWS, 10/19/07. **WASH. POST, 4/12/01, ***WASHINGTON WATCH, 6/00).

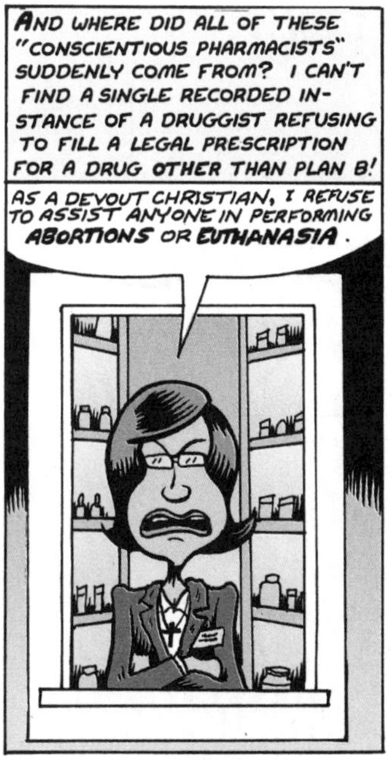
AND WHERE DID ALL OF THESE "CONSCIENTIOUS PHARMACISTS" SUDDENLY COME FROM? I CAN'T FIND A SINGLE RECORDED INSTANCE OF A DRUGGIST REFUSING TO FILL A LEGAL PRESCRIPTION FOR A DRUG **OTHER** THAN PLAN B!
AS A DEVOUT CHRISTIAN, I REFUSE TO ASSIST ANYONE IN PERFORMING **ABORTIONS** OR **EUTHANASIA**.

EUTHANASIA? TAKEN IN THE RIGHT (OR WRONG) DOSE, WOULDN'T THAT INCLUDE **MOST** OF WHAT A PHARMACY SELLS?

PLAN B'S CRITICS CLAIM IT WILL ENCOURAGE **PROMISCUITY** AMONG TEENAGERS, THOUGH THERE'S NO EVIDENCE TO BACK UP THIS CLAIM...

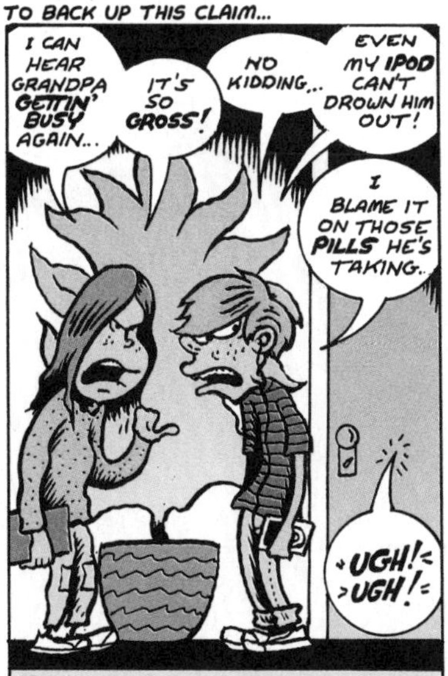
I CAN HEAR GRANDPA **GETTIN' BUSY** AGAIN...
IT'S SO **GROSS**!
NO KIDDING...
EVEN MY **IPOD** CAN'T DROWN HIM OUT!
I BLAME IT ON THOSE **PILLS** HE'S TAKING...
UGH! UGH!

MEANWHILE, VIAGRA HAS CONTRIBUTED TO THE SPREAD OF S.T.D.S AMONG THE **ELDERLY**, YET AS FAR AS I KNOW NO PHARMACIST HAS EVER REFUSED TO FILL A PRESCRIPTION FOR **THAT** DRUG!

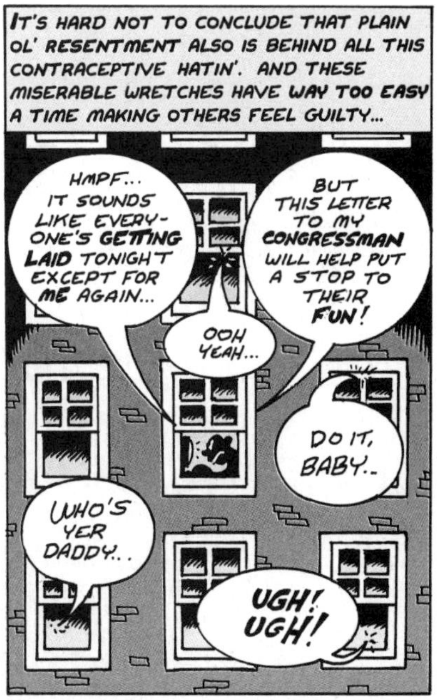
IT'S HARD NOT TO CONCLUDE THAT PLAIN OL' **RESENTMENT** ALSO IS BEHIND ALL THIS CONTRACEPTIVE HATIN'. AND THESE MISERABLE WRETCHES HAVE **WAY TOO EASY** A TIME MAKING OTHERS FEEL GUILTY...
HMPF... IT SOUNDS LIKE EVERYONE'S **GETTING LAID** TONIGHT EXCEPT FOR **ME** AGAIN...
BUT THIS LETTER TO MY **CONGRESSMAN** WILL HELP PUT A STOP TO THEIR **FUN**!
OOH YEAH...
DO IT, BABY...
WHO'S YER DADDY...
UGH! UGH!

TO THIS I SAY, **DON'T GIVE UP THE FIGHT**! STICK IT TO THE MAN BY **FORNICATING YOUR HEAD OFF**! AND ALWAYS HAVE PLENTY OF PLAN B ON HAND, JUST IN CASE!

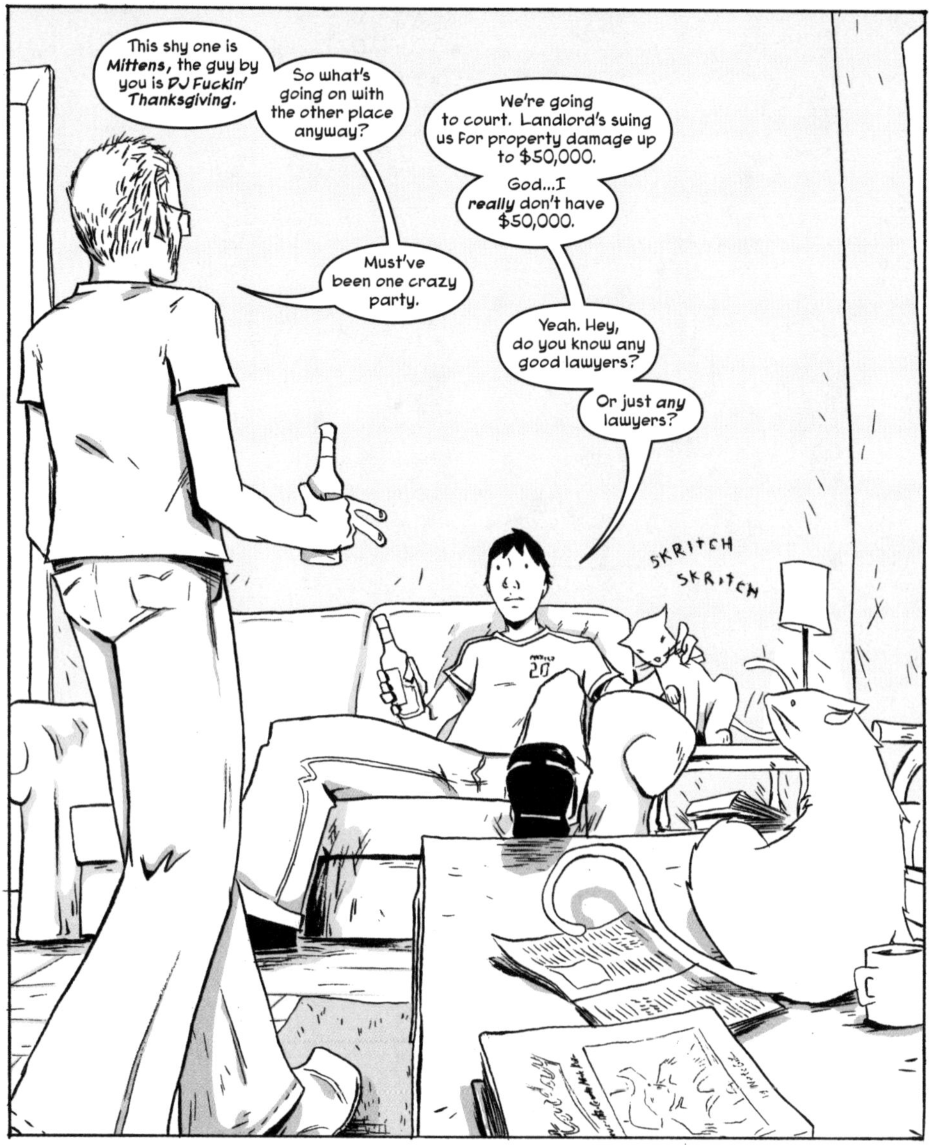
This shy one is *Mittens*, the guy by you is *DJ Fuckin' Thanksgiving*.
So what's going on with the other place anyway?
Must've been one crazy party.
We're going to court. Landlord's suing us for property damage up to $50,000.
God...I *really* don't have $50,000.
Yeah. Hey, do you know any good lawyers?
Or just *any* lawyers?
SKRITCH
SKRITCH

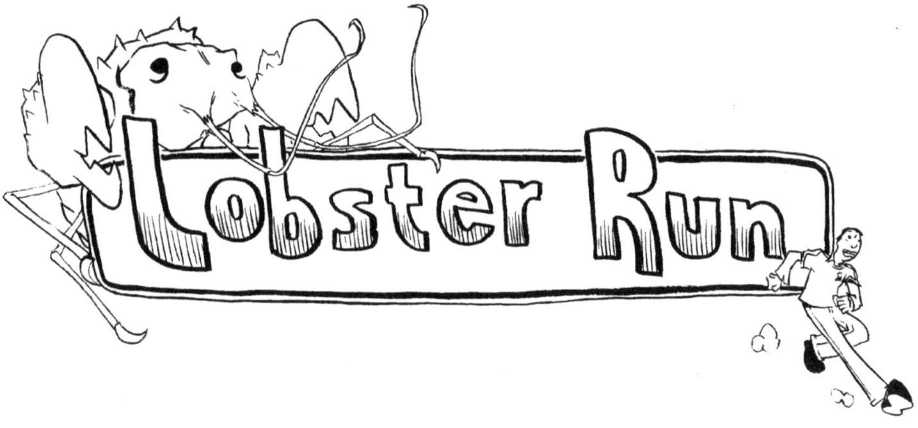
Lobster Run

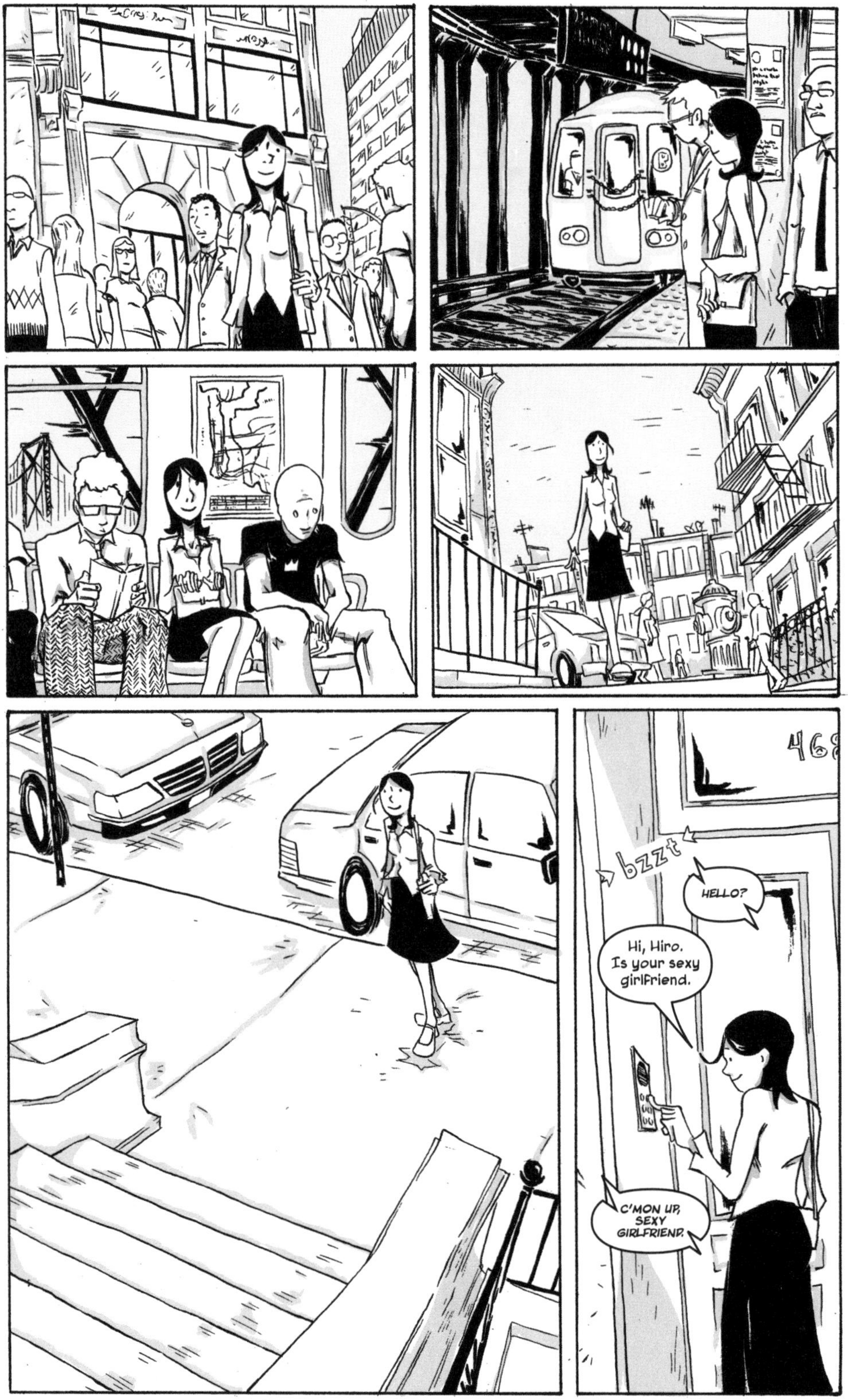

bzzt
HELLO?
Hi, Hiro. Is your sexy girlfriend.
C'MON UP, SEXY GIRLFRIEND.

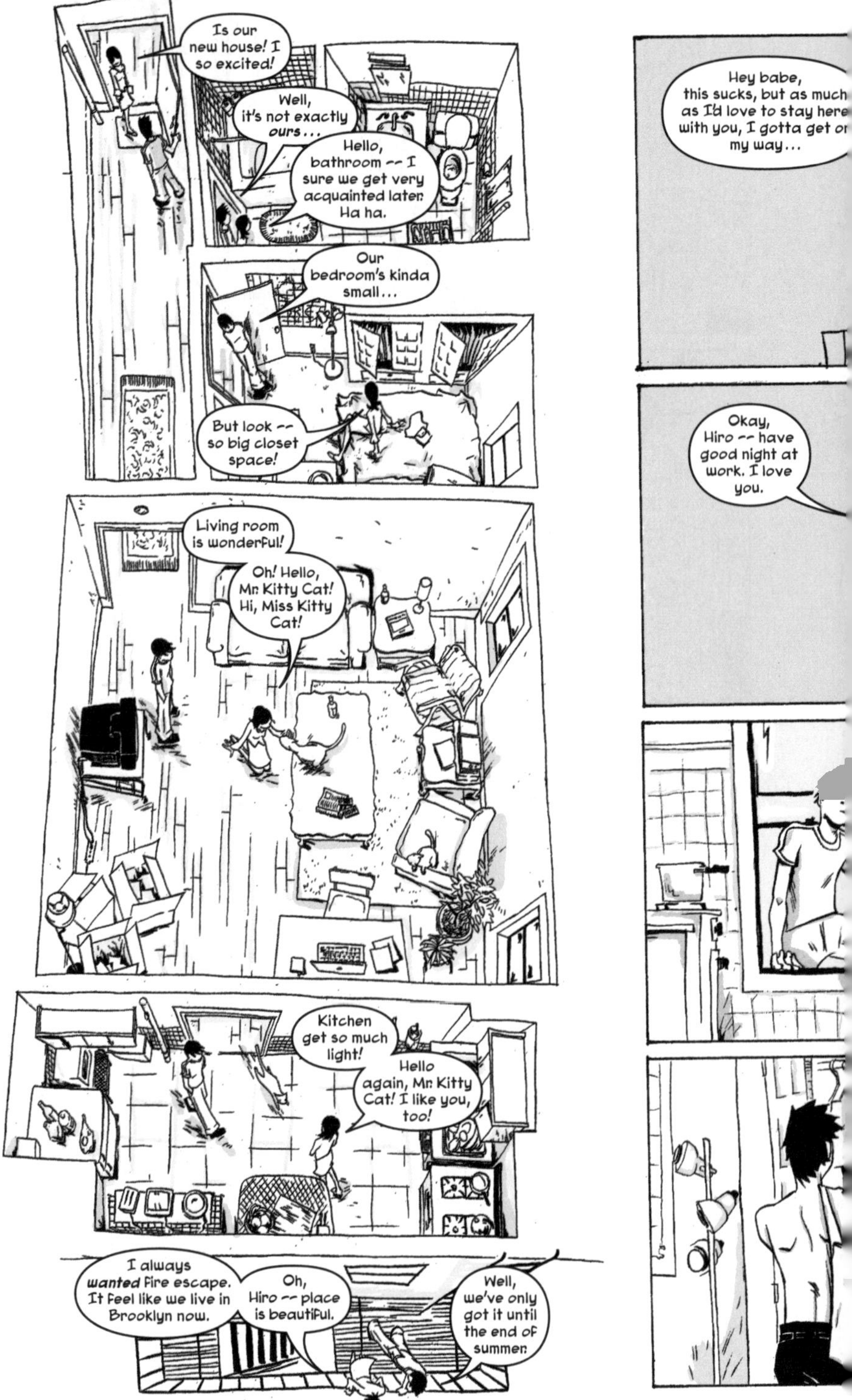
Is our new house! I so excited!
Well, it's not exactly *ours*...
Hello, bathroom -- I sure we get very acquainted later. Ha ha.
Our bedroom's kinda small...
But look -- so big closet space!
Living room is wonderful!
Oh! Hello, Mr. Kitty Cat! Hi, Miss Kitty Cat!
Kitchen get so much light!
Hello again, Mr. Kitty Cat! I like you, too!
I always *wanted* fire escape. It feel like we live in Brooklyn now.
Oh, Hiro -- place is beautiful.
Well, we've only got it until the end of summer.
Hey babe, this sucks, but as much as I'd love to stay here with you, I gotta get
my way...
Okay, Hiro -- have good night at work. I love you.

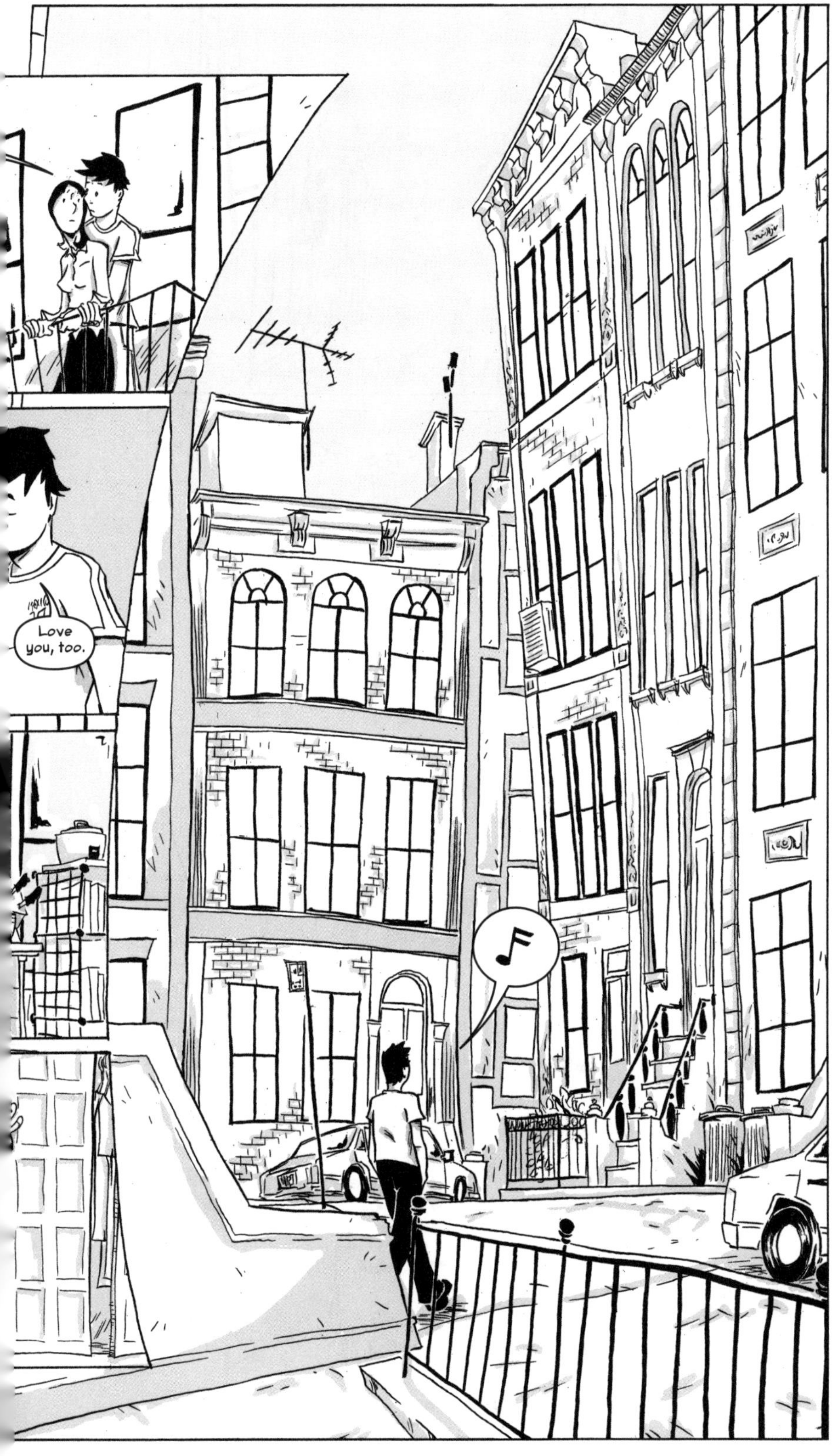
Love you, too.

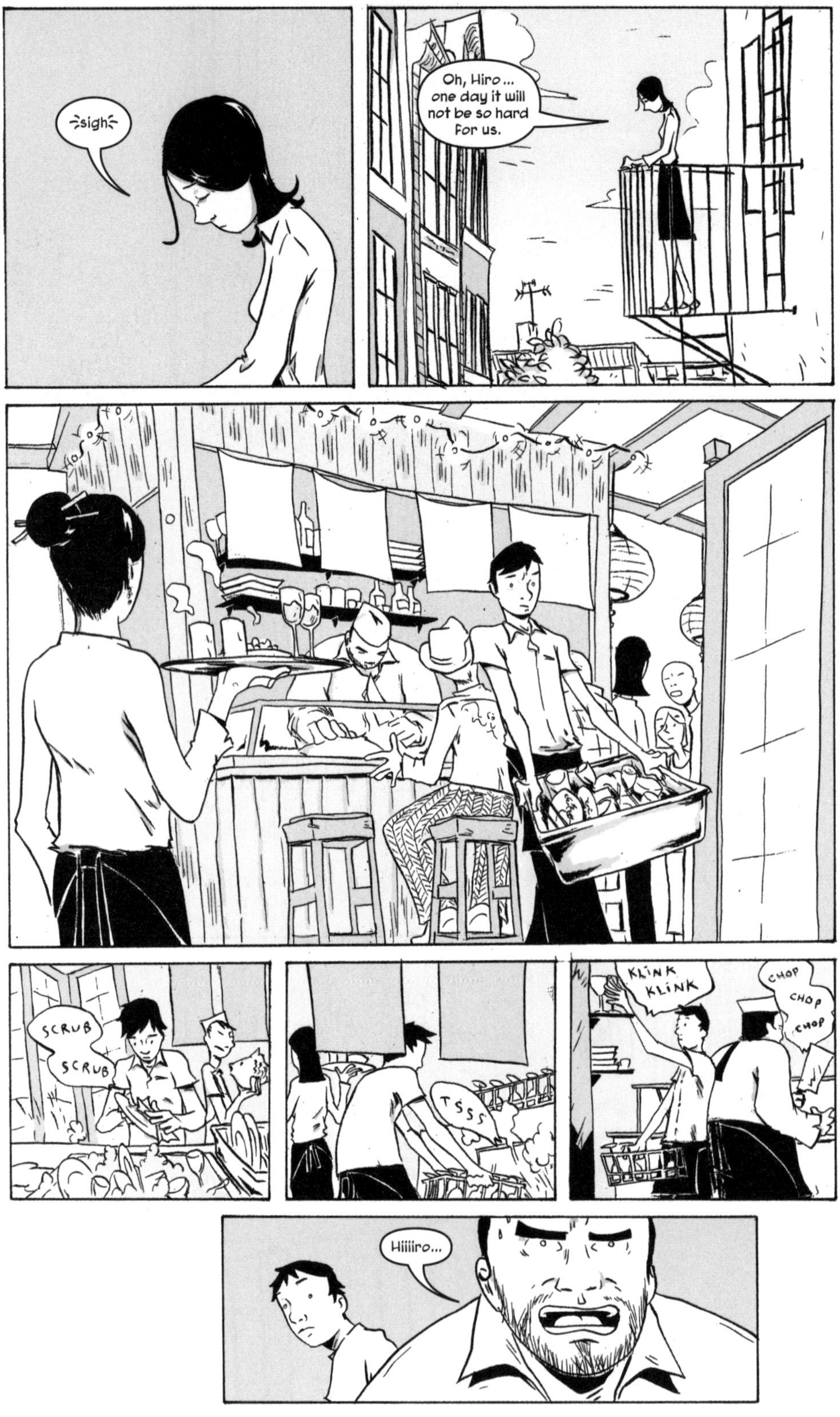
sigh
Oh, Hiro... one day it will not be so hard for us.
SCRUB
SCRUB
TSSS
KLINK
KLINK
CHOP
CHOP
CHOP
Hiiiiro...

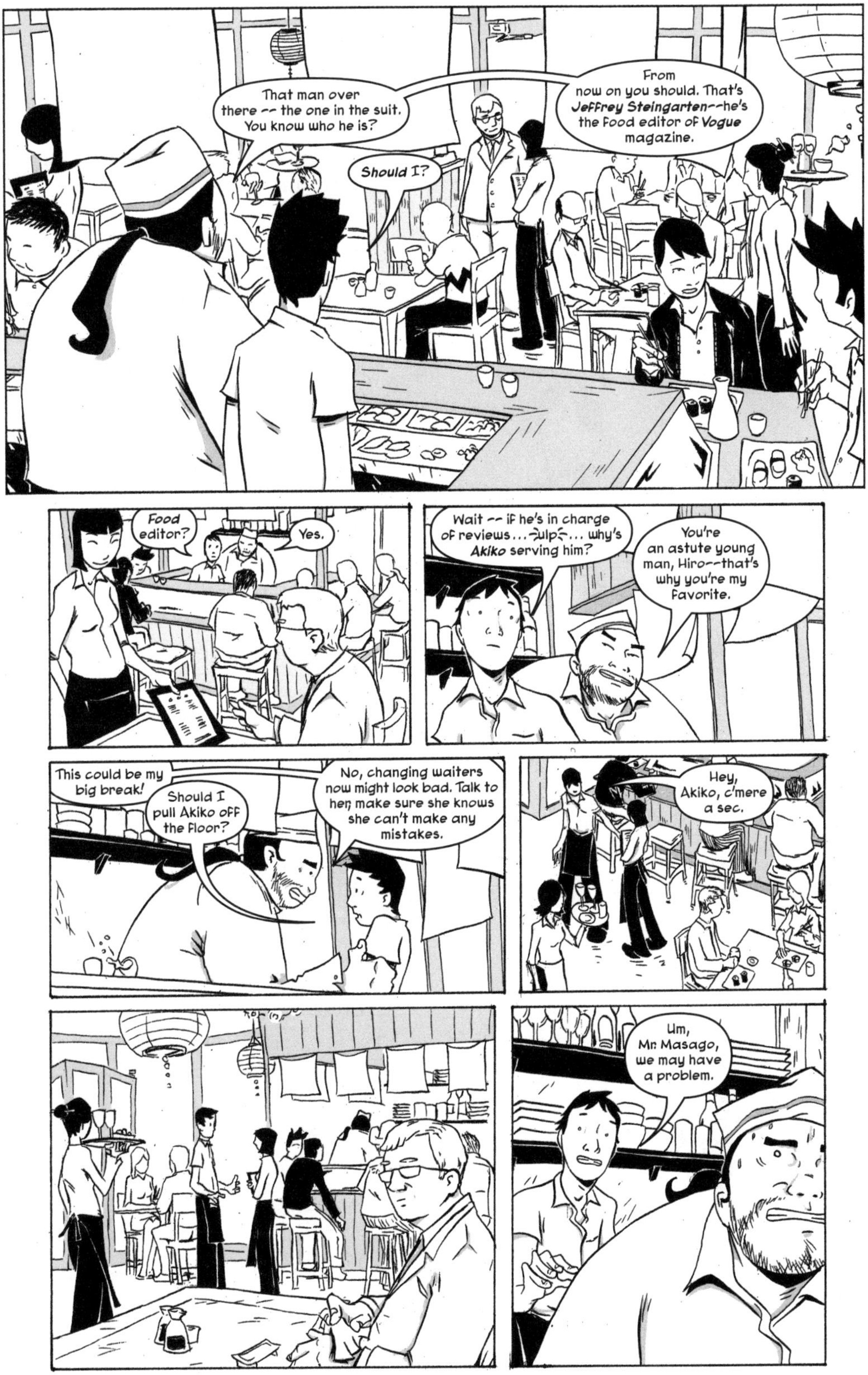

That man over there -- the one in the suit. You know who he is?
Should I?
From now on you should. That's Jeffrey Steingarten--he's the food editor of Vogue magazine.
Food editor?
Yes.
Wait -- if he's in charge of reviews... gulp... why's Akiko serving him?
You're an astute young man, Hiro--that's why you're my favorite.
This could be my big break!
Should I pull Akiko off the floor?
No, changing waiters now might look bad. Talk to her, make sure she knows she can't make any mistakes.
Hey, Akiko, c'mere a sec.
Um, Mr. Masago, we may have a problem.

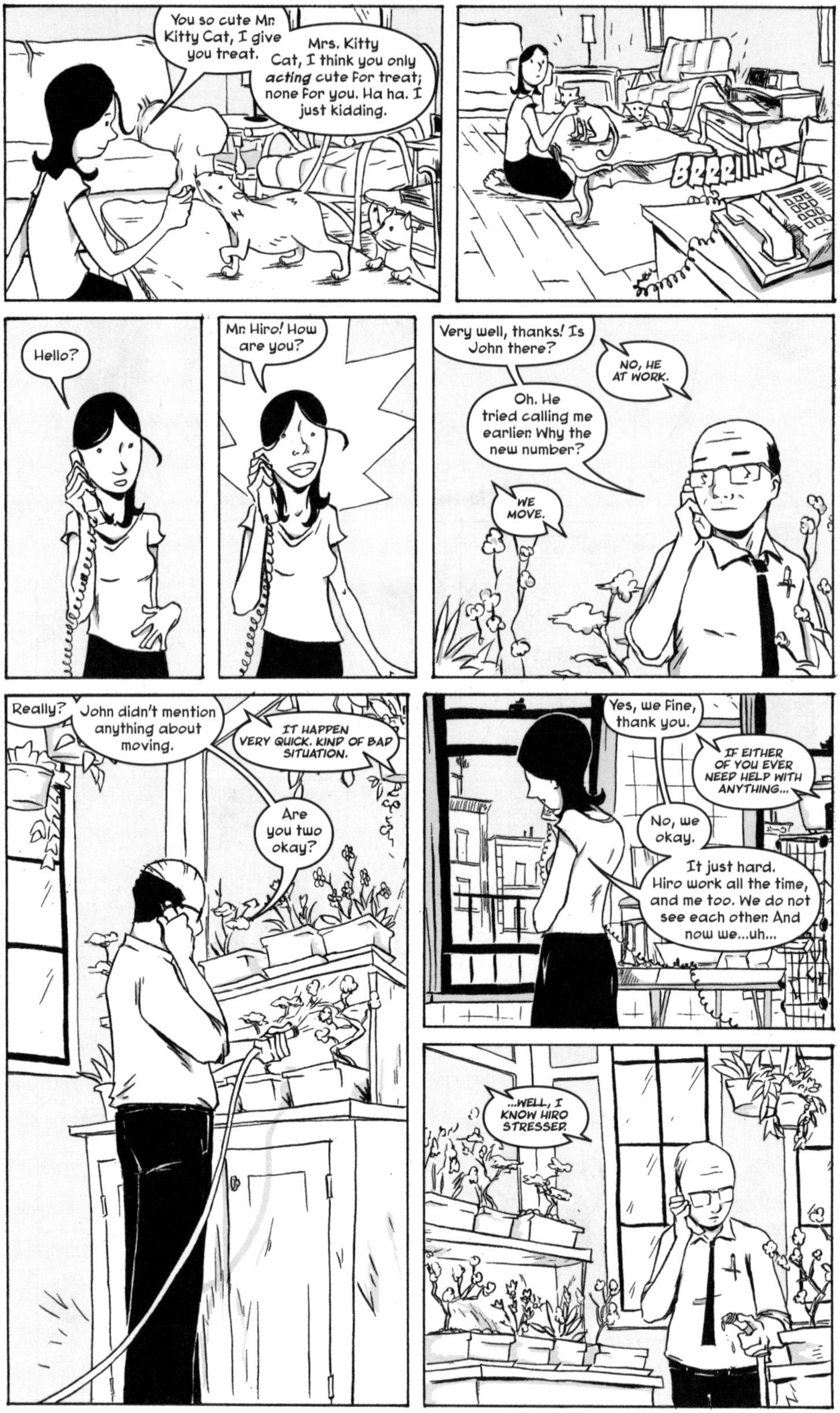
You so cute Mr. Kitty Cat, I give you treat.
Mrs. Kitty Cat, I think you only *acting* cute for treat; none for you. Ha ha. I just kidding.
BRRRIIING
Hello?
Mr. Hiro! How are you?
Very well, thanks! Is John there?
NO, HE AT WORK.
Oh. He tried calling me earlier. Why the new number?
WE MOVE.
Really?
John didn't mention anything about moving.
IT HAPPEN VERY QUICK. KIND OF BAD SITUATION.
Are you two okay?
Yes, we fine, thank you.
IF EITHER OF YOU EVER NEED HELP WITH ANYTHING...
No, we okay.
It just hard. Hiro work all the time, and me too. We do not see each other. And now we...uh...
...WELL, I KNOW HIRO STRESSED.

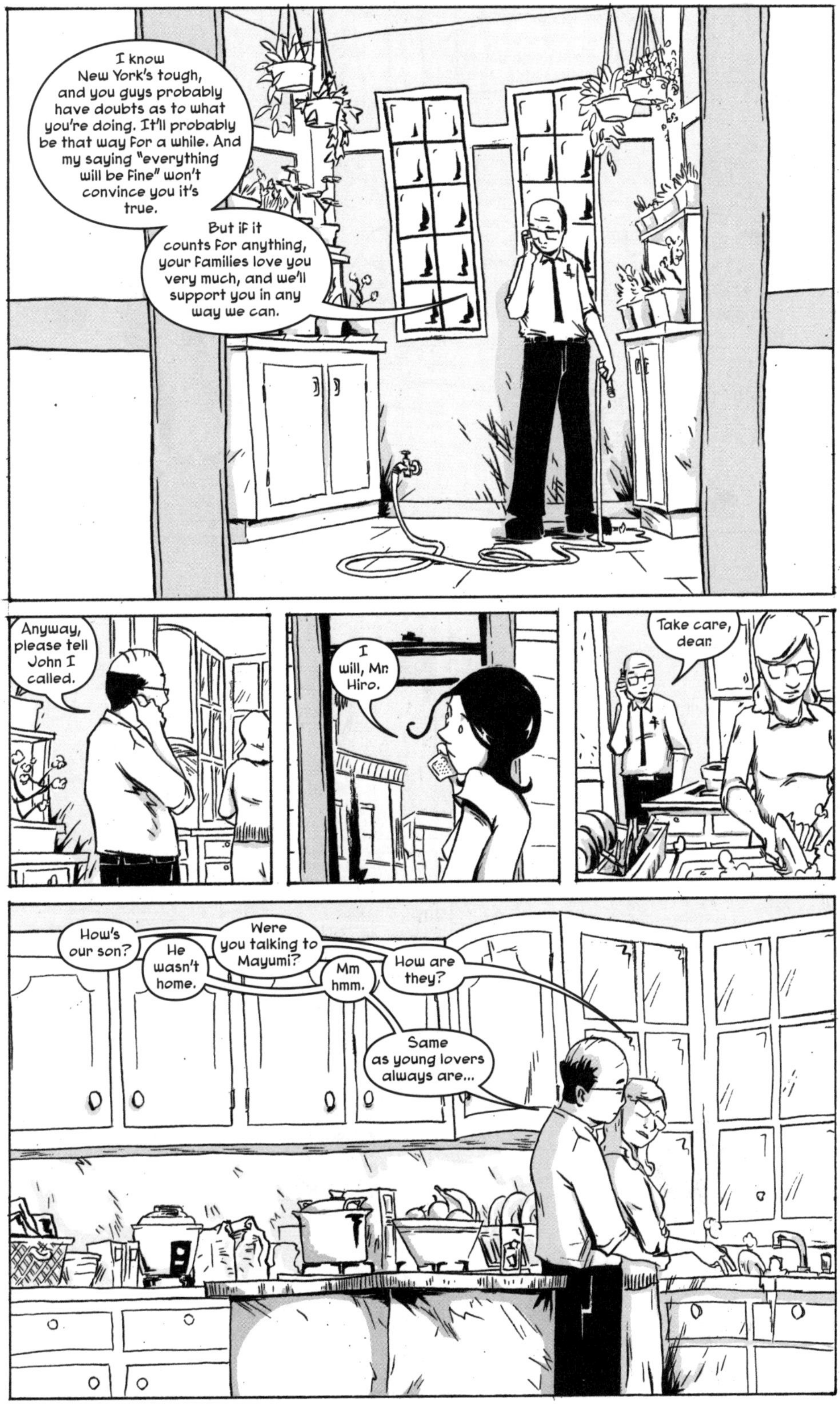

I know New York's tough, and you guys probably have doubts as to what you're doing. It'll probably be that way for a while. And my saying "everything will be fine" won't convince you it's true.
But if it counts for anything, your families love you very much, and we'll support you in any way we can.
Anyway, please tell John I called.
I will, Mr. Hiro.
Take care, dear.
How's our son?
He wasn't home.
Were you talking to Mayumi?
Mm hmm.
How are they?
Same as young lovers always are...

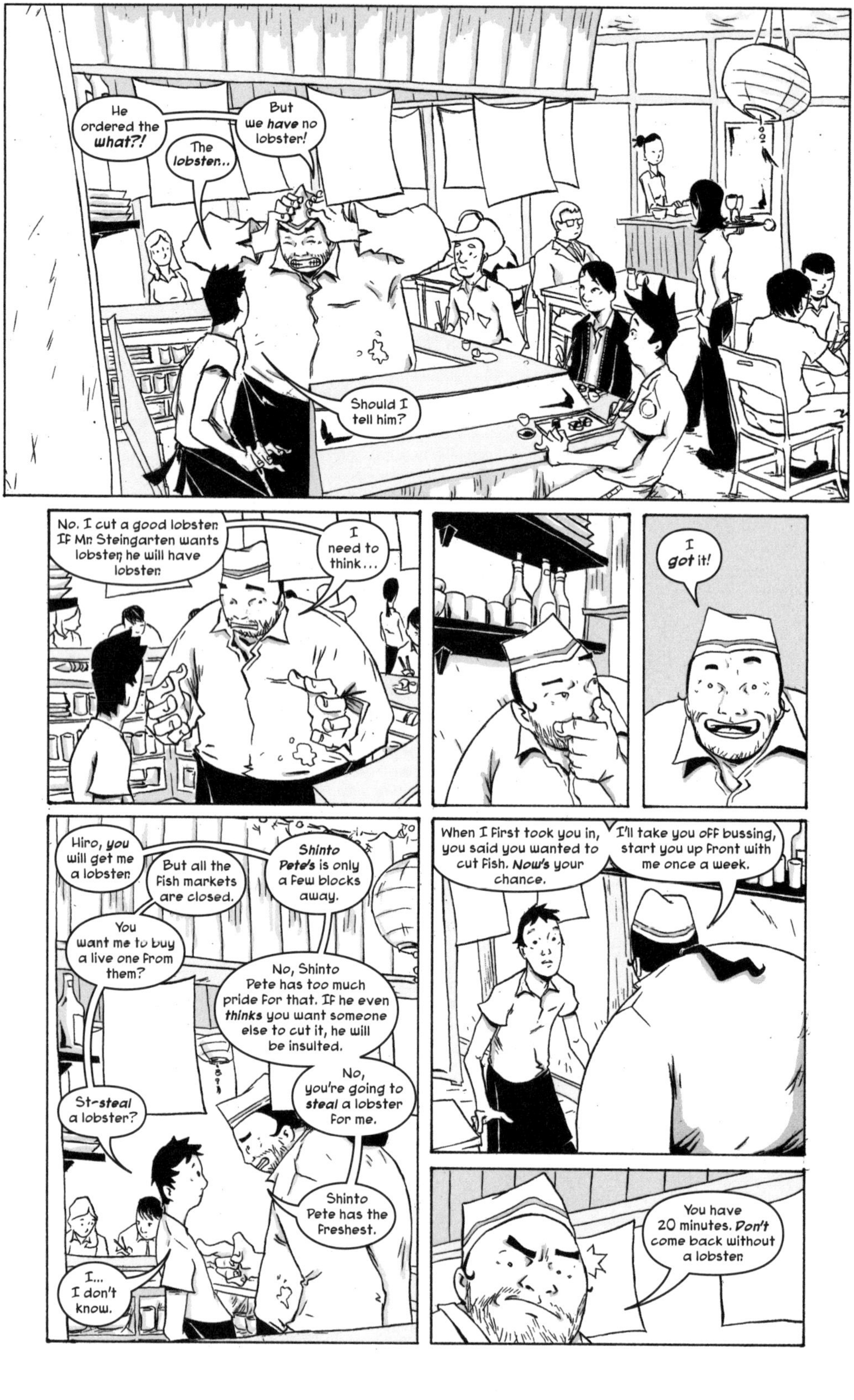
He ordered the *what?!*
But we *have* no lobster!
The *lobster...*
Should I tell him?
No. I cut a good lobster. If Mr. Steingarten wants lobster, he will have lobster.
I need to think...
I *got* it!
Hiro, *you* will get me a lobster.
But all the fish markets are closed.
Shinto Pete's is only a few blocks away.
You want me to buy a live one from them?
No, Shinto Pete has too much pride for that. If he even *thinks* you want someone else to cut it, he will be insulted.
No, you're going to *steal* a lobster for me.
St-*steal* a lobster?
Shinto Pete has the freshest.
I... I don't know.
When I first took you in, you said you wanted to cut fish. *Now's* your chance.
I'll take you off bussing, start you up front with me once a week.
You have 20 minutes. *Don't* come back without a lobster.

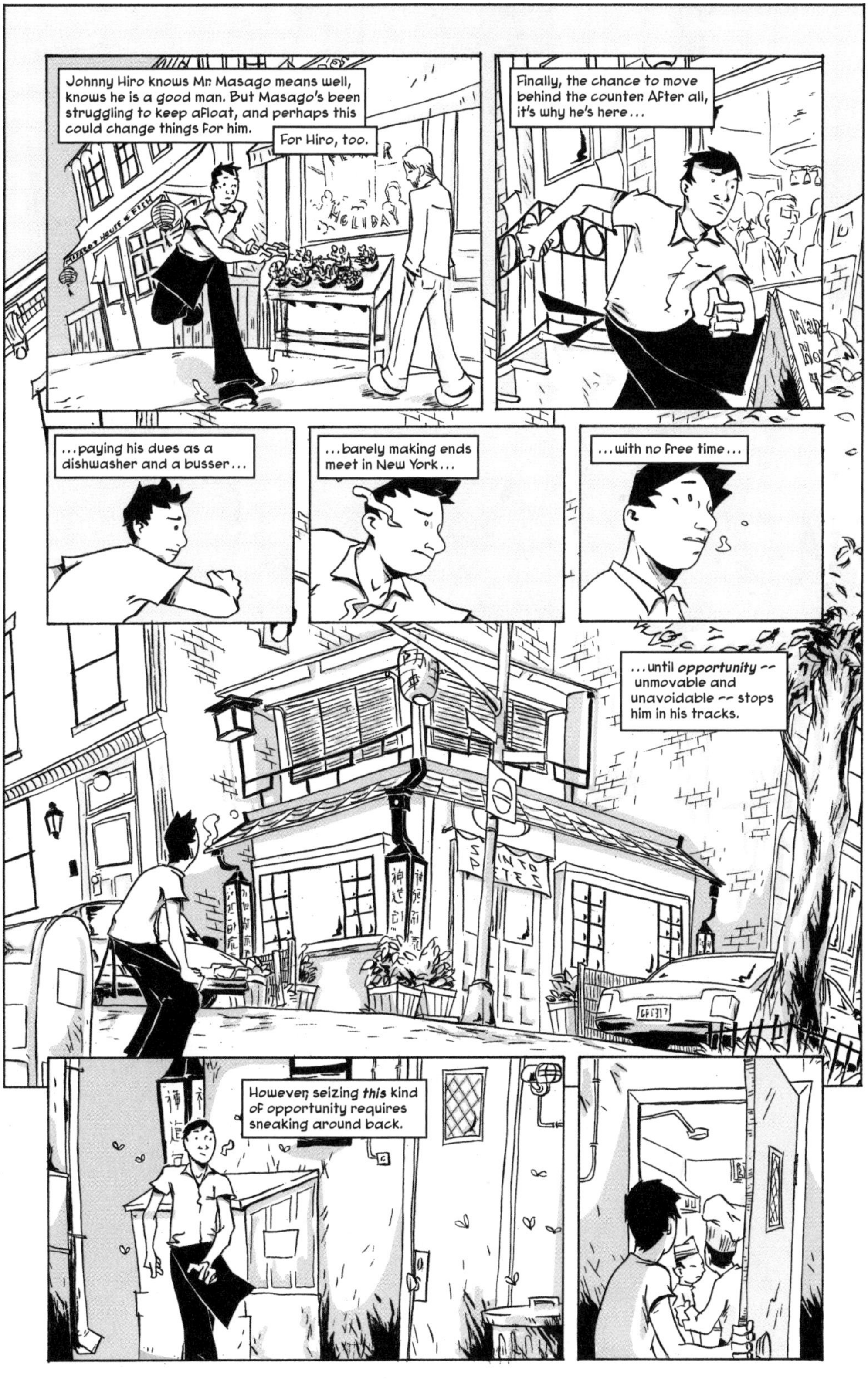
Johnny Hiro knows Mr. Masago means well, knows he is a good man. But Masago's been struggling to keep afloat, and perhaps this could change things for him.
For Hiro, too.
Finally, the chance to move behind the counter. After all, it's why he's here...
...paying his dues as a dishwasher and a busser...
...barely making ends meet in New York...
...with no free time...
...until *opportunity* -- unmovable and unavoidable -- stops him in his tracks.
However, seizing *this* kind of opportunity requires sneaking around back.

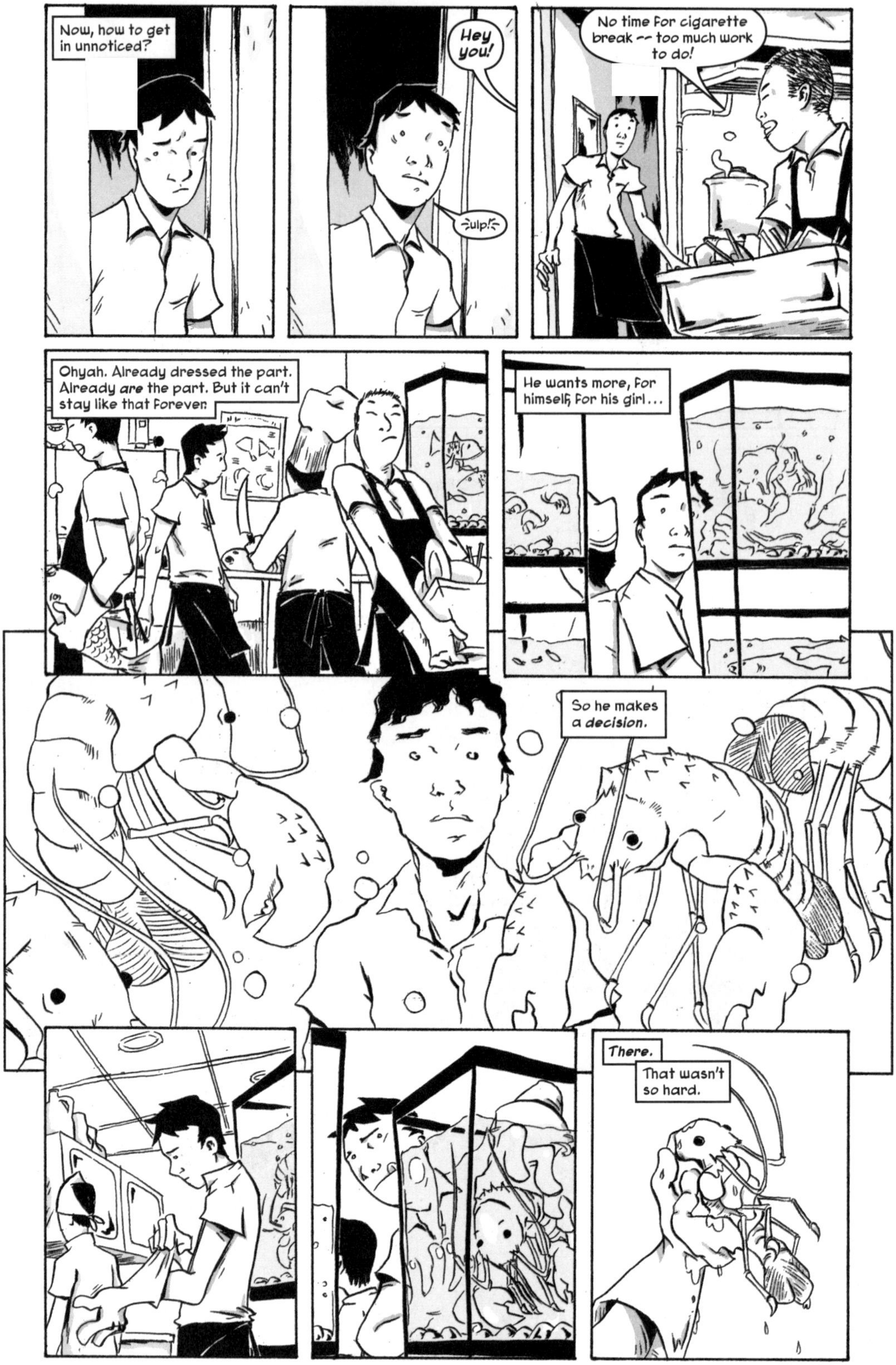
Now, how to get in unnoticed?
Hey you!
ulp!
No time for cigarette break -- too much work to do!
Ohyah. Already dressed the part. Already *are* the part. But it can't stay like that forever.
He wants more, for himself, for his girl...
So he makes a *decision.*
There.
That wasn't so hard.

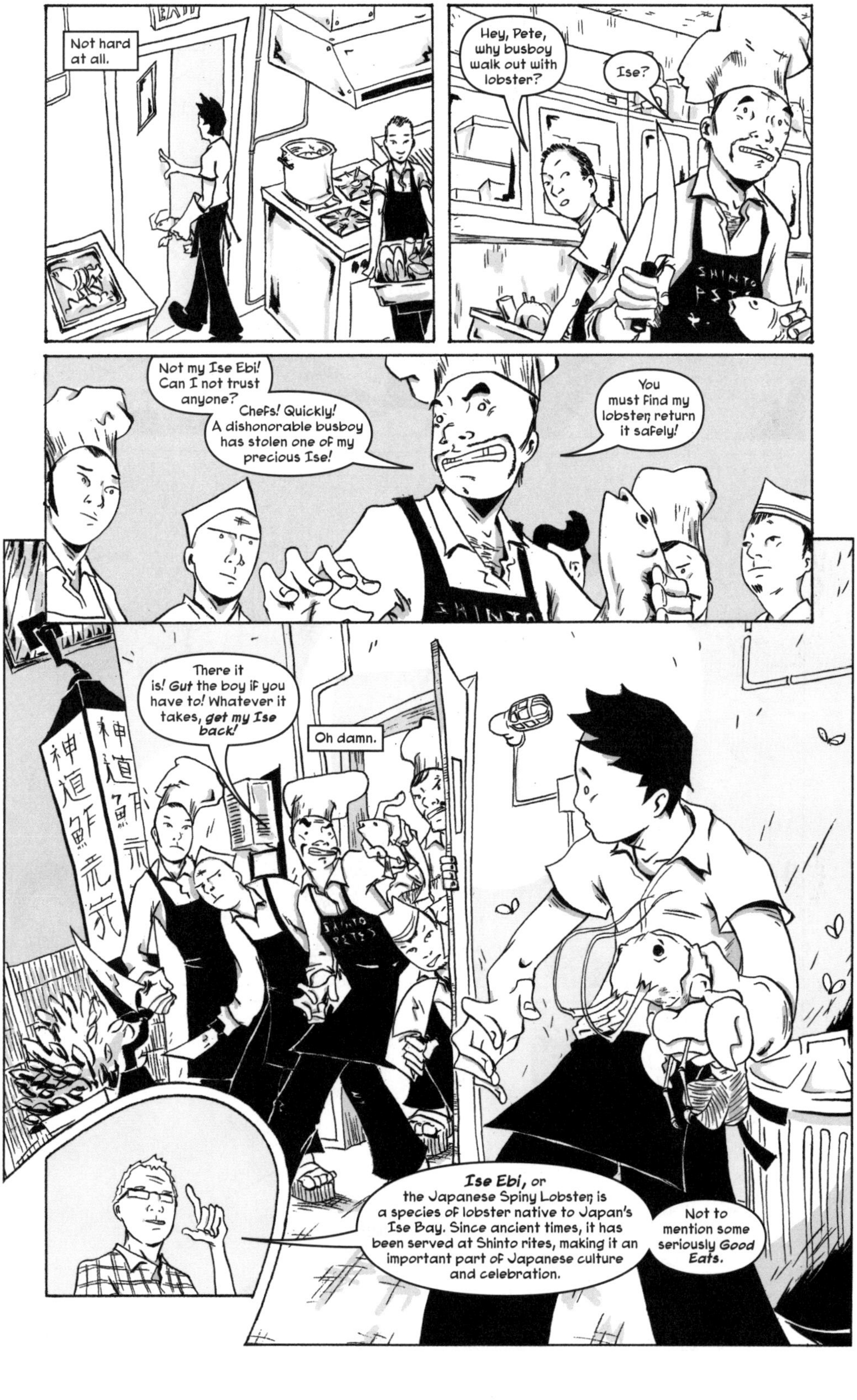

Not hard at all.
Hey, Pete, why busboy walk out with lobster?
Ise?
Not my Ise Ebi! Can I not trust anyone?
Chefs! Quickly! A dishonorable busboy has stolen one of my precious Ise!
You must find my lobster, return it safely!
There it is! Gut the boy if you have to! Whatever it takes, get my Ise back!
Oh damn.
Ise Ebi, or the Japanese Spiny Lobster, is a species of lobster native to Japan's Ise Bay. Since ancient times, it has been served at Shinto rites, making it an important part of Japanese culture and celebration.
Not to mention some seriously Good Eats.

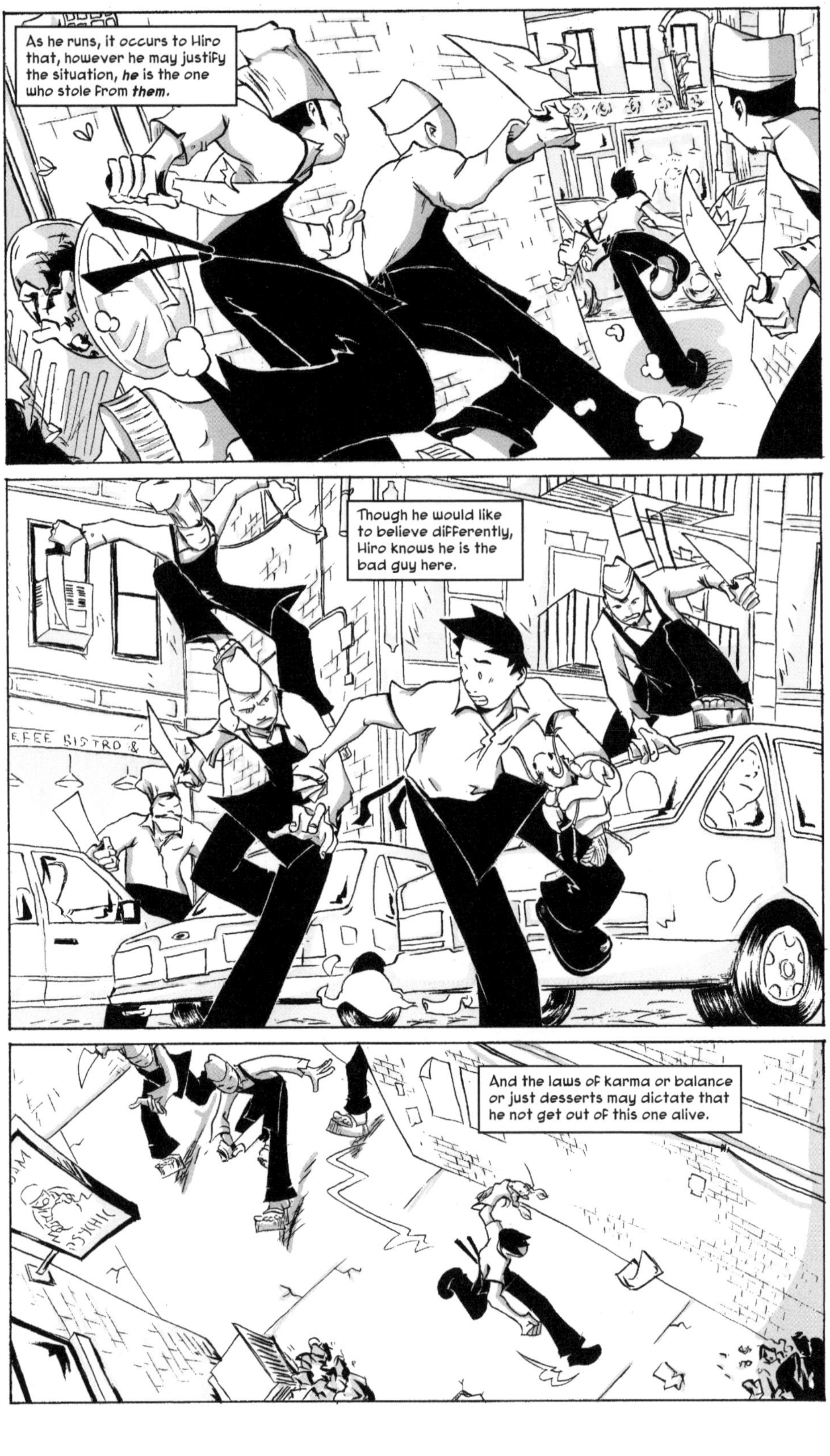
As he runs, it occurs to Hiro that, however he may justify the situation, ***he*** is the one who stole from ***them***.
Though he would like to believe differently, Hiro knows he is the bad guy here.
And the laws of karma or balance or just desserts may dictate that he not get out of this one alive.

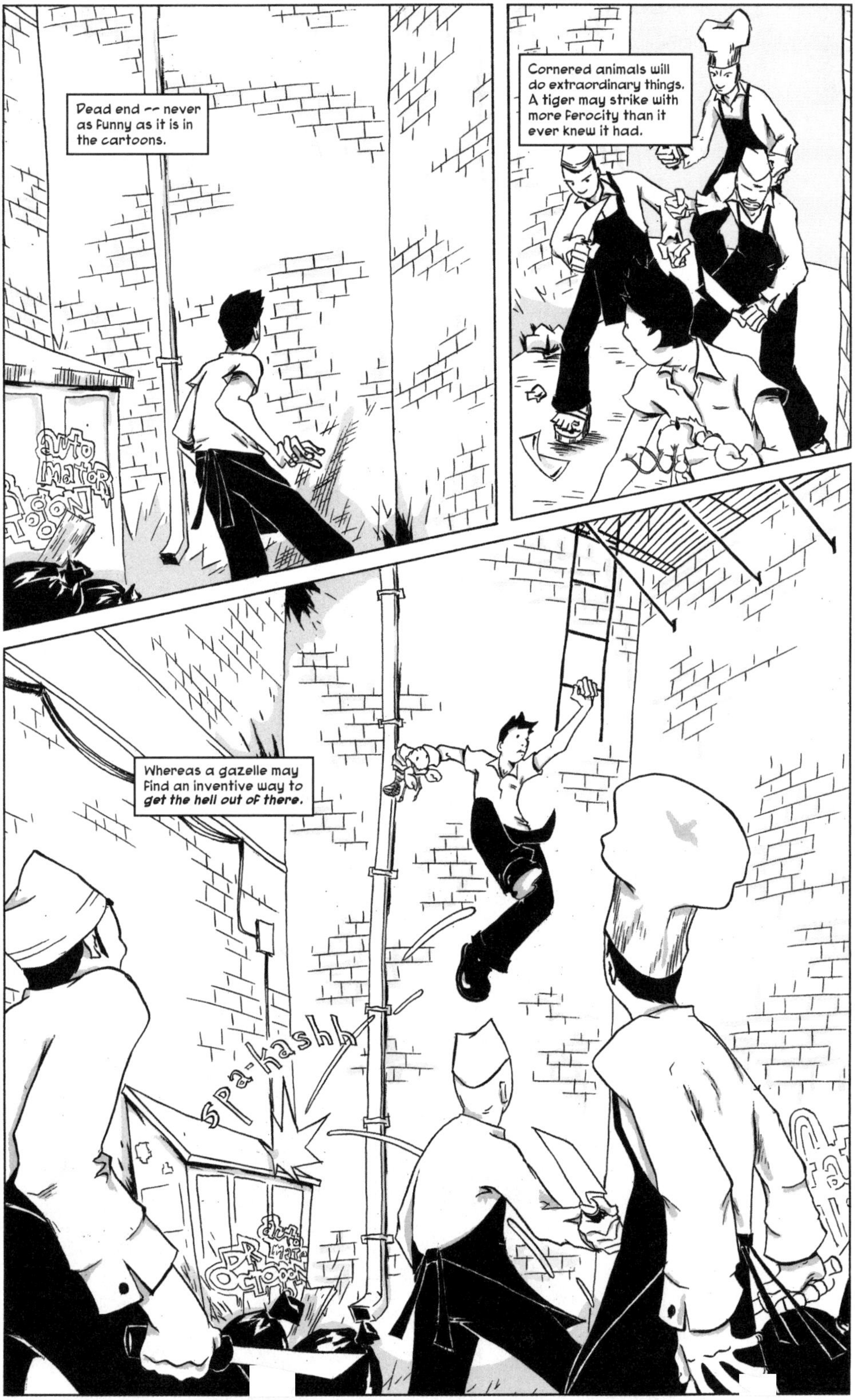
Dead end -- never as funny as it is in the cartoons.
Cornered animals will do extraordinary things. A tiger may strike with more ferocity than it ever knew it had.
Whereas a gazelle may find an inventive way to *get the hell out of there.*
spa-kashh

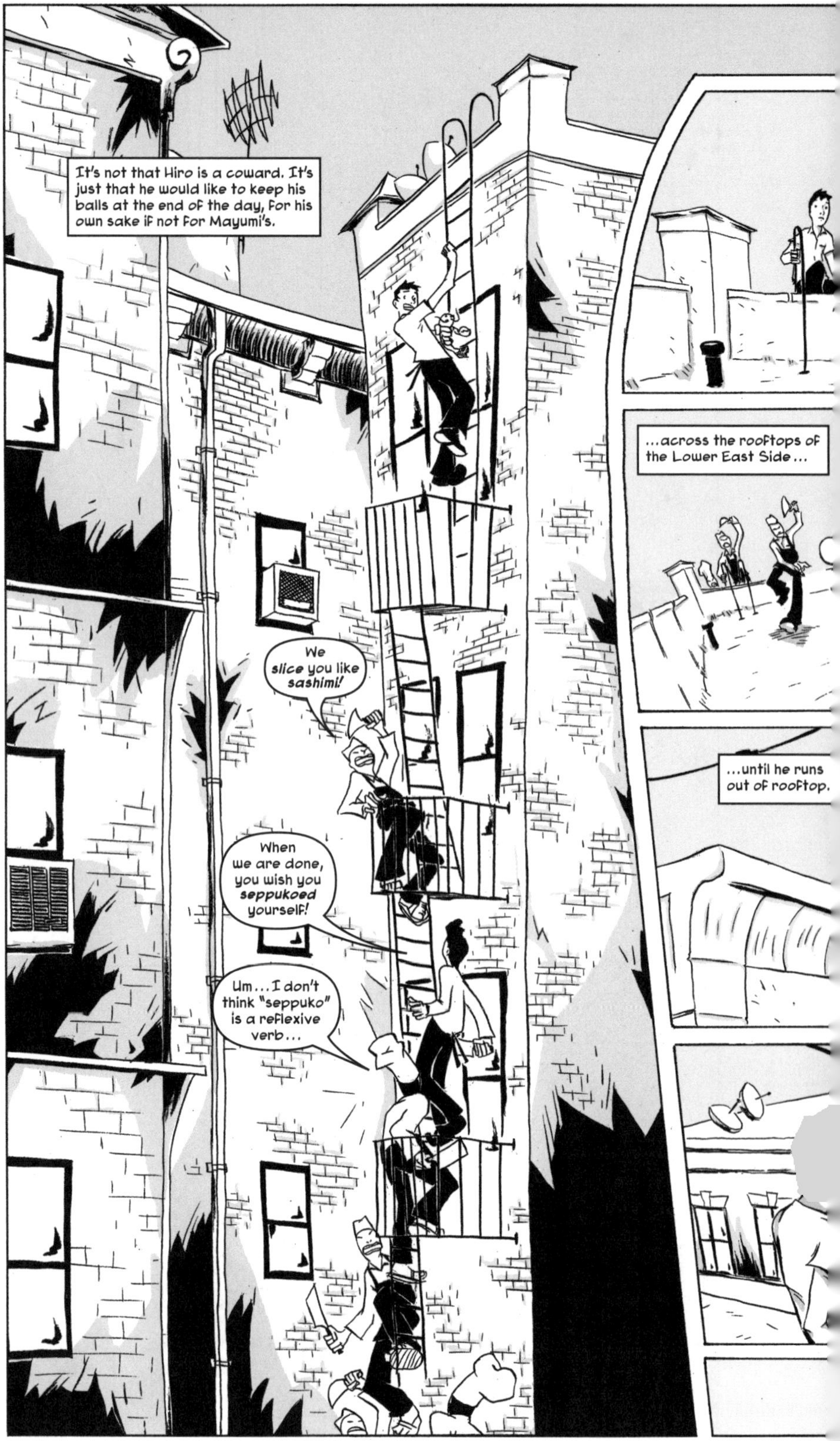
It's not that Hiro is a coward. It's just that he would like to keep his balls at the end of the day, for his own sake if not for Mayumi's.
We slice you like sashimi!
When we are done, you wish you seppukoed yourself!
Um... I don't think "seppuko" is a reflexive verb...
...across the rooftops of the Lower East Side...
...until he runs out of rooftop.

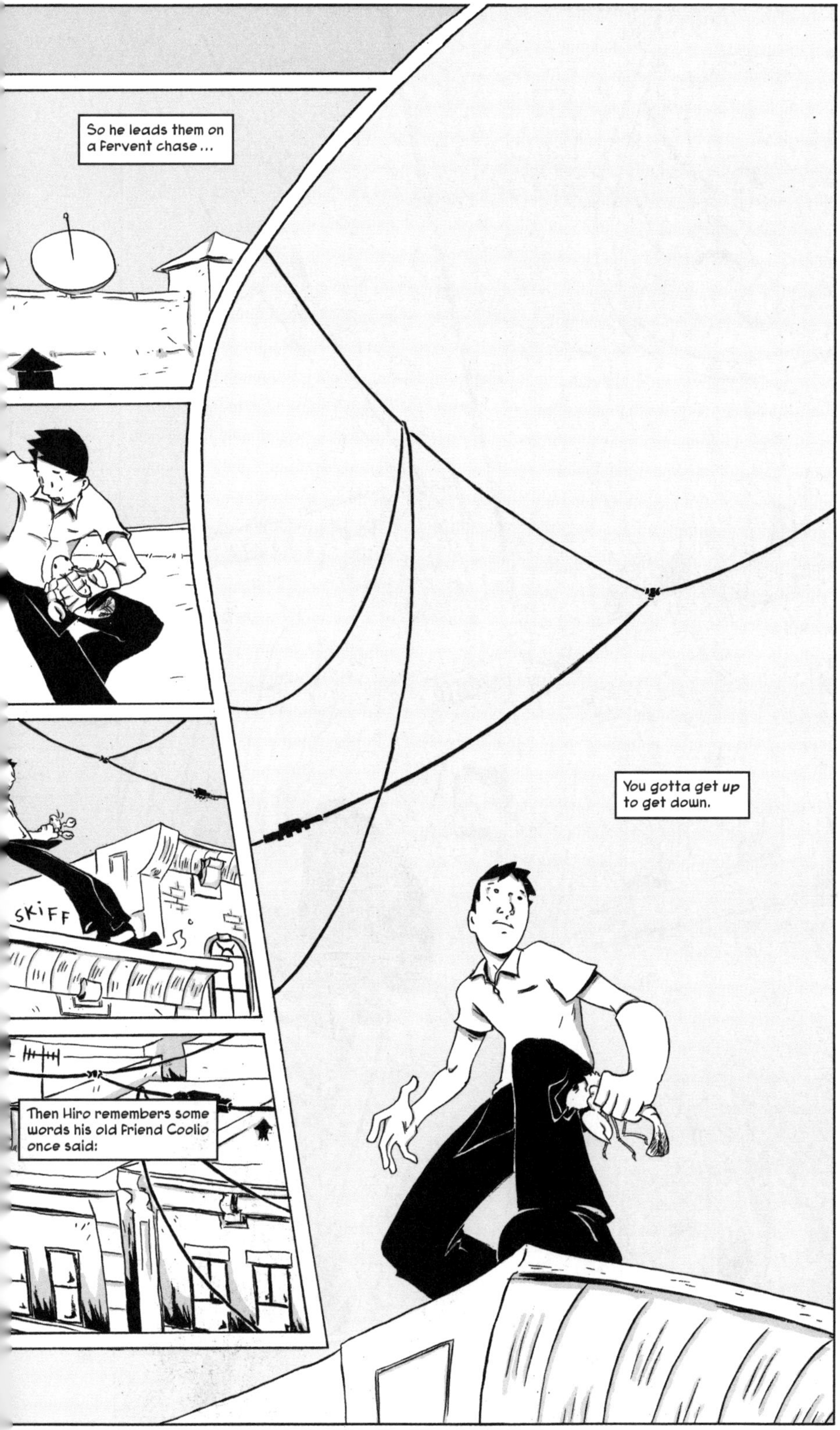
So he leads them on a fervent chase...
SKIFF
Then Hiro remembers some words his old friend Coolio once said:
You gotta get up to get down.

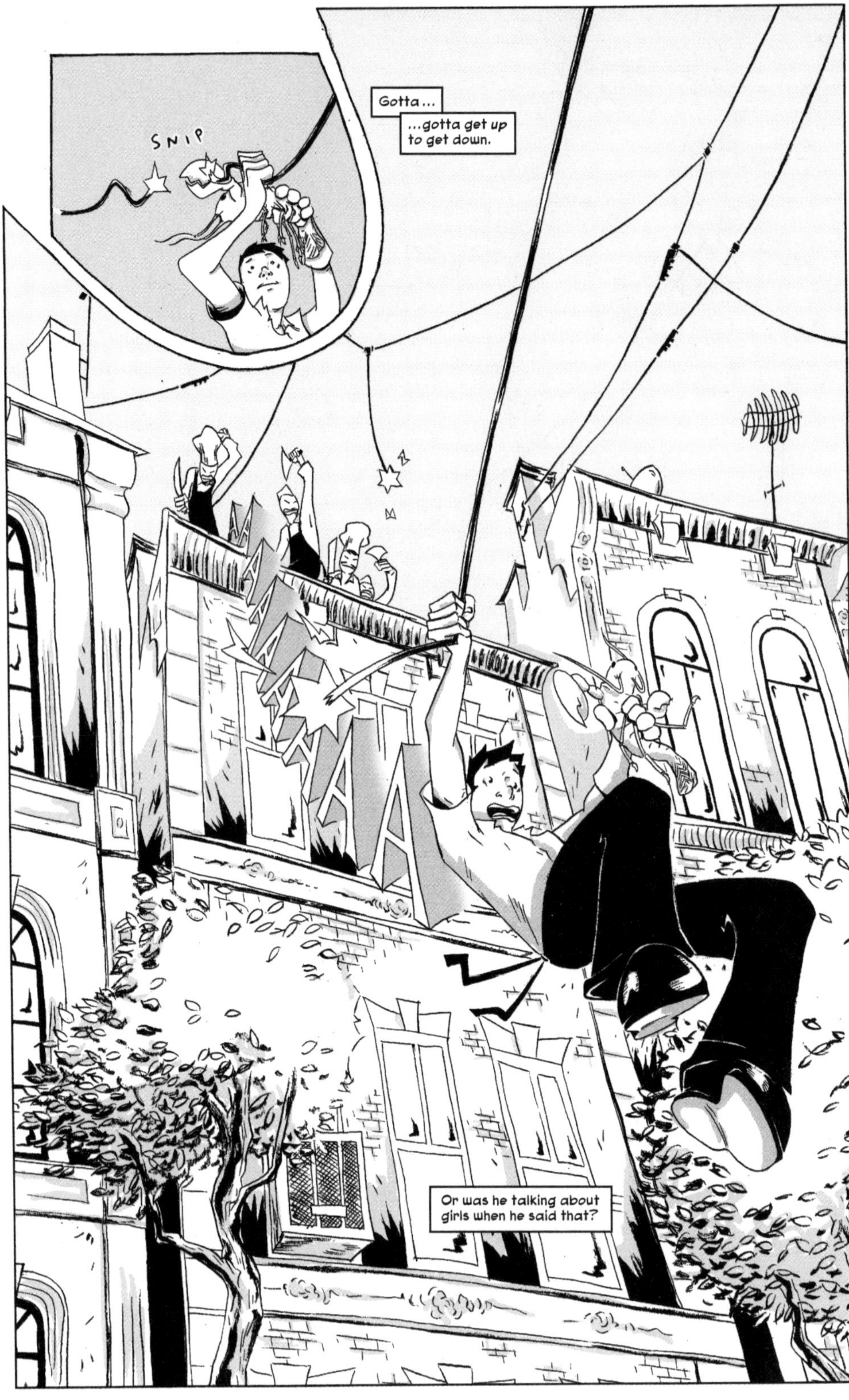
SNIP
Gotta...
...gotta get up to get down.
Or was he talking about girls when he said that?

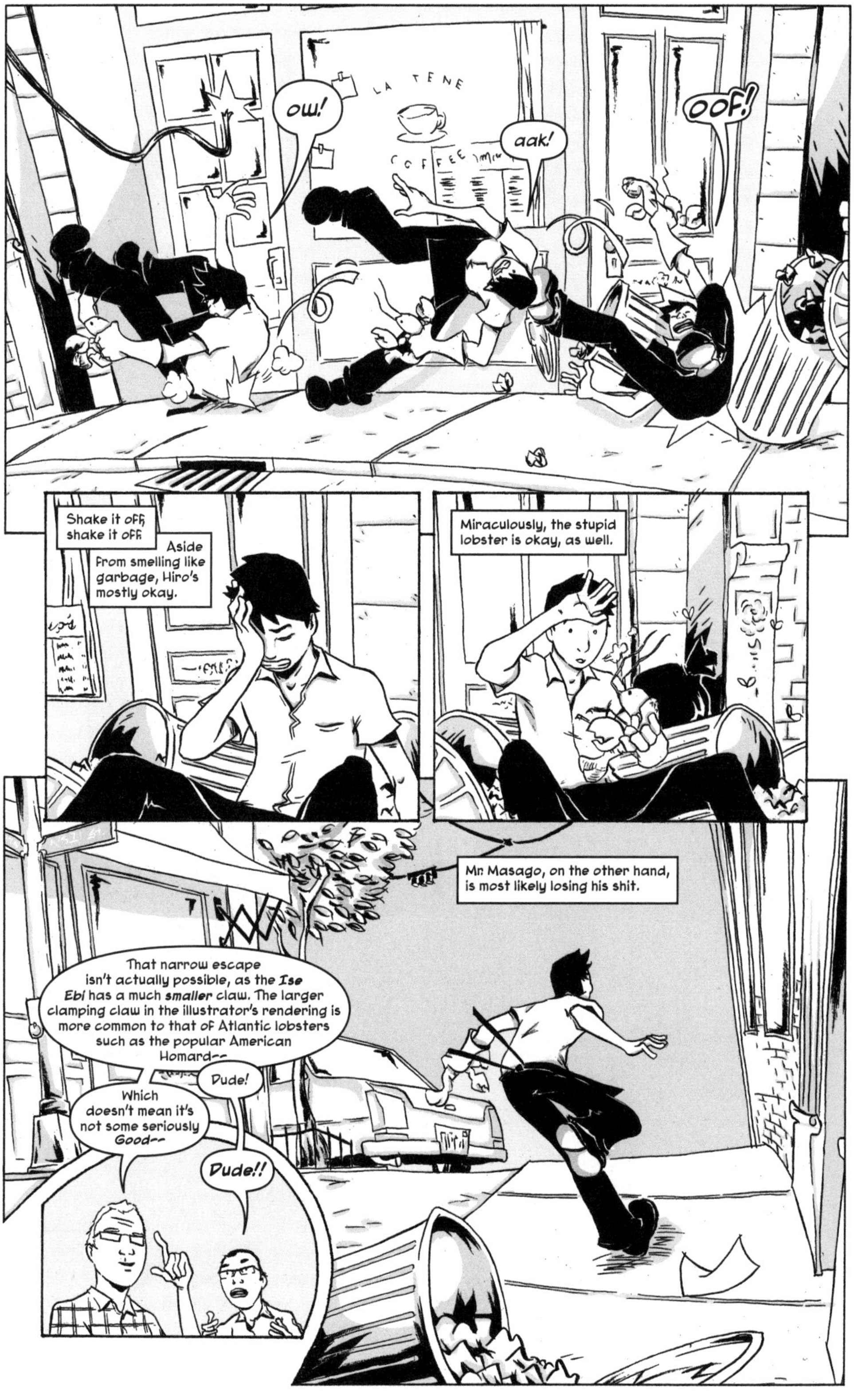

LA TENE
COFFEE
ow!
aak!
OOF!
Shake it off, shake it off.
Aside from smelling like garbage, Hiro's mostly okay.
Miraculously, the stupid lobster is okay, as well.
Mr. Masago, on the other hand, is most likely losing his shit.
That narrow escape isn't actually possible, as the *Ise Ebi* has a much *smaller* claw. The larger clamping claw in the illustrator's rendering is more common to that of Atlantic lobsters such as the popular American Homard--
Dude!
Which doesn't mean it's not some seriously *Good*--
Dude!!

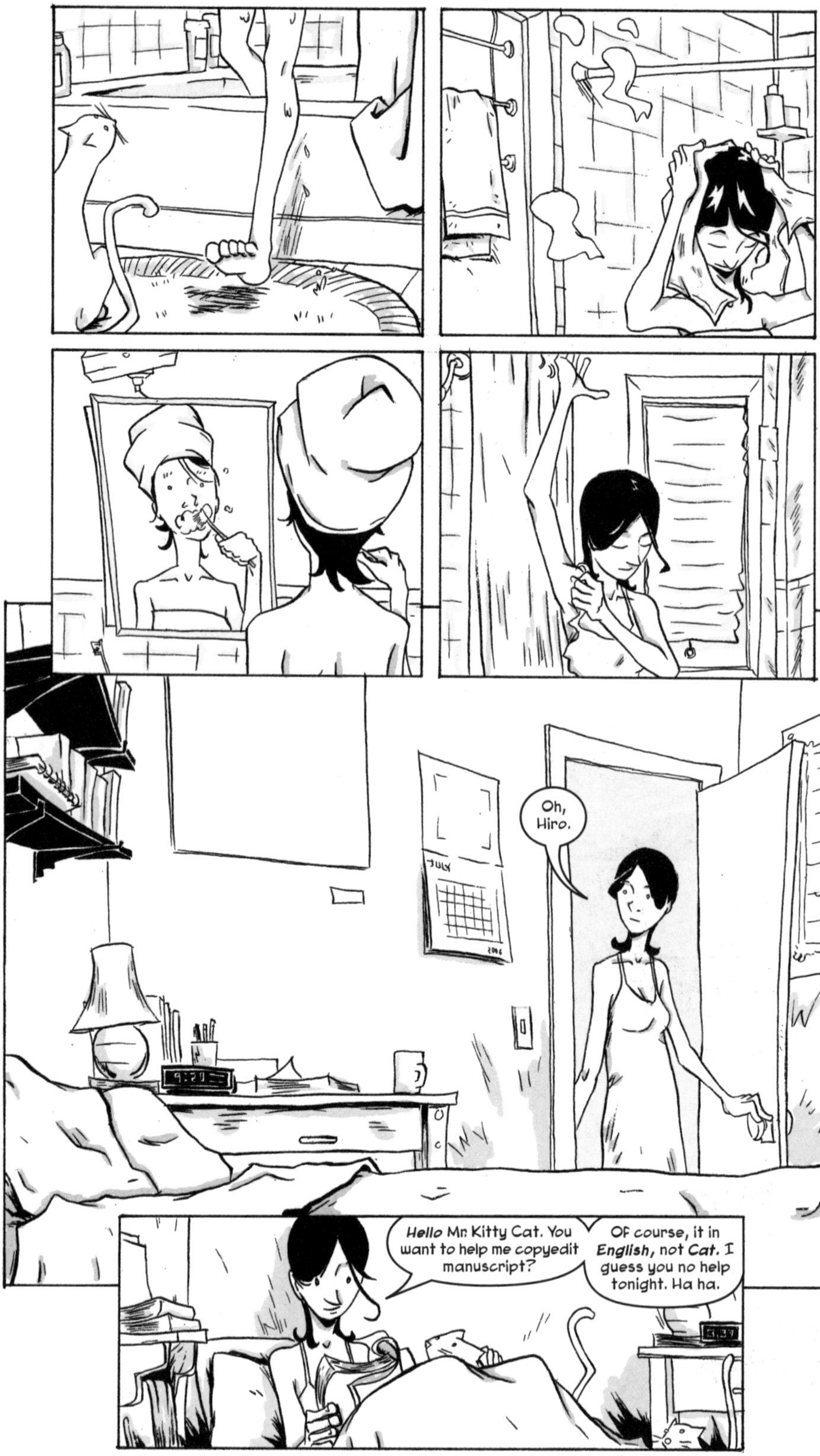

Oh, Hiro.
Hello Mr. Kitty Cat. You want to help me copyedit manuscript?
Of course, it in English, not Cat. I guess you no help tonight. Ha ha.

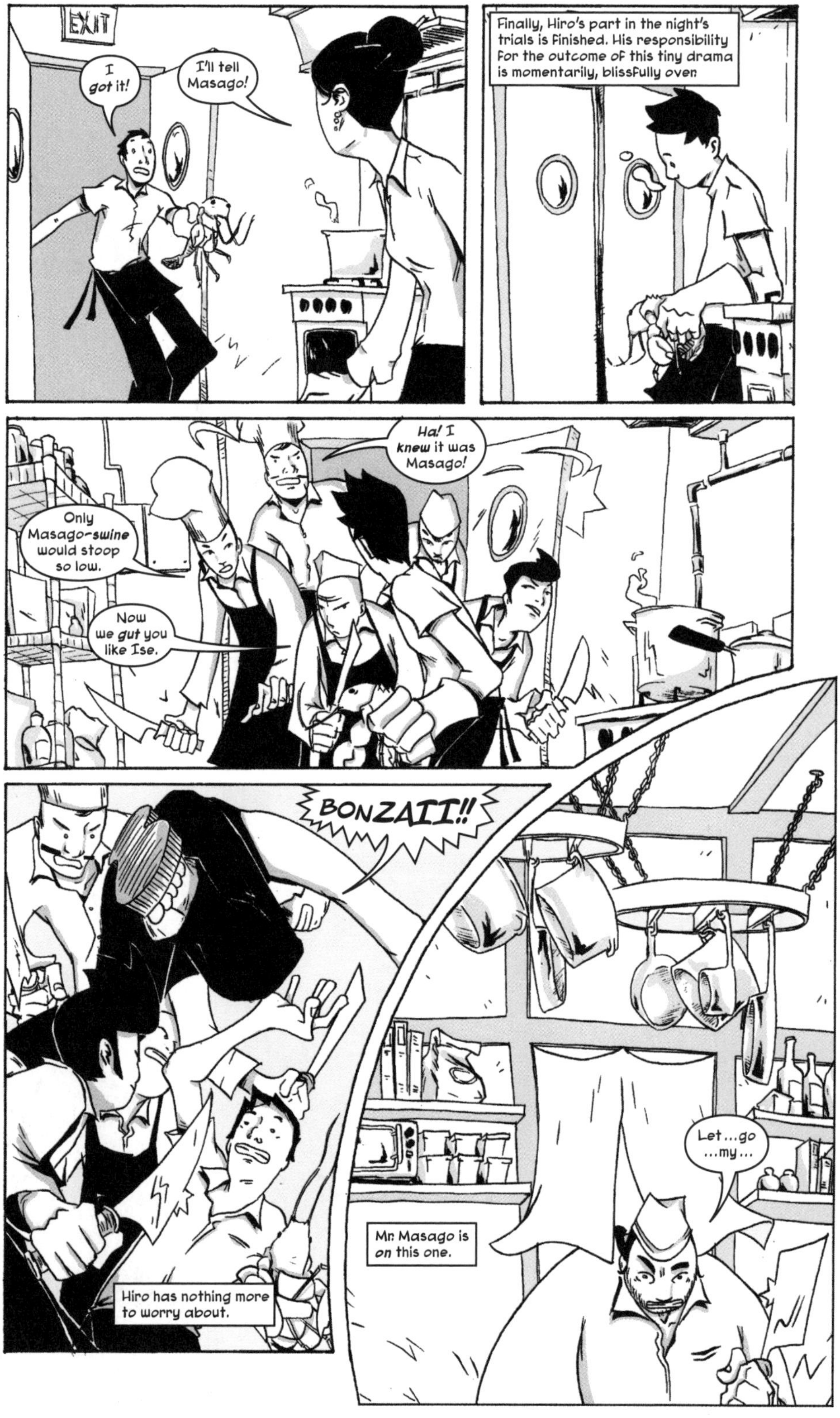
EXIT
I got it!
I'll tell Masago!
Finally, Hiro's part in the night's trials is finished. His responsibility for the outcome of this tiny drama is momentarily, blissfully over.
Ha! I knew it was Masago!
Only Masago-swine would stoop so low.
Now we gut you like Ise.
BONZAII!!
Hiro has nothing more to worry about.
Mr. Masago is on this one.
Let…go …my…

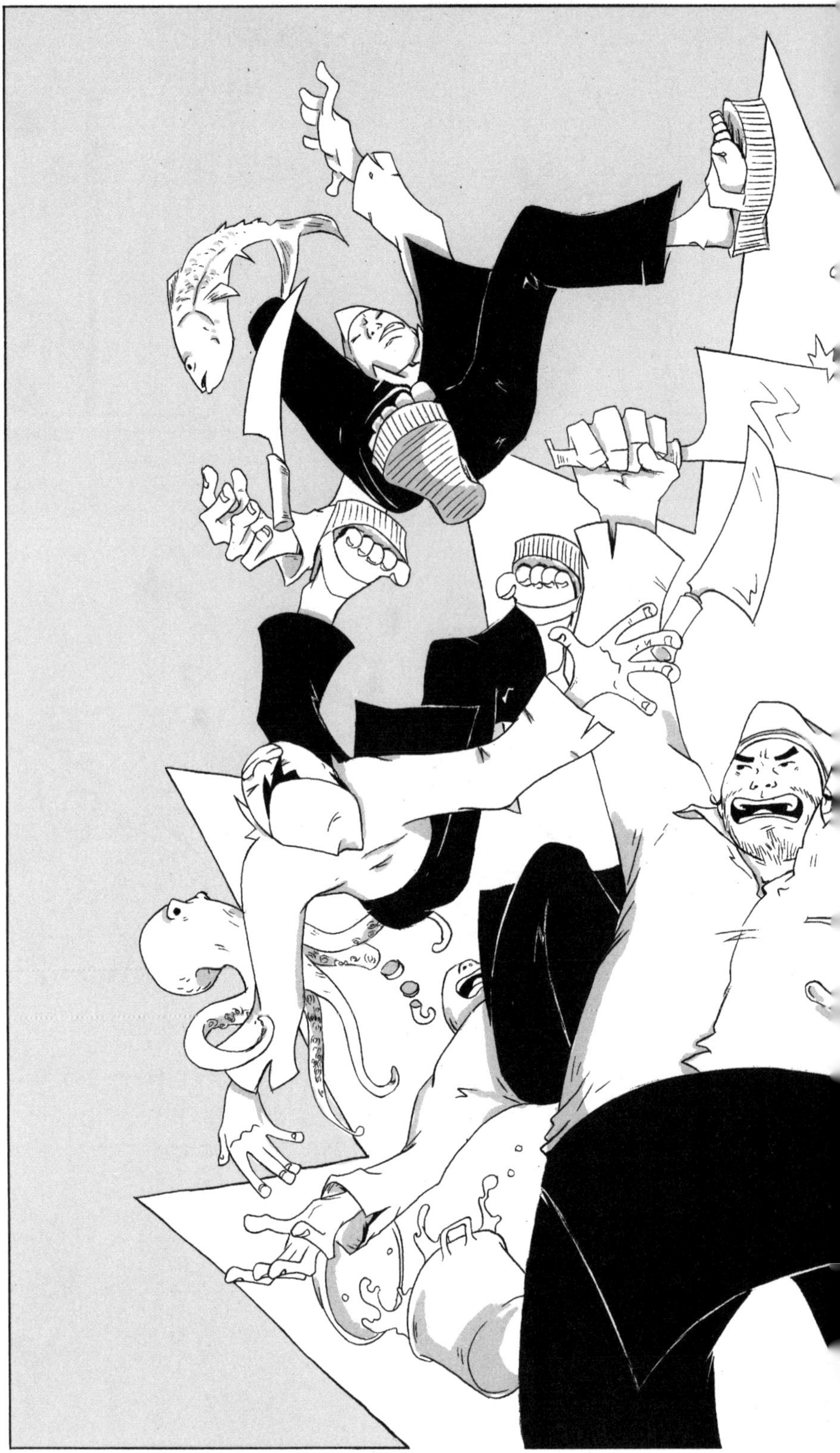

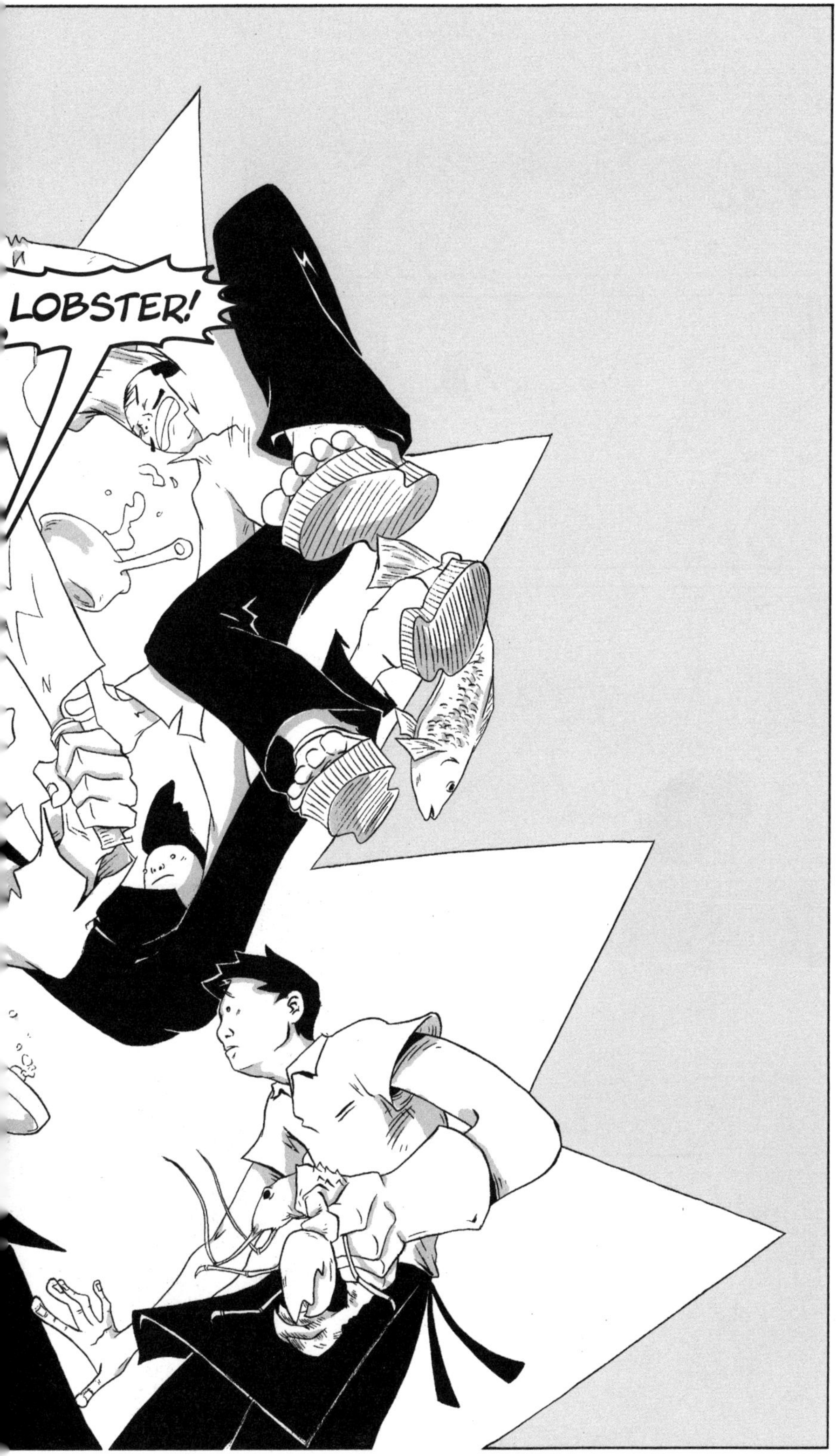
LOBSTER!

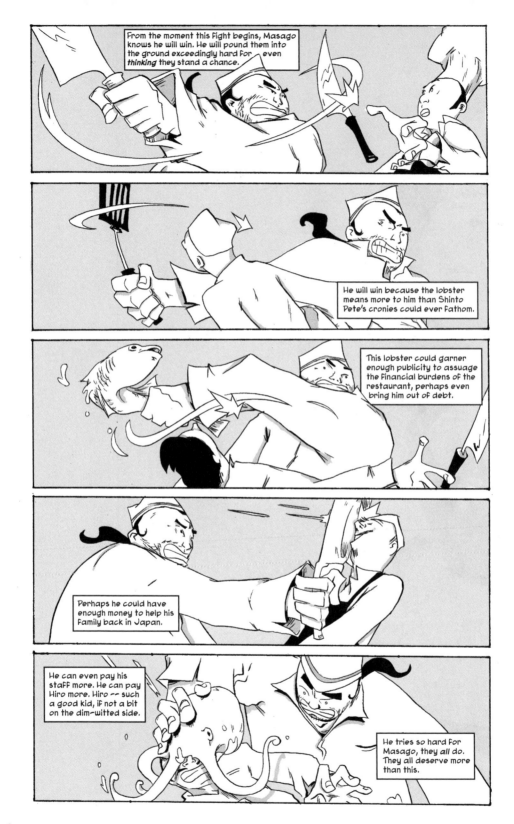

From the moment this fight begins, Masago knows he will win. He will pound them into the ground *exceedingly hard* for even *thinking* they stand a chance.

He will win because the lobster means more to him than Shinto Pete's cronies could ever fathom.

This lobster could garner enough publicity to assuage the financial burdens of the restaurant, perhaps even bring him out of debt.

Perhaps he could have enough money to help his family back in Japan.

He can even pay his staff more. He can pay Hiro more. Hiro -- such a good kid, if not a bit on the dim-witted side.

He tries so hard for Masago, they *all do.* They all deserve more than this.

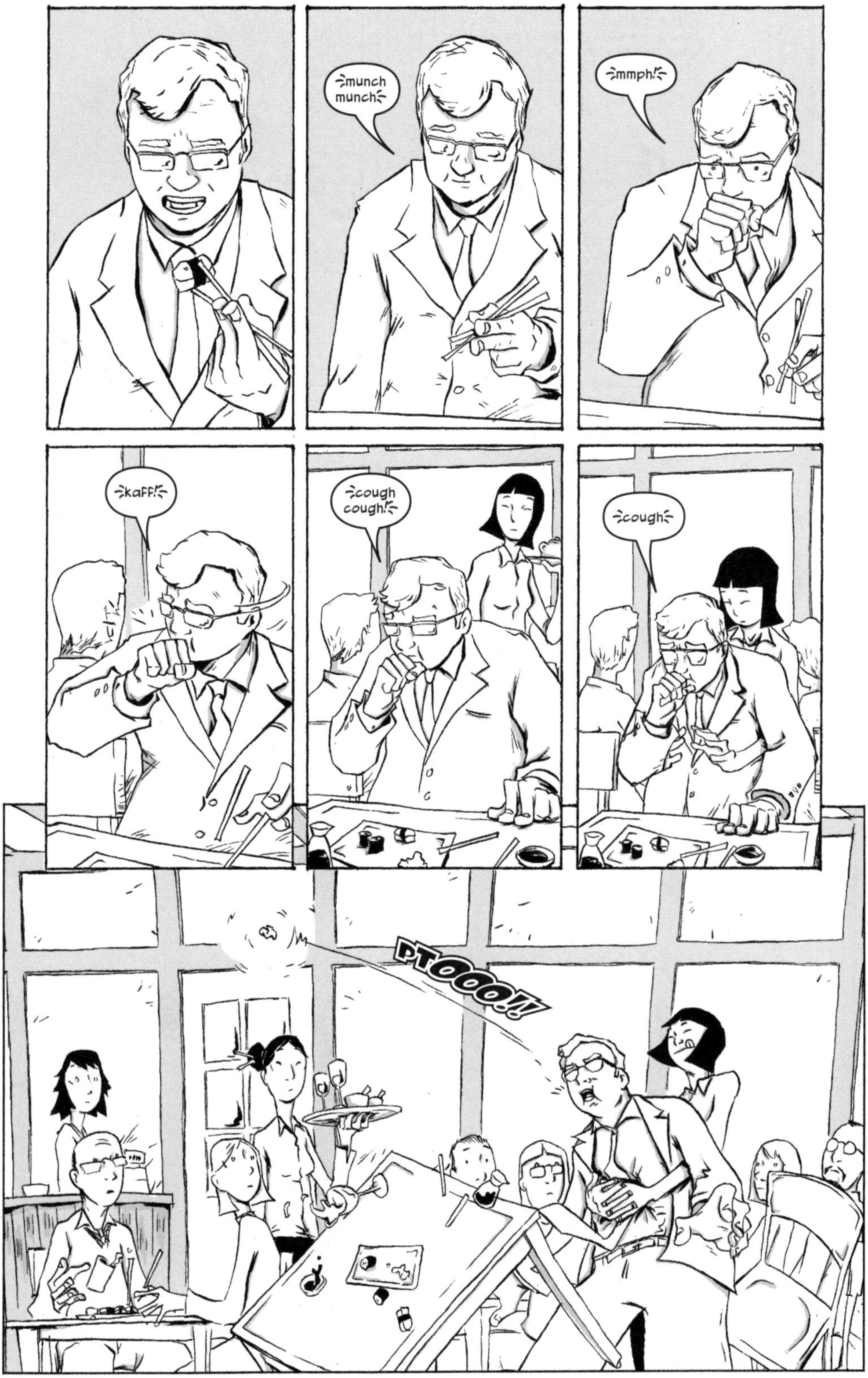
munch munch
mmph!
kaff!
cough cough!
cough
PTOOO!!

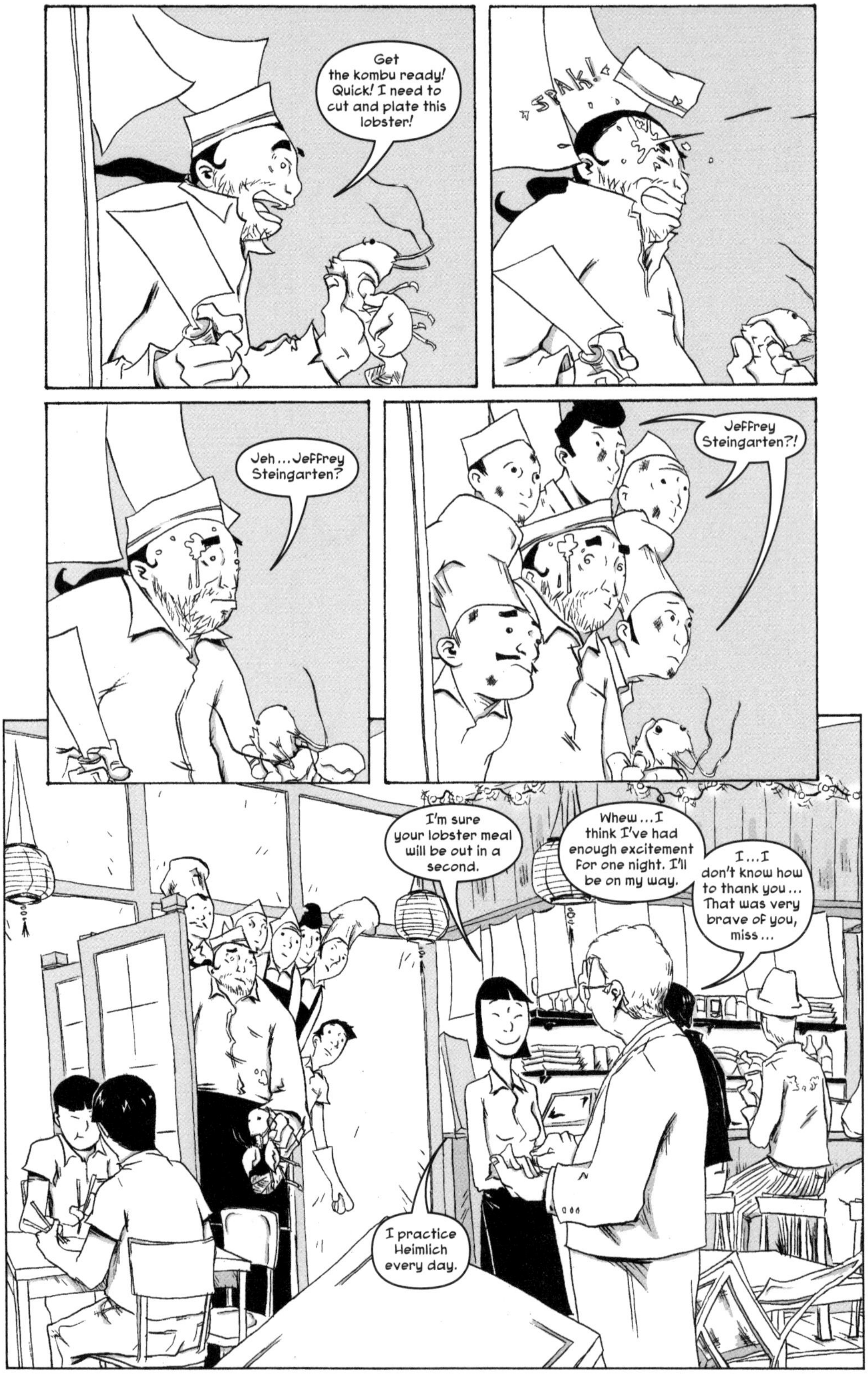
Get the kombu ready! Quick! I need to cut and plate this lobster!
SPAK!
Jeh... Jeffrey Steingarten?
Jeffrey Steingarten?!
I'm sure your lobster meal will be out in a second.
Whew... I think I've had enough excitement for one night. I'll be on my way.
I... I don't know how to thank you... That was very brave of you, miss...
I practice Heimlich every day.

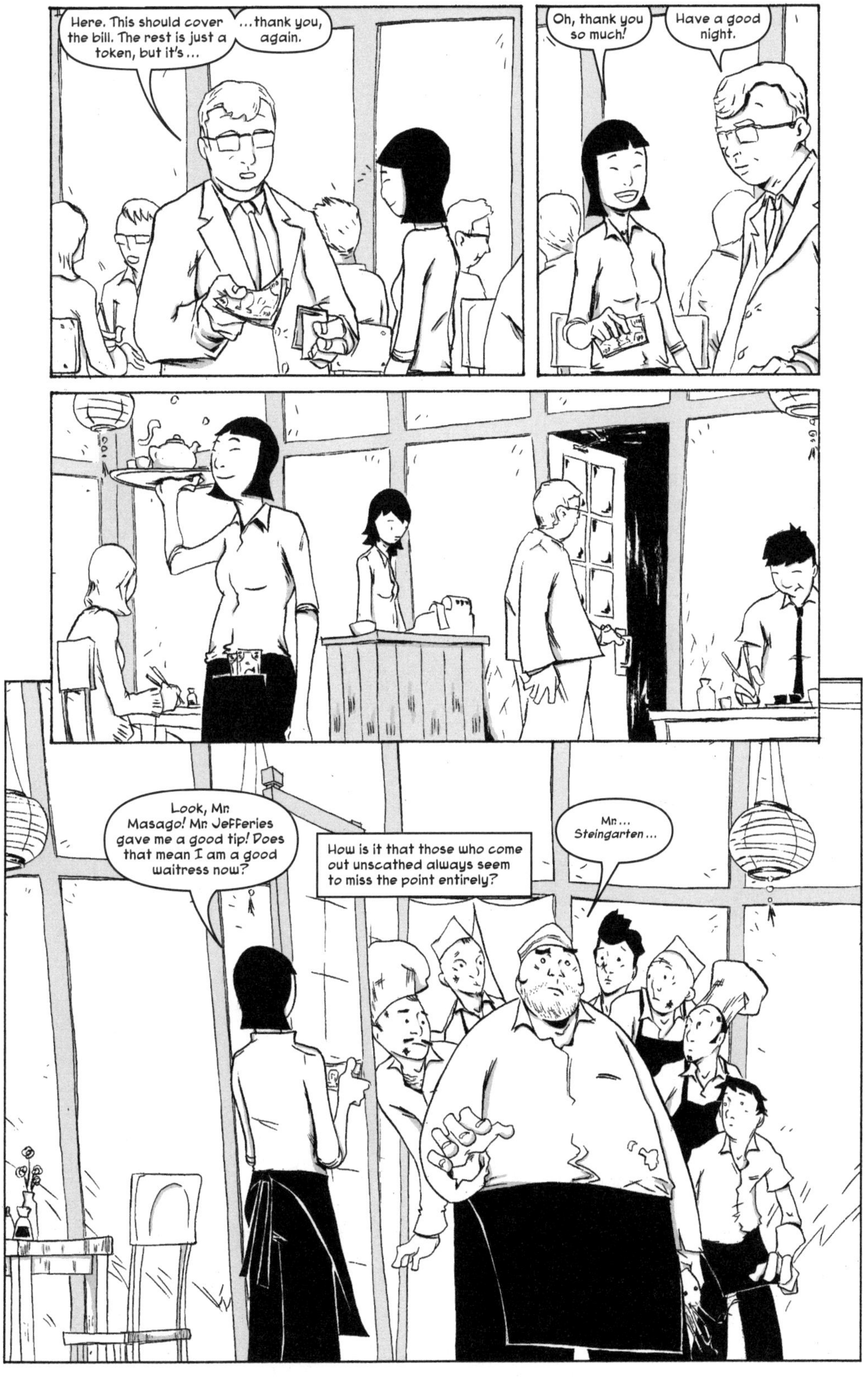
Here. This should cover the bill. The rest is just a token, but it's ...
...thank you, again.
Oh, thank you so much!
Have a good night.
Look, Mr. Masago! Mr. Jefferies gave me a good tip! Does that mean I am a good waitress now?
How is it that those who come out unscathed always seem to miss the point entirely?
Mr. ... Steingarten ...

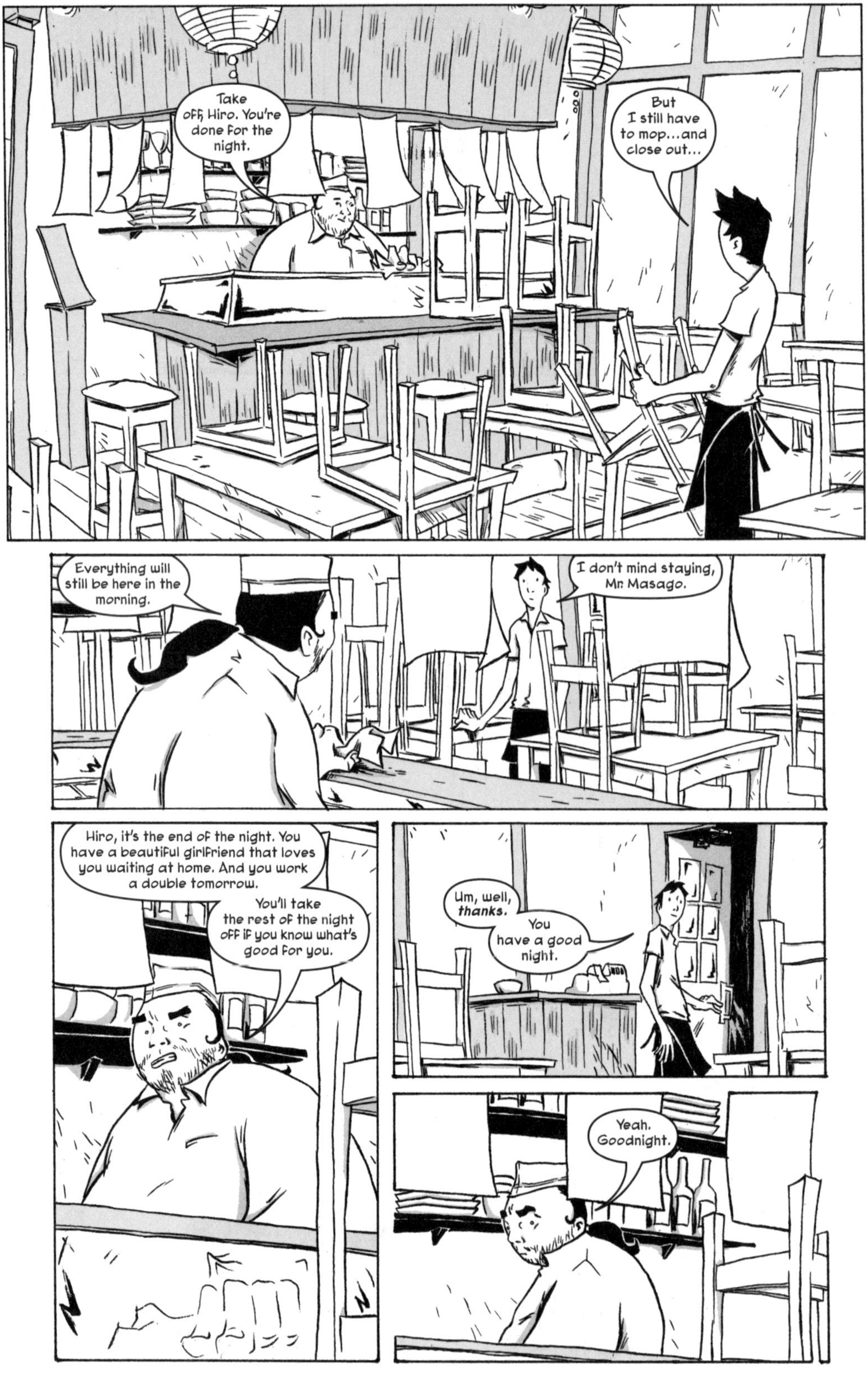
Take off, Hiro. You're done for the night.
But I still have to mop...and close out...
Everything will still be here in the morning.
I don't mind staying, Mr. Masago.
Hiro, it's the end of the night. You have a beautiful girlfriend that loves you waiting at home. And you work a double tomorrow.
You'll take the rest of the night off if you know what's good for you.
Um, well, *thanks.*
You have a good night.
Yeah. Goodnight.

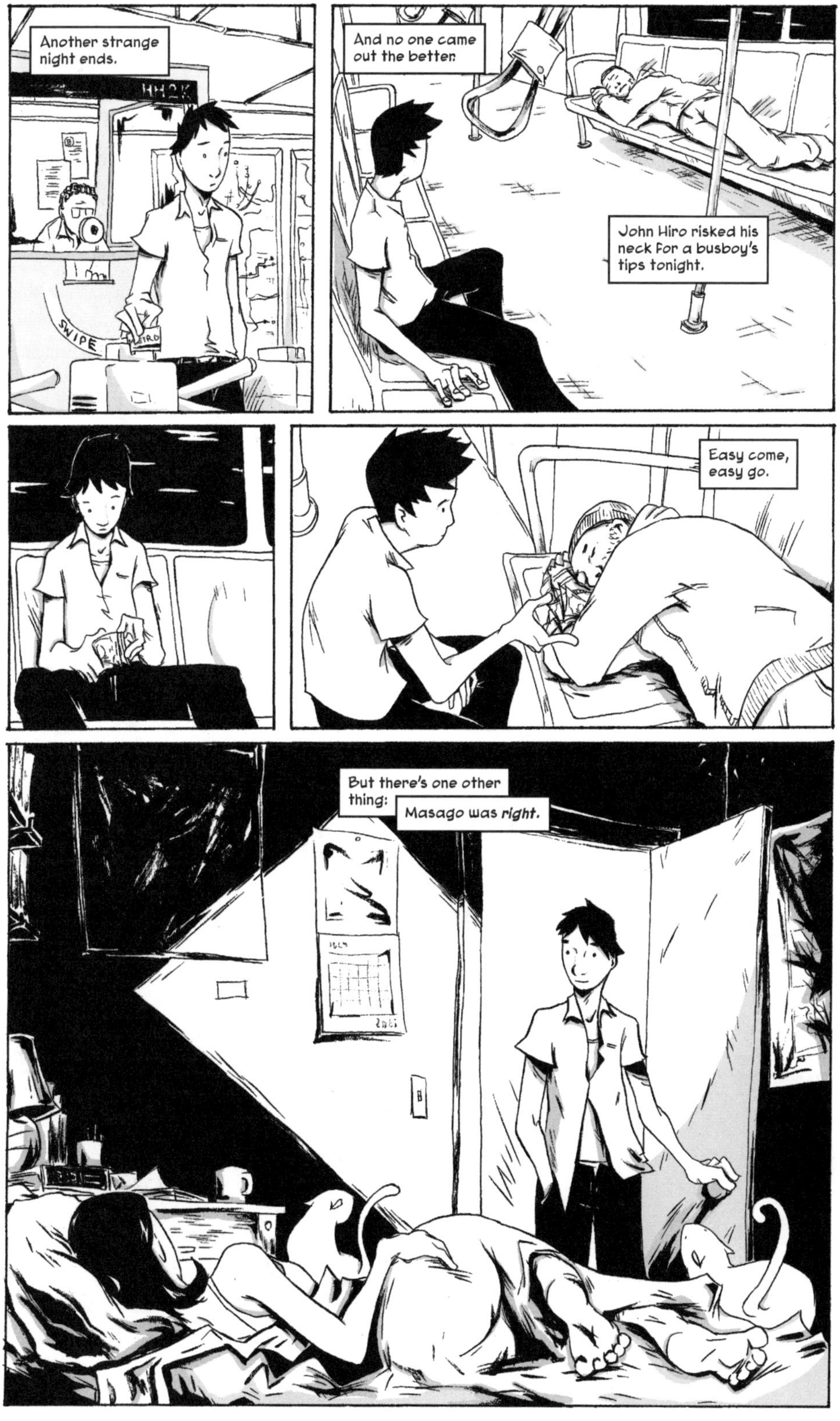
Another strange night ends.
SWIPE
And no one came out the better.
John Hiro risked his neck for a busboy's tips tonight.
Easy come, easy go.
But there's one other thing:
Masago was *right.*

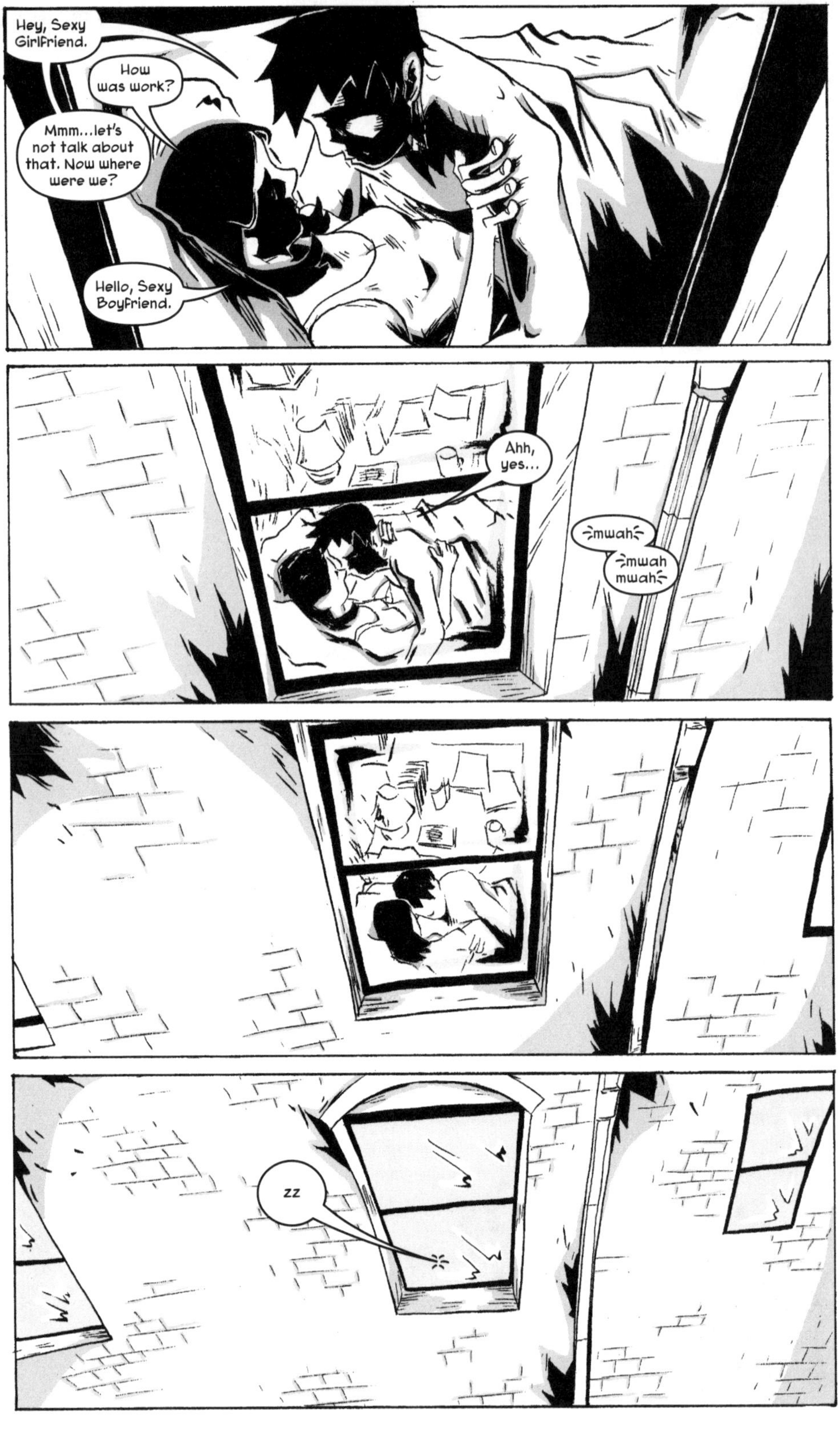
Hey, Sexy Girlfriend.
How was work?
Mmm...let's not talk about that. Now where were we?
Hello, Sexy Boyfriend.
Ahh, yes...
mwah
mwah mwah
zz

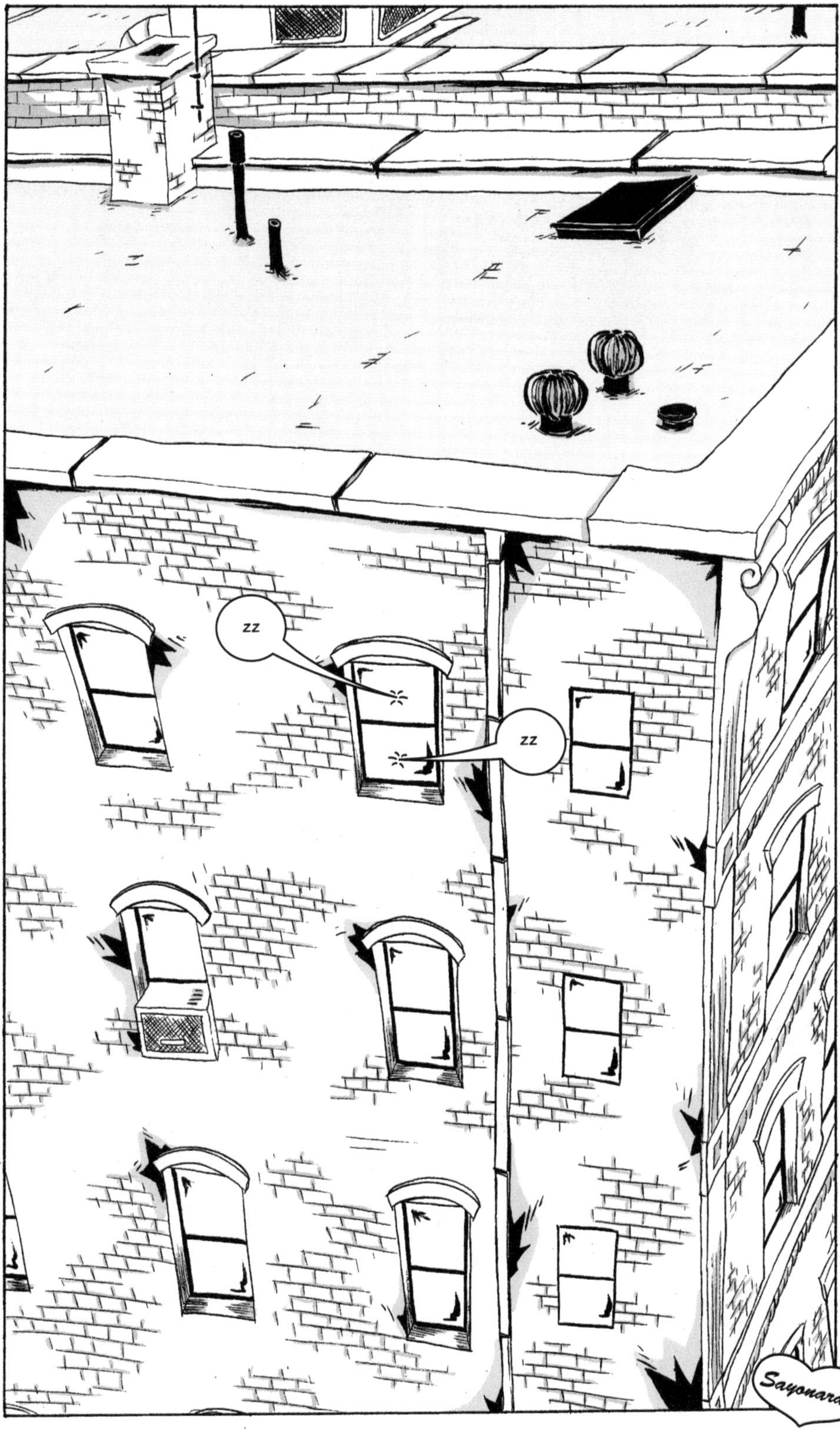
zz
zz
Sayonara!

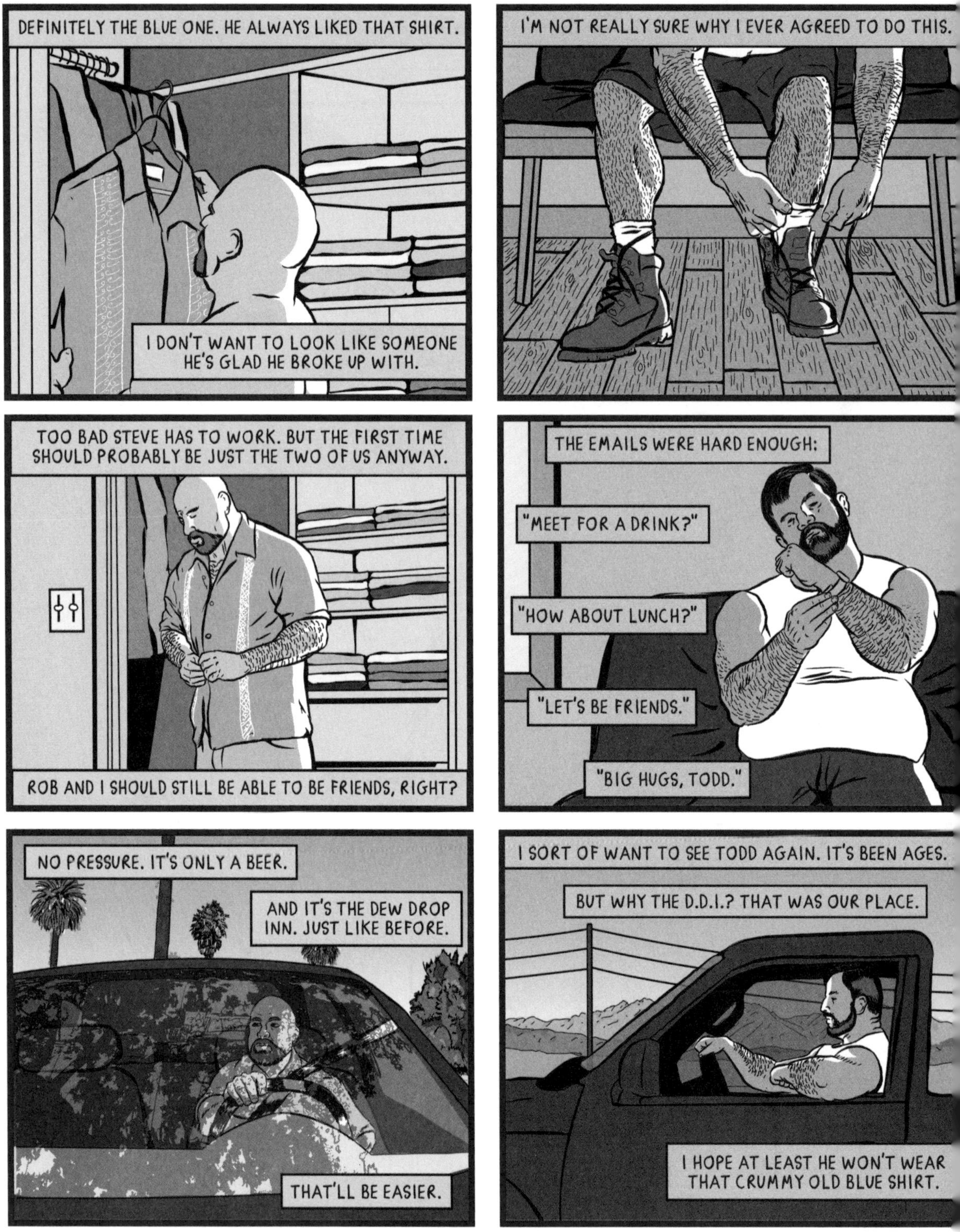
DEFINITELY THE BLUE ONE. HE ALWAYS LIKED THAT SHIRT.
I DON'T WANT TO LOOK LIKE SOMEONE HE'S GLAD HE BROKE UP WITH.
I'M NOT REALLY SURE WHY I EVER AGREED TO DO THIS.
TOO BAD STEVE HAS TO WORK. BUT THE FIRST TIME SHOULD PROBABLY BE JUST THE TWO OF US ANYWAY.
ROB AND I SHOULD STILL BE ABLE TO BE FRIENDS, RIGHT?
THE EMAILS WERE HARD ENOUGH:
"MEET FOR A DRINK?"
"HOW ABOUT LUNCH?"
"LET'S BE FRIENDS."
"BIG HUGS, TODD."
NO PRESSURE. IT'S ONLY A BEER.
AND IT'S THE DEW DROP INN. JUST LIKE BEFORE.
THAT'LL BE EASIER.
I SORT OF WANT TO SEE TODD AGAIN. IT'S BEEN AGES.
BUT WHY THE D.D.I.? THAT WAS OUR PLACE.
I HOPE AT LEAST HE WON'T WEAR THAT CRUMMY OLD BLUE SHIRT.

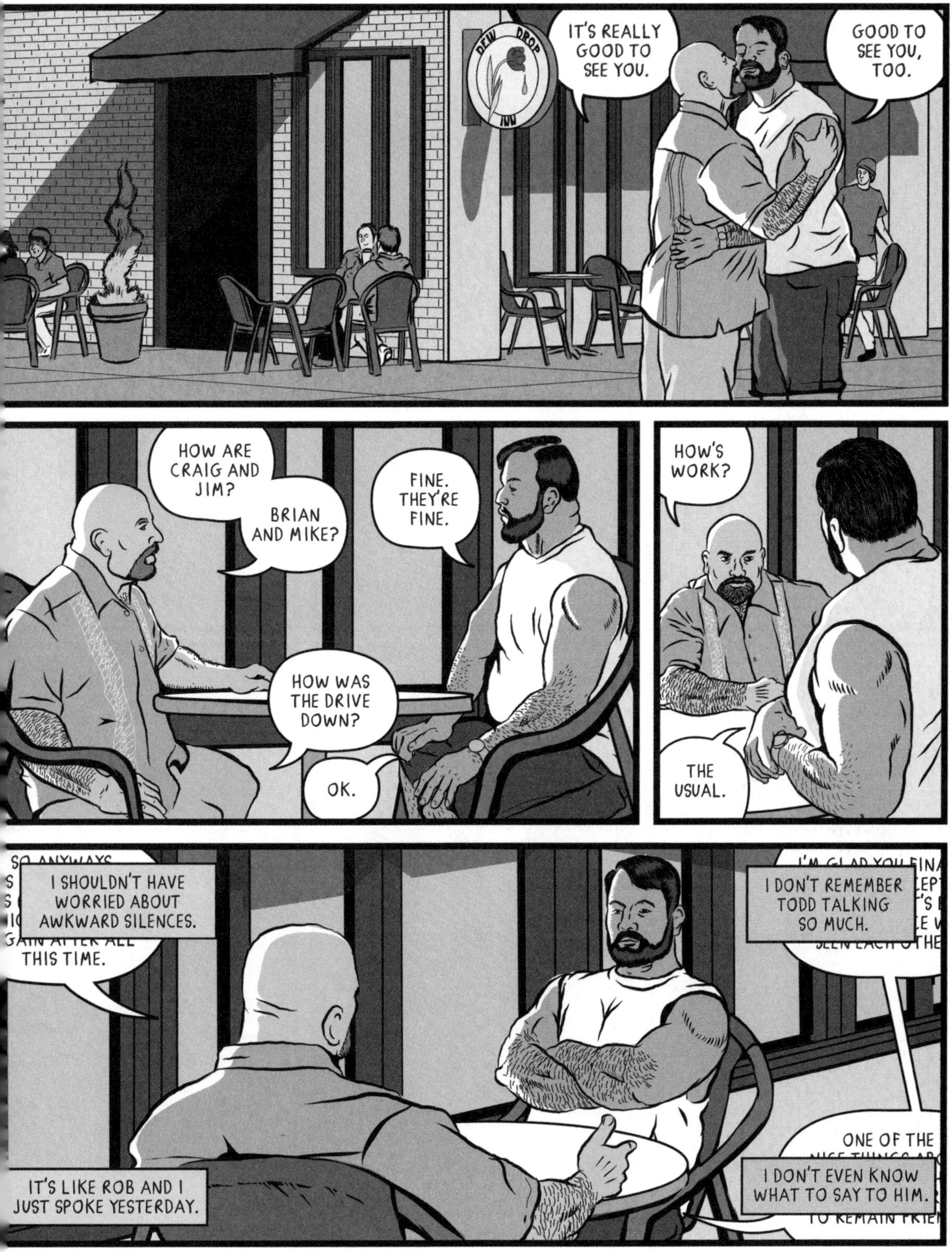
DEW DROP INN
IT'S REALLY GOOD TO SEE YOU.
GOOD TO SEE YOU, TOO.
HOW ARE CRAIG AND JIM?
FINE. THEY'RE FINE.
BRIAN AND MIKE?
HOW WAS THE DRIVE DOWN?
OK.
HOW'S WORK?
THE USUAL.
I SHOULDN'T HAVE WORRIED ABOUT AWKWARD SILENCES.
THIS TIME.
I DON'T REMEMBER TODD TALKING SO MUCH.
ONE OF THE
IT'S LIKE ROB AND I JUST SPOKE YESTERDAY.
I DON'T EVEN KNOW WHAT TO SAY TO HIM.

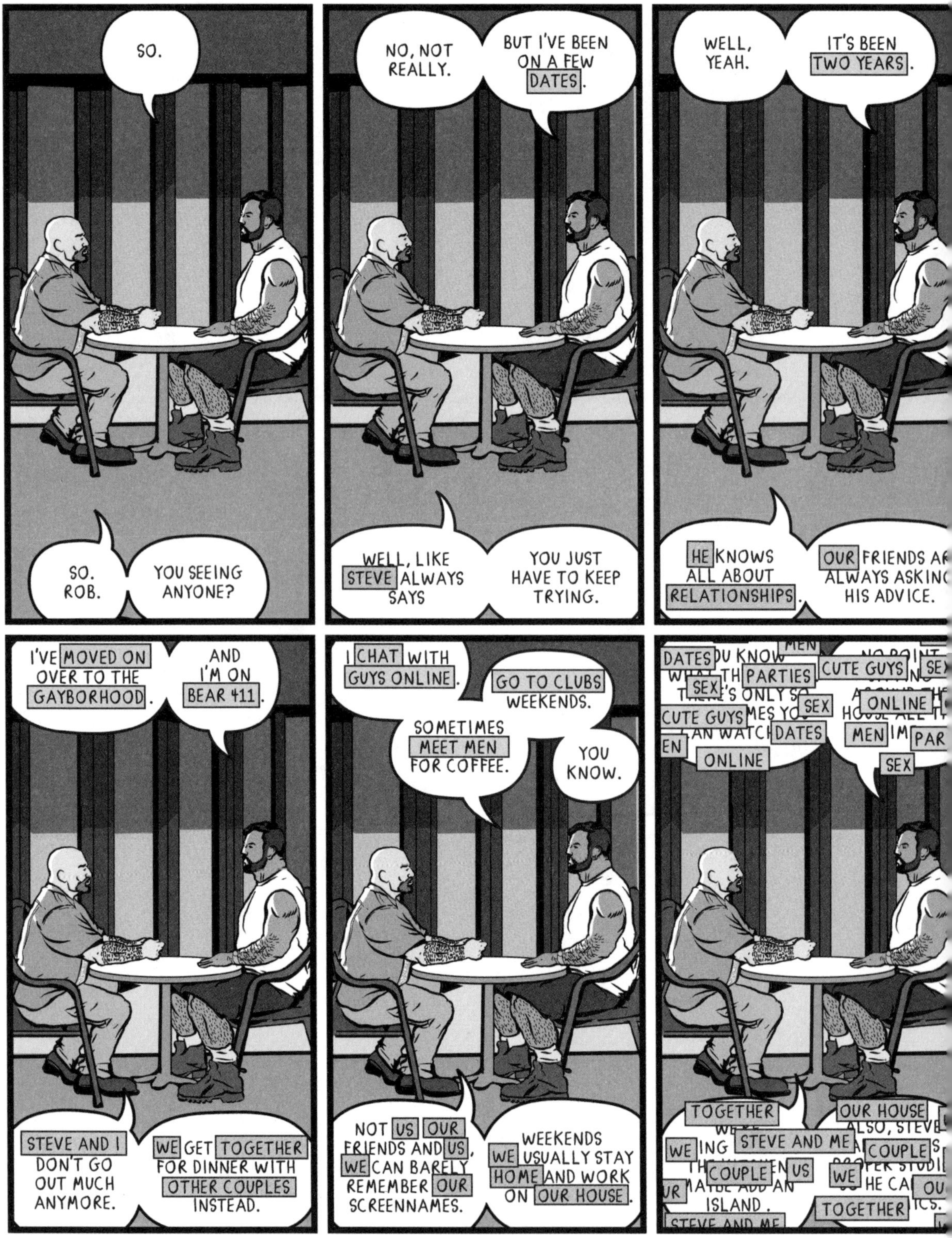

SO.
SO. ROB.
YOU SEEING ANYONE?
NO, NOT REALLY.
BUT I'VE BEEN ON A FEW DATES.
WELL, LIKE STEVE ALWAYS SAYS
YOU JUST HAVE TO KEEP TRYING.
WELL, YEAH.
IT'S BEEN TWO YEARS.
HE KNOWS ALL ABOUT RELATIONSHIPS.
OUR FRIENDS A
ALWAYS ASKIN
HIS ADVICE.
I'VE MOVED ON OVER TO THE GAYBORHOOD.
AND I'M ON BEAR 411.
STEVE AND I DON'T GO OUT MUCH ANYMORE.
WE GET TOGETHER FOR DINNER WITH OTHER COUPLES INSTEAD.
I CHAT WITH GUYS ONLINE.
GO TO CLUBS WEEKENDS.
SOMETIMES MEET MEN FOR COFFEE.
YOU KNOW.
NOT US OUR FRIENDS AND US, WE CAN BARELY REMEMBER OUR SCREENNAMES.
WEEKENDS WE USUALLY STAY HOME AND WORK ON OUR HOUSE.
DATES MEN PARTIES SEX CUTE GUYS SEX CUTE GUYS SEX ONLINE DATES MEN EN ONLINE SEX
TOGETHER OUR HOUSE WE STEVE AND ME COUPLE COUPLE US WE ISLAND. TOGETHER

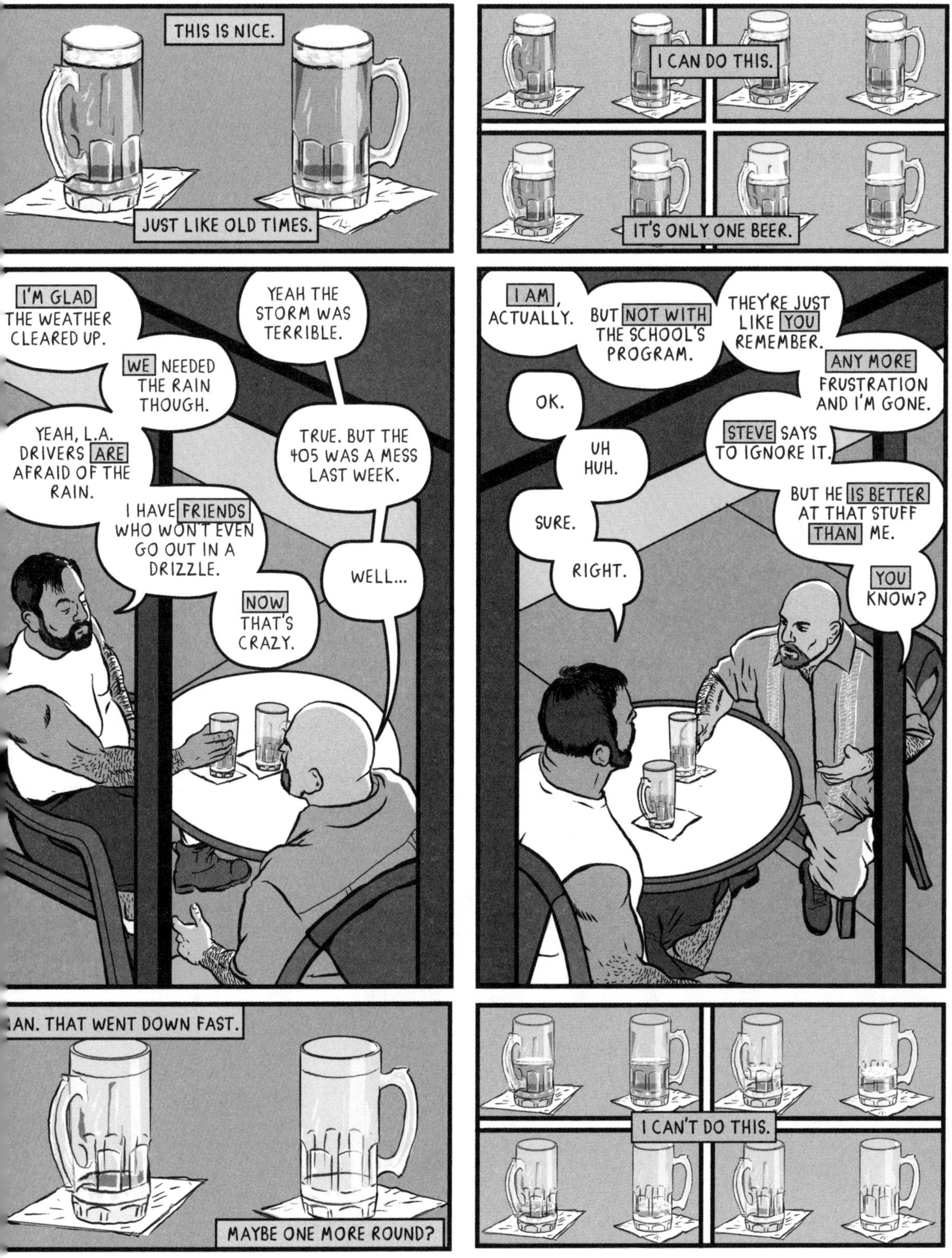
THIS IS NICE.
JUST LIKE OLD TIMES.
I CAN DO THIS.
IT'S ONLY ONE BEER.
I'M GLAD THE WEATHER CLEARED UP.
YEAH THE STORM WAS TERRIBLE.
WE NEEDED THE RAIN THOUGH.
TRUE. BUT THE 405 WAS A MESS LAST WEEK.
YEAH, L.A. DRIVERS ARE AFRAID OF THE RAIN.
I HAVE FRIENDS WHO WON'T EVEN GO OUT IN A DRIZZLE.
WELL...
NOW THAT'S CRAZY.
I AM, ACTUALLY.
BUT NOT WITH THE SCHOOL'S PROGRAM.
THEY'RE JUST LIKE YOU REMEMBER.
ANY MORE FRUSTRATION AND I'M GONE.
OK.
UH HUH.
STEVE SAYS TO IGNORE IT.
BUT HE IS BETTER AT THAT STUFF THAN ME.
SURE.
RIGHT.
YOU KNOW?
AN. THAT WENT DOWN FAST.
MAYBE ONE MORE ROUND?
I CAN'T DO THIS.

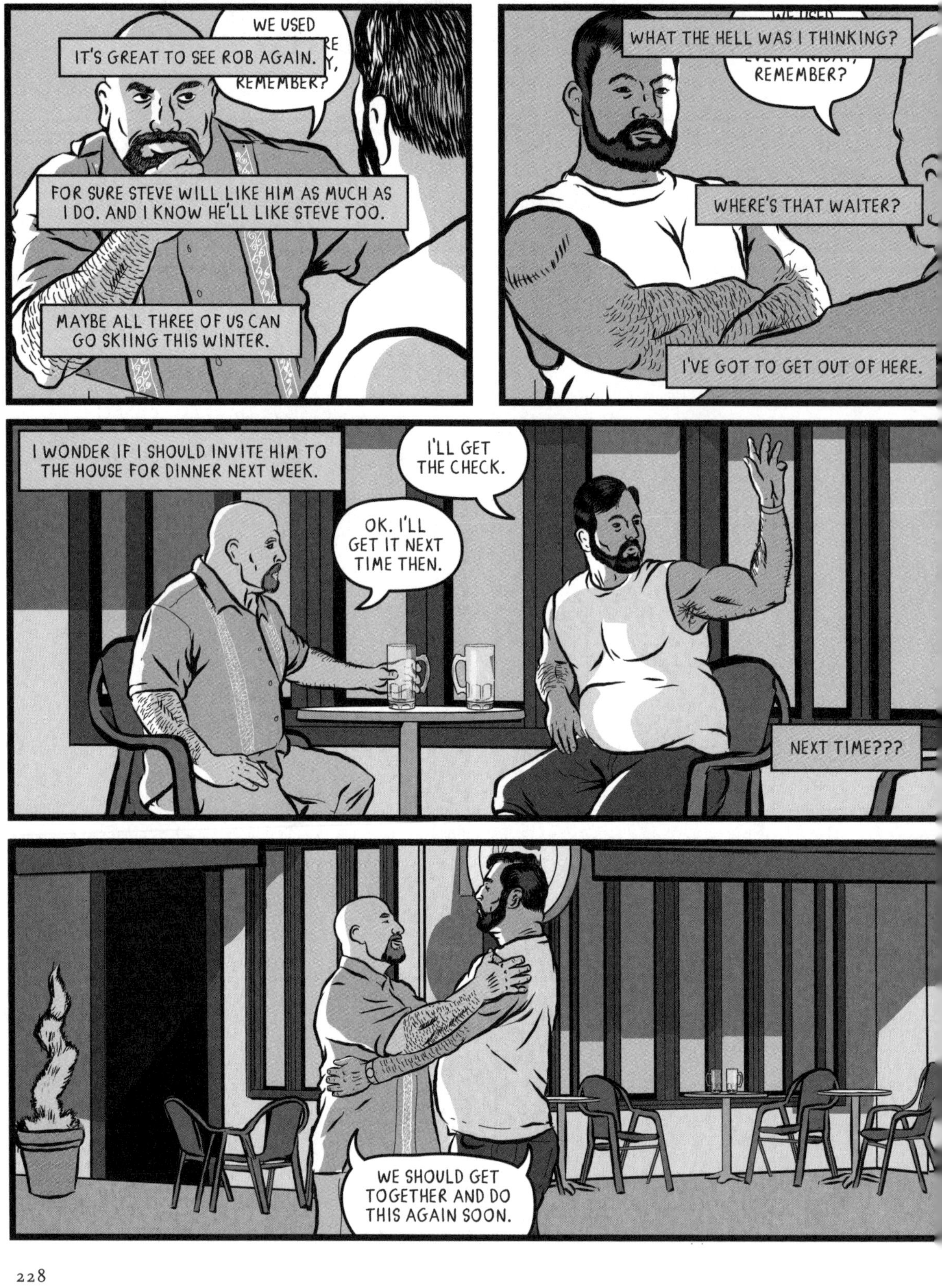
IT'S GREAT TO SEE ROB AGAIN.
WE USED
REMEMBER?
FOR SURE STEVE WILL LIKE HIM AS MUCH AS I DO. AND I KNOW HE'LL LIKE STEVE TOO.
MAYBE ALL THREE OF US CAN GO SKIING THIS WINTER.
WHAT THE HELL WAS I THINKING?
REMEMBER?
WHERE'S THAT WAITER?
I'VE GOT TO GET OUT OF HERE.
I WONDER IF I SHOULD INVITE HIM TO THE HOUSE FOR DINNER NEXT WEEK.
I'LL GET THE CHECK.
OK. I'LL GET IT NEXT TIME THEN.
NEXT TIME???
WE SHOULD GET TOGETHER AND DO THIS AGAIN SOON.

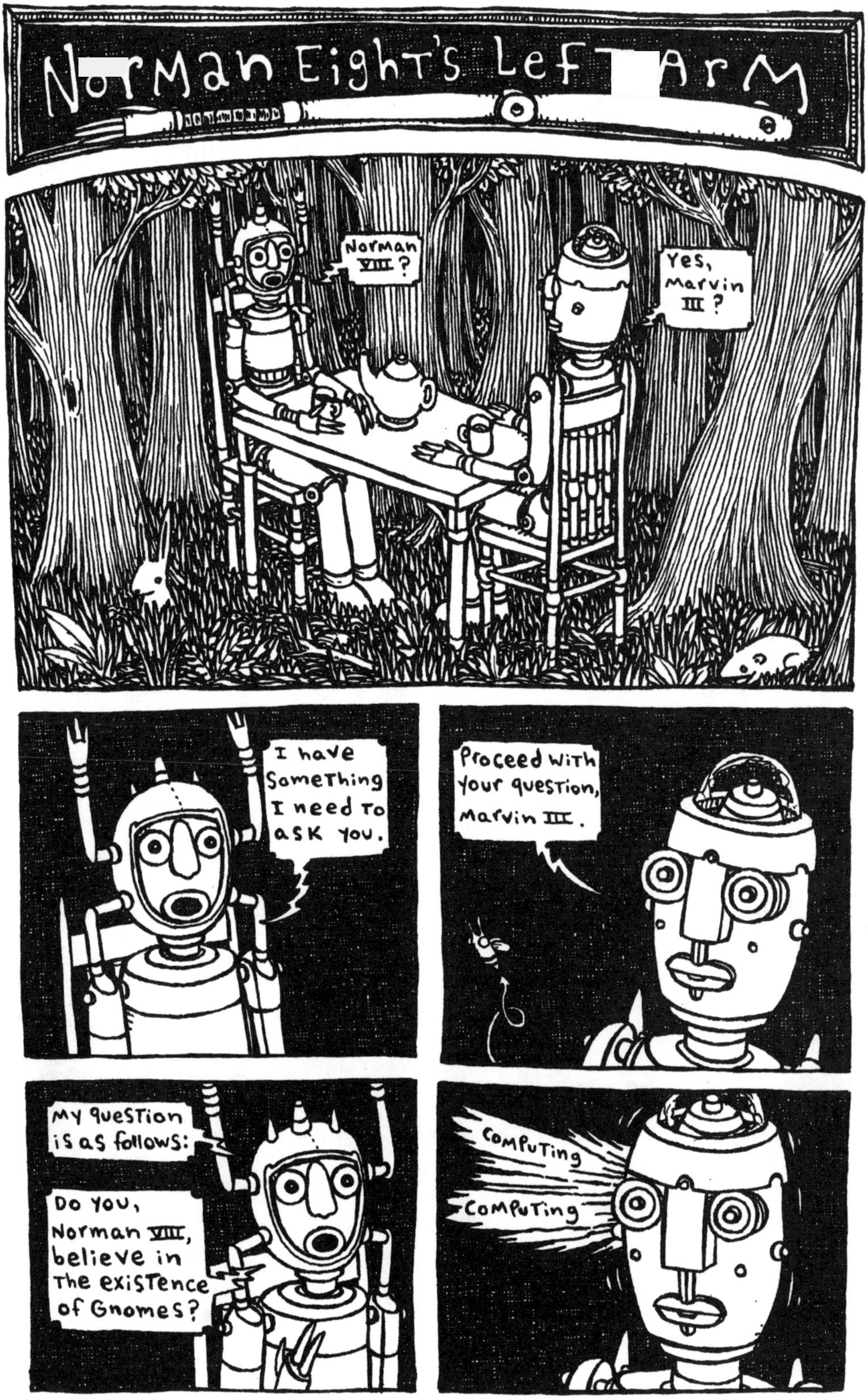
Norman Eight's Left Arm
Norman VIII?
Yes, Marvin III?
I have something I need to ask you.
Proceed with your question, Marvin III.
My question is as follows:
Do you, Norman VIII, believe in the existence of Gnomes?
Computing
Computing

THEO ELLSWORTH

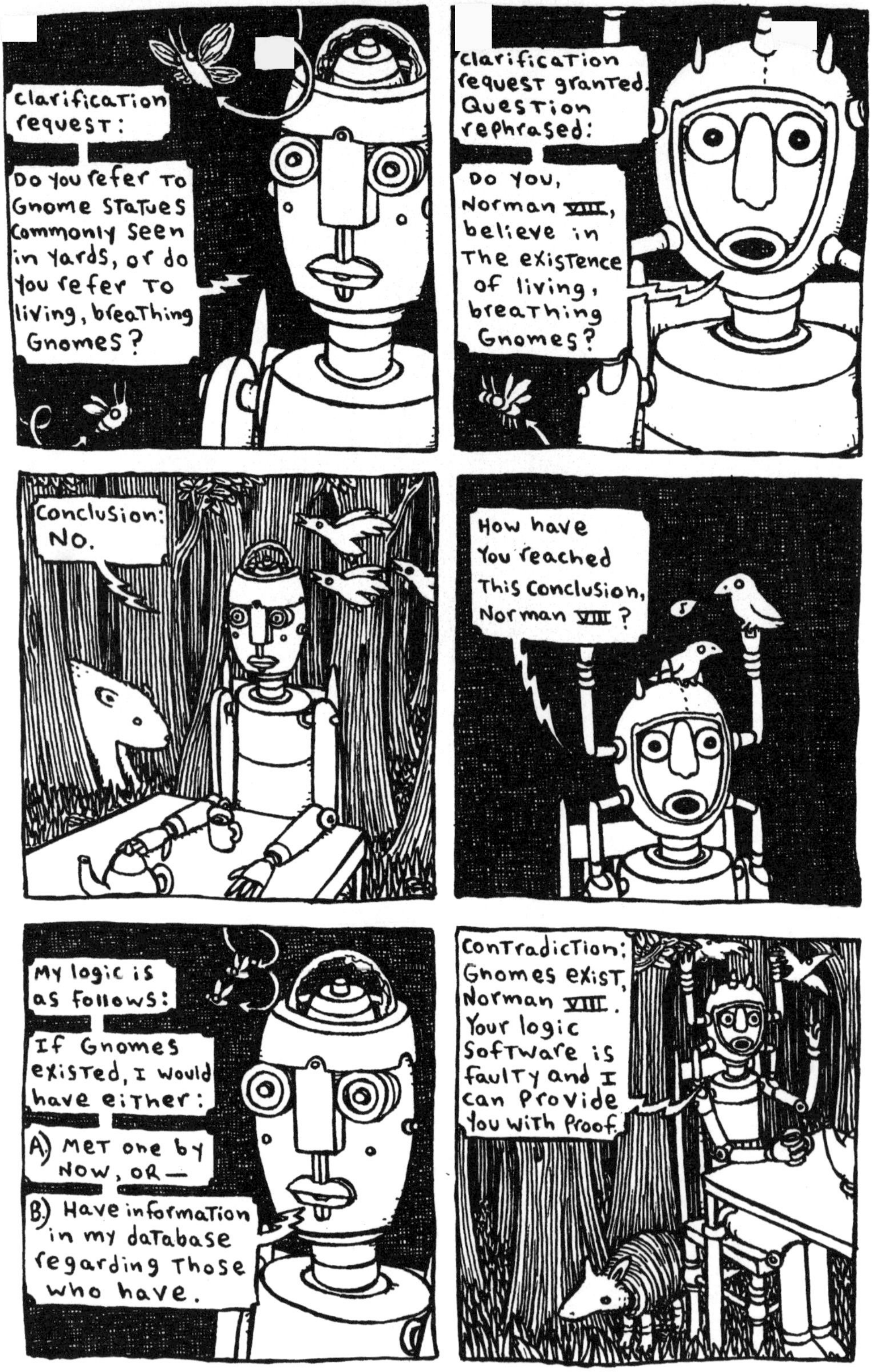
Clarification request:
Do you refer to Gnome statues commonly seen in yards, or do you refer to living, breathing Gnomes?
Clarification request granted. Question rephrased:
Do you, Norman VIII, believe in the existence of living, breathing Gnomes?
Conclusion: No.
How have you reached this conclusion, Norman VIII?
My logic is as follows:
If Gnomes existed, I would have either:
A) Met one by now, or—
B) Have information in my database regarding those who have.
Contradiction: Gnomes exist, Norman VIII. Your logic software is faulty and I can provide you with proof.

Panel 1:

If you seek to challenge my logic, Marvin III, suitable consequences must be decided for each possible outcome.

Agreed. Let the conditions be as follows:

Panel 2:

If within the next five (5) days, I can produce for you at least one (1) Gnome for your inspection, you must relinquish your left arm to me for thirty (30) days.

Panel 3:

The short-term possession of my left arm holds no logical purpose.

ALARM!   ALARM!

Panel 4:

Explanation: Witnessing you go without one of your appendages for a set amount of time has considerable entertainment value.

Robotic laugh track

HA HA

Panel 5:

This entertainment value will be further enhanced by photographing your arm in various locations while it is in my possession.

click   FLASH

Panel 6:

And if you fail to produce said Gnome (s) within the proposed time-frame?

I will grant you complete access to my memory files for thirty (30) seconds.

This is what I have always wanted, but I must not betray signs of eagerness.
Activate internal cooling systems
I suppose I can find it in myself to consider your terms acceptable.
Let us then partake in a symbolic gesture of agreement.
RRRR
Screeee
I shall return within the proposed time-frame. Please guard my body during its period of headlessness.
POP

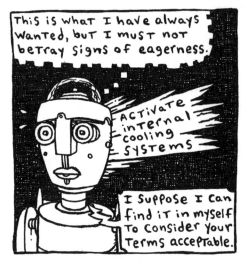

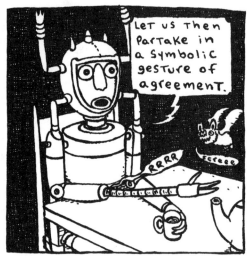

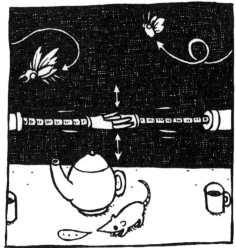

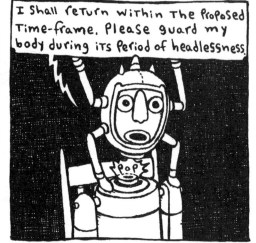

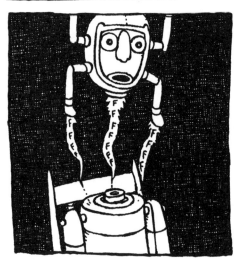

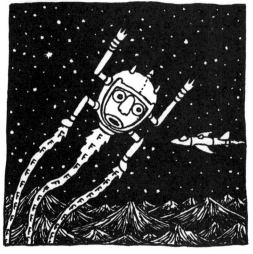

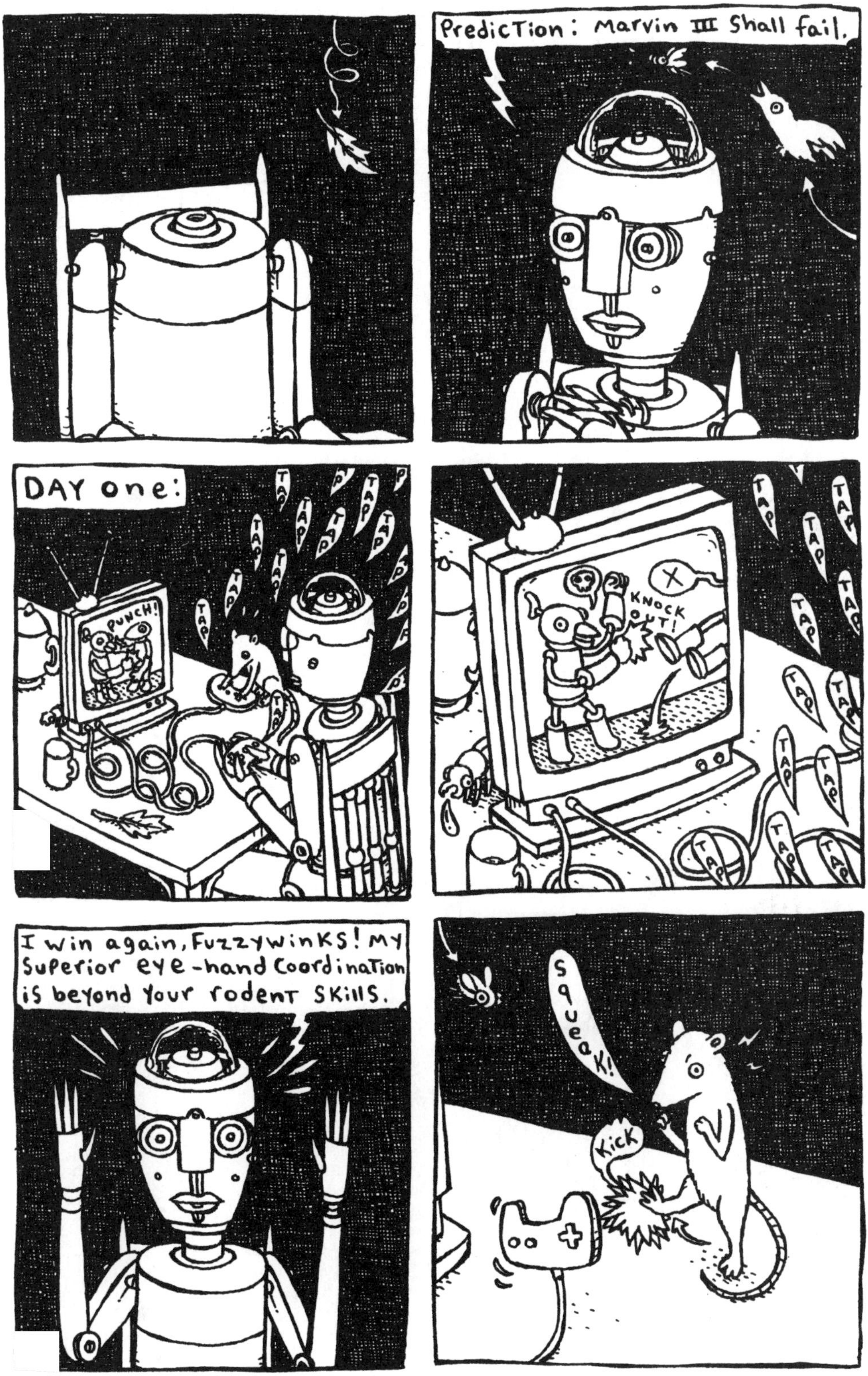
Prediction: Marvin III Shall fail.
DAY one:
PUNCH!
TAP
KNOCK OUT!
I win again, Fuzzywinks! My Superior eye-hand Coordination is beyond your rodent Skills.
Squeak!
Kick

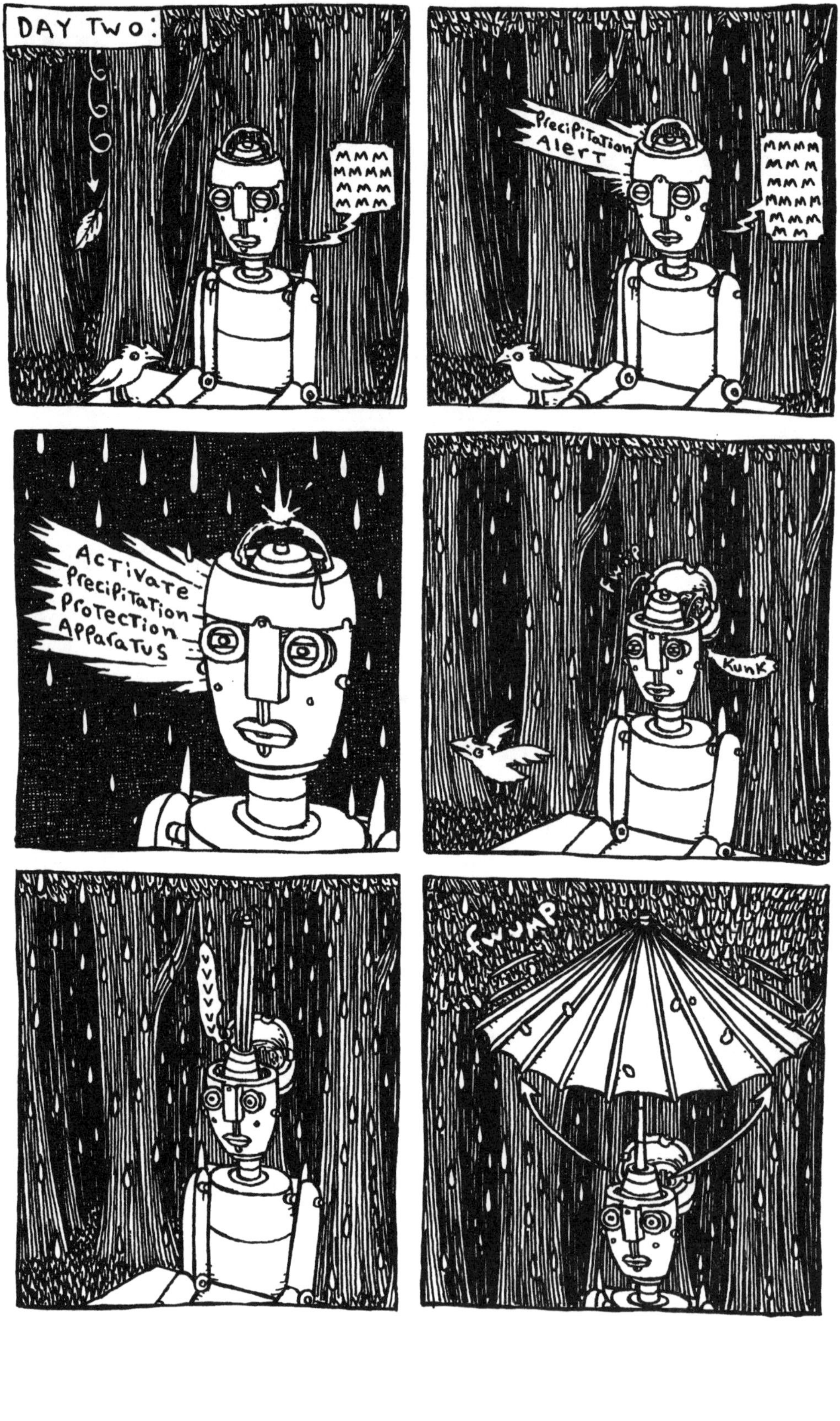

DAY TWO:
MMM MMMM MMM MMM
Precipitation Alert
MMMM MMM MMM MMMM MMM MM
Activate Precipitation Protection Apparatus
Kunk
fwump

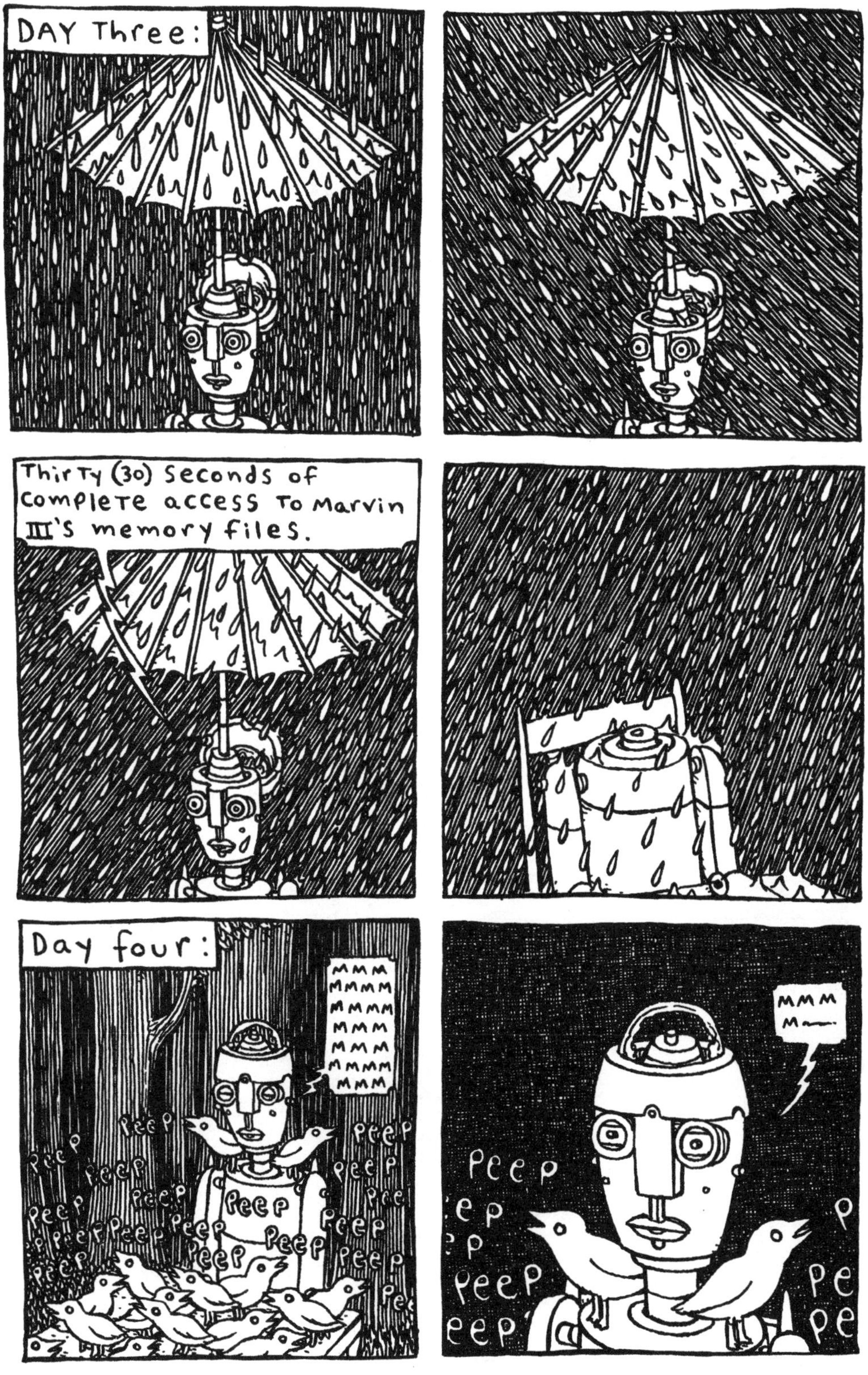
DAY Three:
Thirty (30) seconds of complete access to Marvin III's memory files.
Day four:
MMM MMMM MMMM MMM MMM MMMM MMM
Peep
MMM M—
Peep

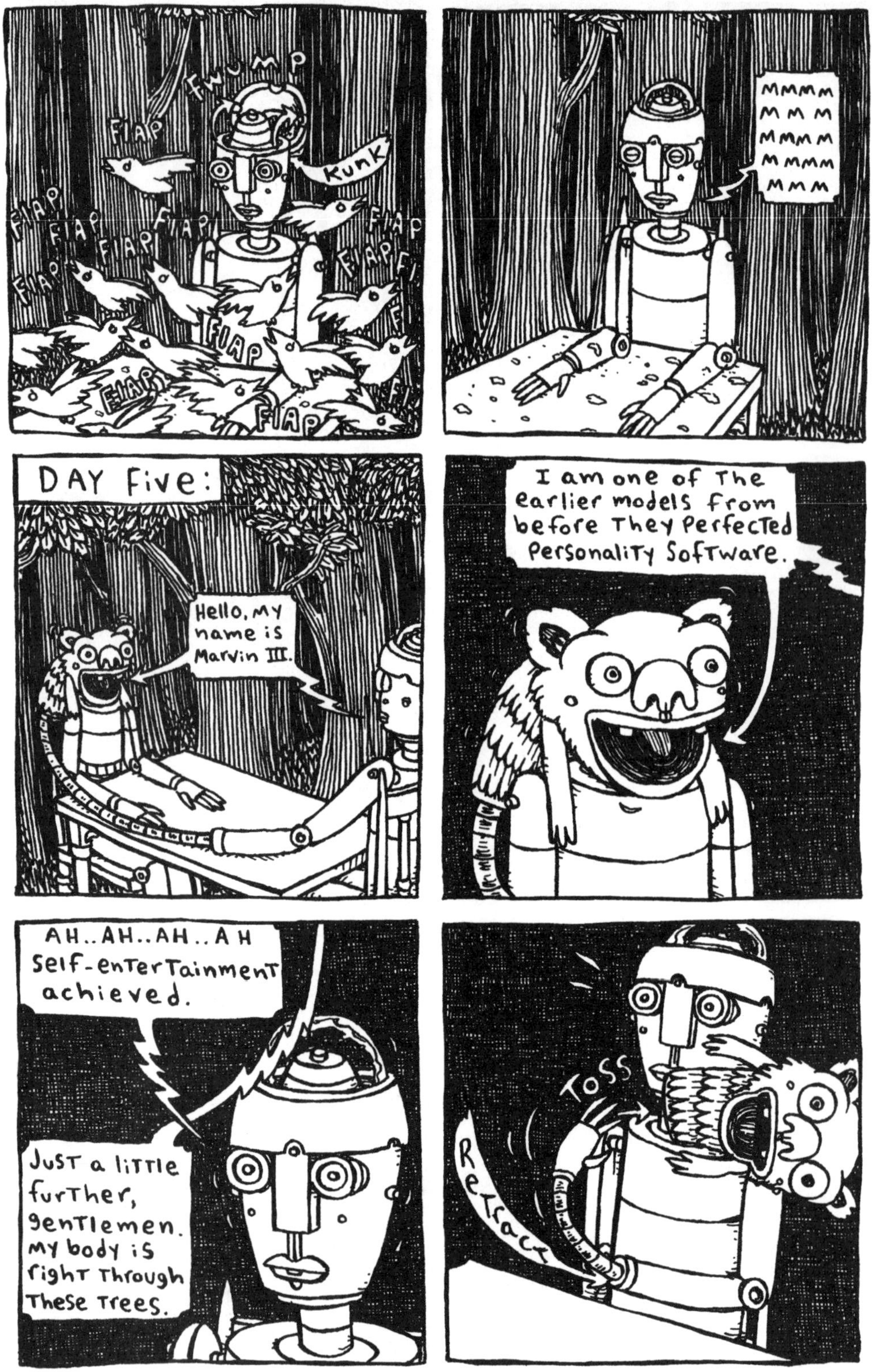
FWUMP
FlAP
KUNK
FlAP FlAP FlAP FlAP FlAP FlAP FlAP FlAP
FlAP
FlAP
FlAP
MMMM
M M M
MMMM
MMMM
MMM
DAY Five:
Hello, My name is Marvin III.
I am one of The earlier models from before They Perfected Personality Software.
AH..AH..AH..AH
Self-enterTainmenT achieved.
JusT a little furTher, genTlemen. My body is right Through These Trees.
TOSS
ReTracT

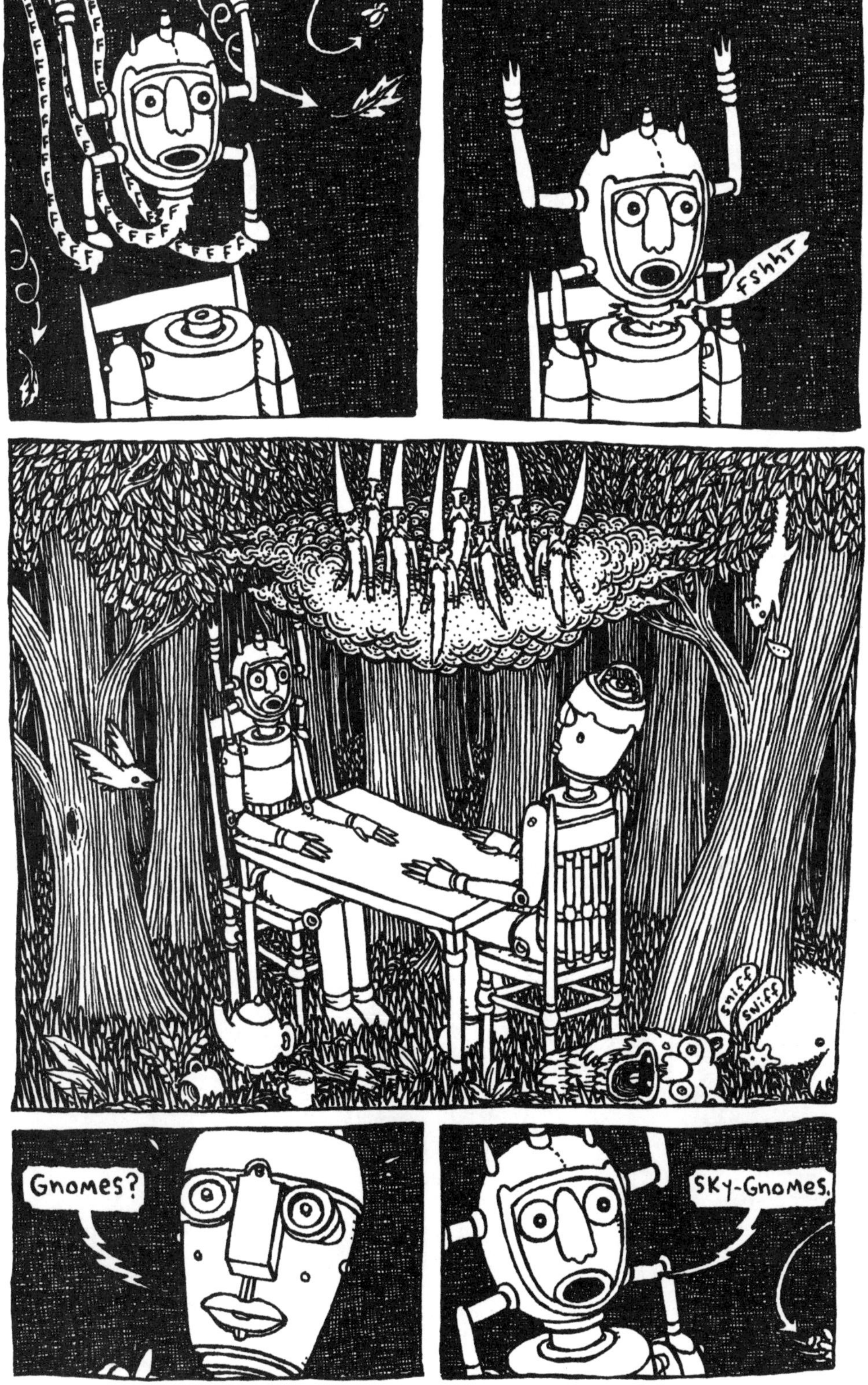
FSHHT
sniff
sniff
Gnomes?
SKy-Gnomes.

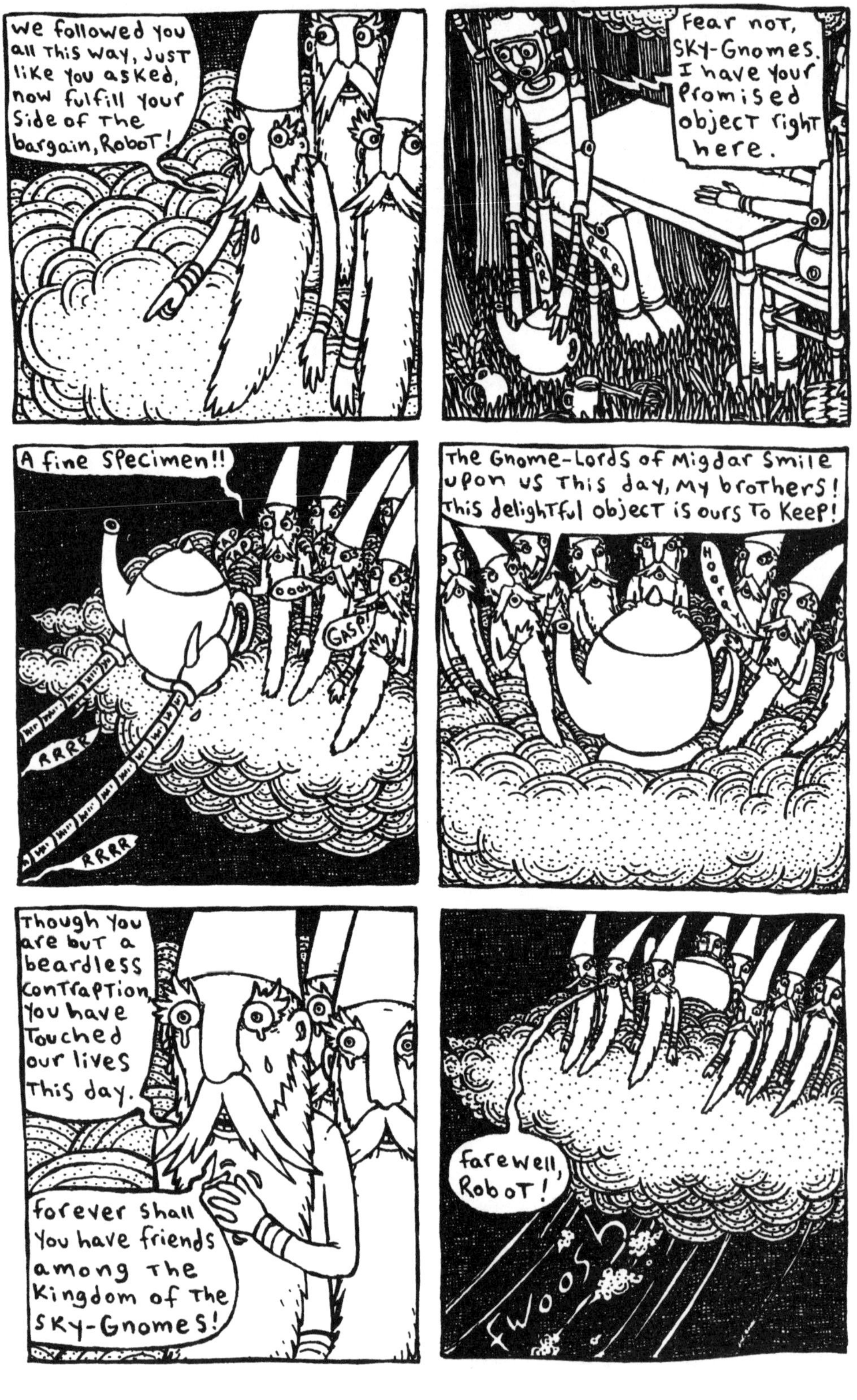
we followed you all this way, just like you asked, now fulfill your side of the bargain, Robot!
Fear not, Sky-Gnomes. I have your promised object right here.
A fine specimen!!
ooh
GASP!
RRRR
RRRR
The Gnome-Lords of Migdar smile upon us this day, my brothers! This delightful object is ours to keep!
Hooray
Though you are but a beardless contraption, you have touched our lives this day.
forever shall you have friends among the Kingdom of the Sky-Gnomes!
farewell, Robot!
FWOOSH

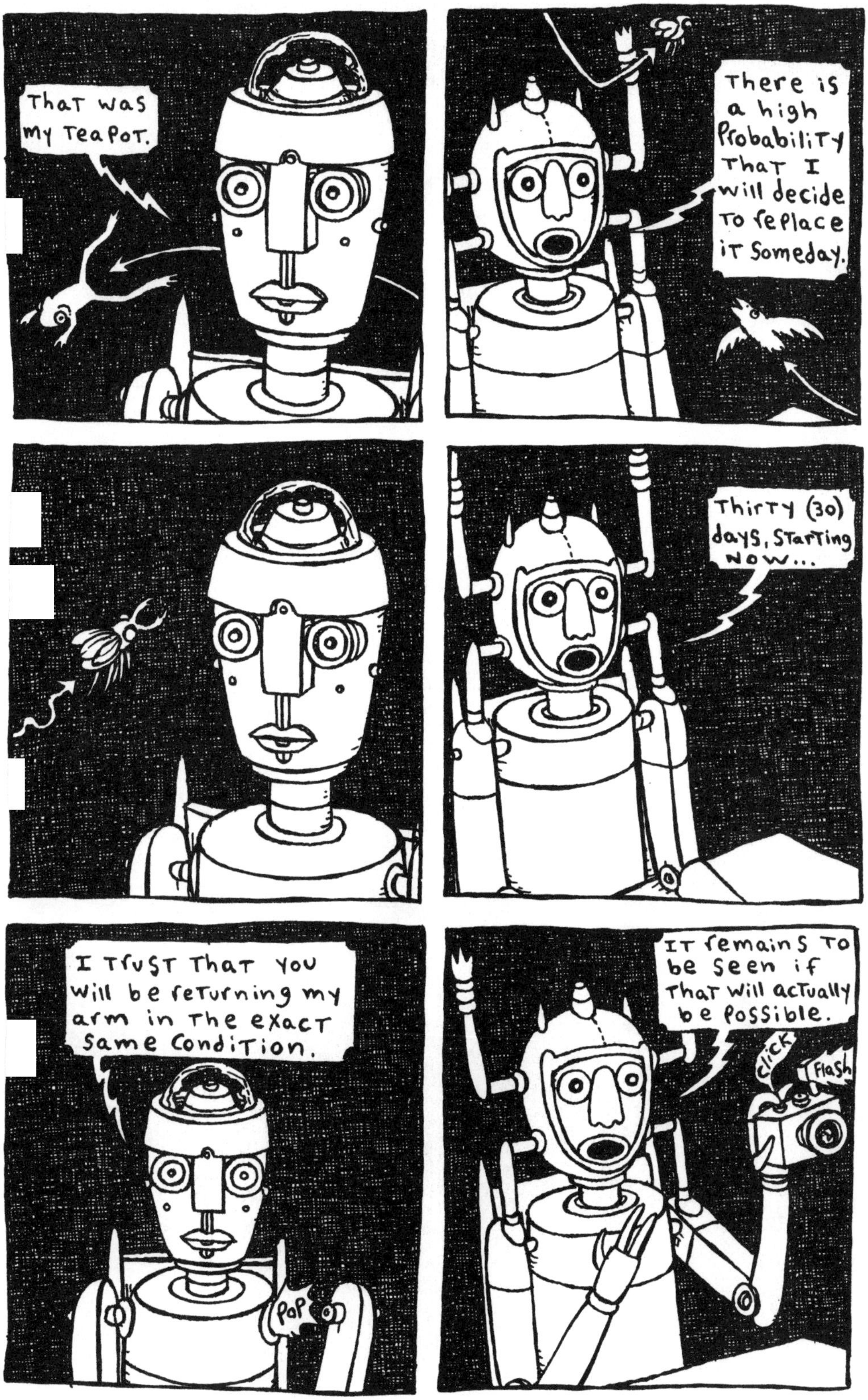
That was my teapot.
There is a high probability that I will decide to replace it someday.
Thirty (30) days, starting now...
I trust that you will be returning my arm in the exact same condition.
POP
It remains to be seen if that will actually be possible.
CLICK
FLASH

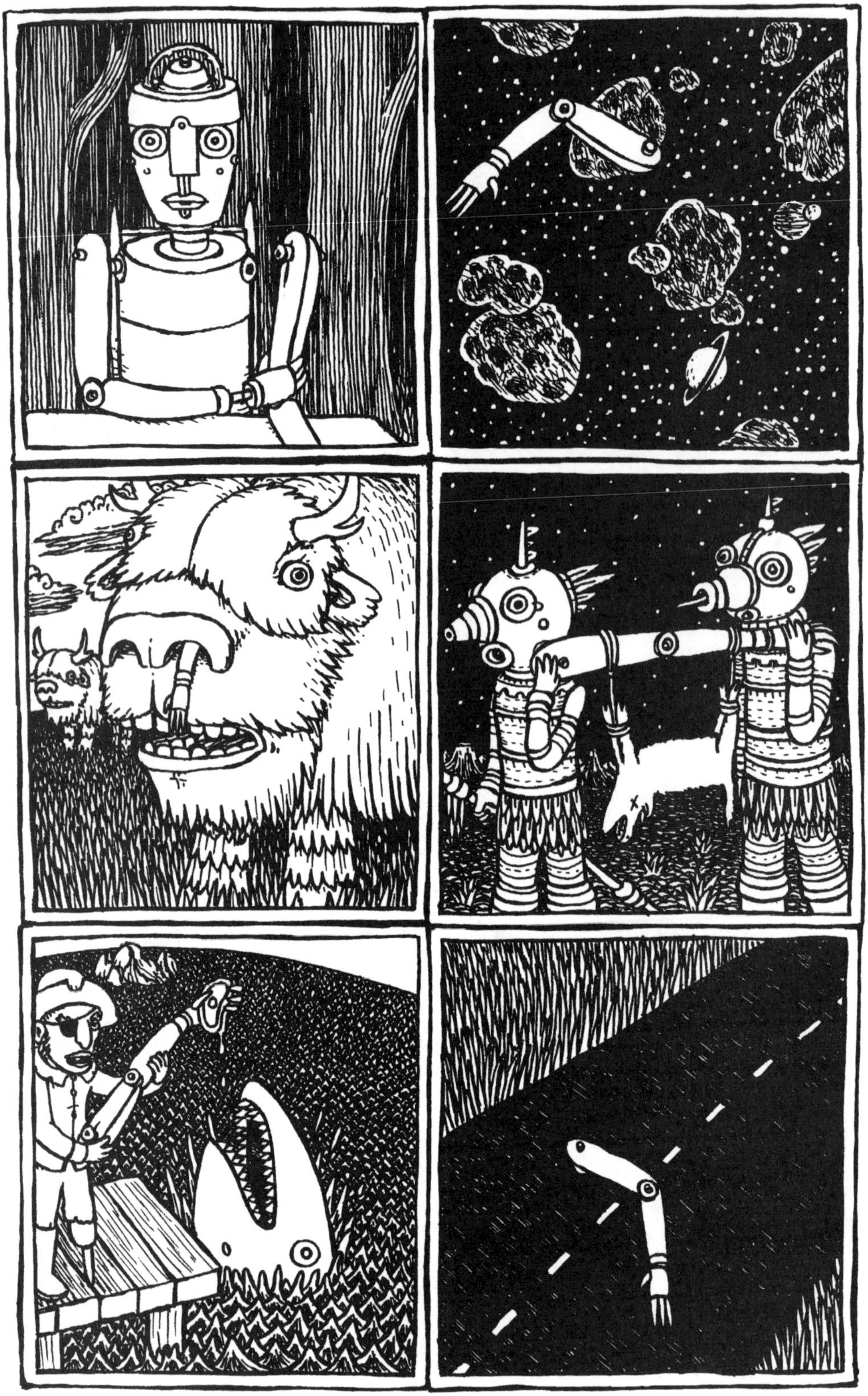

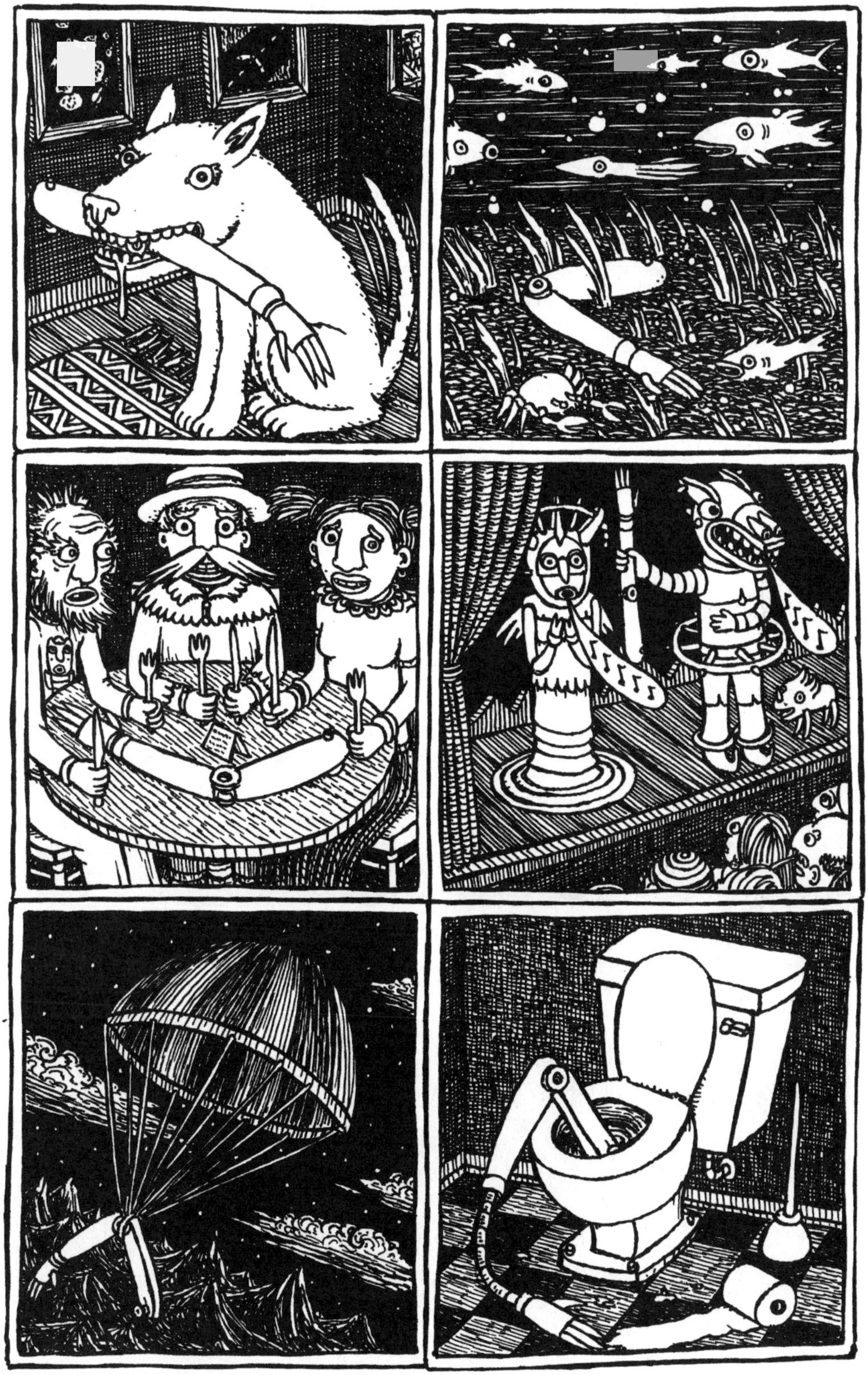

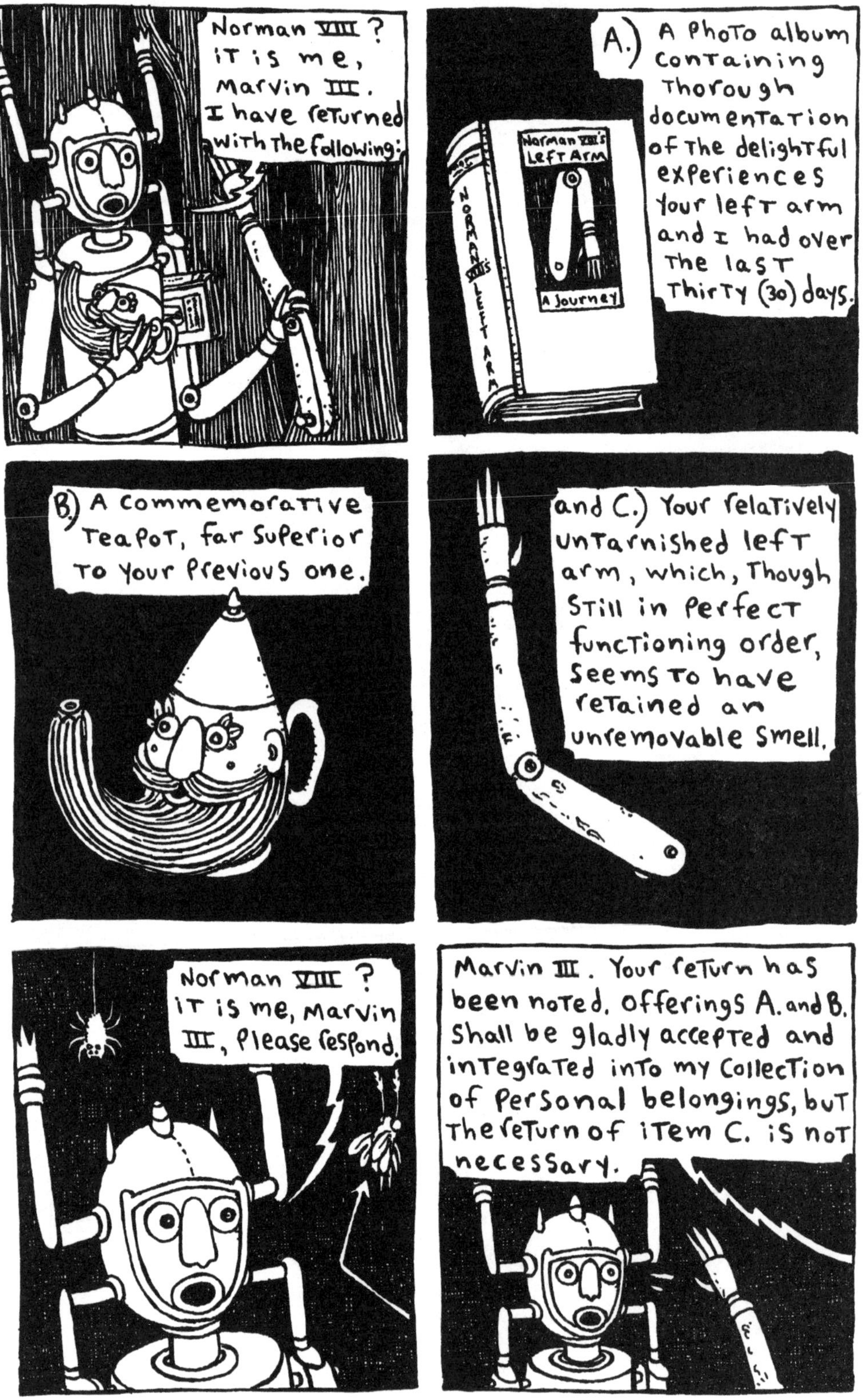
Norman VIII? It is me, Marvin III. I have returned with the following:
A.) A photo album containing thorough documentation of the delightful experiences your left arm and I had over the last thirty (30) days.
Norman VIII's Left Arm
A Journey
B.) A commemorative teapot, far superior to your previous one.
and C.) Your relatively untarnished left arm, which, though still in perfect functioning order, seems to have retained an unremovable smell.
Norman VIII? It is me, Marvin III, please respond.
Marvin III. Your return has been noted. Offerings A. and B. shall be gladly accepted and integrated into my collection of personal belongings, but the return of item C. is not necessary.

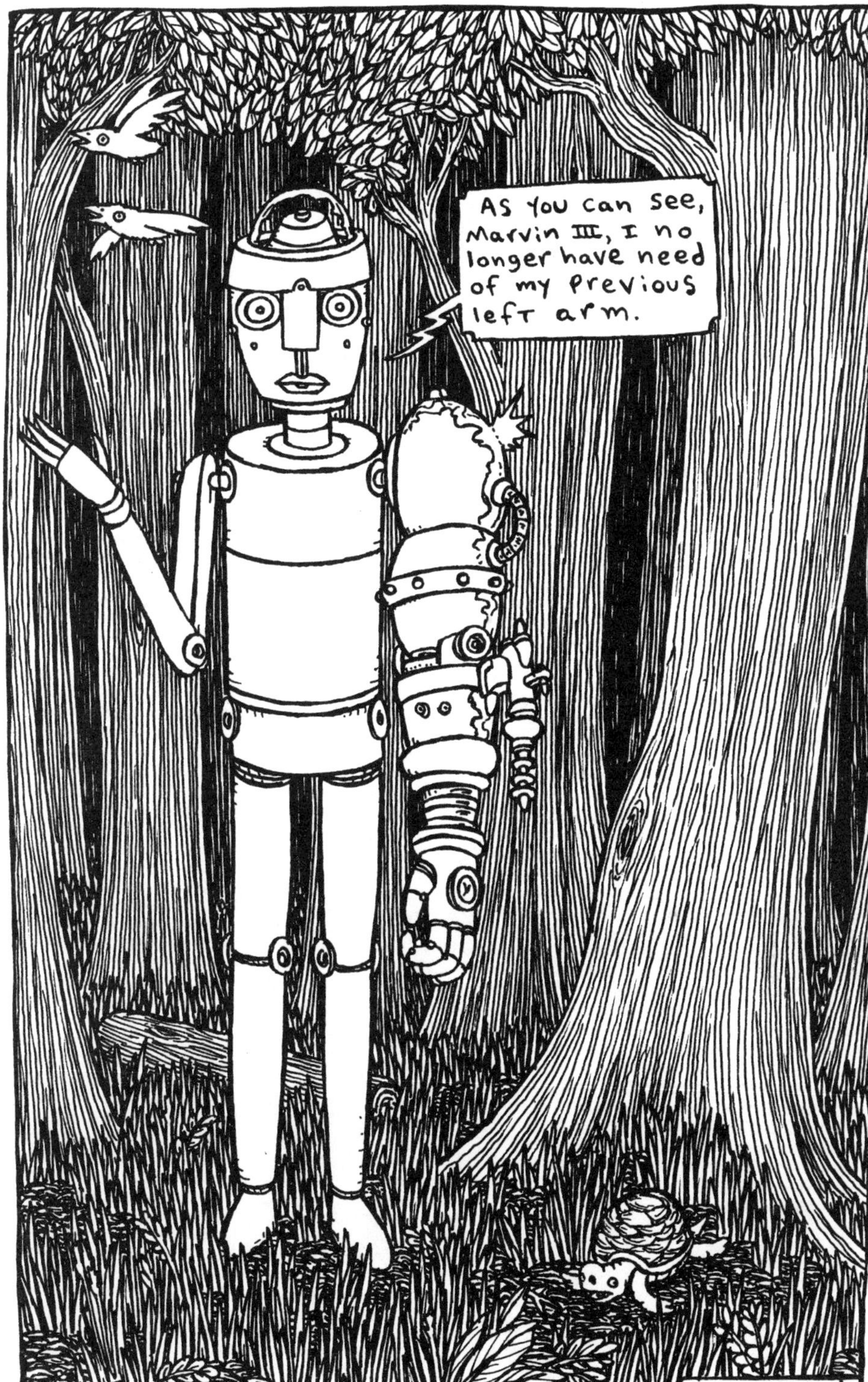
As you can see, Marvin III, I no longer have need of my previous left arm.
Completed

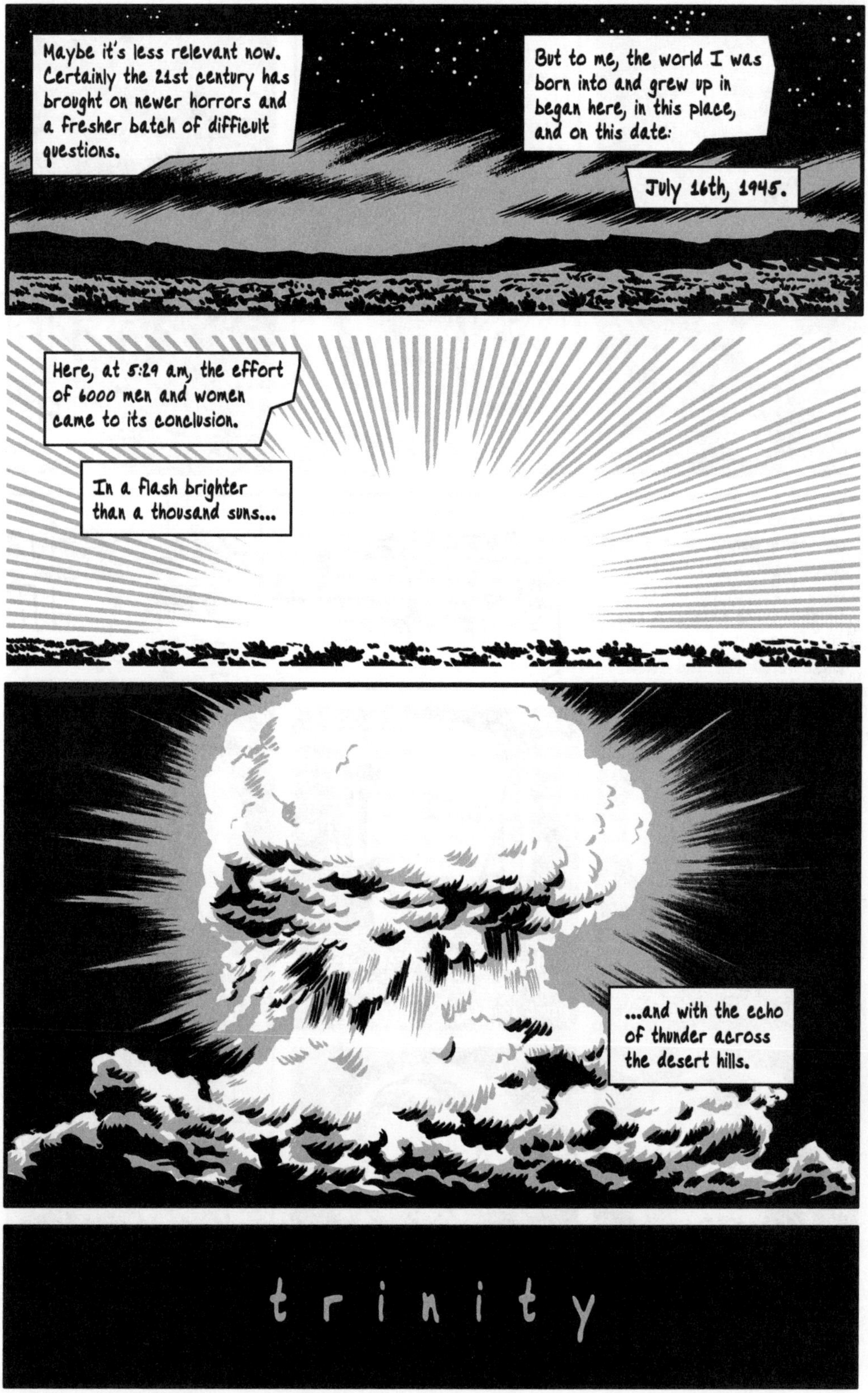

Maybe it's less relevant now. Certainly the 21st century has brought on newer horrors and a fresher batch of difficult questions.
But to me, the world I was born into and grew up in began here, in this place, and on this date:
July 16th, 1945.
Here, at 5:29 am, the effort of 6000 men and women came to its conclusion.
In a flash brighter than a thousand suns...
...and with the echo of thunder across the desert hills.
trinity

December, 1938: fission is discovered by scientists in Germany, splitting the atom and unleashing undreamt of amounts of energy. As the news spreads around the world, top physicists immediately grasp the possibility of creating an atomic bomb.

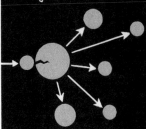

August, 1939: fearing that Nazi scientists may already be working on it, Leo Szilard convinces Albert Einstein to write to President Roosevelt, urging the start of an American-led atomic project.

December, 1941: Pearl Harbor plunges the U.S. into World War II, and the bomb program picks up momentum. Now code named the Manhattan Project, it's headed by General Leslie Groves; the man who built the Pentagon.

At a top secret complex built on the grounds of a former boys school in Los Alamos, New Mexico, the best and brightest scientific minds of the free world are assembled for the task.

Among them:

Hans Bethe: principal theoretician, driven to join in an effort to stop the Nazis.

Niels Bohr: "the Great Dane", Nobel Prize winner and father figure to many of the assembled.

Enrico Fermi: chief experimentalist, who works on the atomic chain reaction.

Ernest O. Lawrence: inventor of the cyclotron, which produces fissionable material.

Edward Teller: the physicist who advocates the construction of a hydrogen "super" bomb.

And overseeing them all, **J. Robert Oppenheimer,** chief physicist and director of operations.

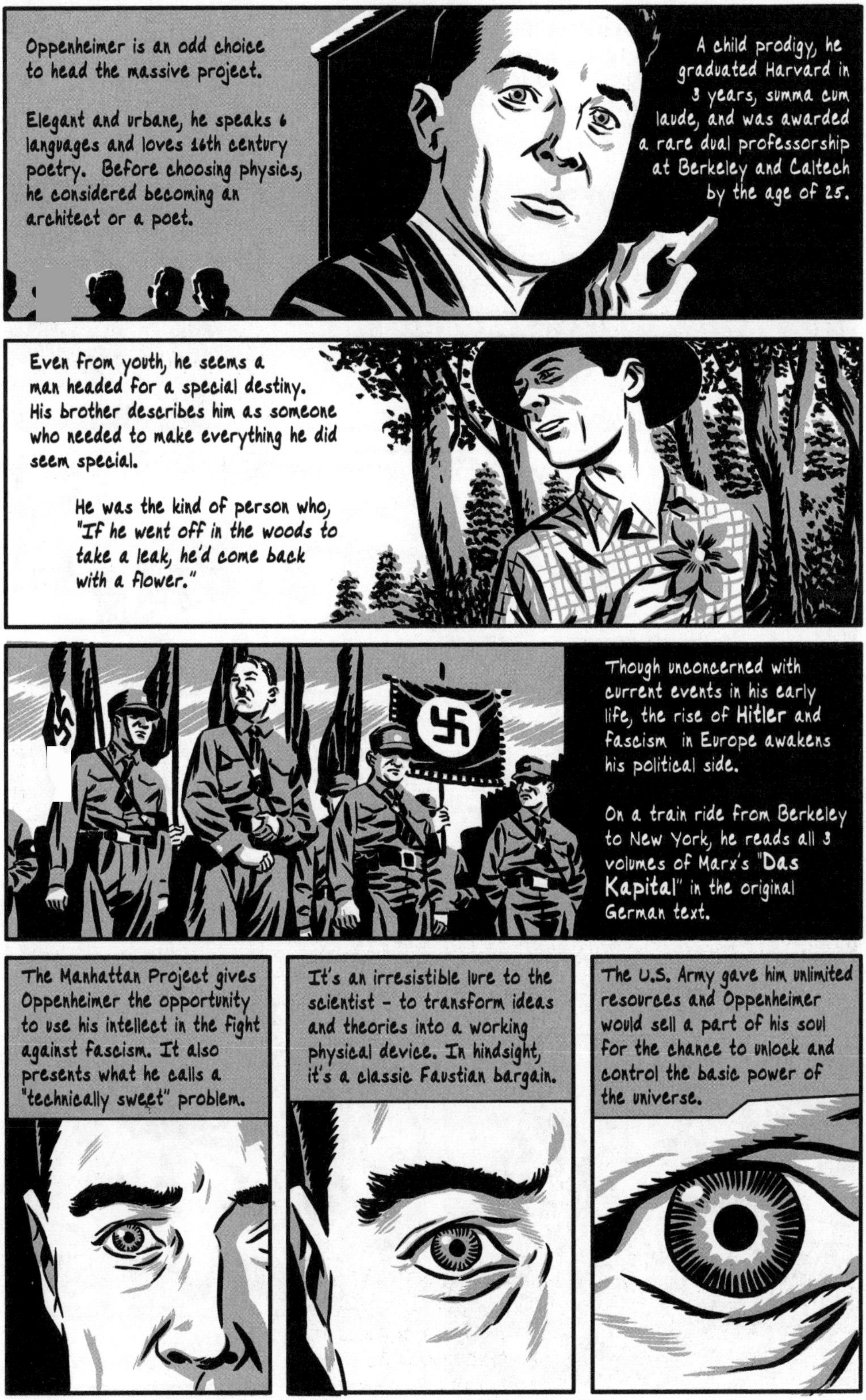

Oppenheimer is an odd choice to head the massive project.
Elegant and urbane, he speaks 6 languages and loves 16th century poetry. Before choosing physics, he considered becoming an architect or a poet.
A child prodigy, he graduated Harvard in 3 years, summa cum laude, and was awarded a rare dual professorship at Berkeley and Caltech by the age of 25.
Even from youth, he seems a man headed for a special destiny. His brother describes him as someone who needed to make everything he did seem special.
He was the kind of person who, "If he went off in the woods to take a leak, he'd come back with a flower."
Though unconcerned with current events in his early life, the rise of Hitler and fascism in Europe awakens his political side.
On a train ride from Berkeley to New York, he reads all 3 volumes of Marx's "Das Kapital" in the original German text.
The Manhattan Project gives Oppenheimer the opportunity to use his intellect in the fight against fascism. It also presents what he calls a "technically sweet" problem.
It's an irresistible lure to the scientist - to transform ideas and theories into a working physical device. In hindsight, it's a classic Faustian bargain.
The U.S. Army gave him unlimited resources and Oppenheimer would sell a part of his soul for the chance to unlock and control the basic power of the universe.

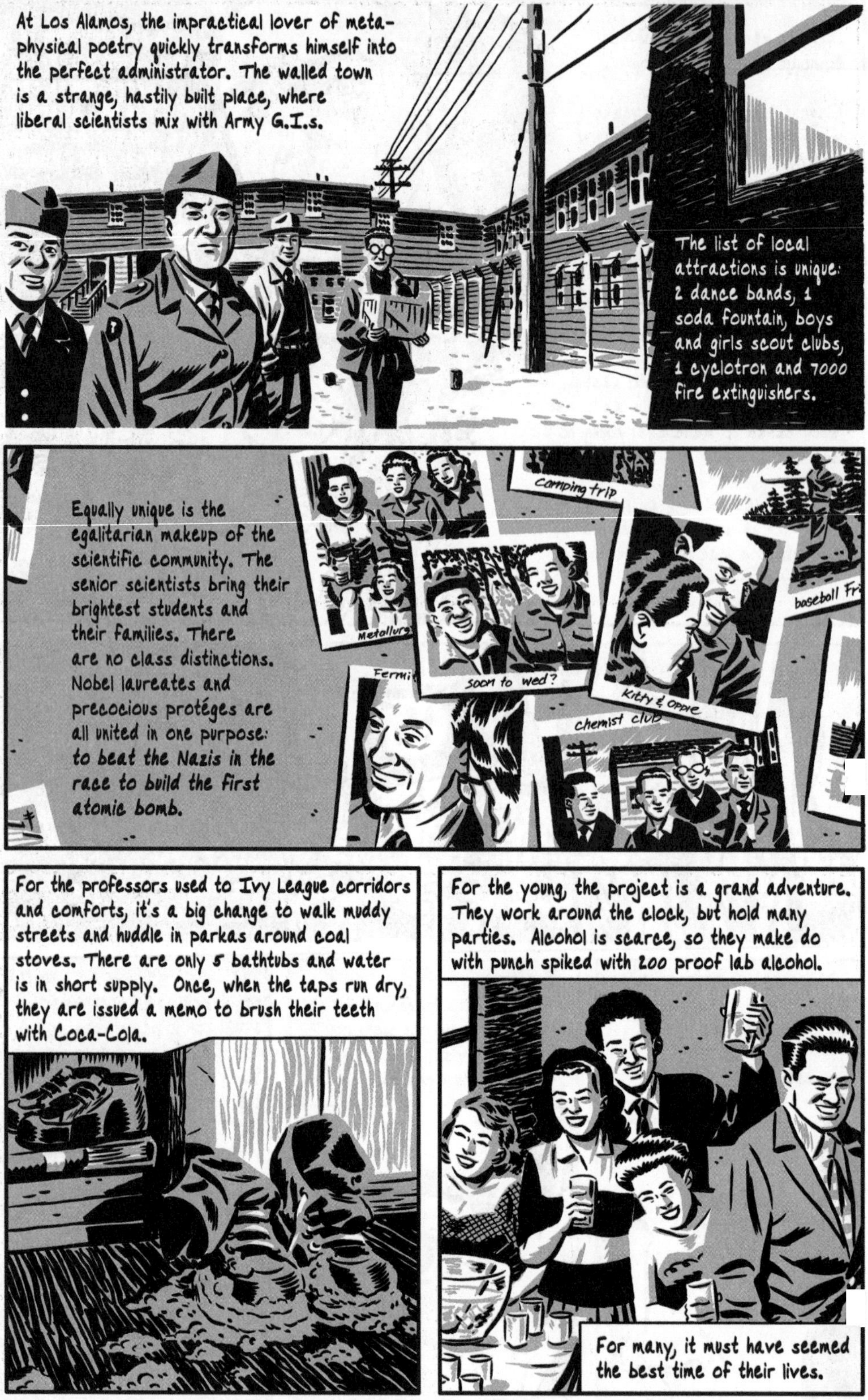
At Los Alamos, the impractical lover of metaphysical poetry quickly transforms himself into the perfect administrator. The walled town is a strange, hastily built place, where liberal scientists mix with Army G.I.s.
The list of local attractions is unique: 2 dance bands, 1 soda fountain, boys and girls scout clubs, 1 cyclotron and 7000 fire extinguishers.
Equally unique is the egalitarian makeup of the scientific community. The senior scientists bring their brightest students and their families. There are no class distinctions. Nobel laureates and precocious protéges are all united in one purpose: to beat the Nazis in the race to build the first atomic bomb.
Camping trip
soon to wed?
Kitty & Oppie
chemist club
For the professors used to Ivy League corridors and comforts, it's a big change to walk muddy streets and huddle in parkas around coal stoves. There are only 5 bathtubs and water is in short supply. Once, when the taps run dry, they are issued a memo to brush their teeth with Coca-Cola.
For the young, the project is a grand adventure. They work around the clock, but hold many parties. Alcohol is scarce, so they make do with punch spiked with 200 proof lab alcohol.
For many, it must have seemed the best time of their lives.

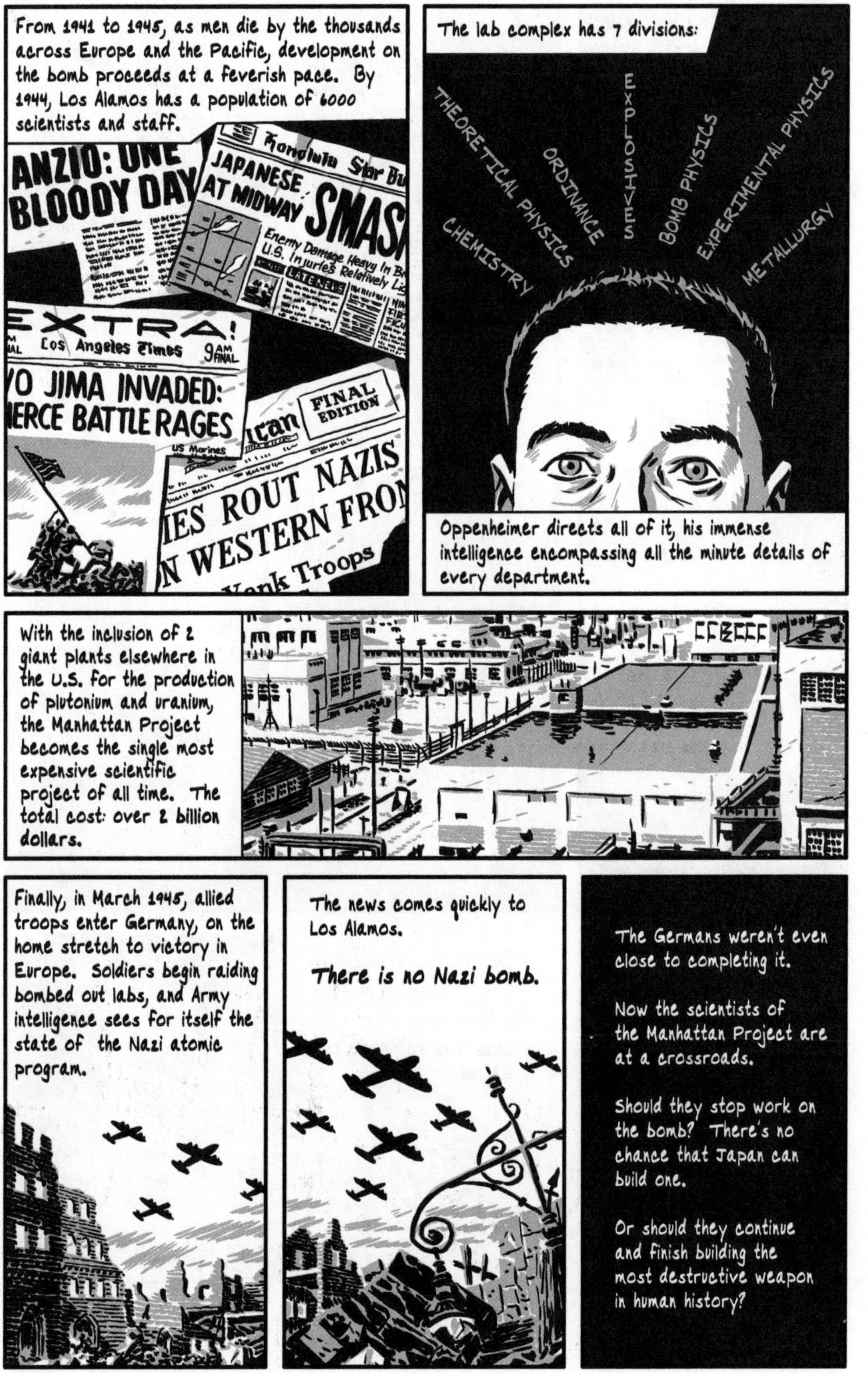

From 1941 to 1945, as men die by the thousands across Europe and the Pacific, development on the bomb proceeds at a feverish pace. By 1944, Los Alamos has a population of 6000 scientists and staff.
ANZIO: ONE BLOODY DAY
Honolulu Star Bu
JAPANESE AT MIDWAY SMASH
Enemy Damage Heavy In B
U.S. Injuries Relatively Li
LATE NEWS
EXTRA!
Los Angeles Times
9AM FINAL
O JIMA INVADED: IERCE BATTLE RAGES
US Marines
FINAL EDITION
IES ROUT NAZIS N WESTERN FRON
Yank Troops
The lab complex has 7 divisions:
CHEMISTRY
THEORETICAL PHYSICS
ORDINANCE
EXPLOSIVES
BOMB PHYSICS
EXPERIMENTAL PHYSICS
METALLURGY
Oppenheimer directs all of it, his immense intelligence encompassing all the minute details of every department.
With the inclusion of 2 giant plants elsewhere in the U.S. for the production of plutonium and uranium, the Manhattan Project becomes the single most expensive scientific project of all time. The total cost: over 2 billion dollars.
Finally, in March 1945, allied troops enter Germany, on the home stretch to victory in Europe. Soldiers begin raiding bombed out labs, and Army intelligence sees for itself the state of the Nazi atomic program.
The news comes quickly to Los Alamos.
There is no Nazi bomb.
The Germans weren't even close to completing it.
Now the scientists of the Manhattan Project are at a crossroads.
Should they stop work on the bomb? There's no chance that Japan can build one.
Or should they continue and finish building the most destructive weapon in human history?

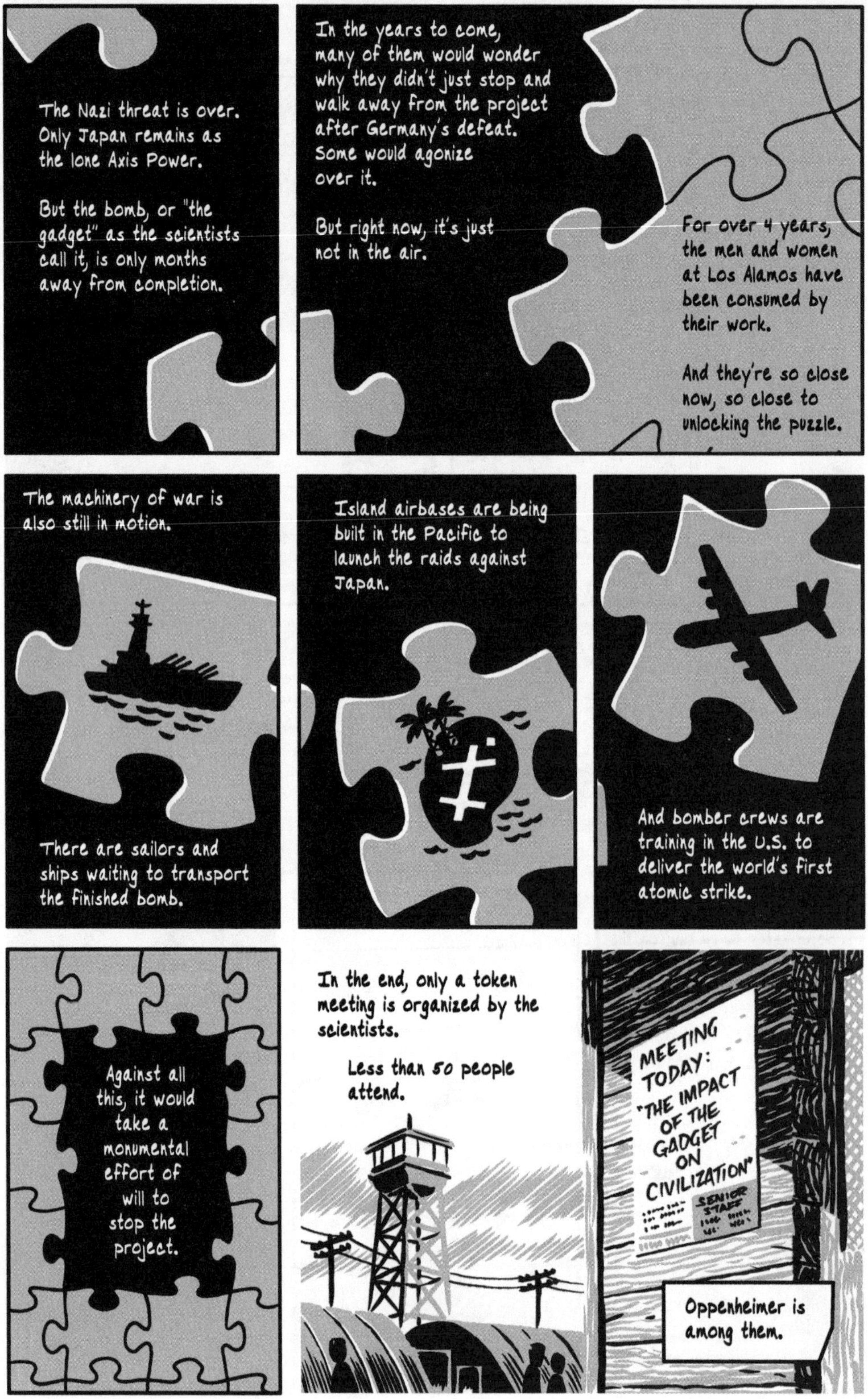
The Nazi threat is over. Only Japan remains as the lone Axis Power.
But the bomb, or "the gadget" as the scientists call it, is only months away from completion.
In the years to come, many of them would wonder why they didn't just stop and walk away from the project after Germany's defeat. Some would agonize over it.
But right now, it's just not in the air.
For over 4 years, the men and women at Los Alamos have been consumed by their work.
And they're so close now, so close to unlocking the puzzle.
The machinery of war is also still in motion.
There are sailors and ships waiting to transport the finished bomb.
Island airbases are being built in the Pacific to launch the raids against Japan.
And bomber crews are training in the U.S. to deliver the world's first atomic strike.
Against all this, it would take a monumental effort of will to stop the project.
In the end, only a token meeting is organized by the scientists.
Less than 50 people attend.
MEETING TODAY: "THE IMPACT OF THE GADGET ON CIVILIZATION"
SENIOR STAFF
Oppenheimer is among them.

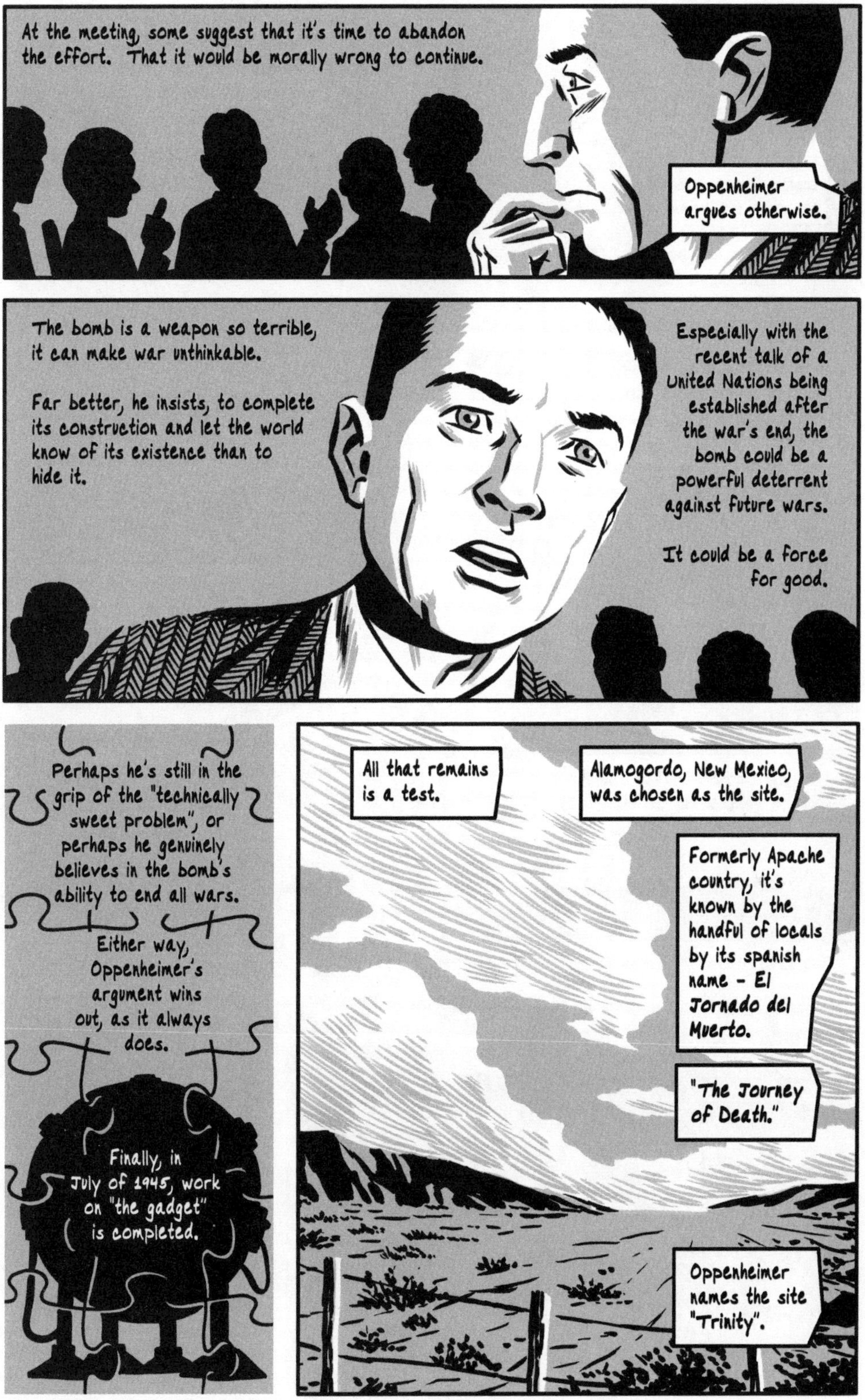
At the meeting, some suggest that it's time to abandon the effort. That it would be morally wrong to continue.
Oppenheimer argues otherwise.
The bomb is a weapon so terrible, it can make war unthinkable.
Far better, he insists, to complete its construction and let the world know of its existence than to hide it.
Especially with the recent talk of a United Nations being established after the war's end, the bomb could be a powerful deterrent against future wars.
It could be a force for good.
Perhaps he's still in the grip of the "technically sweet problem", or perhaps he genuinely believes in the bomb's ability to end all wars.
Either way, Oppenheimer's argument wins out, as it always does.
Finally, in July of 1945, work on "the gadget" is completed.
All that remains is a test.
Alamogordo, New Mexico, was chosen as the site.
Formerly Apache country, it's known by the handful of locals by its spanish name - El Jornado del Muerto.
"The Journey of Death."
Oppenheimer names the site "Trinity".

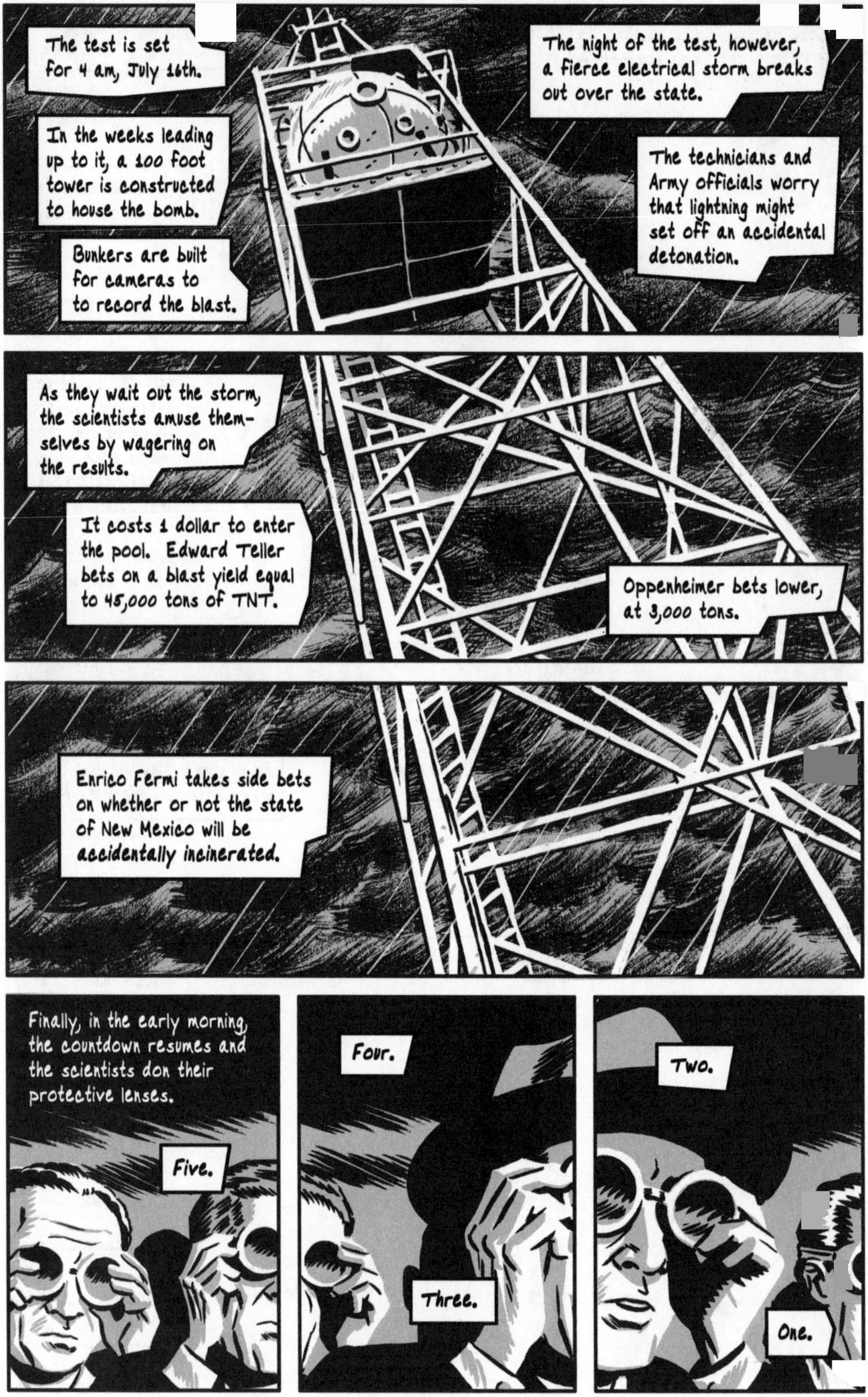
The test is set for 4 am, July 16th.
In the weeks leading up to it, a 100 foot tower is constructed to house the bomb.
Bunkers are built for cameras to to record the blast.
The night of the test, however, a fierce electrical storm breaks out over the state.
The technicians and Army officials worry that lightning might set off an accidental detonation.
As they wait out the storm, the scientists amuse themselves by wagering on the results.
It costs 1 dollar to enter the pool. Edward Teller bets on a blast yield equal to 45,000 tons of TNT.
Oppenheimer bets lower, at 3,000 tons.
Enrico Fermi takes side bets on whether or not the state of New Mexico will be accidentally incinerated.
Finally, in the early morning, the countdown resumes and the scientists don their protective lenses.
Five.
Four.
Three.
Two.
One.

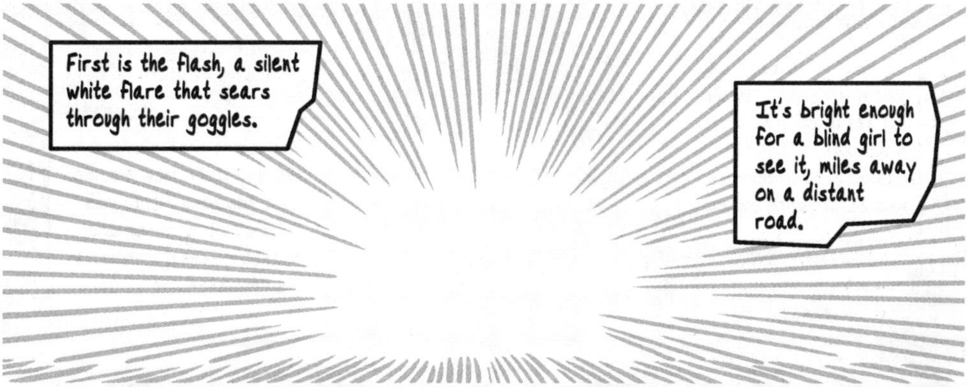
First is the flash, a silent white flare that sears through their goggles.
It's bright enough for a blind girl to see it, miles away on a distant road.

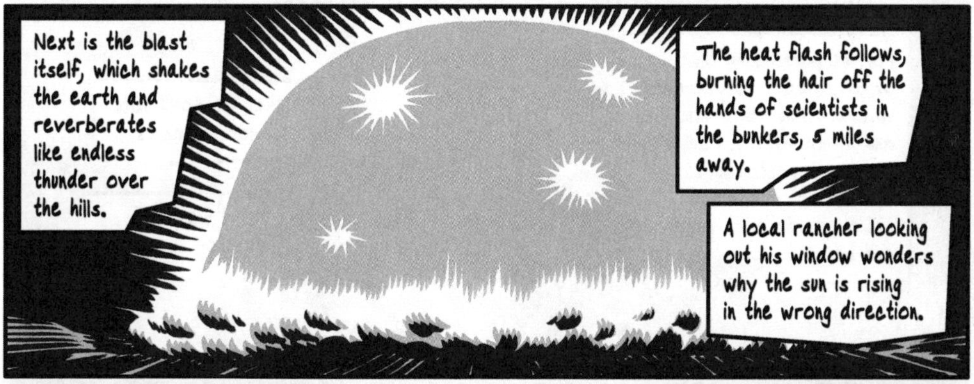
Next is the blast itself, which shakes the earth and reverberates like endless thunder over the hills.
The heat flash follows, burning the hair off the hands of scientists in the bunkers, 5 miles away.
A local rancher looking out his window wonders why the sun is rising in the wrong direction.

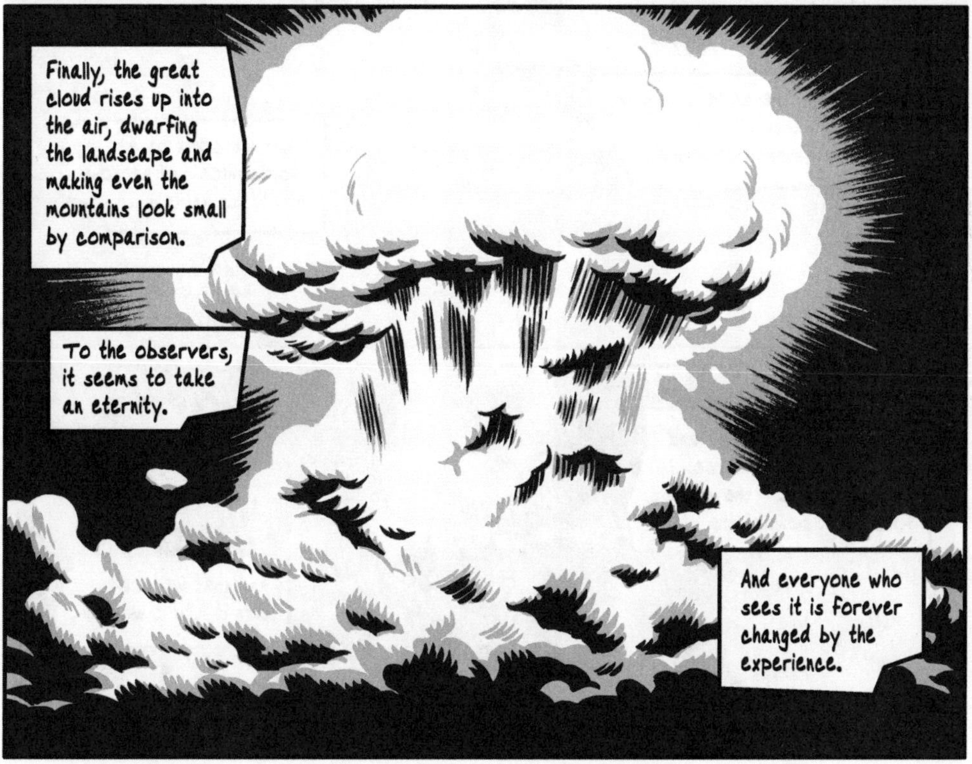
Finally, the great cloud rises up into the air, dwarfing the landscape and making even the mountains look small by comparison.
To the observers, it seems to take an eternity.
And everyone who sees it is forever changed by the experience.

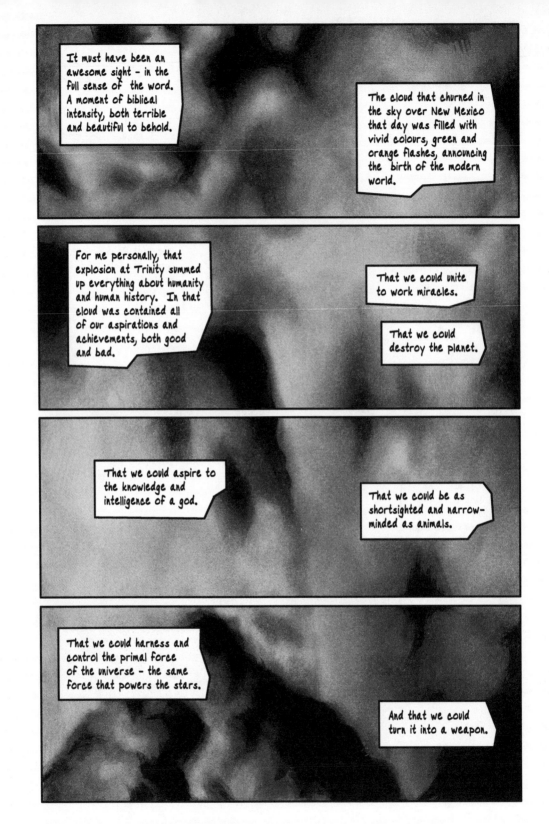

It must have been an awesome sight - in the full sense of the word. A moment of biblical intensity, both terrible and beautiful to behold.

The cloud that churned in the sky over New Mexico that day was filled with vivid colours, green and orange flashes, announcing the birth of the modern world.

For me personally, that explosion at Trinity summed up everything about humanity and human history. In that cloud was contained all of our aspirations and achievements, both good and bad.

That we could unite to work miracles.

That we could destroy the planet.

That we could aspire to the knowledge and intelligence of a god.

That we could be as shortsighted and narrow-minded as animals.

That we could harness and control the primal force of the universe - the same force that powers the stars.

And that we could turn it into a weapon.

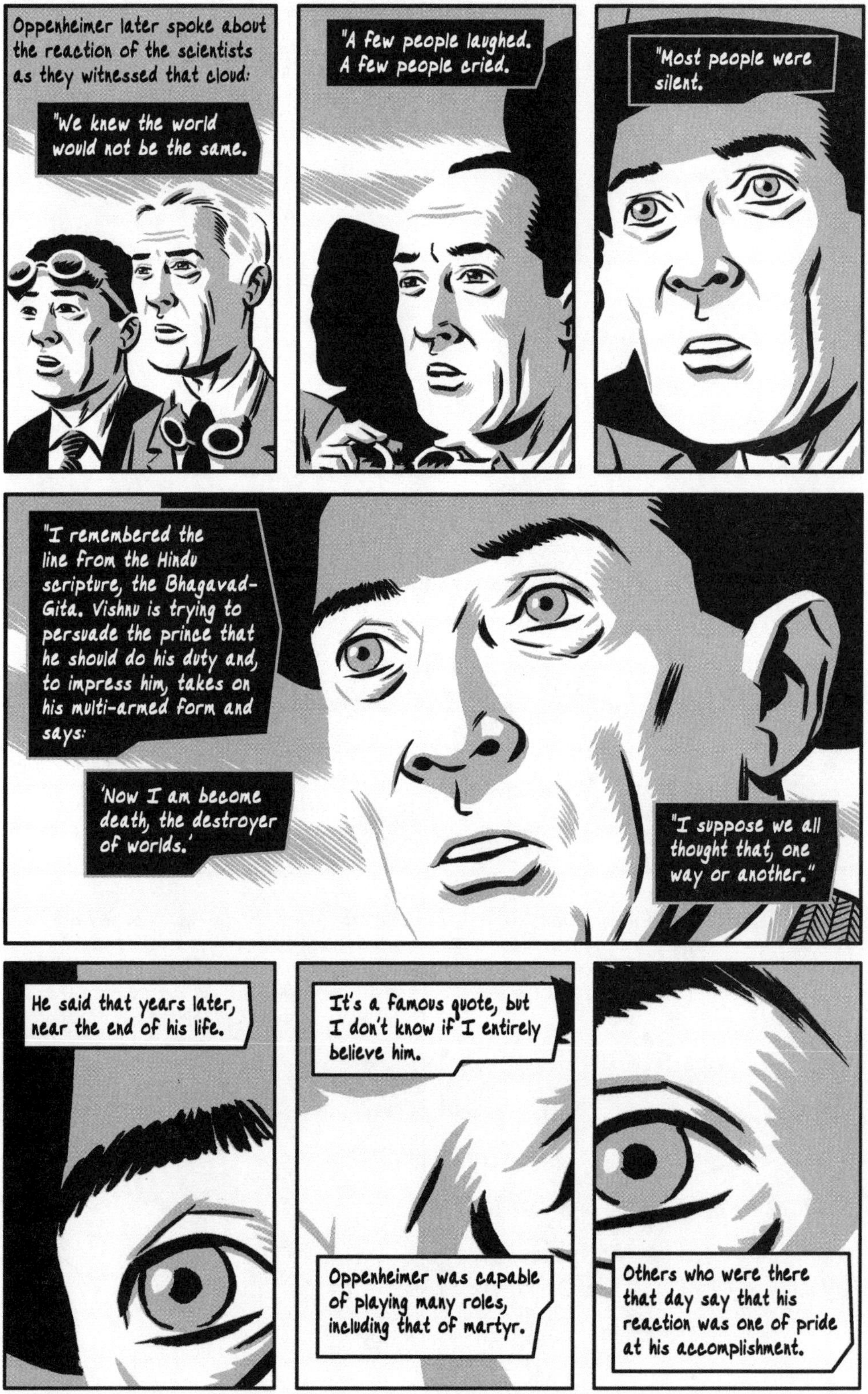
Oppenheimer later spoke about the reaction of the scientists as they witnessed that cloud:
"We knew the world would not be the same.
"A few people laughed. A few people cried.
"Most people were silent.
"I remembered the line from the Hindu scripture, the Bhagavad-Gita. Vishnu is trying to persuade the prince that he should do his duty and, to impress him, takes on his multi-armed form and says:
'Now I am become death, the destroyer of worlds.'
"I suppose we all thought that, one way or another."
He said that years later, near the end of his life.
It's a famous quote, but I don't know if I entirely believe him.
Oppenheimer was capable of playing many roles, including that of martyr.
Others who were there that day say that his reaction was one of pride at his accomplishment.

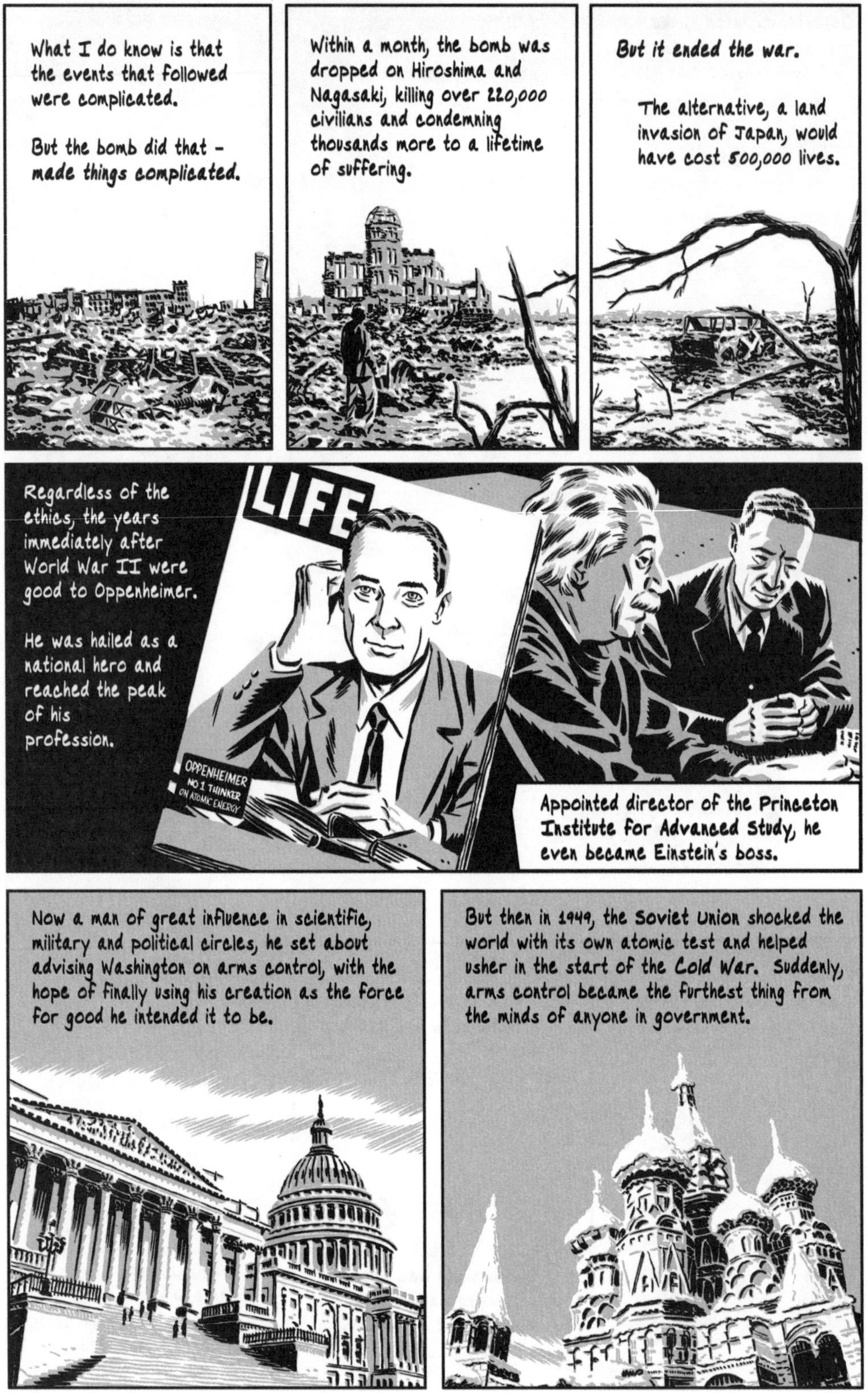
What I do know is that the events that followed were complicated.
But the bomb did that - made things complicated.
Within a month, the bomb was dropped on Hiroshima and Nagasaki, killing over 220,000 civilians and condemning thousands more to a lifetime of suffering.
But it ended the war.
The alternative, a land invasion of Japan, would have cost 500,000 lives.
Regardless of the ethics, the years immediately after World War II were good to Oppenheimer.
He was hailed as a national hero and reached the peak of his profession.
LIFE
OPPENHEIMER NO 1 THINKER ON ATOMIC ENERGY
Appointed director of the Princeton Institute for Advanced Study, he even became Einstein's boss.
Now a man of great influence in scientific, military and political circles, he set about advising Washington on arms control, with the hope of finally using his creation as the force for good he intended it to be.
But then in 1949, the Soviet Union shocked the world with its own atomic test and helped usher in the start of the Cold War. Suddenly, arms control became the furthest thing from the minds of anyone in government.

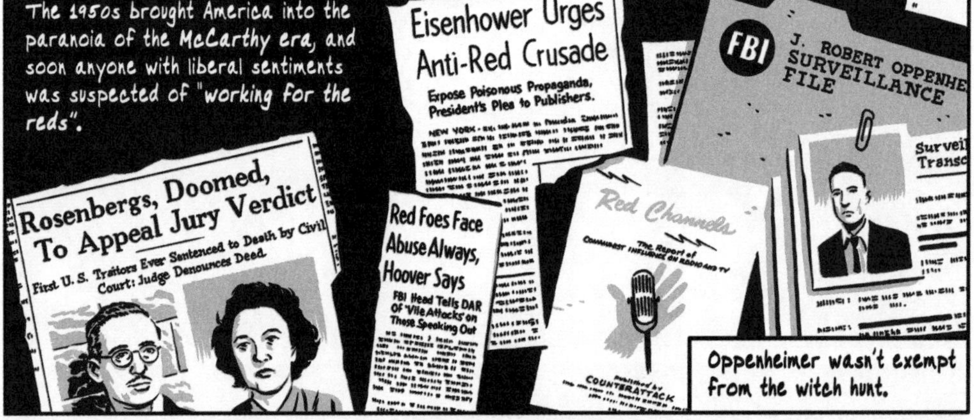
The 1950s brought America into the paranoia of the McCarthy era, and soon anyone with liberal sentiments was suspected of "working for the reds".
Eisenhower Urges Anti-Red Crusade
Expose Poisonous Propaganda, President's Plea to Publishers.
FBI
J. ROBERT OPPENHE
SURVEILLANCE FILE
Rosenbergs, Doomed, To Appeal Jury Verdict
First U.S. Traitors Ever Sentenced to Death by Civil Court: Judge Denounces Deed.
Red Foes Face Abuse Always, Hoover Says
FBI Head Tells DAR Of 'Vile Attacks' on Those Speaking Out
Red Channels
The Report of Communist Influence on Radio and TV
Published by COUNTERATTACK
Oppenheimer wasn't exempt from the witch hunt.

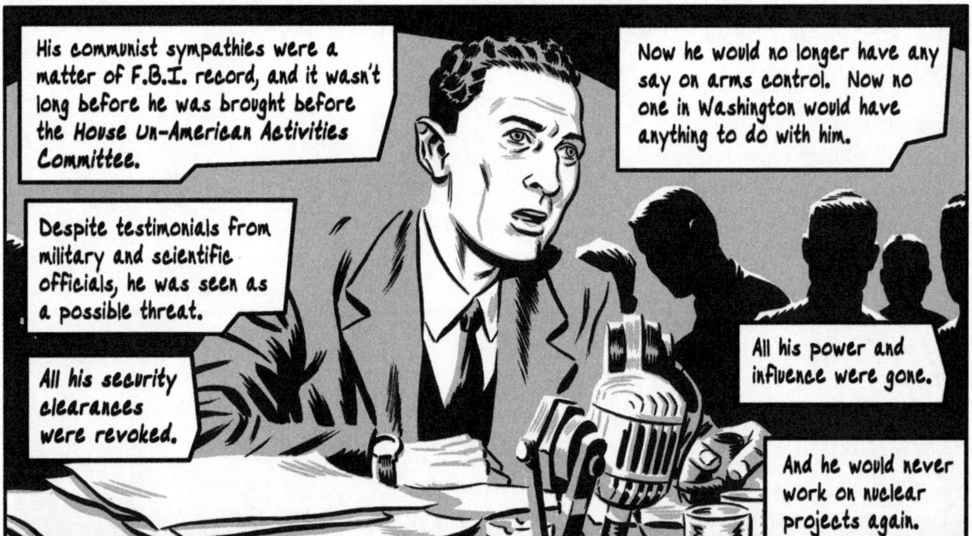
His communist sympathies were a matter of F.B.I. record, and it wasn't long before he was brought before the House Un-American Activities Committee.
Now he would no longer have any say on arms control. Now no one in Washington would have anything to do with him.
Despite testimonials from military and scientific officials, he was seen as a possible threat.
All his security clearances were revoked.
All his power and influence were gone.
And he would never work on nuclear projects again.

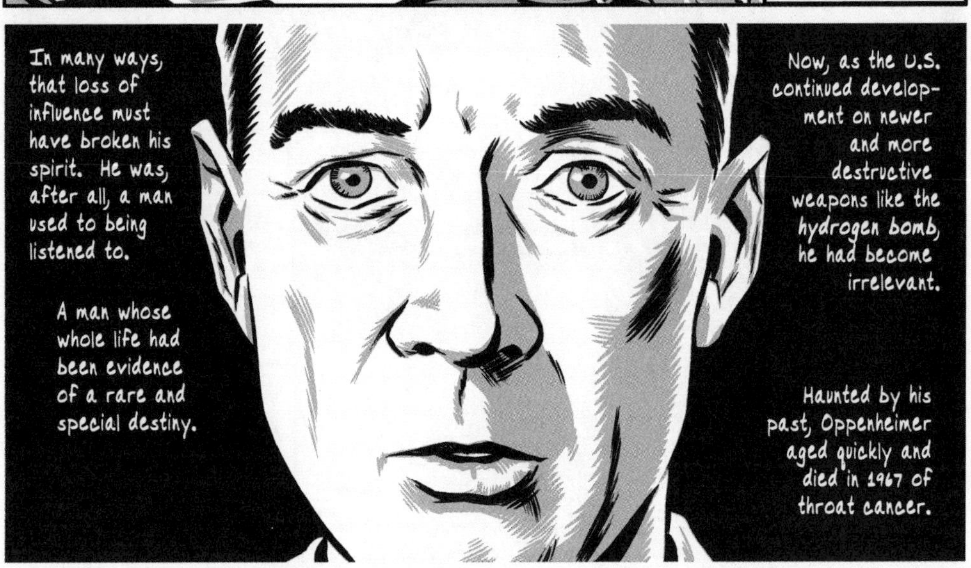
In many ways, that loss of influence must have broken his spirit. He was, after all, a man used to being listened to.
A man whose whole life had been evidence of a rare and special destiny.
Now, as the U.S. continued development on newer and more destructive weapons like the hydrogen bomb, he had become irrelevant.
Haunted by his past, Oppenheimer aged quickly and died in 1967 of throat cancer.

Since that first test in 1945, there have been over 2050 nuclear detonations.

Some were conducted at sea, others deep underground.

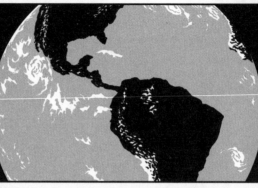

The largest of them carried more than 4000 times the destructive power of the bomb dropped on Hiroshima.

As a result of the fallout from all those tests, everyone on earth now carries trace elements of radioactivity - of *strontium and tritium* in our bodies.

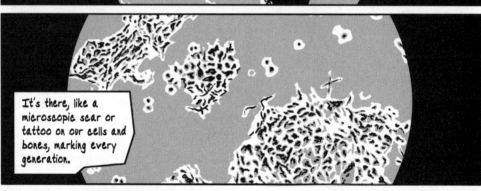

It's there, like a microscopic scar or tattoo on our cells and bones, marking every generation.

TRINITY SITE
WHERE
THE WORLD'S FIRST
NUCLEAR DEVICE
WAS EXPLODED ON
JULY 16, 1945

A tiny reminder of the efforts of 6000 men and women...

...of a fierce and terrible cloud that rose up into the morning air...

...and all the unanswerable questions that rose up with it, on that fateful day at *Trinity.*

EXCERPT FROM

SCOTT PILGRIM
vs. THE UNIVERSE

BRYAN LEE O'MALLEY

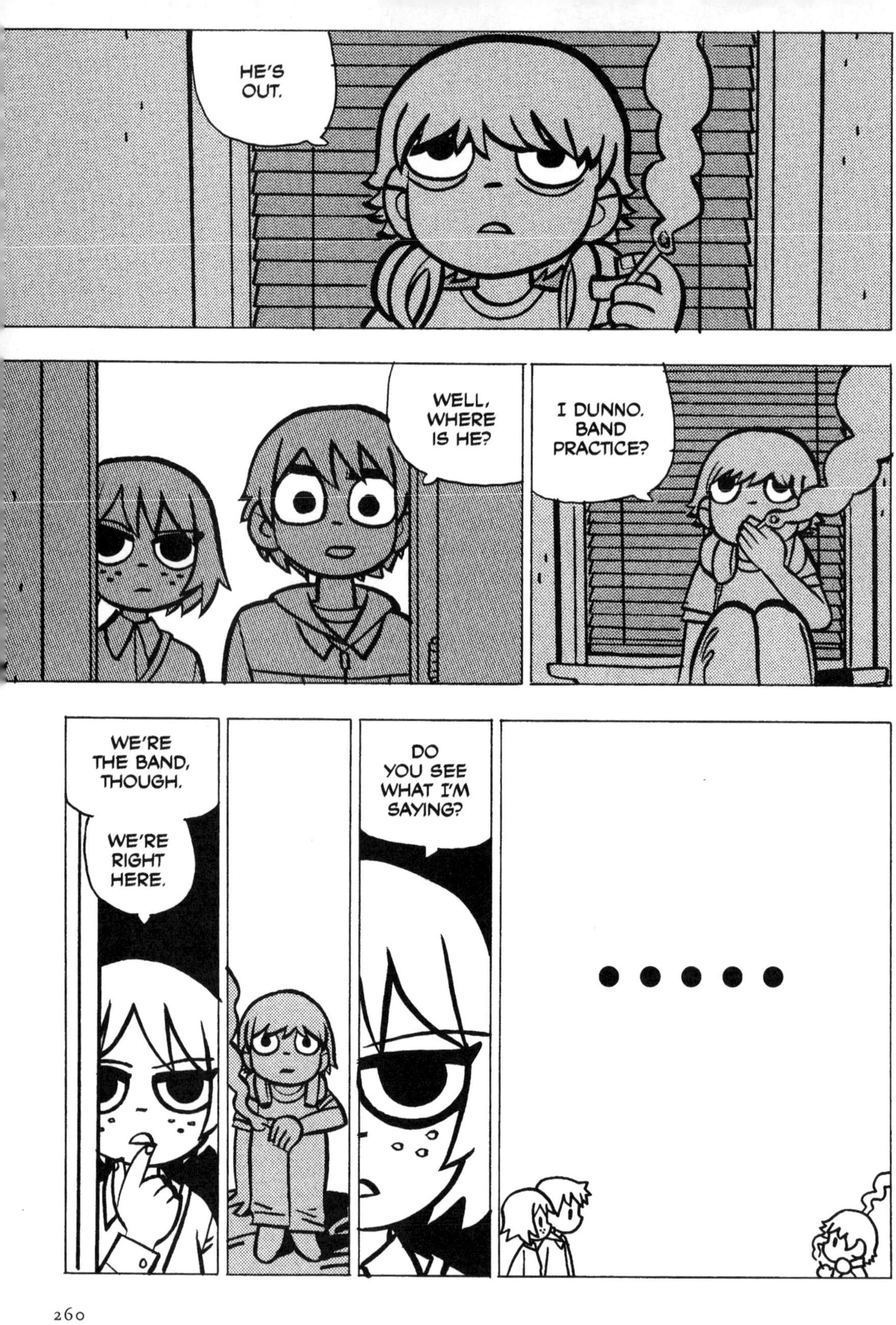
HE'S OUT.
WELL, WHERE IS HE?
I DUNNO. BAND PRACTICE?
WE'RE THE BAND, THOUGH.
WE'RE RIGHT HERE.
DO YOU SEE WHAT I'M SAYING?
• • • • •

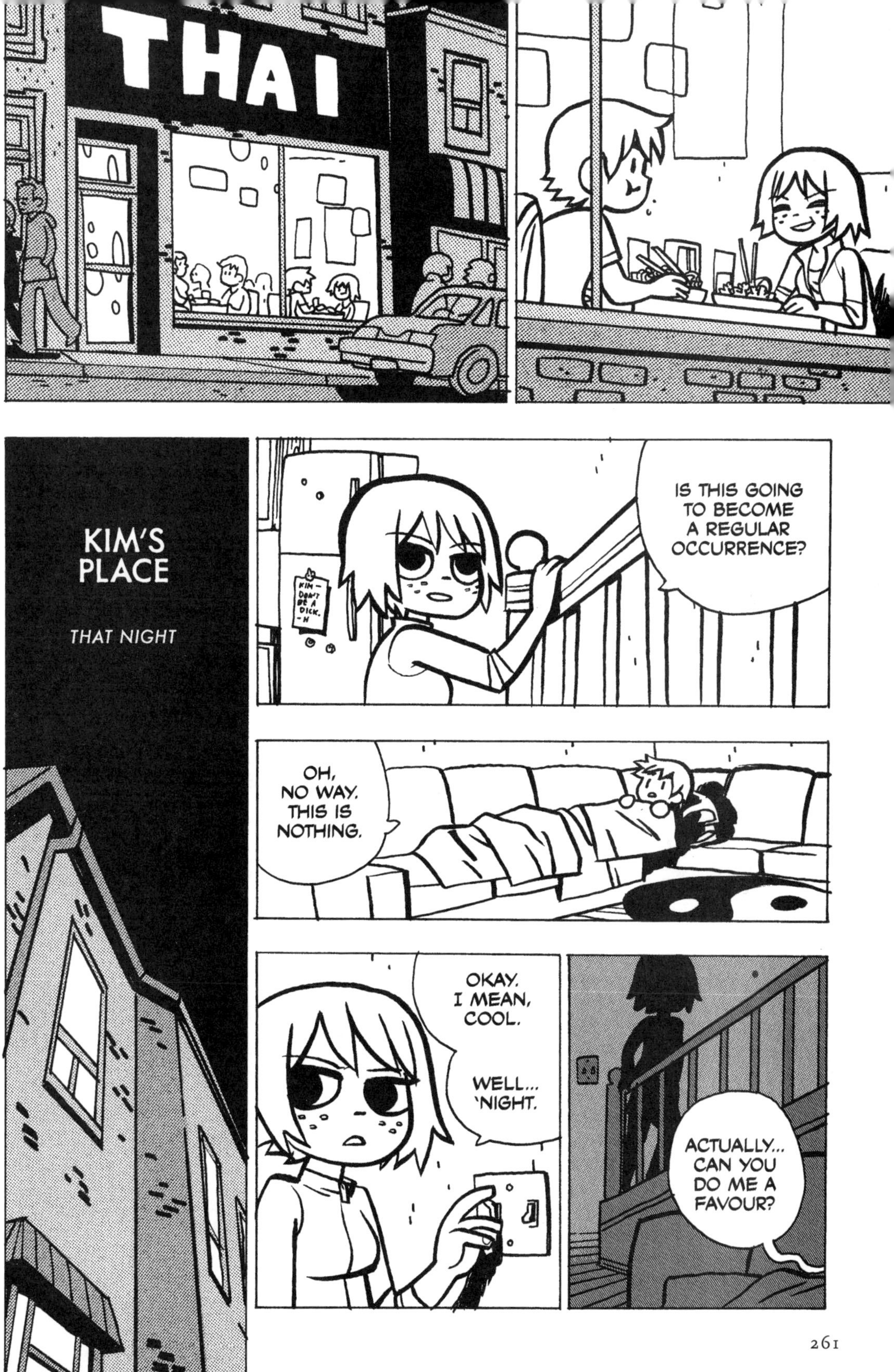
THAI
KIM'S PLACE
THAT NIGHT
KIM — DON'T BE A DICK. -N
IS THIS GOING TO BECOME A REGULAR OCCURRENCE?
OH, NO WAY. THIS IS NOTHING.
OKAY. I MEAN, COOL.
WELL... 'NIGHT.
ACTUALLY... CAN YOU DO ME A FAVOUR?

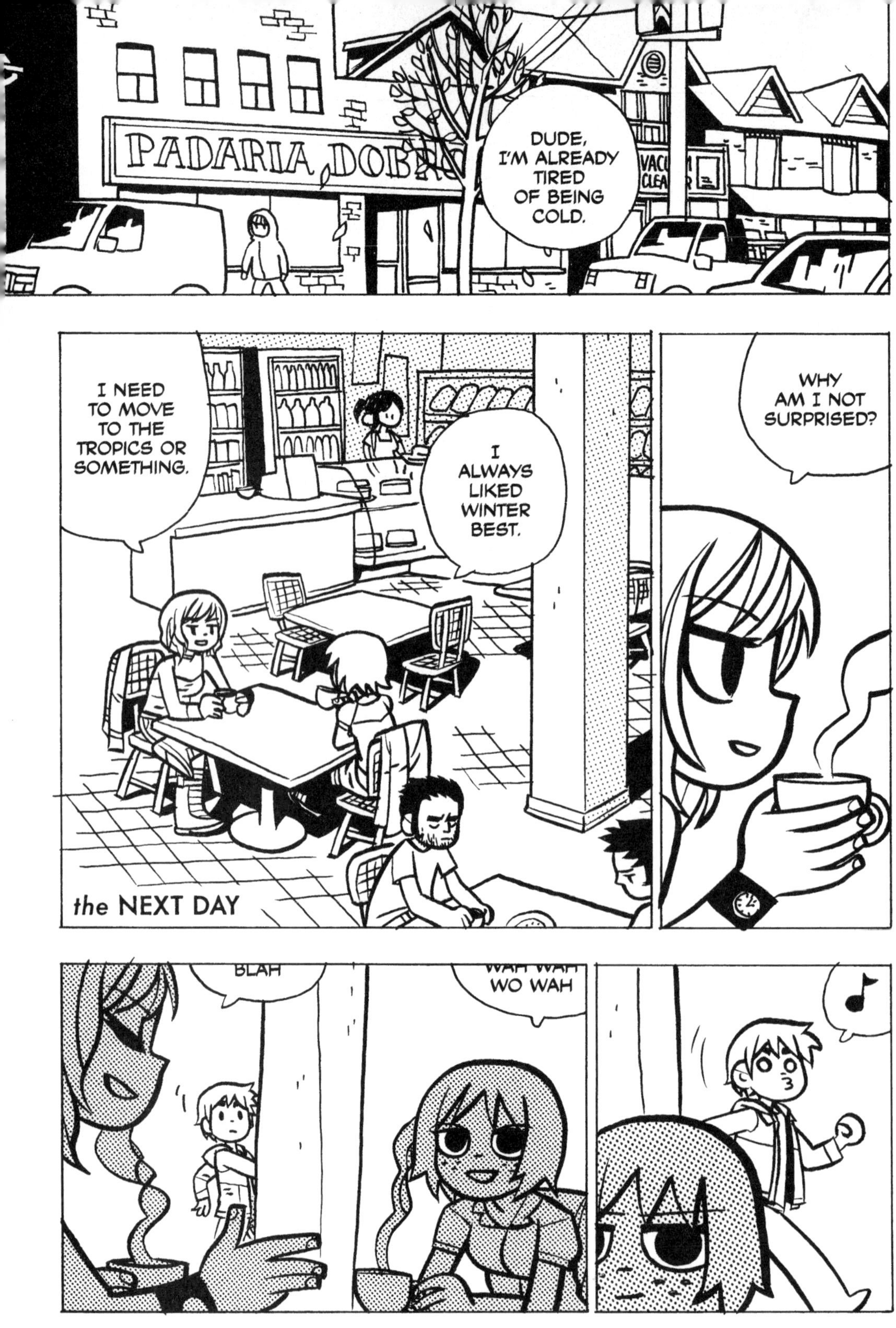
PADARIA DOB
DUDE, I'M ALREADY TIRED OF BEING COLD.
I NEED TO MOVE TO THE TROPICS OR SOMETHING.
I ALWAYS LIKED WINTER BEST.
the NEXT DAY
WHY AM I NOT SURPRISED?
BLAH
WO WAH
♪

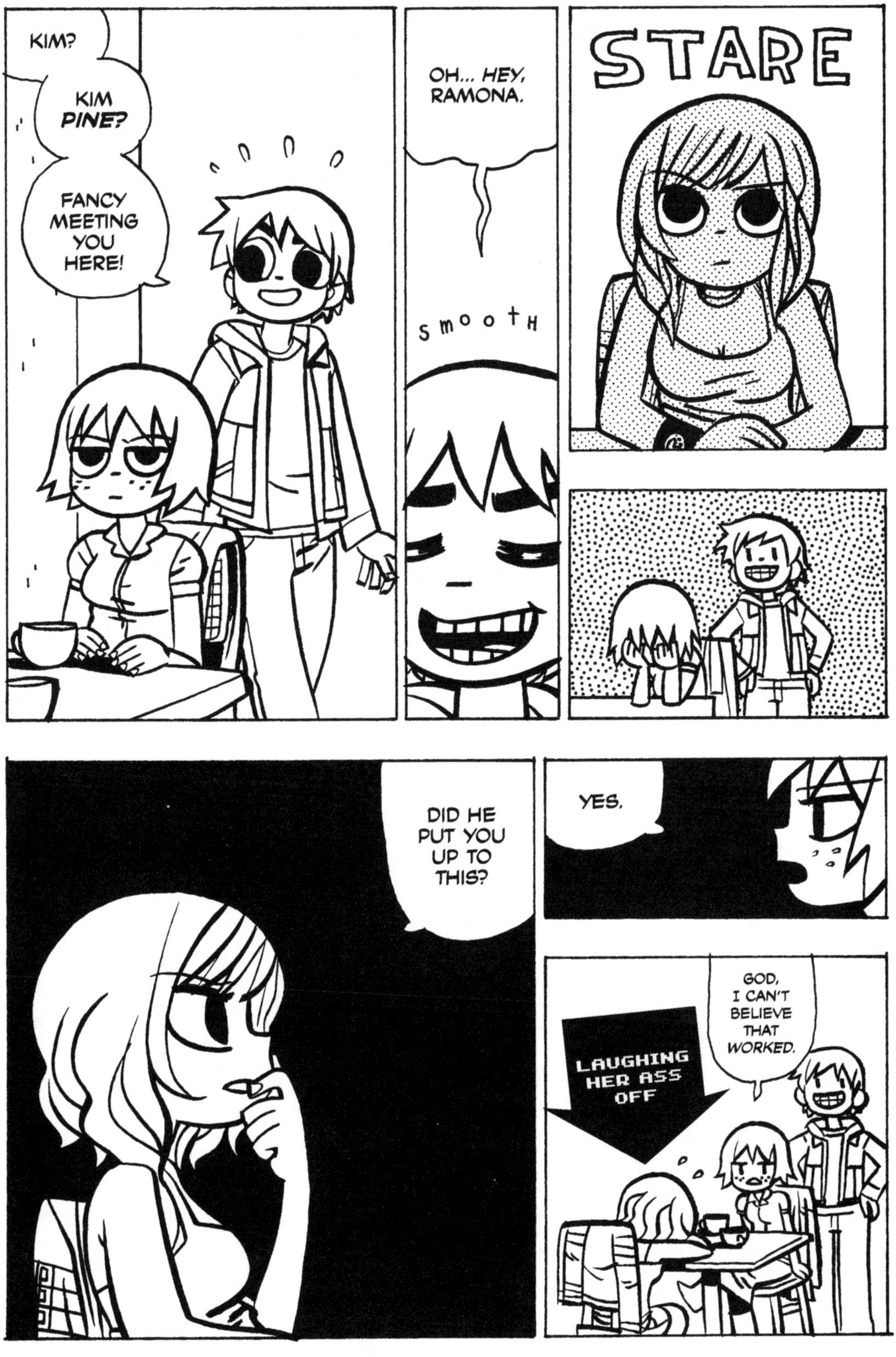

KIM?
KIM PINE?
FANCY MEETING YOU HERE!
OH... HEY, RAMONA.
SMOOTH
STARE
DID HE PUT YOU UP TO THIS?
YES.
LAUGHING HER ASS OFF
GOD, I CAN'T BELIEVE THAT WORKED.

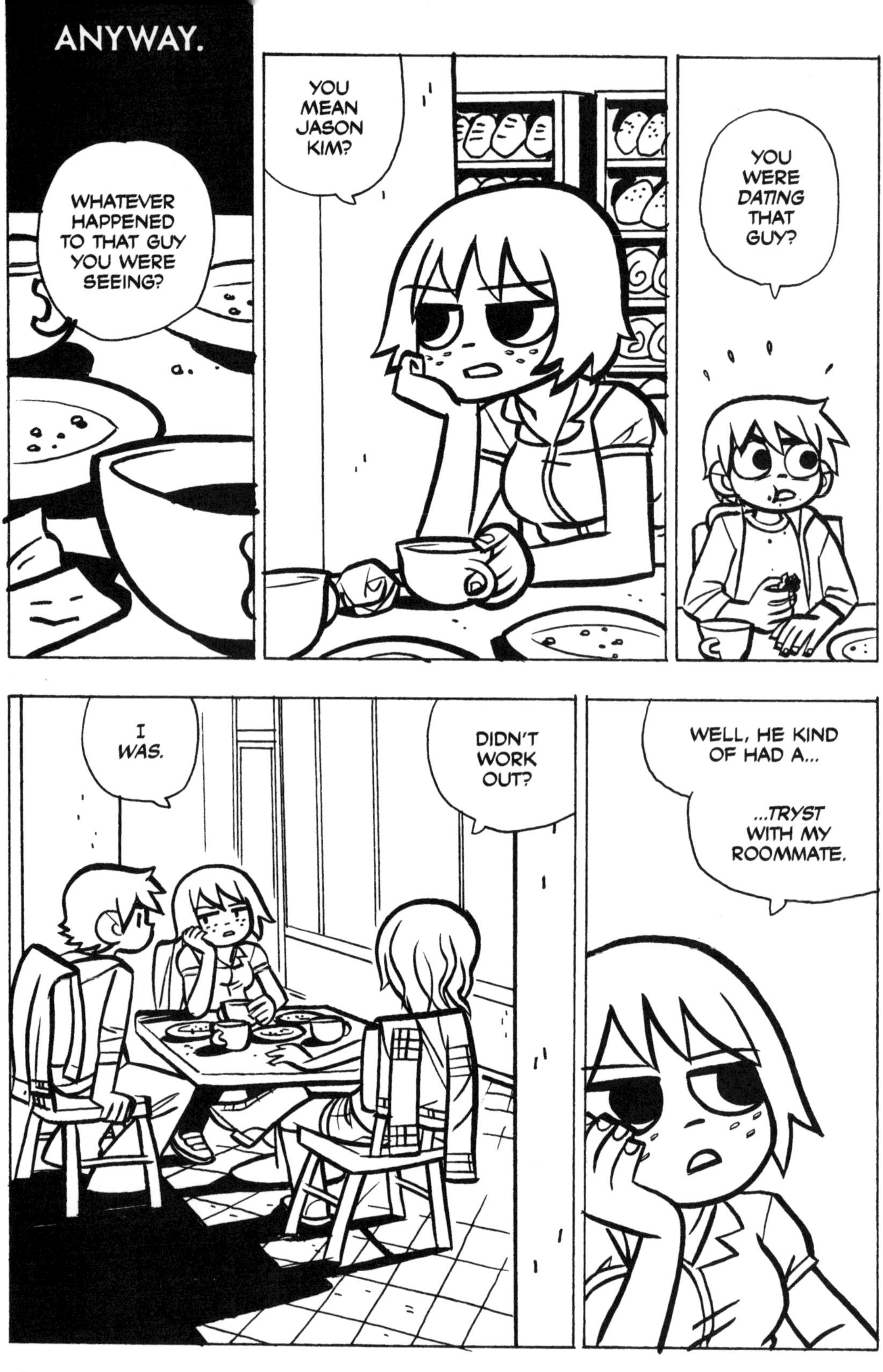
ANYWAY.
WHATEVER HAPPENED TO THAT GUY YOU WERE SEEING?
YOU MEAN JASON KIM?
YOU WERE *DATING* THAT GUY?
I *WAS.*
DIDN'T WORK OUT?
WELL, HE KIND OF HAD A...
...*TRYST* WITH MY ROOMMATE.

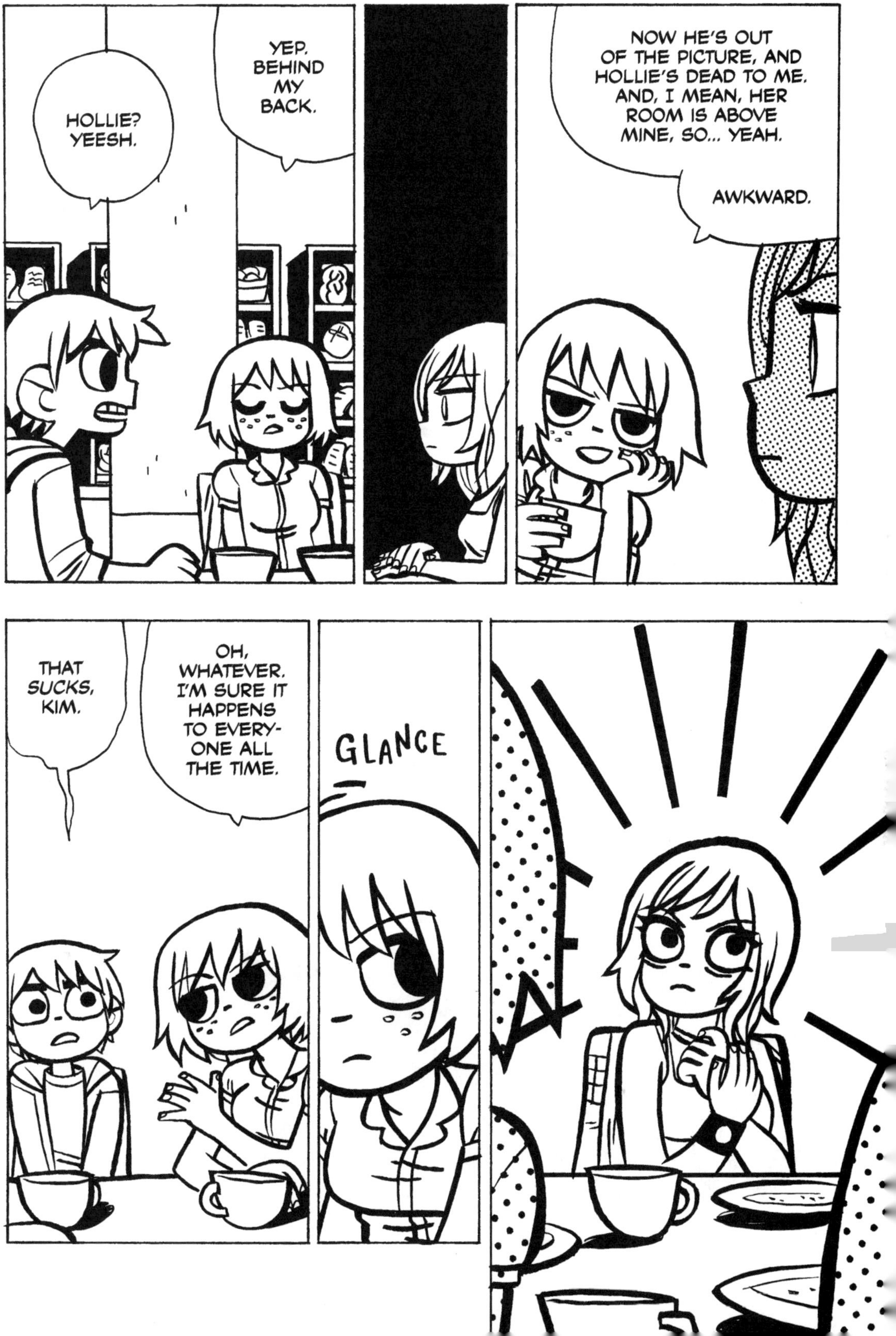
HOLLIE? YEESH.
YEP. BEHIND MY BACK.
NOW HE'S OUT OF THE PICTURE, AND HOLLIE'S DEAD TO ME. AND, I MEAN, HER ROOM IS ABOVE MINE, SO... YEAH.
AWKWARD.
THAT SUCKS, KIM.
OH, WHATEVER. I'M SURE IT HAPPENS TO EVERY-ONE ALL THE TIME.
GLANCE

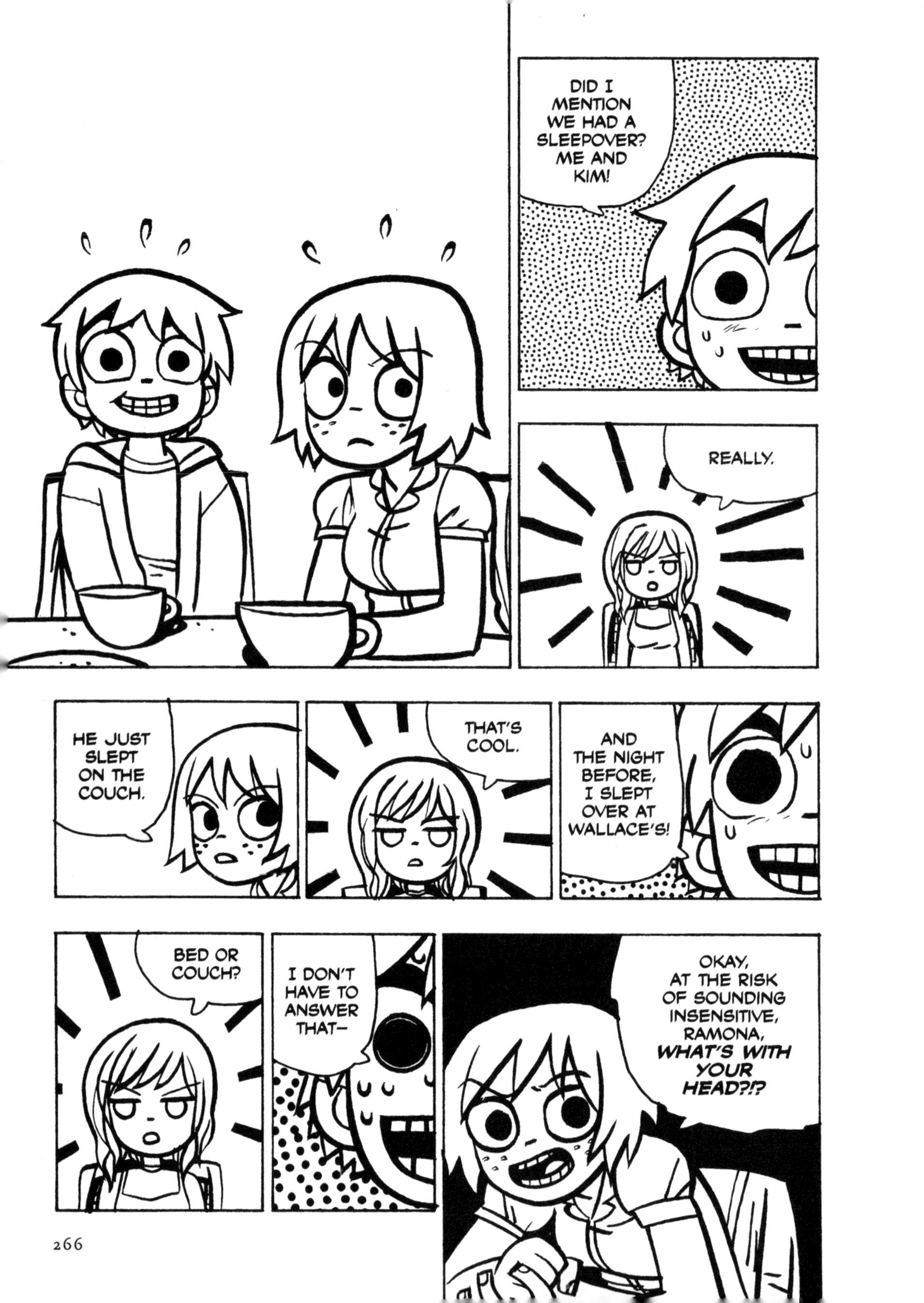
DID I MENTION WE HAD A SLEEPOVER? ME AND KIM!
REALLY.
HE JUST SLEPT ON THE COUCH.
THAT'S COOL.
AND THE NIGHT BEFORE, I SLEPT OVER AT WALLACE'S!
BED OR COUCH?
I DON'T HAVE TO ANSWER THAT–
OKAY, AT THE RISK OF SOUNDING INSENSITIVE, RAMONA, ***WHAT'S WITH YOUR HEAD?!?***

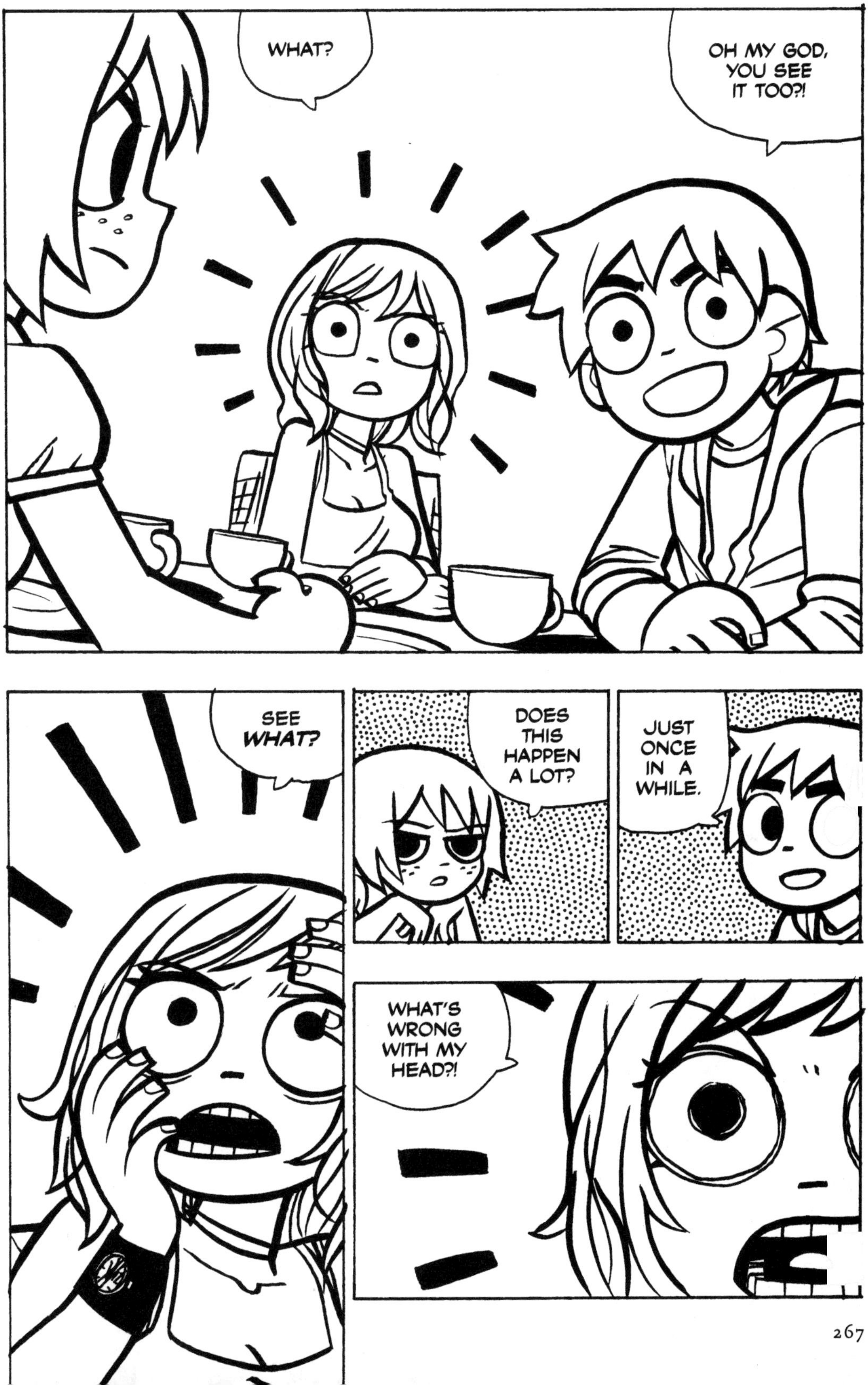
WHAT?
OH MY GOD, YOU SEE IT TOO?!
SEE WHAT?
DOES THIS HAPPEN A LOT?
JUST ONCE IN A WHILE.
WHAT'S WRONG WITH MY HEAD?!

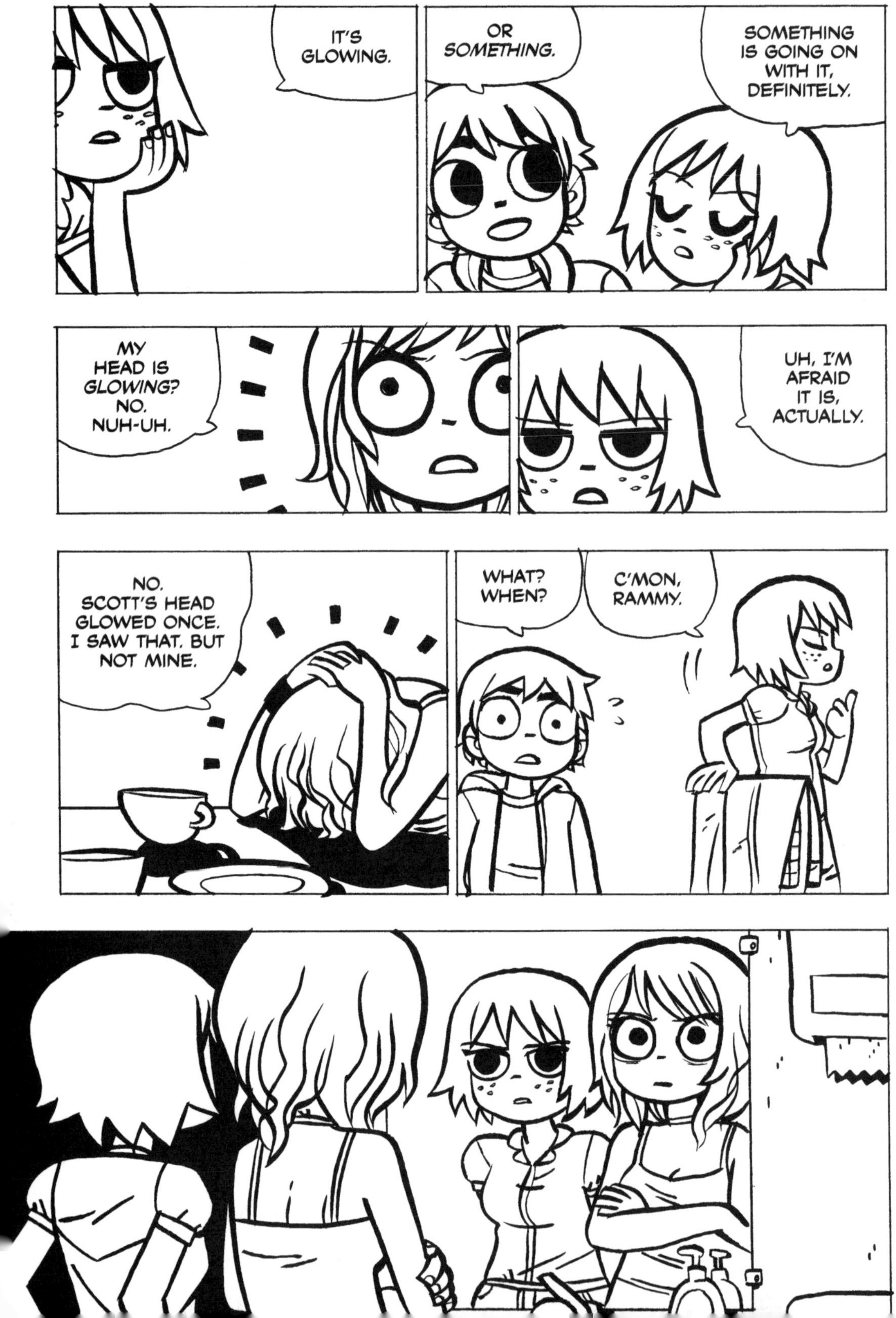
IT'S GLOWING.
OR SOMETHING.
SOMETHING IS GOING ON WITH IT, DEFINITELY.
MY HEAD IS GLOWING? NO. NUH-UH.
UH, I'M AFRAID IT IS, ACTUALLY.
NO. SCOTT'S HEAD GLOWED ONCE. I SAW THAT. BUT NOT MINE.
WHAT? WHEN?
C'MON, RAMMY.

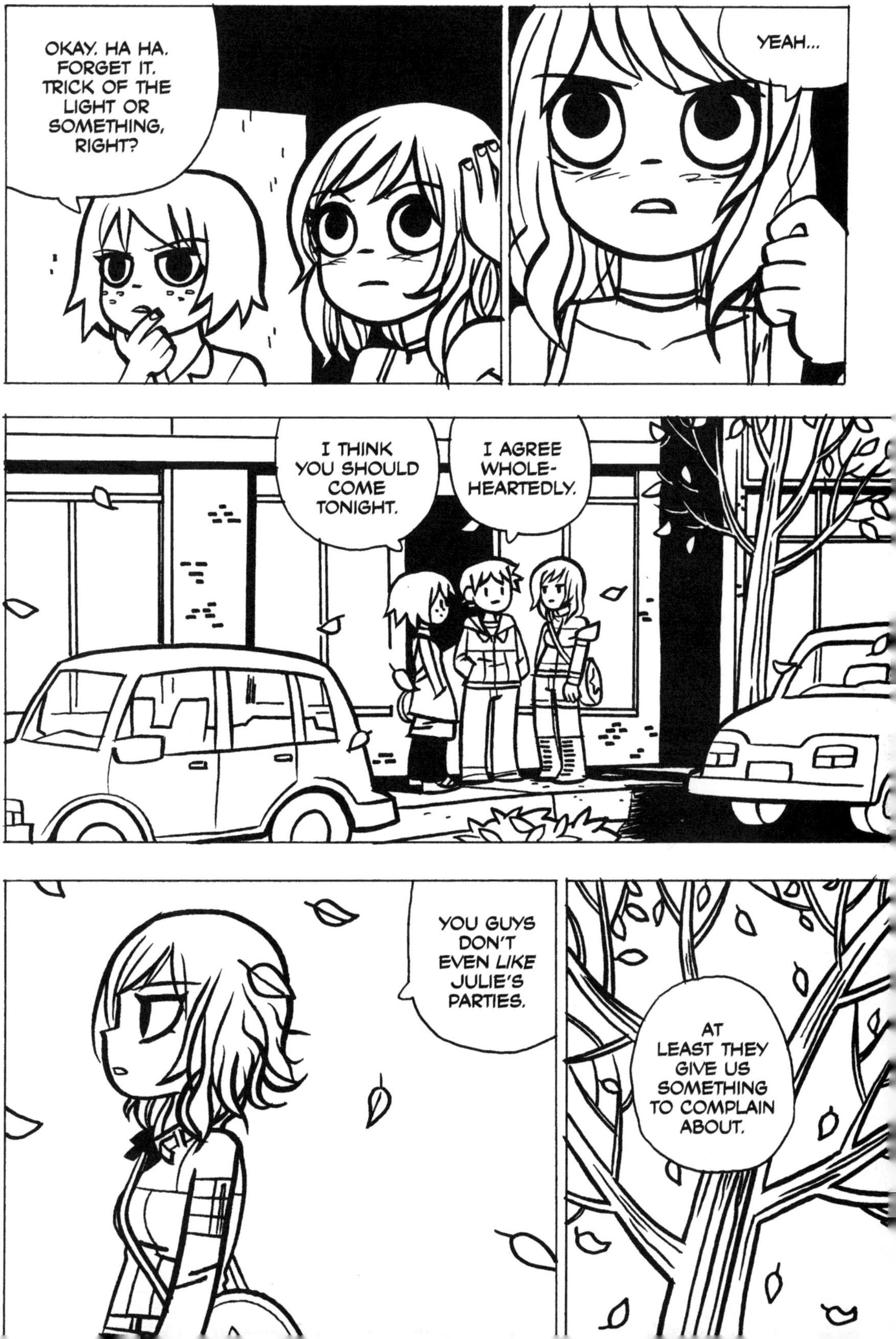
OKAY. HA HA. FORGET IT. TRICK OF THE LIGHT OR SOMETHING, RIGHT?
YEAH...
I THINK YOU SHOULD COME TONIGHT.
I AGREE WHOLE-HEARTEDLY.
YOU GUYS DON'T EVEN *LIKE* JULIE'S PARTIES.
AT LEAST THEY GIVE US SOMETHING TO COMPLAIN ABOUT.

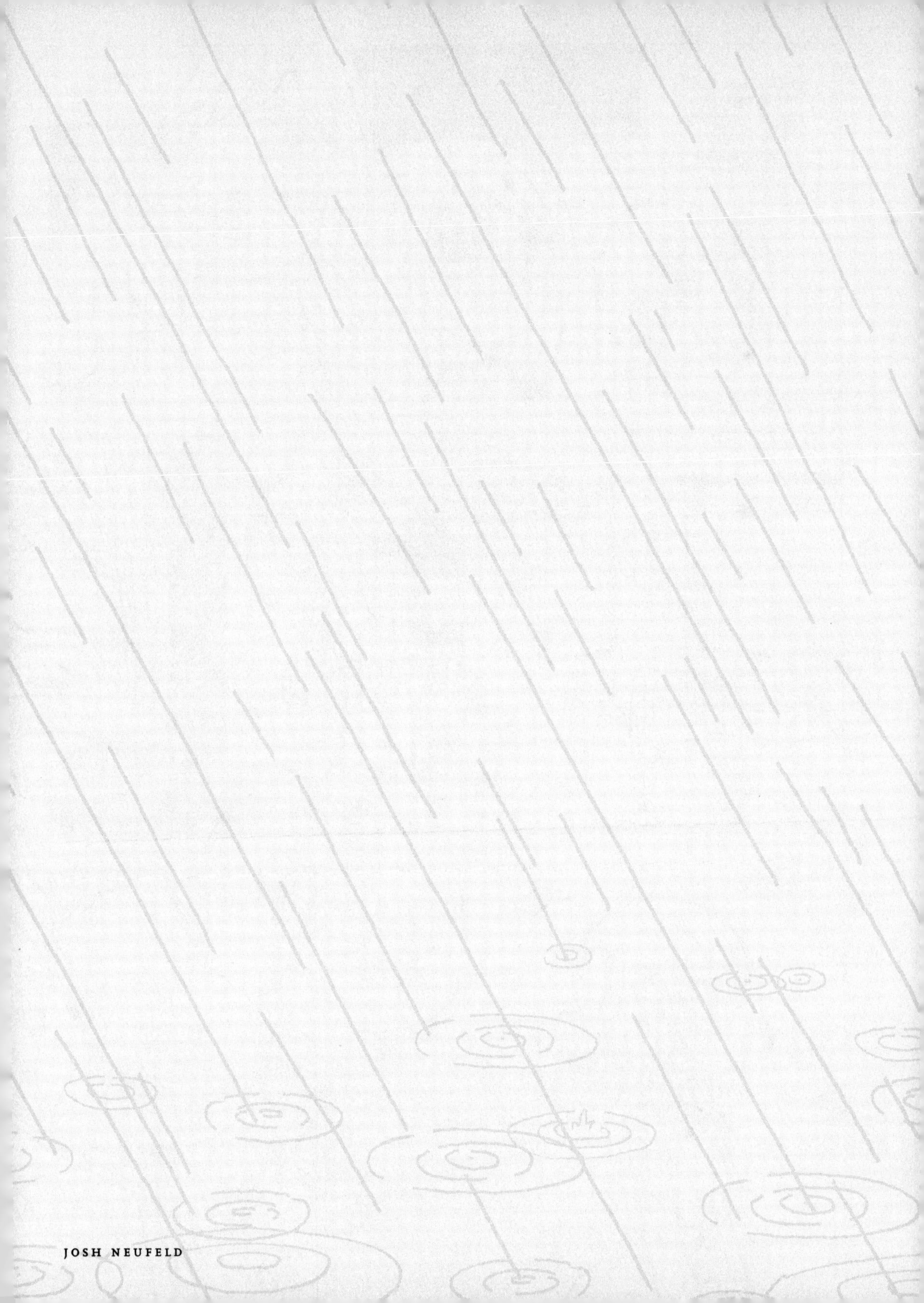

JOSH NEUFELD

THE FLOOD

EXCERPT FROM A.D.: NEW ORLEANS AFTER THE DELUGE

MONDAY
2005
August
29

Monday, August 29, 3:49 p.m. Uptown.
CALHOUN

...reports of widespread power outages and some localized flooding. Now the damage assessment and cleanup begins.
But the worst appears to be over.
Kaito

Darnell, it's really over. No more rain... and the sky is clear!

Yah, Katrina! You ain't so bad!

Heh. C'mon, let's check the store for damage.

5:03 p.m.

Hunh.

CALHOUN SUPERETTE AND

FRESH MEATS
HOT LUNCHES
SEAFOOD PO-BOY
CIGARETTES · BEER
MAJOR CREDIT CARDS ACCEPTED

OPEN

SAINTS

MONDAY 2005
August
29
It's no use. I can't get through. Keeps sayin' all the lines are busy.
Aw, man... I'm sure Habeeba and the kids are fine. Look, they'll get the power back up, and you'll be back in touch with 'em in no time.
And check it out--we still got gas for the grill, baby!
SAINTS
CLINK
Okay--let's break open some steaks and pass a good time!

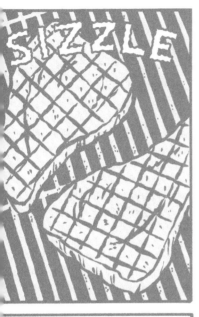

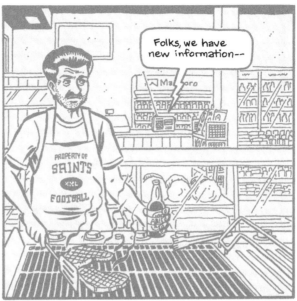

SIZZLE
Folks, we have new information--
PROPERTY OF SAINTS XXL FOOTBALL
--about a possible levee breach in the 17th Street Canal. Right now details are sketchy. We'll be sure to update this story as it develops...
Sure, like a couple of hours ago, when they said the CBD was floodin'!
...However, police have confirmed isolated incidents of looting since the storm passed.
Oh shit, Abbas! Come look outside!

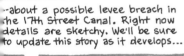

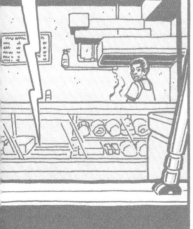

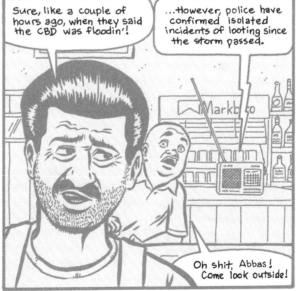

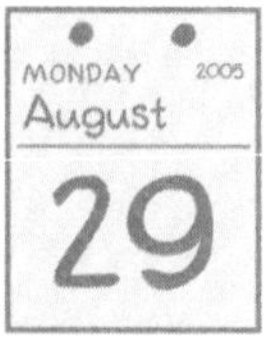
MONDAY 2005
August
29

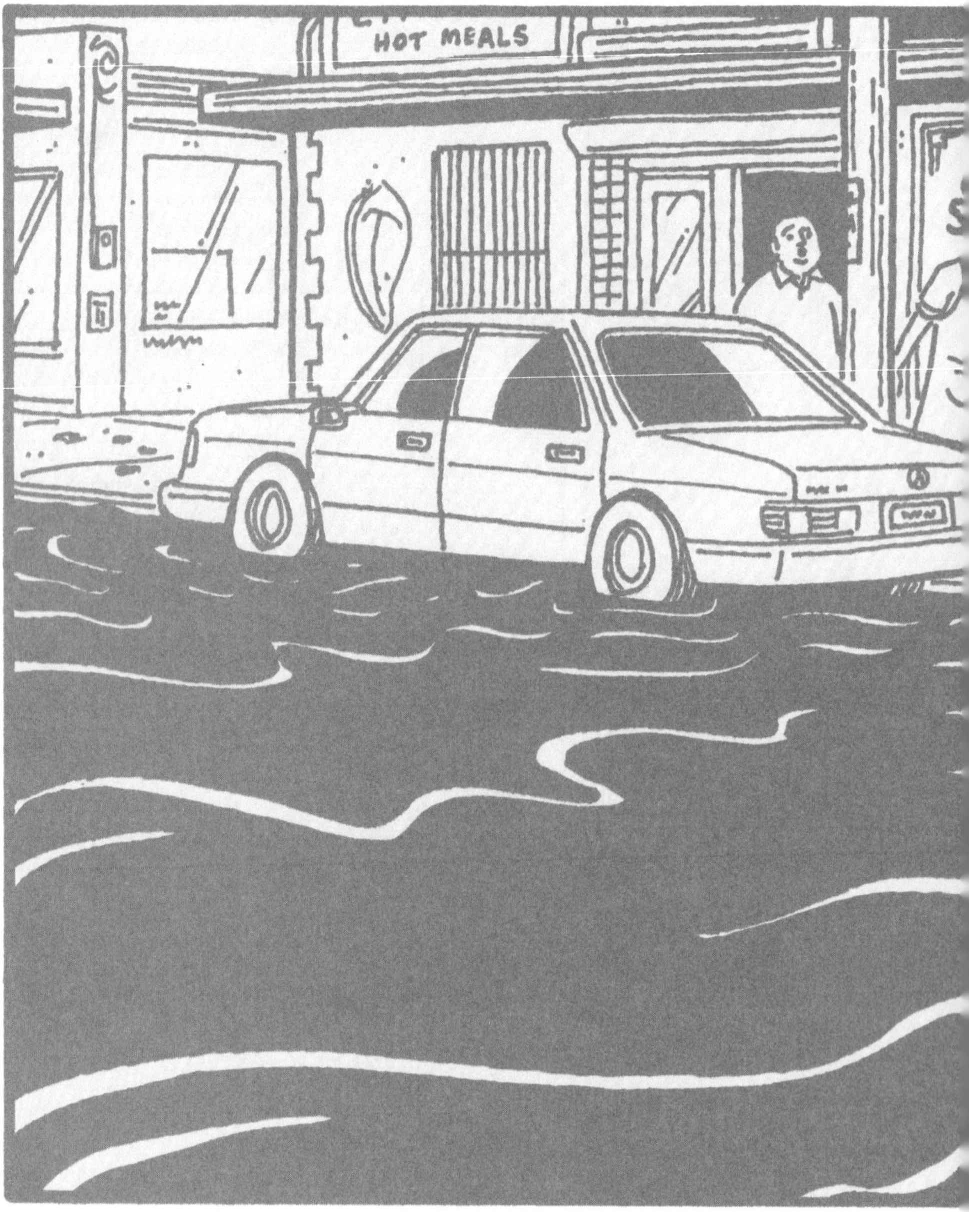
HOT MEALS

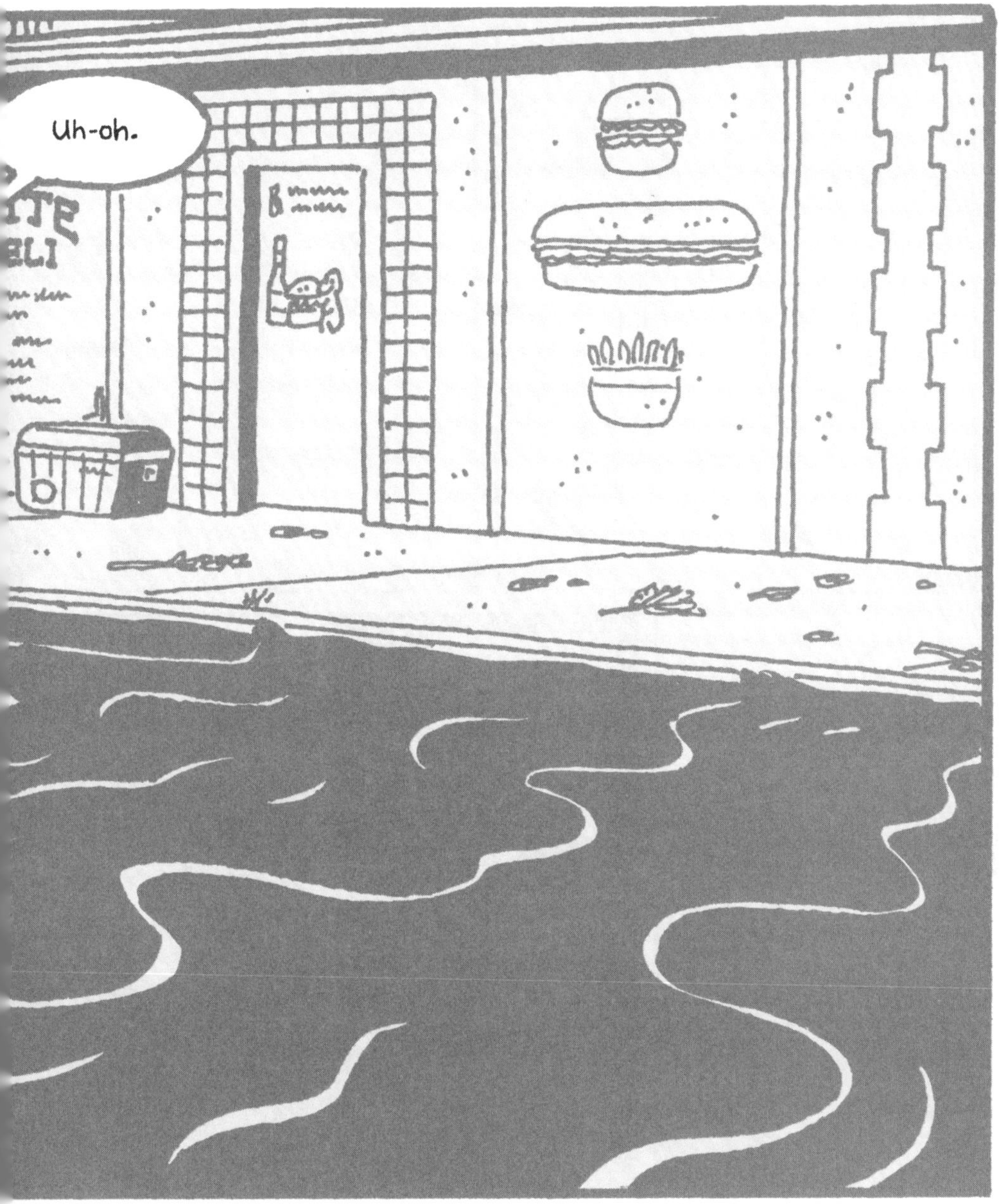
Uh-oh.
ITE
ELI

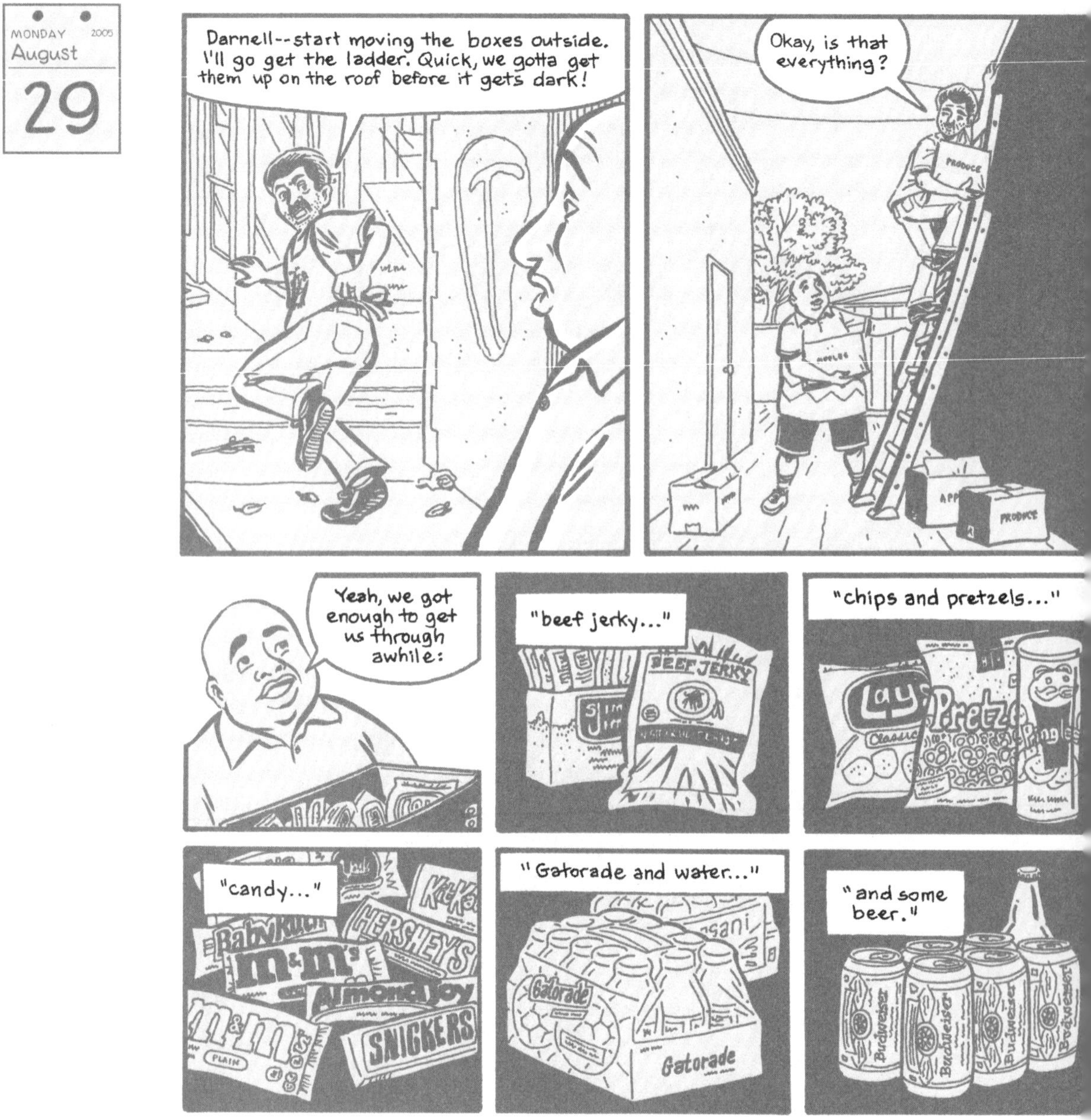
MONDAY 2005
August
29
Darnell--start moving the boxes outside. I'll go get the ladder. Quick, we gotta get them up on the roof before it gets dark!
Okay, is that everything?
PRODUCE
PRODUCE
Yeah, we got enough to get us through awhile:
"beef jerky..."
BEEF JERKY
"chips and pretzels..."
Lay's
Classic
Pretzels
Pringles
"candy..."
Kit Kat
Baby Ruth
HERSHEY'S
m&m's
Almond Joy
m&m's
PLAIN
SNICKERS
"Gatorade and water..."
Gatorade
Gatorade
"and some beer."
Budweiser
Budweiser
Budweiser
Budweiser

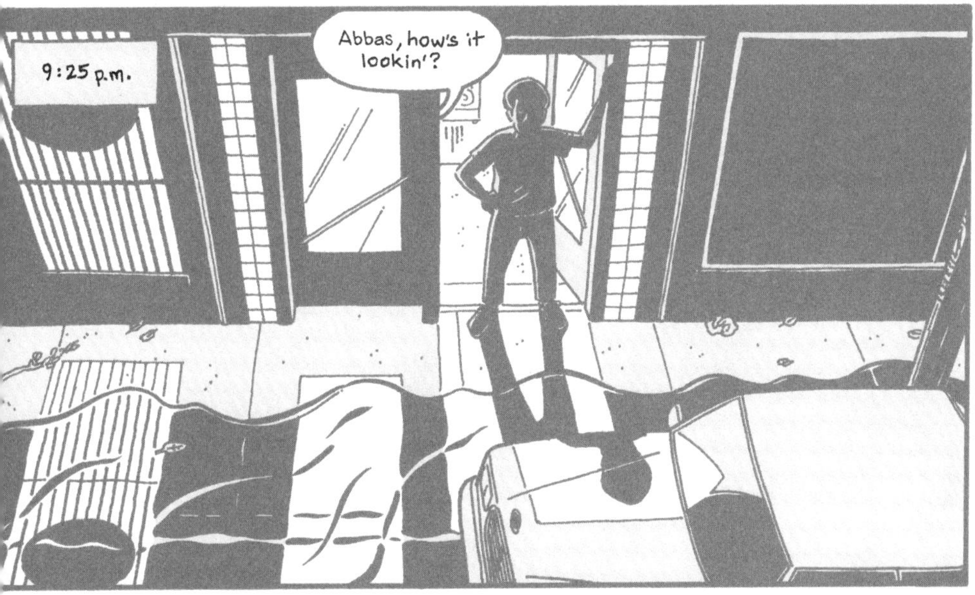
9:25 p.m.
Abbas, how's it lookin'?

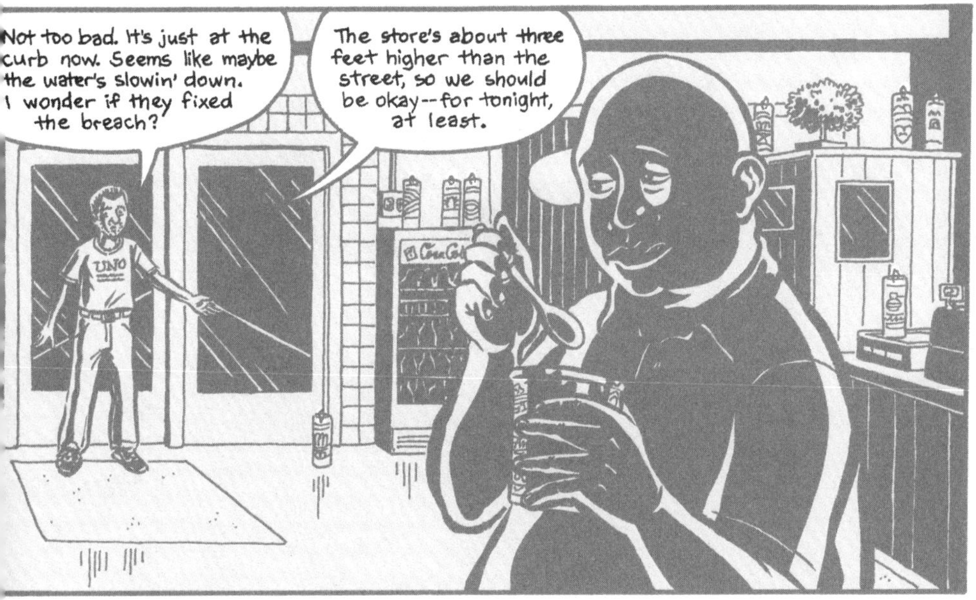
Not too bad. It's just at the curb now. Seems like maybe the water's slowin' down. I wonder if they fixed the breach?
The store's about three feet higher than the street, so we should be okay--for tonight, at least.
UNO

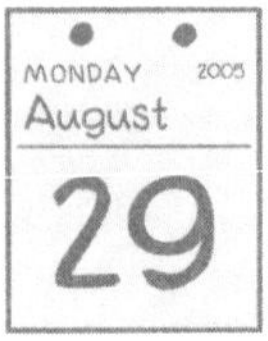
MONDAY 2005
August
29

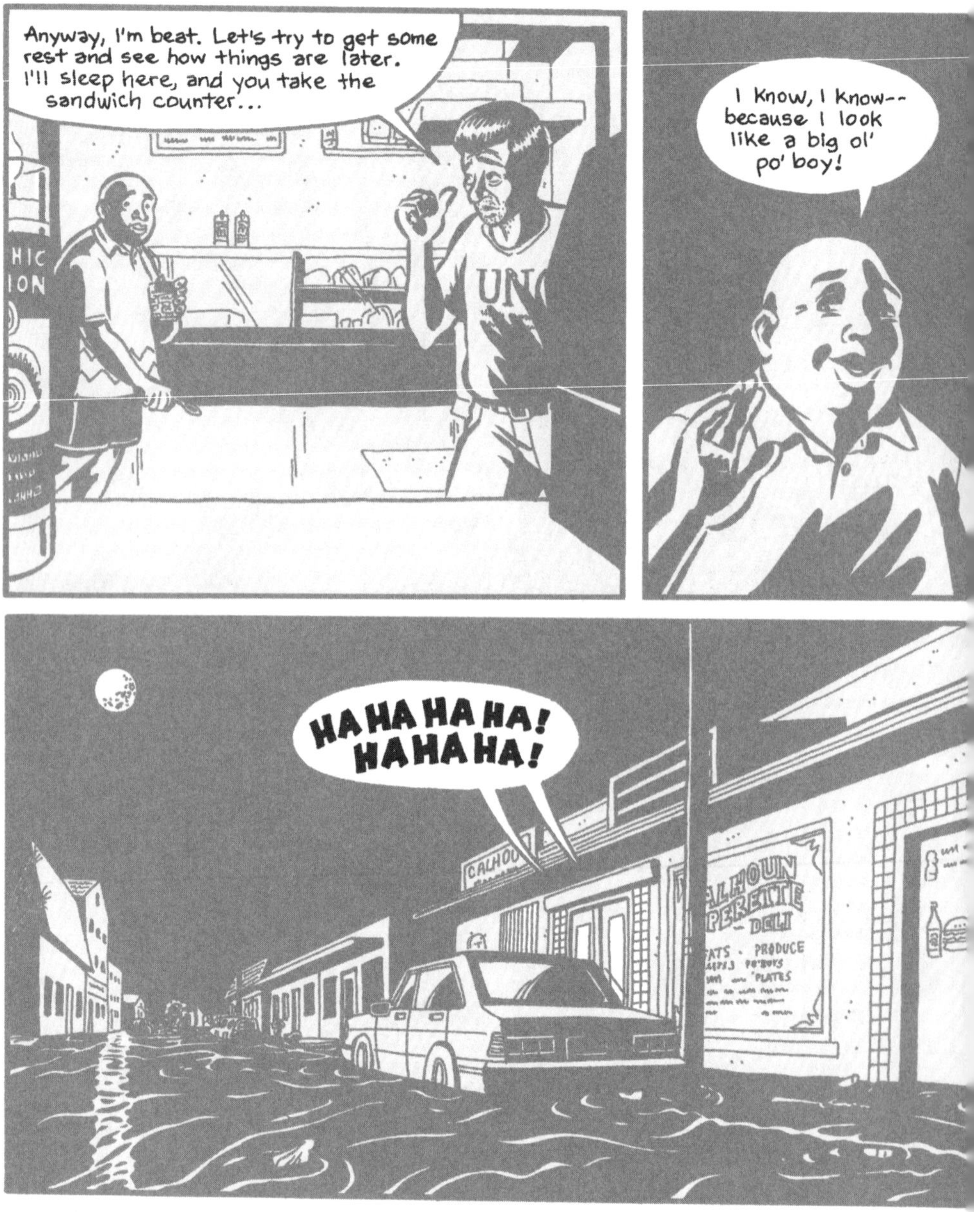
Anyway, I'm beat. Let's try to get some rest and see how things are later. I'll sleep here, and you take the sandwich counter...
I know, I know-- because I look like a big ol' po' boy!
HAHAHAHA! HAHAHA!

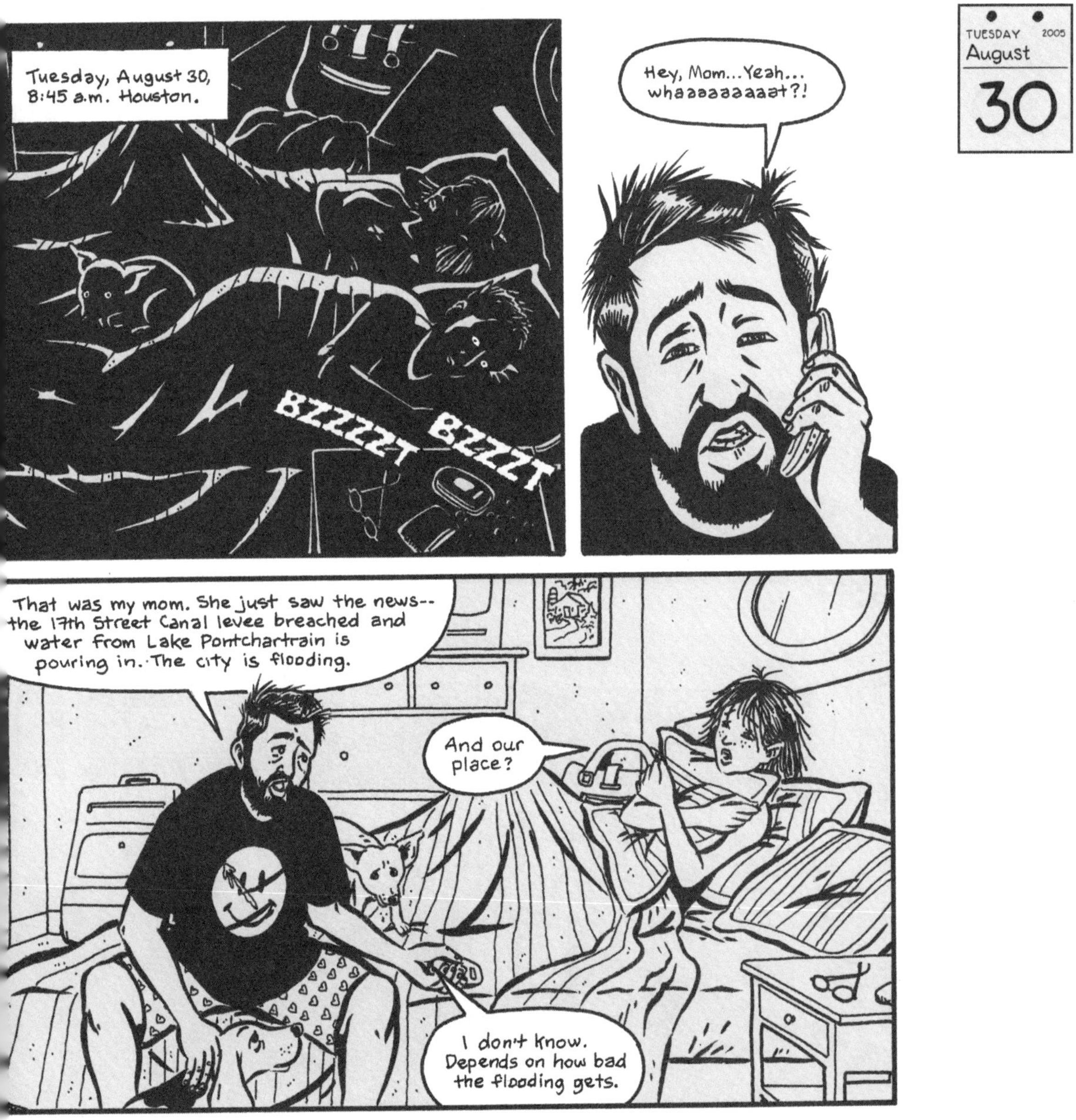
TUESDAY 2005
August
30
Tuesday, August 30, 8:45 a.m. Houston.
BZZZZT BZZZT
Hey, Mom...Yeah... whaaaaaaaaat?!
That was my mom. She just saw the news-- the 17th Street Canal levee breached and water from Lake Pontchartrain is pouring in. The city is flooding.
And our place?
I don't know. Depends on how bad the flooding gets.

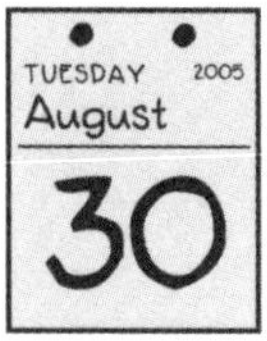
TUESDAY 2005
August
30

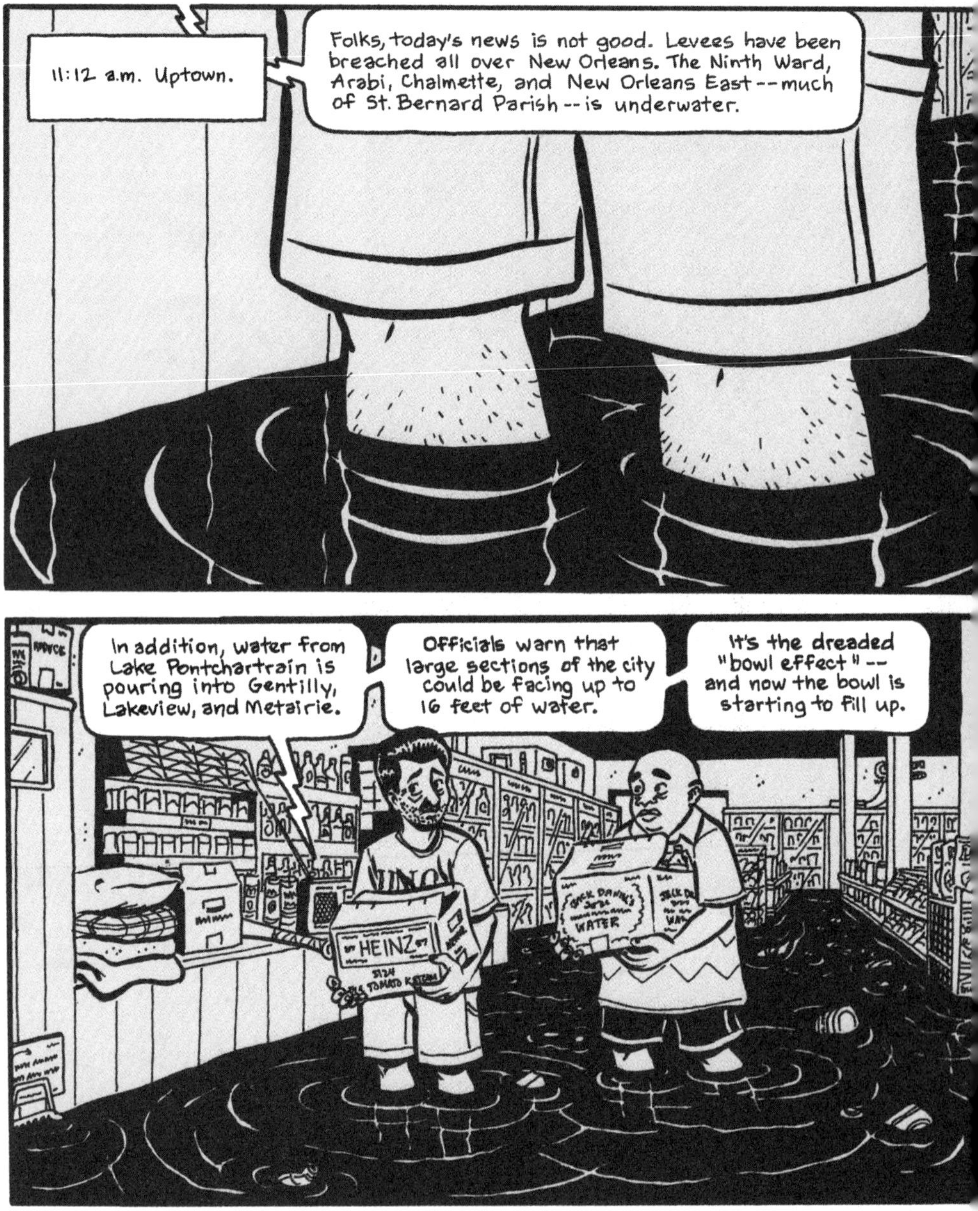
11:12 a.m. Uptown.
Folks, today's news is not good. Levees have been breached all over New Orleans. The Ninth Ward, Arabi, Chalmette, and New Orleans East -- much of St. Bernard Parish -- is underwater.
In addition, water from Lake Pontchartrain is pouring into Gentilly, Lakeview, and Metairie.
Officials warn that large sections of the city could be facing up to 16 feet of water.
It's the dreaded "bowl effect" -- and now the bowl is starting to fill up.
HEINZ
WATER

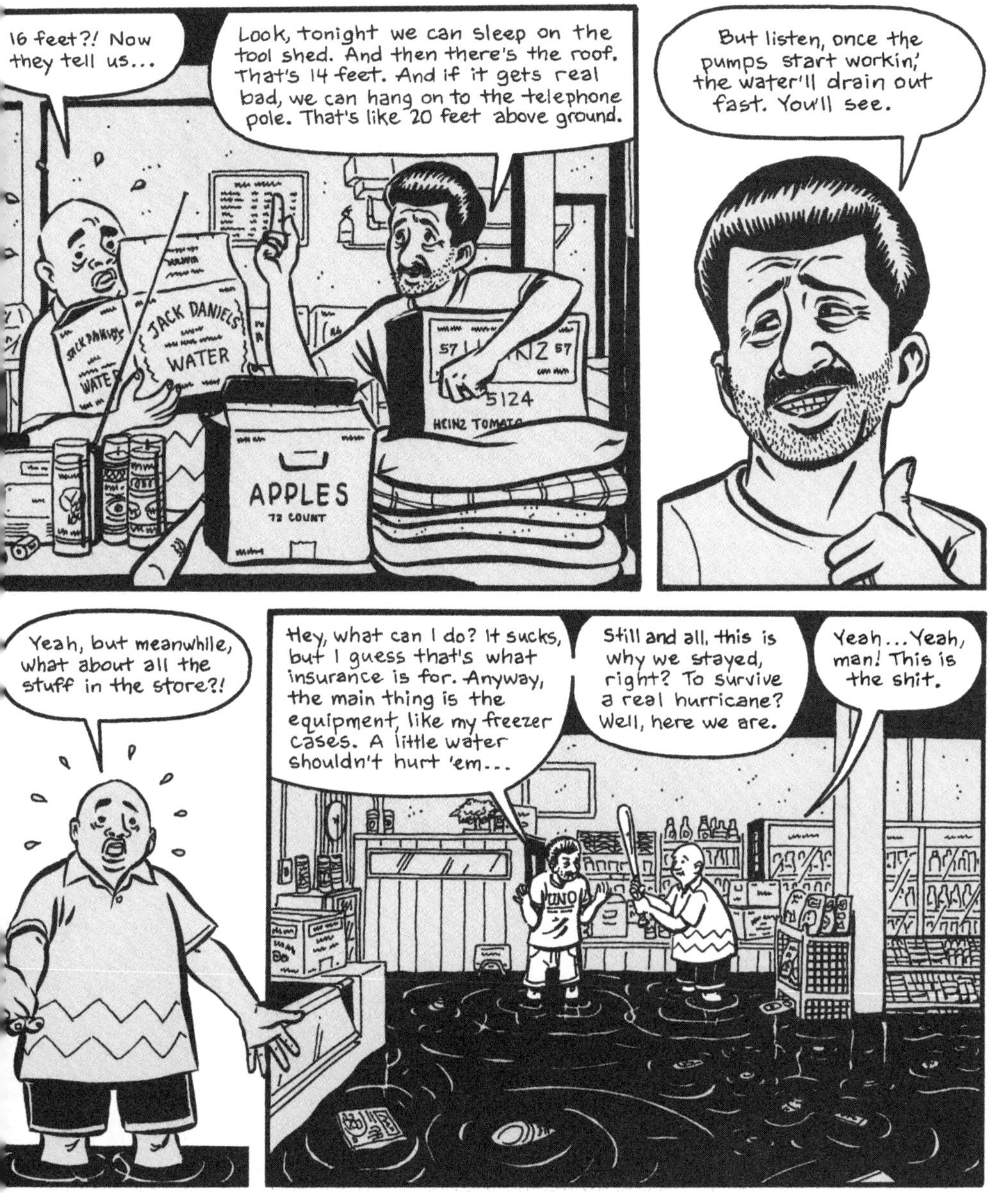
16 feet?! Now they tell us...
Look, tonight we can sleep on the tool shed. And then there's the roof. That's 14 feet. And if it gets real bad, we can hang on to the telephone pole. That's like 20 feet above ground.
JACK DANIELS
WATER
57 57
5124
HEINZ TOMATO
APPLES
72 COUNT
But listen, once the pumps start workin', the water'll drain out fast. You'll see.
Yeah, but meanwhile, what about all the stuff in the store?!
Hey, what can I do? It sucks, but I guess that's what insurance is for. Anyway, the main thing is the equipment, like my freezer cases. A little water shouldn't hurt 'em...
Still and all, this is why we stayed, right? To survive a real hurricane? Well, here we are.
Yeah... Yeah, man! This is the shit.
UNO

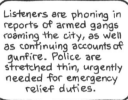

Listeners are phoning in reports of armed gangs roaming the city, as well as continuing accounts of gunfire. Police are stretched thin, urgently needed for emergency relief duties.

See? Just in case, that's why I have this...

And I got 34 ounces of pain right here, baby!

Thing is, it don't look like there is anyone else. Seems like we're the only ones left...

Oh shit, Abbas -- your Mercedes!

Well, it ain't too bad right now. But if it gets in the electrical in the dashboard, then I'm screwed...

3:45 p.m.

≥sigh≥

Hey, Abbas--them folks still up there?

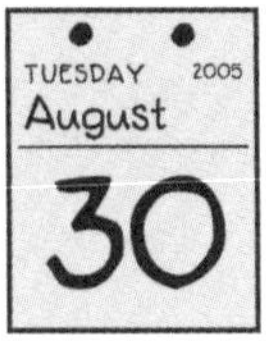
TUESDAY 2005
August
30

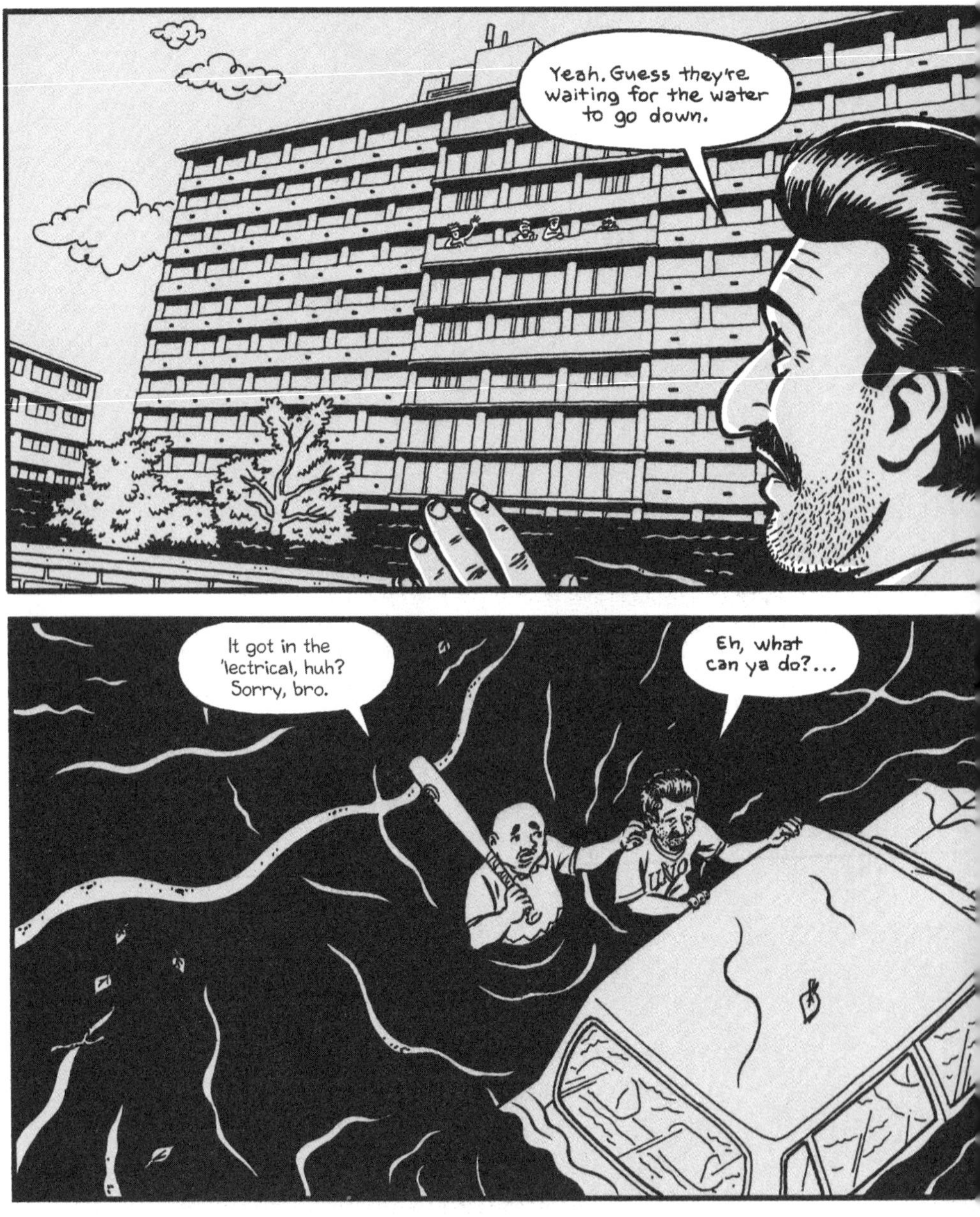
Yeah. Guess they're waiting for the water to go down.
It got in the 'lectrical, huh? Sorry, bro.
Eh, what can ya do?...

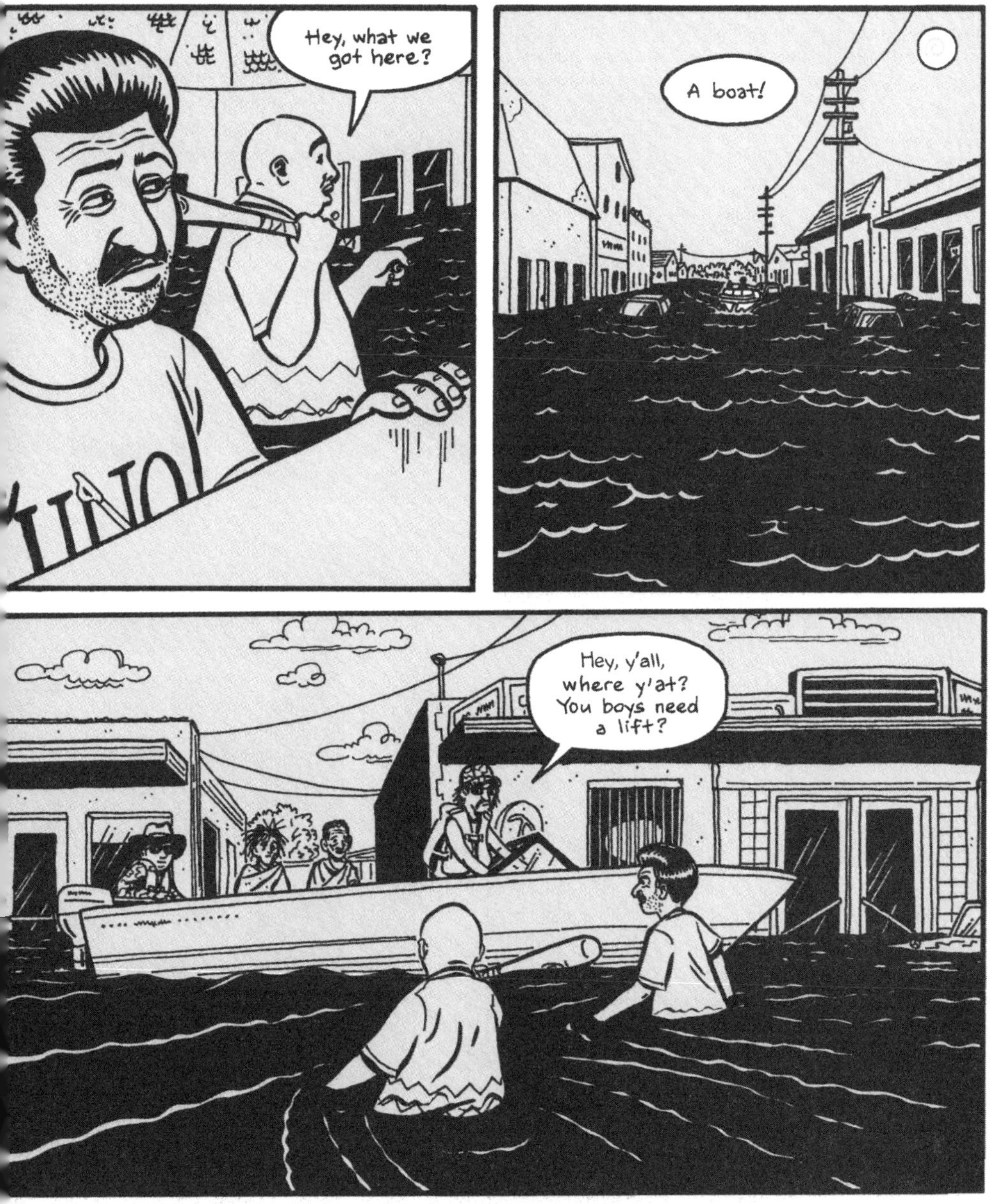
Hey, what we got here?
A boat!
Hey, y'all, where y'at? You boys need a lift?

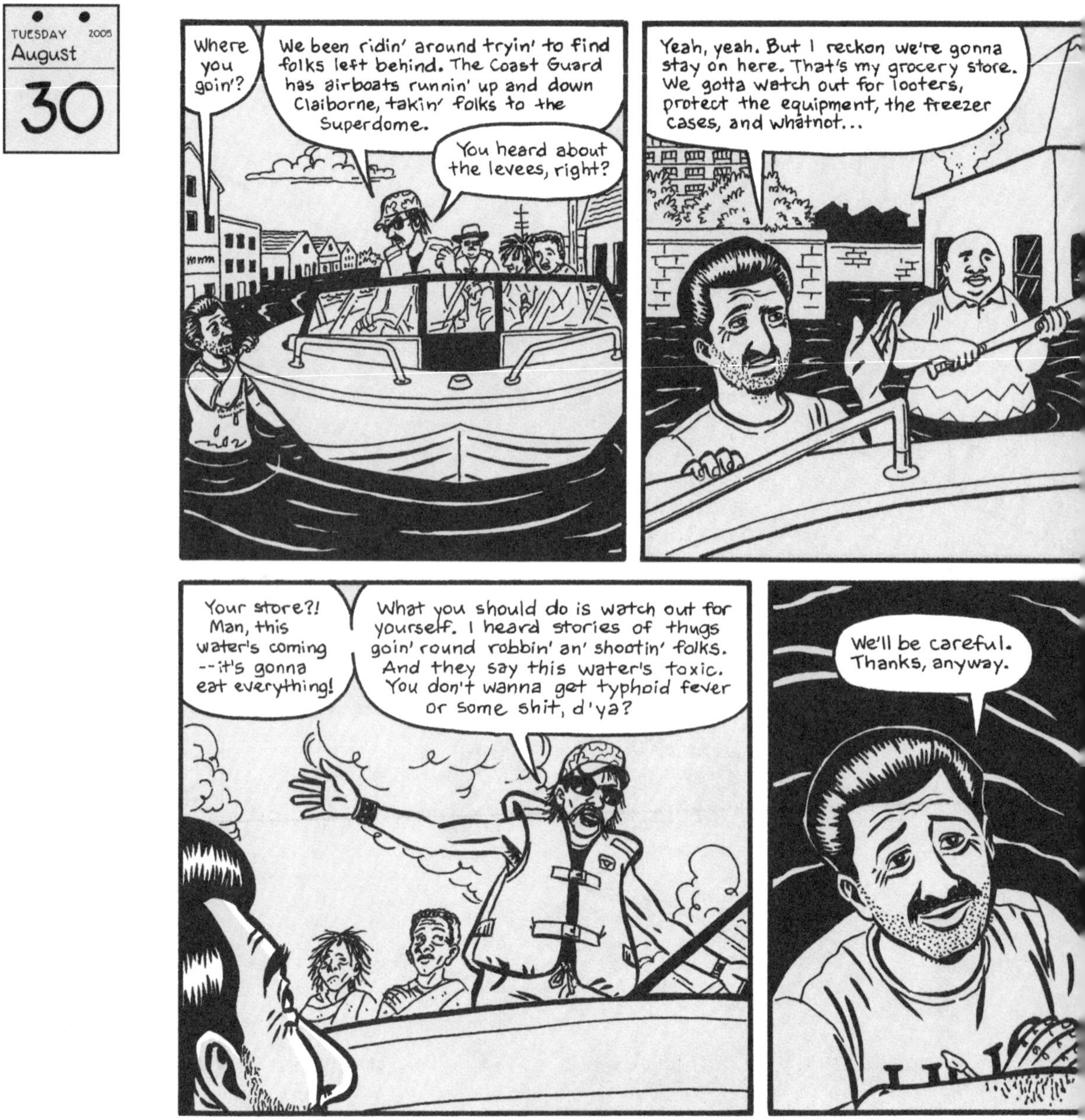
TUESDAY 2005
August
30
Where you goin'?
We been ridin' around tryin' to find folks left behind. The Coast Guard has airboats runnin' up and down Claiborne, takin' folks to the Superdome.
You heard about the levees, right?
Yeah, yeah. But I reckon we're gonna stay on here. That's my grocery store. We gotta watch out for looters, protect the equipment, the freezer cases, and whatnot...
Your store?! Man, this water's coming --it's gonna eat everything!
What you should do is watch out for yourself. I heard stories of thugs goin' round robbin' an' shootin' folks. And they say this water's toxic. You don't wanna get typhoid fever or some shit, d'ya?
We'll be careful. Thanks, anyway.

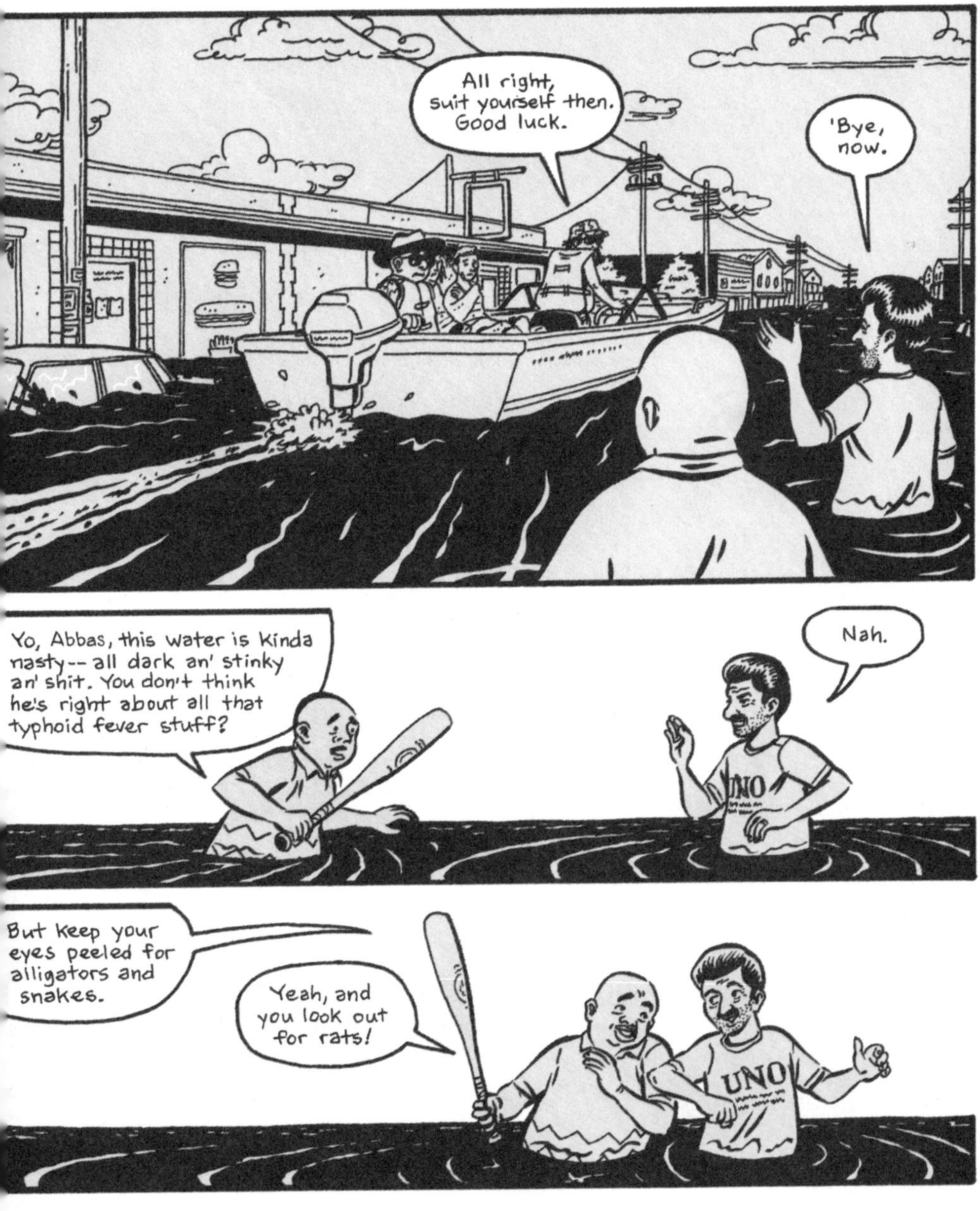
All right, suit yourself then. Good luck.
'Bye, now.
Yo, Abbas, this water is kinda nasty-- all dark an' stinky an' shit. You don't think he's right about all that typhoid fever stuff?
Nah.
But keep your eyes peeled for alligators and snakes.
Yeah, and you look out for rats!

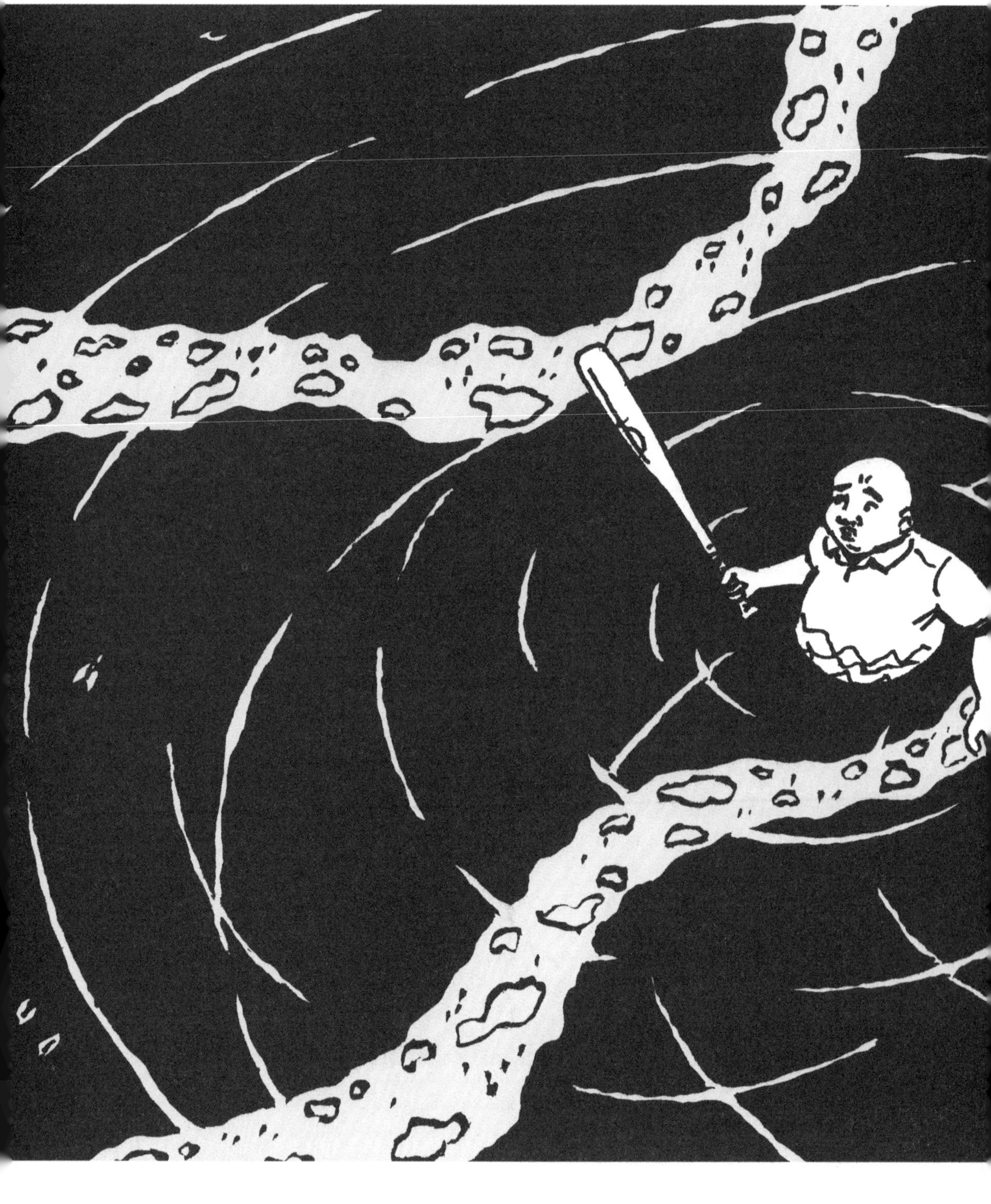

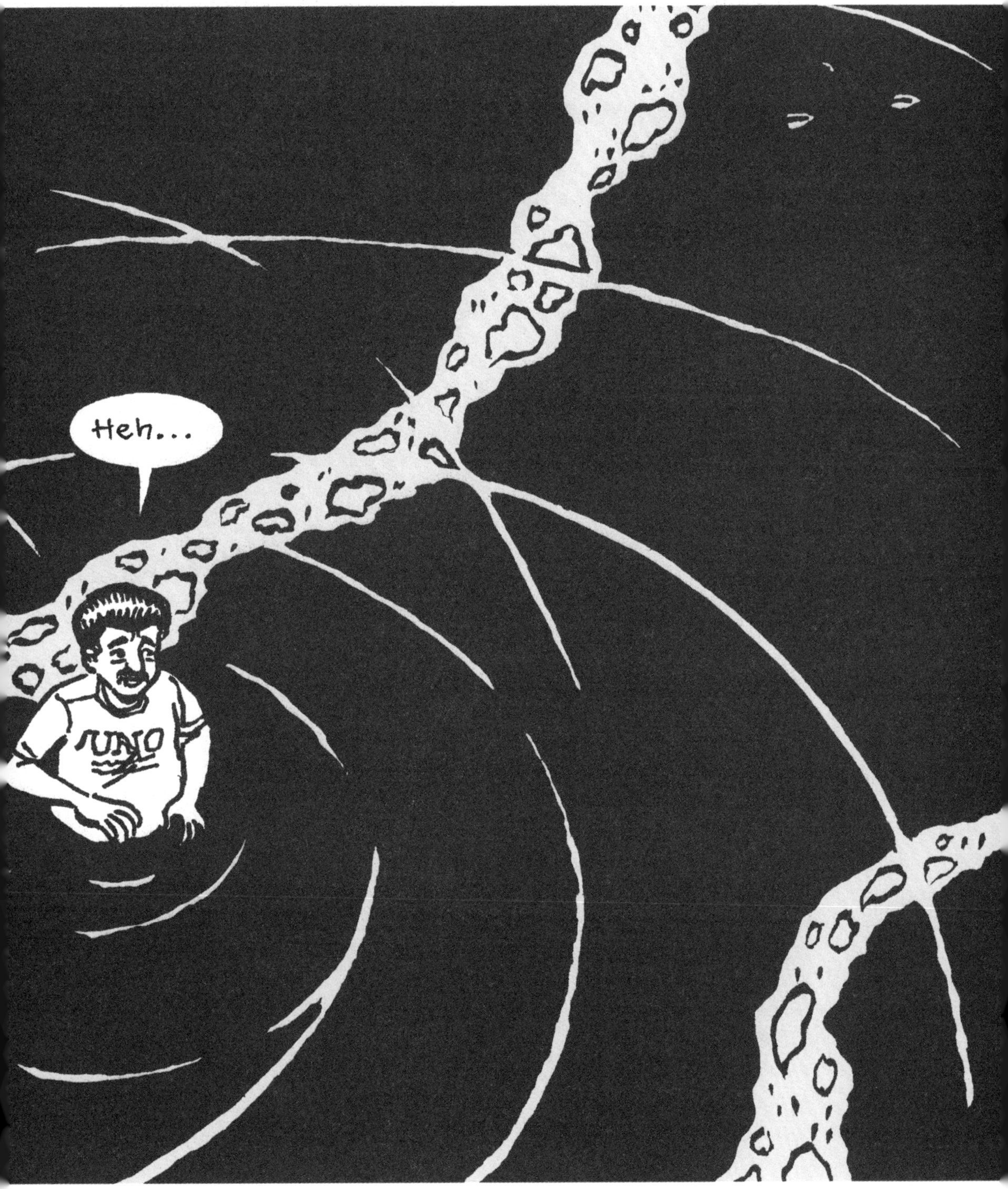
Heh...

TUESDAY 2005
August
30

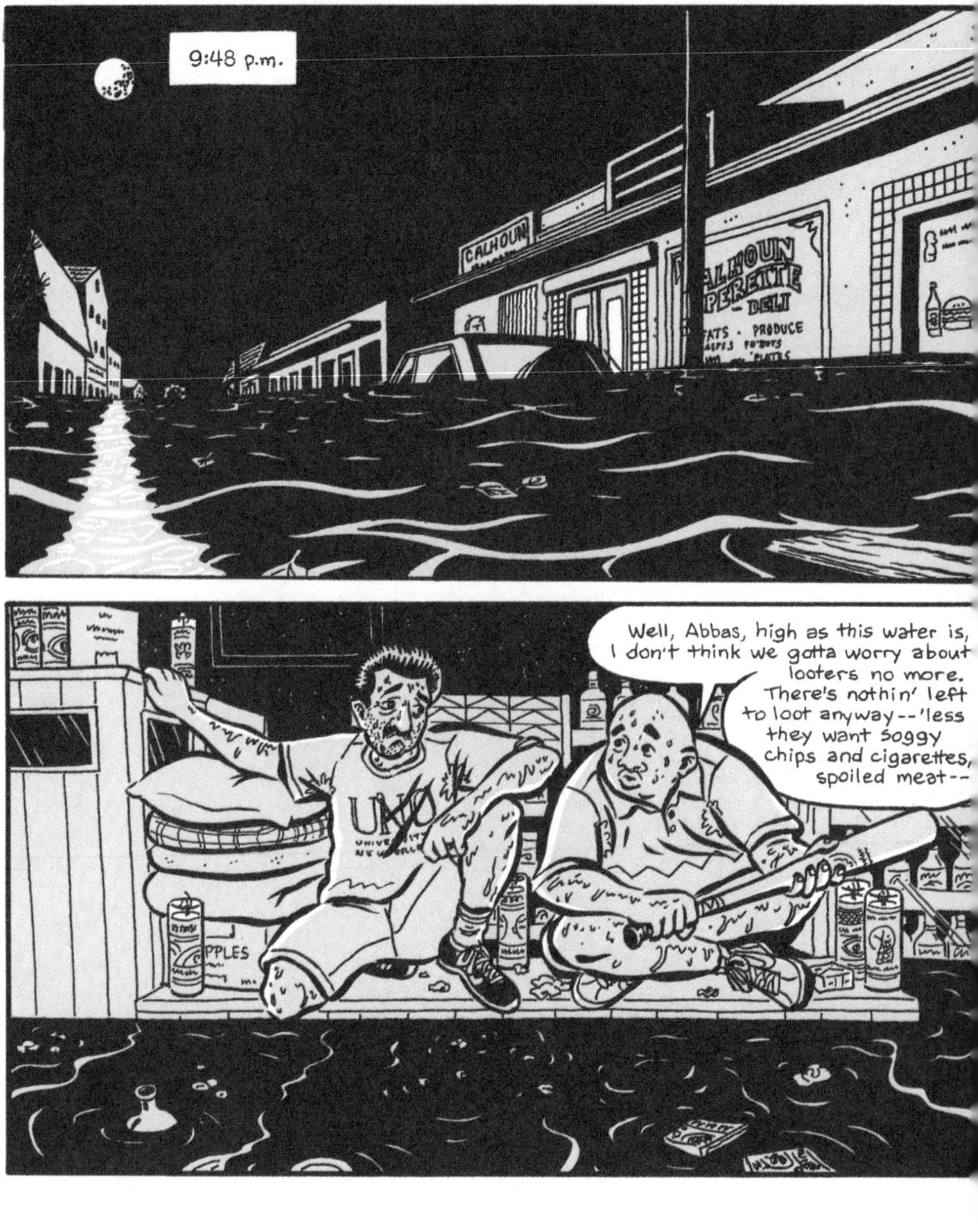
9:48 p.m.
CALHOUN
CALHOUN SUPERETTE DELI
MEATS · PRODUCE
Well, Abbas, high as this water is, I don't think we gotta worry about looters no more. There's nothin' left to loot anyway--'less they want soggy chips and cigarettes, spoiled meat--

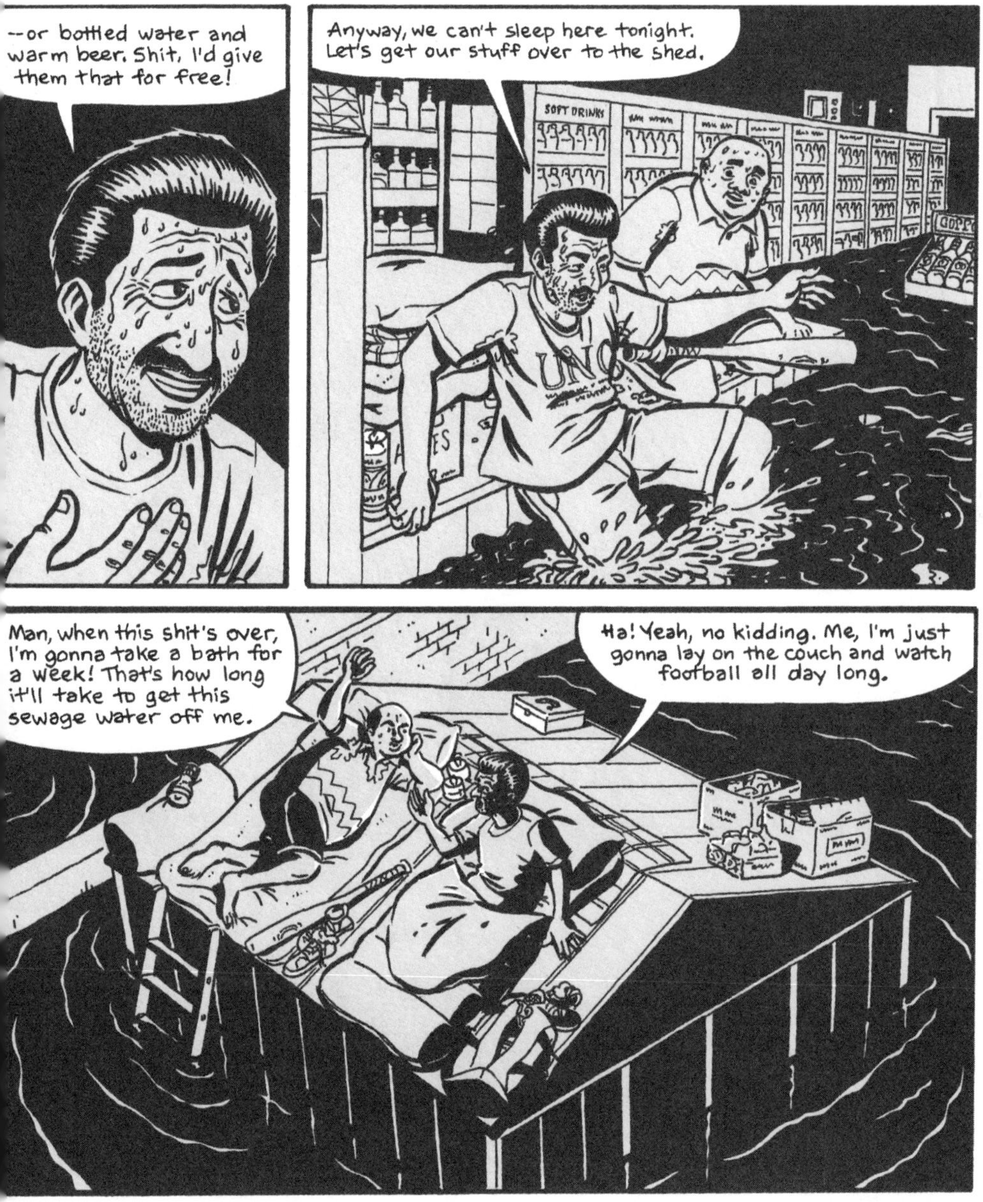
--or bottled water and warm beer. Shit, I'd give them that for free!
Anyway, we can't sleep here tonight. Let's get our stuff over to the shed.
SOFT DRINKS
UNO
Man, when this shit's over, I'm gonna take a bath for a week! That's how long it'll take to get this sewage water off me.
Ha! Yeah, no kidding. Me, I'm just gonna lay on the couch and watch football all day long.

TUESDAY 2005
August
30

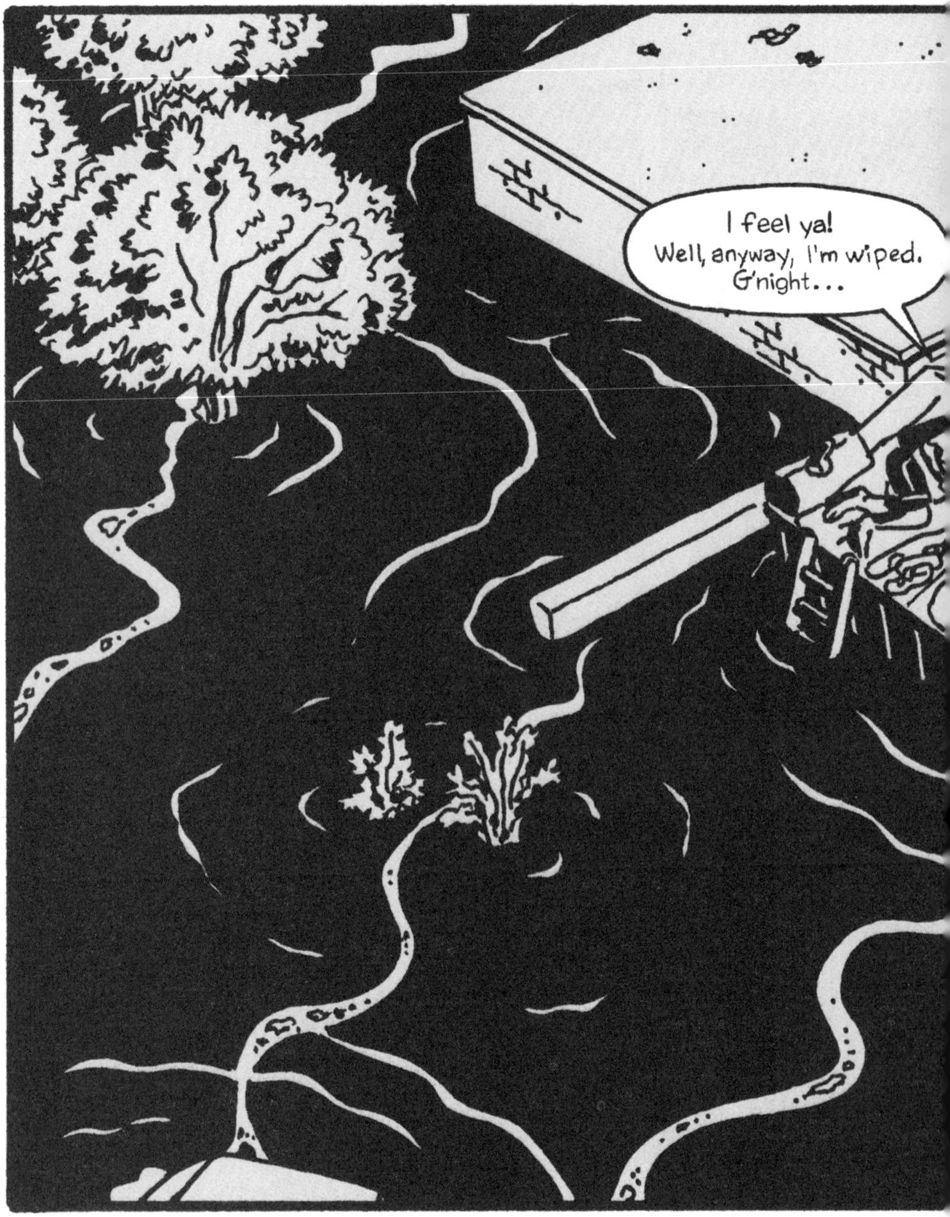
I feel ya!
Well, anyway, I'm wiped.
G'night...

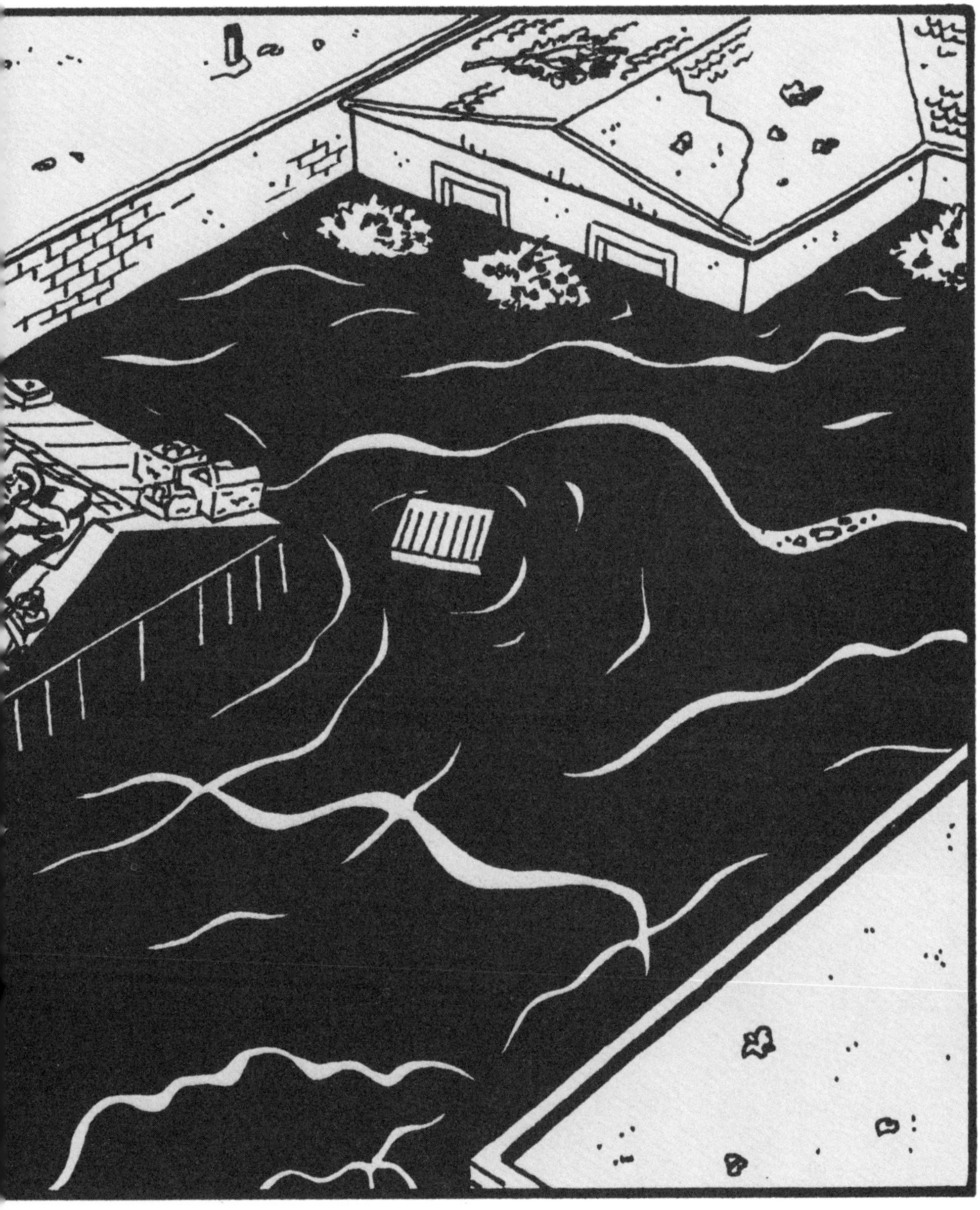

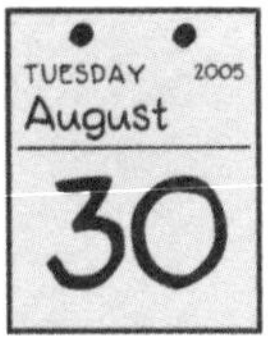
TUESDAY 2005
August
30

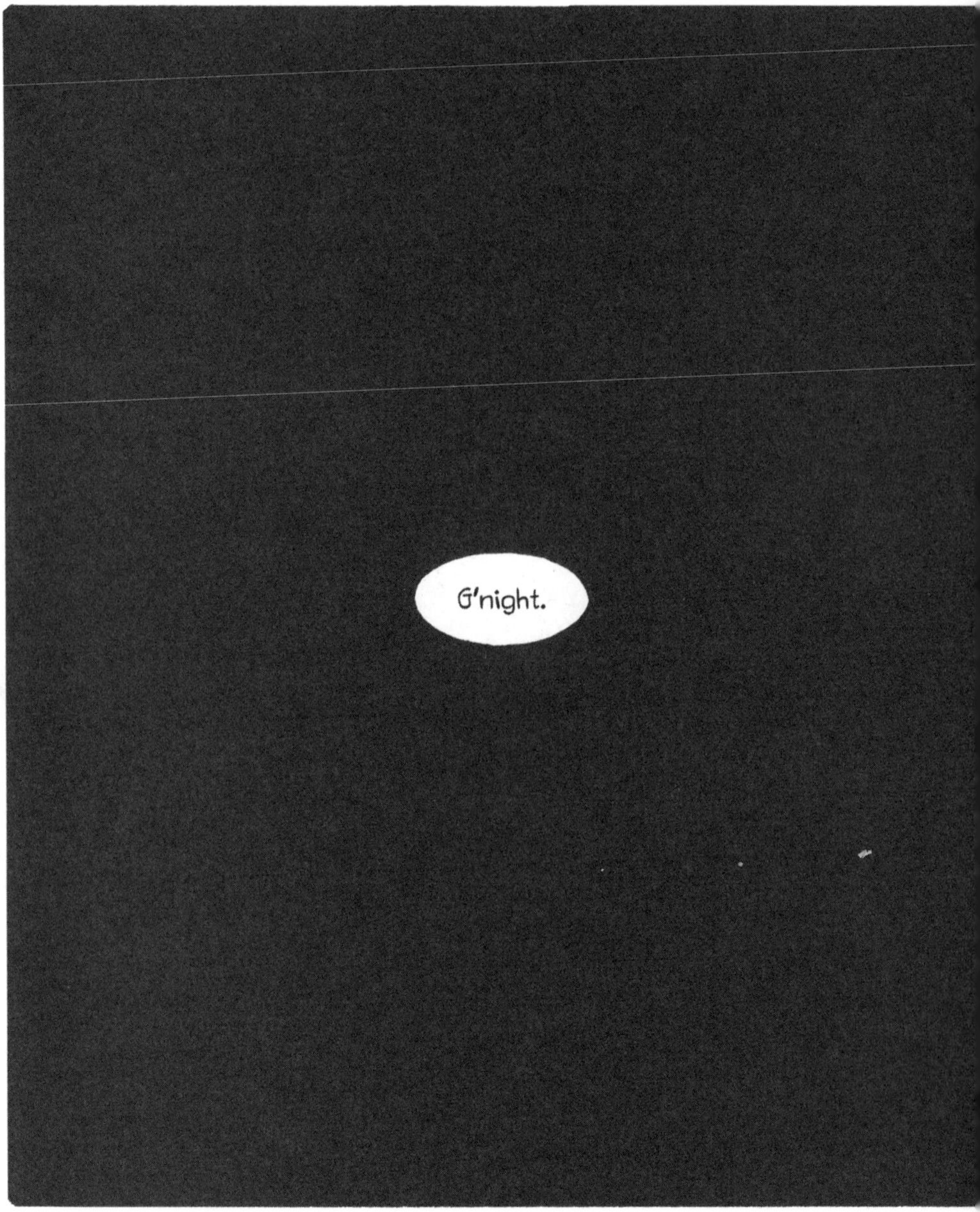
G'night.

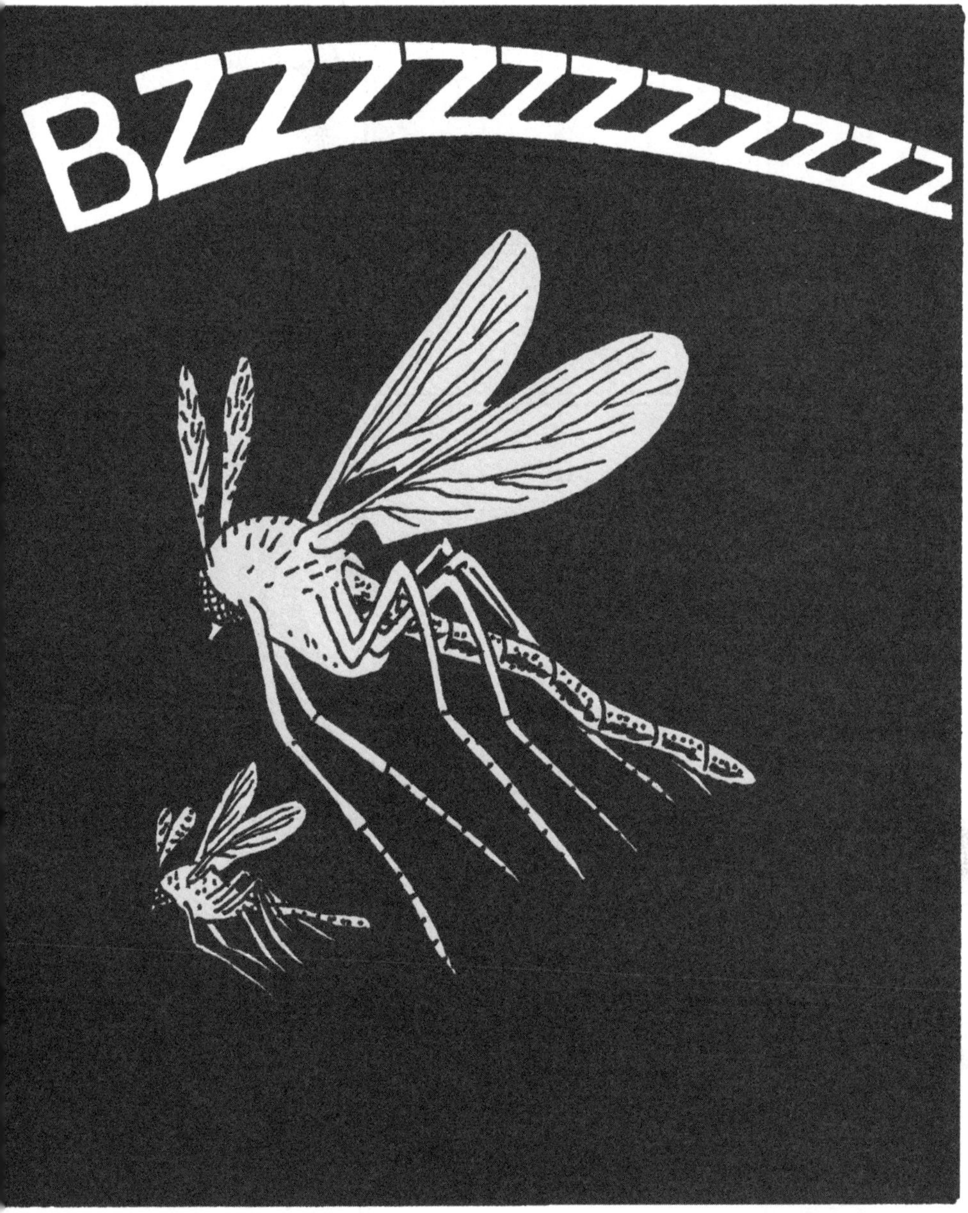
BZZZZZZZZZZZZ

I HEARD SOME DISTANT MUSIC

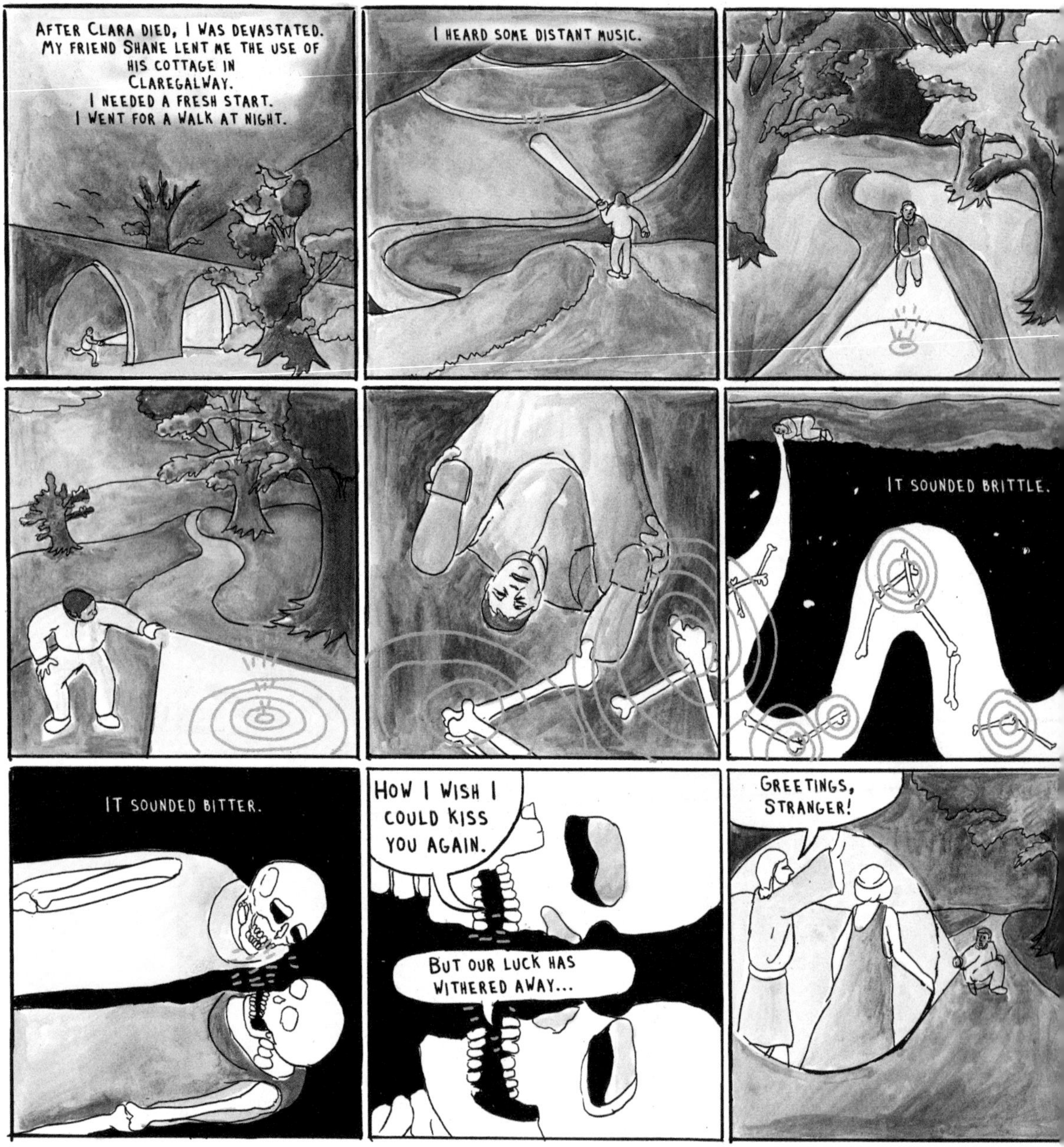

AFTER CLARA DIED, I WAS DEVASTATED. MY FRIEND SHANE LENT ME THE USE OF HIS COTTAGE IN CLAREGALWAY. I NEEDED A FRESH START. I WENT FOR A WALK AT NIGHT.
I HEARD SOME DISTANT MUSIC.
IT SOUNDED BRITTLE.
IT SOUNDED BITTER.
HOW I WISH I COULD KISS YOU AGAIN.
BUT OUR LUCK HAS WITHERED AWAY...
GREETINGS, STRANGER!

LAUREN WEINSTEIN

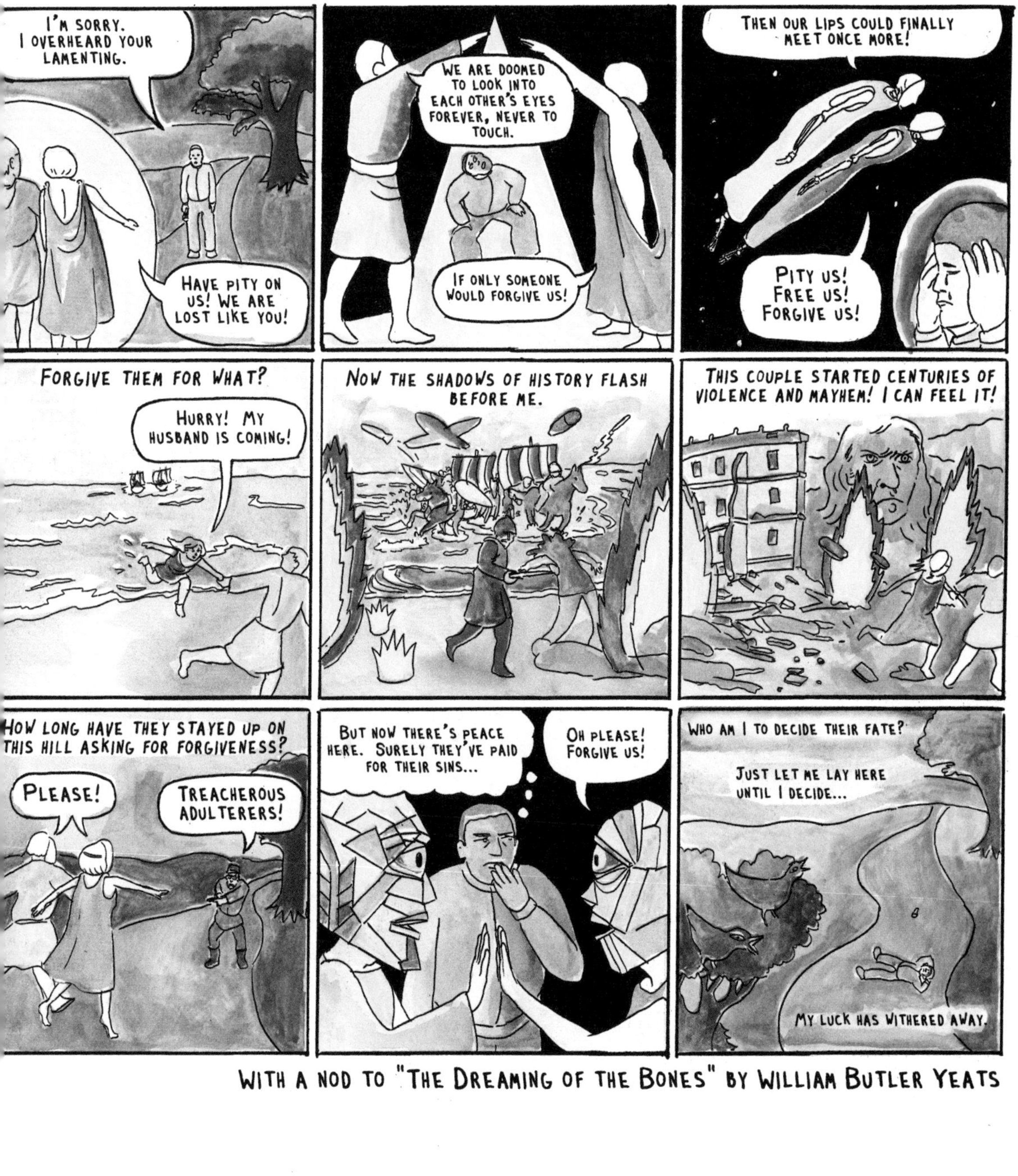
I'M SORRY. I OVERHEARD YOUR LAMENTING.
HAVE PITY ON US! WE ARE LOST LIKE YOU!
WE ARE DOOMED TO LOOK INTO EACH OTHER'S EYES FOREVER, NEVER TO TOUCH.
IF ONLY SOMEONE WOULD FORGIVE US!
THEN OUR LIPS COULD FINALLY MEET ONCE MORE!
PITY US! FREE US! FORGIVE US!
FORGIVE THEM FOR WHAT?
HURRY! MY HUSBAND IS COMING!
NOW THE SHADOWS OF HISTORY FLASH BEFORE ME.
THIS COUPLE STARTED CENTURIES OF VIOLENCE AND MAYHEM! I CAN FEEL IT!
HOW LONG HAVE THEY STAYED UP ON THIS HILL ASKING FOR FORGIVENESS?
PLEASE!
TREACHEROUS ADULTERERS!
BUT NOW THERE'S PEACE HERE. SURELY THEY'VE PAID FOR THEIR SINS...
OH PLEASE! FORGIVE US!
WHO AM I TO DECIDE THEIR FATE?
JUST LET ME LAY HERE UNTIL I DECIDE...
MY LUCK HAS WITHERED AWAY.

WITH A NOD TO "THE DREAMING OF THE BONES" BY WILLIAM BUTLER YEATS

excerpt from

"YOU'LL NEVER KNOW"

by C. Tyler

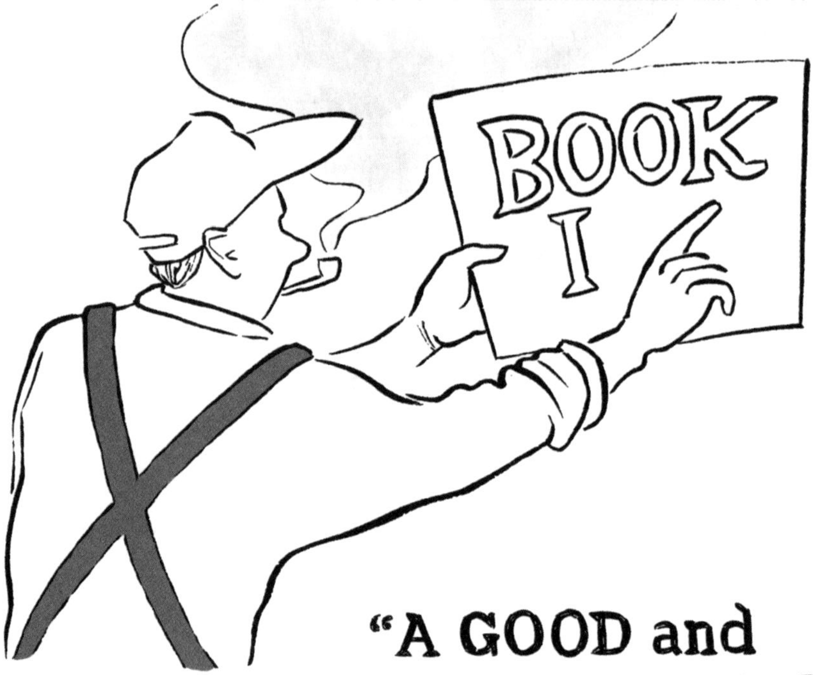
BOOK
I

"A GOOD and DECENT MAN"

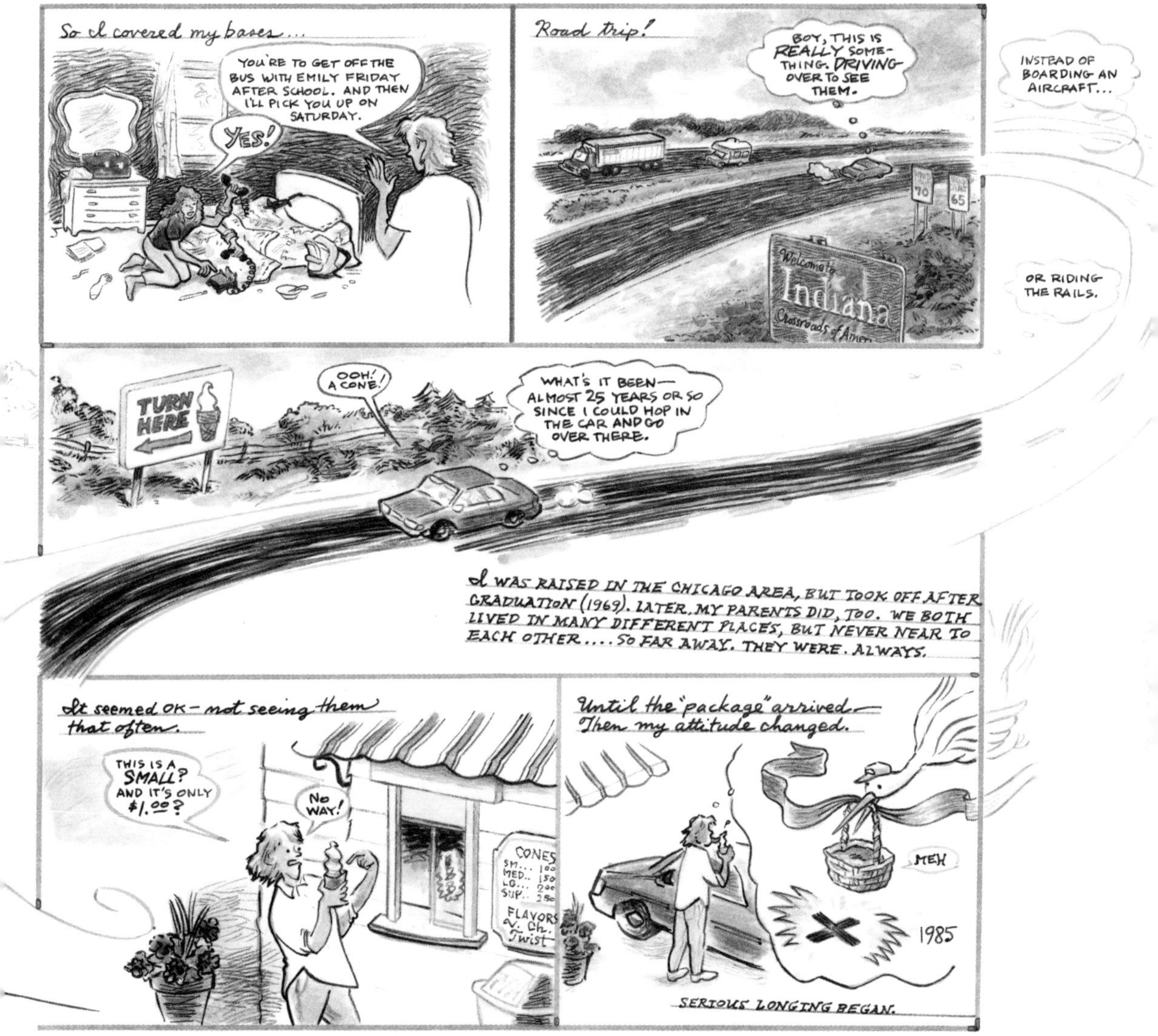

So I covered my bases...
YOU'RE TO GET OFF THE BUS WITH EMILY FRIDAY AFTER SCHOOL. AND THEN I'LL PICK YOU UP ON SATURDAY.
YES!
Road trip!
BOY, THIS IS REALLY SOMETHING. DRIVING OVER TO SEE THEM.
70
65
Welcome to Indiana
Crossroads of Amer
INSTEAD OF BOARDING AN AIRCRAFT...
OR RIDING THE RAILS.
TURN HERE
OOH! A CONE!
WHAT'S IT BEEN— ALMOST 25 YEARS OR SO SINCE I COULD HOP IN THE CAR AND GO OVER THERE.
I WAS RAISED IN THE CHICAGO AREA, BUT TOOK OFF AFTER GRADUATION (1969). LATER, MY PARENTS DID, TOO. WE BOTH LIVED IN MANY DIFFERENT PLACES, BUT NEVER NEAR TO EACH OTHER.... SO FAR AWAY, THEY WERE. ALWAYS.
It seemed OK— not seeing them that often.
THIS IS A SMALL? AND IT'S ONLY $1.00?
NO WAY!
CONES
FLAVORS
Twist
Until the "package" arrived— Then my attitude changed.
MEH
1985
SERIOUS LONGING BEGAN.

It bothered me that my child would not be influenced by them.
California 1985
HE FIXED THEIR GATE. THEY'VE GOT ALL THOSE KIDS. Y'KNOW.
Mom in Tennessee
AND I TAUGHT THE OLDER GIRLS TO MAKE APRONS.
OH..IT SOUNDS GREAT.
SORE
THE 'POVERTY PLUS' YEARS.
All things "Tyler" were missing from my life. I didn't have a dog,
Kitt-ee!
STOP!
WRONG SPECIES
Still Calif., 1987
I didn't own a power saw
AAH!
MUSIC TO MY EARS!
NEIGHBOR
Calif. 1988 and so on
and going to Mass brought up too many issues.
IT'S THE MOMMY CRIES PLACE!
ex Catholic
No money to fly home.
HELEN!
HOW 'BOUT SOME LEMONADE
Sale TODAY
SO MUCH LIKE MY PARENTS
Garage sale folks made great surrogates.
IT'S YOURS, HONEY
DO I LOOK LIKE A WAITRESS TO YOU?
MOM HAS A Nesco!
MAKE AN OFFER
Nesco

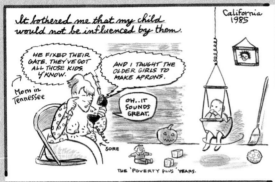

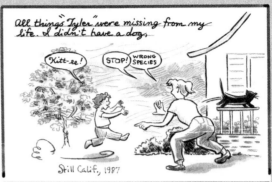

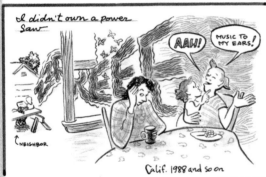

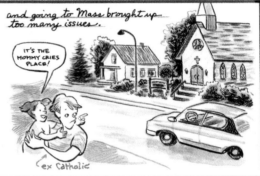

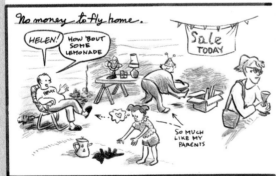

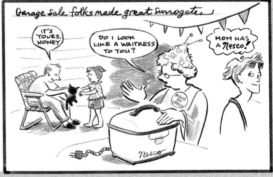

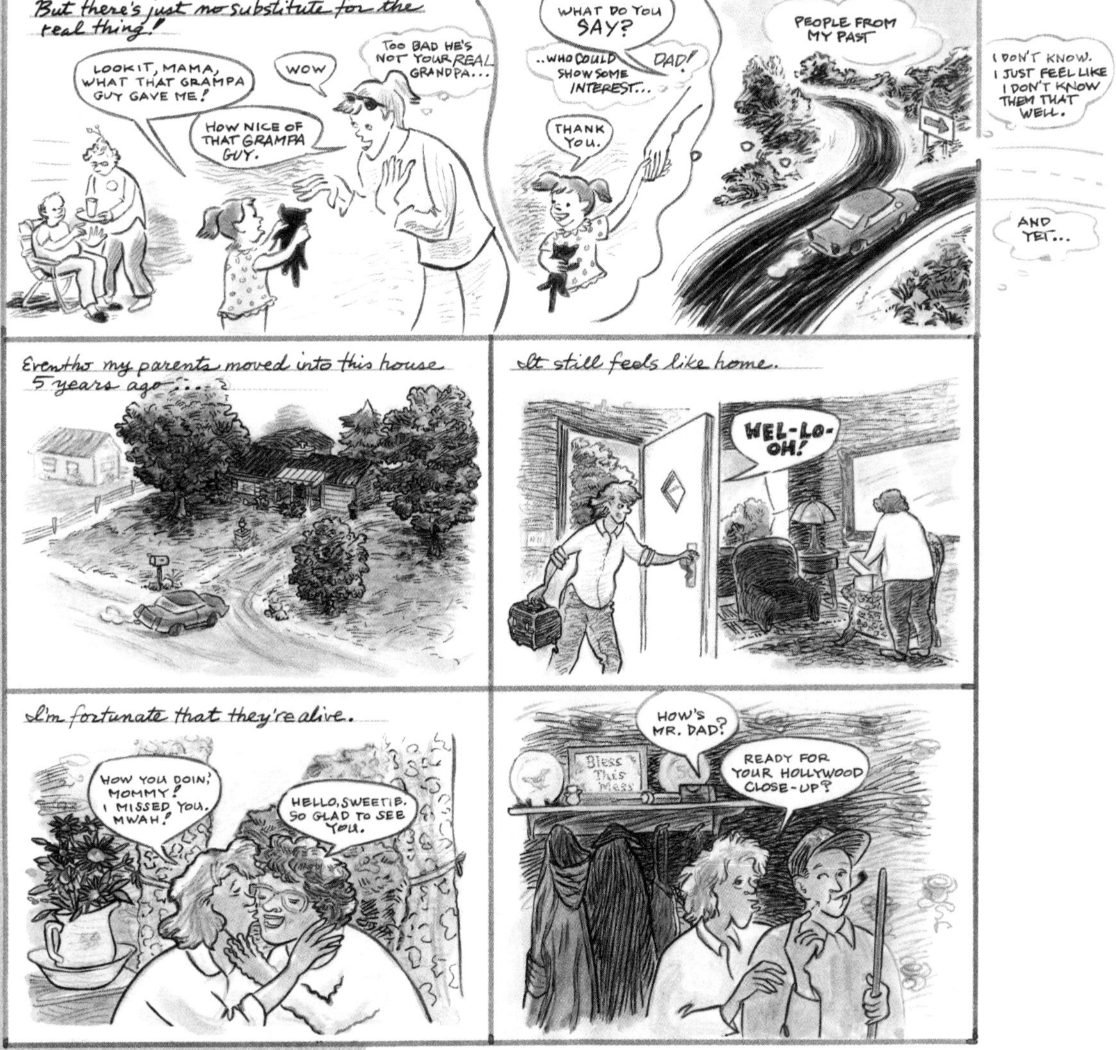
But there's just no substitute for the real thing!
LOOKIT, MAMA, WHAT THAT GRAMPA GUY GAVE ME!
WOW
HOW NICE OF THAT GRAMPA GUY.
TOO BAD HE'S NOT YOUR REAL GRANDPA...
WHAT DO YOU SAY?
..WHO COULD SHOW SOME INTEREST...
DAD!
THANK YOU.
PEOPLE FROM MY PAST
I DON'T KNOW. I JUST FEEL LIKE I DON'T KNOW THEM THAT WELL.
AND YET...
Eventho my parents moved into this house 5 years ago...
It still feels like home.
WEL-LO-OH!
I'm fortunate that they're alive.
HOW YOU DOIN', MOMMY? I MISSED YOU. MWAH!
HELLO, SWEETIE. SO GLAD TO SEE YOU.
HOW'S MR. DAD?
READY FOR YOUR HOLLYWOOD CLOSE-UP?
Bless This Mess

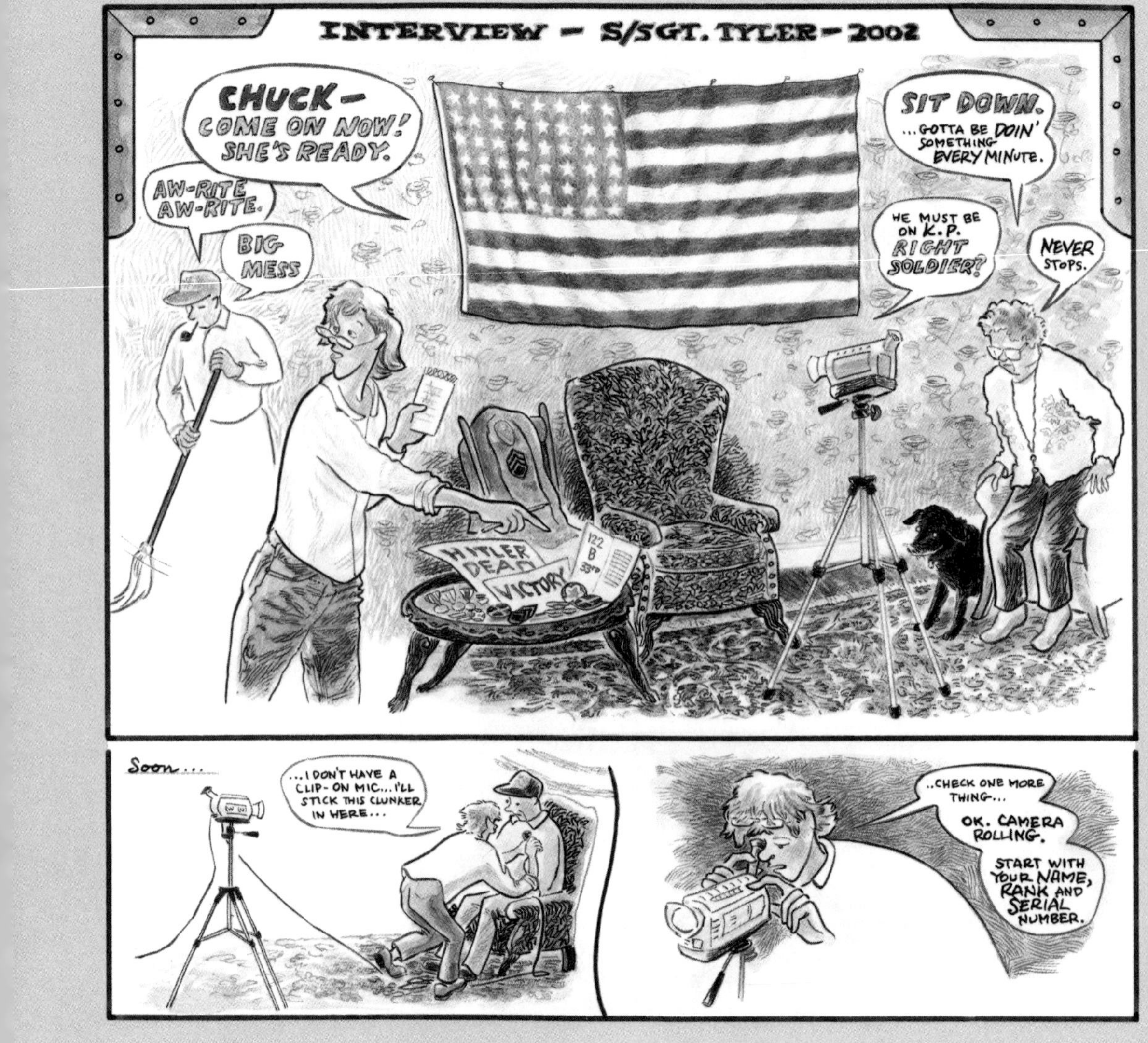
INTERVIEW – S/SGT. TYLER – 2002
CHUCK– COME ON NOW! SHE'S READY.
AW-RITE AW-RITE.
BIG MESS
SIT DOWN. ...GOTTA BE DOIN' SOMETHING EVERY MINUTE.
HE MUST BE ON K.P. RIGHT SOLDIER?
NEVER STOPS.
HITLER DEAD
VICTORY
Soon...
...I DON'T HAVE A CLIP-ON MIC...I'LL STICK THIS CLUNKER IN HERE...
..CHECK ONE MORE THING...
OK. CAMERA ROLLING.
START WITH YOUR NAME, RANK AND SERIAL NUMBER.

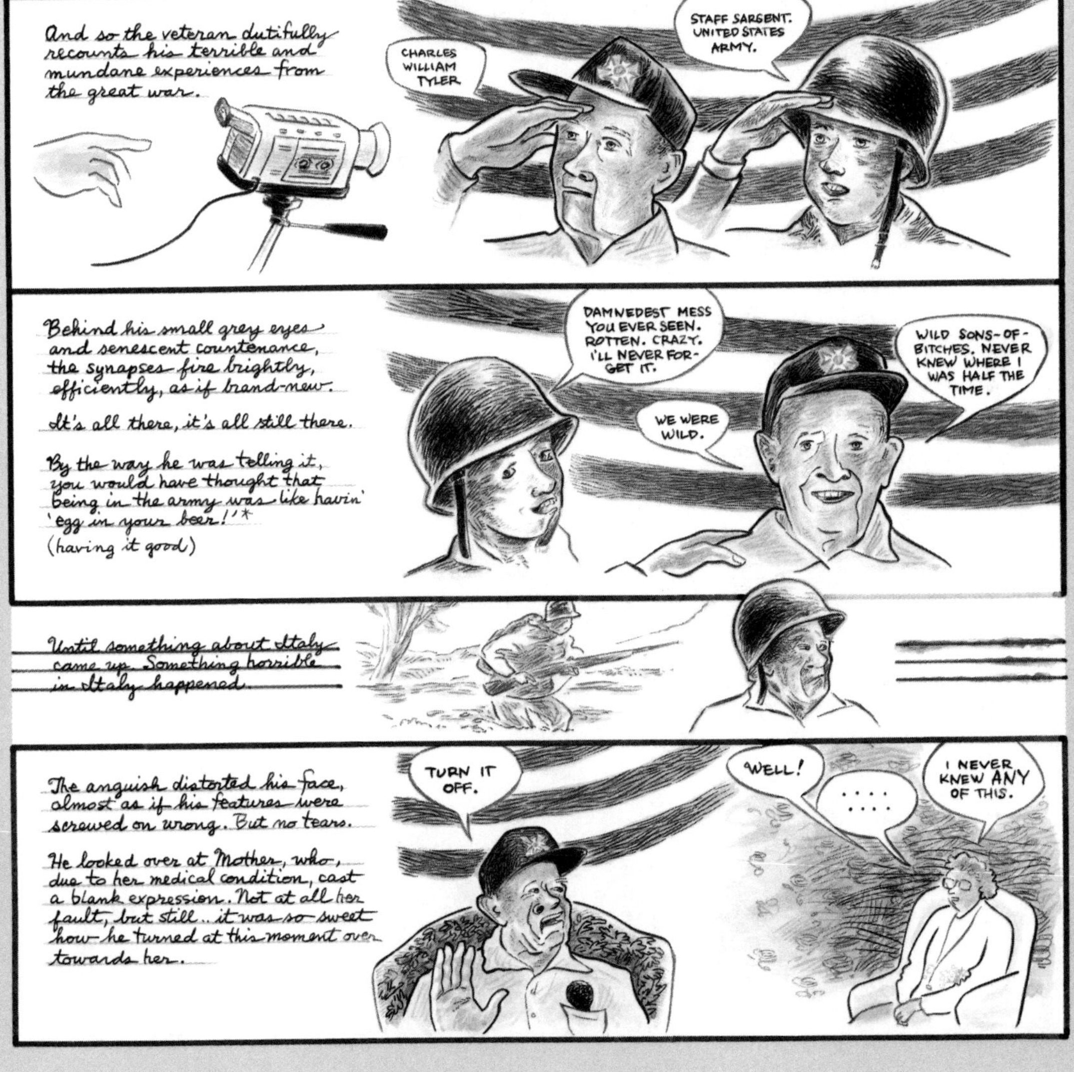
And so the veteran dutifully recounts his terrible and mundane experiences from the great war.
CHARLES WILLIAM TYLER
STAFF SARGENT. UNITED STATES ARMY.
Behind his small grey eyes and senescent countenance, the synapses fire brightly, efficiently, as if brand-new.
It's all there, it's all still there.
By the way he was telling it, you would have thought that being in the army was like havin' 'egg in your beer!'* (having it good)
DAMNEDEST MESS YOU EVER SEEN. ROTTEN. CRAZY. I'LL NEVER FORGET IT.
WE WERE WILD.
WILD SONS-OF-BITCHES. NEVER KNEW WHERE I WAS HALF THE TIME.
Until something about Italy came up. Something horrible in Italy happened.
The anguish distorted his face, almost as if his features were screwed on wrong. But no tears.
He looked over at Mother, who, due to her medical condition, cast a blank expression. Not at all her fault, but still.. it was so sweet how he turned at this moment over towards her.
TURN IT OFF.
WELL!
. . . .
I NEVER KNEW ANY OF THIS.

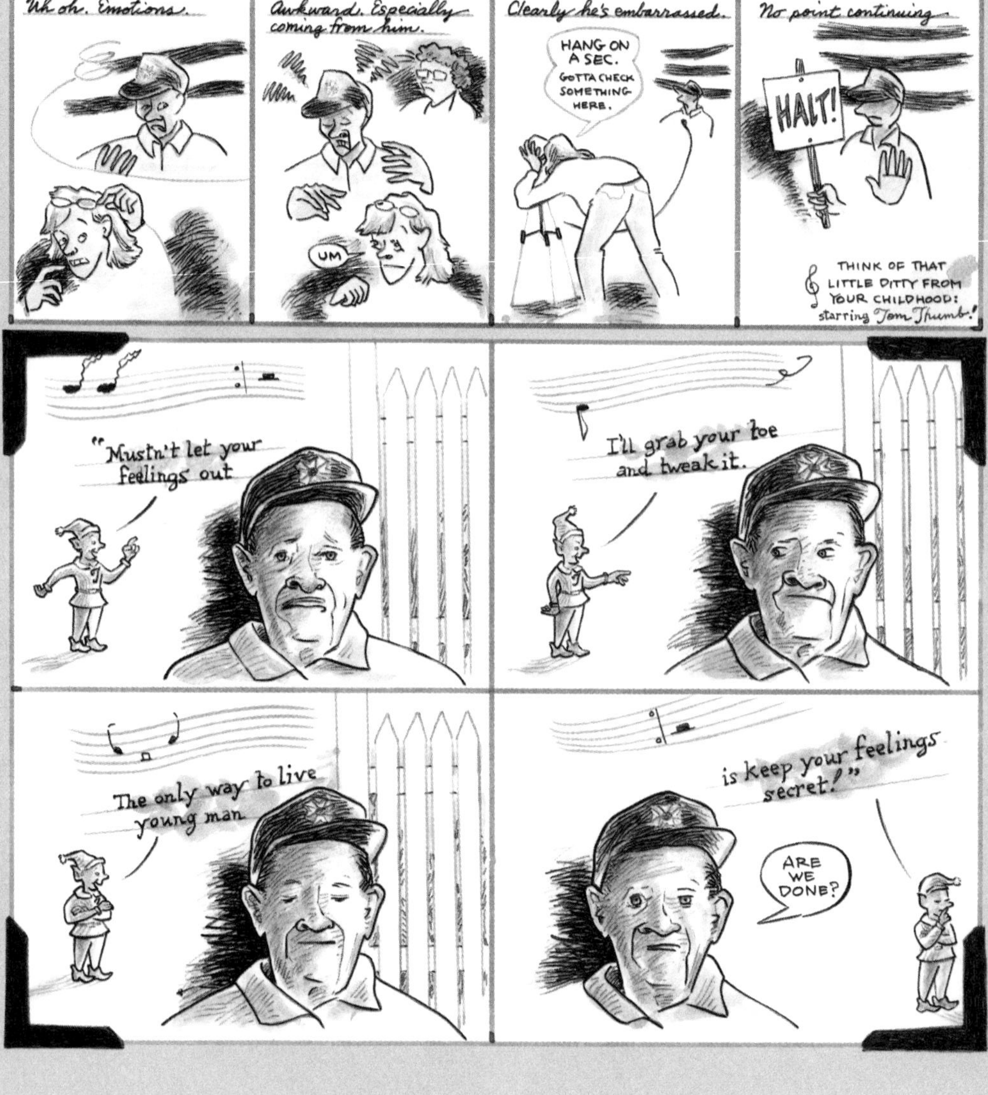

Uh oh. Emotions.
Awkward. Especially coming from him.
UM
Clearly he's embarrassed.
HANG ON A SEC. GOTTA CHECK SOMETHING HERE.
No point continuing
HALT!
THINK OF THAT LITTLE DITTY FROM YOUR CHILDHOOD: starring Tom Thumb!
"Mustn't let your feelings out
I'll grab your toe and tweak it.
The only way to live young man
is keep your feelings secret!"
ARE WE DONE?

Now I was even MORE curious.
ARE WE DONE? 'CAUSE I'M DONE.
WE'RE DONE.
HITLER DEAD
VICTORY
Sure, he had gone over all the facts and details—
HOW COME YOU NEVER TOLD ME ANY OF THIS?
YOU NEVER ASKED, DOLL.
STILL LOVE ME EVEN THOUGH I STOLE A JEEP?
but Italy, you bad boy, what did you do to my Dad.
YES I DID ASK— YEARS AGO.
YOU MIGHT HAVE.
I DON'T KNOW
Vague Discharge Papers
I HAD to know what happened!
PERHAPS THAT STUFF ON THE TABLE WILL PROVIDE A CLUE—
HITLER DEAD
VICTORY
VICTORY
WORLD WAR II
5 FRANCS 5
US
Charles W. Tyler T42 Chicago, Ill.
60331
HITLER DEAD!

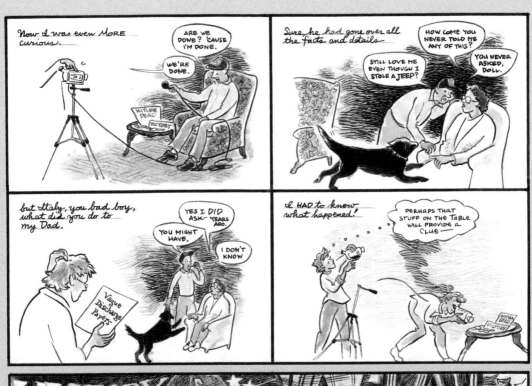

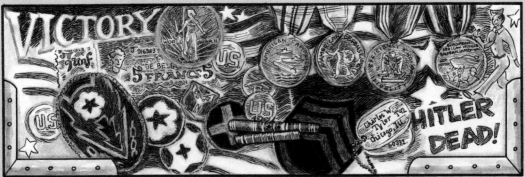

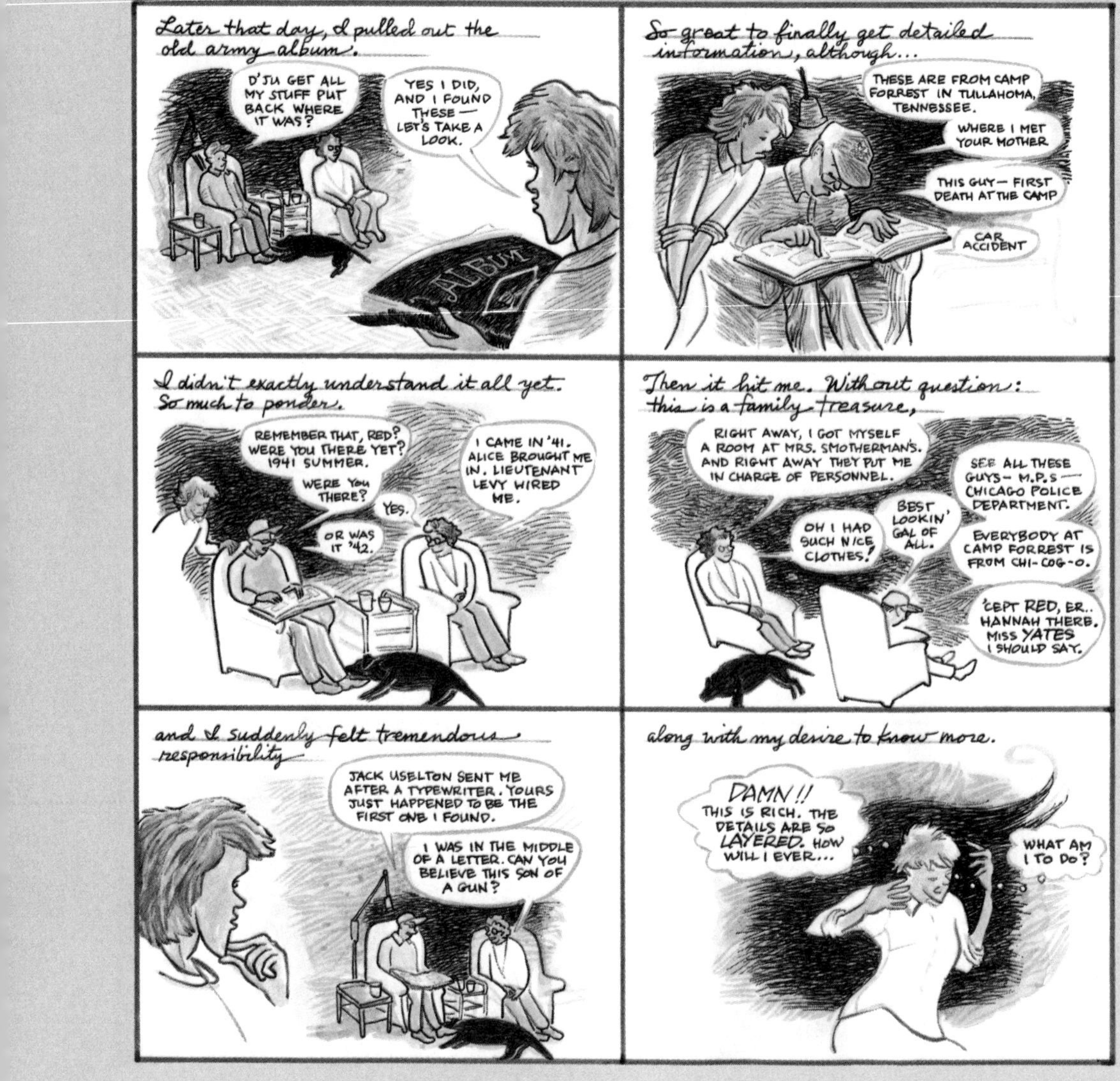

Later that day, I pulled out the old army album.
D'JU GET ALL MY STUFF PUT BACK WHERE IT WAS?
YES I DID, AND I FOUND THESE — LET'S TAKE A LOOK.
ALBUM
So great to finally get detailed information, although...
THESE ARE FROM CAMP FORREST IN TULLAHOMA, TENNESSEE.
WHERE I MET YOUR MOTHER
THIS GUY— FIRST DEATH AT THE CAMP
CAR ACCIDENT
I didn't exactly understand it all yet. So much to ponder.
REMEMBER THAT, RED? WERE YOU THERE YET? 1941 SUMMER.
WERE YOU THERE?
OR WAS IT '42.
YES.
I CAME IN '41. ALICE BROUGHT ME IN. LIEUTENANT LEVY HIRED ME.
Then it hit me. Without question: this is a family treasure,
RIGHT AWAY, I GOT MYSELF A ROOM AT MRS. SMOTHERMAN'S. AND RIGHT AWAY THEY PUT ME IN CHARGE OF PERSONNEL.
OH I HAD SUCH NICE CLOTHES!
BEST LOOKIN' GAL OF ALL.
SEE ALL THESE GUYS— M.P.S — CHICAGO POLICE DEPARTMENT.
EVERYBODY AT CAMP FORREST IS FROM CHI-COG-O.
'CEPT RED, ER.. HANNAH THERE. MISS YATES I SHOULD SAY.
and I suddenly felt tremendous responsibility
JACK USELTON SENT ME AFTER A TYPEWRITER. YOURS JUST HAPPENED TO BE THE FIRST ONE I FOUND.
I WAS IN THE MIDDLE OF A LETTER. CAN YOU BELIEVE THIS SON OF A GUN?
along with my desire to know more.
DAMN!! THIS IS RICH. THE DETAILS ARE SO LAYERED. HOW WILL I EVER...
WHAT AM I TO DO?

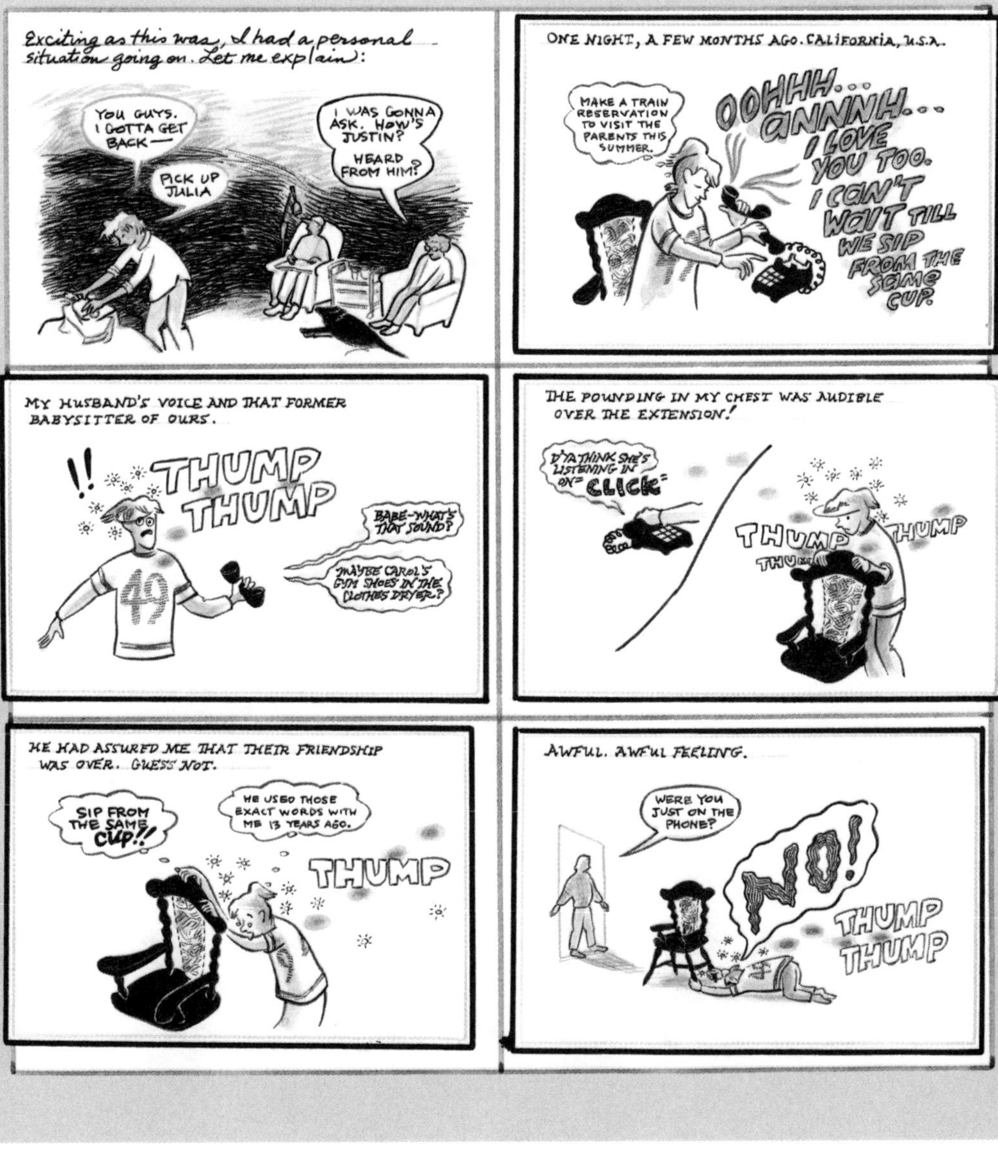
Exciting as this was, I had a personal situation going on. Let me explain:
YOU GUYS. I GOTTA GET BACK—
PICK UP JULIA
I WAS GONNA ASK. HOW'S JUSTIN?
HEARD FROM HIM?
ONE NIGHT, A FEW MONTHS AGO. CALIFORNIA, U.S.A.
MAKE A TRAIN RESERVATION TO VISIT THE PARENTS THIS SUMMER.
OOHHH... ANNNH...
I LOVE YOU TOO. I CAN'T WAIT TILL WE SIP FROM THE SAME CUP.
MY HUSBAND'S VOICE AND THAT FORMER BABYSITTER OF OURS.
!!
THUMP THUMP
BABE—WHAT'S THAT SOUND?
MAYBE CAROL'S GYM SHOES IN THE CLOTHES DRYER?
THE POUNDING IN MY CHEST WAS AUDIBLE OVER THE EXTENSION!
D'YA THINK SHE'S LISTENING IN ON=
CLICK
THUMP
THUMP
HE HAD ASSURED ME THAT THEIR FRIENDSHIP WAS OVER. GUESS NOT.
SIP FROM THE SAME CUP!!
HE USED THOSE EXACT WORDS WITH ME 13 YEARS AGO.
THUMP
AWFUL. AWFUL FEELING.
WERE YOU JUST ON THE PHONE?
NO!
THUMP THUMP

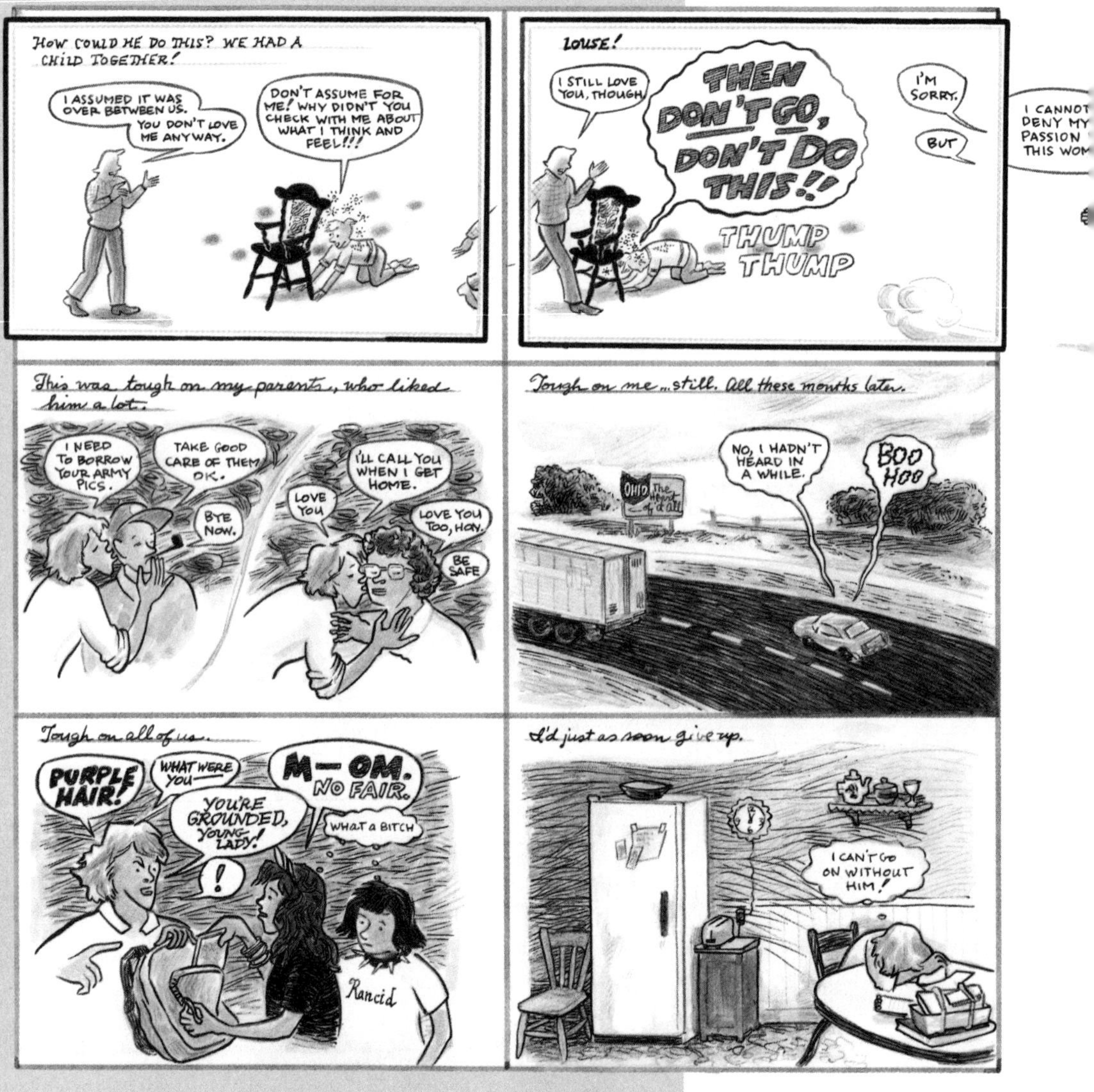
HOW COULD HE DO THIS? WE HAD A CHILD TOGETHER!
I ASSUMED IT WAS OVER BETWEEN US.
YOU DON'T LOVE ME ANYWAY.
DON'T ASSUME FOR ME! WHY DIDN'T YOU CHECK WITH ME ABOUT WHAT I THINK AND FEEL!!!
LOUSE!
I STILL LOVE YOU, THOUGH.
THEN DON'T GO, DON'T DO THIS!!
I'M SORRY.
BUT
I CANNOT DENY MY PASSION
THUMP THUMP
This was tough on my parents, who liked him a lot.
I NEED TO BORROW YOUR ARMY PICS.
TAKE GOOD CARE OF THEM, OK.
BYE NOW.
LOVE YOU
I'LL CALL YOU WHEN I GET HOME.
LOVE YOU TOO, HON.
BE SAFE
Tough on me ... still. All these months later.
OHIO The Heart of it All
NO, I HADN'T HEARD IN A WHILE.
BOO HOO
Tough on all of us.
PURPLE HAIR!
WHAT WERE YOU—
M—OM. NO FAIR.
YOU'RE GROUNDED, YOUNG LADY!
WHAT a BITCH
!
Rancid
I'd just as soon give up.
I CAN'T GO ON WITHOUT HIM!

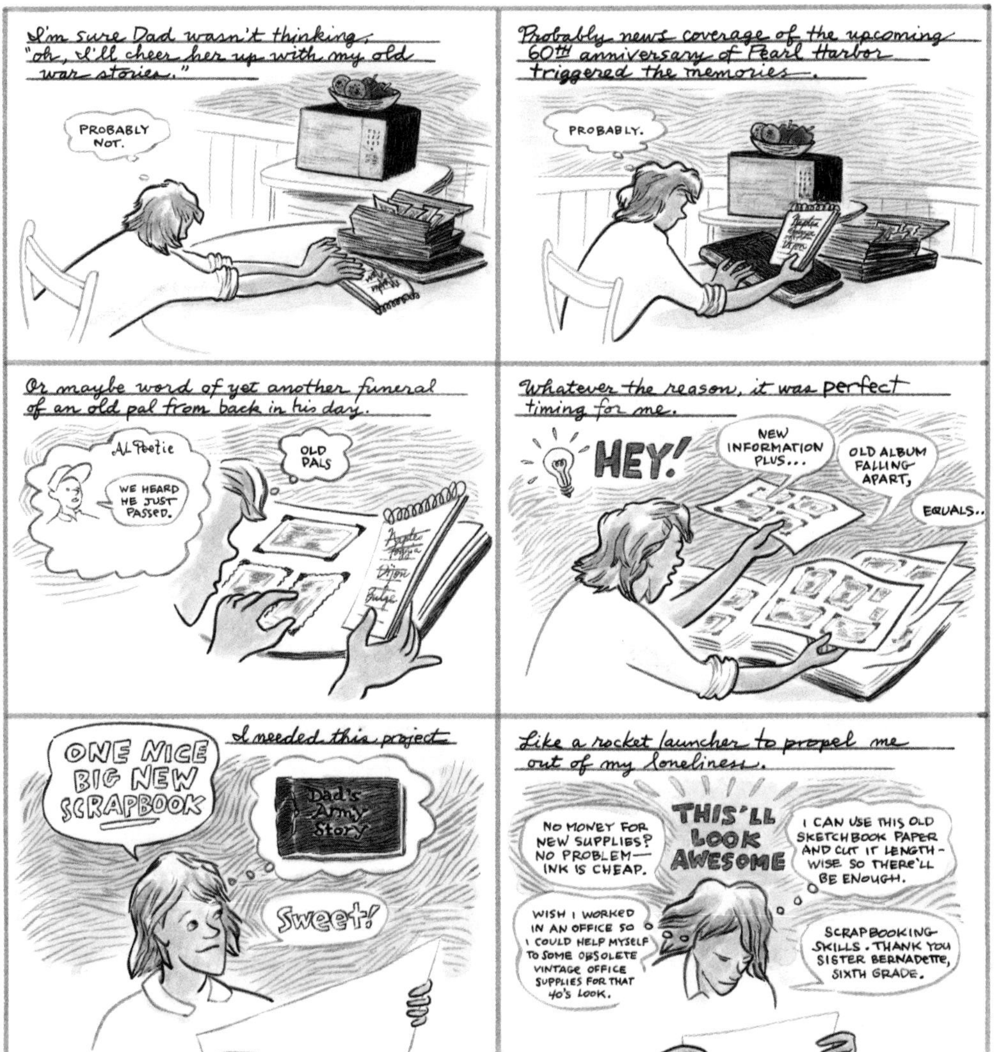
I'm sure Dad wasn't thinking, "oh, I'll cheer her up with my old war stories."
PROBABLY NOT.
Probably news coverage of the upcoming 60th anniversary of Pearl Harbor triggered the memories.
PROBABLY.
Or maybe word of yet another funeral of an old pal from back in his day.
Al Peetie
WE HEARD HE JUST PASSED.
OLD PALS
Whatever the reason, it was perfect timing for me.
HEY!
NEW INFORMATION PLUS...
OLD ALBUM FALLING APART,
EQUALS..
I needed this project.
ONE NICE BIG NEW SCRAPBOOK
Dad's Army Story
Sweet!
Like a rocket launcher to propel me out of my loneliness.
NO MONEY FOR NEW SUPPLIES? NO PROBLEM— INK IS CHEAP.
THIS'LL LOOK AWESOME
I CAN USE THIS OLD SKETCHBOOK PAPER AND CUT IT LENGTH-WISE SO THERE'LL BE ENOUGH.
WISH I WORKED IN AN OFFICE SO I COULD HELP MYSELF TO SOME OBSOLETE VINTAGE OFFICE SUPPLIES FOR THAT 40'S LOOK.
SCRAPBOOKING SKILLS. THANK YOU SISTER BERNADETTE, SIXTH GRADE.

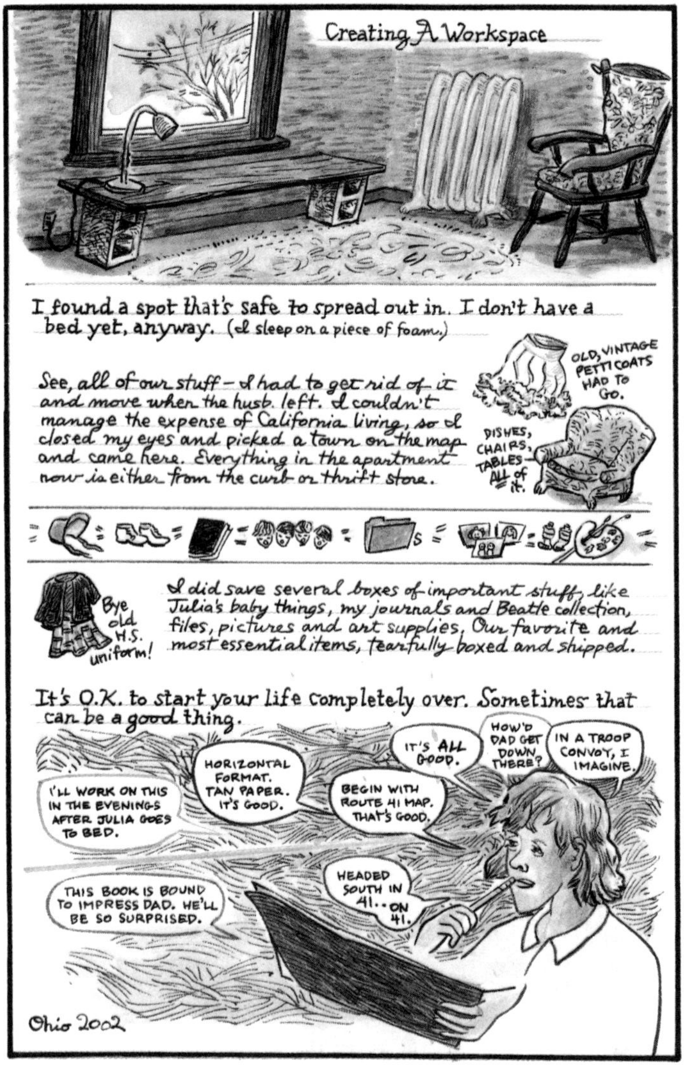
Creating A Workspace
I found a spot that's safe to spread out in. I don't have a bed yet, anyway. (I sleep on a piece of foam.)
See, all of our stuff - I had to get rid of it and move when the husb. left. I couldn't manage the expense of California living, so I closed my eyes and picked a town on the map and came here. Everything in the apartment now is either from the curb or thrift store.
OLD, VINTAGE PETTICOATS HAD TO GO.
DISHES, CHAIRS, TABLES ALL of it.
I did save several boxes of important stuff, like Julia's baby things, my journals and Beatle collection, files, pictures and art supplies. Our favorite and most essential items, tearfully boxed and shipped.
Bye old H.S. uniform!
It's O.K. to start your life completely over. Sometimes that can be a good thing.
I'LL WORK ON THIS IN THE EVENINGS AFTER JULIA GOES TO BED.
HORIZONTAL FORMAT. TAN PAPER. IT'S GOOD.
BEGIN WITH ROUTE 41 MAP. THAT'S GOOD.
IT'S ALL GOOD.
HOW'D DAD GET DOWN THERE?
IN A TROOP CONVOY, I IMAGINE.
THIS BOOK IS BOUND TO IMPRESS DAD. HE'LL BE SO SURPRISED.
HEADED SOUTH IN 41.. ON 41.
Ohio 2002

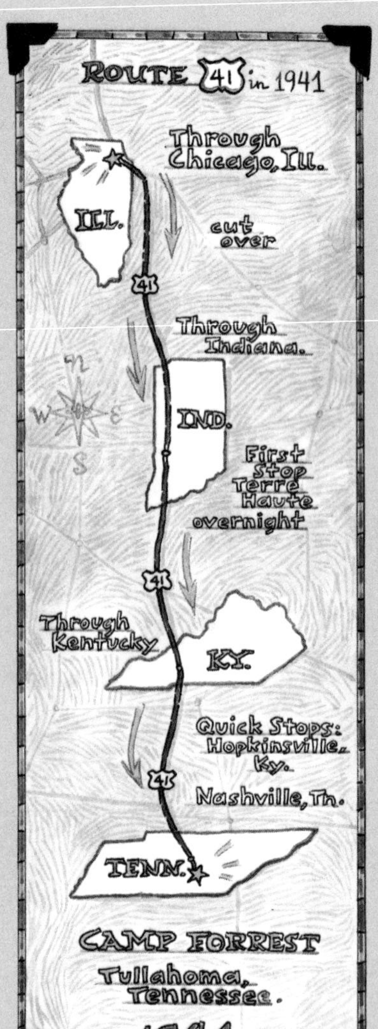
ROUTE 41 in 1941
Through Chicago, Ill.
ILL.
cut over
41
Through Indiana.
N
W
E
S
IND.
First stop Terre Haute overnight
41
Through Kentucky
KY.
Quick Stops: Hopkinsville, Ky.
41
Nashville, Tn.
TENN.
CAMP FORREST
Tullahoma, Tennessee.
- 1941 -

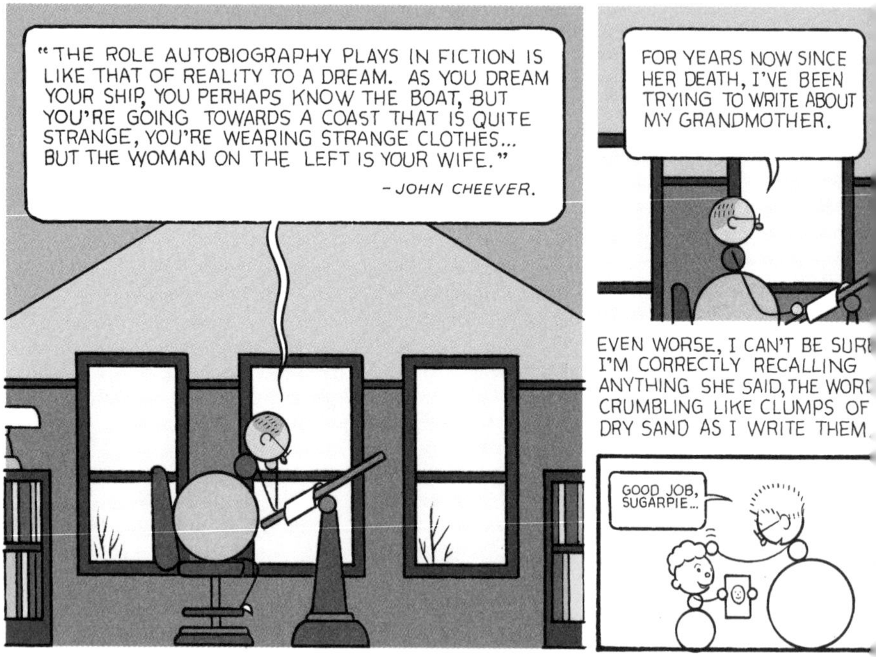
"THE ROLE AUTOBIOGRAPHY PLAYS IN FICTION IS LIKE THAT OF REALITY TO A DREAM. AS YOU DREAM YOUR SHIP, YOU PERHAPS KNOW THE BOAT, BUT YOU'RE GOING TOWARDS A COAST THAT IS QUITE STRANGE, YOU'RE WEARING STRANGE CLOTHES... BUT THE WOMAN ON THE LEFT IS YOUR WIFE."
- JOHN CHEEVER.
FOR YEARS NOW SINCE HER DEATH, I'VE BEEN TRYING TO WRITE ABOUT MY GRANDMOTHER.
EVEN WORSE, I CAN'T BE SUR
I'M CORRECTLY RECALLING ANYTHING SHE SAID, THE WOR
CRUMBLING LIKE CLUMPS OF DRY SAND AS I WRITE THEM
GOOD JOB, SUGARPIE...

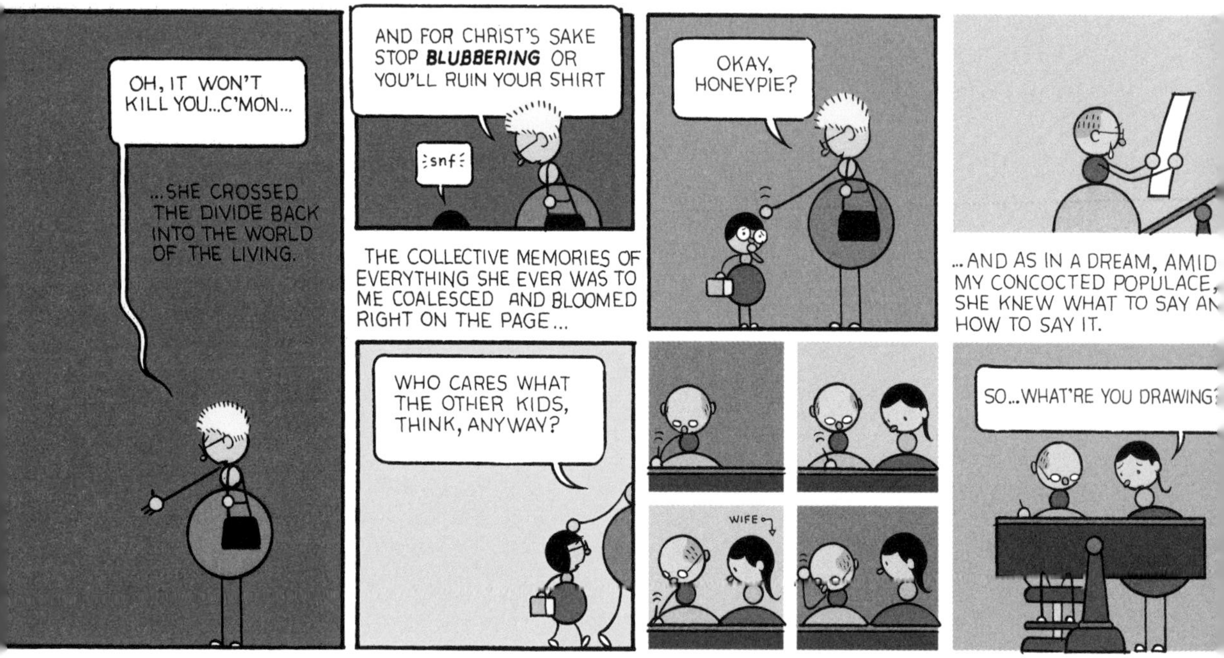
OH, IT WON'T KILL YOU...C'MON...
...SHE CROSSED THE DIVIDE BACK INTO THE WORLD OF THE LIVING.
AND FOR CHRIST'S SAKE STOP **BLUBBERING** OR YOU'LL RUIN YOUR SHIRT
snf
THE COLLECTIVE MEMORIES OF EVERYTHING SHE EVER WAS TO ME COALESCED AND BLOOMED RIGHT ON THE PAGE...
WHO CARES WHAT THE OTHER KIDS, THINK, ANYWAY?
OKAY, HONEYPIE?
WIFE
...AND AS IN A DREAM, AMID MY CONCOCTED POPULACE, SHE KNEW WHAT TO SAY A
HOW TO SAY IT.
SO...WHAT'RE YOU DRAWING

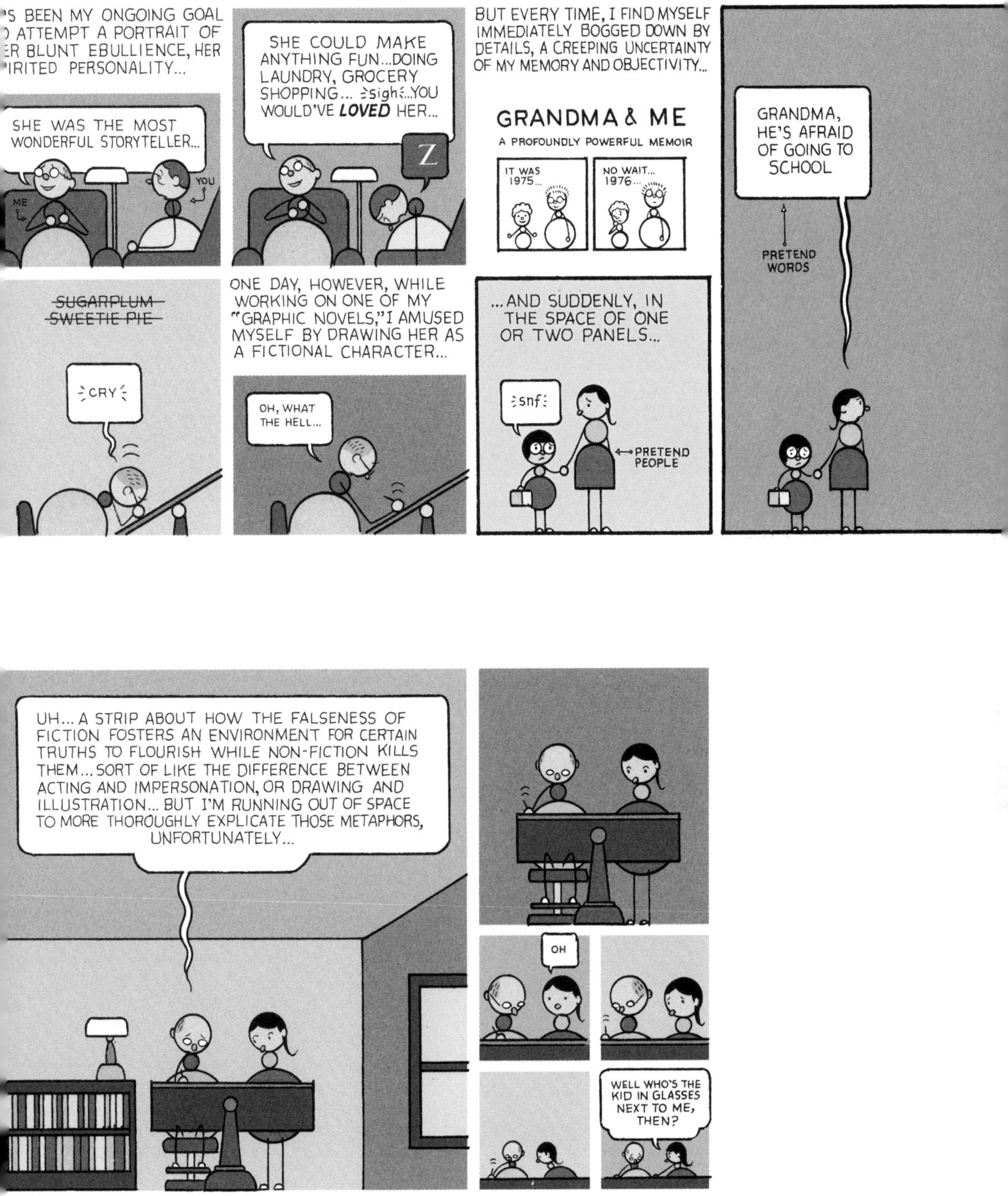
'S BEEN MY ONGOING GOAL
) ATTEMPT A PORTRAIT OF
ER BLUNT EBULLIENCE, HER
IRITED PERSONALITY...
SHE WAS THE MOST WONDERFUL STORYTELLER...
ME
YOU
SHE COULD MAKE ANYTHING FUN...DOING LAUNDRY, GROCERY SHOPPING... sigh ...YOU WOULD'VE ***LOVED*** HER...
Z
BUT EVERY TIME, I FIND MYSELF IMMEDIATELY BOGGED DOWN BY DETAILS, A CREEPING UNCERTAINTY OF MY MEMORY AND OBJECTIVITY...
GRANDMA & ME
A PROFOUNDLY POWERFUL MEMOIR
IT WAS 1975...
NO WAIT... 1976...
GRANDMA, HE'S AFRAID OF GOING TO SCHOOL
PRETEND WORDS
~~SUGARPLUM~~
~~SWEETIE PIE~~
CRY
ONE DAY, HOWEVER, WHILE WORKING ON ONE OF MY "GRAPHIC NOVELS," I AMUSED MYSELF BY DRAWING HER AS A FICTIONAL CHARACTER...
OH, WHAT THE HELL...
...AND SUDDENLY, IN THE SPACE OF ONE OR TWO PANELS...
snf
PRETEND PEOPLE
UH... A STRIP ABOUT HOW THE FALSENESS OF FICTION FOSTERS AN ENVIRONMENT FOR CERTAIN TRUTHS TO FLOURISH WHILE NON-FICTION KILLS THEM... SORT OF LIKE THE DIFFERENCE BETWEEN ACTING AND IMPERSONATION, OR DRAWING AND ILLUSTRATION... BUT I'M RUNNING OUT OF SPACE TO MORE THOROUGHLY EXPLICATE THOSE METAPHORS, UNFORTUNATELY...
OH
WELL WHO'S THE KID IN GLASSES NEXT TO ME, THEN?

Contributors' Notes

Jonathan Ames is the author of eight books, including *Wake Up, Sir!* and *The Alcoholic*. His novel, *The Extra Man*, has been adapted as a film starring Kevin Kline and Paul Dano. Ames is the creator of the HBO series *Bored to Death*, and he's been in two amateur boxing matches, fighting as "The Herring Wonder."

▪ I wrote my graphic novel, *The Alcoholic*, because of my friendship with Dean Haspiel. For several years, he kept urging me to do a project with him, and so to honor our friendship, I wrote this book for him to draw. In doing so, it gave me the opportunity to explore some things that I had not written about in prose — what I witnessed on 9/11 and, unrelated to 9/11, the loss of a childhood friend. Dean was a beautiful collaborator — he would take my words and create the pictures that were in my mind. I am very grateful to him.

Peter Bagge is best known for the '90s alternative comic *Hate*. More recently, he's written and drawn two graphic novels: *Apocalypse Nerd* (Dark Horse, 2008) and *Other Lives* (DC/Vertigo, 2010), as well as a collection of journalistic/social commentary strips for *Reason* magazine titled *Everybody Is Stupid Except for Me* (Fantagraphics, 2009), from which this featured strip has been reprinted.

▪ This comic is one of several I wrote and drew this past decade for the libertarian-leaning commentary magazine *Reason*. It deals specifically with the debates surrounding Plan B, or the so-called Morning After contraceptive pill, and more generally with the ever-present need on the part of some to control other people's sex lives and limit their reproductive rights.

Gabrielle Bell writes and draws the wildly popular autobiographical comic blog *Lucky*. Her latest book is *Cecil and Jordan in New York*, available from Drawn and Quarterly.

▪ Whenever I put my mother in my comics, they always seem to be a success. This is the third time my work has been included the Best American Comics series, and all three stories have had my mother in them, advocating the reading of books in conversation or by example. She was the humanity in the household, and I owe my success to her.

Todd Brower is a law professor in southern California. He has written several academic articles in U.S. and international journals, although he has been reading comics since he was a child. Even back then, he liked comics that did more than just tell a story or joke, like "Smokey Stover" by Bill Holman, in which the screwball plots were mainly a hook on which to hang puns, sight gags, fourth-wall references, and odd dialogue. He has finally found someone who understands and tolerates his sense of humor, his collaborator and partner, Steve MacIsaac.

▪ What has always interested me about comics is the ability to do things in this medium that cannot be done (or not easily done) in other forms. The middle panels of page four were the first pages I sketched out, because I liked the idea of reading a different message in another person's speech. Then I went back and wrote a provisional script with the concepts and some of the dialogue for the some pages or panels. Steve turned my stick figures into rough drawings and layouts that approximated what I wanted to accomplish in the panels. We then bounced ideas back and forth. My original idea was to have the hidden meaning words be different sizes; he thought that was awkward. I responded by using words color-coded to refer to the different characters' inner thoughts, which Steve modified with different colored boxes. That then allowed me to use the colored boxes earlier in the strip and have them overwhelm the spoken dialogue on page three. Our goal was to use comics' distinct formal properties and storytelling methods to suit the different ways in which people perceive the same situation.

Lilli Carré was born in 1983 in Los Angeles and currently lives in Chicago, where she stays inside all winter and works on comics and animation and smudging her face against the windows. Her films have screened around the globe, and her books of comics are *Tales of Woodsman Pete*, *The Lagoon*, and *Nine Ways to Disappear*. She also contributes comics to the Fantagraphics anthology *Mome* and to *The Believer*. Bits of her work can be seen at www.lillicarre.com.

▪ This part of *The Lagoon* was the section I enjoyed drawing and thinking about the most. Mood is a main focus of the book as a whole, and in this moment of the story I tried to have the mood feel spooky and goofy and ominous and sweet all at once, with a heartbeat rhythm leading the father to the bottom of the lagoon.

Fred Chao was born in San Francisco in 1978. His comics have appeared in *Found: Requiem for a Paper Bag*, as well as the *Awesome* and *Awesome 2: Awesomer* anthologies. He is hard at work on a children's comic book.

Nominated for four Will Eisner Comic Industry awards including Best New Series, his *Johnny Hiro* comics have recently been collected into one volume.

He currently lives in Brooklyn. He has no cats.

▪ I grew up reading a lot of superhero comics, and as much as I love them, as I get older, their high-drama situations have become less identifiable to me. Often, the characters' lives are filled with revenge killings, super-powered love triangles, and megalomaniacal global conquest. Still, the comics medium is so conducive to those high-action sequences — people who lift cars and throw lightning bolts, people who dive out of exploding buildings, a kiss while flying through the air.

I moved to New York at twenty-five and felt like getting through my daily responsibilities was action enough. I didn't create any drama, somehow it just happened around me and I was inevitably swept into the development. And all I wanted to do was return to my loving girlfriend, open a beer, and watch *Boston Legal*. The Johnny Hiro series was very much born from that feeling.

I'm constantly amazed at how attached I've grown to these characters, how much I care about them. I've heard other authors talk about that experience but have never had it until Johnny and Mayumi. I hope only that one day I'm given the opportunity to tell more stories with them.

I'd like to give a quick "thank you" to Jesse Post, Dylan Babb, and Chris Pitzer of AdHouse Books — this comic would not be the same without their effort and support.

Michael Cho was born in Seoul, South Korea, but moved to Canada when he was six. He's had a lifelong love of comics and art and does his best to combine the two in his job as an illustrator and cartoonist. He currently lives in Toronto with his wife and baby daughter, and his illustrations have appeared in the *New York Times Book Review, Nickelodeon*, and other periodicals. He's also painted book covers for Random House/Knopf and Penguin Books, including the recent twenty-fifth-anniversary edition of Don DeLillo's *White Noise*. His comics work has been published by Marvel, DC, Image, and AdHouse Books, among others. Michael is currently hard at work on an art book of urban landscapes to be published by Drawn & Quarterly and a long-form graphic novel that is taking him forever to finish. He also painted the jacket art for this collection and had a great time doing so.

   • Being a child of the late Cold War years, the subject of nuclear weapons and the circumstances of their creation has always fascinated me. Trinity was my attempt to explore, in comics form, specific aspects of that subject and what they meant to me. For this fourteen-page story, I took down about seventy pages of notes and research, and I am indebted to Conan Tobias, the editor of *Taddle Creek* magazine (where this comic originally ran), for his tireless fact-checking.

   Robert Dennis Crumb (born August 30, 1943), often credited simply as R. Crumb, is an American artist and illustrator recognized for the distinctive style of his drawings and his critical, satirical, subversive view of the American mainstream. He currently lives in Southern France.

   Crumb was a founder of the underground comix movement and is regarded as its most prominent figure. Though one of the most celebrated of comic book artists, Crumb's entire career has unfolded outside the mainstream comic book publishing industry. One of his most recognized works is the *Keep on Truckin'* comic, which became a widely distributed fixture of pop culture in the '70s. Others are the characters of Devil Girl, Fritz the Cat, and Mr. Natural. He also illustrated the album covers for *Cheap Thrills* by Big Brother and the Holding Company and the compilation album *The Music Never Stopped: Roots of the Grateful Dead*.

   Society of Illustrators Gold Medal–winning cartoonist **Farel Dalrymple** has been producing his own comics since 1999, after graduating from the School of Visual Arts in New York City. The first issue of his ongoing series, *Pop Gun War*, was published with the help of a Xeric grant. In 2003, *Pop Gun War* was collected into a trade paperback by Dark Horse Comics. Farel co-founded, coedits, and contributes to the comic book anthology *Meathaus*.

   In this volume, Farel did the art on *Omega the Unknown*, written by Jonathan Lethem for Marvel Comics. He is currently living in Portland, Oregon, and working on an original graphic novel, *The Wrenchies,* for First Second. He can be found online at http://fareldal.livejournal.com/.

   • My work process is fourteen-hour workdays filled with ecstasy, torment, and procrastination.

   The character was originally created in 1975 by Steve Gerber and Mary Skrenes, then reimagined by Lethem. I am still happily surprised that Marvel Comics let us do a story like that. Those guys went out on a limb but I think it paid off in quality. And I am really grateful and happy to have gotten to work with the excellent Jonathan Lethem, Karl Rusnak, Paul Hornschemeier, and Gary Panter.

   Derf was raised in a small town in Ohio and attended school with future serial killer Jeffrey Dahmer. After high school, Derf worked as a garbage man, an experience that was the basis for his first graphic novel, *Trashed,* published in 2002, a memoir that Time.com called "the funniest book of the year." His latest book is *Punk Rock and Trailer Parks,* which *Booklist* hails as "one of the stand-out graphic novels of the year." Currently he is working on a graphic novel based on his teenage friendship with Dahmer, titled *My Friend Dahmer*. Following his sanitation stint, Derf earned a degree in journalism from Ohio State University and embarked on a newspaper career. For the past twenty years, his cranky comic strip, *The City,* has appeared in weekly city rags coast to coast. He has twice been nominated for Eisner Awards for his comic book work, and his political cartoons have won a host of honors, including a Robert F. Kennedy Award in 2007.

A collection of his work and papers was established at the Ohio State Cartoon Museum in 2008. Derf lives in bucolic Cleveland with his wife, the newspaper columnist and NPR commentator Sheryl Harris, and their two children.

▪ When I started working on this book, I had nothing but my protoganist, Otto "The Baron" Pizcok. He took form very quickly and I knew immediately he was something special. But I had little else: no story, no conflict, no ending, zilch. After a summer of fruitless writing, I shelved the project in frustration.

A few months later, I was asked to help out with a benefit concert in Akron for a couple of musicians from the punk era who were having health problems and facing large medical bills. I supplied a poster and T-shirt for the show, which quickly evolved into a huge reunion of bands, many reuniting after two decades, from the glory days of the Rubber City's legendary punk club, The Bank. The shows themselves (the event had to be split into two concerts it got so big) were magic, with an enthusiastic packed house, terrific music, and a vibe that took me straight back to 1980, when I was a pimply punk rocker. And that's when I had my epiphany. Of course! I'll put Otto in The Bank at the peak of the punk era! Once that inspirational flash hit, I wrote the entire book in a matter of days.

I like telling stories that haven't been told. There has never really been a comic book devoted to the punk counterculture, and the Akron scene, famous in its day for spawning Devo and Chrissie Hynde and a host of other quirky artists, has now been completely forgotten. I could have set this book in the more-renowned CBGBs and the Lower East Side of New York, but I felt that putting it in Akron, which I know intimately, would give the story that vital element of truth that comes with firsthand observation. I've heard from many readers who think this story —and specifically this excerpt!—actually happened! So I guess I succeeded in nailing that truthful chord.

Theo Ellsworth is a self-taught artist and cartoonist living in Portland, Oregon. His first book, *Capacity*, was released from Secret Acres in 2008, followed by the comic *Sleeper Car* in 2009. The pages of his next book have been slowly piling up on his drawing table and are regularly walked on by his cat. He has a website: www.thoughtcloudfactory.com.

▪ "Norman Eight's Left Arm" is a story that came to me while riding my bike. Sometimes scenes will just play out inside of my head like that. When it's really clear, I feel like I'm spying on people in another world. Sometimes the characters notice me spying and the story comes to a grinding halt. Stay invisible, take good notes: that is my mission. Once I have a story, then comes the even harder work of rendering it in visible form. It's not satisfying enough to simply ride my bike around daydreaming. The work is my proof. I have been blessed (or cursed) with the insatiable need to document these kinds of things, and comics seems to be the purest form I've found to get the job done.

Dean Haspiel is a native New Yorker and the creator of *Billy Dogma*, *Street Code*, and *Act-i-vate*. Dino has drawn comics for the *New York Times*, Marvel, DC/Vertigo, Dark Horse, Scholastic, Toon Books, and other publishers, but is best known for his semiautobiographical collaborations with Harvey Pekar on *The Quitter* and *American Splendor*, and with Jonathan Ames on *The Alcoholic* and HBOs *Bored to Death*.

Gilbert Hernandez is the cocreator of *Love and Rockets* and was born with a comic book in his hand. Growing up reading just about every kind of comic book there was in the '60s and '70s, he developed such an appreciation for the medium that it led him to believe comics could be a place for personal expression. The only type of comics that he didn't read were romance comics, and he has ironically been considered mostly a writer of, well, girly comics.

▪ Drawing *Citizen Rex* was a nice change for me, as it gave me the chance to draw just about anything I could think of for the story.

Mario Hernandez is the oldest of the three brothers who breathed life into *Love and Rockets*. He has been sticking and moving around comics most of his life, first collecting then producing. He's been published in various forms and has a million stories to tell.

▪ This story has been knocking around my head for years. I tried to convey the feeling of a cheesy foreign movie you watched late one drunken night and were kind of hazy about in the morning.

Ben Katchor's picture-stories appear in *Metropolis* magazine. His upcoming collection of weekly strips, *The Cardboard Valise,* will be published by Pantheon Books. His most recent music-theater collaboration with Mark Mulcahy, *A Checkroom Romance,* was commissioned and work-shopped in 2009 at the Cullman Center for Scholars and Writers at the New York Public Library and will be performed at the Lincoln Center in 2010. He is an associate professor at Parsons The New School for Design in New York City. For more information, visit www.katchor.com.

▪ These picture-stories were originally published in *Metropolis* magazine (http://www.metropolismag.com) on a 10-by-12-inch page. They are self-contained and self-explanatory. Only painters who have not figured out how to incorporate text into their work need to write statements that explain what's missing.

James Kochalka lives in Burlington, Vermont, with his wife and two boys. He draws a daily diary comic strip called *American Elf,* an absurdist superhero comic series called *SuperF*ckers,* and a series for children called *Johnny Boo.* He also makes crazy, catchy rock music under the name James Kochalka Superstar. His song "Britney's Silver Can" was named one of the top one hundred songs of 2006 by *Rolling Stone,* and his song "Hockey Monkey" was used as the theme song to the Fox TV sitcom, *The Loop.*

▪ I've been keeping a daily diary in comic strip form since October 1998. Just a short little comic strip each day about something that happened to me. My hope was that something amazing about the human experience would be revealed by chronicling my life in this way. This excerpt is mainly about the birth of my second son. I had not read these since I originally drew them, not even when the book was published. I think I don't read my own work out of some sort of fear of seeing myself too closely, perhaps? Anyhow, I just read this section and I'm actually sort of stunned ... the strips seem to vibrate and pulse with life in a rather astonishing way. And then I'm reminded that all our lives vibrate and pulse in this astonishing way. Life is simply amazing.

Peter Kuper is the cofounder of the political 'zine *World War 3 Illustrated.* His illustrations and comics have appeared in *Time,* the *New York Times,* and *MAD,* where he has illustrated "SPY vs. SPY" every month since 1997. He has written and illustrated over twenty books, including *The System* and *Stop Forgetting to Remember,* and adapted Franz Kafka's *The Metamorphosis.* His latest book, *Diario de Oaxaca,* is a sketchbook journal of two years he spent in Oaxaca, Mexico.

More of his work can be found at www.peterkuper.com.

▪ This is not an artist's statement.

I've learned a lot about the use of images and language from eight years of the Bush administration and I humbly request you listen to my insight (please ignore the hood and the ropes that bind you to your chair). Fair and balanced news from the no-spin zone has informed me that it is better to obey like man's best friend than question questionable actions. Who are we to say what's right and wrong if might makes right and evildoers are hiding behind every water bottle? Since every dog has his day, then surely the inheriting meek will fix everything on Earth. So Madoff made off with fifty billion, so what? After giving billions of dollars to bail out multi-multinationals, our titanic nation is shipshape and ready to take on the icebergs (thanks to global warming, they're much smaller). Please don't misunderestimate me—I for one am optimistic. After all, the world always needs comics.

Dave Lapp is a teacher and cartoonist living in Toronto, Canada. He has been doing some form of alternate comics for over a decade. His first graphic novel, *Drop-In*, is a collection of stories about his work as an art teacher in an inner-city drop-in center. *Drop-In* received Best Graphic Novel nominations from the Ignatz and Doug Wright awards. Dave's new book, *Children of the Atom*, is a collection of 240 strange, sweet, sorrowful, weekly strips starring Franklin-Boy and Jim-Jam Girl.

▪ The drop-in center I work at is located in one of the poorest urban locations in Canada, and "Flytrap" is about one of the students I knew there. "Dominic" was excellent at drawing animals and very quiet. He spoke when spoken to and very rarely offered any information about himself. I was really surprised and touched when he offered to show me his little plant. Dominic was soon to enter high school and I was curious about his plans for the future, so I asked him a few questions ...

Jonathan Lethem is the author of eight novels and several collections of stories and essays. His writing has been translated into nearly thirty languages. He lives in Brooklyn and Maine.

▪ When Marvel invited me to plunder their character archives to create my first attempt—well, my first since I was fourteen years old—at writing a comic book, I knew right away, before they'd even finished inviting, which character I'd want to write. Steve Gerber and Mary Skrenes's *Omega the Unknown* was the principal cipher-lodestone gleaming in the back corridors of my memory palace, and in fact I'd already used some of its neglected energies to inspire the combination of "ineffectual superhero" and "alienated kid in public school" in my novel *The Fortress of Solitude*. The thwarted ten-issue run of the original *Omega* in 1975 and '76 (Gerber and Skrenes weren't even permitted or able to write each of those scant ten issues, nor to develop the story in the direction they'd wished) nonetheless managed to convey a tremendous eccentric power, and, if you ask me, were a significant foreshadowing of the "graphic-novel" revolution in superhero stories that was to explode a decade or so later with *Watchmen* and its many successors. But for me, part of the power of *Omega* was in its ruins, its ragged-ended, unfulfilled quality—it was for me a zone of implication and potential. I didn't propose to "repair" the old *Omega* story so much as capitalize on the power a ruin can hold over the imagination. And, compared to Marvel's other characters, about whom so many hundreds of stories have been told, Omega wasn't plumbed-out in the least. The first thing I knew, though, after taking their offer home and chewing on it, was that just as Gerber had Skrenes, I'd need another writer, my old(est) friend Karl Rusnak, with whom I'd been enraptured and disappointed by *Omega the Unknown* the first time out. This seemed more than natural, it was kismet. The kind of comics Karl and I had loved as teenagers had always been like Hollywood studio films: ad hoc corporate collaborations full of borrowed concepts, and with multiple auteurs. So I'd build a little Bullpen of my own.

Yet this would have led nowhere if I hadn't found someone whose drawings could activate the story I had stirring in mind, art being where the action is in a comic book, after all. I'd been way out of touch with contemporary comics of the type I was now supposed to be creating, and my search was initially a fumbling one. When I found (thanks to Bob Fingerman) Farel Dalrymple's *Pop Gun War,* I suddenly could really believe in my own nascent *Omega.* For one thing, this kid had the patience to draw a million crumbling brownstone facades, which I was sure I needed drawn. And the bodies he drew were homely and humane yet still capable of flight, like the ones in my old superhero dreams.

Thanks to Farel, we drew the superb and excellently opinionated Paul Hornschemeier into this mix, and Paul was immediately more than a colorist, but a kind of secret weapon, energizing us from the sidelines. It seemed criminal to keep him contained as merely the colorist, so I found a good excuse to have Paul draw a few panels in issue six. And when I figured out that Omega, that autistic, supersensitive, godlike stick of wood from another planet, was going to draw a little mini-comic of his own, the only living human I believed capable of channeling him was, needless to say, Gary Panter. That I was able to enlist the Jack Kirby of the '80s underground under the banner of Marvel Enterprises is now one of my life's great accomplishments—sort of like if Robert Benton really had succeeded in persuading Godard to direct *Bonnie and Clyde.* In my mind, at least, it was that big a deal.

An expat Canadian living in Los Angeles after several years in Japan, **Steve MacIsaac**'s comics explore contemporary gay culture, identity, and sexuality. To date, MacIsaac has released three issues of his solo series *Shirtlifter,* with the fourth due in 2010. His work has appeared in a number of anthologies, including *I Like It Like That* (Arsenal Pulp), all three volumes of *Best Erotic Comics* (Last Gasp), and several volumes of *Boy Trouble* (Green Candy Press), from which the story "Ex Communication" is taken. He is perhaps best known for his wordless collaboration with Dale Lazarov, *Sticky,* published by Bruno Gmuender.

▪ One of the dangers of living with a cartoonist is being pressed into service as a de facto editor. Pretty early in our relationship, Todd became my sounding board and ideal reader. Even though he doesn't draw, he's perceptive, has a good eye, and unfailingly spots the unconventional spellings, logical inconsistencies, and anatomical awkwardness that pepper my first drafts. While I usually listen to most of his suggestions (albeit with a soupçon of defensiveness …), occasionally we'd disagree on some modification or other. With diplomatic aplomb, I then trotted out a line usually guaranteed to silence criticism: "That sounds like a great idea. Why don't YOU write a comic strip and I'll draw it?" I never expected that he'd, you know, actually do it. Or that it would be so damn good. I had to give him a few suggestions, though. He even listened to me about most of them. Perhaps there's a lesson in that somewhere.

David Mazzucchelli has been making comics his whole life. Known chiefly for his collaborations—with Frank Miller on seminal Batman and Daredevil stories, and with Paul Karasik on an adaptation of Paul Auster's novel, *City of Glass*—he began publishing his own stories in 1991 in his anthology magazine, *Rubber Blanket.* Since then, his short comics have been published in books and magazines around the world. *Asterios Polyp* is his first graphic novel.

Josh Neufeld works primarily in the realm of nonfiction comics, In addition to *A.D.,* his projects include the Xeric Award–winning graphic travelogue *A Few Perfect Hours (and Other Stories from Southeast Asia and Central Europe).* Neufeld is currently collaborating with the National Public Radio host Brooke Gladstone on a book called *The Influencing Machine,* due out from W. W. Norton in 2011. His work has been featured in *The Vagabonds, Keyhole,* and *Titans of Finance,* as well as in numerous comics anthologies, newspapers, magazines, and literary journals. He is a longtime artist for Harvey Pekar's *American Splendor,* and his art has been exhibited in gallery and museum shows in the United States and Europe. Neufeld lives in Brooklyn, New York, with his wife, the writer Sari Wilson, and their daughter.

▪ In October 2005, shortly after Hurricane Katrina, I spent three weeks as an American Red Cross volunteer in Biloxi, Mississippi, delivering hot meals to sections of the city without power. While I was there, I met many folks who had lost everything in the hurricane. The blog entries I kept about that experience turned into a self-published book, *Katrina Came Calling* (and gave me a sense of connection that later provided vital background and context for *A.D.*).

In the summer of 2006, I was approached by the storytelling website *Smith* magazine to tell the Katrina story in comics form. I conceived of the project as a journalist. I felt it was important to tell the story from the perspectives of a range of real people with different backgrounds and experiences: from those who evacuated and those who stayed behind, people who were greatly affected by the flooding and even some who weren't. Eventually, seven people emerged as *A.D.*'s "characters": Denise, Leo, Michelle, Abbas, Darnell, Kwame, and The Doctor—all of whom I finally met in person in January 2007. (The section excerpted here mostly features Abbas and Darnell.) It was then up to me to weave the characters' stories together in comics form, illustrating the storm and their disparate paths into and through it—while periodically fact-checking with them and keeping up with their changing fortunes. *A.D.* was serialized online on *Smith* magazine in 2007–2008. The book edition of *A.D.*, which was published by Pantheon in 2009, has about 25 percent more story and art than what appeared online; I also made significant changes and revisions to large chunks of the original material.

Bryan Lee O'Malley is a Canadian cartoonist and the creator of the popular Scott Pilgrim series. He has written and drawn five volumes, with the sixth and final volume set to debut in the summer of 2010, alongside a major feature film from Universal Pictures (by writer/director Edgar Wright). He has won numerous awards, including Harvey, Shuster, and Doug Wright awards, and has been nominated for the Eisner Award and the National Cartoonists Society Reuben Award. His future plans include naps.

▪ I don't really remember anything about this particular stretch of pages. I've been working on comics in two-hundred-page segments for the past six years, which requires full-blown obsession during the process. Afterward, when the books are finally in print, all that remains is mild bemusement at the barely remembered contents and vague irritation at all the mistakes made. I look forward to trying to make comics some other way, later.

John Pham was born in Saigon, Vietnam, in 1974 and subsequently raised in the United States. He currently lives in Los Angeles, where he is working on *Sublife*, his anthology series for Fantagraphics, as well as other noncomics-related projects.

▪ The first issue of *Sublife* was composed almost entirely of an episode of *221 Sycamore St*, an ongoing serial. As the book was nearing completion, I realized that there was room for two more pages' worth of material. I wanted to do something that provided a good contrast stylistically to the rest of the issue, so I figured a soft sci-fi story would be kind of fun.

221 Sycamore St is typical autobiography-as-fiction. I'm taking experiences and emotional events from my own life and filtering them through the lens of contrived characters and settings. I didn't quite intend it this way, but I suppose *Deep Space* is somewhat autobiographical, too. I worked on most of *Sublife #1* in the solitude of my apartment, and it made for a rough experience. Fortunately, I was able to eventually rent a studio space with another comics colleague, which helped a great deal in relieving some of the characteristic pressure of working on comics all day. Deek somehow saves the astronauts from themselves with just his presence; I guess this may relate to my experience of sharing a workspace with a friend and how it helped restore my professional sanity. One person can make a difference!

Jesse Reklaw has been drawing the self-syndicated, weekly comic strip *Slow Wave* since 1995. It is currently printed by six newspapers around the United States, and two collections have been published, *Dreamtoons* (Shambhala, 2000) and *The Night of Your Life* (Dark Horse, 2008). Currently Jesse is working on a comics memoir called *Couch Tag,* one chapter of which was published in *The Best American Comics 2006.*

▪ I receive about twenty dream submissions per week, mostly through a form on the *Slow Wave* website. I read them, rate them, and enter them in a database (12,000 dreams and counting). When it comes time to draw new strips, I read over the top-rated dreams and choose the one that feels right to me that week. I ask the dreamers for a photo or a personal description and try to stay as close to the dream narrative as I can, though I often edit a little for clarity or humor.

C. Tyler is an award-winning, autobiographical comic book artist/writer, whose work R. Crumb describes as having "the extremely rare quality of genuine, authentic heart. Hers are the only comics that ever brought me to the verge of tears."

Her stories first appeared in *Weirdo* in 1987 and numerous publications over the years, most recently the Yale anthologies and *Kramers Ergot #7.* She has been nominated for Harvey, Eisner, and Ignatz awards and was listed as one of the Top 100 Cartoonists of the Twentieth Century.

She has three solo books, *The Job Thing* (1993), *Late Bloomer* (2005), and *You'll Never Know: A Good and Decent Man* (2009).

▪ This excerpt is from Book I of the trilogy *You'll Never Know.* The series is about my dad's lifetime silence about his war service and the effect that had on me. I started this project thinking I could get it all done in two years, maybe three. But in reality, it's taking that long for each book—so much to research, so many details! I do everything by hand using a dip pen and a sable brush. Also, I wanted to challenge myself technically, so I work only with ink, no watercolor, no colored pencil, and no computer bucket fills. Fifty-three custom mixed colors. Fun, huh? (What was I thinking!) Because of occasional tendonitis flare-ups, I'm back to a sport I learned in kindergarten: baton twirling. It seems to help.

Chris Ware lives in Oak Park, Illinois, with his wife, Marnie, a high school science teacher, and their daughter, Clara, and is the author of *Jimmy Corrigan—The Smartest Kid on Earth,* which was recently selected as one of the hundred best books of the decade by the *London Times.* A contributor to *The New Yorker,* his work will also be the subject of an exhibit at the Gävle Konstcentrum in Gävle, Sweden, in 2010.

▪ In my early days as an aspiring cartoonist, I feared that if I attempted fiction, I'd be branded a liar. Now I know that's not true, and that fiction is, in fact, one way of actually approaching the truth more finely than reportage—sort of like not looking directly at the sun (or, for that matter, a dim star) to better see either. Fiction is also a direct conduit to the nuts and bolts of the mysterious manner by which we remember and distort the world. (In school lunchroom parlance, that means giving up on trying to remember exactly what somebody said and simply imitating their annoying mannerisms instead. Everyone knows which approach is more believable, and funnier.)

Not incongruously, in the lengthy Rusty Brown excerpt, the romantic memories of failed science-fiction writer Woodward Brown supersede a rereading of his own sophomoric early work (not shown). Now a high school English teacher in a midwestern private school, Brown realizes his early ambitions were nothing more than a blip, despite his clinging to them as a still-open portal to his unfinished youth.

Ignatz Award–winning cartoonist **Lauren R. Weinstein** lives in Brooklyn with her dog, Dr. Buddy, her husband, Tim, and her new baby daughter, Ramona. She has published three books. The Xeric-winning, self-published *Inside Vineyland* is a collection of surreal, psychologically charged one-panel comics and stories, which she drew mostly in her early twenties. *Girl Stories* gathers loosely autobiographical strips about preadolescent life. It was published by Henry Holt. Her latest book, *The Goddess of War,* is a bombastic, large-format sci-fi/fantasy/Western/romance comic available from PictureBox. In 2009, Weinstein exhibited her work at the Fumetto Festival in Lucerne, Switzerland. Her work has also appeared in *Kramers Ergot, The Ganzfeld, An Anthology of Graphic Fiction, Glamour,* and *The Best American Comics 2007.* Currently she is working on a graphic novel sequel to *Girl Stories.*

▪ Not long before *Bookforum* asked me to contribute a literary themed comic, I read a section of *The Dreaming of the Bones,* a verse play written by William Butler Yeats. It inspired me to try to create a comic that read like a poem. I tried to be as economical as possible with form, pictures, and words, while still alluding to a much bigger story. Yeats writes, "At the grey round of the hill/ Music of a lost kingdom/Runs, runs and is suddenly still." These lines perfectly described a feeling that I got while staying in a Victorian farmhouse in the Catskills one recent summer: I saw the remains of a stone wall out in the woods and was overwhelmed by ghosts.

Notable Comics

from September 1, 2008, to August 31, 2009

Selected by Jessica Abel and Matt Madden

DERIK BADMAN
Flying Chief. *Abstract Comics,* 2009.
NICK BERTOZZI
How and Why to Bale Hay. *Syncopated,* 2009.
RAY BRADBURY AND TIM HAMILTON
Ray Bradbury's Fahrenheit 451: The Authorized Adaptation, 2009.
NICHOLAS BREUTZMAN
My Town. *The Good Minnesotan,* 2008. *Yearbooks,* 2009.
MAT BRINKMAN
Multiforce, 2009.
KEVIN CANNON
Far Arden, 2009.
C.F.
Powr Mastrs, no. 2.
MARK CHIARELLO, EDITOR
Wednesday Comics, nos. 1–6.
BECKY CLOONAN
I See the Devil in My Sleep. *MySpace Darkhorse Presents,* no. 3.
BECKY CLOONAN AND STEVEN T. SEAGLE
American Virgin, 2008.
DARWYN COOKE AND RICHARD STARK
Parker: The Hunter, 2009.
JP COOVERT, STEPHEN FLOYD, JAMES HINDLE, ALEXIS FREDERICK-FROST, AND JOSEPH LAMBERT
Sword, 2008.
WARREN CRAGHEAD III
Un Caligramme. *Abstract Comics,* 2009. This Is a Ghost. *Ghost Comics,* 2009.
JORDAN CRANE
Vicissitude. *Uptight,* no. 3.

JONATHAN DALTON
Lil' Ulysses in Chicago. *Funday Sunnies,* 2009.
TRAVIS DANDRO
Journal, 2009.
EZRA CLAYTAN DANIELS
A Circuit Closed. *MySpace Darkhorse Presents,* no. 1.
MIKE DAWSON
Boy Scout Troop 142. *Awesome,* no. 2.
WILL DINSKI
Errand Service, 2009.
JOSH DYSART AND RON WIMBERLY
The Stain. *MySpace Darkhorse Presents,* no. 3.
THEO ELLSWORTH
Capacity, 2008.
JESS FINK
We Can Fix It: A Time Travel Memoir, 2009.
HILARY FLORIDO
Prescription Strength. *Hey! 4-Eyes,* no. 3.
JOHN HANKIEWICZ
The Offering. *Ghost Comics,* 2009.
FAITH ERIN HICKS
The War at Ellsmere, 2008.
ALEX HOLDEN
West Side Improvements. *Syncopated,* 2009.
PAUL HOPPE
The Horror. *Horror of Rabid Rabbit,* no. 9.
DAMIEN JAY
Willy. *Papercutter,* no. 10.
HELEN JO
Jin and Jan, no. 1.
AYA KAKEDA
Delicious Soup of Horror. *Horror of Rabid Rabbit,* no. 9.

JOE KELLY AND JM KIN MIIMURA
I Kill Giants, 2009.

VICTOR KERLOW
Falling Sky.
The Lumberjack. *Gutter*, 2009.

NEIL KLEID AND NICHOLAS CINQUEGRANI
The Big Kahn, 2009.

KEITH KNIGHT
The K Chronicles. *MySpace Darkhorse Presents*, no. 3.

JOESEPH LAMBERT
Food/Fall, 2008.

DAVID LAPHAM
Young Liars, 2008.

MIRIAM LIMBICKI
Jobnik!, 2008.

ELLEN LINDNER
Shams, Scams and Blind Faith. *Hey! 4-Eyes*, no. 3.

MAGGIE MCKNIGHT
Swingin'. *The Iowa Review*, 2009.

ADAM MEUSE
Social Insect, 2009.

MIKE MIGNOLA AND BEN STENBECK
Murderous Intent. *MySpace Darkhorse Presents*, no. 3.

ANDREI MOLOTIU
Otherwise Untitled. *Nautilus*, 2008.

TOM MOTLEY, EDITOR
Made Out of "Mac," 2009.

JESSE MOYNIHAN
Follow Me, 2009.

CORINNE MUCHA
Growing Up Haunted. *Papercutter*, no. 8.

NATHAN NEAL
Delia's Love. *Mome*, no. 15.

ANDERS NILSEN
Monologues for Calculating the Density of Black Holes, 2009.
Big Questions, no. 12.

DANICA NOVGORODOFF
Slow Storm, 2008.

SARAH OLEKSYK
Previously Possessed. *MySpace Darkhorse Presents*, no. 3.

CHRIS ONSTAD
The Great Outdoor Fight, 2008.

JASON OVERBY
Exploding Head Man, 2008.

LAURA PARK
Sleep Is for Suckers. *Mome*, no. 13.
Office 32F. *Mome*, no. 14.

JOHN PORCELLINO
Silent Birds. *King Cat*, no. 69.

NATE POWELL
Swallow Me Whole, 2008.

HENRIK REHR
Reykjavik, 2009.

JESSE REKLAW
Ten Thousand Things to Do, no. 1–4.

SIMON ROY
Jan's Atomic Heart, 2009.

STAN SAKAI
Traitors of the Earth. *Usagi Yojimbo*, no. 117–9.
Saya. *MySpace Darkhorse Presents*, no. 3.

DASH SHAW
Satellite CMYK. *Mome*, no. 13.

ANUJ SHRESTHA
American Cat. *Rabid Rabbit*, no. 10.

JOSH SIMMONS
Jesus Christ. *Mome*, no. 13.

JEFF SMITH
RASL, no. 3.

ALEXEY SOKOLIN
Life, Interwoven. *Abstract Comics*, 2009.

ADAM SUERTE
Aprendiz, no. 3.

GARY SULLIVAN
Am I Emo? *Poetry*, 2009.

JEREMY TINDER
Pete at Night. *Papercutter*, no. 8.

JONATHAN VANKIN AND SETH FISHER
Tokyo Days. *Vertigo Pop: Tokyo Days, Bangkok Nights*, 2009.

RICK VEITCH AND GARY ERSKINE
Army @ Love: Generation Pwned, 2008.

JASON VIOLA
Sunward, 2009.

BRIAN WOOD AND NATHAN FOX
Random Fire. *DMZ: The Hidden War*, 2008.

J.T. YOST
Losers Weepers, 2009

CREDITS

"The Alcoholic (Excerpt)" by Jonathan Ames, art by Dean Haspiel. First published in *The Alcoholic*. Copyright © 2008 by Jonathan Ames and DC Comics. All rights reserved. Reprinted by permission of Jonathan Ames and DC Comics. "The War on Fornication" by Peter Bagge. First published in *Everybody Is Stupid Except for Me*. Copyright © 2009 by Peter Bagge and *Reason* magazine. Reprinted by permission of *Reason*. "Mixed Up Files" by Gabrielle Bell. First published in *Bookforum*. Copyright © 2009 by Gabrielle Bell. Reprinted by permission of the author. "Ex Communication" by Todd Brower and Steve MacIsaac. First published in *Book of Boy Trouble, Volume 2*. Copyright © 2009 by Todd Brower and Steve MacIsaac. Reprinted by permission of Todd Brower and Steve MacIsaac. "The Lagoon (Hiding in the Water)" by Lilli Carré. First published in *The Lagoon*. Copyright © 2008 by Lille Carré. Reprinted by permission of Fantagraphics Books and Lilli Carré. "Lobster Run" by Fred Chao. First published in *Johnny Hiro*. Copyright © 2009 by Fred Chao. Reprinted by permission of the author. "Trinity" by Michael Cho. First published in *Taddle Creek*, Summer 2009. Copyright © 2009 by Michael Cho. Reprinted by permission of the author. "The Book of Genesis Illustrated (Excerpts)." First published in *The New Yorker*, June 8 and 15, 2009. Copyright © 2009 by Robert Crumb. Used by permission of the author. From *Genesis: Translation and Commentary*, translated by Robert Alter. Copyright © 1996 by Robert Alter. Used by permission of W. W. Norton and Company, Inc. "The Bank" by Derf. First published in *Punk Rock and Trailer Parks*. Copyright © 2009 by John Backderf. Reprinted by permission of John Backderf. "Norman Eight's Left Arm" by Theo Ellsworth. First published in *Sleeper Car*. Copyright © 2009 by Theo Ellsworth. Reprinted by permission of the author. "Water! Electricity! Meat!" by Gilbert and Mario Hernandez. First published in *Citizen Rex*, Dark Horse Comics. Copyright © 2009 by Gilbert and Mario Hernandez. Reprinted by permission of the authors. "The Daily Grand Prix" and "Forbidden Rooms" by Ben Katchor. First published in *Metropolis*, February/April 2009. Copyright © 2009 by Ben Katchor. Reprinted by permission of the author. "November 8–28, 2007" by James Kochalka. First published in *American Elf*, Book Three. Copyright © 2008 by James Kochalka. Reprinted by permission of James Kochalka and Top Shelf Productions. "Ceci N'est Pas Une Comic" by Peter Kuper. First published in *Virginia Quarterly Review*, Winter 2009. Copyright © 2009 by Peter Kuper. Reprinted by permission of the author. "Flytrap" by Dave Lapp. First published in *Drop-In*. Copyright © 2010 by Dave Lapp. Reprinted by permission of the author. "Omega the Unknown (Chapter Seven)" by Jonathan Lethem with Karl Rusnak, art by Farel Dalrymple and Gary Panter, coloring by Paul Hornschemeier. First published in *Omega the Unknown*. Copyright © 2010 by Marvel Characters, Inc. Used with permission. "Asterios Polyp (Excerpt)" by David Mazzucchelli. First published in *Asterios Polyp*. Copyright © 2009 by David Mazzuccelli. Used by permission of Pantheon Books, a division of Random House, Inc. "The Flood (Excerpt)" by Josh Neufeld. First published in *A.D.: New Orleans After the Deluge* by Josh Neufeld. Copyright © 2009 by Josh Neufeld. Used by permission of Pantheon Books, A Division of Random House, Inc. "Scott Pilgrim vs. The Universe (Excerpt)" by Bryan Lee O'Malley. First published in *Scott Pilgrim, Volume 5*. Copyright © 2009 by Bryan Lee O'Malley. Reprinted by permission of the author. "Deep Space" by John Pham. First published in *Sublife*. Copyright © 2009 by John Pham. Reprinted by permission of the author. "Titanic Urination," "Hooker Cookies," "Duck Mom," "Carrot Romance," "Pumpkin Drummer," and "Sleep Multiplication" by Jesse Reklaw. First published in *The Night of Your Life*. Copyright © 2008 by Jesse Reklaw. Reprinted by permission of the author. "A Good and Decent Man (Excerpt)" by C. Tyler. First published in *You'll Never Know, Book One*. Copyright © 2009 by C. Tyler. Reprinted by permission of the author. "Fiction versus Nonfiction" by Chris Ware. First published in *Bookforum*. Copyright © 2009 by Chris Ware. Reprinted by permission of the author. "Acme Novelty Library (Excerpt)" by Chris Ware. First published in *Acme Novelty Library*. Copyright © 2009 by Chris Ware. Reprinted by permission of the author. "I Heard Some Distant Music" by Lauren Weinstein. First published in *Bookforum*. Copyright © 2009 by Lauren Weinstein. Reprinted by permission of the author.

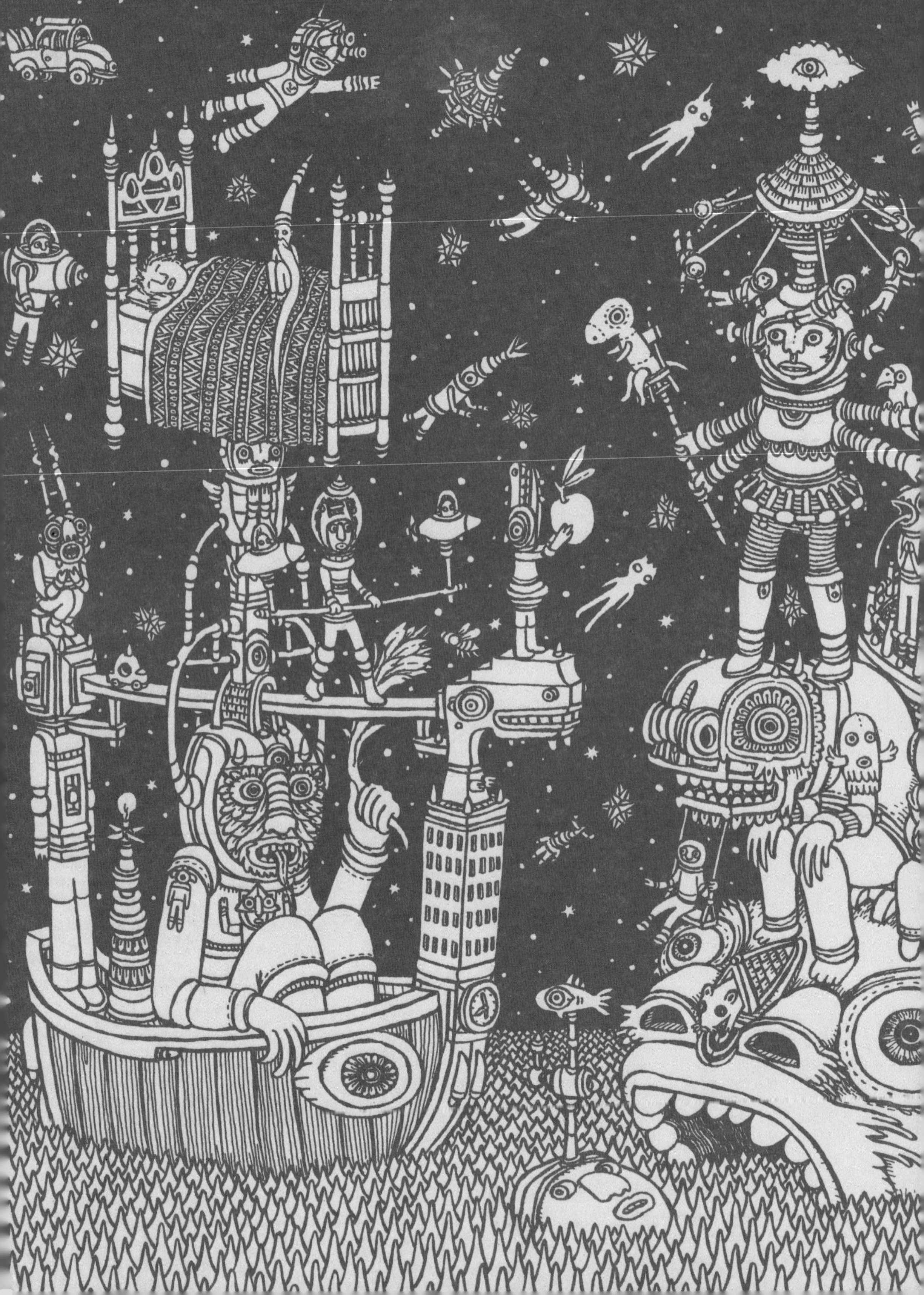